DIVERSITY AND EUROPEAN HUMAN RIGHTS

Through redrafting the judgments of the ECHR, *Diversity and European Human Rights* demonstrates how the Court could improve the mainstreaming of diversity in its judgments. Eighteen judgments are considered and rewritten to reflect the concerns of women, children, LGB persons, ethnic and religious minorities and persons with disabilities, in turn. Each redrafted judgment is accompanied by a paper outlining the theoretical concepts and frameworks that guided the approaches of the authors and explaining how each amendment to the original text is an improvement. Simultaneously, the authors demonstrate how difficult it can be to translate ideas into judgments, whilst also providing examples of what those ideas would look like in judicial language. By rewriting actual judicial decisions in a wide range of topics, this book offers a broad overview of diversity issues in the jurisprudence of the ECHR and aims to bridge the gap between academic analysis and judicial practice.

EVA BREMS is a professor of human rights law at Ghent University, where she co-founded the Human Rights Centre. Her research interests include most areas of human rights law (Belgian law, European law, international law, comparative law), with special emphases on women's rights, children's rights and cultural diversity.

DIVERSITY AND EUROPEAN HUMAN RIGHTS

Rewriting Judgments of the ECHR

Edited by

EVA BREMS

CAMBRIDGE
UNIVERSITY PRESS

CAMBRIDGE
UNIVERSITY PRESS

University Printing House, Cambridge CB2 8BS, United Kingdom

Cambridge University Press is part of the University of Cambridge.

It furthers the University's mission by disseminating knowledge in the pursuit of education, learning and research at the highest international levels of excellence.

www.cambridge.org
Information on this title: www.cambridge.org/9781107538047

© Cambridge University Press 2013

First published 2013
First paperback edition 2015

A catalogue record for this publication is available from the British Library

Library of Congress Cataloguing in Publication data
Diversity and European human rights : rewriting judgments of the ECHR / Edited by Eva Brems.
p.   cm.
ISBN 978-1-107-02660-5
1. Human rights – Europe – Cases.   2. European Court of Human Rights.
3. Multiculturalism – Law and legislation – Europe.   I. Brems, Eva.
KJC5132.D58   2012
342.408′5–dc23
2012020515

ISBN 978-1-107-02660-5 Hardback
ISBN 978-1-107-53804-7 Paperback

CONTENTS

v

TABLES

NOTES ON THE CONTRIBUTORS

PETER BARTLETT is Nottinghamshire Healthcare NHS Trust Professor of Mental Health Law in the School of Law and Institute of Mental Health at the University of Nottingham. With Oliver Lewis and Oliver Thorold, he is author of *Mental Disability and the European Convention on Human Rights* (2006).

PIERRE BOSSET is Professor of Human Rights and Public Law at the Université du Québec à Montréal (UQAM). The relationship between law and religion is one of his major research interests. For the Québec Human Rights Commission, he has authored influential policy papers on religion in the public sphere, secularism, reasonable accommodation, and the right to wear headscarves in schools.

EVA BREMS is a professor of human rights law at Ghent University (Belgium). Her research interests include most areas of human rights law, in European and international law as well as in Belgian and comparative law.

MARIS BURBERGS is a PhD candidate at the Human Rights Centre of Ghent University. He holds a BA from the University of Latvia and a European Master's Degree in Human Rights and Democratisation from EIUC (Italy). Prior to his PhD studies, he was a lecturer on human rights at the University of Latvia and a legal adviser to the Ombudsman of Latvia.

AEYAL GROSS is Associate Professor of Law at Tel Aviv University. He is also a visiting reader at the School of Oriental and African Studies (SOAS) at the University of London. He holds an LLB from Tel Aviv University and an SJD from Harvard Law School. He is a board member of the Association for Civil Rights in Israel (ACRI).

MICHAEL KAVEY, a writer and attorney in New York, recently served as an Associate-in-Law at Columbia Law School, where he taught legal practice workshop and assisted in teaching legal methods and employment discrimination law; he also worked with Columbia's Sexuality and Gender Law Clinic. He previously practised law with Lambda Legal, and served as a law clerk to the Honorable Sonia Sotomayor (US Court of Appeals, Second Circuit) and the Honorable Gerard E. Lynch (US District Court, Southern District of New York).

URSULA KILKELLY is a professor of law at University College Cork where she directs the Child Law Clinic and the LLM in Child and Family Law. She has published widely on children's rights and youth justice, and on the European Convention on Human Rights. The second edition of her book, *The Child and the ECHR*, will be published in 2012.

HOLNING LAU is an associate professor of law at the University of North Carolina, where he teaches family law and law and sexuality. He has held fellowships at UCLA's Williams Institute on Sexual Orientation and Gender Identity Law and Public Policy, and at the University of Hong Kong's Centre for Comparative and Public Law.

PATRICIA LONDONO is a barrister (Lincoln's Inn) and a lecturer in law at Brunel Law School (2011 to present). Before that, she was a John Collier Fellow in Law at Trinity Hall, Cambridge (2007–10), a lecturer in law (non-stipendiary) at Jesus College, Oxford (2006–7), a graduate teaching assistant at the Faculty of Law, Oxford University (2006) and a lecturer in law (non-stipendiary) at Lincoln College, Oxford (2004–5 and 2005–6).

SAÏLA OUALD CHAIB is a PhD researcher at the Human Rights Centre of Ghent University. In her research she aims at integrating a minority perspective in the case law of the European Court of Human Rights, with a main focus on religious minorities. She obtained her LLB (Kandidaat in de Rechten) from KU Leuven Kulak and her LLM from Ghent University.

LOURDES PERONI is a PhD candidate at the Human Rights Centre of Ghent University. Her research focuses on issues of recognition and equality in ECHR case law concerning religious and ethnic minorities. She received her LLB from the National University of Asunción and her LLM from Harvard Law School. She was a fellow at the Inter-American Commission on Human Rights and at Yale Law School.

JULIE RINGELHEIM is a researcher with the Belgian National Fund for Scientific Research (FRS-FNRS) and Lecturer in Human Rights Law at Louvain University. Her publications include *Ethnic Monitoring. The Processing of Racial and Ethnic Data in Anti-Discrimination Policies* (with O. De Schutter, 2010) and *La protection des minorités par la Convention européenne des droits de l'homme* (2006).

EDUARDO J. RUIZ VIEYTEZ is Director of the Human Rights Institute of the University of Deusto (Bilbao, Basque Country, Spain) and associate professor of constitutional law at the same university. He has been a legal adviser to the Basque Ombudsman and member of the Spanish Official Council for Integration of Immigrants. His activities and publications are related to immigration policies and the rights of national, religious or linguistic minorities.

JULIE RYNGAERT is a PhD researcher at the Law and Development Research Group, University of Antwerp Law Research School. She studies the interaction between children's rights and human rights, with a particular emphasis on migration.

SIA SPILIOPOULOU ÅKERMARK, JUR. DR., is an associate professor in international law (Uppsala, Sweden) and Director of the Åland Islands Peace Institute (Finland). Her research focuses on minorities, autonomies, treaty law, use of force, and development issues. Among her latest major works are the edited volumes, *International Obligations and National Debates: Minorities around the Baltic Sea* (2006) and *The Åland Example and Its Components – Relevance for International Conflict Resolution* (2011).

ALEXANDRA TIMMER is a PhD candidate at the Human Rights Centre of Ghent University. Her research explores issues of equality and discrimination in the case law of the ECHR, with a specific focus on the concepts of stereotyping and vulnerability. She studied both history and law at Leiden University, and obtained an LLM from Columbia Law School.

YOFI TIROSH is a member of the Tel Aviv University Faculty of Law. Her research focuses on anti-discrimination law and on cultural legal analysis, with a particular emphasis on body, gender, language and identity. She teaches labour and employment law, jurisprudence, anti-discrimination law and food law.

RENATA UITZ is professor and chair of the comparative constitutional law program at the Legal Studies Department of Central European University, Budapest. She works on the protection of individual autonomy as a human right, in contexts ranging from religious liberty to sexual autonomy.

WOUTER VANDENHOLE teaches human rights and holds the UNICEF Chair in Children's Rights at the Faculty of Law of the University of Antwerp, where he co-directs the Law and Development research group. He is the chair of the Research Networking Programme GLOTHRO: *Beyond Territoriality: Globalisation and Transnational Human Rights Obligations*.

LISA WADDINGTON holds the European Disability Forum Chair in European Disability Law at Maastricht University, the Netherlands. She is the joint editor of the *European Yearbook of Disability Law*. Professor Waddington is a coordinator of the European Network of Legal Experts in the Non-Discrimination Field and a member of the Core Research Team of the Academic Network of European Disability experts (ANED).

FOREWORD

I am pleased to welcome an original, audacious and courageous initiative. Under the capable and dynamic leadership of Professor Eva Brems – undoubtedly one of the most brilliant academics of her generation in the human rights field – a group of international researchers have tackled the 'magic mountain' of the case law of the European Court of Human Rights. But they have not just done so any old how, and that is precisely why this publication is of such interest.

First of all, they have chosen an *angle* which is especially important and sensitive but which, it has to be acknowledged, is very often – indeed all too often – neglected, namely, the particular situation of non-dominant groups: children, gender, religious, sexual and cultural minorities, and disability. While we all recognise that the question of minorities is at the heart of a democratic society, are the experience and perspectives of these groups clearly visible in the case law of the European Court of Human Rights? How, in the judgments selected, have their specific concerns been taken into account in our reasoning, if at all? The vigilance and sensitivity of the various contributors are particularly acute since they are all experts, in their respective fields, on the matter under discussion, both nationally and at a European and international level. They also have a shared concern: the emancipation of non-dominant groups through a change in culture.

Next, the researchers have invented a *new method*. Rather than sticking to the traditional method of external scientific analysis, they have chosen 'to put themselves in the Court's shoes'. Taking the no doubt legitimate view that the Court's case law could still be improved in its approach to different forms of diversity, the authors have had no hesitation in revisiting and rewriting the judgments subjected to their critical analysis. They have done so intelligently and humanely. Some might find the whole exercise ambitious, if not somewhat impertinent; I disagree entirely. The fundamental idea is the translation of academic, scholarly views into judicial language, an approach which is rarely encountered. Personally, I find it a helpful and necessary means of bridging the gap between theory and practice, between what we know and what we do. How can we clarify theory through practice and practice through theory? I am convinced that steps need to be taken on both sides to work progressively towards this goal.

As far as the judicial decision-makers are concerned, I think that they should be reminded of the famous quip that 'there is nothing more practical than a good theory'. Analyses and interpretations of the Court's judgments by academics, with the special tools and critical distance that are characteristic of their work, are of vital importance for judges. Because of the responsibility they assume, an attitude of openness on the judges' part is, in my view, essential and, moreover, they have everything to gain from it. As far as the researchers are concerned, it is a pity that, very often, they pay little attention to the practical use of their research. They have a tendency to look at matters out of context and only rarely offer alternative solutions to the situations they criticise.

These are precisely the traditional obstacles which the initiators of the project behind this publication boldly set out to address and overcome. In a further effort to break down the barriers between these two worlds, they also submitted their reflections and analyses to the scrutiny of the judges themselves at a seminar in Strasbourg in February 2011. Of course, certain 'rewritings' of judgments of the European Court of Human Rights may in turn attract criticism, not least from the judges. But that is not what matters here. The background to this publication, and the contributions it contains, pave the way for enhanced *mutual understanding* between judges and academics, for the greater benefit of human rights, our common heritage.

Françoise Tulkens
Vice-President of the European Court of Human Rights

ACKNOWLEDGMENTS

The trajectory from a 'wild idea' over an amazing conference to the present volume was made possible thanks to a number of people and institutions, who deserve a heartfelt thanks.

Thanks to the European Research Council, the Research Fund of Ghent University and the Flemish Fund for Scientific Research, we have a great team at the Human Rights Centre of Ghent University working on the legal reasoning of the European Court of Human Rights. It is a privilege to work with such capable and dynamic young people. Together, we planned and realised the conference as well as the book. Alexandra, Laurens, Lourdes, Maris, Saïla and Stijn, thank you very much!

We are obliged also to the European Court of Human Rights, which hosted our conference. Special thanks are due to judge Françoise Tulkens, to her assistant Sylvie Ruffenach, and to Deputy Registrar Michael O'Boyle.

We thank all contributors to this volume for taking up the challenge, and for bearing with the constraints of the format. And we thank the respondents at the conference, who, through their comments on first drafts, enriched the rewritten judgments and accompanying papers: Judges Egbert Myjer, Ann Power, Christos Rozakis and András Sajó, Aida Grgic, Professor Marie-Bénédicte Dembour, and NGO representatives Nuala Mole (AIRE Centre), Gauri Van Gulik (Human Rights Watch), Lucy Claridge (Minority Rights Group International), Helmut Graupner, and Constantin Cojocariu (Interights).

Academic work is not possible without excellent supporting staff. For this and other projects, I am much indebted to Anne Van Beversluys and in particular Martine Dewulf, who accompanied us to Strasbourg and finalised the manuscript.

Finally, we thank Nienke van Schaeverbeke at Cambridge University Press for her friendly, flexible and efficient professionalism.

GUIDE TO UNDERSTANDING THE
REWRITTEN JUDGMENTS

Each chapter of this volume consists of commentaries on a specific judgment of the European Court of Human Rights, followed by a rewritten version of that judgment. This deliberate choice of format comes with unique challenges at the level of presentation. To assist the reader in understanding the rewritten judgments, an explanation is given below of all style elements that have been used in the presentation of the rewritten judgments. To further improve the reading experience, we advise the reader to keep the original judgment close by when reading the rewritten judgments.

Plain text	Indicates passages of the original judgment that have been kept intact by the author.
Bold text	Indicates new passages, written by the author as part of the rewriting exercise.
[Paragraph deleted]	Indicates that a paragraph from the original judgment has been deleted, because the author disagrees with its content.
[Original paragraph deleted]	Indicates that a paragraph from the original judgment has been deleted, because the author disagrees with its content, and a new paragraph with the same numbering has been inserted in place of the original paragraph.
[Fragment deleted]	Indicates that a passage from the original judgment has been deleted, either because the author disagrees with its content or for purposes of coherence of the rewritten judgment (e.g. for grammatical reasons).
[References deleted]	Indicates that references to other cases as represented in the original judgment have been deleted by the author to ease the reading of the rewritten judgment.
. . .	Indicates that passages or paragraphs from the original judgment have not been reproduced in the rewritten judgment. The author agrees with these passages or paragraphs, but their reproduction is not necessary to understand the rewritten judgment.

ABBREVIATIONS

CEDAW	Convention on the Elimination of All Forms of Discrimination Against Women
CPA 2004	Civil Partnership Act 2004 (UK)
CPT	Committee for the Prevention of Torture (Council of Europe)
CRC	Convention on the Rights of the Child
CRPD	Convention on the Rights of Persons with Disabilities (UN)
DR	Decisions and Reports of the European Commission of Human Rights
ECHR	European Court of Human Rights
ECJ	European Court of Justice
ECommHR	European Commission of Human Rights
EHRR	European Human Rights Reports
ETS	European Treaty Series
FCNM	Framework Convention for the Protection of National Minorities
GC	Grand Chamber
HPAT	Homosexual Policy Assessment Team (UK)
HRC	Human Rights Committee (UN)
ICCPR	International Covenant on Civil and Political Rights
ICD	International Classification of Diseases (UN)
LGB	lesbian, gay and bisexual
MHRT	Mental Health Review Tribunal (UK)
MoD	Ministry of Defence (UK)
RADAR	reciprocal anti-discrimination argument
UNHRC	Human Rights Committee (UN)
UNTS	United Nations Treaty Series

~

Introduction

EVA BREMS*

The contributors to this volume have rewritten a judgment or decision of the European Court of Human Rights, with a view to improving the way the Court addresses the specific concerns of members of non-dominant groups. Contributors were selected on the basis of their academic expertise on the rights of the particular group concerned, in addition to relevant diversity factors, including gender, academic seniority and the geographic location of their institution. They were invited to select a case and put themselves in the Court's shoes. In the accompanying papers, authors have outlined the theoretical concepts and frameworks that guided their approaches and have explained the amendments they made to the original text and how, in their opinion, each of these improves the reasoning.

While the initiators of this project worked on the assumption that there is room for improvement in the Court's approach to diversities, we have refrained from offering substantive guidelines to the contributors. Rather than promoting one way of doing justice for non-dominant groups, we want to explore how different approaches can be translated into judicial practice. The focus of the book is therefore on the translation of – sometimes diverging – academic views into judicial language.

First drafts of the papers were presented at the conference, 'Mainstreaming Diversity: Rewriting Judgments of the European Court of Human Rights', held at the European Court of Human Rights in Strasbourg on 3–4 February 2011. The event brought together academics from around the world, judges of the European Court of Human Rights, and practitioners from across Europe. Presentations were organised in six panels covering gender, disability, religion, culture, sexual orientation and children. In each panel, three legal scholars presented the rewritten passages of the selected judgments and decisions and two discussants – generally a practitioner and a judge of the European Court of Human Rights – reacted to the proposals giving crucial insights into their practical feasibility.

* The research for this paper was conducted within the framework of the ERC Starting Grant project 'Strengthening the European Court of Human Rights: More Accountability Through Better Legal Reasoning'.

The rewriting concept has been practised by top scholars in other jurisdictions such as Canada,[1] the United States[2] and the United Kingdom.[3] Compared to these other projects, the current book is wider in scope, covering six types of diversity. Moreover, while some judgments were selected because of their 'landmark' status, other judgments and decisions have been redrafted for different reasons, as set out by the authors of the redrafts.

With this rewriting concept, the book seeks to bridge the gap between academic analysis and judicial practice. This is not about academics telling judges that they can or must do better. It is not even certain whether this exercise can be labelled 'academic activism'.[4] If anything, it has been a humbling experience for the scholars involved. They were forced out of their comfort zones, and had to make the jump from theoretical analysis to technical solutions. Reading this book may provide an *Aha-Erlebnis* for both academics and judges. To academics, the book shows that the translation of ideas into judgments is fraught with complications, and that it may be worth spending some time on this issue, especially for those who wish their work to impact on judicial practice. At the same time, judges will find in this book numerous examples of what endorsing a theoretical analysis may look like in the text of a judgment.

Redrafting eighteen judgments/decisions

This volume presents eighteen redrafted judgments/decisions. Among them are ten Chamber judgments, four Grand Chamber judgments and four decisions in which the Court finds the applicant's complaint inadmissible. The eighteen judgments/decisions are listed and categorised in Table 1.

With respect to two of the four inadmissibility decisions (*Phull* and *De La Cierva Osorio*), the redraft finds a violation of the Convention, resulting in the conversion of the decision into a judgment on the merits.

The large majority of the redrafts concern judgments/decisions that are less than a decade old. None is older than two decades. Some authors have deliberately selected a somewhat older landmark judgment, with a view to updating it in light of developments that have occurred in the Court's case law, and/or in the broader legal environment, in society or science. While a historical approach, working with the sources available at the time of the original

---

[1] The Women's Court of Canada, 'Rewriting Equality', available at www.womenscourt.ca.
[2] Jack Balkin (ed.), *What Brown v. Board of Education Should Have Said: The Nation's Top Legal Experts Rewrite America's Landmark Civil Rights Decision* (New York University Press, 2002); Jack Balkin (ed.), *What Roe v. Wade Should Have Said: The Nation's Top Legal Experts Rewrite America's Most Controversial Decision* (New York University Press, 2005).
[3] Rosemary Hunter, Clare McGlynn and Erika Rackley (eds.), *Feminist Judgments, From Theory to Practice* (Oxford and Portland, OR: Hart Publishing, 2010).
[4] *Ibid.*, p. 8.

Table 1 *Typology of redrafted judgments/decisions*

Case name	Chapter
Chamber judgment	
A, B and C v. Ireland	4
Herczegfalvy v. Austria	14
Kemal Taşkın	18
and others v. Turkey	
Kolanis v. United Kingdom	15
Konstantin Markin v. Russia	6
Lustig-Prean and Beckett	12
v. United Kingdom	
Muñoz Díaz v. Spain	16
Muskhadzhiyeva and others	3
v. Belgium	
Schalk and Kopf v. Austria	10
V v. United Kingdom	1
Grand Chamber judgment	
Burden v. United Kingdom	11
Chapman v. United Kingdom	17
DH and others v. Czech	2
Republic	
Leyla Şahin v. Turkey	8
Inadmissibility decision	
De La Cierva Osorio De	5
Moscoso v. Spain	
Deschomets v. France	7
Sentges v. Netherlands	13
Suku Phull v. France	9

judgment,[5] has its own value, several authors have preferred a redraft from today's perspective.[6] Table 2 sets out the chronology of the eighteen judgments/decisions.

Doing justice for non-dominant groups is not only a matter of outcomes, it concerns first and foremost ways of reasoning that take into account minority experiences and worldviews. About half of the redrafts in this volume change the outcome of the case – invariably in the sense of finding a violation where the

---

[5] See Michael Kavey, in Chapter 12, p. 317, below.
[6] See Pierre Bosset, in Chapter 8, p. 196, below; Ursula Kilkelly, in Chapter 1, p. 95, below; and Julie Ringelheim, in Chapter 17, below.

Table 2 *Chronology of redrafted judgments/decisions*

	2010	2009	2008	2007	2006	2005	2003	2001	1999	1992
A, B and C	X									
Burden			X							
Chapman								X		
De La Cierva Osorio De Moscoso									X	
Deschomets					X					
DH				X						
Herczegfalvy										X
Kemal Taşkın	X									
Kolanis						X				
Konstantin Markin	X									
Leyla Şahin						X				
Lustig-Prean and Beckett									X	
Muñoz Díaz		X								
Muskhadzhiyeva	X									
Schalk and Kopf							X			
Sentges	X									
Suku Phull						X				
V									X	

Court found none. Six authors selected a judgment in which the Court had found in favour of the applicant. Keeping this outcome unaltered, the redrafts improve the Court's reasoning, and in several cases find additional violations on top of those found by the Court. In three cases, the redrafters agree with the finding that there is no violation – two of those even agree with the finding of inadmissibility – yet they change the reasoning in a way that, to their mind, reflects a better integration of diversity concerns. Table 3 sets out the results of the redrafted judgments/decisions.

There is an interesting range of diversity among the redrafts in this volume. Interventions vary from the changing of a single word[7] to the near-total replacement of the Court's reasoning on the merits.[8]

Some authors have explicitly attempted to keep the redraft as realistic as possible, so that it 'appears like it could have been written by the European

---

[7] See Lisa Waddington, in Chapter 13, below.   [8] See Holning Lau, in Chapter 10, below.

Table 3 *Outcome of original judgments/decisions and redrafts*

	Non-violation becomes violation	Violation stays violation	Non-violation stays non-violation
A, B and C	X		
Burden	X		
Chapman	X		
De La Cierva Osorio De Moscoso	X		
Deschomets			X
DH		X	
Herczegfalvy	X		
Kemal Taşkın	X		
Konstantin Markin		X	
Leyla Şahin	X		
Lustig-Prean and Beckett		X	
Muñoz Díaz		X	
Muskhadzhiyeva		X	
Schalk and Kopf	X		
Sentges			X
Suku Phull			X
V		X	

Court of Human Rights',[9] and/or that the changes do not go further than the author anticipates the Court might be willing to go along with.[10] In that sense, several authors have strategically built their proposals for change on existing lines of reasoning in the Court's case law.[11] Authors generally have provided 'appropriate grounding in (and citations to) Convention jurisprudence',[12] selecting references that support their argument, or distinguishing cases whenever appropriate. The separate (concurring or dissenting) opinions attached to

[9] Alexandra Timmer, in Chapter 6, p. 166, below.
[10] Holning Lau, in Chapter 10, pp. 257–8, below; and Eduardo J. Ruiz Vieytez, in Chapter 16, p. 408, below.
[11] E.g. Lourdes Peroni, in Chapter 18, pp. 458–9, below (dimensions of a substantive notion of equality); Patricia Londono, in Chapter 4, p. 96, below (developing positive obligations); Renata Uitz, in Chapter 7, p. 180, below (general intention); Holning Lau, in Chapter 10, p. 247, below (general intention); Pierre Bosset, in Chapter 8, p. 199, below ('practical and effective') and p. 206, below (self-determination); and Michael Kavey, in Chapter 12, p. 311, below (multi-faceted character of private law).
[12] Michael Kavey, in Chapter 12, p. 314, below.

some of the original judgments have proven to be a source of inspiration for several redrafts.[13] Yet some authors have not hesitated to propose drastic changes based on innovative reasoning, such as the creation of a new (sub-) right[14] or the adoption of a new approach to relations and family life.[15]

Some authors have made up additional factual information, when that was not available, yet felt to be needed for the new line of argument.[16] Others have refrained from doing so, preferring to work within the limits of the available information.[17] Similarly, some authors have chosen to raise issues and bring up arguments that were not brought forward by the applicants in the case.[18] This reveals that, to the extent that a redraft can be seen as a criticism of the original judgment, such criticism is not *per se* addressed to the Court alone. A judgment is the result of an interplay between the judges, the applicant, the defendant, their representatives, and all other intervening parties – such as other States and NGOs intervening as third parties. If an issue that is crucial to the case was not raised during the proceedings, this is in the first place the responsibility of the applicants and their representatives.[19] Conversely, some objectionable aspects of the Court's reasoning may be traced to the applicants themselves.[20]

In the course of redrafting judgments and decisions, the contributors to this volume have made numerous improvements that are specifically tailored to diversity and minority issues, as well as others that are more generally aimed at improving the Court's reasoning. In what follows, the two types of interventions will be presented separately.

Improving judicial reasoning

In most cases, the redrafts are animated not only by a desire to do (better) justice for minorities, but also by broader ambitions, for example for judgments that are 'intellectually satisfying',[21] or for the development by the Court of human rights norms that provide guidance to the Contracting States and beyond.

---

[13] Patricia Londono, in Chapter 4, below; Sia Spiliopoulou Åkermark, in Chapter 2, pp. 53–4, below; Julie Ringelheim, in Chapter 17, p. 434, below; and Pierre Bosset, in Chapter 8, p. 200, below. In one case, a parallel case had been brought before the Human Rights Committee of the United Nations, and the redraft was inspired by the dissenting opinion attached to the views of the Committee: Yofi Tirosh, in Chapter 5, below.

[14] Maris Burbergs, in Chapter 15, below.

[15] Aeyal Gross, in Chapter 11, pp. 288–9, below.

[16] Sia Spiliopoulou Åkermark, in Chapter 2, p. 51, below (information on views and experience of each individual applicant).

[17] Peter Bartlett, in Chapter 14, p. 353, below.

[18] E.g. Lourdes Peroni, in Chapter 18, pp. 459–60, below; Maris Burbergs, in Chapter 15, pp. 382–3, below; Eduardo J. Ruiz Vieytez, in Chapter 16, p. 408, below.

[19] See Sia Spiliopoulou Åkermark, in Chapter 2, p. 55, below.

[20] Michael Kavey, in Chapter 12, p. 294, below.

[21] Pierre Bosset, in Chapter 8, p. 200, below.

Several authors have shifted emphases in their redrafts compared to the original texts, so as to *better reflect the applicant's perspective.* They express the wish to focus on the real, fundamental issues, pertaining to the harm as it is experienced by the individuals concerned. They claim that the Court either failed to identify some core human rights issues or identified them inadequately.[22] This may be blamed on a reliance on analytical schemes that do not grasp what parties are trying to convey,[23] and in that case may be remedied through the improvement of such schemes. A variant of this is the opinion that the Court's labelling of the harm as pertaining to a particular Convention provision does not send the right message – the answer to this is requalification of the issue under a different provision.[24] A related claim wants the Court to take certain types of harm more seriously, by bringing something within the scope of a Convention right that in the eyes of the Court was too light or not sufficiently linked to that right.[25] A lighter intervention in cases where an interference is found is one that dwells in more detail on that interference, painting a richer picture of the harm in all its aspects.[26] Under Article 3, specifying whether the treatment is 'inhuman', 'degrading' or 'torture', rather than leaving this open, may do more justice to the applicant's suffering and add moral force to the judgment.[27]

From a different – yet complementary – angle, several authors propose that the Court broaden its perspective *beyond the applicants' case.* They may wish the Court to acknowledge a systemic problem underlying the violation in the individual case and to suggest general measures that would bring legislation and administrative practice into conformity with the Convention.[28] Or they may want the Court to choose wording that broadens the impact of the judgment, addressing other scenarios than the one before the Court or issuing clear general statements that allow for a better assessment of the relevance of the judgment for similar yet not identical cases.[29]

In most cases, the core of the Court's reasoning consists of a *proportionality analysis.* Most contributors make suggestions that apply to this part of the judicial analysis. In particular, some authors take issue with the use of the margin of appreciation. When the Court leaves a wide margin of appreciation to the

[22] Lourdes Peroni, in Chapter 18, pp. 451–3, below; Peter Bartlett, in Chapter 14, p. 364, below; Ursula Kilkelly, in Chapter 1, p. 24, below.
[23] Lourdes Peroni, in Chapter 18, pp. 451–2, below.
[24] Michael Kavey, in Chapter 12, p. 310, below.   [25] Yofi Tirosh, in Chapter 5, below.
[26] Michael Kavey, in Chapter 12, pp. 315–16, below.
[27] Wouter Vandenhole and Julie Ryngaert, in Chapter 3, p. 79, below.
[28] Julie Ringelheim, in Chapter 17, p. 438, below; Alexandra Timmer, in Chapter 6, p. 158, below.
[29] Wouter Vandenhole and Julie Ryngaert, in Chapter 3, p. 77, below; Patricia Londono, in Chapter 4, p. 108, below; and Eduardo J. Ruiz Vieytez, in Chapter 16, pp. 416–17, below.

Member States, it exercises only light scrutiny. Authors may disagree with this, claiming that the Court should play a more active role in norm-setting, exercising more leadership.[30] Several authors have more specific criticisms with respect to margin-of-appreciation analysis. For example, Bosset emphasises correct interpretation of the consensus among the Member States[31] – which is an important line in the Court's reasoning: if an infringement is widely practised throughout Europe, the Court is less likely to find it violates human rights, and *vice versa*. Londono argues against conflating the margin of appreciation with respect to the beginning of life, with the margin of appreciation in balancing conflicting rights.[32] And Lau develops a different approach to the margin of appreciation, where the room for flexibility shifts from whether, to how and when.[33]

Nearly the opposite of a wide margin of appreciation, is a 'less restrictive alternative' test, obliging States to choose among several options the one that least restricts Convention rights. Several authors promote a version of this test. Ouald Chaib[34] uses a procedural interpretation – the obligation to examine whether less restrictive alternatives are available – coupled with a shift of the burden of proof. Bosset promotes 'a general obligation to design public policy so as to mitigate its impact on fundamental rights'.[35] And Vandenhole and Ryngaert include the less restrictive alternative test in their redraft in a context of positive obligations.[36] Other proposals aimed at correct proportionality reasoning concern 'asking the right necessity question':[37] the question is not whether the legitimate aim of the interference is necessary, but whether the interference is necessary for the aim – and avoiding analysis at an overly abstract level.[38]

A majority of contributors include in their redraft *references to other international human rights standards*, beyond the Convention, and/or to the output of other international human rights bodies. This is a technique that is particularly suited for the integration of minority concerns, in those cases where specific texts exist that target this particular group, 'for the latter can be assumed to accommodate more and better the specificities of that particular group'.[39] Yet the integration of the Convention within the broader world of human rights law is an issue that goes beyond diversity concerns. This is about ensuring harmony within international human rights law[40] – indeed, it should be avoided that the

---

[30] Holning Lau, in Chapter 10, pp. 244–5, below.
[31] Pierre Bosset, in Chapter 8, pp. 109–200, below.
[32] Patricia Londono, in Chapter 4, p. 112, below.
[33] Holning Lau, in Chapter 10, pp. 255–6, below.
[34] Saïla Ouald Chaib, in Chapter 9, pp. 234–5, below.
[35] Pierre Bosset, in Chapter 8, p. 202, below.
[36] Wouter Vandenhole and Julie Ryngaert, in Chapter 3, p. 82, below.
[37] Saïla Ouald Chaib, in Chapter 9, p. 231, below.
[38] Pierre Bosset, in Chapter 8, pp. 198–9, below.
[39] Wouter Vandenhole and Julie Ryngaert, in Chapter 3, p. 83, below.
[40] Pierre Bosset, in Chapter 8, p. 197, below.

proliferation of norms and supervising bodies leads to conflicting guidelines for States and individuals.[41] Moreover, cross-referencing may serve to emphasise the indivisibility of human rights.[42] References in the redrafts include the Convention on the Elimination of All Forms of Discrimination Against Women (CEDAW), and related general recommendations,[43] the United Nations Convention on the Rights of Persons with Disabilities,[44] the Convention on the Rights of the Child (CRC) and related general recommendations,[45] general comments of the Committee on Economic, Social and Cultural Rights,[46] general comments and case law of the Human Rights Committee,[47] concluding observations of the CRC Committee[48] and the CEDAW Committee,[49] case law of the Inter-American Court of Human Rights,[50] the Charter of Fundamental Rights of the European Union,[51] the work of the Advisory Committee on the Framework Convention for the Protection of National Minorities,[52] the work of the European Committee of Social Rights,[53] the Standards of the Committee for the Prevention of Torture,[54] and soft law standards of the United Nations[55] and the Council of Europe.[56]

In some cases, these references constitute supportive arguments that strengthen a line of reasoning, yet, in others, they have implications for the outcome of the case.[57] One way in which the outcome may be affected, is through the 'consensus argument': the fact that the large majority of States Parties ratified a specific treaty can be seen as evidence of a consensus with respect to that treaty's approach, and hence should restrict the States' margin of appreciation.[58]

---

[41] Peter Bartlett, in Chapter 14, pp. 358–9, below.

[42] Pierre Bosset, in Chapter 8, p. 215, below.

[43] Alexandra Timmer, in Chapter 6, pp. 166 and 168, below.

[44] Maris Burbergs, in Chapter 15, below; and Peter Bartlett, in Chapter 14, below.

[45] Wouter Vandenhole and Julie Ryngaert, in Chapter 3, below.

[46] Pierre Bosset, in Chapter 8, p. 196, below.

[47] Pierre Bosset, in Chapter 8, pp. 192 and 208, below.

[48] Ursula Kilkelly, in Chapter 1, p. 39, below.

[49] Pierre Bosset, in Chapter 8, p. 203, below.

[50] Alexandra Timmer, in Chapter 6, pp. 167 and 168, below.

[51] Maris Burbergs, in Chapter 15, p. 391, below.

[52] Julie Ringelheim, in Chapter 17, p. 427, below.

[53] Julie Ringelheim, in Chapter 17, p. 435, below.

[54] Peter Bartlett, in Chapter 14, below; and Wouter Vandenhole and Julie Ryngaert, in Chapter 3, below.

[55] Maris Burbergs, in Chapter 15, p. 382, below; and Pierre Bosset, in Chapter 8, p. 208, below.

[56] Maris Burbergs, in Chapter 15, p. 391, below; Julie Ringelheim, in Chapter 17, p. 436, below; Peter Bartlett, in Chapter 14, p. 365, below; and Ursula Kilkelly, in Chapter 1, p. 39, below.

[57] This is the case in Julie Ringelheim, in Chapter 17, below; Peter Bartlett, in Chapter 14, below; and Pierre Bosset, in Chapter 8, p. 196, below.

[58] Julie Ringelheim, in Chapter 17, pp. 434–5, below.

Against this tendency, however, Spiliopoulou Åkermark points out that broad references to international standards risk depersonalising a case – whereas, in her approach, personalising the case is crucial.[59]

A number of concerns addressed in the redrafts concern *procedural justice*. Ouald Chaib places procedural justice at the centre of her paper. Based on social psychology research, she checks the original decision against four procedural justice criteria: representation, neutrality, respect and trustworthiness.[60] Several other authors discuss related issues. Bosset takes a critical look at the process of 'dialogue' that had preceded the measure allegedly violating Convention rights.[61] Kilkelly wants to promote the clarity and coherence of the judgment.[62] And Uitz argues that detailed guidance from the Court is needed to improve the perception of impartiality and neutrality in domestic court decisions.[63] In fact, several authors expect more detailed guidance from the Court on specific issues, such as clarifying the threshold for establishing an interference in a particular field[64] or creating substantive criteria for interpreting a concept (*in casu* 'therapeutic necessity').[65]

Additionally, some amendments simply want to strengthen the Court's reasoning, by adding more and better arguments,[66] adding references to recent research,[67] and avoiding circular argumentation.[68]

Dealing with diversity

The focus of this volume is on approaches to diversity in human rights cases. Hence, most of the interventions in the redrafts aim at improving justice for non-dominant groups: women, children, ethnic or religious minority members, persons with disabilities, and lesbian, gay and bisexual (LGB) individuals. These groups were chosen by the initiators of the project, yet, in many cases, judicial tools that are suited for one type of diversity may be applied equally to other types. The conference preceding this volume had 'mainstreaming diversity' in its title. The term 'mainstreaming' refers to the integration of specific attention for the concerns of minority or non-dominant groups in a general human-rights-protection mech-anism – as opposed to a mechanism that is specifically tailored to that group. However, within the 'general' European Convention on Human Rights, some provisions target specific groups. Article 9, on religious freedom, is the obvious

---

[59] Sia Spiliopoulou Åkermark, in Chapter 2, pp. 42 and 58, below.
[60] Saïla Ouald Chaib, in Chapter 9, below.   [61] Pierre Bosset, in Chapter 8, p. 203, below.
[62] Ursula Kilkelly, in Chapter 1, p. 24, below.
[63] Renata Uitz, in Chapter 7, pp. 178 and 188, below.
[64] Lisa Waddington, in Chapter 13, pp. 330–1, below.
[65] Peter Bartlett, in Chapter 14, p. 365, below.
[66] Wouter Vandenhole and Julie Ryngaert, in Chapter 3, pp. 69 and 73, below.
[67] Ursula Kilkelly, in Chapter 1, p. 37, below.   [68] Aeyal Gross, in Chapter 11, p. 278, below.

recourse for religious minorities;[69] while under Article 8, a right of members of cultural minorities to live according to their cultural tradition has been identified,[70] and a right of disabled people to community living may be found.[71] Moreover, the anti-discrimination provisions of Article 14 and Protocol 12 offer protection against both direct and indirect discrimination on all the grounds that are relevant to the groups considered here, and more. In a more narrow sense of the term, relying on minority-targeted Convention provisions concerning special rights or anti-discrimination is not quite 'mainstreaming' of minority concerns. In that sense, mainstreaming diversity takes place when minority perspectives are integrated within the interpretation and application of Convention provisions that do not as such have a minority focus. The mainstreaming argument is, then, that, whenever a case concerns minority members, the Court should integrate the relevant specific minority concerns, experiences and perspectives in its reasoning. This may include also scientific insights with respect to the group concerned.[72]

The crucial issue for several contributors is therefore to make the Court recognise the minority concerns that are at stake in a case, which in the original judgment may have been overlooked. This should go beyond a formal acknowledgment, as it should affect the Court's perception of the harm that was done to the applicant.[73] This may imply carefully scrutinising States' purposes in search of 'assimilationist bias' and unveiling illegitimate attempts to suppress cultural distinctiveness,[74] as well as exposing possible discriminatory implications of *prima facie* neutral measures on account of this distinctiveness.[75] For several authors, it is essential to bring context into the Court's reasoning: information on the historical context of injustice and marginalisation suffered by the group concerned, and on the systemic nature of the problem brought before the Court.[76] Both types of information bring in the group dimension: the individual case represents harm done to many people belonging to the same non-dominant group. Contributors have introduced in the judgment contextual elements coming from applicants' submissions, from reports by international organisations and from literature.[77]

---

[69] See Chapter 8 below on *Leyla Şahin* and Chapter 9 below on *Suku Phull*.

[70] See Chapter 17 below on *Chapman*.   [71] See Chapter 15 below on *Kolanis*.

[72] Maris Burbergs, in Chapter 15, below; and Wouter Vandenhole and Julie Ryngaert, in Chapter 3, p. 69, below.

[73] Cf. Lourdes Peroni, in Chapter 18, pp. 445, 446 and 448–9, below; Julie Ringelheim, in Chapter 17, pp. 432–3, below; and Eduardo J. Ruiz Vieytez, in Chapter 16, pp. 401–2, below.

[74] Lourdes Peroni, in Chapter 18, pp. 446 and 453–4, below. Peroni borrows the expression 'assimilationist bias' from Kenji Yoshino: K. Yoshino, 'Assimilationist Bias in Equal Protection: The Visibility Presumption and the Case of "Don't Ask, Don't Tell"' (1998–9) 108 *Yale Law Journal* 485.

[75] Lourdes Peroni, in Chapter 18, pp. 446 and 453–4, below.

[76] Julie Ringelheim, in Chapter 17, pp. 432–3, below; Lourdes Peroni, in Chapter 18, below; Alexandra Timmer, in Chapter 6, below; and Eduardo J. Ruiz Vieytez, in Chapter 16, p. 414, below.

[77] Lourdes Peroni, in Chapter 18, pp. 455–7, below; Alexandra Timmer, in Chapter 6, below.

They emphasise moreover that, in light of the historical context, seemingly trivial issues of mainly symbolic value (such as titles or the spelling of names) should be recognised as valuable for minorities; as they 'have been traditionally excluded from representation in the symbolic order'.[78] Peroni, discussing ethnic minority rights, proposes a procedure for the mobilisation of group-related contextual information: '(1) take into account the broader context of disadvantage [of the minority in the state concerned]; (2) explore the links between their historical disadvantage and their present vulnerability; and (3) underscore the particularly harmful effects the disputed restriction may have on the applicants given their vulnerable status.'[79] Next, she wants this analysis to be given considerable weight in the proportionality analysis.

Emphasising vulnerability of non-dominant groups as the core factor arising from past and present contexts is, however, not without risk. Vandenhole and Ryngaert[80] – writing about children's rights – point out that a one-sided emphasis on vulnerability is reductionist where it coincides with stereotypes concerning that group. In order to avoid this reductionist effect which risks denying agency to the group's members, they prefer to use the term 'contextual vulnerability'.

At a general level, Ouald Chaib inserts the need to accommodate minorities as a new principle in the Court's case law.[81] More concretely, several authors state that the interpretation of human rights in light of minority status creates new positive obligations for the State.[82] Others adapt the Court's reasoning, for example by proposing a strict proportionality test in some cases,[83] or joint reading of several Convention provisions.[84] Taking minorities seriously more-over means that the Court should avoid defining culture, religion or other shared characteristics from the outside.[85]

Moreover, emphasising difference is not the only way of doing minority justice. In some situations, the challenge may be defined as undoing a perception of difference, and emphasising sameness instead. In that sense, Kavey rejects any perception of special protection based on LGB people's supposedly

---

[78] Yofi Tirosh, in Chapter 5, p. 124, below; cf. Lourdes Peroni, in Chapter 18, p. 452, below.

[79] Lourdes Peroni, in Chapter 18, p. 456, below.

[80] Wouter Vandenhole and Julie Ryngaert, in Chapter 3, p. 70, below.

[81] Saïla Ouald Chaib, in Chapter 9, p. 229, below.

[82] Eduoardo J. Ruiz Vieytez, in Chapter 16, p. 414, below; cf. also Patricia Londono, in Chapter 4, below.

[83] Wouter Vandenhole and Julie Ryngaert, in Chapter 3, p. 81, below (strict proportionality test under Article 5 when children are concerned) and p. 82, below (introduction of a family perspective into the evaluation of the detention of the mother, leading to a strict necessity test).

[84] Renata Uitz, in Chapter 7, pp. 174, 187 and 188, below, bridging the gap between Articles 8 and 9 by inserting a concept of personal autonomy with religious connotation in the analysis of Articles 8 and 14.

[85] Saïla Ouald Chaib, in Chapter 9, p. 230, below (subjective approach to religious practice).

unique needs[86] – for him, a non-discrimination approach is key to challenging the 'transparency' of heterosexuality.[87] This applies to other diversities as well: majority culture is so deeply entrenched and pervading everyone's life on a near daily basis that we tend not to notice it. Changing this – cultural norms, people's attitudes and worldviews – is ultimately what the emancipation of non-dominant groups is about.

Such change does not happen overnight. As non-dominant groups emancipate, and some States Parties adapt their laws and policies accordingly, pressure builds on the Court to enforce similar change in the remaining States Parties. In practice, the Court takes up this role only at a late stage – when the large majority of States Parties have already turned – referring to the States' margin of appreciation before that time. Authors who want the Court to make this move at an earlier stage argue the existence of a strong consensus where the Court ignores or denies it (cf. above). Yet an alternative approach is possible, in which the Court guides incremental reform in the States Parties. Such an approach is proposed by Lau, who applies it to the case of gay marriage. He uses the consensus doctrine to determine the minimum pace of reform, and in his redraft grants the State Party a 'grace period'.[88]

Several redrafts add an increased emphasis on discrimination. This can be done by adding an Article 14 analysis where there was none in the original judgment,[89] or by using Article 14 as an interpretation aid to another provision.[90] Several authors promote specific approaches to non-discrimination or equality analysis. In particular, some take issue with formal conceptions of equality,[91] and promote instead substantive or transformative equality. With substantive equality, redrafters want to 'remove the detrimental consequences attached to differences rather than differences themselves',[92] and promote equal results on the ground.[93] It is recognised that the Court's case law contains a basis for substantive equality, in particular with *Thlimmenos*,[94] finding discrimination where States fail to treat differently persons whose situations are significantly different, without objective and reasonable justification.[95] Authors who aim for transformative equality want to address also the underlying norms and structures of discrimination;[96] an example is Gross' questioning of the concepts of marriage and family life.[97]

---

[86] Michael Kavey, in Chapter 12, p. 309, below.
[87] Michael Kavey, in Chapter 12, p. 308, below.   [88] Holning Lau, in Chapter 10, below.
[89] E.g. Michael Kavey, in Chapter 12, p. 309, below.
[90] E.g. Peter Bartlett, in Chapter 14, p. 368, below, with respect to Article 3.
[91] E.g. Eduardo J. Ruiz Vieytez, in Chapter 16, p. 401, below.
[92] Lourdes Peroni, in Chapter 18, p. 459, below, quoting Sandra Fredman.
[93] Lourdes Peroni, in Chapter 18, p. 459, below; Aeyal Gross, in Chapter 11, p. 273, below.
[94] ECHR (GC), *Thlimmenos* v. *Greece*, 6 April 2000, para. 44.
[95] Julie Ringelheim, in Chapter 17, pp. 433–4, below; Lourdes Peroni, in Chapter 18, p. 459, below.
[96] Alexandra Timmer, in Chapter 6, p. 149, below.
[97] Aeyal Gross, in Chapter 11, pp. 281–2 and 288, below.

From a different angle, Tirosh addresses (and criticises) what she calls 'reciprocal anti-discrimination arguments'; these may be seen as an informal and light variant of the abuse clause: they dismiss an anti-discrimination claim when it concerns access to something that is in itself discriminatory. She points out that such arguments tend to unequally burden minorities.[98]

In a number of redrafts, the issue of discriminatory stereotypes is raised. Timmer addresses this in most detail, stressing firstly the importance of naming stereotypes and the harm they do, and suggesting furthermore that stereotypes should not be allowed to function as justifications for State conduct.[99] Other authors have redrafted passages in order to avoid the Court reproducing stereotypes in its judgment – in particular with respect to societal conditions of oppression that are presented as group characteristics. They have solved this either by changing the terminology,[100] or by alternative framing of the issues.

The conference that was the first step in this redrafting project was organised in six panels, representing six types of diversity. The present volume is similarly organised. One major drawback of this approach is the risk of downplaying intersectionality. Several authors, however, have incorporated this concern in their redrafts. Individuals who belong to several non-dominant groups may experience a focus on their membership of one group as a misrepresentation of their experience. In their lives, it may actually be the interaction between different grounds that leads to marginalisation.[101] Yet legal reasoning, with its penchant towards categorisation, does not easily accommodate these complex realities. In the words of Spiliopoulou Åkermark, 'in situations of multiple diversities, or intersectionality, the Court seems in recent years, to be giving precedence to racial or ethnic ascription over other aspects of diversity and vulnerability, such as gender or age. The particular needs of children or women are thus subsumed under what is perceived as the dominant understanding about a particular group or minority.'[102] This author deliberately selected a judgment that is famous as a minority (Roma) rights case for analysis from a different angle, i.e. children's rights. Highlighting intersectionality acts as a corrective for the emphasis on group characteristics by pointing back to intersections between groups, and possibly also to unique individual situations. Bosset links intersectionality to agency: his redraft wants to make the voices of the relevant individuals

---

[98] Yofi Tirosh, in Chapter 5, pp. 132 *et seq.*, below.

[99] Alexandra Timmer, in Chapter 6, pp. 156 and 160–2, below.

[100] Wouter Vandenhole and Julie Ryngaert, in Chapter 3, below; Michael Kavey, in Chapter 12, p. 303, below.

[101] Alexandra Timmer, in Chapter 6, pp. 162–3, below.

[102] Sia Spiliopoulou Åkermark, in Chapter 2, p. 59, below.

heard – resulting in language on the multi-layered meaning of the Islamic headscarf.[103] Moreover, he translates intersectionality into a finding of discrimination on multiple grounds, adding gender discrimination where the original judgment mentioned only discrimination on the ground of religion.[104] For Spiliopoulou Åkermark, the answer lies in taking into account the particularities of the experiences and capabilities of different applicants.[105]

The process of writing this book was enriching and rewarding for all involved. It is our sincere hope that the reader will have a similar experience.

---

[103] Pierre Bosset, in Chapter 8, pp. 204–6, below.
[104] Pierre Bosset, in Chapter 8, p. 207, below.
[105] Sia Spiliopoulou Åkermark, in Chapter 2, p. 54, below.

PART I

Children

Rewriting V v. United Kingdom: building on a ground-breaking standard

URSULA KILKELLY

Introduction

The judgment of the European Court of Human Rights (ECHR) in the case of *V* v. *United Kingdom*[1] concerned the trial of an eleven-year-old boy (with his co-accused, considered in *T* v. *United Kingdom*)[2] for the notorious murder of a two-year-old boy, James Bulger, in Liverpool, England, in 1993. The case made headlines around the world for various reasons: its shocking facts, the public outrage and anger that erupted around the murder and the trial, and the wave of punitive measures introduced as a response by the United Kingdom government.[3]

From the perspective of ECHR case law, the judgment, which found that the boys' trial was unfair and contrary to Article 6 of the Convention, was ground-breaking. Although it was not the first time the Court had addressed the application of Article 6 to children,[4] the judgment broke new ground in its development of the concept of 'effective participation' of children in criminal proceedings against them. Mirroring Article 12 of the Convention on the Rights of the Child, which guarantees the right of the child to be heard in matters that affect him/her, the judgment makes a unique contribution to our understanding of children's treatment by the criminal justice system. The judgment raised awareness about a range of issues in youth justice. In particular, *V* v. *United Kingdom* cast important light on the role of the media and publicity in the trial of children, and raised concern about the harm that can be caused by the trial of children in adult court. It stressed the need to ensure that children in the

[1] ECHR, *V* v. *United Kingdom*, 16 December 1999.
[2] *T* v. *United Kingdom*, 16 December 1999, was an almost identical judgment. Although the facts and other circumstances are largely similar, for the purposes of simplicity the focus is solely on the Court's judgment in *V* in this exercise.
[3] See Haydon and Scraton, '"Condemn a Little More, Understand a Little Less": The Political Context and Rights' Implications of the Domestic and European Rulings in the Venables–Thompson Case' (2000) 27(3) *Journal of Law and Society* 416–48.
[4] See *Nortier* v. *Netherlands*, concerning the trial of children in a youth court and its compliance with Article 6. *Nortier* v. *Netherlands*, judgment of 24 August 1993, Series A no. 267, 17 EHRR 273. See the more recent case of *Adamkiewicz* v. *Poland*, judgment of 2 March 2010.

criminal justice system are treated in a manner that takes full account of their age, maturity and intellectual and emotional capacities, and it linked this clearly to the child's right to understand and participate in proceedings against him/her. These issues have been developed in subsequent international instruments like the Council of Europe's Guidelines on Child-Friendly Justice, and the Strasbourg court's findings are echoed in recent criminology and neuroscience research.[5]

However, while the judgment is very strong on fundamental principles, it is not entirely clear as to what additional steps the UK authorities should have taken to avoid violating V's fair trial rights. In this way, the judgment can be criticised for not addressing head-on the compatibility with Article 6 of the trial of children in adult court, and it was not entirely definitive as to whether such proceedings need to be held in private and the identities of the accused kept confidential. It is these positive and negative aspects of the judgment that make it an excellent subject for this rewriting project.

The aim of this chapter is to reconsider the judgment of the Strasbourg Court in *V* v. *United Kingdom* in this context. It begins with an outline of the facts and a brief description of the Court's judgment before going on to evaluate the impact of the judgment, including on subsequent developments in international youth justice. It then points to recent research that reinforces the principles underpinning the Court's approach, and, finally, it considers how all of this evidence might be incorporated into the judgment so as to promote its clarity and coherence.

V v. United Kingdom: relevant facts

V was born in August 1982. On 12 February 1993, when he was just ten years old, he and another ten-year-old boy, T, played truant from school and abducted a two-year-old boy from a shopping mall. T and V took the little boy on a journey of over two miles before battering him to death, leaving him on a railway line to be run over. The boys were arrested shortly afterwards and charged with murder. They were detained pending their trial in the (adult) Crown Court in November 1993. They were eleven years old when they were tried before a judge and jury, and they were convicted of murder and abduction after a trial that lasted three weeks. They did not appeal their conviction.

In the months before the trial, each applicant was taken by social workers to visit the courtroom and was introduced to trial procedures and personnel 'by way of a "child witness pack" containing books and games'.[6] The trial was preceded by massive international publicity, and the boys' arrival in court every day was greeted by a 'hostile crowd' with occasional attempts being made to attack the vehicles which transported them. In the courtroom, 'the press

---

[5] These issues are discussed below.   [6] ECHR, *V* v. *United Kingdom*, para. 9.

benches and public gallery were full'.[7] Although the trial was conducted with all the formality of an adult court, certain modifications were made to the procedure to take into account the age of the accused. In particular, they were seated next to social workers in a specially raised dock with their parents and lawyers nearby. The hearing times were shortened to reflect the school day (10.30 am to 3.30 pm, with an hour's break for lunch), and a ten-minute interval was taken every hour. During adjournments, the defendants were allowed to spend time with their parents and social workers in a play area. The judge made it clear that he would adjourn whenever the social workers or defence lawyers told him that one of the defendants was showing signs of tiredness or stress. This occurred on one occasion.[8]

At the opening of the trial, the judge made an order that there should be no publication of the names, addresses or other identifying details, including photographs, of either defendant. On the same day, the judge rejected the application of counsel seeking a stay on the proceedings on the ground that the trial would be unfair due to the nature and extent of the media coverage. The judge found that it was not established that the defendants would suffer serious prejudice to the extent that no fair trial could be held.[9]

Following the conviction, the judge modified the order previously made to allow the boys' names to be published. The following day – 25 November 1993 – their names, photographs and other particulars were published in newspapers throughout the country. However, on 26 November 1993, the judge granted an injunction restraining, inter alia, the publication of the addresses where the boys were being detained or any other detail which could lead to information about their whereabouts, care or treatment being revealed.[10]

According to a medical assessment of V conducted by Dr Bentovim on behalf of the defence, V showed 'post-traumatic effects and extreme distress and guilt, with fears of punishment and terrible retribution'. V 'found it very difficult and distressing to think or talk about the events in question' and the doctor found that it was not possible to ascertain many aspects, identifying in V evidence of immaturity, as he behaved 'in many ways like a younger child emotionally'.[11]

V was interviewed again by Dr Bentovim in 1995, in relation to a judicial review of his sentence.[12] The doctor found that when the trial was mentioned V described his shock when he had seen the public being let into the courtroom, and his considerable distress when his name and photograph were published subsequently. He described being 'terrified of being looked at in court' and 'had frequently found himself worrying what people were thinking about him'. According to the Strasbourg Court's account, the doctor found that:

---

[7] *Ibid.*   [8] *Ibid.*   [9] *Ibid.*, para. 10.   [10] *Ibid.*, para. 16.   [11] *Ibid.*   [12] *Ibid.*, para. 17.

[m]ost of the time he had not been able to participate in the proceedings and had spent time counting in his head or making shapes with his shoes because he could not pay attention or process the whole proceedings. He did not follow when he heard his and T's interviews with the police being played in court and he recalled crying at that time.[13]

In 1997, Dr Bailey, who assessed V on behalf of the prosecution, considered that it took him twelve months to get over the trial and he still thought of it every night. He had been scared initially, but, after the first three days at the Crown Court, 'he had felt all right because he played with his hands and stopped listening'. He remembered the press 'laughing at him and he could tell from the faces of the jury that they would find him guilty. He still did not understand why the trial had been so long.'[14] Concern about the length of the trial was also expressed in a 1998 report by Sir Michael Rutter, Professor of Child Psychiatry at the Institute of Psychiatry, University of London.[15] Commenting on the likely mental and emotional effects on children in general, and on V in particular, of the prolonged trial process being in public, he observed two negative aspects: the first was the inevitable delay in providing the psychological care and therapeutic help that such a young accused needs. Accordingly, he submitted: 'the child cannot begin to come to terms with the reality of what he has done when a trial is still under way and guilt has still to be decided by the court.' Thus, 'the very prolonged nature of the trial process is bound to be deleterious for a child as young as ten or eleven (or even older)'.[16] The second concern related to the fact that the trial process was held in public, meaning that the negative public reactions (often extreme negative reactions) constituted a further potentially damaging factor. Rutter considered that, '[w]hile it is crucially important for young people who have committed a serious act to accept both the seriousness of what they have done and the reality of their own responsibilities in the crime, this is made more difficult by the public nature of the trial process'.[17]

It was clear from the medical evidence, therefore, that the nature of the trial process, notably the public nature of the proceedings, had a particularly damaging effect on V's capacity to follow and participate effectively in the proceedings against him. The extent to which this formed part of the Court's judgment is dealt with further below.

V v. United Kingdom: summary of the judgment

Before the European Court of Human Rights, the applicant made a number of complaints under Articles 3, 5 and 6 of the Convention.[18] The Article 3 claim

---

[13] *Ibid.*   [14] *Ibid.*, para. 18.   [15] *Ibid.*, para. 19.   [16] *Ibid.*, para. 19.   [17] *Ibid.*, para. 19.
[18] The applicants were successful in complaining under Article 5 (right to liberty) that the setting of the tariff (the set, punitive element of the indeterminate life sentence) by the Home Secretary was contrary to this provision.

concerning the question of whether the prosecution and trial of the applicant constituted inhuman and degrading treatment is clearly relevant and is addressed briefly below.[19] However, it is the Article 6 complaint – upheld by the Court – that is the principal focus of this critique.

Article 6 provides in relevant part as follows:

> In the determination of ... any criminal charge against him, everyone is entitled to a fair and public hearing within a reasonable time by an independent and impartial tribunal established by law. Judgment shall be pronounced publicly but the press and public may be excluded from all or part of the trial in the interests of morals, public order or national security in a democratic society, where the interests of juveniles or the protection of the private life of the parties so require, or to the extent strictly necessary in the opinion of the court in special circumstances where publicity would prejudice the interests of justice.

According to the applicant, his right to a fair trial was violated by the failure to ensure that he was able to participate effectively in the conduct of his case.[20] In particular, he referred to the evidence that he was no more emotionally mature than an eight- or nine-year-old, that he did not fully attend to or understand the proceedings and that he was too traumatised and intimidated to give his own account of events, either to his lawyers, the psychiatrist who interviewed him, or to the court.[21] The government submitted that the public trial was important and in the public interest given the serious nature of the charges, that the applicant had been represented by experienced lawyers and that efforts had been made to modify the formality and the intimidating nature of the proceedings in order to take his young age into account.[22]

The Court agreed with the view of the European Commission of Human Rights that, 'having regard to the applicant's age, the application of the full rigours of an adult, public trial deprived him of the opportunity to participate effectively in the determination of the criminal charges against him, in breach of Article 6 para. 1'.[23] In respect of a young child charged with a grave offence attracting high levels of media and public interest, the Court held that it was necessary to conduct the hearing in such a way as to reduce as far as possible his or her feelings of intimidation and inhibition. The Court concluded that this standard had not been met. In particular, the Court found fault with the failure to restrict public access and media reporting of the proceedings and it also noted that some of the measures taken to make the proceedings more child-appropriate (e.g. raising the dock so that V could see what was going on) had

---

[19] This was addressed in paras. 62–80 of the judgment. See below.
[20] In this respect, he relied on EHRR, *Stanford* v. *United Kingdom*, 23 February 1994, para. 26.
[21] ECHR, *V* v. *United Kingdom*, para. 82.   [22] *Ibid.*, para. 83.   [23] *Ibid.*, para. 84.

the effect of increasing rather than decreasing his anxiety. Taken together with the medical evidence relating to V's capacity to participate in the proceedings, the 'tense courtroom' and 'public scrutiny' to which V was subjected led the Court to conclude that there had been a violation of Article 6(1).

Having outlined the facts of the case and explained the judgment of the Court, this chapter will now proceed to a critical analysis of the Court's judgment. In particular, it will consider the impact of the judgment by considering subsequent developments in international youth justice. It will then revisit the judgment with a view to identifying how the Court's reasoning could be improved in order to maximise its coherence and clarity. In particular, although the judgment has significant merit in elucidating the concept of the child's 'effective participation' in his/her criminal trial, it is submitted that the Court missed the opportunity here both to comment directly on the compatibility with the Convention of the trial of the applicant in adult court and to address the inability of the applicant to challenge the decision to try him in an adult court.[24]

Subsequent developments: viewing the judgment in hindsight

In finding that V had been denied his right to a fair trial under Article 6 of the Convention, the judgment of the Strasbourg Court made an important contribution to the law on youth justice.[25] For example, even though several international instruments address youth justice, few, if any, consider the child's fair trial rights or how they can be secured in adult court.[26] Moreover, although the US Supreme Court had defended the child's due process rights in its seminal

---

[24] See C. Van Dijk, A. Nuytiens and C. Eliaerts, 'The Referral of Juvenile Offenders to the Adult Court in Belgium: Theory and Practice' (2005) 44(2) *Howard Journal of Criminal Justice* 125; J. Junger-Tas, 'Youth Justice in the Netherlands' (2004) 31 *Crime and Justice* 293; J. A. Arteaga, 'Juvenile (In)Justice: Congressional Attempts to Abrogate the Procedural Rights of Juvenile Defendants' (2002) 102(4) *Columbia Law Review* 1051–88; and S. Green, 'Prosecutorial Waiver into Adult Criminal Court: A Conflict of Interests Violation Amounting to the States' Legislative Abrogation of Juveniles' Due Process Rights' (2005) 110 *Penn State Law Review* 233.

[25] See U. Kilkelly, 'The Human Rights Act 1998: Implications for the Detention and Trial of Young People' (2000) 51(3) *Northern Ireland Legal Quarterly* 466.

[26] The Convention on the Rights of the Child and the Council of Europe Guidelines on Child-Friendly Justice are considered below. In addition, see, for example: the United Nations Standard Minimum Rules for the Administration of Juvenile Justice (the 'Beijing Rules') adopted by General Assembly Resolution 40/33, 29 November 1985; the United Nations Guidelines for the Prevention of Juvenile Delinquency (the 'Riyadh Guidelines') adopted by General Assembly Resolution 45/112, 14 December 1990; the United Nations Rules for the Protection of Juveniles Deprived of Their Liberty (the 'Havana Rules'), adopted by General Assembly Resolution 45/113, 14 December 1990; and Council of Europe Recommendation Rec(2008)11 of the Committee of Ministers of the Council of Europe on the European Rules for juvenile offenders subject to sanctions or measures,

judgment *In re Gault* in 1967,[27] the European Court's judgment in *V* was the first international pronouncement on this issue.

Reflecting on the Court's judgment in the *V* case, it is apparent that a number of subsequent developments – in the law and in research – have taken place that are relevant to this contemporary analysis of the Court's approach. These developments, which are examined below, support the principles underpinning the Court's ruling, while also suggesting that the Court might have gone further by finding fault not just with the failure to manage the public nature of V's trial but in ruling definitively both on V's trial in adult court and his inability to seek trial in a more specialised, child-friendly environment. The sections that follow deal with these three issues in this context: the first outlines research that proves that children are different from adults; the second considers legal developments on the protection of the child's identity; and the third details developments relating to the child-friendly court, including the requirement for specialised proceedings and the mechanism of transferring children to and from adult court.

The special circumstances of young offenders

The Court was clear in its judgment in *V* that additional measures must be taken to ensure that a child charged with a criminal offence enjoys his/her fair trial rights under the Convention.[28] In this regard, the Court showed awareness that children, by virtue of their vulnerability and their immaturity, face particular challenges when defending criminal charges. In recent years, scientific research has confirmed that there are differences between children and adults that are relevant to their treatment in the criminal justice process. Moreover, this has begun to be taken into account by the US Supreme Court in its review of the constitutionality of the treatment of young accused.[29] In addition, research in the field of criminology has clarified that children who commit violence are especially vulnerable. Given the relevance of this evidence to the offender's circumstances in *V*, reliance is placed on this research in the rewriting of the judgment in order to reinforce the Court's conclusion that children need additional protection and support in the enjoyment of their fair trial rights. An explanation of this research elaborates this point.

which was adopted on 5 November 2008. On the use of these standards, see U. Kilkelly, 'Youth Justice and Children's Rights: Measuring Compliance with International Standards' (2008) 8(3) *Youth Justice* 187–92; and T. Hammarberg, 'A Juvenile Justice Approach Built on Human Rights Principles' (2008) 8(3) *Youth Justice* 193–6.

[27] In *Re Gault*, 387 US 1 (1967). See further C. Manfredi, *The Supreme Court and Juvenile Justice* (Lawrence, KS: University Press of Kansas, 1998).

[28] See paras. 88 and 90.

[29] *Roper* v. *Simmons*, 543 US 551 (2005); *Graham* v. *Florida*, 560 US (2010); and, more recently, *JDB* v. *North Carolina*, US Supreme Court, 16 June 2011.

The Brain Science evidence first came to international prominence when it was submitted by the American Medical Association and others in their intervention as an *amicus curiae* in the US Supreme Court case of *Roper* v. *Simmons* in 2005.[30] What this evidence shows is that a juvenile's brain is anatomically different to that of an adult because the frontal lobe – the part of the brain responsible for reasoning, impulse control, considering consequences and good judgment – is not fully developed. This, the interveners argued, supported the case for less punitive punishment for juveniles who were, as a matter of scientific fact, less responsible and therefore less culpable than adults.[31] The weight of this evidence helped to persuade the US Supreme Court to find the eligibility of sixteen- and seventeen-year-olds for the death penalty to be contrary to the ban on cruel and unusual punishment under the US Constitution.[32] In 2010, the US Supreme Court extended this reasoning to the eligibility of children to the sentence of life without parole in non-homicide cases in *Graham* v. *Florida*,[33] making it clear that it accepts the diminished culpability of juveniles for their criminal acts. Furthermore, in its 2011 judgment in *JBD* v. *North Carolina*, the US Supreme Court held that the age of the accused must be taken into account by police officers when taking steps to protect the accused child's Miranda rights.[34] In short, therefore, evidence as to the difference between children and adults is now well established by science and its relevance to the treatment of children in the juvenile justice system is well accepted by one of the world's leading courts. Although it came much later than the Strasbourg Court's judgment in *V*, it nonetheless serves retrospectively to underpin the basis for the Strasbourg Court's conclusion that special measures are necessary to secure the right to a fair trial for young accused.

Research emanating from an entirely different source has highlighted the additional vulnerabilities experienced by children who commit violent crime. The Edinburgh Study of Youth Transition and Crime is a longitudinal study of

---

[30] *Roper* v. *Simmons*, 543 US 551 (2005). See the *amicus curiae* brief submitted by the American Psychological Association to the US Supreme Court in *Roper* v. *Simmons*. For a discussion of the implications of this science for juvenile justice, see E. Scott and L. Steinberg, 'Adolescent Development and the Regulation of Youth Crime' (2008) 18(2) *Future of Children* 15–34. See also A. Haider, 'Roper v. Simmons: The Role of the Brain Science Brief' (2005–6) 3 *Ohio State Journal of Criminal Law* 369. For a broader perspective, see T. A. Maroney, 'The False Promise of Adolescent Brain Science in Juvenile Justice' (2009) 85(1) *Notre Dame Law Review* 89–176.

[31] For a discussion on the issues of youth and culpability see I. Weijers, 'The Moral Dialogue: A Pedagogical Perspective on Juvenile Justice', in I. Weijers and A. Duff (eds.), *Punishing Juveniles: Principle and Critique* (Oxford: Hart Publishing, 2002), pp. 135–54.

[32] *Roper* v. *Simmons*, 543 US 551 (2005).   [33] *Graham* v. *Florida*, 560 US (2010).

[34] According to *Miranda*, the accused must be warned prior to questioning that he/she has the right to remain silent, that any statement he does make may be used as evidence against him, and that he has a right to the presence of an attorney, either retained or appointed. *Miranda* v. *Arizona*, 384 US 436, 444 (1966).

pathways into and out of offending for a cohort of 4,300 young people who began secondary school in Edinburgh in 1998. Analysis from the Study has found that those involved in violent offending were 'the most vulnerable and victimized young people in the cohort'.[35] While there were other relevant factors, the evidence shows that violence among those aged fifteen years is predicted by elements of 'sustained adversity over time'.[36] Moreover, this relationship between violence and vulnerability runs both ways, in that boys involved in violence at age fifteen were more than twice as likely as other boys to be self-harming.[37] The research notes also that many of the adversities faced by violent young people 'more often stem from close interactions in respect of peers, family and other adults in the young person's milieu and the mechanisms which they use to cope with the negative consequences of such interactions'.[38] The authors' conclusion on this evidence is to recommend a holistic approach to children in conflict with the law, one that focuses on the welfare needs of young people who offend, rather than prosecuting them through the criminal justice system.[39] It is clear that the applicant in *V* fell within the category of offenders that this research addresses. It is arguable, therefore, that it underpins attempts to ensure a child's fair trial by adopting special measures that take into account the child's particular needs and circumstances.

   In summary, then, it is submitted that this research provides important context to the judgment of the Court in *V* v. *United Kingdom* insofar as it explains why a child's right to a fair trial must be interpreted and applied differently to that of an adult. Adding a statement to this effect (see paragraph 86 below) usefully reinforces the Court's view that special measures are necessary to ensure that children receive a fair trial. More generally, it serves to underpin the judgment as a whole.

Publicity and the protection of the child's identity[40]

On V's conviction, as noted above, the trial judge agreed to permit the media to publish his details (along with that of his co-accused, T) although he later restricted the publication of any details of the boy's place of detention or treatment. The photographs taken in police custody and two other school photographs of the boys remain the only ones in the public domain. T and V were given new identities and, prior to their release in 2001, they sought and were granted a life-long injunction *contra mundum* against the media restraining them from publishing any information about their new identities, current location or the location or circumstances of their time in

---

[35] See L. McAra and S. McVie, 'Youth Crime and Justice: Key Messages from the Edinburgh Study of Youth Transitions and Crime' (2010) 10(2) *Criminology and Criminal Justice* 179–209, especially pp. 185–9.
[36] *Ibid.*, p. 187.   [37] *Ibid.*, p. 188.   [38] *Ibid.*   [39] *Ibid.*   [40] See paras. 85 and 88.

detention.[41] When the application for this extraordinary injunction came before Dame Butler Sloss in the High Court, she was heavily influenced by the obligations to protect the applicants' Convention rights especially under Article 2 (the right to life) in granting the application. According to the judge:

> From all the evidence provided to me, I have come to the clear conclusion that if the new identity of these claimants became public knowledge it would have disastrous consequences for the claimants, not only from intrusion and harassment but, far more important, the real possibility of serious physical harm and possible death from vengeful members of the public or from the Bulger family. If their new identities were discovered, I am satisfied that neither of them would have any chance of a normal life and that there is a real and strong possibility that their lives would be at risk.[42]

A number of newspapers were subsequently prosecuted for contempt of this order,[43] and, in 2010, the matter came to public attention again when V was arrested, prosecuted and convicted on charges of child pornography. This is relevant here because it shows the ongoing risk posed to V's privacy arising from the disclosure of these details at the time of trial. Media organisations sought permission to publish the new identity of V, with arguments based on the principles of open justice and risk to the public.[44] However, this was refused by Bean J in the High Court on the grounds that the relevant fact now in the public domain was that the man known as Jon Venables (V's real name) had been convicted of charges of child pornography.[45] He had been tried in public, thereby satisfying that principle, but, as he was not otherwise assessed to be a risk to the public, making his new identity public could not be justified on this ground. The second and related reason related to the continuing risk that he faced from the public. As Bean J articulated:

> One would have thought that with the passage of 17 years since the murder and 9 years since Lady Butler-Sloss' judgment the threat from members of the public would have diminished. But there is clear evidence that it has not.[46]

It is clear, therefore, that revealing V's identity had very serious consequences for him, such that he was offered a new identity on release and that an

---

[41] *Thompson and Venables* v. *News Group Newspapers* [2001] Fam 340.

[42] *Ibid.*, para. 94.

[43] See, for example, *Venables and Thompson* v. *News Group International and others* [2001] EWHC 53C (QB).

[44] *Venables and Thompson* v. *News Group Newspapers Ltd* [2010] EWHC B18 (QB).

[45] See para. 23.

[46] *Ibid.*, para. 11. Evidence adduced included statements from those mistaken to be Jon Venables suffering constant harassment and abuse including having to move homes multiple times. Paras. 11–12.

extraordinarily wide injunction had to be used to protect him from this being exposed by the media. It is arguable that the trial judge, when releasing the identities of V and his co-accused into the public domain, ought to have anticipated the harm that this would cause and the measures that would subsequently be necessary to minimise the risk of harm on their release. Perhaps surprisingly, the disclosure of V's identity to the public by the trial judge was not raised by V before the Strasbourg Court, possibly because the decision was reversed within a few days and the case of the injunction had not yet arisen.[47] However, it is arguable that the issue should have been included in the application – either under Article 6, which contains special protections in the interests of juveniles (see below), and/ or Article 8, which provides protection for the right to respect for private and family life – with a view to challenging the practice under the Convention of releasing the identity of a child defendant to the public. Consideration of this issue by the Strasbourg Court might have drawn on Article 40(2)(b)(vii) of the Convention on the Rights of the Child which provides that children have a right to have their privacy protected 'at all stages of the proceedings'. According to the Committee on the Rights of the Child, the Convention on the Rights of the Child requires that '[n]o information shall be published that may lead to the identification of a child offender because of its effect of stigmatization, and possible impact on his/her ability to have access to education, work, housing or to be safe'.[48] It also notes that public hearings should be permitted only in 'well-defined cases' 'stated by law', and exceptions must be explained by a written decision of the court and subject to appeal.[49]

Protecting the accused's right to privacy is inextricably linked to the need to ensure child-friendly criminal proceedings. In this regard, it is also relevant that the Council of Europe Guidelines on Child-Friendly Justice[50] (discussed below) consider that the privacy and personal data of children who are or have been involved in judicial or non-judicial proceedings should be protected in accordance with national law. This generally implies that no information or personal data may be made available or published, particularly in the media, which could reveal or indirectly enable the disclosure of the child's identity, including image,

---

[47] If it had, it may well be that an arguable case could have been made out under Article 8, which guarantees the right to respect for private and family life. Further consideration of this issue is beyond the scope of this chapter.

[48] United Nations Committee on the Rights of the Child, General Comment No. 10. Children's Rights in Juvenile Justice CRC/C/GC/10 (2007), available at www.ohchr.org (30 November 2011), para. 64.

[49] *Ibid.*, paras. 65–6.

[50] The Guidelines were adopted in 2010 by the Committee of Ministers of the Council of Europe. See www.coe.int/childjustice.

detailed descriptions of the child or the child's family, names or addresses, audio and video records, etc.[51]

Taking the strength of international law on the issue of privacy into account and reflecting on the consequences that the failure to protect V's privacy had in this case, it is proposed to amend that part of the judgment (paragraph 88) that discusses the impact of publicity on the boy's trial to acknowledge the extra-ordinary injunction that was required to protect his right to life.

A specialist, child-friendly court

Until the Court's judgment in *V v. United Kingdom*, the international community had paid virtually no attention to how children might be facilitated to participate in the criminal justice system, and in criminal proceedings more specifically. Developments in three areas – at the UN, in the Council of Europe and before the European Court of Human Rights itself – illustrate that *V v. United Kingdom* was a starting point for a renewed and more intense focus on the fair trial rights of children.

The idea that children have a right to participate in decisions made about them was recognised as an international legal principle for the first time in the United Nations Convention on the Rights of the Child (CRC), which was adopted in 1989. Moreover, Article 12(2) of the CRC provides that, to this end, a child 'shall be provided the opportunity to be heard in any judicial and administrative proceedings affecting the child, either directly, or through a representative or an appropriate body, in a manner consistent with the procedural rules of national law'. Prior to the Strasbourg Court's ruling in *V*, however, the analysis of this principle had focused primarily on children's participation in public policy decision-making, and in individual decisions that affect them such as in health-care, education and in the family law area, with little regard for the criminal process. Notwithstanding that the Court did not cite Article 12 in its judgment,[52] the judgment can be said to have opened the door to the application of the principle of participation in the criminal context.[53] In this regard, it is submitted

---

[51] *Ibid.*, rule 6.

[52] Reference was made in para. 46 to Article 3 (the best interests principle), Article 37 (the right to liberty) and Article 40 (juvenile justice, including the right to privacy in particular) as well as to the specific provisions of the Beijing Rules (on criminal responsibility, privacy and welfare), para. 45. Reference was also made to Article 14(4) of the International Covenant on Civil and Political Rights which provides that, '[i]n the case of juvenile persons, the procedure shall be such as will take account of their age and the desirability of promoting their rehabilitation'. At para. 48. Finally, reference was made to Recommendation No. R (87) 20 of the Committee of Ministers of the Council of Europe on the right to privacy, and the need to ensure children are not tried in adult courts, where youth courts exist. At para. 49.

[53] See, for example, para. 84 of the judgment.

that it paved the way for subsequent legal developments in this area, including, first, the inclusion of the issue in the Committee on the Rights of the Child's General Comment No. 10 on Children's Rights in Juvenile Justice,[54] and, secondly, the decision by the Council of Europe to draft Guidelines on Child-Friendly Justice in 2010. Both of these developments are now considered in light of the Court's judgment in *V*.

General Comment No. 10 of the Committee on the Rights of the Child

Although the Convention on the Rights of the Child has two core provisions dealing with the rights of children in conflict with the law – Article 37 (right to liberty) and Article 40 (due process) – General Comment No. 10 of the Committee on the Rights of the Child addresses the relevance of the whole Convention to this area. The General Comment is thus a wide-ranging instrument which deals with the prevention of delinquency and the importance of diverting young people from offending, for example, but it also focuses considerable attention on children's rights in the trial process. In doing so, the Committee on the Rights of the Child has clearly built on the ground established by the Strasbourg Court in *V* v. *United Kingdom*. In particular, the Committee notes that:

> A fair trial requires that the child alleged as or accused of having infringed the penal law be able to effectively participate in the trial, and therefore needs to comprehend the charges, and possible consequences and penalties, in order to direct the legal representative, to challenge witnesses, to provide an account of events, and to make appropriate decisions about evidence, testimony and the measure(s) to be imposed. Article 14 of the Beijing Rules provides that the proceedings should be conducted in an atmosphere of understanding to allow the child to participate and to express himself/herself freely. Taking into account the child's age and maturity may also require modified courtroom procedures and practices.[55]

In relation to the application of Article 12, the Committee notes that:

> the child must be given the opportunity to express his/her views freely, and those views should be given due weight in accordance with the age and maturity of the child (art. 12(1)), throughout the juvenile justice process. This means that the child, in order to effectively participate in the proceedings, must be informed not only of the charges ... but also of the juvenile justice process as such and of the possible measures.[56]

In addition to stressing the importance of maintaining respect for the child's privacy throughout criminal proceedings (see also above), the General

---

[54] Committee on the Rights of the Child, General Comment No. 10, Children's Rights in Juvenile Justice, CRC/C/GC/10 (2007) available at www.ohchr.org (30 November 2011).
[55] *Ibid.*, para. 46.   [56] *Ibid.*, para. 45.

Comment thus focuses in an important way on how to ensure that a child's fair trial rights are secured in criminal proceedings. In emphasising the importance of justice for children in this context, the Committee was undoubtedly inspired by the judgment of the Strasbourg Court in *V*.

Guidelines on Child-Friendly Justice

The second, related development that took place after the Court's judgment in *V*, and following its lead, was the adoption by the Council of Europe of an instrument on the rights of children in the justice system. The Council of Europe Guidelines on Child-Friendly Justice were adopted by the Committee of Ministers on 17 November 2010.[57] Although the Guidelines are broader than participation in the criminal process – they extend to children's right to access and participate in a justice system that is child-appropriate in the civil sphere also – they make a number of important statements that build on the Court's judgment in *V*. In particular, section D of the Guidelines deals with children's rights during judicial proceedings and makes provision for the organisation of proceedings, and the importance of ensuring that children encounter a child-friendly environment when they are involved in legal proceedings, including criminal proceedings.[58] In addition to requiring that language appropriate to the age and understanding of the child should be used, the Guidelines require that:

> As far as possible, specialist courts (or court chambers), procedures and institutions should be established for children in conflict with the law. This could include the establishment of specialised units within the police, the judiciary, the court system and the prosecutor's office.[59]

Moreover, in all proceedings, the Guidelines require that children should be treated with respect for their age, their special needs, their maturity and level of understanding, and bearing in mind any communication difficulties they may have. They also provide that cases involving children should be dealt with in non-intimidating and child-sensitive settings with respect for their privacy.[60]

Further developments in the European Court of Human Rights

As highlighted above, the Strasbourg Court denied that the trial of V in an adult court in itself violated Article 6, although it did conclude that it is essential 'that a child charged with an offence is dealt with in a manner which takes full account of his age, level of maturity and intellectual and emotional capacities, and that steps are taken to promote his ability to understand and participate in the proceedings'.[61] A key judgment adopted in 2004 in the case of *SC* v. *United Kingdom* developed this reasoning.[62] This case concerned the trial in the Crown

---

[57] For details, see www.coe.int/childjustice.   [58] See paras. 54–63.   [59] *Ibid.*, Rule 63.
[60] *Ibid.*, Rule 54. See further the discussion of the privacy issue above.
[61] ECHR, *V* v. *United Kingdom*, para. 86.   [62] ECHR, *SC* v. *United Kingdom*, 15 June 2004.

Court of an eleven-year-old boy who had a very low intellectual level for his age, meaning that he could not, it was argued, fully comprehend or participate in the trial process or give adequate instructions. According to the Court, the Convention does not require that a child on trial should understand or indeed be capable of understanding every point of law or evidential detail, not least because, given the sophistication of modern legal systems, many adults of normal intelligence are unable to fully comprehend all the intricacies and exchanges which take place in the courtroom. However, the Court held that 'effective participation' in this context 'presupposes that the accused has a broad understanding of the nature of the trial process and of what is at stake for him or her, including the significance of any penalty which may be imposed'.[63]

Thus, the Court said, the defendant should be able to follow what is said by the prosecution witness, explain to his own lawyers his version of events, point out any statements with which he disagrees, and make them aware of any facts which should be put forward in his defence. On the facts, the Court noted that, although the applicant was tried in public, steps were taken to ensure that the procedure was as informal as possible and many of the intimidating features of the trial in V were absent.[64] Although this judgment had been taken into account when the decision was made to allow the trial to proceed, the Strasbourg Court noted that two experts who assessed the applicant before the hearing concluded that he had a low intellectual level for his age, with one concluding that his understanding of the consequences of his actions 'may have been adversely affected by his learning difficulties and impaired reasoning skills'.[65] Despite the recommendation that the process be explained carefully to him in a manner commensurate with his learning difficulties, and the efforts to that end by the social worker, the Court noted that the applicant seemed to have little comprehension of the role of the jury in the proceedings or the importance of making a good impression on them. 'Even more strikingly', the Court said, 'he does not seem to have grasped the fact that he risked a custodial sentence and once sentence had passed and he was taken to the holding cells he appeared confused and expected to go home with his foster father'.[66] In light of this evidence, the Court found that the applicant had not participated effectively in his trial in violation of Article 6.[67]

According to the Strasbourg Court, certain duties flow from the decision to deal with a child by way of criminal proceedings, rather than some other form of disposal directed primarily at his best interests and those of the community.

---

[63] Ibid., para. 29.   [64] Ibid., para. 32.   [65] Ibid., para. 32.   [66] Ibid., para. 33.

[67] Judge Pelonpaa, joined by Judge Bratza, expressed the dissenting view that the domestic court's assessment of the applicant's ability to proceed and be tried in the Crown Court should have prevailed, inter alia, due to the absence of the aggravating factors present in the cases of T and V, the lack of evidence that the applicant was unfit to plead, and the fact that the domestic judge, who made the assessment which was upheld on appeal, had personal contact with the young defendant.

In particular, where the child risks not being able to participate due to his young age and limited intellectual capacity, 'it is essential that he be tried in a specialist tribunal which is able to give full consideration to and make proper allowance for the handicaps under which he labours and adapt its procedure accordingly'.[68] In this sense, *SC* builds on the judgment in *V* and in fact appears to have gone further in suggesting that a specialist tribunal is necessary to ensure that a child can enjoy his right to a fair trial under Article 6. Admittedly, *SC* concerned a situation where trial in the Youth Court was available (see further below) with the authorities preferring trial in the Crown Court because of the seriousness of the charges, but it is nonetheless an important precedent on the nature of the youth trial.

Overall, then, it is clear that the Court's judgment in *SC*, the adoption of the Council of Europe Guidelines on Child-Friendly Justice and the Committee on the Rights of the Child's General Comment on Juvenile Justice all build on the Court's judgment in *V v. United Kingdom*. In particular, they articulate with greater detail and clarity the obligations that flow from the child's right to be tried in a manner that takes into account his/her special vulnerability and limited capacity to understand and participate in a criminal trial. Although these developments occurred subsequent to the Court's judgment in *V*, revisiting the judgment in the modern context allows the relationship between these developments to be drawn more clearly. Because they strengthen the case under Article 6 for the trial of children in a specialist tribunal, they are incorporated into the Court's reasoning in *V* (see paragraph 90) with a view to completing and improving the coherence of the judgment and to ensure that it is more fully in line with the major international developments in this area.

The clear merits of the Court's judgment in *V* are the articulation of the concept of 'effective participation' and the related criticism of the failure to take measures to reduce the feelings of intimidation and stress experienced by the young defendants, especially due to the public nature of the trial process. However, it is difficult to say from the Court's judgment that holding the proceedings *in camera* would have been sufficient to ensure *V*'s participation in his trial. It is clear that the glare of publicity – both inside and outside the courtroom – under which the trial took place affected the defendant's ability to concentrate. In addition, however, research on child development referred to above and that put before the Strasbourg Court (e.g. paragraph 11) supports the view that *V* was too young and immature to be tried in the ritualistic and formal setting of the Crown Court, with or without publicity. For this reason, it is proposed to rewrite, or supplement, the judgment of the Court in *V* to make this additional finding (paragraphs 86 and 88). It is hoped that these changes make the judgment more consistent both with the evidence before the Court about the children's circumstances, and with the modern international

---

[68] ECHR, *SC* v. *United Kingdom*, para. 35.

standards on youth justice, which increasingly require the trial of children in a specialist tribunal.

Transferring to adult court

V and his co-accused had been tried in the Crown Court – an adult court – rather than in the Youth Court, and much of the judgment of the Strasbourg Court focused on the extent to which V's trial met the demands of Article 6. It has already been submitted above that the Court's judgment would have been more coherent had it concluded that V could not have received a fair trial in the Crown Court, and that Article 6 requires a specialist, child-friendly tribunal for young accused. Another relevant issue, not addressed in the judgment – and not raised by the applicant – was the existence of a mechanism to determine whether V should be tried in the Crown Court or in the Youth Court. Under the law of England and Wales,[69] it is compulsory that children facing certain charges, including murder, are tried in the adult or Crown Court. In these circumstances, there is no discretion and there is no mechanism or process whereby the implications of that situation, including the consequences for the applicant's right to a fair trial, can be considered and return to the Youth Court ordered if there is a risk that the trial would be unfair.

Many jurisdictions have a formal process of sending children forward for trial to an adult court. Mechanisms vary from one country to the next, but most include a system whereby a judge, public prosecutor or other official has the power to decide that a child should be tried in adult court.[70] In many jurisdictions, this process allows for legal challenge whereby consideration is given to the question whether the application of adult criminal procedure and sentencing will have a disproportionately damaging effect on the child concerned. More importantly, perhaps, some jurisdictions, like Germany, allow for a two-way process whereby cases mandated for trial in the adult court can be returned to the youth or children's court in certain circumstances. This mechanism of 'transfer down', where the default position can be challenged, allows maturity and other social factors to be taken into account.[71] It is clear from the analysis above that it is very difficult, if not impossible, to ensure that children tried in adult court receive a fair trial as required by Article 6. On this basis, it is

---

[69] Section 24 of the Magistrates' Courts Act 1980.

[70] See C. Van Dijk, A. Nuytiens and C. Eliaerts, 'The Referral of Juvenile Offenders to the Adult Court in Belgium: Theory and Practice' (2005) 44(2) *Howard Journal of Criminal Justice* 125; J. Junger-Tas, 'Youth Justice in the Netherlands' (2004) 31 *Crime and Justice* 293; J. A. Arteaga, 'Juvenile (In)Justice: Congressional Attempts to Abrogate the Procedural Rights of Juvenile Defendants' (2002) 102(4) *Columbia Law Review* 1051–88; and S. Green, 'Prosecutorial Waiver into Adult Criminal Court: A Conflict of Interests Amounting to the States' Legislative Abrogation of Juveniles' Due Process Rights' (2005) 110 *Penn State Law Review* 233.

[71] A. N. Doob and M. Tonry, 'Varieties of Youth Justice' (2004) 31 *Crime and Justice* 1 at 8.

arguable that a legal system that does not provide a mechanism to determine the merits and necessity of trial in adult court does not meet with the requirements of Article 6. To reflect this, the amended judgment (paragraph 91) contains an additional paragraph asserting that the applicant's inability to challenge his trial in the Crown Court constituted a further violation of his right to a fair trial.

Age of criminal responsibility

This chapter is focused on the fair trial aspect of the Court's judgment in *V* v. *United Kingdom*, and so does not address the Court's related findings under Article 3, under which V argued that the low age of criminal responsibility constituted inhuman and degrading treatment. The Strasbourg Court rejected the applicant's claim under Article 3, finding that any inhuman and degrading treatment suffered was caused by the horrific crime he had committed and not by his trial *per se*. Nor was the Court persuaded that the age of criminal responsibility – ten in England and Wales – was so out of line with European norms as to raise a Convention issue. However, it is notable that five judges dissented from the judgment of the Court on this issue with reference to the relatively higher ages applied by other Council of Europe Member States. Moreover, in 2007, the Committee on the Rights of the Child identified the merits of applying an age of fourteen or sixteen years, and proposed twelve years as a recognised minimum norm.[72] Accordingly, it is proposed to delete the reference in the judgment (paragraph 86) to the absence of a clear common standard among the Member States of the Council of Europe, as well as to highlight where appropriate (paragraph 87) that the high age of criminal responsibility in many European jurisdictions would prevent the trial of ten-year-olds in the first instance.

Conclusion

The above analysis aims to show that the judgment of the European Court of Human Rights in the case of *V* v. *United Kingdom* set an important standard in the fair trial of children in adult court. Research and legal developments subsequent to the judgment serve to consolidate the underlying principle, i.e. that children have different characteristics and needs to adults, and that their treatment in the criminal justice system needs to reflect that difference in a substantial way. This chapter has also sought to show that, notwithstanding its

---

[72] United Nations Committee on the Rights of the Child, *General Comment No. 10, Children's Rights in Juvenile Justice*, CRC/C/GC/10 (2007), paras. 30–5. The Committee has also criticised States' treatment of children as adults and recommends the full application of the juvenile justice regime to children under eighteen years.

merits, the judgment of the Strasbourg Court did not go far enough to send a clear and coherent message as to what is required for children to enjoy their fair trial rights. While limiting the role of the public makes a contribution in this regard, subsequent case law indicates that in fact a child-friendly, specialist tribunal is important to secure adherence to the Article 6 principle of effective participation. The edited judgment also addresses the absence from the law of England and Wales of a transfer mechanism, which can help to ensure that children not capable of participating effectively in an adult court can be tried in a youth court instead. Finally, it addresses in a limited way the Court's finding on the absence of a common age of criminal responsibility in Europe.

Rewriting V v. United Kingdom

. . .

C.   Article 6 § 1 of the Convention

. . .

85. The Court notes that Article 6, read as a whole, guarantees the right of an accused to participate effectively in his criminal trial (see the *Stanford* judgment cited above . . .). **It also notes that under Article 6 § 1 'the press and public may be excluded from all or part of the trial . . . where the interests of juveniles so require'.** It has not until the present time been called upon to consider how [fragment deleted] **these** Article 6 § 1 guarantees apply to criminal proceedings against children, and in particular whether procedures which are generally considered to safeguard the rights of adults on trial, such as publicity, should be abrogated in respect of children in order to promote their understanding and participation (but see the *Nortier* v. *The Netherlands* judgment of 24 August 1993, Series A no. 267, and particularly the separate opinions annexed thereto).

86. The Court recalls its above finding [fragment deleted] that the attribution of criminal responsibility to the applicant does not in itself give rise to a breach of Article 3 of the Convention (see paragraph 74 above) **notwithstanding concerns about the low age of criminal responsibility applied in this case.** Likewise, it cannot be said that the trial on criminal charges of a child, even one as young as eleven, as such violates the fair trial guarantee under Article 6 § 1. The Court does, however, agree with the Commission that it is essential that a child charged with an offence is dealt with in a manner which takes full account of his age, level of maturity and intellectual and emotional capacities, and that steps are taken to promote his ability to understand and participate in the proceedings. **This is supported by extensive research evidence which supports the Court's understanding that**

children are different to adults and must be treated appropriately in the manner of their trial. The question then becomes whether and to what extent this was achieved in the instant case where a child aged 11 was tried in a public adult court.

87. It follows that, in respect of a young child charged with a grave offence attracting high levels of media and public interest, it would be necessary to conduct the hearing in such a way as to reduce as far as possible his or her feelings of intimidation and inhibition **and to take steps to ensure his effective participation in the trial process**. In this connection it is noteworthy that in England and Wales, **as in other jurisdictions**, children charged with less serious crimes are dealt with in special youth courts, from which the general public is excluded and in relation to which there are imposed automatic reporting restrictions on the media (see paragraphs 30 and 31 above). **It is also noteworthy that, in many jurisdictions, children as young as 11 will not be prosecuted at all, regardless of the nature of the offence.** Moreover, the Court has already referred to the **strength** of international standards [fragment deleted] on the protection of the privacy of child defendants (see paragraph 77 [fragment deleted] **and paragraph 86** above). It has considered carefully the Government's argument that public trials serve the general interest in the open administration of justice (see paragraph 83 above), and observes that, where appropriate in view of the age and other characteristics of the child and the circumstances surrounding the criminal proceedings, this general interest could be satisfied by a modified procedure providing for selected attendance rights and judicious reporting.

88. **Even were a better balance to be achieved between the open administration of justice and the right of the child to privacy, as Article 6 § 1 suggests, the Court does not consider that the applicant could have enjoyed a fair trial in an adult court, given his very young age, immaturity and the general vulnerabilities under which he laboured (see paragraphs 17–19 above).** The Court notes that the applicant's trial took place over three weeks in public in the Crown Court. Special measures were taken in view of the applicant's young age and to promote his understanding of the proceedings: for example, he had the trial procedure explained to him and was taken to see the courtroom in advance, and the hearing times were shortened so as not to tire the defendants excessively. Nonetheless, the formality and ritual of the Crown Court must at times have seemed incomprehensible and intimidating for a child of eleven, and there is evidence that certain of the modifications to the courtroom, in particular the raised dock which was designed to enable the defendants to see what was going on, had the effect of increasing the applicant's sense of discomfort during the trial, since he felt exposed to the scrutiny of the press and public. The trial

generated extremely high levels of press and public interest, both inside and outside the courtroom, to the extent that the judge in his summing-up referred to the problems caused to witnesses by the blaze of publicity and asked the jury to take this into account when assessing their evidence (see paragraph 14 above). **It is noteworthy also that subsequent to the trial, the disclosure of the applicant's identity by the media caused a risk to his Convention rights (notably under Article 2) that then fell to be addressed by the High Court in the granting of an injunction against the media of extraordinary scope.**

89. There is considerable psychiatric evidence relating to the applicant's ability to participate in the proceedings ...

90. In such circumstances the Court does not consider that it was sufficient for the purposes of Article 6 § 1 that the applicant was represented by skilled and experienced lawyers ... Here, although the applicant's legal representatives were seated, as the Government put it, 'within whispering distance', it is highly unlikely that the applicant would have felt sufficiently uninhibited, in the tense courtroom and under public scrutiny, to have consulted with them during the trial or, indeed, that, given his immaturity and his disturbed emotional state, he would have been capable outside the courtroom of cooperating with his lawyers and giving them information for the purposes of his defence. **In this regard, the Court recalls the requirements of the Council of Europe Guidelines on Child-Friendly Justice and the recommendations of the Committee on the Rights of the Child's General Comment No. 10 which require that where children face trial, they should appear before a specialist tribunal with a setting, procedure and language that are appropriate to their age, maturity and needs.**

91. **The Court notes that in jurisdictions where children can be tried in adult court, mechanisms exist to transfer the trial of a child from the youth into the adult system. This decision, whether made by prosecutor or judge, is normally reviewable and may be reversed where certain conditions are met. The Court notes, however, that, in England and Wales, the decision to prosecute the applicant in the (adult) Crown Court is automatic, determined by the charge of murder. Accordingly, the fact that the applicant could not avail of any means to challenge the decision to try him in adult court, or to have that decision reversed allowing him to be tried in a specialist tribunal that met his needs, further undermines his right to a fair trial.**

92. **In conclusion, the Court considers that the applicant was unable to participate effectively in the criminal proceedings against him and was, in consequence, denied a fair hearing in breach of Article 6 § 1.**

2

Images of children in education: a critical reading of DH and others v. Czech Republic

SIA SPILIOPOULOU ÅKERMARK

Introduction

The case of *DH and others v. Czech Republic* (which is also referred to as the *Ostrava* case, which was the municipality in which the situation examined by the Court had occurred) was decided by the Grand Chamber of the European Court of Human Rights in November 2007.[1] It is undoubtedly a landmark case in many ways. This case elevated the issue of separate classes for Roma children in Europe to a legal question at the level of the European Court of Human Rights (hereinafter, 'the Court'). In addition, in its judgment, the Court pursued its first major encounter with issues of indirect discrimination and the role of statistics in assessing discrimination cases. The judgment has been welcomed by many observers as a great victory in the fight against indirect discrimination and, more generally, against the exclusion of the Roma in the education systems of many countries around Europe and in European societies.[2]

This is also a landmark case, as it is the first in a series of recent cases concerning the interpretation of Article 2 of Protocol 1 to the European Convention on Human Rights concerning the right to education, and indirectly concerning the rights of children to and in education. The *Ostrava* case was followed by the *Sampanis and others v. Greece* case (2008) and, more recently, by *Oršuš and others v. Croatia* (decided by the Court in Grand Chamber in March 2010).[3]

---

[1] ECHR (GC), *DH and others v. Czech Republic*, 13 November 2007; ECHR (Second Section), *DH and others v. Czech Republic*, 7 February 2006.

[2] See, for example, A. Grgić, 'Recognizing Formal and Substantive Equality in the Oršuš Case' (2010) 9 *European Yearbook of Minority Issues* (forthcoming); R. Medda, 'Dismantling Segregating Education and the European Court of Human Rights. DH and others v. Czech Republic: Towards an Inclusive Education?' (2007/8) 7 *European Yearbook of Minority Issues*; I. E. Koch, 'The Right to Education for Roma Children under the European Convention on Human Rights', in J. Grimheden, D. Karlsson and R. Ring (eds.), *On-line Festschrift in Honour of Katarina Tomasevski*, www.rwi.lu.se/ktfestschrift/On-line_festschrift_in_honour_of_Katarina_Tomasevski.html (last accessed 30 November 2011).

[3] ECHR (GC), *Oršuš and others v. Croatia*, 16 March 2010; ECHR, *Sampanis and others v. Greece*, 5 June 2008.

Another reason for choosing this particular case is the fact that it gives us the opportunity to consider issues of multiple vulnerabilities and of multiple discrimination, i.e. discrimination which is attributed to several interrelated but distinct grounds, in this particular case age and membership of a minority. There are other ways of understanding multiple discrimination, such as discrimination caused by several perpetrators. In a more strict sense, multiple discrimination occurs also when several substantive rights of applicants are affected. In the present chapter, I have chosen to focus on the first of these understandings of the notion of multiple discrimination, sometimes referred to as 'intersectionality', in other words discrimination attributable to multiple, distinct and interrelated grounds.[4] The term 'intersectionality' emphasises the interplay of various identities and characteristics of persons and placing them in a disadvantageous position. This approach is particularly appropriate in a volume dedicated to 'mainstreaming diversity', in that it argues that the legal system is confronted regularly with and needs to address diversities and multiple identities of different kinds and that the singular categorisation of applicants under age, gender, social position, political affiliation, belonging to a minority or any other ground shows little understanding and respect for their factual situation. If the effort of mainstreaming diversity has as its goal not simply to describe multiplicity but to empower individuals within a human rights framework, then such efforts should consciously try to capture and take into account the particularities of experiences of different applicants, who have different personal capabilities, experiences and aspirations.

In the present chapter, I make a critical reading and rewriting of *DH and others v. Czech Republic* from a child perspective. I try to highlight the tension between the prioritisation by the Court of the aspect of group indirect discrimination on the one hand and the legitimate expectation that the views of children shall be heard and in addition that these views shall be taken into account in all decisions affecting them on the other. Indeed, the fact that children should be heard, to the extent appropriate to their capabilities, and that their views should be taken into account is today, at least in Europe, more than a legitimate expectation. It is a legal obligation that has been enshrined in a number of international and European treaties, most notably the European Convention on the Exercise of Children's Rights (1996) and the UN Convention on the Rights of the Child (1989).[5]

---

[4] S. Spiliopoulou Åkermark, 'Minoritetskvinnors rätt till familjeliv och artikel 8 i Europeiska konventionen om de mänskliga rättigheterna' (Minority Women and the Right to Family Life under Article 8 of the European Convention on Human Rights) (2003) 103 *Retfaerd* 76–86; S. Spiliopoulou Åkermark, *Human Rights of Minority Women* (Åland Islands Peace Institute, 2000); S. Spiliopoulou Åkermark, 'Minority Women: International Protection and the Problem of Multiple Discrimination', in L. Hannikainen and E. Nykänen (eds.), *New Trends in Discrimination Law – International Perspectives* (Turku Law School, 1999).

[5] European Convention on the Exercise of Children's Rights, ETS No. 160 (1996), in force since 2000; UN Convention on the Rights of the Child (1989), 1577 UNTS 3.

In my analysis, I shall not be focusing on the rights of minorities as such, and of Roma in particular, or on wider issues of pluralism and diversity under the European Convention on Human Rights.[6] Nor is there any effort to summarise the entire case law of the Court with regard to Article 2 of Protocol 1 concerning the right to education, going back to the *Belgian Linguistic* case of 1968. The purpose of the present argument is to look at how the European Court of Human Rights approaches situations of applicants who are children at the time of the violations of their rights, and at the same time are members of a minority. At this point, I use the term 'violations', since the Court in its final judgments found violations in certain aspects in all three cases (i.e. the *DH* case, the *Sampanis* case and the *Oršuš* case). The argument I make is that it would have been possible for the Court to examine and affirm the particularities and circumstances of individual applicants and their families while at the same time expanding its reasoning on issues of indirect discrimination, segregation policies in education and the quality of education as such.

Most observers have welcomed the increased willingness of the Court in cases such as *DH* to refer to evidence from other international bodies in cases of discrimination and minority rights. It can, however, be argued that, while such information is useful in depicting the general interpretations and understandings of the situation in different countries, it has also in most cases the effect of depersonalising the interpretation of the actual conditions of individual applicants. The focus of attention becomes that of other international instruments, rather than on the factual situation of the applicants and whether this situation entails a violation of the European Convention on Human Rights. So, if the goal of the Court is to move towards more overall, systemic evaluations of the application of individual rights in countries, this seems like a wise choice. If, however, the Court intends to engage in individualised and personalised assessments of particular rights, in specific situations, then this may be a counterproductive avenue if not accompanied by the personal narratives of individual applicants, including children. For those reasons, I have also refrained from adding further references to other international treaties, including those guaranteeing the right of the child to be heard, even though, as argued below, the Court could well have referred to them.

My goal is to explore how the Court is expressing, or not, its effort to document the subjective experience of child applicants in an indirect discrimination case in the field of education and then to propose possible

---

[6] I have dealt with such wider issues in other writings, e.g. S. Spiliopoulou Åkermark, 'The Limits of Pluralism – Recent Jurisprudence of the European Court of Human Rights with Regard to Minorities: Does the Prohibition of Discrimination Add Anything?', *Journal on Ethnopolitics and Minority Issues in Europe*, Issue 3/2002, www.ecmi.de/jemie/download/Focus3-2002_Akermark.pdf (last accessed 30 November 2011); and S. Spiliopoulou Åkermark, 'Multiculturalism in Crisis', in E. Ruiz Vieytez and R. Dunbar (eds.), *Human Rights and Diversity: New Challenges for Plural Societies* (Bilbao, 2007), pp. 37–50.

amendments to this work. To a more limited extent I shall explore the possibilities the Court had in this regard with reference to the right to and in education. This is, however, a secondary and less explored track in the present text.

The chapter is divided into five main parts, after the present Introduction. In the following section, I summarise the main facts of the cases concerned. Thereafter, I identify the complex legal issues that arise once we start examining the cases from an individual child perspective. This examination brings us to the analysis of the images of children encapsulated in the judgments of the Court but also in the arguments of the representatives of the applicants and the governments involved. In the last section, some possible explanations are identified, accompanied by concluding remarks. Finally, the rewritten judgment is presented.

A summary of the facts of the cases discussed

In the *DH* case, the applicants were all born between 1985 and 1991, and they had been placed in so-called 'special schools' between 1996 and 1999 when the applicants were all below the age of fifteen years. The applicants were the children themselves rather than their parents, even though issues of parental consent were important in the reasoning of the Court. The applicants challenged their placement in such special schools as well as their treatment in the education system, and argued that it amounted to discrimination due to a generalised pattern of placement of Roma children in special schools as well as due to the inadequacy of the testing methods applied. The case thus concerned the alleged violation of Article 14 of the Convention (prohibition on discrimination) taken together with Article 2 of Protocol 1 (right to education).

The *DH* case was decided first by a Chamber of the European Court of Human Rights in which the Second Section of the Court held by six votes to one that there had been no violation of Article 14 of the Convention taken together with Article 2 of Protocol 1.[7] The final judgment was rendered by the Grand Chamber of the Court, which reversed the original outcome. The Grand Chamber found, by thirteen votes to four, that there had indeed been a violation of Article 14 in conjunction with the education provision in Article 2 of Protocol 1. In making my argument, I shall be using mainly the Grand Chamber judgment which is the only legally binding outcome of the process and which has legally replaced fully the Second Section judgment. However, reference is going to be made also to the Second Section judgment in order to reveal and understand the choices and assessments made by the Grand Chamber and the context of such assessments in the broader thinking and practice of the Court. I further argue that, even though the Grand Chamber

---

[7] ECHR (Second Section), *DH and others* v. *Czech Republic*, 7 February 2006.

reversed the outcome by finding a violation of the non-discrimination provision, perceptions concerning the position and rights of children applicants in the educational process as well as in legal and judicial proceeding concerning non-discrimination cases remained essentially intact between the Chamber and the Grand Chamber stages.

Further, while the rewriting of the judgment in the present contribution will focus on the *DH* case, this judgment needs to be looked at in its wider context within the jurisprudence of the Court, which includes also two subsequent cases in which the Court fine-tuned some aspects of its views, namely, the *Oršuš* and – to lesser extent – the *Sampanis* cases. The *Oršuš* case concerned three regions in Croatia and the placement of the applicants, fifteen Roma children, in separate classes albeit in most cases within the framework of mixed schools. The main argument of the Croatian government was that the children concerned were unable to follow teaching in mixed classes due to gaps in their knowledge of the Croatian language.

The *Sampanis* case involved actions not only by the educational establishment in Greece but also several attacks and threats against Roma children in one specific region and two elementary schools in a small Greek city. The *Sampanis* case concerned not simply a segregating education system, but also potentially life-threatening conditions for the Roma children and their families. The threats and attacks and the blocking of the school buildings were organised by the parents of non-Roma pupils, rather than by the Greek authorities, so that the legal question was rather whether the authorities had done enough to prevent and condemn such acts and also to ensure effective access to education for Roma children. However, from the perspective of the present enquiry, it is important to note that, in contrast to the *Ostrava* and *Oršuš* cases, the applicants in the Greek case were the parents of the Roma children, rather than the children themselves.

For sure, the Court has been extremely careful in emphasising the important differences in the factual situations concerned in the three cases.[8] In the *Oršuš* judgment, the Court underlined that, in *DH*, the Court had established that between 50 and 70 per cent of Roma children in the Czech Republic attended special schools for pupils with learning difficulties, while in the *Sampanis* case all Roma children attending the school at issue were allocated to a separate establishment. As to the *Oršuš* case, the Court first noted that the applicants, unlike in the *Sampanis* case, attended regular primary schools and that the Roma-only classes were situated in the same premises as other classes. While the differences between the cases is an argument valid to a large extent, in particular as regards the efforts of the authorities to find various types of solutions, the legal questions with regard to both Article 14 and Article 2 of Protocol 1, are largely the same: to what extent are these provisions, as

---

[8] See e.g. para. 85 in the *Sampanis* case; and para. 152 in the *Oršuš* case.

interpreted by the Court today, sensitive to the conditions, needs and views of individual children applicants?

The main legal issues raised in the DH case

The *DH* case raises distinct issues under Article 14 on non-discrimination and under Article 2 of Protocol 1 concerning the rights of children and parents in the education system.

Segregation of Roma pupils

The main legal questions as identified by the Court in the *DH* case were: is the overall evidence of segregation of Roma in the education system of the Czech Republic sufficient enough to entail a breach of Article 14 in conjunction with Article 2 of Protocol 1? Secondly, is the system of separate classes a discriminatory practice as such? Thirdly, did the testing methods used by the Czech authorities prior to the placement of Roma children in separate classes meet the expectations of appropriate and balanced testing? Fourthly, had the parents consented to the placement of their children in special schools?

In addressing these questions, the Court relied heavily on statistics and on a wide range of reports by intergovernmental as well as non-governmental organisations documenting long-standing practices of segregation of Roma as evidence of indirect discrimination. The problem ensuing out of this course of action taken by the Court then becomes the following: is it possible to combine a commitment against indirect discrimination of various groups, e.g. ethnic minorities, with sensitivity for the particularities of individual applicants?

The above problem is important in a human rights system for which the respect of individual dignity is the entire rationale. It is all the more important when the cases concern children who do not have full agency, i.e. full capacity to decide on affairs concerning them but whose views are to be heard and to be taken into account. The right of children to participation has been viewed as a precondition of the human dignity of children, of their empowerment as well as of democratic decision-making.[9] This seems even more relevant with regard to minority children who are regularly excluded from consultative processes and hearings, sometimes both by the authorities as well as, sometimes, by their parents and the minority group to which they belong (or, are ascribed as belonging to).[10]

---

[9] R. Stern, *The Child's Right to Participation – Reality or Rhetoric?* (Uppsala University, 2006); Committee on the Rights of the Child, General Comment No. 12 (2009) on the right of the child to be heard, CRC/C/GC/12 (2009).

[10] L. Krappmann, 'The Weight of the Child's View' (2010) 18 *International Journal of Children's Rights* 501–13 at 511.

The right of children to be heard

The right of children to be heard is based on the legal obligations assumed within and outside the Council of Europe with regard to issues of participation of children in decision-making affecting them as well as in judicial proceedings. The Council of Europe has made efforts to highlight the Court's commitment to children's rights, for instance by the setting up of the Theseus database of case law concerning children between 1968 and 2010.[11] Of course, the European Court of Human Rights interprets and applies the European Convention on Human Rights. However, as the Court chose itself to make extensive reference to a vast number of international conventions and standards, it is remarkable that aspects of the right of children to be informed, to participate and be taken into consideration in their own individuality is absent in the reasoning of the Court.

For instance, the Court referred only to Articles 28 and 30 of the Convention on the Rights of the Child and did not pursue, for instance, the impact of Article 3, third sentence, concerning the responsibility of State authorities in regularly monitoring the respect of the best interest of the child.[12] Even more importantly, the Court did not find it necessary to examine issues concerning the procedural guarantees embedded in the right to education and flowing out of Article 12 of the Convention on the Rights of the Child, concerning the right to be heard, including in educational matters. Czechoslovakia had ratified the Convention on the Rights of the Child in 1992, with no particular declarations or reservations as regards Article 12, and this commitment was succeeded to by the Czech Republic (and Slovakia) in 1993.

The Court could have resorted to Article 3 of the European Convention on the Exercise of Children's Rights (1996) which guarantees the right of the child to be informed and to express his or her views in judicial proceedings.[13]

In rewriting the judgment, I shall focus primarily on the first aspect (non-discrimination), since in the *DH* case the Court was mainly preoccupied with the problem of indirect group discrimination as evidenced through the extensive arguments based on statistics about Roma segregation and the

---

[11] Council of Europe, Theseus Database, www.coe.int/t/dg3/children/caselaw/caselawchild_en. asp? (last accessed 9 May 2011). The database is not a legally binding document; it can, however, be looked at as an outflow of legal obligations of States party to a number of international conventions incorporating the right of children to be heard and the ensuing obligation to take the views of children into account.

[12] See Grand Chamber judgment, para. 100.

[13] ETS No. 160 (1996), in force since 2000. The Czech Republic ratified the Convention in March 2001. The Commissioner for Human Rights of the Council of Europe, Thomas Hammarberg, emphasised in his presentation at the Conference 'International Justice for Children' (Strasbourg, 17–18 September 2007) the need for '[m]aking international and regional human rights complaints and communications mechanisms child-friendly'. Council of Europe CommDH/Speech (2007) 13.

discrimination of Roma as a group and in the Czech education system as a whole. As will be shown, the Court did not consider the individual situation and concerns of the children applicants in terms of discriminatory experiences and effects or with regard to the rights to and in education.[14] By following such an approach, the Court did not explore in any detail the individual position of the applicants with regard to the effects of the discriminatory practices, and at the same time the Court did not have to address issues of positive obligations of States with regard to the rights of children or their parents in matters of education.

The importance of a right for the applicant and the margin of appreciation

A first conclusion flowing from the Court's choice of focus in the *DH* case is that the effects of the situation concerned on individual children take a secondary place in the reasoning of the Court. This is not simply a problem of incorporating the right of children to be heard into the workings of the Court and into the interpretation of the European Convention by the Court. The importance of this matter lies in the role it plays in the legal reasoning of the Court and its theory of the margin of appreciation. The Court has attached legal relevance to the importance of the alleged violation of a particular right for a particular person, in this particular case children and teenagers. In other words, the more important a particular right is for a particular individual, the more limited is the margin of appreciation of States Parties. Thus, in order to assess the limits of the margin of appreciation, the Court needs first to make an assessment of the importance of a right for a particular individual.

In the *DH* case, the Court found in general terms that:

> The present case therefore warrants particular attention, especially as when the applications were lodged with the Court the applicants were minor children for whom the right to education was of paramount importance.[15]

---

[14] The concept of a 'right to education' describes the right to access to education, which is to be free and compulsory as regards primary education, while the concept of 'rights in education' concerns the quality, adaptability and acceptability of education as well as the procedures that need to be in place in decision-making that guarantee the above aspects. See further 'Commentary on Education under the Framework Convention in National Minorities', Advisory Committee on the Framework Convention, Council of Europe, ACFC/25DOC(2006)002; and General Comment 13 (1999) on the Right to Education of the Committee on Economic, Social and Cultural Rights, and Preliminary Report of the UN Special Rapporteur on Education, E/CN.4/1999/49.

[15] Grand Chamber judgment, para. 182. This phrasing was also repeated in the *Oršuš* case, para. 147.

In order to proceed to an examination of discriminatory practices, the Court required in the *Buckley* case (see below) a thick set of statistical as well as narrative evidence concerning the living conditions and everyday experiences of Ms Buckley and her family. In addition to being a challenging task in itself for the applicants – especially in countries where statistical information is not collected regularly and with respect to the various thematic areas of concern – there is a clear tension between on the one hand the structural, collectively oriented, quantifiable proof provided through statistical arguments and on the other hand the subjective perceptions, needs and experiences of the applicants. If this was an issue in a case such as *Buckley* concerning only one adult applicant, it is all the more challenging in cases such as *DH* with eighteen applicants or *Oršuš* with fifteen applicants who were minors at the time of the starting point of the alleged violation, as well as their parents, in terms of issues of consent. In such cases where the Court finds it necessary to rely on statistical evidence, it seems all the more crucial to find ways to accompany this abstract approach with concerns about the individual applicants.

The sensitivity for the particularities and individualities of individual applicants and their situations came to the forefront of the Court's reasoning in the case of *Buckley* v. *United Kingdom*, concerning the intersection of gender and membership in a minority. In this case, first the Commission, and then the Court emphasised that *the special circumstances of every individual applicant and the importance of the right for him or her have to be taken into consideration when assessing the balance between the interests of the individual and other societal interests*, whether financial expedience, the interests of others or other weighing considerations.[16] The Court said further that the scope of the margin of appreciation of States is not identical in each case but will vary according to the context. Relevant factors include, according to the Court, 'the nature of the Convention right in issue, its importance for the individual and the nature of the activities concerned'. In the *Buckley* case, the Court had to assess the right to family and access to a permanent home (Article 8) against the background of planning regulations. On the basis of the above reasoning, the Court said in the *Buckley* case with regard to the procedural guarantees embedded in Article 8 on the right to a home:

> The importance of that right for the applicant and her family must also be taken into account in determining the scope of the margin of appreciation allowed to the respondent State. Whenever discretion capable of interfering with the enjoyment of a Convention right such as the one in issue in the present case is conferred on national authorities, the procedural safeguards available to the individual will be especially material in determining whether the respondent State has, when fixing the regulatory framework, remained within its margin of appreciation. Indeed it is settled case law

[16] *Buckley* v. *United Kingdom*, Judgment, September 1996, paras. 74–6.

that, whilst Article 8 contains no explicit procedural requirements, the decision-making process leading to measures of interference must be fair and such as to afford due respect to the interests safeguarded to the individual by Article 8.[17]

The Court's treatment of the right to education

The positions taken by the Court in the *DH* case and described above could possibly be explained by the structure and wording of Article 2 of Protocol 1. Article 2 provides:

> No person shall be denied the right to education. In the exercise of any functions which it assumes in relation to education and to teaching, the State shall respect the right of parents to ensure such education and teaching in conformity with their own religious and philosophical convictions.

The substantive provision concerned does not have a child-oriented perspective as such, so it is not surprising that the Court cannot go further than the Convention and its interpretation allow for. The first sentence of the education provision refers explicitly to the right to education and is indeed brief. It is followed by the much more elaborate sentence concerning the right of parents to ensure education for their children in conformity with their beliefs and convictions. From the outset of the preparatory works in 1949 concerning this provision, there was apparent tension in the discussions between those viewing this provision within the framework of so-called 'family rights' and then looking at it as the child's right to culturally sensitive education developing its own personality.[18] In the *DH* case, the Court showed more interest in issues and procedures of granting parental consent for the placement of the children in special schools rather than on the substantive and procedural educational rights of children. By substantive rights in education, I mean the right to access to an appropriate education for all children, something which has, however, been guaranteed by the Court to a rather limited extent so far. By procedural rights of children in education, I mean the guarantees afforded to children in decision-making within the education system. There is indeed a fine line between the wide margin of appreciation that the Court seems to accept in the field of education and the requirement for extensive procedural guarantees in the way this right is exercised. In its effort to strike an appropriate balance

---

[17] The Court referred at this point to the *McMichael* v. *United Kingdom* judgment of 24 February 1995, Series A no. 307-B, p. 55, para. 87.

[18] See, for example, the discussions of the Committee on Legal and Administrative Questions of the Consultative Assembly of the Council of Europe on 7th September 1949, Council of Europe, Preparatory Work on Article 2 of the Protocol to the Convention, Doc. CDH (67) 2, 1967, p. 7.

between, on the one hand, judicial assessment of the effects of law and policy on individuals and, on the other hand, the margin of appreciation of States and governments in designing their own responses to societal needs and aspirations, the Court seems to be avoiding pronouncing on any substantive aspects of the right to education for minority children.

Below, I shall therefore expose and challenge the images projected on children by the wording and the workings of the Court as well as by the representatives of the parties with regard to decisions in the education system.

The image of Roma children and their parents in the Ostrava case

Arguing that the Court neglected the individual views, effects on and procedural guarantees of children due to the wording and historical background of Article 2 of Protocol 1, seems, however, not to be a sufficient explanation. Researchers have argued over time that there are similar findings with respect to other material provisions and situations covered by the Convention. They have noted that the image of the child that transpires in cases concerning the headscarf controversies around Europe and the approaches taken by individual countries, but also by the European Court of Human Rights, in cases such as *Şahin* v. *Turkey* (2004) and *Dahlab* v. *Switzerland* (2001), 'is predominantly one of a passive and vulnerable being'.[19] Similarly, it has been argued that the greatest advancement in introducing Article 12 in the Convention on the Rights of the Child is the fact that it is a definitive departure from the long-standing views, which have been stressing the child as incompetent, as lacking responsibility, in need of protection and, therefore, understood as being in a phase of 'preparation for life', thus as 'an incomplete human being'.[20]

Children as incompetent and passive objects

There is a procedural constraint which comes into play in this regard. The Court is bound by the complaints of the applicants and the legal arguments put forward by them. The applicants in the *Ostrava* case were the children themselves and they were represented in domestic proceedings by a lawyer acting on the basis of signed written authorisation from the parents.[21] From the perspective of the applicants, this case is one concerning the rights of the children concerned, rather than of their parents. The representing lawyers themselves,

[19] Eva Brems, 'Above Children's Heads – The Headscarf Controversy in European Schools from the Perspective of Children's Rights' (2006) 14 *International Journal of Children's Rights* 119–36.

[20] Lothar Krappmann, 'The Weight of the Child's View' (2010) 18 *International Journal of Children's Rights* 501–13 at 502.

[21] *DH*, Grand Chamber judgment, para. 22.

and, by consequence, later on the Court, argued mainly along the line of proving an indirect discrimination case through statistical evidence and structural segregation arguments. The representatives of the applicants put much emphasis on issues of the consent given (or not) by the parents of the applicants, thus accepting tacitly an understanding of the children concerned as passive objects, lacking capacity and agency.[22]

Children are looked at by the Court as well as by the disputing parties, as passive objects, subjected to various types of actions.[23] The children concerned are assessed by teachers and experts; they are placed in various types of schools; their parents challenge decisions or not; they are treated as a group rather than as unique individuals; they are considered victims of collective racial prejudice or not. In accounts like these, the autonomy of children is downplayed in favour of conceptualisations of a perceived intellectual deficit of children, and especially Roma children, with regard to the ability to understand their own situation and have meaningful opinions. For those reasons, my rewriting of the judgment assumes that the Court has available before it evidence concerning the views and experience of each individual applicant.

The Second Section of the Court held that there had been no violation of Article 14 of the Convention taken together with the education provision. In its assessment, the Court's Second Section makes reference to the information provided by several international governmental and non-governmental organisations, including the Council of Europe, about 'arrangements whereby Roma children are placed in special schools and about the difficulties they have in gaining access to ordinary schools'.[24] It is clear that this is generalised information, necessary to give the overall picture in a country, region or thematic area, but hardly sufficient to deal with and reflect upon the particularised conditions of the applicants.

The problem of the absence of specific and individualised information on the applicants

The Court observed that, if a policy or a general measure has disproportionately prejudicial effects on a group of people, the possibility of it being considered discriminatory cannot be ruled out even if it is not specifically aimed or directed at that group. The Court spoke about the setting of the curriculum and the tests used for the assessment of children's capacities. However, the only truly

---

[22] Before the European Court the applicants in the *DH and others* case were represented by the European Roma Rights Centre, based in Budapest, by Lord Lester of Herne Hill QC, Mr Goldston of the New York Bar and Mr Strupek, a lawyer practising in the Czech Republic.

[23] *DH v. Czech Republic*. Judgment by the Second Section of the Court, 7 February 2006, paras. 32 *et seq.*

[24] *DH v. Czech Republic*, Second Section judgment, para. 45.

individualised information we get is that, for some of the applicants, the parents failed to take any action, while in two cases the applicants were transferred to an ordinary primary school, on one occasion upon the request of the mother and on another at the initiative of the special school she was attending. A discussion is initiated by the Second Section of the Court on parental consent and whether it was informed or not. The Court concluded, however, that:

> [T]he concrete evidence before the Court does not enable it to conclude that the applicants' placement or, in some cases continued placement, in special schools was the result of racial prejudice, as they have alleged.[25]

So, both the representing lawyers and the Second Section of the Court seem to follow the same main pattern of the image of the child, even though they came to different conclusions about the factual situation.

Is this image changed in the Grand Chamber Judgment a year and a half later? Of course, the Court reversed its previous decision, by thirteen votes to four, and found that there had indeed been a violation of Article 14 in conjunction with the education provision in Article 2 of Protocol 1. Most of the Court's argument concerns, first, the issue of indirect discrimination and, secondly, the issue of whether statistics can constitute evidence of such indirect discrimination. The Court noted, with reference to *Chapman* v. *United Kingdom* and *Connors* v. *United Kingdom* that 'the vulnerable position of Roma/Gypsies means that special consideration should be given to their needs and their different lifestyle both in the relevant regulatory framework and in reaching decisions in particular cases'.[26] As in the Second Section judgment, the Court's summary of facts and principles and its assessment is based on overall assessments of the statistical evidence and of the tests used to assess the intellectual capabilities of children. On this last point, the Court found that 'the tests used to assess the children's learning abilities or difficulties have given rise to controversy and continue to be the subject of scientific debate and research'. The Court stressed that it is not its role to judge the validity of such tests; however, it was able to conclude that 'the tests carried out at the material time were not capable of constituting objective and reasonable justification' for the purposes of Article 14 of the Convention, since the same tests were used for all children and that there is 'at the very least' a danger that the tests were biased and that the results were not analysed in light of the particularities and special characteristics of the Roma children who sat them.[27]

With regard to parental consent, the Court found that 'the parents of the Roma children, who were members of a disadvantaged community and often poorly educated, were capable of weighing up all the aspects of the situation and the consequences of giving their consent'.[28] Also with regard to the parents, the

---

[25] *Ibid.*, para. 52.   [26] Grand Chamber judgment, para. 181.   [27] *Ibid.*, paras. 199–201.
[28] *Ibid.*, para. 203.

Court adopts a collective approach assuming that all concerned are most likely poorly educated and unable to give an informed consent. At the same time, the Court asserts that the choice of parents was guided by the dilemma of a choice between ordinary schools that were ill-equipped to cater for their children's social and cultural differences and in which their children risked isolation and ostracism, and special schools where the majority of the pupils were Roma, but on this point the Court draws no conclusions as to the risks, advantages or disadvantages of segregated schools or, even more, about the experiences of the applicants as such. This is addressed in the rewritten judgment.

On the issue of school models, the Court is rather cryptic and does not offer much guidance on the positive obligations of States. It argued simply that 'the choice between a single school for everyone, highly specialised structures and unified structures with specialised sections is not an easy one. It entails a difficult balancing exercise between the competing interests.'[29] What the competing interests are, is not identified by the Court, nor are the needs of children identified as any privileged concern, in spite of the fact that the Court had made explicit reference to the UN Convention on the Rights of the Child.

The fact that the ages of the applicants varied and some of them had been teenagers at the time of the various measures was not seen as having any particular importance in the eyes of the Court. All of them are looked at as minors, belonging to the Roma minority.

The main concern of the Court is indeed explicitly 'the social and educational integration of the disadvantaged group which the Roma form'.[30] The Court speaks also of the applicants as 'members of a disadvantaged class'. The Court concluded that the applicants 'received an education which compounded their difficulties and compromised their subsequent personal development instead of tackling their real problems or helping them to integrate into the ordinary schools and develop the skills that would facilitate life among the majority population'. But – and this is a crucial point – since the applied legislation had a disproportionately prejudicial effect on the Roma community, the Court considered that the applicants as members of that community 'necessarily suffered the same discriminatory treatment'.

The dissenting opinions raise important questions on the way the Court chose to assess an entire education system of a country, rather than its concrete implementation and effects for the applicants.[31] Judge Borrego Borrego was the most explicit critic of the absence of the examination of the individual applications and moreover of the absence of narratives giving personalised accounts. We learn through the dissenting opinion of Judge Borrego Borrego, that the applicants were not present in the Court's hearings, something that could perhaps be explained by logistical and financial constraints. But Judge Borrego Borrego apparently did not receive any answer to his questions of

---

[29] *Ibid.*, para. 205.   [30] *Ibid.*   [31] Dissenting Opinion of Judge Jungwiert.

whether the representing lawyers had met the applicants, or their parents, or had been to Ostrava.

In other words, while the outcome is the reverse, the view on children is the same in the Chamber as well as in the Grand Chamber reasoning. Children are in essence looked at as parts of an abstract statistical account or as members of an ethnic group which is, by definition, considered unable to form any wise opinions and decisions. Their personalised accounts of experiences, problems, achievements, wishes and goals are astonishingly absent in the facts and arguments by the parties, as well as by the Court.

The core arguments and conclusions in the Grand Chamber Judgment are found in paragraphs 207–9. The following points are highlighted: first of all, the Court found an absence of 'safeguards' in education for Roma children in general. The Court refers in a general manner to the quality of education offered, which in the words of the Court 'compounded their difficulties and compromised their subsequent personal development instead of tackling their real problems or helping them to integrate into the ordinary schools and develop the skills that would facilitate life among the majority population'. With such strong wording, it may be found surprising that the Court did not proceed to the establishment of a violation of Article 2 of Protocol 1 on the right to education. This can possibly be explained by the fact that the Court did not have evidence and sufficient proof concerning the effect of the quality of education for the specific applicants. Instead, the Court proceeds again in general terms and finds that the Czech government has 'implicitly admitted that job opportunities are more limited for pupils from special schools', i.e. not specifically for the applicants themselves.

The main conclusion is found in the next paragraph, where the Court 'is not satisfied that the difference in treatment between Roma children and non-Roma children was objectively and reasonably justified and that there existed a reasonable relationship of proportionality between the means used and the aim pursued'. The Court concluded that 'the relevant legislation as applied in practice at the material time had a disproportionately prejudicial effect on the Roma community', while the Court considered further, as already mentioned above, that 'the applicants as members of that community necessarily suffered the same discriminatory treatment'. Accordingly, said the Court, 'it does not need to examine their individual cases'.[32] This point will be altered in my rewriting of the judgment.

In sum, the reasoning of the Court focuses on the evidence for indirect discrimination at an abstract level and does not make any effort to address the individual experiences, obstacles and opportunities of the children applicants and, as we shall see, also of their parents. The redraft emphasises the need for individualised information and assessment (paragraphs 181 and 200). I also

---

[32] Grand Chamber judgment, para. 209.

introduce substantive proposals with regard to the right of children to be heard in decision-making within the education system (paragraph 193). Further, I clarify that the possibility of waiver is not available to the parents, neither as regards discrimination, nor with regard to the right of children to be heard in the education system (paragraph 204). The final redrafted assessment covers also the right to education and deletes the sentence concluding that the Court does not need to examine the individual cases, since the legislation as such has been found disproportionately prejudicial (paragraphs 207–10).

In other words, I both agree and disagree with Judge Borrego Borrego who compared in rather unusual language the Court's Grand Chamber Judgment with a Formula One car, which is 'hurtling at high speed into the new and difficult terrain of education and, in so doing, has inevitably strayed far from the line normally followed by the Court'. It needs to be re-emphasised that strengthening the child-affirming and child-sensitive approach in the work of the Court is not a task only for the Court itself, but equally for the applicants, their representatives and for all interveners in the Court's proceedings. The cases examined do not give much evidence of such sensitivity.

The images of parents

As regards parental consent, the Court is inconclusive, but notes that, 'under the Court's case law, the waiver of a right guaranteed by the Convention – in so far as such a waiver is permissible – must be established in an unequivocal manner, and be given in full knowledge of the facts, that is to say on the basis of informed consent and without constraint'.[33] The wording leaves open several questions; is a waiver by parents possible in cases of discrimination against their children in education? Or is the waiver only possible with regard to the right of parents to choose an education according to their own beliefs and convictions? Can children, or their parents, waive their right to education, which is at the same time a duty as far as primary education is concerned?

The crucial point in the reasoning of the Court as regards parental consent is found in the following sentence:

> In the circumstances of the present case, the Court is not satisfied that the parents of the Roma children, who were members of a disadvantaged community and often poorly educated, were capable of weighing up all the aspects of the situation and the consequences of giving their consent.[34]

Thus, also with regard to the parents of the applicants, the Court concludes that they are by definition incapable of understanding the consequences of their actions and giving an informed consent. Thereby, children are put by the reasoning of the Court in a doubly disadvantaged position; not only are they

---

[33] *Ibid.*, para. 202.   [34] *Ibid.*, para. 203.

themselves incapacitated to form opinions, to express them and to take wise decisions to the extent appropriate for their age and capacities, but also their parents are found to be in the same situation. They are then doubly disqualified as autonomous individuals. Such a consequence is problematic from the perspective of disadvantaged minorities for whom judicial proceedings often aim at an emancipatory and empowerment potential.

The Court modified its position somewhat in the *Oršuš* case. The Court there gave an extensive account of the individual circumstances of each applicant, even though this information originates from official school records and not from the personalised narratives of individual applicants, something that would normally have been gathered during domestic judicial proceedings.[35]

In the domestic proceedings in the *Oršuš* case, the applicants had also argued that their right to education had been violated as such, on the ground that the teaching organised in the Roma classes was more reduced in volume and in scope than the Curriculum for primary schools, something which reduced significantly their prospects of higher education.[36]

It may therefore be hoped that this shift in the way the Court looked at the young applicants in the *Oršuš* case represents indeed a consistent and conscious effort in a direction sensitive to the difficulties encountered in different ways, but along similar patterns, by Roma children all over Europe. However, also in this judgment, the Court concluded that it was not necessary to examine the complaint under Article 2 of Protocol 1, taken alone, i.e. with regard to the substantive rights of children in education.

In the *Oršuš* case, the Court referred, however, to its case law on the right to education, and found that the length of any proceedings needs to be assessed against the importance of what was at stake for the applicant in the litigation. The Court concluded that Article 6(1) of the Convention had been violated due to the length of proceedings before the Constitutional Court in Croatia which had lasted for more than four years.

With regard to Article 14 in conjunction with Article 2 of Protocol 1, the Court established in the *Oršuš* case a violation, since there had not been any specific testing of the children's command of the Croatian language, nor were any specific measures taken during the first years of schooling in order to improve the linguistic capacities of the pupils.[37] The Court found also that, 'owing to the lack of transparency and clear criteria' as regards the transfer to mixed classes, the applicants had stayed in Roma-only classes for substantial

---

[35] ECHR (GC), *Oršuš and others* v. *Croatia*, 16 March 2010, paras. 18–51. There is a specific subsection under the section concerning the facts of the case which is entitled 'The individual circumstances of each applicant' (paras. 18–51), with information concerning enrolment, assignment to class, academic performance, participation in parents' meetings and school attendance.
[36] *Ibid.*, para. 60.   [37] *Ibid.*, paras. 160 and 162.

periods of time, sometimes even for their entire primary schooling.[38] At the same time, the Court recognised the efforts made by the Croatian government in ensuring schooling for Roma children. Thus, in the *Oršuš* case, the Court developed a test by which the government was expected to show that it is reasonably possible for children in special classes to reintegrate in the mainstream education system.

Concluding remarks

The difficulty in handling the *DH* case and the controversy surrounding it are evident in the number of third-party interventions and in the willingness and extensiveness of the Court in making selective references to other sources of international law, without, however, reflecting upon the role and impact they have or should have in the work of the Court.[39] A high number of third-party interventions are of course positive as such, in that the Court has easy access to rich information and an understanding of the importance attached to a case by a wider audience.

Twenty-nine pages in the Grand Chamber judgment summarise the situation of Roma in Europe and in the Czech Republic in general and in the educational field in particular and give an account of legally binding provisions and recommendations from various treaty regimes, including the UN Convention on the Rights of the Child and EU discrimination legislation. Interventions were made by Interights, Human Rights Watch, Minority Rights Group International, the European Network against Racism and the European Roma Information Office, all making general statements against segregated education. The International Step by Step Association, the Roma Education Fund and the European Early Childhood Education Research Association made more concrete comments with regard to the implementation of assessment tests in the Ostrava region, but that was hardly taken up by the Court in its reasoning on the facts and in the conclusions.[40] These last-mentioned interveners argued that the assessment tests as used in the Ostrava region had not taken into account the language and culture of the children, their prior learning experiences or their unfamiliarity with the demands of the testing situation. Tests had not been done over time and children had not been given the opportunity to demonstrate their learning in realistic or authentic settings. So, the interveners at this point argued precisely that the individual experiences of children were not taken into account in the testing process either.

It is equally remarkable that nowhere in the judgments, nor in the contributions of interveners, is there any differentiation made between younger and older children, or teenagers and how they were integrated in the education

---

[38] *Ibid.*, para. 182.   [39] For the third party interventions, see paras. 161–74.
[40] Grand Chamber, paras. 168–71.

system in principle and in the concrete instances. For example, with regard to the issue of consent, or participation in educational decisions, older children are to have better information and an important say in the process, as also provided in the above-mentioned provisions of the UN Convention on the Rights of the Child and the European Convention on the Exercise of Children's Rights. Neither the facts submitted by the parties, nor the comments of the Court include any reflections in this direction affecting the procedural safeguards of children in decision-making in the educational field.

What was then the purpose of such a thorough account of background norms and facts by the Court, other than trying to convince that the way the case was dealt with and the conclusion reached were 'unavoidable' and 'natural' in light of general opinion in international law? However, it can be argued that the role of the Court is not as such the consolidation of international law views, nor is it ensuring an absolute consistency of legal views in Europe. The Court's primary role is assessing the respect of the rights under the Convention and its Protocol for unique individuals in unique situations, even though it has increasingly made reference to the importance of interpreting the Convention in light of international law.[41] The Court avoided going deeper into the interpretation of the substance of the law under the right to education and its application for minority children and preferred, instead, to move within the international debate about indirect discrimination. This can and should of course be welcomed but is hardly sufficient in light of the complexity of the cases before it.

As Judge Jungwiert noted in the dissenting opinion, there is a risk that 'the implication is that it is probably preferable and less risky to do nothing and to leave things as they are elsewhere, in other words to make no effort to confront the problems with which a large section of the Roma community is faced'. While Judge Jungwiert also argues, like the Court, on the basis of a general assessment of

---

[41] In the *Loizidou* case, with a great number of general international law questions involved, the Court found that, 'unlike the Convention institutions, the role of the International Court is not exclusively limited to direct supervisory functions in respect of a law-making treaty such as the Convention'. ECHR, *Loizidou* v. *Turkey* (Preliminary Objections), 23 March 1995, para. 84. However, in a case concerning torture, i.e. affecting *ius cogens* rules, the Court emphasised that 'the Convention has to be interpreted in the light of the rules set out in the Vienna Convention on the Law of Treaties of 23 May 1969', and that Article 31 § 3(c) of that treaty indicates that account is to be taken of 'any relevant rules of international law applicable in the relations between the parties'. See ECHR, *Al-Adsani* v. *United Kingdom*, 21 November 2001, para. 55. It remains to be seen whether this is a general long-term trend, in view of the fact that, in a very recent case, of a different nature, concerning custody of a child, the Court argued that 'it is primarily for the national authorities, notably the courts, to resolve problems of interpretation of domestic legislation. This also applies where domestic law refers to rules of general international law or to international agreements. The Court's role is confined to ascertaining whether those rules are applicable and whether their interpretation is compatible with the Convention.' See ECHR (GC), *Neulinger and Shuruk* v. *Switzerland*, 6 July 2010, para. 100.

the situation, rather than on the specificities of the cases, he touches upon the soft spot of a reactive rather than a proactive understanding of the obligations of States Parties under the Convention and its Protocols. The Court chose not to go into the positive obligations of States in order to ensure that children are not denied their right to education, in accordance with the first sentence of Article 2 of Protocol 1, or that they themselves have procedural guarantees, adapted to their needs, when decisions concerning their rights to education are taken.

The *Ostrava* case confirmed earlier accounts of the case law of the Court ascribing to children an image of passive, subordinate and vulnerable beings that need to be protected and managed by grown-ups. This image seems slowly starting to be more nuanced, as evidenced in the deeper analysis and arguments of the Court and the applicants in the *Oršuš* case.

While the Court has commenced its reasoning on procedural guarantees in educational matters, the substantive content of the right to education for children remains underexplored in the judgment.

A worrying conclusion may be that, in situations of multiple diversities, or intersectionality, the Court seems to be giving precedence to racial or ethnic ascription over other aspects of diversity and vulnerability, such as gender or age. The particular needs of children or women are thus subsumed under what is perceived as the dominant understanding about a particular group or minority. In the *Ostrava* case, it would have been perfectly possible for the Court both to take a position with regard to indirect discrimination and the role of statistical evidence, as well as looking at the effects of such evidence on the individual applicants and their parents. Such a combined approach would have honoured the modern legal and societal requirements of looking at children as autonomous individuals with their own specific needs, distinct from their parents and siblings, and with a right to be informed and heard at a level appropriate to their intellectual and cognitive capacities.

Rewriting DH and others v. Czech Republic

. . .

C. *The Court's assessment*

1. Recapitulation of the main principles

175. The Court has established in its case law that discrimination means treating differently, without an objective and reasonable justification, persons in relevantly similar situations (*Willis* v. *the United Kingdom*, no. 36042/97, § 48, ECHR 2002-IV; and *Okpisz* v. *Germany*, no. 59140/00, § 33, 25 October 2005) . . . The Court has also accepted that a general policy

or measure that has disproportionately prejudicial effects on a particular group may be considered discriminatory notwithstanding that it is not specifically aimed at that group [references deleted].

176. Discrimination on account of, *inter alia*, a person's ethnic origin is a form of racial discrimination. Racial discrimination is a particularly invidious kind of discrimination and, in view of its perilous consequences, requires from the authorities special vigilance and a vigorous reaction. It is for this reason that the authorities must use all available means to combat racism, thereby reinforcing democracy's vision of a society in which diversity is not perceived as a threat but as a source of enrichment (*Nachova and others* v. *Bulgaria* [GC], nos. 43577/98 and 43579/98, § 145, ECHR 2005- . . . and *Timishev* v. *Russia*, nos. 55762/00 and 55974/00, § 56, ECHR 2005- . . .). The Court has also held that no difference in treatment which is based exclusively or to a decisive extent on a person's ethnic origin is capable of being objectively justified in a contemporary democratic society built on the principles of pluralism and respect for different cultures (*Timishev*, cited above, § 58).

. . .

179. The Court has also recognised that Convention proceedings do not in all cases lend themselves to a rigorous application of the principle *affirmanti incumbit probatio* (he who alleges something must prove that allegation – *Aktaş* v. *Turkey (extracts)*, no. 24351/94, § 272, ECHR 2003-V). In certain circumstances, where the events in issue lie wholly, or in large part, within the exclusive knowledge of the authorities, the burden of proof may be regarded as resting on the authorities to provide a satisfactory and convincing explanation (*Salman* v. *Turkey* [GC], no. 21986/93, § 100, ECHR 2000-VII; and *Anguelova* v. *Bulgaria*, no. 38361/97, § 111, ECHR 2002-IV) . . .

180. As to whether statistics can constitute evidence, the Court has in the past stated that statistics could not in themselves disclose a practice which could be classified as discriminatory (*Hugh Jordan*, cited above, § 154). However, in more recent cases on the question of discrimination, in which the applicants alleged a difference in the effect of a general measure or *de facto* situation (*Hoogendijk*, cited above; and *Zarb Adami*, cited above, §§ 77–78), the Court relied extensively on statistics produced by the parties to establish a difference in treatment between two groups (men and women) in similar situations. [Fragment deleted]

181. Lastly, as noted in previous cases, the vulnerable position of Roma/Gypsies means that special consideration should be given to their needs and their different lifestyle both in the relevant regulatory framework and in reaching decisions in particular cases (*Chapman* v. *the United Kingdom* [GC],

no. 27238/95, § 96, ECHR 2001-I; and *Connors* v. *the United Kingdom*, no. 66746/01, § 84, 27 May 2004).

In *Chapman* (cited above, §§ 93–94), the Court also observed that there could be said to be an emerging international consensus amongst the Contracting States of the Council of Europe recognising the special needs of minorities and an obligation to protect their security, identity and lifestyle, not only for the purpose of safeguarding the interests of the minorities themselves but to preserve a cultural diversity of value to the whole community.

The assessment of the needs of applicants should take into account the particularities and experiences of each individual applicant even when it forms part of an examination of a generalised pattern of alleged discrimination or segregation. Such an assessment is necessary in order to delimit the margin of appreciation of States (Buckley v. the United Kingdom, Judgment, 29 September 1996, §§ 74–76). This is particularly so with regard to the right to education of children which affects the entire lifespan of the applicants.

2.   Application of the aforementioned principles to the instant case

182. The Court notes that as a result of their turbulent history and constant uprooting the Roma have become a specific type of disadvantaged and vulnerable minority [references deleted]. As the Court has noted in previous cases, they therefore require special protection (see paragraph 7 above). As is attested by the activities of numerous European and international organisations and the recommendations of the Council of Europe bodies (see paragraphs 54–61 above), this protection also extends to the sphere of education. The present case therefore warrants particular attention, especially as when the applications were lodged with the Court the applicants were minor children for whom the right to education was of paramount importance.

183. [Paragraph deleted]

184. The Court has already accepted in previous cases that a difference in treatment may take the form of disproportionately prejudicial effects of a general policy or measure which, though couched in neutral terms, discriminates against a group [fragment deleted] [S]uch a situation may amount to 'indirect discrimination', which does not necessarily require a discriminatory intent.

(a)   Whether a presumption of indirect discrimination arises in the instant case

185. It was common ground that the impugned difference in treatment did not result from the wording of the statutory provisions on placements in special schools in force at the material time. Accordingly, the issue in the instant case is whether the manner in which the legislation was applied in

practice resulted in a disproportionate number of Roma children – including the applicants – being placed in special schools without justification, and whether such children were thereby placed at a significant disadvantage.

186. As mentioned above, the Court has noted in previous cases that applicants may have difficulty in proving discriminatory treatment (*Nachova and others*, cited above, §§ 147 and 157). In order to guarantee those concerned the effective protection of their rights, less strict evidential rules should apply in cases of alleged indirect discrimination.

. . .

188. In these circumstances, the Court considers that when it comes to assessing the impact of a measure or practice on an individual or group, statistics which appear on critical examination to be reliable and significant will be sufficient to constitute the *prima facie* evidence the applicant is required to produce. This does not, however, mean that indirect discrimination cannot be proved without statistical evidence.

189. Where an applicant alleging indirect discrimination thus establishes a rebuttable presumption that the effect of a measure or practice is discriminatory, the burden then shifts to the respondent State, which must show that the difference in treatment is not discriminatory (see, *mutatis mutandis*, *Nachova and others*, cited above, § 157). Regard being had in particular to the specificity of the facts and the nature of the allegations made in this type of case (*ibid.*, § 147), it would be extremely difficult in practice for applicants to prove indirect discrimination without such a shift in the burden of proof.

190. In the present case, the statistical data submitted by the applicants was obtained from questionnaires that were sent out to the head teachers of special and primary schools in the town of Ostrava in 1999. It indicates that at the time 56% of all pupils placed in special schools in Ostrava were Roma. Conversely, Roma represented only 2.26% of the total number of pupils attending primary school in Ostrava. Further, whereas only 1.8% of non-Roma pupils were placed in special schools, the proportion of Roma pupils in Ostrava assigned to special schools was 50.3%. According to the Government, these figures are not sufficiently conclusive as they merely reflect the subjective opinions of the head teachers. The Government also noted that no official information on the ethnic origin of the pupils existed and that the Ostrava region had one of the largest Roma populations.

191. The Grand Chamber observes that these figures are not disputed by the Government and that they have not produced any alternative statistical evidence. In view of their comment that no official information on the ethnic origin of the pupils exists, the Court accepts that the statistics submitted by the applicants may not be entirely reliable. It nevertheless considers that these figures reveal a dominant trend that has been confirmed both by the respondent State and the independent supervisory bodies which have looked into the question.

192. In their reports submitted in accordance with Article 25 § 1 of the Framework Convention for the Protection of National Minorities, the Czech authorities accepted that in 1999 Roma pupils made up between 80% and 90% of the total number of pupils in some special schools [references deleted] and that in 2004 'large numbers' of Roma children were still being placed in special schools [references deleted]. The Advisory Committee on the Framework Convention observed in its report of 26 October 2005 that according to unofficial estimates Roma accounted for up to 70% of pupils enrolled in special schools. [Fragment deleted]

193. In the Court's view, the latter figures, which do not relate solely to the Ostrava region and therefore provide a more general picture, show that, even if the exact percentage of Roma children in special schools at the material time remains difficult to establish, their number was disproportionately high. Moreover, Roma pupils formed a majority of the pupils in special schools. Despite being couched in neutral terms, the relevant statutory provisions therefore had considerably more impact in practice on Roma children than on non-Roma children and resulted in statistically disproportionate numbers of placements of the former in special schools. **In decision-making about the transition to the next or other level of schools or in situations of choice of tracks or streams in school, all children, including minority children, should be properly informed and heard and their views should be taken into account, since such choices will influence future education and professional opportunities of the children concerned. The Court notes that some of the applicants had a different age at the time of the tests and their placement in special schools. However, the individual conditions and capabilities of the applicants were not taken into account by the responsible authorities and by the schools concerned. The Court is not convinced that the procedural guarantees provided by the Czech government in important decisions concerning educational choices have been sufficient in the case of the applicants and in general.**

. . .

195. In these circumstances, the evidence submitted by the applicants can be regarded as sufficiently reliable and significant to give rise to a strong presumption of indirect discrimination. The burden of proof must therefore shift to the Government, which must show that the difference in the impact of the legislation was the result of objective factors unrelated to ethnic origin.

(b) Objective and reasonable justification

196. The Court reiterates that a difference in treatment is discriminatory if 'it has no objective and reasonable justification', that is, if it does not

pursue a 'legitimate aim' or if there is not a 'reasonable relationship of proportionality' between the means employed and the aim sought to be realised (see, among many other authorities, *Larkos* v. *Cyprus* [GC], no. 29515/95, § 29, ECHR 1999-I; and *Stec and others*, cited above, § 51). Where the difference in treatment is based on race, colour or ethnic origin, the notion of objective and reasonable justification must be interpreted as strictly as possible.

...

198. The Court accepts that the Government's decision to retain the special-school system was motivated by the desire to find a solution for children with special educational needs. However, it shares the disquiet of the other Council of Europe institutions who have expressed concerns about the more basic curriculum followed in these schools and, in particular, the segregation the system causes.

199. The Grand Chamber observes, further, that the tests used to assess the children's learning abilities or difficulties have given rise to controversy and continue to be the subject of scientific debate and research. While accepting that it is not its role to judge the validity of such tests, various factors in the instant case nevertheless lead the Grand Chamber to conclude that the results of the tests carried out at the material time were not capable of constituting objective and reasonable justification for the purposes of Article 14 of the Convention.

200. In the first place, it was common ground that all the children who were examined sat the same tests, irrespective of their ethnic origin. The Czech authorities themselves acknowledged in 1999 that 'Romany children with average or above-average intellect' were often placed in such schools on the basis of the results of psychological tests and that the tests were conceived for the majority population and did not take Roma specifics into consideration [references deleted]. As a result, they had revised the tests and methods used with a view to ensuring that they 'were not misused to the detriment of Roma children' [references deleted].

The applicants have demonstrated that the tests to which they were subjected did not relate to any experiences relevant to them and they were in many cases unable to understand what was expected of them. The purpose of the tests was not clear to them nor did they receive full information about the consequences of the tests. Further, several individual applicants have indicated that education in special schools is not supportive of their cognitive, intellectual and emotional development as it is adapted to children with very weak intellectual capacities and does not take into account the cultural context and the life experiences of Roma children. Therefore, the education offered to them in special schools is, according to the applicants, not felt as meaningful,

appropriate and productive. In addition, the applicants have been intimidated within and outside the special schools for the fact that they attend such a school. Such a situation aggravates their experiences of discrimination and anti-Gypsyism. Finally, the Government has failed to prove to the Court that there have been regular reassessments of the progress of Roma pupils and that they have been given the opportunity to integrate into other forms of primary education.

In addition, various independent bodies have expressed doubts over the adequacy of the tests [references deleted]. Lastly, in the submission of some of the third-party interveners, placements following the results of the psychological tests reflected the racial prejudices of the society concerned.

201. The Court considers that, at the very least, there is a danger that the tests were biased and that the results were not analysed in the light of the particularities and special characteristics of the Roma children who sat them. In these circumstances, the tests in question cannot serve as justification for the impugned difference in treatment.

202. As regards parental consent, the Court notes the Government's submission that this was the decisive factor without which the applicants would not have been placed in special schools. In view of the fact that a difference in treatment has been established in the instant case, it follows that any such consent would signify an acceptance of the difference in treatment, even if discriminatory, in other words a waiver of the right not to be discriminated against. However, under the Court's case law, the waiver of a right guaranteed by the Convention – in so far as such a waiver is permissible – must be established in an unequivocal manner, and be given in full knowledge of the facts, that is to say on the basis of informed consent (*Pfeifer and Plankl* v. *Austria*, judgment of 25 February 1992, Series A no. 227, §§ 37–38) and without constraint (*Deweer* v. *Belgium*, judgment of 27 February 1980, Series A no. 35, § 51).

203. In the circumstances of the present case, the Court is not satisfied that the parents of the Roma children, who were members of a disadvantaged community and often poorly educated, were **given adequate information and were consulted in an appropriate manner so as to ensure that they were** capable of weighing up all the aspects of the situation and the consequences of giving their consent. The Government themselves admitted that consent in this instance had been given by means of a signature on a pre-completed form that contained no information on the available alternatives or the differences between the special-school curriculum and the curriculum followed in other schools. Nor do the domestic authorities appear to have taken any additional measures to ensure that the Roma parents received all the information they needed to make an informed decision or were aware of the consequences that

giving their consent would have for their children's futures. It also appears indisputable that the Roma parents were faced with a dilemma: a choice between ordinary schools that were ill-equipped to cater for their children's social and cultural differences and in which their children risked isolation and ostracism and special schools where the majority of the pupils were Roma.

204. In view of the fundamental importance of the prohibition of racial discrimination (see *Nachova and others*, cited above, § 145; and *Timishev*, cited above, § 56), the Grand Chamber considers that, even assuming the conditions referred to in paragraph 28 above were satisfied, no waiver of the right not to be subjected to racial discrimination can be accepted, as it would be counter to an important public interest (see, *mutatis mutandis, Hermi* v. *Italy* [GC], no. 18114/02, § 73, ECHR 2006- . . .). **In other words, neither the parents nor the children could waive the right of the children not to be discriminated in their right to education; nor is it possible to waive the right of the parents not to be discriminated in their parental rights with regard to the education of their children. Furthermore, the Court has not received any evidence that the children applicants had been specifically informed and heard by the Czech authorities before the tests to which they had been subjected.**

(c) Conclusion

. . .

207. The facts of the instant case indicate that the schooling arrangements for Roma children were not attended by safeguards (see paragraph 28 above) that would ensure that, in the exercise of its margin of appreciation in the education sphere, the State took into account their special needs as members of a disadvantaged class (see, *mutatis mutandis, Buckley*, cited above, § 76; and *Connors*, cited above, § 84). **The Court has found that the facts of the instant cases show that the schooling arrangements for the applicants did not safeguard their right to a safe and culturally sensitive education which offers them the necessary preconditions to develop their personality. The children have given evidence of how they were effectively kept segregated from other children and the wider population and how their needs, views and wishes were hardly taken into account in the education system and in the schools and classes they attended.** Furthermore, as a result of the arrangements the applicants were placed in schools for children with mental disabilities where a more basic curriculum was followed than in ordinary schools and where they were isolated from pupils from the wider population. As a result, they received an education which compounded their difficulties and compromised their subsequent personal development instead of tackling their real problems or helping them to integrate into

the ordinary schools and develop the skills that would facilitate life among the majority population. Indeed, the Government have implicitly admitted that job opportunities are more limited for pupils from special schools **and this has also been the case for the applicants.**

208. In these circumstances and while recognising the efforts made by the Czech authorities to ensure that Roma children receive schooling, the Court is not satisfied that the difference in treatment between Roma children and non-Roma children was objectively and reasonably justified and that there existed a reasonable relationship of proportionality between the means used and the aim pursued. **The relevant legislation as applied in practice at the material time and affecting the applicants had a disproportionately prejudicial effect on the Roma community.** In that connection, it notes with interest that the new legislation has abolished special schools and provides for children with special educational needs, including socially disadvantaged children, to be educated in ordinary schools.

209. [Paragraph deleted][42]

210. Consequently, there has been a violation in the instant case of **Article 2 of Protocol 1 as well as of** Article 14 of the Convention, read in conjunction with Article 2 of Protocol 1, as regards each of the applicants **examined individually and as a group.**

---

[42] The author emphasises that paragraph 209 has been deleted because it is in conflict with the spirit of the revisions.

3

Mainstreaming children's rights in migration litigation: Muskhadzhiyeva and others v. Belgium

WOUTER VANDENHOLE* AND JULIE RYNGAERT

The case of *Muskhadzhiyeva and others* v. *Belgium* concerns the detention of five Russian citizens of Chechnyan origin, Ms Aina Muskhadzhiyeva and her four children, Alik, Liana, Khadizha and Louisa, at the time of the events respectively seven years, five years, three and a half years and seven months old. They applied for asylum in Belgium on 12 October 2006. After it had been established that they had entered the Schengen area through Poland, and that the Polish authorities had declared to be willing to take care of them, they were ordered to leave Belgian territory, and were detained for more than a month in Centre 127*bis* with a view to their deportation to Poland. They were put on a plane to Poland on 24 January 2007. The European Court of Human Rights (hereinafter the Court or the ECHR) held that a violation had taken place of Articles 3 and 5(1)(f) of the European Convention on Human Rights (hereinafter 'the Convention') concerning the children, but not concerning the mother. The violations arose from the living conditions in detention and the absence of reasonable necessity for their detention. The Court rejected the claim of a violation of Article 8 as manifestly ill-founded.

With regard to the *children*, we do not disagree as such with the findings of the Court on Articles 3 and 5. Our concerns lie rather with the lack of elaboration of arguments and justification for these findings. The Court seems to have over-relied on the *Tabitha* case[1] and on the question whether the current case was relevantly distinctive, at the expense of an analysis of this case in its own right. While this may be an understandable approach in a politically sensitive case for a Court that is suffering from an excessive workload and that is under increasing, often politically inspired criticism, it does not necessarily do justice to the complainants, nor to the cause of the group (in our case, children) they belong to. We do disagree with the findings of the Court that a violation neither of Article 3 nor of Article 5 has taken place with regard

---

* Wouter Vandenhole holds the UNICEF Chair in Children's Rights. UNICEF respects the academic freedom of the chair holder. Opinions expressed by the chair holder do not commit UNICEF.

[1] ECHR, *Mubilanzila Mayeka and Kaniki Mitunga v. Belgium*, 12 October 2006.

to the *mother*. That disagreement is at least partly related to the fact that the mother was accompanied by (young) children. In addition, we argue that Article 8 should have been held applicable, and that a violation of the right to respect of family life should have been found.

In our understanding, mainstreaming diversity with regard to children means that the specificity of children and of their rights is taken into account. In particular, insights gained in the multidisciplinary field of children's rights need to be fully incorporated in the Court's case law. We consciously do not rely on the notion of the best interests of the child in our analysis, as we believe that this notion is not particularly helpful – at least from a conceptual point of view – to elucidate the specificity of their rights. Notwithstanding recent efforts of the Court to clarify how the best interests of the child may be operationalised in migration cases,[2] it remains a very vague and open-ended concept that is often invoked as a trump card without clarification of its meaning. Given the fundamental uncertainty about the notion's meaning due to the absence of solid criteria to substantiate it,[3] the notion of best interests of the child may be invoked to justify basically *whatever* decision is reached.

We have chosen this case precisely because it raises many of the fundamental issues that are at stake in children's rights' scholarship, such as different images of the child (with the central notions of agency and vulnerability); the relationship between human rights of children and adults; the question whether the situation of children can be disconnected from that of their parent(s); and how parental responsibility and State obligations for care and protection interact. In addition, we believe that the relevance of children's rights law, and by extension of human rights law, is particularly put to the test in migration control policies, given the blend of human suffering and States' reliance on sovereignty arguments.

Our comments and suggestions are situated at two levels: some relate to paragraphs of the judgment that are amenable to improvement in wording or argument; other comments go to the heart of the mainstreaming diversity exercise, and take the specificity of children and of their human rights as a starting point.

---

[2] See, in particular, ECHR (GC), *Maslov* v. *Austria*, 23 June 2008, paras. 82–3; and ECHR (GC), *Neulinger and Shuruk* v. *Switzerland*, 6 July 2010, paras. 135–6. See also the references to 'best interests' in recent cases on the detention of accompanied minors: ECHR, *Kanagaratnam and others* v. *Belgium*, 13 December 2011, para. 67; ECHR, *Rahimi* v. *Greece*, 5 April 2011, para. 109.

[3] See, *inter alia*, M. Freeman, 'Article 3: The Best Interests of the Child', in A. Alen, J. Vande Lanotte, E. Verhellen, F. Ang, E. Berghmans and M. Verheyde (eds.), *A Commentary on the United Nations Convention on the Rights of the Child* (Leiden/Boston: Martinus Nijhoff, 2007); P. Alston, 'The Best Interests Principle: Towards a Reconciliation of Culture and Human Rights' (1994) 8 *International Journal of Law and the Family* 1–25; S. Parker, 'The Best Interests of the Child – Principles and Problems' (1992) 8 *International Journal of Law and the Family* 26–41.

Quite some of the issues that we raise are underlying our analysis *as a whole* rather than that of a specific Article of the Convention. This chapter is therefore not so much structured Article-by-Article, but addresses seven issues, namely: images of the child; a rationale for the irrelevance of the distinction between accompanied and unaccompanied children; the relationship between human rights of children and adults; the minimum level of severity threshold under Article 3; the absence-of-arbitrariness requirement in Article 5(1)(f); positive obligations under the right to family life; and the role of other instruments in the interpretation of the Convention.

Image of the child: vulnerability and agency

In paragraph 56 of the judgment, while referring to the *Tabitha* case, the Court recalls the situation of extreme vulnerability of a child which is paramount to and takes precedence over the status as an alien. In other provisions of this judgment too, the Court takes the situation of extreme vulnerability of children as the starting point (see, for example, paragraphs 73–4). While it refers to a *situation of* extreme vulnerability rather than to vulnerability as a personal characteristic of children, it does not clarify the rationale for that wording, nor does it contextualise vulnerability in its relationship with agency.

Considering the situation of extreme vulnerability of a child as paramount in relation to its rights as asylum-seeker is absolutely correct *in this particular case*. However, from a more general children's rights perspective, the one-sided emphasis on extreme vulnerability is reductionist, as it shows only one dimension of the image of children, who are first and foremost to be seen as fully fledged human beings with agency.[4] Secondly, vulnerability is not only attributable to personal factors such as age, but has to do with a complex web of both internal and external factors, so that the degree of vulnerability and agency heavily depends on each particular child and context. In order to reflect this complexity of factors that constitute vulnerability, as well as the interface with the countervailing notion of agency, we propose to refer systematically to 'contextual vulnerability' rather than to 'situation of vulnerability'.

To answer the question of which characteristics are attributed to children as fully fledged human beings is rather complex.[5] It was not until the adoption of the 1989 Convention on the Rights of the Child (CRC) that human rights doctrine paid attention to the question how a child was perceived. Before, to the extent that provisions of the general human rights treaties addressed children in particular, they did so from an exclusively protectionist agenda, and often by

---

[4] See e.g. B. Mayall, 'The Sociology of Childhood in Relation to Children's Rights' (2000) 8 *International Journal of Children's Rights* 243–59.

[5] We take a non-essentialist approach: see O. Nieuwenhuys, 'Editorial: The Ethics of Children's Rights' (2008) 15 *Childhood* 4–11.

protecting the family (see, for example, Article 10 of the International Covenant on Economic, Social and Cultural Rights).

Two schools of thought on children, i.e. child protection and child liberation theories, have influenced the CRC to some extent. Child protection theorists mainly emphasise the welfare and special needs of the child. From this paternalistic point of view, children are approached as irrational and dependent individuals whose decisions should be made by rational autonomous adults. Child liberation theorists, on the other hand, draw attention predominantly to children as autonomous individuals and 'fully fledged beneficiaries of human rights'.[6] This strand of thinking acknowledges that children do possess a competence for rational thought by means of which informed choices can be made. Moreover, the lack of competence in decision-making on the part of children is not of overriding importance to exclude them from participation in decision-making.[7]

The approach adopted by the CRC stands midway between a protection and a liberation approach.[8] A child is considered as 'an initially highly vulnerable person in need of protection, nurturing and care who under parental guidance gradually prepares for an independent life in a social setting of rights and duties when reaching eighteen'.[9] Two key principles frame the characteristics of the child as constructed by the CRC, namely, Article 3 and Article 12. On the one hand, there is the State obligation to take the child's 'best interests' into account as a primary consideration in all matters affecting the child (Article 3 CRC). From this perspective, the child tends to be seen as a dependent human being in need of protection against harm. At the same time, the CRC recognises the agency of children through the right to voice, to be heard and to participation (Article 12 CRC).[10] These two principles forge a balanced image of the child, namely, that of a vulnerable child yet with agency.[11] The degree of agency and vulnerability differs from child to child and arises from the interaction of multiple factors. In some cases, children may be (considered) especially in

---

[6] N. Cantwell, 'The Origins, Development and Significance of the United Nations Convention on the Rights of the Child', in S. Detrick (ed.), *The United Nations Convention on the Rights of the Child: A Guide to the 'Travaux Préparatoires'* (Dordrecht/Boston/London: Martinus Nijhoff, 1992), p. 27.

[7] C. Breen, *Age Discrimination and Children's Rights* (Leiden/Boston: Martinus Nijhoff, 2006), pp. 2–8.

[8] *Ibid.*, p. 8; W. Vandenhole, 'A Children's Rights Perspective on Poverty', in W. Vandenhole, J. Vranken and K. De Boyser (eds.), *Why Care? Children's Rights and Child Poverty* (Antwerp/Oxford/Dordrecht: Intersentia, 2010), p. 19.

[9] A. Eide, 'Article 27: The Right to an Adequate Standard of Living', in A. Alen, J. Vande Lanotte, E. Verhellen, E. Berghmans and M. Verheyde (eds.), *A Commentary on the United Nations Convention on the Rights of the Child* (Leiden/Boston: Martinus Nijhoff, 2006), p. 3.

[10] J. Bhabha, 'The Child – What Sort of Human?' (2006) 121 *The Humanities in Human Rights: Critique, Language, Politics* 1526–35.

[11] For further elaboration, see D. Archard and M. Skivenes, 'Balancing a Child's Best Interests and a Child's Views' (2009) 17 *International Journal of Children's Rights* 1–21.

need of protection. In other cases, children themselves can be best placed to judge what they really need or want.

There is an often mistaken claim of inherent, personal or automatic vulnerability of a child. Due to the status of 'being a child', it is assumed that children need special attention. This concept of vulnerability is based on personal factors only, i.e. the simple fact of age, of 'being a child'.

A recent study by STEPS Consulting Social,[12] commissioned by the European Parliament, has argued that vulnerability does not only result from personal factors, but should be understood as a mechanism governed by the *interaction between different factors*. In that study, 'vulnerability' arises from three factors: personal factors, environmental factors and risk factors. Personal factors result from the specific conditions of a person, such as physical and mental conditions, age, genetic composition or knowledge. Environmental factors are external to the person. Risk factors are external too, but concern more specifically characteristics or circumstances that if present, reduce the chance of a positive outcome. These factors all interact to constitute vulnerability.[13] Applied to the specific context of migration, *risk factors* were defined as experiences of asylum-seekers prior to arrival, whether in their country or as a consequence of their migration. In the case under review, mention can be made of the war in Chechnya, and their flight to Poland and subsequently to Belgium. *Personal factors* relate to the person's individual history and condition (physical and psychological constitution). In this case, the young age of the four children, their health state (serious physical and psychosomatic symptoms as a consequence of trauma, respiratory problems), their exposure to an apparently violent father, and the absence of the father – who is often considered as very important in models of child development – can be flagged. *Environmental factors* were defined as the experiences of the asylum-seeker after his arrival in Europe. More specifically, detention in an ill-suited environment; the duration of detention and the prison-like regime are external, contextual elements that may exacerbate personal vulnerability.

In conclusion, from a childhood studies and children's rights perspective, a child is regarded as being vulnerable and endowed with agency at the same time. The degree of vulnerability and agency depends on the interaction between different factors. In the particular case under discussion, the vulnerability of the children prevails over their agency. However, their vulnerability should not exclusively be seen as personal or inherent to childhood. Risk and environmental

---

[12] STEPS Consulting Social, 'The Conditions in Centres for Third Country National (Detention Camps, Open Centres as well as Transit Centres and Transit Zones) with a Particular Focus on Provisions and Facilities for Persons with Special Needs in the 25 EU Member States' (December 2007).

[13] For a discussion of risk factors and the interplay between vulnerability and resilience, see I. Derluyn, *Emotional and Behavioural Problems in Unaccompanied Refugee Minors* (Ghent: Academia Press, 2005), in particular pp. 22–34.

factors related to migration and reception may add to or worsen personal vulnerability, and amount to extreme vulnerability. We therefore suggest referring to *contextual* vulnerability. In addition, it would be helpful to elucidate the sources of vulnerability (personal, risk, environment) whenever possible, so as not to create the impression that vulnerability is purely resulting from personal or inherent characteristics (see paragraph 56 of the rewritten judgment).

A rationale for the irrelevance of the distinction between unaccompanied and accompanied migrant children regarding (positive) State obligations

In paragraphs 57–8, the Court recalls that Belgium has already been found in violation of the Convention in the *Tabitha* case, for the detention of an *unaccompanied* minor asylum-seeker in a closed detention centre. In the case under scrutiny, the children were detained *together with* their mother. They therefore were accompanied minors. In the Court's view, the fact that in the present case the four children have not been separated from their mother, unlike *Tabitha*, does not exempt the authorities from their positive obligations to protect under Article 3.

Regrettably, the Court does not explain why the difference of circumstances (accompanied/non-accompanied) is considered irrelevant for a State's positive obligation to protect children under Article 3. While we agree with the principle, it would have been preferable for the Court to explain its position, including whether and which particular positive obligations are incumbent on States with regard to accompanied *immigrant* children as compared to *national* children, or with regard to *unaccompanied* immigrant children as compared to *accompanied* ones.

Generally, human rights are situated in the vertical relationship between a State – as the duty-holder – and an individual under its jurisdiction – the rights-holder. Children's rights, i.e. the human rights of children, come to play within that same relationship. However, the situation is more complex and sophisticated as there is an intermediary level of parents and care-givers. Although parents have not been assigned legally binding obligations, they do hold a number of responsibilities under some human rights instruments, and in particular under the CRC. Article 18 CRC states that parents or legal guardians have the primary responsibility for the upbringing and development of the child. The best interests of the child should be their basic concern. Article 3(2) CRC refers to the undertaking of States to ensure the child's protection and care as necessary for its well-being, although they have to take the rights and duties of the child's parents into account. Article 27 CRC stipulates that parents have the primary responsibility to secure proper living conditions for their children. In summary, the primary responsibility for the upbringing and the development of the child lies with the parents, and the ultimate responsibility with the State.

While international human rights law respects the rights and duties of the parents, the State is under a duty to intervene where there is a risk that members of the family do not exercise their parental responsibility in the best interests of the child.[14]

The positive obligation to intervene may also imply that a State needs to protect children *against their parent(s)*. Therefore, a State may be required to provide effective deterrence against corporal punishment,[15] or to place children into care when they are victims of abuse or neglect.[16]

In the present case, the mother of the four children had the primary responsibility for the upbringing and development of her children. However, due, *inter alia*, to her detention (environmental factor) in Centre 127*bis*, the relationship between the mother and her children may have been disrupted, and, as has been documented (see below), the conditions and regime of detention did not allow parents to assume and exercise their parental responsibilities (e.g. to provide a safe environment, material conditions etc.). Although the mother had the primary responsibility for the upbringing and the development of her children, she was unable or prevented from taking up that responsibility, all the more so as the State contributed to that inability, hence the State should have assumed fully its protection obligations. That positive obligation of protection applies regardless of whether a child is accompanied by parents or not, though it may be assumed that it will be an even stronger obligation when a child comes under the power of the State in the absence of its parents (see paragraph 58 of the redraft).

Moreover, as they were seeking asylum, the four children came under the scope of application of Article 22 CRC, which imposes an obligation on States to take appropriate measures to ensure that children seeking asylum, whether unaccompanied or accompanied by their parents or by any other person, receive appropriate protection in the enjoyment of applicable rights set forth in the CRC and in other international human rights instruments to which the States are party. So there is an additional protection obligation towards asylum-seeking children.

In sum, an explanation should have been given as to why the difference in circumstances (accompanied/non-accompanied) did not affect the positive obligation incumbent on States to protect children under Article 3. That explanation relates to the State's ultimate responsibility for children when parents are unable to take up their responsibility, all the more so when the State has contributed to that inability (see paragraph 58 of the rewritten judgment).

---

[14] J. C. M. Willems, 'What May Parents Be Asked to Pledge', in H. Van Crombrugge, W. Vandenhole and J. C. M. Willems (eds.), *Shared Pedagogical Responsibility* (Antwerp/ Oxford/ Portland, OR: Intersentia, 2008), pp. 17–36.

[15] ECHR, *A v. United Kingdom*, 23 September 1998, para. 22.

[16] ECHR, *Z and others v. United Kingdom*, 10 May 2001, paras. 73–4.

The relationship between the human rights of children and adults

With regard to both Articles 3 and 5, the Court concludes that these rights have been violated on account of the children, but not of the mother. This may create the impression that children and their rights are somehow of higher value than adults and their rights. This tension between the human rights of children and those of adults (in the present case, the mother) seems to be based on a perception of children as inherently or automatically more vulnerable than adults. The European Court of Human Rights seems to recognise only certain predefined categories or classes of vulnerable persons such as minors as persons in need of special protection.

Due to their status of 'being a child', children may for sure have special needs that require special attention. However, persons with special needs are not automatically or inherently vulnerable in every respect. Moreover, as explained earlier, vulnerability is not an inherent quality of a particular class of human beings, such as those aged under eighteen, but rather results from the inter-action between internal and external factors, such as personal factors, risk factors and environmental factors. If vulnerability is defined as contextual, not every child may be particularly vulnerable, while many adult asylum-seekers or undocumented migrants may be extremely vulnerable. This more advanced understanding of vulnerability may considerably loosen the apparent tension between the human rights of children and adults.

Strategically, one may want to create political space for debating sensitive human rights issues by raising them (initially) as children's rights issues. A good case in point is migration policies. In recent years, complaints in the field of migration policies have been dealt with by both the European Committee of Social Rights (ECSR) and the European Court of Human Rights. In *International Federation of Human Rights Leagues (FIDH) v. France*, the ECSR examined a complaint about the denial of medical assistance to undocumented migrants, adults and children alike.[17] In *Defence for Children International (DCI) v. Netherlands*, the issue at stake was the exclusion of children not lawfully on Dutch territory from the right to housing.[18] In both cases, a violation was found.

The ECHR has been confronted with some cases in which the treatment of undocumented minor migrants was at stake. In both the *Tabitha* case and the *Muskhadzhiyeva* case here under discussion, a complaint was lodged by both the minor(s) concerned and the mother. In the current case, it is surprising to note that the Court does not examine whether the detention of the mother, together with her children, reaches the minimum level of severity to come within the scope of Article 3. The Court confines itself to examining whether

[17] European Committee of Social Rights, Complaint No. 14/2003, 8 September 2004.
[18] European Committee of Social Rights, Complaint No. 47/2008, 20 October 2009.

the mother has undergone treatment that reaches the minimum level of severity because of the treatment of her children in violation of Article 3.

There are two potential risks with strategically mobilising the human rights of children to raise a broader human rights issue that also concerns adults. A first risk is that, while children's rights are used as a stepping stone for mobilisation and advocacy, children ultimately may hardly or not at all benefit from the outcome of the litigation undertaken on behalf of their rights. A second risk is that in such cases of strategic mobilisation of children's rights as leverage for raising a broader issue, the violation of children's rights is recognised indeed, but almost at the expense of the human rights of adults. The latter seems to have been the case in some of the cases mentioned, and a similar risk is discernible in the case under discussion here.

Towards parameters for the 'minimum level of severity' threshold in Article 3[19]

In order for treatment to fall within the scope of Article 3, a minimum level of severity has to be reached. That minimum level of severity is an issue of fact, which depends on the specific circumstances of the case. The assessment of the minimum is relative. Elements to be taken into account are the nature and context of the treatment, the duration of the treatment, its physical or mental effects, the sex, age and state of health of the person concerned etc.[20]

Once it has been established that the minimum threshold of severity has been reached, the Court may hold that Article 3 generally speaking has been violated, or it may clarify whether the violation amounts to degrading treatment, inhuman treatment, or torture. Since its early case law, the Court has tried to clarify what kind of treatment amounts to each of the categories. The distinction derives mainly from a difference in the intensity of the suffering. In particular, 'a special stigma to deliberate inhuman treatment causing very serious and cruel suffering' is attached to torture.[21]

In the present case, the Court invokes the low age of the children, the duration of their detention and their health status to conclude that the living conditions in the Centre have reached the minimum threshold of severity and amount to a violation of Article 3. Regrettably, the Court does not explain nor justify that finding, and refrains from qualifying the treatment as degrading or

---

[19] See paras. 60–1 and 65 of the redraft.
[20] ECHR, *Ireland v. United Kingdom*, 18 January 1978, para. 162; ECHR, *A v. United Kingdom*, 23 September 1998, para. 20.
[21] ECHR, *Ireland v. United Kingdom*, 18 January 1978, para. 167.

inhuman treatment, or torture. In order to be able to draw somewhat more general principles from this case, it would be important to know in particular what the relative weight of each element is, and whether the conditions apply cumulatively, i.e. whether *all* conditions of a low age, a long period and a worrying and deteriorating health status need to be fulfilled in order to reach the minimum level of severity. Admittedly, the Court has emphasised in its case law on Article 3 that the assessment is relative. While that is undoubtedly true, it does not mean by necessity that no clarification and more general principles are possible, so as to allow for a better assessment of the relevance of this judgment for similar, though not identical, cases. The Court has, for example, clarified by way of *obiter dictum* that the principles that it developed on the expulsion of a person with an HIV and AIDS-related condition equally applied in relation to any person 'afflicted with any serious, naturally occurring physical or mental illness which may cause suffering, pain and reduced life expectancy and require specialised medical treatment which may not be so readily available in the applicant's country of origin or which may be available only at substantial cost'.[22] In the context of Article 8, where it has developed criteria to assess the proportionality of the expulsion of foreign offenders with their private and family life,[23] the Court has identified more recently which criteria are of relevance in cases 'where the person to be expelled is a young adult who has not yet founded a family of his own'.[24]

We shall now look into more general principles that the Court may want to apply under Article 3 in order to assess the living conditions in closed centres where migrant children are held. As to the criterion of age, the Court sends out confusing signals. On the one hand, it points out that, out of the four children – aged seven months, three and a half years, five years and seven years at the time of the events – at least two were of an age at which one can be aware of one's environment (paragraph 59). That seems to suggest that, for children below the age of five, their age is not a constitutive element to reach the minimum level of severity. On the other hand, when summarising its assessment in paragraph 63, the Court refers to the low age of the children, without any differentiation in accordance with their age. In that paragraph, having a low age (i.e. seven or lower) seems to be the relevant issue, and a constitutive element for reaching the minimum level of severity. What does this mean? Most likely, the suggestion is that the lower the age, the more likely it is that unsuitable living conditions in a closed centre will reach the mini-mum level of severity. While the Court may have hinted at a minimum age from which that principle applies, we would like to argue that such a

---

[22] ECHR, *N* v. *United Kingdom*, 27 May 2008, para. 45.
[23] ECHR, *Boultif* v. *Switzerland*, 2 August 2001; ECHR, *Üner* v. *Netherlands*, 18 October 2006.
[24] ECHR, *Maslov* v. *Austria*, 23 June 2008, para. 71.

minimum age is questionable. There is, for example, a solid body of evidence that the context in which very young children (three years or under) grow up, i.e. in a family environment or in an institution, does affect children and their development in multiple ways.[25] Although the Court is silent on a maximum cut-off age, we would equally advise against such an age, for there is no conclusive scientific evidence on the relevance of a particular age limit.

The duration of detention is a second element to assess whether the minimum level of severity has been reached. In this case, it amounted to more than a month. The Court does not engage with either the argument of the government that the duration of the detention is to be attributed to the applicants, who opposed their removal from the territory (paragraph 70), nor with the argument of the applicants, who submitted that the length of detention could not be attributed to their own behaviour, as they did not want to return to the violent father in Poland (paragraph 54). It is impossible to say which number of days might be considered still acceptable, and which not. Rather, the principle seems to be that the longer the treatment (in this case, detention) lasts, the more it contributes to reaching the minimum level of severity. Secondly, the duration is not to be assessed in isolation, but in conjunction with the other criteria, in particular of age and state of health.

A third element is the worrying state of health of the children. Although the Court, in paragraph 60, focuses on the state of health of two of the children in particular – the three-and-a-half year old and the five year old – in its summary in paragraph 63 it refers to their state of health without any differentiation. Two points seem to be of particular importance. First of all, the Court itself emphasises in this case that their state of health had been established in medical certificates during their detention (paragraphs 60–1 and 63). The authorities therefore knew of their state of health. The rich case law of the Court on the obligation incumbent on the State to provide adequate health care and medical assistance to ill prisoners can and should be applied to the case of detention of asylum-seekers too,[26] with even more force as they have not committed criminal offences but look for international protection. We would like to add as a second element the *evolution* of their state of health, i.e. deterioration, in a time span of eleven days only. First, the Court has submitted that a considerable deterioration of the health condition in detention raises doubts about the adequacy of the health care provided.[27] Secondly, it has considered the medical condition and the dynamics of the health condition as relevant criteria

---

[25] K. Browne, *The Risk of Harm to Young Children in Institutional Care* (2009), www.crin. org/docs/The_Risk_of_Harm.pdf.

[26] See, in particular, ECHR, *Mouisel* v. *France*, 14 November 2002; ECHR, *Aleksanyan* v. *Russia*, 22 December 2008; and ECHR, *Sławomir Musiał* v. *Poland*, 20 January 2009.

[27] ECHR, *Farbtuhs* v. *Latvia*, 2 December 2004, para. 57.

(amongst others) for assessing the permissibility of detention of seriously ill people.[28]

Somehow contradictory to the consideration that at least the two oldest children (of five and seven years old) must have been aware of the environment they lived in, here attention is primarily paid to the worrying psychological state of health of the three-and-a-half year old. That she hid under the table as soon as she noticed a man in uniform cannot be interpreted otherwise than that she was all too aware of her environment.

The nature of the treatment, i.e. detention, which takes place moreover in infrastructure that has been judged unsuitable for the reception of children in more than one expert report, gets rather superficial and inconsistent treatment in the judgment. It is not addressed in a separate paragraph (which is admittedly also the case for age and duration) (paragraph 59). Moreover, detention of very young children does not seem to be a relevant element in itself in the assessment of the minimum level of severity. While reference is made to the *conditions of detention* (not to detention itself) in paragraph 59, the summary in paragraph 63 contains only a reference to the *living conditions* in the centre, and not to detention nor even to the conditions of detention (see paragraphs 59*bis*, 59*ter* and 63 of the redraft).

An explanation, though not justification, for this less argued part of the judgment is most likely to be found in the fact that the core question at stake was whether the same positive obligations to protect the children and to adopt adequate measures applied to children *accompanied* by one of the parents, i.e. the mother, as to an unaccompanied minor – the latter situation had been assessed in the *Tabitha* case (paragraphs 57–8).

In the *Muskhadzhiyeva* case, the Court has refrained from qualifying the treatment in violation of Article 3 as either degrading or inhuman treatment, or torture. In the *Tabitha* case, the Court held that the detention of the five year old amounted to inhuman treatment (paragraph 58). Albeit weakly argued (detention amounted to *inhuman* treatment because it demonstrated a *lack of humanity*), the qualification as inhuman treatment could have added moral force to the judgment (see paragraph 63 of the rewritten judgment).

As far as the assessment of the mother's situation in light of Article 3 is concerned, we would like to make two points. First of all, from a technical point of view the Court argues erroneously that her feelings of powerlessness (*impuissance*) did not reach the level of severity that is required in order to be qualified as *inhuman treatment* (paragraph 66). The level of severity that is required has nothing to do with the qualification as inhuman treatment, but with the question whether the treatment complained of comes within the scope of Article 3. Treatment within the scope of Article 3 may then be qualified as either degrading treatment, inhuman treatment or torture. Secondly, the

---

[28] ECHR, *Aleksanyan v. Russia*, 22 December 2008, para. 137.

impact of both her own detention and that of her children on her state of mental health is not appropriately examined (see paragraph 64 of the redraft).

Strict necessity of detention in order to be free from arbitrariness (Article 5)

Article 5(1)(f) allows for the deprivation of liberty in the case of lawful detention of a person against whom action is being taken with a view to deportation or extradition.

Lawfulness of detention extends beyond compliance with national law, and requires that detention is not arbitrary.[29] This absence of arbitrariness implies that there should be no element of bad faith or deception on the part of the authorities; that the order to detain and the execution of the detention must genuinely conform with the purpose of the restrictions permitted by the relevant sub-paragraph of Article 5(1) (namely, in the case of sub-paragraph (f), deportation); and that there is some relationship between the ground of permitted deprivation of liberty and the place and conditions of detention (paragraph 69). As regards the latter condition in relation to sub-paragraph (f), the Court has pointed out that it should be borne in mind that detention takes place with regard 'not to those who have committed criminal offences but to aliens who, often fearing for their lives, have fled from their own country'.[30]

With regard to Article 5(1)(f) in particular, the Court has held that there is no requirement of necessity, i.e. the detention does not need to be reasonably considered necessary in order to be free from arbitrariness. The principle of proportionality merely requires that the detention does not last for an unreasonably long period of time.[31]

In the present case, the Court simply aligns itself with the arguments and finding in the *Tabitha* case as far as the four children are concerned. The five-year-old child in *Tabitha* had been detained in a closed centre intended for adult illegal immigrants, under the same conditions as adults; 'these conditions were consequently not adapted to the position of extreme vulnerability in which she found herself as a result of her position as an unaccompanied foreign minor.'[32] As far as the mother is concerned, the Court points out that there is no requirement of reasonable necessity for detention with a view to deportation. A violation is therefore found on account of the children, but not of the mother.

---

[29] ECHR, *Saadi* v. *United Kingdom*, 29 January 2008, para. 67.
[30] ECHR, *Amuur* v. *France*, 25 June 1996, para. 43.
[31] ECHR, *Chahal* v. *United Kingdom*, 15 November 1996, paras. 112 and 113; ECHR, *Saadi* v. *United Kingdom*, 29 January 2008, para. 73.
[32] ECHR, *Mubilanzila Mayeka and Kaniki Mitunga* v. *Belgium*, 12 October 2006, para. 103.

We submit that the absence of arbitrariness as required by the notion of lawfulness imposes a strict proportionality test with regard to children, i.e. a condition of necessity. As the Court has pointed out with regard to the sub-paragraphs (b), (d) and (e), '[t]he detention of an individual is such a serious measure that it is justified only as a last resort where other, less severe measures have been considered and found to be insufficient to safeguard the individual or public interest which might require that the person concerned be detained'.[33] Moreover, the principle of Article 37(b) CRC holds that the deprivation of liberty of a child 'shall be used only as a measure of last resort and for the shortest appropriate period of time'. Regard must also be had to the best interests of the child. There is an emerging common ground in international instruments on the centrality of the best interests of the child and the undesirability of detention of asylum-seekers in general, and of (unaccompanied) minors in particular. Only in very exceptional circumstances, as a measure of last resort, can minors be deprived of their liberty, on condition that their detention is of the shortest possible duration[34] (see paragraph 73 of the rewritten judgment).

As far as the mother is concerned, we argue that a family perspective is required in order to be able to appropriately deal with this question. A literal reading of the current judgment could result in the conclusion that, in the future, States should no longer detain children in such centres, but that they can continue to do so with regard to their parents. Obviously, such a practice would be highly problematic in light of Article 8. The Committee on the Prevention of Torture has accepted that there may be exceptional situations, with explicit reference to children and parents being held as immigration detainees, 'in which it is plainly in the best interests of juveniles not to be separated from particular adults'.[35] So, in practice, the only option left seems to be indeed to either detain children and their parent(s) together in places and under conditions of detention that are adapted to children – if such places and conditions can exist – or not to detain them anymore.[36] Conceptually, the wording of the judgment does not acknowledge the importance of family and family life in its assessment of the lawfulness of the detention with a view to deportation. From a

---

[33] ECHR, *Saadi* v. *United Kingdom*, 29 January 2008, para. 70.
[34] See, *inter alia*, the Council of Europe Parliamentary Assembly Resolution 1707 and Recommendation 1900 of 28 January 2010 on the detention of asylum-seekers and irregular migrants in Europe; CPT Standards 2009; the Committee of Ministers' Twenty Guidelines on Forced Return of 2005; the UNHCR Recommendations as Regards Harmonisation of Reception Standards for Asylum Seekers in the European Union, July 2000; UNHCR Guidelines on Protection and Care of Refugee Children; UNHCR Guidelines on Detention, etc.
[35] CPT Standards, p. 74.
[36] See our earlier argument on the necessity test with regard to the deprivation of liberty of children.

children's rights perspective, this is a regrettable omission. In light of respect for family life, for detention of an adult immigrant accompanied by children in view of their deportation to be devoid of arbitrariness, a strict necessity test is to be applied (see paragraphs 74–6 of the rewritten judgment).

Positive obligations to promote and facilitate family life

Under Article 8, the applicants complain of the conditions of detention in Centre 127*bis*, and of the absence of any effort by the State to find alternatives to detention. The Court does not see any issue under the right to family life, for there is no issue of family reunification, as the mother and her four children were detained together in the same place. Neither does it consider that the absence of steps to find alternative solutions to detention raises an issue under the right to respect for private life. It declares the complaints under Article 8 manifestly ill-founded, and therefore inadmissible.

Quite surprisingly, the Court narrows down the meaning of respect for family life here to family reunification. Again, this approach seems to be informed by taking the *Tabitha* case as a starting point, so that the Court only examines whether there is any similarity or difference. In its case law, the Court has clearly given a broader meaning to the right to respect of family life, and identified a number of positive obligations. The question can be raised whether there are any positive obligations incumbent on the State under the right to respect for family life to guarantee living conditions that allow for a genuine enjoyment of the right to family life. The Court has refrained from determining whether the promotion of family unity may entitle a family to a particular *standard of living* at public expense, probably because of the resource implications.[37] However, it should take a more affirmative stance on a positive obligation to promote and facilitate family life by allowing for *living conditions* that are the least intrusive and harmful to/ most respectful of family life in the circumstances, in particular when these alternatives are available.[38] Here, too, the notion of best interests of the child needs to be taken into account, which justifies a strict proportionality test for any limitations to the right to respect for family life. A similar reasoning has been developed with regard to negative obligations, in cases in which children had been taken into care exclusively because of the material living conditions of the family. The Court has argued that, in light of the principle of proportionality, less radical means should have been explored.[39] With regard to positive obligations, the Court has held the following factors to be relevant for the assessment of the content of positive obligations: in the first place, factors concerning the applicant,

---

[37] ECHR, *Saviny* v. *Ukraine*, 18 December 2008, para. 57.

[38] In our view, the positive obligation to promote and facilitate family-friendly living conditions should extend beyond detention.

[39] ECHR, *Wallová and Walla* v. *Czech Republic*, 26 October 2006, paras. 73–4.

such as the importance of the interest at stake and whether fundamental values or essential aspects of the right are involved, as well as the impact on a person of a discordance between social reality and the law (coherence); and, secondly, factors concerning the position of the State, i.e. whether the alleged obligation is defined or indeterminate, and the extent of any burden the obligation would impose on the State.[40] In the present case, factors militating in favour of a positive obligation to promote and facilitate family life are certainly those related to the importance of the interest at stake (i.e. allowing parents and children to play their respective role in the family in avoidance of the de-structuring of family life), and the all-in-all limited burden the obligation would impose on the State (family-life-friendly infrastructure and arrangements).

So, as a minimum, infrastructure adapted to families and allowing for family life should be made available. Reports on the infrastructure and regime of Centre 127*bis* have revealed that both were completely unsuitable for families. The detention conditions corresponded to a prison regime, with an infrastructure that was completely unsuitable for family life and education, lack of privacy, and therefore potentially provoking de-parentisation (as parents were not allowed to take up their parental responsibilities) and de-structuring of family life.[41]

Since October 2008, the Belgian State has decided in principle not to detain families anymore, but to house them in open living units, thereby recognising the harmful effects of the living circumstances in closed detention centres for children and families (see paragraphs 98–100 of the redraft).

The role of other instruments in the interpretation of the Convention

The Court increasingly relies on international law standards or domestic law standards of European States in its interpretation of the Convention. This is particularly warranted when a certain group, such as children, has been the particular focus of attention in other instruments, for the latter can be assumed to accommodate more and better the specificities of that particular group. In the case under review, the Court limits itself to mentioning Articles 3, 10, 22 and 37 CRC as relevant international law in the facts part of the judgment (paragraph 43). In the operative part of the judgment, it refers in its examination of a violation of Article 3 only to Article 22 CRC, but not to any of the other provisions in the examination of the alleged violations of other convention provisions.

---

[40] ECHR (GC), *A, B and C* v. *Ireland*, 16 December 2010, para. 248.
[41] SumResearch, 'Study on Alternatives for Detention of Families with Children in Closed Centres', Part 1 (February 2007), pp. 43–8 and pp. 74–7; STEPS Consulting Social, 'The Conditions in Centres for Third Country National (Detention Camps, Open Centres as well as Transit Centres and Transit Zones) with a Particular Focus on Provisions and Facilities for Persons with Special Needs in the 25 EU Member States' (December 2007), p. 59.

A grand chamber of the Court has submitted that the Court never considers the provisions of the Convention as the sole framework of reference for the interpretation of the rights enshrined therein, but has to take into account 'any relevant rules and principles of international law applicable in relations between the Contracting Parties'.[42] It draws on a diversity of international texts and instruments of general international law and Council of Europe instruments, amongst others. The Court thereby seeks to identify common ground among norms of international law, while not distinguishing between sources of law according to whether they have been signed or ratified by the State concerned.[43]

The Court may thus draw on specialised treaties and their interpretation, general principles of law, peremptory norms of international law, as well as on non-binding instruments of Council of Europe organs (e.g. recommendations and resolutions of the Committee of Ministers, the Parliamentary Assembly and other bodies) and EU instruments.

When it comes in particular to the determination of the breadth of the margin of appreciation in deciding on the proportionality of an interference with the aim pursued, the existence of a relevant consensus among a substantial majority of Contracting States of the Council of Europe may narrow the broad margin of appreciation of a State. If that is the case, the Court does not think it necessary to examine international trends and views.[44] In another case, in which a common European approach was lacking, the Court argued that it attached 'less importance to the lack of evidence of a common European approach', 'than to the clear and uncontested evidence of a continuing international trend'.[45] In our case, under both of these tests to determine the breadth of the margin of appreciation, the detention of minor asylum-seekers would fall under a *narrower* margin of appreciation for the State. For, in both EU and Council of Europe instruments as well as in international instruments, an emerging common ground can be identified with regard to the undesirability of the detention of minor asylum-seekers in particular (see above; and see paragraph 73 of the redraft).

Conclusion

The *Muskhadzhiyeva* case touches on some of the ongoing debates in the children's rights community. We have highlighted these debates and have made suggestions on how they could have been better accommodated in this case, so as to mainstream children's rights in the case law of the Court. We have argued in particular for a more nuanced presentation of children as vulnerable

---

[42] ECHR (GC), *Demir and Baykara* v. *Turkey*, 12 November 2008, para. 67.
[43] *Ibid.*, para. 78.   [44] ECHR, *A, B and C* v. *Ireland*, 16 December 2010, paras. 234–5.
[45] ECHR, *Goodwin* v. *United Kingdom*, 11 July 2002, para. 85.

and endowed with agency – by introducing the concept of contextual vulnerability; for recognition of a State's ultimate responsibility for children when
parents fail to take up their responsibility, all the more so when the State has
contributed to the parents' inability; for the identification of a positive obligation to promote and facilitate family life by allowing for *living conditions* that
are the least intrusive and harmful to/most respectful of family life in the
circumstances; and for a strict proportionality test for the detention of minor
asylum-seekers and the parent(s) accompanying them. We have also flagged
the tensions and potential in the relationship between the human rights of
children and adults. Children's rights may be strategically used to create
political space for debating sensitive human rights issues, provided that children do benefit from it, and that children's rights are not pitched against the
human rights of adults. All in all, while the Court has increasingly engaged
more explicitly with children's rights norms in recent years, full mainstreaming
of children's rights in the Court's case law has not yet taken place.

Rewriting Muskhadzhiyeva and others v. Belgium[46]

. . .

1. On the alleged violation of Article 3 of the Convention

. . .

2. The Court's assessment

a) Concerning the applicant children

. . .

Relevant principles

56. In the previous judgment [**i.e. ECHR, *Mubilanzila Mayeka and
Kaniki Mitunga* v. *Belgium*, 12 October 2006**], the Court concluded that
Article 3 had been violated because of the detention of a minor in Centre
'127', situated close to the airport of Brussels, which served as a detention
centre for foreigners awaiting their deportation. The Court noted that the
conditions of detention of the applicant, who was five years old at the time,
were the same as for adults, that the child had been detained for two months
in a centre that had initially been designed for adults, even though she was
unaccompanied by her parents, no one had been assigned to look after her
and no measures had been taken to ensure that she received proper

---

[46] The following text is a non-official translation of the judgment, which has only been issued
in French.

counselling and educational assistance from qualified personnel specially mandated for that purpose (*ibid.*, para. 50). [Fragment deleted] **The Court fully acknowledges that a child is to be regarded as vulnerable and endowed with agency at the same time. The degree of vulnerability and agency depends on the interaction between different factors. In this particular case, however, there is no denial that the children were in an extremely vulnerable situation that prevailed over their agency. That vulnerability should be seen as contextual, as it was the result of personal factors (e.g. very young age, mental state), and external risk and environmental factors related to migration and reception. The Court stresses that the contextual vulnerability of the children concerned is the decisive factor, and takes precedence over considerations relating to the applicants' status as an illegal immigrant.**

57. The Court does not lose sight of the fact that the present case differs from the previous judgment in one important regard: in the present case, the applicants' children have not been separated from her.

58. Nevertheless, in the Court's view, this element is not sufficient to exempt the authorities from their obligation to protect children and to take adequate measures as part of their positive obligations under Article 3 of the Convention (*Ibid.*, para. 55).

Similar to the *Tabitha* case, the mother, who has the primary responsibility for the upbringing and development of her children, could not assume her parental responsibility due to the intervention of the State. In the current case, the mother was submitted to conditions and a regime of detention that prevented her from assuming her parental responsibility. The State therefore has to assume that responsibility.

59. According to the Court's well-established case law, treatment must attain a minimum level of severity if it is to fall within the scope of Article 3. The assessment of this minimum level of severity is relative; it depends on all the circumstances of the case, such as the duration of the treatment, its physical and mental effects and, in some cases, the sex, age and state of health of the victim (*Jalloh* v. *Germany*, 11 July 2006, para. 67).

59 *bis*. When assessing conditions of detention, account has to be taken of the cumulative effects of those conditions (*A* v. *UK*, 23 September 1998, para. 128). Furthermore, one of the factors which the Court must take into account when assessing whether the threshold of Article 3 was attained is whether any stress caused by the treatment was sufficiently serious and enduring to affect the mental health of the applicant (*A* v. *UK*, para. 130). The Court has held on many occasions that the detention of a person who is ill may raise issues under Article 3 of the Convention. In particular, the assessment of whether the particular conditions of detention are incompatible with the standards of Article 3 has, in the case of

mentally ill persons, to take into consideration their vulnerability. Detained persons who suffer from a mental disorder are more susceptible to the feeling of inferiority and powerlessness. Because of that, an increased vigilance is called for in reviewing whether the Convention has been complied with (*Sławomir Musiał* v. *Poland*, 20 January 2009, para. 96).

59 *ter*. Article 3 requires that the health and well-being of detainees are adequately ensured by providing them the requisite medical assistance. While the Court reserves sufficient flexibility in defining the required standard of health care, it should be compatible with the human dignity of a detainee and in cases other than that of convicted prisoners, it should be of the same level of that in the outside community (*Aleksanyan* v. *Russia*, 22 December 2008, paras. 139–140; European Committee for the Prevention of Torture and Inhuman or Degrading Treatment or Punishment CPT Standards, CPT/Inf/E (2002) 1 – Rev. 2009, p. 29). In addition, the CPT has clarified that, when children of foreign nationals are detained, an assessment should be made 'of their particular vulnerabilities, including from the standpoints of age, health, psychosocial factors and other protection needs, including those deriving from violence, trafficking or trauma'. In addition, the regular presence of, and individual contact with, a psychologist needs to be ensured (CPT Standards, p. 55). Just as the very nature of the medical and psychological condition of an ill person makes that person more likely to be contextually vulnerable and therefore requires detention in a specialised setting, the condition of childhood at least requires detention in a specialised and adapted setting in order to avoid that potential personal vulnerability due to age is exacerbated by external factors. Failure to do so unnecessarily exposes the child to a risk to its development and must result in stress and anxiety (*mutatis mutandis*, *Sławomir Musiał* v. *Poland*, 20 January 2009, para. 96).

59 *quater*. In conclusion, health and age are to be taken into account in assessing a person's suitability for continued detention (*Mouisel* v. *France*, 14 November 2002, para. 38).

Application of these principles to the present case
   [Original paragraphs 59–62 deleted]
   60. The Court notes that the four applicant children were at the age of seven months, three-and-a-half years, five years and seven years at the time of detention. They were all at a very young age, at which a high degree of dependence and potential contextual vulnerability can be presumed. Detention may impact differently on each child, depending on its mental health state, resilience, past experience or age. It should not be assumed that the impact is automatically lower or negligible the younger a child is. The adverse consequences of detention may have a serious

impact on the health, development and well-being of very young children too, and possibly even to a greater extent, similar to the profound and comparatively more severe impact of institutional care on young children. While the presence of one of the parents, i.e. the mother, may mitigate that negative impact, that has not been the case here: as it appears from the medical certificate of 22 January 2007, the mother experienced such a degree of stress that it rather intensified the children's own distress, for they felt that their mother was unable to protect them.

61. Whereas detention of very young children in such circumstances may reach *per se* the minimum level of severity to bring it within the scope of Article 3, it surely does so when it takes place for a protracted period of time and under material conditions and a regime of detention that is inadequate for children, given the role of these environmental factors on their contextual vulnerability. The children were kept for more than a month in Centre 127*bis*, the facilities of which and the prison-like regime applicable there have been judged inadequate for children and families in a number of reports (paras. 31–35 above). This finding is of itself a sufficient basis on which to conclude that the applicant children were subjected to treatment that falls within the scope of Article 3. However, the Court considers it appropriate to examine the case also in light of the state of health of the applicant children.

62. The state of mental health of the four children gave cause for concern, as all four showed serious signs of mental and physical trauma. No appropriate and adapted health care seemed to be available. While medical services were available in Centre 127*bis*, they were mainly supplied by nurses and a general practitioner. No specialised health care, either for children or for mental illness, was made available by the State. The medical certificates on the applicant's health were issued by a medical doctor of Médécins sans Frontières, one of the non-governmental organisations that were allowed to visit the centre. Nor was an assessment made of the children's particular vulnerabilities, in particular also from the standpoints of health and psychosocial factors, including those deriving from violence or trauma (CPT Standards, p. 55). In light of their undoubtedly traumatic experiences with violence in Chechnya, compounded by domestic violence (para. 54) and the feeling that their mother was unable to protect them, the absence of an initial assessment as well as of appropriate and specialised mental health care must have aroused strong feelings of inferiority, vulnerability and powerlessness, and affected their mental health even further. While that situation may in itself come already within the scope of Article 3, it definitely did so as of 22 January 2007, when a second medical certificate was issued. That certificate pointed out that the state of mental health of the children

had deteriorated, and that they had to be released in order to minimise mental damage. This state of mental health did not leave in fact any other option to the State than to discontinue detention. Not doing so amounts to inhuman treatment. Consequently, Article 3 has also been violated by the failure to release the children following a medical certificate that pointed out the deterioration of their mental state of health, in combination with the absence of specialised mental health care.

Conclusion

63. Assessing the facts of the case as a whole, the very young age of the applicants (personal factor) and the cumulative effects of ill-adapted material conditions and the regime of detention in which they were held for more than a month (environmental factor), the Court considers that the treatment to which the applicants were subjected is to be qualified as inhuman. In addition, the Court would also have been prepared to find a violation on account of the failure to release the children following a medical certificate that pointed out the increasingly detrimental effect of detention on their mental health, well-being and development, in combination with the absence of specialised mental health care.

b) Concerning the first applicant
[Original paragraphs 64–66 deleted]
64. The mother experienced a high level of stress as she realised that her family and herself continuously ran the risk of being deported to Poland, where she might be confronted with her violent husband, who had applied for asylum there. In addition, she directly and continuously witnessed how the state of (mental) health of her four young children deteriorated, but felt completely powerless and unable to change their detention situation, let alone to improve their state of mental health. That must have aroused feelings of stress and anxiety of such a nature so as to reach the minimum level of severity. Article 3 has consequently been breached.

II. *On the alleged violation of Article 5 § 1 of the Convention*

. . .
[Original paragraphs 73–75 deleted]

a) Concerning the applicant children

73. The cardinal principles regarding the deprivation of minors of their liberty are twofold: one, deprivation of liberty should be a measure of last resort; and, secondly, it should be for the shortest appropriate period of time – which implies a strict proportionality test. These

principles have been codified in Article 37 of the Convention on the Rights of the Child, and reiterated by the CRC Committee (e.g. in its General Comment No. 10 on children's rights in juvenile justice, para. 79). While these principles have emerged in the context of juvenile justice, they equally and with even more force apply to minor asylum-seekers whose application has been rejected, for detention in such a situation takes place with regard 'not to those who have committed criminal offences but to aliens who, often fearing for their lives, have fled from their own country' (*Amuur* v. *France*, 25 June 1996, para. 43). The CPT has argued, based on the principle of the 'best interests of the child', as formulated in Article 3 of the Convention on the Rights of the Child, that every effort should be made to avoid the deprivation of liberty of an irregular migrant who is a minor, and that it can 'certainly not be motivated solely by the absence of residence status'. Also, in line with Article 37 CRC, it has held that, when a child is exceptionally detained, the deprivation of liberty should be for the shortest possible period of time (CPT Standards, p. 54). The Council of Europe Commissioner for human rights has recommended that '[n]o migrant child should ever be subject to detention' (Commissioner for human rights, February 2010).

In the present case, no necessity for detention of the children has been demonstrated. While it is true that they had escaped earlier on from the reception centre where they were staying, alternative and less intrusive measures could have been pursued. The Court therefore concludes that Article 5 § 1(f) has been violated.

b) Concerning the mother

74. It is established case law that, for detention to be lawful, it should not be arbitrary. Moreover, as the Court has pointed out with regard to the sub-paragraphs (b), (d) and (e), '[t]he detention of an individual is such a serious measure that it is justified only as a last resort where other, less severe measures have been considered and found to be insufficient to safeguard the individual or public interest which might require that the person concerned be detained' (*Saadi* v. *United Kingdom*, 29 January 2008, para. 70). A strict proportionality test thus applies, which requires the absence of less far-reaching alternatives. With regard to Article 5 § 1(f), however, the Court has held that there is no requirement of necessity, i.e. the detention does not need to be reasonably considered necessary in order to be free from arbitrariness.

75. The present case concerns the situation of a mother who is accompanied by four very young children. The Commissioner for human rights has recommended that having a dependent child must be ground for an adult migrant not to be detained except in accordance with the lawful

order of a criminal court (Commissioner for human rights, February 2010). While no European consensus can be identified in this regard, in light of respect for family life and the principle of best interests of the child, for detention of an adult immigrant accompanied by children in view of their deportation to be devoid of arbitrariness, a strict proportionality test is to be applied. The fact that the family had run away once from the reception centre where they were staying is not sufficient in itself to consider the detention to have been necessary, as less far-reaching measures could have been taken.

76. The Belgian State has acknowledged moreover that the detention of parents and their young children with a view to their deportation is not desirable, let alone strictly needed. This is illustrated by the putting in place of a system of return homes. The deprivation of liberty of the mother has not been demonstrated to be strictly necessary. The Court therefore concludes that Article 5 § 1(f) has been violated.

V.   On the alleged violation of Article 8 of the Convention

. . .

[Original paragraphs 98 and 99 deleted]

98. The Court has given a broad meaning to the right to respect of family life, and identified a number of positive obligations. So far, the Court has not examined whether there are any positive obligations incumbent on the State under the right to respect for family life, i.e. to guarantee living circumstances that allow for a genuine enjoyment of the right to family life. With regard to positive obligations, the Court has held the following factors to be relevant for the assessment of their content: factors concerning the applicant, such as the importance of the interest at stake and whether fundamental values or essential aspects of the right are at stake, as well as the impact on a person of a discordance between social reality and the law (coherence); and factors concerning the position of the State, i.e. whether the alleged obligation is defined or indeterminate, and the extent of any burden the obligation would impose on the State (*A, B and C* v. *Ireland*, 16 December 2010, para. 248).

99. While the Court has refrained from determining whether the promotion of family unity may entitle a family to a particular standard of living at public expense (*Saviny* v. *Ukraine*, 18 December 2008, para. 57), because of the resource implications, it has emphasised that a State needs to allow parents to assume their parental role and responsibilities (*Wallová and Walla* v. *Czech Republic*, 26 October 2006, para. 73; *Saviny* v. *Ukraine*, 18 December 2008, para. 57). A positive obligation can be said to exist to promote and facilitate family life by allowing for living

conditions that are the least intrusive and harmful to family life in the concrete circumstances of the case, in particular when these alternatives are available. As a minimum, infrastructure adapted to families and allowing for family life should be made available. This is in line with the Committee on the Prevention of Torture's position on keeping children with their parents during detention, and in particular on the need to ensure that appropriate conditions (including accommodation) are foreseen 'under which parents can continue to provide parental care' (CPT, Greece CPT/Inf (2010) 33).

100. In the case under consideration, the applicant mother and her four very young children stayed for more than a month in Centre 127 *bis*. While they stayed in a family wing of this centre, the conditions and the regime of detention did not allow the mother to assume her parental role, or rendered it extremely difficult, as has been concluded in several studies undertaken in the period during which the applicants resided in the centre (See SumResearch, 'Study on Alternatives for Detention of Families with Children in Closed Centres', Part 1, February 2007, pp. 74–7; STEPS Consulting Social, 'The Conditions in Centres for Third Country National (Detention Camps, Open Centres as well as Transit Centres and Transit Zones) with a Particular Focus on Provisions and Facilities for Persons with Special Needs in the 25 EU Member States', December 2007, p. 59). The Court therefore concludes that Article 8 has been violated.

PART II

Gender

4

Redrafting abortion rights under the Convention: A, B and C v. Ireland

PATRICIA LONDONO

Introduction

Access to safe abortion services continues to be a problem worldwide. Recent statistics by the World Health Organization (WHO) show that deaths due to unsafe abortions make up approximately 13 per cent of all maternal deaths, some 47,000 in 2008. Approximately 21.6 million unsafe abortions were performed worldwide in this period, representing some 14 for every 1,000 women of reproductive age, the overwhelming majority in developing regions. The WHO states that 'the numbers of unsafe abortions will continue to increase unless women's access to safe abortion and contraception – and support to empower women (including their freedom to decide whether and when to have a child) are put in place and further strengthened'.[1] International human rights bodies have increasingly recognised women's access to safe abortion as a human rights issue[2] and have expressed concerns about Ireland's abortion laws in their individual reports.[3] It is in this contact that the decision in *A, B and C v. Ireland*[4] stands out as being particularly unsatisfactory.

Despite the fact that reproductive rights and abortion services in particular have been of considerable concern in relation to women's human rights, the jurisprudence of the European Court of Human Rights (ECHR) has been disappointing. The ECHR does not recognise an entitlement to abortion, and, on the case law as it stands so far, States with highly restrictive abortion laws will not, without more, be found to breach the Convention. I chose this case because

---

[1] World Health Organization, *Unsafe Abortion: Global and Regional Estimates of the Incidence of Unsafe Abortion and Associated Mortality in 2008* (6th edn, WHO, 2011), p. 1.

[2] See the next section below.

[3] 'Report of the Commissioner for Human Rights on His Visit to Ireland, 26–30th November 2007, Adopted on the 30th April 2008', CommDH (2008) 9; Office of the High Commissioner for Human Rights, Committee on the Elimination of Discrimination Against Women ('CEDAW'), July 2005, A/60/38 (SUPP); Human Rights Committee, Concluding Comments on the Third Periodic Report of Ireland on the Observance of the UN Covenant on Civil and Political Rights, CCPR/C/IRL/CO/3, 30 July 2008. All are referred to at paras. 109 and 111 of the judgment.

[4] ECHR (GC), *A, B and C v. Ireland*, 16 December 2010.

it is a good illustration of the manner in which human rights decisions do not always reflect women's interests. Furthermore, it is important in that it illustrates the way in which, in relation to abortion rights, the European human rights system is out of step with other human rights bodies.

The chapter starts from the premise that developing abortion rights under the Convention would be a positive development. The importance of developing human rights jurisprudence in relation to abortion rights is crucial to the development of women's human rights. There are significant health risks associated with a lack of safe abortion facilities. In addition, reproductive freedom is an important aspect of privacy. Finally, the lack of reproductive services has knock-on effects on other rights such as women's ability to participate in public spheres of life. The Convention should thus reflect these issues in the decision-making of its bodies to give further effect to women's rights.

In redrafting the judgment, this chapter aims to bolster Convention jurisprudence in relation to abortion rights and develop positive obligations on States to provide abortion facilities by applying pre-existing principles and case law under Articles 2, 3 and 8. It will also apply Article 14 jurisprudence to the issue of whether a failure to provide abortion facilities discriminates against women. It thus seeks to develop pre-existing principles in a manner that assists women. The autonomy associated with personal choice in the field of reproduction facilitates the enjoyment of other rights such as the ability to participate in the public sphere which in turn has the effect of bringing the diverse experiences of women into the mainstream.

A global problem

Whilst unsafe abortions are entirely preventable, 'they continue to pose undue risks to a woman's health and may endanger her life'.[5] Abortions to save the woman's life are permitted in the overwhelming majority of countries, although the numbers fall quite dramatically when it comes to protecting the physical and mental health of the women in Africa, Asia and Oceania.[6] These numbers

---

[5] World Health Organization, *Unsafe Abortion: Global and Regional Estimates of the Incidence of Unsafe Abortion and Associated Mortality in 2008* (6th edn, WHO, 2011), p. 2.

[6] Abortions to save a woman's life are permitted in 100 per cent of countries in Africa, Asia, Oceania and 'other developed countries' (Australia, Canada, Japan, New Zealand and the United States), 98 per cent of countries in Europe and 91 per cent of countries in Latin America and the Caribbean. Abortions to preserve the physical health of the woman are permitted in 58 per cent of African countries, 67 per cent of Asian countries, 88 per cent of European countries, 100 per cent of other developed countries, 58 per cent of Latin American and Caribbean countries, and 50 per cent of Oceania countries. Abortions to preserve the mental health of the mother are permitted in 55 per cent of African countries, 62 per cent of Asian countries, 88 per cent of European countries, 80 per cent of other developed countries, 58 per cent of Latin American and Caribbean countries, and 50 per cent of Oceania countries. *Ibid.*, pp. 3–6.

decrease further in cases of rape and incest.[7] The lowest rates for entitlement to lawful abortions are for those carried out for 'social or economic' reasons.[8] In countries with restrictive abortion laws, the majority of abortions are unsafe.[9] In Europe, the annual unsafe abortion rate is 6 for every 1,000 women aged between fifteen and forty-four.[10]

International human rights bodies have increasingly recognised the failure to provide abortion services as a violation of the rights of women.[11] The Special Rapporteur on Violence against Women states that '[a]cts deliberately restraining women ... from having an abortion constitute violence against women by subjecting women to excessive pregnancies and childbearing against their will, resulting in increased and preventable risks of maternal mortality and morbidity'.[12] She emphasises the need for access to abortion that is both safe and affordable.[13]

> [Reproductive rights] rest on the recognition of the basic right of all couples and individuals to decide freely and responsibly the number, spacing and timing of their children and to have the information and means to do so, and the right to attain the highest standard of sexual and reproductive health. It also includes their right to make decisions concerning reproduction free of discrimination, coercion and violence, as expressed in human rights documents.[14]

The Report of the Fourth World Conference on Women echoed similar sentiments stating that '[t]he human rights of women include their right to have

---

[7] Abortions are permitted following rape or incest in 30 per cent of African countries, 49 per cent of Asian countries, 84 per cent of European countries, 100 per cent of other developed countries, 42 per cent of Latin American and Caribbean countries, and 7 per cent of Oceania countries. *Ibid.*

[8] Terminations on the grounds of social or economic reasons are permitted in 8 per cent of African countries, 40 per cent of Asian countries, 79 per cent of European countries, 80 per cent of other developed countries, 15 per cent of Latin American and Caribbean countries, and 7 per cent of Oceania countries. Focusing on Europe alone, 90 per cent of countries in Eastern and Northern Europe, 64 per cent of Southern European, and 78 per cent of Western European countries permit abortions for social and economic reasons. Abortions on request are permitted in 90 per cent of Eastern European countries, 60 per cent of Northern European countries, 64 per cent of Southern European countries, and 67 per cent of Western European countries. *Ibid.*

[9] *Ibid.*, pp. 3 and 6. [10] *Ibid.*, p. 16.

[11] C. Zampas and J. M. Gher, 'Abortion as a Human Right: International and Regional Standards' (2008) 8(2) *Human Rights Law Review* 249.

[12] Report of the Special Rapporteur on violence against women, its causes and consequences, Ms Radihka Coomaraswamy, in accordance with Commission on Human Rights Resolution 1997/44, 'Integration of the Human Rights of Women and the Gender Perspective', Addendum, 'Policies and Practices That Impact Women's Reproductive Rights and Contribute to, Cause or Constitute Violence Against Women', E/CN.4/1999/68/Add.4, 21 January 1999, paras. 57 and 63.

[13] *Ibid.* [14] A/CONF.171/13: Report of the ICPD (94/10/18) (385k)[7.3].

control over and decide freely and responsibly on matters related to their sexuality, including sexual and reproductive health, free of coercion, discrimination and violence'.[15] Referring to, amongst other things, the health problems associated with unsafe abortions, it notes that:

> [i]n most countries, the neglect of women's reproductive rights severely limits their opportunities in public and private life, including the opportunities for education and economic and political empowerment. The ability of women to control their own fertility forms an important basis for the enjoyment of other rights.[16]

CEDAW General Recommendation 24 is couched in comparable terms:

> It is discriminatory for a State Party to refuse to legally provide for the performance of certain reproductive health services for women . . . if health service providers refuse to perform such services based on conscientious objection, measures should be introduced to ensure that women are referred to alternative healthcare providers.[17]

Recommendations include amending legislation that criminalises abortion to ensure that women who have terminations are not subject to 'punitive provisions'.[18]

General Comment 28 of the Human Rights Committee requires States to provide details on measures undertaken to assist women in preventing unwanted pregnancies and of measures to ensure 'that they do not have to undergo life-threatening clandestine abortions'.[19] It also asks States to report on whether safe abortion facilities are provided to victims of rape if they have become pregnant as a consequence.[20] In *KNLH* v. *Peru*, the Human Rights Committee found violations of Article 2 (failure to provide an effective remedy), 7 (prohibition of inhuman and degrading treatment), 17 (protection of privacy) and 24 (protection of minors) of the International Covenant on Civil and Political Rights (ICCPR) in a case where a seventeen-year-old carrying an anencephalic foetus was unable to secure a therapeutic abortion, and was forced to carry the foetus to term in the knowledge that the baby would not survive more than a few days.[21] Following the birth of the child (who survived for four

---

[15] United Nations 'Report of the Fourth World Conference on Women' (Beijing, 4–15 September 1995), A/CONF.177/20, para. 95.

[16] *Ibid.*, para. 97.

[17] General Recommendation No. 24 (20th Session 1999) (Article 12: Women and Health), para. 11.

[18] *Ibid.*, para. 31c.

[19] General Comment No. 28: Equality of Rights Between Men and Women (Article 3), 29 March 2000, CCPR/C/21/Rev.1/Add.10, para. 10.

[20] *Ibid.*, para. 11.

[21] Human Rights Committee, 85th Session, Communication No. 1153/2003.

days), the mother had to breast-feed her and subsequently fell into a state of deep depression.

There have also been moves within the Council of Europe to ensure Europe-wide access to abortion. A Parliamentary Assembly resolution notes that, while abortion is available in most European countries:

> [t]he Assembly is nonetheless concerned that, in many of these states, numerous conditions are imposed and restrict the effective access to safe, affordable, acceptable and appropriate abortion services. These restrictions have discriminatory effects, since women who are well informed and possess adequate financial means can often obtain legal and safe abortions more easily.[22]

It also notes that:

> abortion should not be banned within reasonable gestational limits. A ban on abortions does not result in fewer abortions but mainly leads to clandestine abortions, which are more traumatic and increase maternal mortality and/or lead to abortion 'tourism' which is costly, and delays the timing of an abortion and results in social inequities. The lawfulness of abortion does not have an effect on a woman's need for an abortion, but only on her access to a safe abortion.[23]

The Resolution recommends that abortion be decriminalised within 'reasonable gestational limits' and that women be guaranteed 'effective exercise of their right of access to a safe and legal abortion'.[24]

It is clear that international human rights thinking has moved towards access to abortion as part of reproductive freedom to preserve the well-being of the woman, and to promote equality. It is in the context of these concerted efforts both internationally and Europe-wide that the decision in *A, B and C* is particularly disappointing.

Factual background

The highly restrictive abortion laws in Ireland are well known. Abortion is prohibited by sections 58 (as amended) and 59 of the Offences against the Person Act 1861 with a maximum penalty of 'penal servitude for life'. Following the decision in *Attorney General* v. *X and others*, women who have been raped and are suicidal are able to obtain an abortion.[25] It is unclear, however, whether this applies to other life-threatening situations. Section 40.3.3 of the Irish Constitution provided that 'the State acknowledges the right of life of the unborn and, with due regard to the equal right to life of

---

[22] Resolution 1607 (2008), Access to Safe and Legal Abortion in Europe, para. 2.
[23] *Ibid.*, para. 4. [24] Resolution 1607 (2008), para. 7. [25] [1992] 1 IR 1.

the mother, guarantees in its laws to respect, and, as far as is practicable, by its laws to defend and vindicate that right', although this had not been implemented.

The three applicants in *A, B and C* had obtained abortions in the United Kingdom, two on 'well-being' grounds, and one on health grounds.[26] The first applicant became pregnant unintentionally, was living in impoverished circumstances, and was unmarried and unemployed. She had suffered from alcoholism and her four young children, the youngest of whom was disabled, were in foster care as a consequence. She borrowed €650 at a high interest rate to cover the costs of her travel and the termination procedure, which she did in secret. She obtained medical care on her return to Ireland.[27] The second applicant also became pregnant unintentionally in 2005 after having taken the 'morning after pill'. She did not wish to continue with the pregnancy because she did not feel able to raise a child as a single mother at that point in her life.[28] She also had difficulty meeting the costs of her travel, and attended alone to have the procedure undertaken. To ensure secrecy, she did not give details of a next-of-kin or an Irish address. Uncertain of her legal position with regard to travelling to the United Kingdom for her termination, she sought follow-up medical attention in an Irish clinic that was associated with the English clinic that she had attended.[29] The third applicant had suffered a rare form of cancer prior to becoming pregnant in 2005, and had been treated with chemotherapy for three years. During her treatment, she had been advised that, were she to become pregnant, it would be dangerous for the foetus for her to have chemotherapy during the first trimester. When the cancer fell into remission, she had a number of tests 'contraindicated during pregnancy'.[30] She was unaware that she was already pregnant at that time. She claimed that, because of 'the chilling effect' of Ireland's abortion laws, she was unable to receive sufficient information regarding the implications 'of the pregnancy on her health and life' as well as the implications of the tests she had had on the foetus.[31] She travelled to the UK for a termination.

The judgment

The three applicants argued that the highly restrictive access to abortion in the Republic of Ireland violated their rights under Articles 2 (the third applicant), 3, 8 and 14 of the Convention. In determining the parameters of the claim,

---

[26] The court distinguished between abortions obtained on health grounds and those obtained on well-being grounds: see p. 100 above.

[27] ECHR (GC), *A, B and C v. Ireland*, 16 December 2010 paras. 13–17.

[28] She had also been advised of a 'substantial risk' that the pregnancy was ectopic, although, by the time she travelled to the United Kingdom, she had received confirmation that this was not the case: *ibid.*, para. 19.

[29] *Ibid.*, paras. 18–21.   [30] *Ibid.*, para. 24.   [31] *Ibid.*, para. 24.

the ECHR distinguished 'between health (physical and mental) and other well-being reasons to describe why the applicants choose to obtain abortions [*sic*]'.[32] In addition, it considered that there was 'a significant psychological burden on each applicant'. This was as a result of 'the weight of a considerable stigma' of having to travel to the United Kingdom for an abortion.[33] They were doing something that was a serious criminal offence in their country of residence, and contrary to 'the profound moral values of the majority of Irish people'.[34] This was in contrast to being able to secure an abortion 'in the security of their own country and medical system'.[35] There were also significant financial burdens on the first applicant, and 'a considerable expense' for the other applicants associated with travelling to secure an abortion.[36] Nevertheless, the ECHR held that the claims under Articles 2 and 3 were manifestly ill-founded, and, by majority (eleven votes to six) that there had been no breach of Article 8, or Article 8 in combination with Article 13 in relation to the first and second applicants. In determining whether the measures were 'necessary in a democratic society', the Court granted Ireland a wide margin of appreciation in determining the balance to be struck between the rights of the mother and those of the unborn child given the strong views held on the subject by the Irish people.

The ECHR held that there had been a violation of Article 8 in relation to the third applicant. Although women who had been raped and were suicidal were able to obtain an abortion in Ireland, it was unclear whether the same applied in other life-threatening situations. Ireland had failed to implement section 40.3.3 of the Constitution which had placed the life of the mother on an equal footing with that of the unborn child.[37] This created uncertainty for the legal position of the third applicant. This, combined with the 'chilling factor' associated with the criminal provisions, meant that she was unable to establish her entitlement to a lawful abortion in Ireland. In relation to all the claims, the Court held that no separate issue arose under Article 14.

The decision of the majority in this case is unsatisfactory in its over-cautiousness. While the majority of States provide abortion facilities, it appears that those that have highly restrictive abortion facilities will not, without more, be found to breach the Convention. The only basis upon which a violation will be found is where a State has already made abortion legally available and the applicant is denied the procedural measures to establish that entitlement. This exceptionally limited approach marginalises entirely the reproductive rights of women in terms of substantive human rights protections and is out of keeping with international and European moves in this regard.

The judgment will now be considered Article by Article.

---

[32] *Ibid.*, para. 125.   [33] *Ibid.*, para. 126.   [34] *Ibid.*   [35] *Ibid.*, para. 126.
[36] *Ibid.*, para. 128.   [37] See pp. 99–100 above.

Article 2

In relation to the claim under Article 2, the Court found that, because the third applicant was not prevented from travelling to England to have an abortion, nor were the post-abortion complications associated with a risk to her life, the Article 2 claim was 'manifestly ill-founded'.[38]

The right to life of the foetus

One of the issues that emerges in this judgment is whether the foetus is entitled to the protection of Article 2. Previous cases concerning abortion have demonstrated a reluctance to grant the foetus Article 2 protection. In *X* v. *United Kingdom*, the European Commission of Human Rights held that the provision of abortion under British law of a foetus of ten weeks' gestation did not breach Article 2, holding that:

> [i]f Article 2 were held to cover the foetus and its protection under this Article were, in the absence of any express limitation, seen as absolute, an abortion would have to be considered as prohibited even where the continuance of the pregnancy would involve a serious risk to the life of the pregnant woman. This means that the 'unborn life' of the foetus would be regarded as being of higher value than the life of the pregnant woman.[39]

Abortion for social as opposed to health reasons was found not to breach Article 2 in *H* v. *Norway*.[40] Here, it was held that 'national laws on abortion vary considerably', so 'contracting states must have a certain discretion'. While Norway had not fallen foul of this discretion, it is unclear from this judgment the circumstances that would.[41] In *Vo* v. *France*,[42] the applicant brought a claim under Article 2 following an unintentional injury on the part of a doctor necessitating a therapeutic abortion. In that case, the Court held that it was 'neither desirable, nor even possible as matters stand, to answer in the abstract the question whether the unborn child is a person for the purposes of Article 2 of the Convention'.[43] This was reiterated in *A, B and C* v. *Ireland*. In its judgment in relation to Article 8, the Court made the point that, because there was no European consensus as to when life began, it was impossible to determine whether the foetus was a person protected under Article 2. The dissenting judges qualified this position slightly, holding that, while they agreed that it was not desirable to determine the issue of when foetal life began, it was the case that the mother is 'a person already participating, in an active manner, in social interaction'.[44] The foetus, however, is 'within the mother's body, whose

---

[38] ECHR (GC), *A, B and C* v. *Ireland*, 16 December 2010, para. 159.
[39] ECommHR, *X* v. *United Kingdom*, 13 May 1980, para. 19.
[40] ECommHR, *H* v. *Norway*, 19 May 1992.
[41] *Ibid.*, para. 1. See also ECHR, *Boso* v. *Italy*, 5 September 2002.
[42] ECHR (GC), *Vo* v. *France*, 8 July 2004.   [43] *Ibid.*, para. 85.
[44] ECHR (GC), *A, B and C* v. *Ireland*, 16 December 2010, para. 2 of dissenting opinion.

life has not been definitively determined as long as the process leading to the birth is not yet complete, and whose participation in social interaction has not even started'.[45]

The right to life of the mother

On the facts before the Court in *A, B and C*, there appeared to be little evidence of a risk to the life of the mother. However, in circumstances where the mother's life is in danger, Article 2, and the positive duties that emerge from it, may well be engaged. In *KNLH* v. *Peru*, the author claimed a violation of Article 6 of the ICCPR (the right to life) in that the State's refusal to provide her with a therapeutic abortion placed her in the position where she had to choose between one of two options, both of which put her life in danger. She could either seek a clandestine abortion (with all the risks to her life that that entailed) or continue with a pregnancy that was both traumatic and dangerous and which also posed a risk to her life.[46] In the event, the Human Rights Committee found that the treatment complained of violated Article 7 (the prohibition on torture and inhuman and degrading treatment) and did not believe it was necessary to make a finding under Article 6.[47] However, such an interpretation of the right to life is not ruled out, and the dissenting view by Hipólito Solari-Yrigoyen was that a violation of Article 6 had taken place. Refusing to provide the author with a therapeutic abortion endangered her life and 'had grave consequences ... It is not only taking a person's life that violates article 6 ... but also placing a person's life in grave danger, as in this case.'[48]

In light of this and in light of the ambiguity concerning the point at which foetal life begins, it is possible to determine that a failure on the part of a State to provide abortion facilities to women where there is evidence of a risk to their lives should the pregnancy continue would be a violation of the positive obligations associated with Article 2. Such an approach would be consistent with the reasoning of the ECHR in relation to the positive duties emerging under that Article. In *LCB* v. *United Kingdom*, the ECHR held that Article 2 requires the State 'not only to refrain from the intentional and unlawful taking of life, but also to take appropriate steps to safeguard the lives of those within its jurisdiction'.[49] In these circumstances, the State must do 'all that could have been required of it to prevent the applicant's life from being avoidably put at risk'.[50] In *Osman* v. *United Kingdom*, the Court held that the positive duty

---

[45] *Ibid.*

[46] Human Rights Committee, 85th Session, Communication No. 1153/2003, para. 3.3.

[47] *Ibid.*, para. 6.3.

[48] *Ibid.*, Appendix, Dissenting Opinion by Committee Member Hipólito Solari-Yrigoyen.

[49] ECHR, *LCB* v. *United Kingdom*, 9 June 1998, para. 360.   [50] *Ibid.*

under Article 2 can also entail 'in certain well-defined circumstances a positive obligation on the authorities to take preventive operational measures to protect an individual whose life is at risk from the criminal acts of another individual'.[51] In order to establish a breach of the positive duty to protect life, it must be shown 'that the authorities knew or ought to have known at the time of the existence of a real and immediate risk to the life' of an individual 'and that they failed to take measures within the scope of their powers which, judged reasonably, might have been expected to avoid that risk'.[52] The positive duty is 'construed as applying in the context of any activity, whether public or not, in which the right to life may be at stake'.[53] Furthermore, abortion facilities may involve the provision of healthcare services on the part of the State. In *Cyprus* v. *Turkey*, the ECHR held that issues 'may arise under Article 2 . . . where it is shown that the authorities of a Contracting State put an individual's life at risk through the denial of health care which they have undertaken to make available to the population generally'.[54] This case appears to indicate that the withholding of treatment needs to be deliberate.[55] The case law thus suggests that where a real and immediate risk to the life of the mother in continuing with the pregnancy can be established, the State will be failing in its positive duties if they are aware or ought to be aware of such a risk and fail to take measures to avert it. This is clarified in the redrafted judgment with some additional reasoning at paragraphs 157–9.

Article 3

The three applicants argued that the positive and negative obligations associated with Article 3 had been violated because criminalising abortion represented a 'crude stereotyping and prejudice against women', was thus discriminatory, violated women's dignity and stigmatised them, leading to 'increasing feelings of anxiety'.[56] They also argued that the options available to women in these circumstances, namely, 'overcoming taboos' and seeking an abortion abroad with aftercare back in Ireland, or continuing with their pregnancies, 'were degrading and a deliberate affront to their dignity'.[57] They argued that there was considerable evidence as to the effects of criminalisation on women in the form of stigma and taboo. The Court held however that whether or not the effects were as the applicants submitted, this did not reach the 'minimum level of severity' required for a claim under Article 3 to succeed.[58]

[51] ECHR (GC), *Osman* v. *United Kingdom*, 28 October 1998, para. 115.
[52] *Ibid.*, para. 116.   [53] ECHR (GC), *Öneryildiz* v. *Turkey*, 30 November 2004, para. 71.
[54] ECHR (GC), *Cyprus* v. *Turkey*, 10 May 2001, para. 219.
[55] *Ibid.* Cf. ECHR, *Pentiacova* v. *Moldova*, 4 January 2005.
[56] ECHR (GC), *A, B and C* v. *Ireland*, 16 December 2010, para. 162.   [57] *Ibid.*
[58] ECHR, *Ireland* v. *UK*, 18 January 1978, para. 162; ECHR, *Lotarev* v. *Ukraine*, 8 April 2010.

Whilst it appears that the treatment complained of did not reach the level of suffering required to meet the standards of Article 3,[59] it is possible to envisage circumstances where the failure to provide abortion facilities would reach the threshold. For example, the Court has held on a number of occasions that sexual assault or rape reaches the threshold of Article 3.[60] It seems likely therefore that being forced to continue with a pregnancy following rape or incest would also be found to reach the level of severity required for Article 3. Articulating matters in this way is of crucial importance given that there are a number of countries (including in Europe) that do not provide abortions in cases of rape or incest. In *LMR* v. *Argentina*, a young woman with a mental age of between eight and ten became pregnant as a result of a suspected rape.[61] Despite the legality of such a procedure in these circumstances, the family could not find anyone to perform the abortion and the procedure was undertaken illegally. The author suffered mental and psychological suffering, including post-traumatic stress disorder with predominantly phobic symptoms.[62] She claimed that she had been forced to continue with her pregnancy, causing days of physical anguish and mental suffering, forcing her to have an illegal abortion, thus endangering her life and well-being, as well as being subjected to opprobrium from a variety of sources. The Human Rights Committee found, *inter alia*, a violation of Article 7 of the ICCPR. The author had been denied a termination to which she was lawfully entitled, causing 'physical and mental suffering constituting a violation of article 7 of the Covenant that was made especially serious by the victim's status as a young girl with a disability'.[63]

There are further arguments that could be made in relation to Article 3. As we have seen above, abortion services to protect the physical and mental well-being of the woman vary. Where continuing with a pregnancy causes severe mental and physical effects (other than the normal process of giving birth), it is possible that a failure to provide abortion services could reach the threshold of Article 3. This would be consistent with the decision on the part of the Human Rights Committee in *KNLH* v. *Peru*,[64] and would resonate with existing case law in relation to Article 3 and the provision of medical care. In principle, there should be no difficulty if the claim related simply to mental harm, provided that the Article 3 threshold was reached.

---

[59] Cf. ECHR (GC), *Cyprus* v. *Turkey*, 10 May 2001, para. 302–11; ECHR, *Moldovan* v. *Romania (No. 2)*, 12 July 2005, paras. 102–14, where discriminatory treatment was held to fall within the remit of Article 3.

[60] ECHR (GC), *Aydin* v. *Turkey*, 25 September 1997; ECHR, *E* v. *United Kingdom*, 26 November 2002; ECHR, *MC* v. *Bulgaria*, 4 December 2003; ECHR, *Maslova* v. *Russia*, 24 January 2008.

[61] CCPR, Comm. No. 1608/2007, 29 March 2011.   [62] *Ibid.*, para. 3.1.

[63] *Ibid.*, para. 9.2.

[64] Human Rights Committee, 85th Session, Communication No. 1153/2003.

In *Tanko* v. *Finland*, the European Commission of Human Rights did not rule out the possibility that Article 3 could be breached in circumstances where an individual 'is suffering from a serious illness' and does not receive medical care.[65] In *D* v. *United Kingdom*, a prisoner who had been convicted of drugs offences, had advanced AIDS and was being threatened with deportation succeeded in his claim that his removal would breach Article 3. The Court was influenced by the fact that D had no accommodation, would not have received a proper diet, would be lacking in 'moral or social support' as well as the fact that the removal of his AIDS treatment would have drastically hastened his death.[66] In *Pretty* v. *United Kingdom*, the ECHR held that 'suffering which flows from naturally occurring illness, physical or mental, may be covered by Article 3, where it is, or risks being, exacerbated by treatment . . . for which the authorities can be held responsible'.[67] The Article 3 claim was unsuccessful in part because the applicant was receiving adequate medical care.

In relation to abortion cases specifically, the ECHR held in *Tysiąc* v. *Poland* that the failure to provide an abortion to a young mother of two whose eyesight had deteriorated seriously as a consequence of a pregnancy causing considerable distress and hardship as well as significant disability did not reach the threshold of Article 3.[68] It is possible that, in that case, a higher threshold was being used than that of the Human Rights Committee in *KNLH*. In *RR* v. *Poland*, decided after *A, B and C*, the ECHR did find a violation of Article 3.[69] Following a scan during the eighteenth week of pregnancy, the applicant was informed of the likelihood that the foetus was suffering an 'unidentified malformation'.[70] She became concerned that the foetus had a genetic disorder, but, through the prevarication and procrastination of the hospital authorities, she could not obtain access to genetic tests to confirm these suspicions. The tests were eventually carried out and the results obtained after the time limit for a lawful abortion in these circumstances had passed. The Court made its finding in relation to Article 3 on a number of grounds. The applicant was already in a position of 'great vulnerability', given the distress caused by the knowledge that the foetus could be suffering some abnormality.[71] Furthermore,

> [a]s a result of the procrastination of the health professionals . . . she had to endure weeks of painful uncertainty concerning the health of the foetus, her own and her family's future and the prospect of raising a child suffering from an incurable ailment. She suffered acute anguish through having to think about how she and her family would be able to ensure the child's welfare, happiness and appropriate long-term medical care.[72]

---

[65] ECommHR, 14 September 1995.
[66] ECHR, *D* v. *United Kingdom*, 2 May 1997, para. 52.
[67] ECHR, *Pretty* v. *United Kingdom*, 29 April 2002, paras. 52–3.
[68] ECHR, *Tysiąc* v. *Poland*, 20 March 2007, para. 66.
[69] ECHR, *RR* v. *Poland*, 26 May 2011.   [70] *Ibid.*, para. 153.   [71] *Ibid.*, para. 159.   [72] *Ibid.*

These concerns were not addressed or acknowledged in the proper way by those responsible for her care and the results of the test came too late to obtain an abortion lawfully. The conduct of the State in this case was aggravated by the fact that the testing she had requested was 'at all times available and that she was entitled as a matter of domestic law to avail herself of them'.[73] The redraft endeavours to articulate the principles set out here at paragraphs 163–6 of the new judgment.

Article 8

All three applicants brought claims under Article 8. The Court treated the claim brought by the first and second applicant as a possible breach of the negative obligations associated with Article 8, namely, whether the prohibition of abortion in Ireland represented a disproportionate interference with their private lives. The Court's approach in relation to the first and second applicant is consistent with previous case law, which does not recognise a *prima facie* entitlement to abortion.[74] In contrast, in relation to the third applicant, the Court treated her claim as a violation of the positive obligations associated with Article 8, namely, to provide effective and accessible procedures enabling her to determine her right to a lawful termination.[75] Her claim is not redrafted here.

Private life

In relation to Article 8, the Court in *A, B and C* recalled that the concept of 'private life' includes, *inter alia*, 'decisions both to have and not to have a child or to become genetic parents'.[76] In addition, the Court also referred to previous decisions which held that while the issue of pregnancy does come within the remit of the private life of the woman, it does not create an absolute right to privacy in relation to 'pregnancy and its termination' given the interconnection between the private life of the pregnant woman and that of the foetus. The woman's right to privacy in these circumstances had to be weighed against 'competing rights and freedoms, including those of the unborn child'.[77] Thus,

---

[73] *Ibid.*, para. 160.

[74] ECommHR, *Brüggeman and Scheuten* v. *Germany*, 19 May 1976. In this case, the applicants complained that their rights under Article 8 were infringed by a law that curtailed entitlement to abortion in Germany. The Commission held that such interference did not breach Article 8. The alleged interference fell within the remit of Article 8(2) given that it was provided by law and 'a measure necessary in a democratic society for prevention of crime and . . . the protection of the rights of others' (*ibid.*, para. 107). The discretion that a State had to punish abortion had not been used arbitrarily, and 'the rights and freedoms of others' included 'the life growing in the mother's womb, this being independent property protected by law' (*ibid.*, para. 107).

[75] ECHR (GC), *A, B and C* v. *Ireland*, 16 December 2010, para. 246.

[76] ECHR (GC), *Evans* v. *United Kingdom*, 10 April 2007.

[77] ECHR, *Tysiąc* v. *Poland*, 20 March 2007; and ECHR (GC), *Vo* v. *France*, 8 July 2004.

while Article 8 did not confer 'a right to abortion', the matters raised by the applicants did engage that Article. In relation to the first and second applicants, the legislative provision prohibiting abortion did constitute an interference with their private lives, the interference was in accordance with the law, and 'pursued the legitimate aim of the protection of morals of which the protection in Ireland of the right to life of the unborn was one aspect'.[78] The judgment turned on whether the measures were necessary in a democratic society.

Positive and negative obligations

The application of positive obligations to give effect to substantive rights under Article 8 is problematic in abortion cases. The Court appears to be protecting solely the positive entitlement to procedure where States have already made some arguable legislative provision for abortion in certain circumstances, as opposed to obliging States either to extend abortion facilities in the shape of permissive legislation or to make resources available to give effect to any substantive entitlement. The effect of this reasoning is that, as it stands, legislation that outlaws abortion will not, without more, engage Article 8. This was illustrated in *Tysiąc v. Poland*.[79] Here, the Court held that legislation regulating the termination of pregnancy touched on the private life of the woman, and that States were under a positive duty to protect their physical and psychological integrity.[80] However, the Court would not consider whether the refusal to provide an abortion *per se* interfered with the applicant's rights under Article 8. Rather, once the legislature had determined that abortion was lawful in some circumstances, 'it must not structure its legal framework in such a way which would limit real possibilities to obtain it'.[81] This structure in relation to positive and negative duties is replicated in *A, B and C v. Ireland*.

The argument presented here is two-fold. First, it is argued that the right to privacy should entail a positive duty to provide termination facilities in certain circumstances in order to comply with the duty to 'fulfil' rights under Article 1. Even if the Court had accepted that legislation outlawing abortion disproportionately interfered with the applicants' private lives in *A, B and C*, the repeal of such legislation would not necessarily mean that the State would be willing to make financial provision for abortion facilities within its healthcare system. Given the interests at stake, a better approach would be to make the privacy right effective by requiring States to put permissive legislation into place backed up by appropriate resources to provide abortions in some circumstances. Secondly, it is argued that the case concerning the first and second applicants

---

[78] ECHR (GC), *A, B and C v. Ireland*, 16 December 2010, para. 227.
[79] ECHR, *Tysiąc v. Poland*, 20 March 2007.
[80] *Ibid*. In cases of abortion, the balancing exercise was one of privacy, the public interest, and the positive duty to protect 'the physical integrity of mothers to be': *ibid.*, para. 107.
[81] *Ibid.*, paras. 108 and 116.

would have been better viewed as one of positive obligations given that their position was not dissimilar to that of the third applicant in terms of the social consequences of unwanted pregnancies. Indeed, the Court does not provide any reasoning as to why the cases of the first and second applicants were treated as involving solely negative obligations.[82]

Positive obligations place duties on States to take action to secure human rights, and emerge from the duty to 'secure' Convention rights that emerge under Article 1. They tend to be 'associated with economic, social and cultural rights'.[83] Whilst the Court continues to rely on the dichotomy of positive and negative duties that tend to dominate debates concerning civil and political rights, 'the tripartite typology, to respect, protect and fulfil' is regarded as more apt in dealing with rights that tend to have this type of character.[84] Negative obligations correlate to the duty to 'respect'. Positive duties relate to the duty on States to 'protect' rights from the actions of others, and to fulfil by 'legislative, budgetary, judicial and other measures towards the full realisation of such rights'.[85] Whilst the distinction between positive and negative duties is retained here, it is argued that the *fulfilment* of the privacy right under Article 8 for women in relation to reproductive freedom entails a positive duty to take legal and financial measures to provide abortions in certain circumstances.

Positive duties as they relate to the duty to fulfil rights started to emerge in *X and Y* v. *Netherlands*. Here, it was established that positive duties

> may involve the adoption of measures designed to secure respect for private life ... including both the provision of a regulatory framework of adjudicatory and enforcement machinery protecting individuals' rights and the implementation, where appropriate, of specific measures.[86]

In that case, the Court found that the Netherlands was under a positive duty to enact legislation in order to criminalise sexual assaults against those with mental disabilities. In *Marckx* v. *Belgium*, it was held that Belgium was under a positive duty to enact laws to recognise children born out of wedlock as a member of the mother's family.[87] Cases with financial implications have included *Airey* v. *Ireland*. Here, it was held that the State was under a positive duty under Article 8 to provide resources to give effective access to a court for a

---

[82] ECHR (GC), *A, B and C* v. *Ireland*, 16 December 2010, para. 216.
[83] D. J. Harris, M. O'Boyle, E. P. Bates and C. M. Buckley, *Harris, O'Boyle and Warbrick: Law of the European Convention on Human Rights* (2nd edn, Oxford University Press, 2009), p. 18.
[84] I. D. Koch, 'Dichotomies, Trichotomies or Waves of Duties?' (2005) 5(1) *Human Rights Law Review* 81–103, 81.
[85] *Ibid.*, p. 82.
[86] ECHR, *X and Y* v. *Netherlands*, 26 March 1985, para. 23. See also ECHR, *A* v. *United Kingdom*, 23 September 1998.
[87] ECHR, 13 June 1979.

woman who had claimed she had been the victim of domestic violence in order to petition for judicial separation.[88]

In its determination of the claim raised by the third applicant, the Court made a number of observations concerning positive obligations which could apply equally to the first and second applicants, given the very real personal and financial difficulties they faced in either carrying the pregnancy to term or having to travel to secure an abortion. It held that although the application of the principles in relation to positive and negative obligations is similar, the concept of 'respect' is less clear given the wide variety of practices and circumstances under which such obligations will arise.[89] In the absence of a negative obligation, the following factors were regarded as relevant in determining whether a positive duty existed, and these were applied to the circumstances concerning the third applicant:[90]

(1) 'the importance of the interest at stake and whether "fundamental values" or "essential aspects" of private life are in issue';[91]
(2) 'the impact on an applicant of a discordance between the social reality and the law, the coherence of the administrative and legal practices within the domestic system being regarded as an important factor in the assessment carried out under Article 8';[92]
(3) whether the obligation is 'narrow and defined or broad and indeterminate';[93] and
(4) 'the extent of any burden the obligation would impose on the State'.[94]

As noted above, once a legal framework is in existence to protect that right, it should be 'shaped in a coherent manner which allows the different legitimate interests involved to be taken into account adequately and in accordance with the obligations deriving from the Convention'.[95]

First, it is unclear from this why these principles apply only to the procedural right to establish entitlement to an abortion, and not to the substantive right to an abortion itself, i.e. the fulfilment of the right. Secondly, the principles articulated here could equally be applied to the circumstances of the first and second applicants. The difference between the positions of the applicants was

---

[88] ECHR, 9 October 1979.
[89] Referring to ECHR (GC), *Goodwin* v. *United Kingdom*, 11 July 2002.
[90] ECHR (GC), *A, B and C* v. *Ireland*, 16 December 2010, para. 248.
[91] Referring to ECHR, *Gaskin* v. *United Kingdom*, 7 July 1989; and ECHR, *X and Y* v. *Netherlands*, 26 March 1985.
[92] Referring to ECHR, *B* v. *France*, 25 March 1992; and ECHR (GC), *Goodwin* v. *United Kingdom*, 11 July 2002.
[93] Referring to ECHR, *Botta* v. *Italy*, 24 February 1998.
[94] ECHR, *Rees* v. *United Kingdom*, 17 October 1986; ECHR (GC), *Goodwin* v. *United Kingdom*, 11 July 2002.
[95] ECHR, *SH and others* v. *Austria*, 1 April 2010, para. 74.

that the third applicant was arguably already entitled to an abortion under the existing law. However, the division between the first and second and the third applicants does not stand up to scrutiny. As seen above, the Court held that the privacy right was engaged in relation to the first and second applicants.[96] The effects of an unwanted pregnancy on a poor single mother with four children in care as a result of alcoholism and who suffers from depression are not substantially different in terms of serious hardship from a mother who gives birth to a child with disabilities. The difficulties caused to pregnant women are not limited to those associated with the potential for giving birth to a seriously disabled child. Both have serious consequences for the mothers concerned. Thus, the disconnection between social reality and the law given the hardship inflicted on these women is not inconsiderable. What is required (namely, access to an abortion) is specific enough to meet the requirement that the obligation is 'narrow and defined' and the burdens on the State could not be said to be excessive.

The redrafting of the judgment thus seeks to frame the claims of the first and second applicants in terms of positive obligations at paragraphs 216–18 of the redraft, providing the basis for the substantive entitlement.

Were the measures 'necessary in a democratic society'?

In relation to whether the restrictions were necessary in a democratic society, the Court considered a number of factors in determining the breadth of the margin of appreciation. It recalled that if a particularly significant aspect of an applicant's identity or existence is at stake, the margin of appreciation will be narrow.[97] However, the margin will be wider where no consensus exists within Europe as to the significance of the interest or the manner in which it should be achieved, especially when they entail 'sensitive moral and ethical issues'.[98]

Crucially, and despite the consensus amongst European countries in the provision of abortion, the Court gave Ireland a *wide* margin of appreciation on the grounds of the sensitivity of the issues at stake. The wide consensus amongst European countries in the provision of abortion did not narrow the broad margin of appreciation. The basis of this finding was the decision in *Vo* v. *France* (cited above) under *Article 2* concerning the lack of consensus about the point at which life began. This, according to the Court, translated into a margin of appreciation under Article 8 as to how a State balances the rights of the mother with those of the unborn. The Court said that it did not under-estimate

---

[96] See p. 108 above.
[97] Citing ECHR (GC), *Evans* v. *United Kingdom*, 10 April 2007, para. 232.
[98] ECHR (GC), *A, B and C* v. *Ireland*, 16 December 2010, para. 232, citing: ECHR (GC), *Evans* v. *United Kingdom*, 10 April 2007; ECHR (GC), *X, Y and Z* v. *United Kingdom*, 22 April 1997; ECHR, *Frette* v. *France*, 26 February 2002; and ECHR (GC), *Goodwin* v. *United Kingdom*, 11 July 2002.

the significant impact of the abortion restrictions as they affected the first and second applicants in the shape of the physically and psychologically arduous task of having to travel abroad for an abortion. It nevertheless found that in light of their ability to travel abroad, in combination 'with appropriate information and medical care in Ireland', the restriction on abortion achieved 'a fair balance between the right of the first and second applicants to respect for their private lives and the rights invoked on behalf of the unborn'.[99]

Six of the judges disagreed with the views of the majority. They argued that regardless of when life begins, 'an undeniably strong consensus' exists within Europe that the mother's right to life and, in the majority of countries, her health and well-being are regarded as of greater importance 'than the right to life of the foetus'.[100] As a result of this, they took the view that it was incorrect to conflate the margin of appreciation in determining the point at which life began (and therefore the right to life) with the margin of appreciation in relation to 'weighing the right to life of the foetus against the right to life of the mother'.[101] Given the inappropriate conflation, the dissenting view is adopted in the redraft.

The dissenting judges reiterated the view that a consensus exists within Europe concerning the provision of abortion. However, in cases of this nature, the Court usually concludes that such a 'consensus decisively narrows the margin of appreciation'.[102] The dissenting judges strongly disagreed with the finding that, in light of the fact that the applicants were able to travel to procure an abortion, Ireland was entitled to prohibit abortion on the grounds of 'the profound moral views of the Irish people as to the nature of life'.[103] They considered both of these premises in permitting a wide margin of appreciation to be 'disputable'.

The dissenting judges then addressed how the balancing exercise should have been tackled. In relation to the first premise, the ability to travel, the majority reasoning was inadequate because the applicants' complaint related to the prohibition on having an abortion in their own country. They considered rightly that having to travel abroad 'is not only financially costly but also entails a number of practical difficulties'. The result is that the Court dodges 'the real issue of unjustified interference'. In relation to the second premise, even if the 'profound moral views' indeed existed, it was 'a real and dangerous departure' in existing case law to conclude that this can take precedence over a European consensus which points in an entirely different direction.[104] Such case law has

---

[99] ECHR (GC), *A, B and C v. Ireland*, 16 December 2010, para. 241.
[100] Joint partly dissenting opinion of Judges Rozakis, Tulkens, Fura, Hirvela, Malinverni and Poalelungi. See also the discussion pertaining to Article 2 above.
[101] ECHR (GC), *A, B and C v. Ireland*, 16 December 2010, para. 2 of the dissenting judgment.
[102] *Ibid.*, para. 5 of the dissenting judgment.
[103] ECHR (GC), *A, B and C v. Ireland*, 16 December 2010, para. 241.
[104] *Ibid.*, paras. 8–10 of the dissenting judgment.

not, to date, differentiated 'between moral and other beliefs' in considering the margin of appreciation accorded to States where such consensus exists.[105] The dissenting judges also regarded the 'severity of the (rather archaic) law' to be a factor in determining whether the measures are proportionate.

The dissenting view is a much more plausible interpretation of the existing law and leads to a result more conducive to giving women effective protection over their well-being, their reproductive lives and therefore their privacy (see paragraphs 229–42 of the redraft). Whilst the ECHR has been criticised for its lack of clear and consistent use of the margin of appreciation doctrine,[106] the debate here is about what Lestas calls the 'structural' aspect of the margin of appreciation, namely, 'the limits or intensity of the review of [the ECHR] in view of its status as an international tribunal.'[107] This translates into the argument that the ECHR 'should often *defer* to the judgment of national authorities on the basis that the [Convention] is an *international* convention, not a national bill of rights. The ideas of subsidiarity and state consensus are usually invoked to support the structural use of the margin of appreciation.'[108] However, State consensus was clearly evident in this case. Both the process of national decision-making and 'the substantive outcome' should conform to 'the object and purpose of the governing norm'.[109] The governing norm both in terms of Member States and in terms of international law is that of greater entitlement of abortion rights as an important aspect of women's human rights.

Article 14

It is in relation to this Article that the approach of the European Court of Human Rights is perhaps the most disappointing, given the manner in which the international human rights bodies are approaching the issue.[110] As noted above, CEDAW has articulated access to abortion facilities as an issue of equality.[111] In *LMR* v. *Argentina*, the author claimed that the State had failed 'to exercise due diligence in safeguarding a legal right to a procedure required solely by women, coupled with the arbitrary action of the medical staff, resulted in discriminatory conduct' against her.[112] This was aggravated by her status 'as a poor, disabled woman'.[113] The Human Rights Committee

---

[105] *Ibid.*, para. 9 of the dissenting judgment.
[106] R. MacDonald, 'The Margin of Appreciation', in R. St J. Macdonald, F. Matscher and H. Petzold (eds.), *The European System for the Protection of Human Rights* (1993), p. 85; G. Lestas, 'Two Concepts of the Margin of Appreciation' (2006) *Oxford Journal of Legal Studies* 705.
[107] *Ibid.*, p. 706.   [108] *Ibid.*
[109] Y. Shany, 'Towards a General Margin of Appreciation Doctrine in International Law?' (2005) *European Journal of International Law* 907 at 911.
[110] See pp. 96–9 above.   [111] *Ibid.*
[112] CCPR, Comm. No. 1608/2007, 29 March 2011, para. 3.5.   [113] *Ibid.*

found violations, *inter alia*, of Article 3, although it does not state the basis for this finding.[114] The redraft attempts to articulate the failure to provide abortion facilities as an issue of discrimination against women (paragraphs 269–72 of the redraft).

Limiting women's reproductive freedom has an impact on their ability to participate in public life, including education and employment.[115] The need for an abortion is gender-specific, so that failure to recognise the gendered nature of abortion provision fails to do justice to the gendered nature of the compromise to other rights (privacy, inhuman or degrading treatment) where States do not make suitable provision. Given the highly gendered nature of the issues at stake, and the fact that women disproportionately continue to bear most of the responsibility for child-rearing, articulating this as an issue of discrimination is both important and in line with moves in the international human rights community to secure abortion rights.

Conclusions

In conclusion, the redraft contains a number of findings that would bolster women's entitlement to abortion facilities. In circumstances where the life of the woman is in danger and the State has failed to provide abortion facilities, this could breach the positive obligations owed by States under Article 2 to protect life. Similarly, in circumstances where there are serious consequences compromising the physical and mental well-being of the mother, this could breach the positive duties owed by States to ensure that its citizens are not subjected to inhuman or degrading treatment. The provision of abortions on social, economic or well-being grounds should be regarded as a breach of the positive duty to protect privacy and the margin of appreciation should be a narrow one. Finally, failure to provide abortion facilities should be treated as an issue of discrimination.

Rewriting A, B and C v. Ireland

. . .

C.   Article 2 of the Convention

157. The third applicant complained under Article 2 that abortion was not available in Ireland even in a life threatening situation because of the failure to implement Article 40.3.3 of the Constitution. The Government argued that no issue arose under Article 2 of the Convention.

---

[114] *Ibid.*, paras. 9.4 and 10.   [115] See the text accompanying note 15 above.

158. The Court has previously held that Article 2 protects individuals against the intentional and unlawful taking of life on the part of the State, but also a positive obligation to 'take appropriate steps to safeguard the lives of those within its jurisdiction' and to do all that can be 'required of it to prevent the applicant's life being unavoidably put at risk' (*LCB* v. *United Kingdom* (9 June 1998), § 36, Reports and Judgments of Decisions 1998-III; and *Osman* v. *United Kingdom* (28 October 1998), § 116, Reports 1998-VIII). The Court has also previously held that 'an issue may arise under Article 2 of the Convention where it is shown that the authorities of a Contracting State put an individual's life at risk through the denial of healthcare which they have undertaken to make available to the population generally' (*Cyprus* v. *Turkey* (10 May 2001), § 219).

The Court notes that, as in previous cases, there is no Europe-wide consensus concerning the point at which life begins. It is therefore not desirable, under these circumstances, for the Court to seek to make a determination in relation to whether a foetus is a person for the purpose of Article 2. Nevertheless, it is indisputable that the mother is entitled to the protection of Article 2 in circumstances where there is a serious risk to her life (including self-destruction) as a result of continuing with a pregnancy.

159. Applying these principles in the present case, had there been evidence of a real and serious risk to the third applicant's life as a result of continuing with the pregnancy, the failure to provide termination services could have constituted a breach of that Article. However, such evidence has not been presented to the Court.

160. The Court recalls that, just as for the first and second applicants, there was no legal impediment to the third applicant travelling for an abortion abroad [reference deleted]. The third applicant did not refer to any other impediment to her travelling to England for an abortion and none of her submissions about post-abortion complications concerned a risk to her life. [Fragment deleted] Her complaint that she was required to travel abroad for an abortion given her fear for her life falls to be examined under Article 8 of the Convention.

D. *Article 3 of the Convention*

. . .

163. The Court considers it evident [fragment deleted] that travelling abroad for an abortion was both psychologically and physically arduous for each of the applicants. It was also financially burdensome for the first applicant [reference deleted].

164. [Fragment deleted] The Court reiterates its case law to the effect that ill-treatment must attain a minimum level of severity if it is to fall within the scope of Article 3. The assessment of this minimum depends on all the circumstances of the case, such as the duration of the treatment, its physical or mental effects and, in some cases, the sex, age and state of health of the victim (*Ireland* v. *the United Kingdom*, 18 January 1978, § 162, Series A no. 25; and, more recently, *Lotarev* v. *Ukraine*, no. 29447/04, § 79, 8 April 2010).

165. There are circumstances under which it is possible to envisage the failure to provide termination services to be a breach of the positive and negative obligations associated with Article 3. The Court has previously held that sexual assaults reach the minimum level of severity required to meet the Article 3 threshold (*Aydin* v. *Turkey* (1998) 25 EHRR 251; *E* v. *UK* (2003) 36 EHRR 31; *MC* v. *Bulgaria* (2005) 40 EHRR 20; *Maslova* v. *Russia* (2009) 48 EHRR 37). In these circumstances, a failure to provide abortion services to women who become pregnant as a result of rape and who require them could breach the positive obligations associated with Article 3, regardless of whether the woman's life was at risk as a consequence. Furthermore, it is also possible to envisage circumstances that do not involve a sexual assault where continuing with a pregnancy causes physical and mental effects severe enough to reach the threshold, other than the effects normally associated with childbirth, such as, for example, a very serious deterioration in a pre-existing physical or mental condition (*İlhan* v. *Turkey* [GC], no. 22277/93, § 87, ECHR 2000-VII; *D* v. *UK* (1997) EHRR 423; *Pretty* v. *UK* (2002) 25 EHRR 1 §§ 51–52).

166. However, in the above-described factual circumstances (paragraphs 124–129 above) and whether or not such treatment would be entirely attributable to the State, the Court considers that the facts alleged do not disclose a level of severity falling within the scope of Article 3 of the Convention. The Court rejects the applicants' complaints under Article 3 of the Convention as manifestly ill-founded pursuant to Article 35 §§ 3 and 4 of the Convention.

. . .

II.   Alleged violation of Article 8 of the Convention

. . .

(a)   **Positive or negative obligations under Article 8 of the Convention?**
216. [Fragment deleted] **As** there are positive obligations inherent in effective respect for private life (see paragraphs 244–246 below), the Court considers it appropriate to analyze the first and second applicants' complaints as concerning [fragment deleted] **positive** obligations. [Fragment

deleted] **The Court must consider whether the failure to provide abortion on health and well-being grounds falls foul of the positive obligations on States to secure effectively the privacy of those within its jurisdiction to give practical effect to those rights.**

217. The Court has previously found States to be under a positive obligation to secure to its citizens their right to effective respect for their physical and psychological integrity (*Glass* v. *United Kingdom*, no. 61827/00, §§ 74–83, ECHR 2004-II; *Sentges* v. *Netherlands* (dec.) no. 27677/02, 8 July 2003; *Pentiacova and others* v. *Moldova* (dec.), no. 14462/03, ECHR 2005- . . . *Nitecki* v. *Poland* (dec.), no. 65653/01, 21 March 2002; *Odièvre* v. *France* [GC], cited above, § 42). In addition, these obligations may involve the adoption of measures, including the provision of an effective and accessible means of protecting the right to respect for private life (*Airey* v. *Ireland*, 9 October 1979, § 33, Series A no. 32; *McGinley and Egan* v. *United Kingdom*, 9 June 1998, § 101, Reports of Judgments and Decisions 1998-III; and *Roche* v. *United Kingdom* [GC], no. 32555/96, § 162, ECHR 2005-X) including both the provision of a regulatory framework of adjudicatory and enforcement machinery protecting individuals' rights and the implementation, where appropriate, of specific measures in an abortion context (*Tysiąc* v. *Poland*, cited above, § 110).[116] The difficulties facing the applicants must therefore be viewed as whether the State has failed in its positive duties to give effect to their right to privacy under Article 8.

218. The Court has previously noted, citing with approval the case law of the former Commission in *Bruggemann and Scheuten* v. *Germany*, that not every regulation of the termination of pregnancy constitutes an interference with the right to respect for the private life of the mother *(Vo* v. *France* [GC], cited above, § 76). Nevertheless, having regard to the broad concept of private life within the meaning of Article 8 including the right to personal autonomy and to physical and psychological integrity (see paragraphs 212–214 above), the Court finds that the prohibition of the termination of the first and second applicants' pregnancies sought for reasons of health and/or well being amounted to an interference with their right to respect for their private lives. The essential question which must be determined is whether the prohibition is an unjustified interference with their rights under Article 8 of the Convention.

[Paragraphs 222–41 deleted]

---

[116] This paragraph is taken from para. 245 of the judgment which deals with the positive duties owed to the third applicant and with the way in which the Court has treated positive obligations. As argued above, these can be said to apply equally to the first and second applicants.

241. The Court cannot ignore the real difficulties created for the first and second applicants in having to travel abroad to secure abortions. In addition, the profound moral views of the Irish people cannot override the consensus that exists in other European States to provide abortions on health and well-being grounds. It is also the case that the burden of childcare falls disproportionately on the mother so that the interference with her privacy in relation to a pregnancy that is not conducive with her health or well-being is considerable. The Convention protects the physical integrity of individuals, including reproductive freedom. Giving effect to that right cannot entail only refraining from preventing women from having abortions. It requires a positive duty to provide access to abortions in certain circumstances. In this regard, the Court does not consider it material that the applicants were able to travel to the UK to secure an abortion. The issue is whether the State is under a positive duty to protect the privacy of those living within its jurisdiction, an obligation that cannot be evaded by the applicant's ability to travel abroad. The Court concludes that such an obligation does indeed exist.

In addition, the penalties on the applicants had they been able to procure an abortion in Ireland on these grounds would have been severe. The Court also views this as a breach of the negative obligation to refrain from undue interference with the privacy right. In light of this, the Court believes that the Irish State has exceeded its margin of appreciation and violated the rights of both the first and second applicants in prohibiting abortions on health and well-being grounds. This is not to give the first and second applicants an unlimited entitlement to abortion given the competing interests at stake, but rather a conclusion that, in these circumstances, the prohibition in light of the Europe-wide consensus in relation to the provision of abortion, and on pain of severe prison sentences if breached, exceeds the narrow margin of appreciation that exists in securing the applicants' rights under Article 8.

(f)   The Court's conclusion as regards the first and second applicants

242. It concludes that there has been [fragment deleted] a violation of Article 8 of the Convention as regards the first and second applicants.

. . .

III.   Alleged violation of Article 14 in conjunction with Article 8 of the Convention

269. The applicants also complained that the above-described restrictions and limitations on lawful abortion in Ireland were discriminatory and in breach of Article 14 in conjunction with Article 8 in that they placed an

excessive burden on them as women and, in particular, on the first applicant as an impoverished woman. The Government argued that there was no basis for considering that the impugned legal framework discriminated against women on grounds of sex. Even if it did constitute a difference of treatment on that ground, it was justifiable and proportionate for the reasons referred to under Article 8 of the Convention. That the first applicant would have been adversely affected by virtue of her financial status was insufficient to ground a complaint under Article 14 of the Convention.

[Original paragraph 270 deleted]

The Court's Assessment

270. The Court recalls previous case law on the principles to be observed in determining whether a State has acted contrary to Article 14 in the determination of one of the substantive Convention rights. Any differential treatment between individuals 'in relatively similar situations' can be discriminatory if it has no 'objective and reasonable justification' (*Willis* v. *United Kingdom*, no. 36042/97, § 48, ECHR 2002-IV; and *Okpisz* v. *Germany*, no. 59140/00, § 33, 25 October 2005). In addition, discrimination can occur where States 'without an objective and reasonable justification fail to treat differently persons whose situations are significantly different' (*Thlimmenos* v. *Greece* (2001) 31 EHRR 411 § 44). Furthermore, 'a general policy or measure that has disproportionately prejudicial effects on a particular group may be considered discriminatory notwithstanding that it is not specifically aimed at that group' (*DH* v. *Czech Republic* (2008) 47 EHRR 59). Differential treatment must pursue a legitimate aim and be a proportionate means of achieving that aim (*Belgian Linguistics* case (1968) 1 EHRR 252 PC § 10). Member States enjoy a considerable margin of appreciation in determining whether differences in treatment are justified (*Somerfield* v. *Germany* (2004) 38 EHRR 756). However, it should be noted that equality between the sexes 'is today a major goal in the member states of the Council of Europe. This means that very weighty reasons would have to be advanced before a difference of treatment on the ground of sex could be regarded as compatible with the Convention' (*Abdulaziz, Cabales and Balkandali* v. *UK* (1985) 7 EHRR 163 § 78).

271. It is clear that a policy of refusing to perform abortions affects women disproportionately, even if the intention is to protect the unborn. Thus, weighty reasons need to be advanced before a difference in treatment on the grounds of sex is justified. Given the effects of pregnancy continued despite the risks to the well-being of the mother, the intimate issues at stake and the burdens placed on women in terms of child-rearing as a result of continuing with an unwanted pregnancy, such a policy

cannot be a proportionate means of protecting the interests of the unborn. It is further to be noted that women's ability to participate in public life, including education and employment, can be significantly curtailed by unwanted pregnancies, and that reproductive freedom is key to the enjoyment of other rights.

272. The Court accordingly finds that there has been a breach of Article 8 in combination with Article 14.

5

A noble cause: a case study of discrimination, symbols and reciprocity

YOFI TIROSH*

Introduction

In *De La Cierva Osorio De Moscoso* v. *Spain*,[1] four Spanish women challenged the succession rule of nobility titles in their country in an application to the European Court of Human Rights (hereinafter ECHR). The rule in question gives precedence to male heirs of the title, such that women inherit the title only if there are no male heirs. All applicants were the oldest offspring of the deceased title-bearer, and would have inherited the title had they not been women: their younger male relatives (mostly siblings) won the titles. The applicants argued that this rule had violated their right to private and family life under Article 8 of the European Convention on Human Rights (hereinafter 'the Convention'),[2] taken together with the prohibition of discrimination laid down in Article 14. The applicants also based their claim on Article 1 of Protocol 1 to the Convention,[3] which protects the right to peaceful enjoyment of one's possessions. The ECHR accepted Spain's reasoning and declared the complaint inadmissible.

Two reasons lead me to discuss this case in a volume dedicated to diversity. First, the case raises the question of accessibility of *symbols of prestige* to traditionally discriminated social groups. Spain replied to the ECHR that the applicants' claim should be rejected since nobility titles do not fall under Article 8 because they have long lost their actual importance in determining one's social rank, property, wealth, or legal status, and remain merely a

* I am grateful to Eva Brems and the Human Rights Centre at Ghent University for their intriguing and original invitation to rethink and rewrite a case of the European Court of Human Rights. I am also thankful to Daniel Drenger, Seyda Emek, Zohar Kohavi and Alexandra Timmer for their comments on earlier versions of this chapter. Tami Yakira provided excellent editorial assistance.
1 ECHR, *De La Cierva Osorio De Moscoso* v. *Spain*, 28 October 1999.
2 Convention for the Protection of Human Rights and Fundamental Freedoms, 4 November 1950, 213 UNTS 222.
3 Paris, 20 March 1952.

symbolic relic of bygone times. As such, nobility titles are not a material part of the right protected in Article 8 (i.e. they do not shape one's sense of affiliation with one's family as names do). This argument is intriguing because it raises questions about the intersections between law and semiotics. Should the argument that titles were 'merely' symbolic have appeased the Court, and should it have led it to the conclusion that there was no need for legal intervention in this case?

Secondly, underlying the ECHR's ruling was a theory of anti-discrimination that merits critical examination. I shall argue that this theory is problematic in that it unnecessarily narrowed the scope of protection of traditionally discriminated groups. Spain argued that, by their very nature, titles represented an old social regime of hierarchy and discrimination, which was discordant with the contemporary liberal nature of Spanish law and society. It would therefore be paradoxical, Spain continued, to sustain the practice of passing on titles (which were inherently discriminatory and were based on social hierarchies that were often arbitrary, having nothing to do with merits) while suddenly injecting a sex-equality component to that practice. This, then, was an argument about the *authenticity*, or the *integrity*, of the institution of nobility titles: such titles would be distorted and emptied of their essence if they are to be shaped and reshaped according to changing times. Spain's argument was also one of *reciprocity*: according to Spain, the female applicants could not focus their argument on sex-based discrimination while ignoring other forms of discrimination that are inherent to the titles, namely, the arbitrary biological fact of being born to an aristocratic family, and the fact that one is older than other potential competitors to the title (primogeniture). It would be inappropriate to invoke anti-discrimination law to allocate something that is in itself unequal and discriminatory.

Moreover, continued Spain, by fine-tuning the succession line so that it would reflect the contemporary commitment to sex equality, nobility titles might gain social resonance, or become even more normalised and legitimate than they have been.

This chapter addresses, then, two challenging issues emanating from *De La Cierva Osorio De Moscoso* v. *Spain* (hereinafter '*De Moscoso*'). First, I shall discuss the inherent tension typifying signs such as nobility titles – as merely symbolic or as carrying substantive content. I shall argue that the distinction between form and substance collapses in this case, as in many other cases that involve allocation of allegedly merely symbolic signifiers – particularly to underprivileged groups. Secondly, I shall examine the idea that a party that presents an anti-discrimination claim cannot seek equal allocation of matters that are in themselves inherently discriminatory. This fascinating characteristic of nobility titles – as relics of an old world of rank and social hierarchy – is one of the reasons that the applicants' discrimination claim was rebutted. I dub such claims 'reciprocal anti-discrimination arguments', or RADARs, and sketch guidelines for thinking about this type of claims.

Five years after this case was decided in Strasbourg, a very similar communication, *Barcaiztegui* v. *Spain*, was decided by the UN's Human Rights Committee (hereinafter UNHRC). This time the applicants based their sex discrimination argument on the fact that the succession rule of nobility titles violated the International Covenant on Civil and Political Rights (hereinafter ICCPR).[4] Similarly to the ECHR, the UNHRC found that Spain did not violate the ICCPR (but, unlike the Strasbourg decision, in the latter decision there were three dissenting opinions). Since the parties' arguments in the UNHRC were very similar to the arguments in *De Moscoso*, I shall at times refer to the UNHRC decision as another reference for understanding the legal questions of *De Moscoso*.

My analysis begins by exploring the role of symbols in socio-legal life, and reaches the conclusion that the line between symbolic and material is often blurred, arbitrary, and not as important as we tend to think.

The discussion then moves to the arguments that the application lacks reciprocity and would strip the tradition of titles of their authenticity. A critical examination of these arguments questions their merits in the context of antidiscrimination law.

Finally, the chapter ends with the rewritten opinion in *De Moscoso*.

Nobility titles: between form and substance

A central part of Spain's defence in *De Moscoso* was that, today, nobility titles are insignificant, and therefore the applicants suffered no deprivation. In one of the domestic proceedings which preceded the application to Strasbourg, Spain's Constitutional Court wrote:

> The distinction on the ground of sex . . . is now only of purely symbolic value, since it no longer has any substantive content within our legal order. On the contrary, the social and legal values enshrined in our Constitution and which, therefore, are fully applicable today would necessarily come into play if the legal distinction had a substantive content, which it certainly does not here.[5]

---

[4] UNHRC, *Mercedes Carrión Barcaiztegui* v. *Spain*, 30 March 2004. Another case raising a similar discrimination claim, this time as a communication to the CEDAW Committee (under the Convention on the Elimination of All Forms of Discrimination against Women (1979), 1249 UNTS 13), was decided in 2007. A majority of the Committee found the communication inadmissible on procedural grounds, but a concurring opinion and a dissent were also written. I shall return to these latter opinions below. See CEDAW, *Munoz-Vargas y Sainz de Vicuna* v. *Spain*, 9 August 2007. As this chapter was written, the Commonwealth cancelled the priority given to males in royal succession. See Nicholas Watt, 'Royal Succession Gender Equality Approved by Commonwealth', *Guardian*, 28 October 2011.

[5] ECHR, *De La Cierva Osorio De Moscoso* v. *Spain*, 28 October 1999, p. 2.

The fact that the titles are (allegedly) merely symbolic guided the Strasbourg Court in finding that access to titles or lack thereof did not violate any of the rights protected in Article 8. This section of the chapter addresses the various questions emanating from the semiotic nature of titles. I shall argue that the symbolic functions of titles are important – especially for women and other minority groups, who have been traditionally excluded from representation in the symbolic order.

Are nobility titles merely symbolic?

The applicants argued that their right to inherit the nobility titles falls within the scope of Article 8 of the Convention, which protects the right to respect for private and family life. They based their argument on the similarity between nobility titles and names. The ECHR had recognised that first names and surnames sometimes fell within the right protected under Article 8 because a name is 'a means of personal identification and of linking to a family'.[6] In order to understand why the Court rejected the claim that nobility titles should also be considered protected under Article 8, we need to understand how exactly the Court sees the connection between Article 8 and names, and why this connection was not extendable to nobility titles.

In discussing this question in *De Moscoso*, the Court said Article 8 includes the right to a name. Although Article 8 'does not contain any explicit provisions on names, as a means of personal identification and of linking to a family, a person's name nonetheless concerns his or her private and family life'.[7]

Names therefore fulfil the role of personal identifiability and linkage to the family. In *Burghartz* v. *Switzerland*,[8] a leading case on the linkage between names and Article 8, the European Commission of Human Rights referred to the connection between names and identity. But the Commission framed the right to identity narrowly – as the right to identifiability.[9]

But note that 'identity' here is used in the narrow sense of the term, as technical identifiability. In the terminology of semiotics theory, the function of names here would be described as indexical:[10] they work as labels, to point to the person and differentiate him or her from others and to link him or her to a family. But, if the function of names is merely to provide individual and familial identifiability, then we could hypothesise that in principle, names can be replaced by more impersonal and bureaucratic means of identifications, such

---

[6] *Ibid.*, p. 8. See A. M. Gross, 'Rights and Normalization: A Critical Study of European Human Rights Case Law on the Choice and Change of Names' (1996) 9 *Harvard Human Rights Journal* 269–70.

[7] ECHR, *De La Cierva Osorio De Moscoso* v. *Spain*, 28 October 1999, p. 8.

[8] ECommHR, *Burghartz* v. *Switzerland*, 22 February 1994.   [9] *Ibid.*, p. 37.

[10] See D. Chandler, *Semiotics: The Basics* (2nd edn, Routledge, 2002), pp. 42–4.

as social security numbers or even barcode chips implanted under our skins, if technological circumstances facilitate easy and efficient use of such chips. The ECHR seems to provide a reductive account of the function of names: one that does not encompass the meaning of names, their connotation, or the ideological, religious or aesthetic worlds that they come from.

But names are, of course, much more than a means of identifiability. If names are essential to 'the right to development and fulfilment of one's personality', as the Court recognises, then names cannot be merely understood as arbitrary and random signs that serve the technical function of identifiability or identification.[11] Self-fulfilment and personality require that names do more than provide the technical ability to differentiate between person X and person Y, or membership in family A or in family B.

Like barcodes or ID numbers, names are a specific combination of signs (alphabetical letters) that are attached to a person (although they are less specific than ID numbers or barcodes, because they are not unique or exclusive: different people can have the same name, and even the same first name and surname).[12] But, unlike ID numbers or barcodes, names also carry meaning that extends beyond the technical.[13] Names are laden with cultural associations. They invoke, for example, connotation to a certain religion (e.g. names of saints), to a historical role model, or to a certain language (consider the difference between Jamila and Bella – both meaning 'beautiful', one in Arabic and one in Italian); they may invoke the memory of a beloved ancestor or express a desire for certain moral convictions or personal traits (consider the names Grace, Chastity, Sophie or Fortuna).

I posit that this wider meaning of names falls within the right to personal development and fulfilment under Article 8. A convincing interpretation of the scope of the right to private life under Article 8 would not end at the point of the ability to identify a person correctly through their name (although this is certainly an essential aspect of the right to private life). If the right to private life includes the right to self-fulfilment, then it must include the right to a name that would be meaningful for its bearer.

My suggested understanding of the scope of names under Article 8 is extendable to titles. If surnames tell us something about the affiliation of a person to his or her family and culture, then so do nobility titles.

---

[11] I develop this point extensively in Y. Tirosh, 'A Name of One's Own: Gender and Symbolic Legal Personhood in the European Court of Human Rights' (2010) 33 *Harvard Journal of Law and Gender* 247.

[12] For a brilliant mapping of names on the axis of tattoos on the one hand and State registers on the other hand, see D. Riley, 'Your Name Which Isn't Yours', in D. Riley, *Impersonal Passion: Language as Affect* (Durham, NC: Duke University Press, 2005), pp. 115–28.

[13] See e.g. J. Kaplan and A. Bernayse, *The Language of Names: What We Call Ourselves and Why It Matters* (Simon & Schuster, 1999).

In the case at hand, the applicants

> submitted that nobiliary titles constituted the heritage of their lineage's honour and a blood tie with their ascendants, and that they had been deprived of those attributes solely because they were females, not males.[14]

The applicants argued, then, that, although their names were sufficient for the purpose of simple identifiability (i.e. the ability to tell that this individual belongs to family X), titles should fall under Article 8 because they tell a richer story about the applicants' familial heritage. The title connected them to their family in a way that a name did not and could not, for it added a layer of allusion to the glorious past of their ancestors. This interpretation reflects a notion of development of personhood that is much more akin to the spirit and purpose of Article 8 than the ECHR's narrow interpretation.

To the question posited in the title to this section ('Are nobility titles merely symbolic?'), my answer would be negative, because they have the meaning and function of conveying familial history and other content that is important to the development of personhood[15] (see paragraph 1 of the rewritten judgment).

Finally, the Court based its reasoning that titles do not fall within Article 8 on the notion that nobility titles are merely honorary signifiers, lacking any substantial importance. *But this claim loses its convincing force by the very act of positing it.* For every time that a party claims that something (in this case, nobility titles) is not worth our time and attention because it is merely symbolic, a paradox emerges: if titles are so marginal and insignificant, if they really are meaningless, then why fight so hard about maintaining the order of their succession (or about any of their other aspects, for that matter)? The very fact that the Spanish government defended its position through domestic courts and all the way up to the ECHR is a strong indication that titles are apparently not *merely* symbolic but *very* symbolic.

Do titles fall within the scope of Article 8?

The applicants added that the fact that, according to Spanish law at the time, titles of nobles and dignitaries would be entered into a civil register means that

---

[14] ECHR, *De La Cierva Osorio De Moscoso* v. *Spain*, 28 October 1999, p. 7.

[15] At this point of the analysis, once we have established that Spain interfered with the right to private and family life under Article 8 § 1, we should have normally moved to analysing whether this interference was necessary in a democratic society according to Article 8 § 2. However, since this discussion did not occur in the case itself (because the Court did not find that the complaint fell within the scope of Article 8), it seems unnecessary to conduct this hypothetical discussion in the present context. On the bifurcation between the definition and scope of the Convention's rights, and the review of the justification for interfering with them, see J. Gerards and H. Senden, 'The Structure of Fundamental Rights and the European Court of Human Rights' (2009) 7(4) *International Journal of Constitutional Law* 619–53.

the title serves 'as an additional element identifying and linking the holder with the founder's lineage for transmission to future generations'.[16]

To this argument Spain replied that nobiliary titles do not fall within the scope of the right protected in Article 8, because:

> [i]dentity with a family was expressed through the surname and not through a nobiliary title ... A person's surname and first names, which were indisputably elements of the right to respect for private and family life, could not be confused with a nobiliary title.[17]

The Court recognised that its jurisdiction indeed considered first names and family names as part of Article 8, but it laconically stated that the case law relating to names is simply irrelevant, because the dispute is not over names:

> Identity with a family was expressed through the surname and not through a nobiliary title. That was made clear by section 53 of the [Spanish] Law on the Civil Register, which provided statutory protection for surnames. A person's surname and first names, which were indisputably elements of the right to respect for private and family life, could not be confused with a nobiliary title.[18]

This formalistic statement is disappointing, because it does not offer a theory to justify why the Court draws the lines of Article 8's scope between surnames and nobiliary titles. After all, both surnames and titles are signs of identification; both are registered by the State; and both signify a connection to one's family. It is therefore unclear why the Court so offhandedly rejected the analogy between names and titles, by stating that titles are simply not names and that was that.

The applicants argued, further, that, even if Article 8 did not include the right to inherit a nobility title, the fact that Spain regulated this practice obligated it to ensure that it was done equally:

> [W]hile it was true that 'the enjoyment of a nobiliary title' did not constitute a human right, once a person's right to use the title had been recognised, it necessarily concerned Article 8 of the Convention since it constituted an element of identification of the holder of the right with their parents, their lineage and their ancestors, one that was not unconnected with the holder's family life. Consequently the holder could not be subjected to discrimination on the ground of sex.[19]

In *Barcaiztegui* v. *Spain* (the similar case from the UNHRC mentioned earlier), the State's involvement in regulating titles is depicted more elaborately (albeit by a dissenting opinion):

> The distribution of family titles in Spain is regulated by public law. Decisions on succession to titles of honor or nobility are published as official acts of state in the *Boletin Oficial del Estado*. The order of succession

---

[16] ECHR, *De La Cierva Osorio De Moscoso* v. *Spain*, 28 October 1999, p. 8.

[17] *Ibid.*, pp. 7–8.   [18] *Ibid.*, pp. 7–8.   [19] *Ibid.*, p. 8.

is not a matter of private preference of the current titleholder. Rather, female descendants are statutorily barred from any senior claim to a title, pursuant to the preference for males regardless of the wishes of the ascendant titleholder. Such a statutory rule … would seem to be a public act of discrimination.[20]

While the argument about the State's involvement was rejected in *De Moscoso*,[21] subsequent Strasbourg jurisprudence did accept this argument and developed a doctrine that broadens the application of Article 14. In *EB* v. *France* (hereinafter *EB*),[22] the Grand Chamber held that, if the State guaranteed rights that go far beyond the scope of what was guaranteed in Article 8, then it must do so without discrimination. In *EB*, France guaranteed the right to adoption to its citizens. There was no doubt that the right to adoption fell outside the scope of the Convention's Article 8 – but there was also no doubt that the right to adopt fell within the ambit of the right to private and family life that Article 8 guaranteed. The Court held:

> The prohibition of discrimination enshrined in Article 14 thus extends beyond the enjoyment of the rights and freedoms which the Convention and the Protocols thereto require each State to guarantee. It applies also to those additional rights, falling within the general scope of any Convention Article, for which the State has voluntarily decided to provide.[23]

Applying the doctrine of *EB* to our case, once the Spanish State enabled registration of nobility titles, it operated within the ambit of Article 8 (because, even under the narrow interpretation of Article 8, there can be no doubt that nobility titles are also means of identifiability, which associate their bearer with his or her family). In granting the right to register titles and operating within the ambit of Article 8, Spain was obligated to provide this right without discrimination. Otherwise, it would be operating in violation of Article 14 in conjunction with Article 8.

---

[20] *Barcaiztegui* v. *Spain*, 30 March 2004, Individual Opinion by Committee member Ms Ruth Wedgwood. A dissenting opinion with a similar reasoning was written in the CEDAW Committee case of *Munoz-Vargaz y Sainz de Vicuna* v. *Spain*, 9 August 2007 (para. 13, Individual Opinion by Committee member Mary Shanthi Dairiam) (holding that States must in no context provide for a differential treatment of women and men in a manner that establishes the superiority of men over women, and that historical grounds or the perceived immaterial consequence of a differential treatment are a violation of women's right to equality).

[21] ECHR, *De La Cierva Osorio De Moscoso* v. *Spain*, 28 October 1999, p. 9.

[22] ECHR (GC), *EB* v. *France*, 22 January 2008. For further discussion of the ambit requirements of the ECHR see R. O'Connell, 'Substantive Equality in the European Court of Human Rights?' (2009) 107 *Michigan Law Review First Impressions* 129 at 215 and 225.

[23] ECHR (GC), *EB* v. *France*, 22 January 2008, para. 48 of the majority judgment.

So far, I have argued against the notion that titles are merely symbolic. In the next section, I will argue that, even if titles have only a symbolic function, they still mattered, and the Court should have dealt with the issue of their succession rules on its merit (see paragraph 4 of the rewritten judgment).

And what if titles are 'merely' symbolic? On the importance of the semiotic

Spain successfully argued that titles lost their 'density' in contemporary Spanish society, in that they no longer actually determined status, formally or informally. Spain and the Court operated on the assumption that what mattered was the reality 'behind' or 'under' the symbols, and that, once this reality is uncertain – once we establish that titles did not determine status – then the conversation is over and the case should be closed. But much important activity happens on the symbolic or semiotic level itself.[24] Even if symbols such as titles operate only on the symbolic level without clear manifestations in the 'reality behind the symbols' – even if persons carrying a nobility title are not necessarily richer or more privileged than others in their social or legal status – the symbolic level still matters, and the way symbols are allocated should not be dismissed as a matter so trivial and petty that the law should not intervene in it.

Elsewhere, I dubbed symbolic aspects of identity such as physical appearance, names or titles as the poetics of personhood.[25] I argued that a lot of meaning-making occurs on the level of representation of self or appearance. Names, dress, accent, and in our case titles, make up the semiotic domain of personhood: the interface through which individuals are perceived by others and by which they constitute their identity and personhood. I further argued that the fact that we cannot stably anchor every signifier to a stable signified 'behind' it (or an appearance to an identity that supposedly lies underneath it) does not mean that we should ignore or dismiss this semiotic level of personhood.[26]

If, as I suggest, nobility titles are not to be expected to function as accurate depictions of wealth or status, then the argument that they are *merely* symbolic loses its grip. *De Moscoso* is indeed a case about symbols, and the Court was asked to determine the allocation of access to symbols, but that the drama and the conflict occurred on the symbolic level does not mean that there was no drama and conflict at all. Spain knew this, the Court knew this, and the applicants knew this. The applicants knew that their identity was not accurately *represented* by the nobility title, but, rather, the relationship between the title and its bearer is one of allusion or connotation. Nobility titles certainly suggested a connection of their bearers to certain familial relations, to a past of

---

[24] See Y. Tirosh, 'Adjudicating Appearance: From Identity to Personhood' (2007) 19 *Yale Journal of Law and Feminism* 49.
[25] *Ibid.*   [26] *Ibid.*, pp. 56–7.

aristocratic status, etc., but in today's Spain, they did not guarantee such connection, nor did they constitute it.

The Court was therefore wrong to accept Spain's argument that, because nobility titles no longer constituted a special, privileged status, they were meaningless and unworthy of judicial attention. Titles should fall within the scope of the right protected in Article 8 because they serve to connote affiliation to and identification with one's family[27] (see paragraph 2 of the rewritten judgment).

A note before proceeding with the analysis: the applicants also argued that denying their right to inherit nobility titles violates their right to peaceful enjoyment of their possessions under Article 1 of Protocol 1 to the Convention. Because I am willing to accept, for the sake of the argument, Spain's claim that titles were symbolic and had no pecuniary value, the question of violation of Article 1 of Protocol 1 indeed becomes irrelevant, and I shall not elaborate on it.

Gender and signs

So far, I have offered a semiotic analysis of the case at hand, but the picture would not be complete without adding the gender component to our understanding of the case. Historically, women have been particularly vulnerable regarding access to social visibility, and the reasoning in De Moscoso echoes the patriarchal notions that have traditionally denied women access to symbols of public prestige.

In an article that analysed the ECHR's case law on gender and surnames, I showed that the prevailing patrilineal surname customs made it hard for women to remain socially visible and present as stable and independent individuals.[28] Bearing the surname of their fathers when they are born, they receive a different surname in every transition from one patriarch to another. Once they marry, it is hard to trace them because their surnames change (all the more so when they divorce or remarry). This invisibility is true not only in women's own lifetime: it is also hard to trace women in historical records, even when they were significant figures, because they appeared as Mrs John Smith, or were mentioned only by their first names – a practice that was rarely the case for men.[29]

---

[27] Cf. the author's argument in Barcaiztegui: '[T]he lack of any financial value of the titles is without importance since for the holders they possess great emotional value.' Barcaiztegui v. Spain, 30 March 2004, para. 5.6.

[28] Y. Tirosh, 'A Name of One's Own: Gender and Symbolic Legal Personhood in the European Court of Human Rights' (2010) 33 Harvard Journal of Law and Gender 247.

[29] Ibid., p. 283.

Article 8, protecting the right to private life, is also problematic and some-what paradoxical when women are concerned. In protecting the private sphere, Article 8 imagines a legal subject who is active in the public sphere, and needs a safe haven of discreteness in the shelter of his home and his correspondence, where the long arm of the government or society would not reach. But, when it comes to women, who have been placed in traditional liberal theory in the private rather than the public sphere, Article 8 seems almost redundant, if not nonsensical: how can the private sphere be demarcated and distinguished as an especially protected space for someone who barely exists outside of it? Moreover, privacy clauses such as Article 8 do not provide an answer to the question of what happens when a man's right to private life conflicts with that of his wife, daughter or sister.

A vicious circle is at play here: the more women are denied access to signs such as surnames or nobility titles, the harder it becomes to recognise their stake in such signs and the harder it is to assess the wrong in denying them such access. An analogy from tort law would illustrate my point. One of the biggest challenges in tort theory is how to avoid compensating the rich more than the poor for the same damage: if a person with a high salary loses his ability to work, the court might assess his loss in higher sums than the low-earning plaintiff who suffered a similar damage. It is easy for courts to assess the damage suffered by the wealthy as higher than that suffered by the impoverished. And yet, tort doctrine and theory recognise this problem and try to mitigate its effects so that compensation for torts would not be regressive, thereby widening the gap between the 'haves' and 'have nots'.[30]

Going back to our case, in the matter of access to signs, men have been the 'haves'. They were the ones who had primary access to signs such as surnames and to nobility titles. Women were the 'have nots', who have been denied convenient and uninterrupted access to such signs. It is therefore understand-able that the Spanish courts could more readily recognise the damage that would be caused to males if they were no longer the first heirs of nobility titles (for something that was theirs for centuries would suddenly be denied to them). It is also unsurprising that the ECHR did not recognise the unequal allocation of titles as a human right. Women, according to this view, would not lose much, because what they asked for in *De Moscoso* was never theirs.

In cases such as *De Moscoso*, women face a greater challenge than men in demonstrating that their rights have been impaired by blocking their access to

---

[30] See T. Keren-Paz, *Torts, Egalitarianism, and Distributive Justice* (Ashgate Publishing, 2007), pp. 23–160; A. Porat, 'Misalignments in Tort Law' (2012) *Yale Law Journal* (forthcoming). Tort scholars suggest ways to achieve the equalisation of compensation by relying on objective and uniform assessments of lost income, that would mitigate factors such as the social class, ethnicity or gender of the injured party. Such ways include, for example, relying on the scope of physical disability after the injury, or relying on average income rather than on concrete past income.

signs that grant their bearer social visibility. Men, who have had such access for generations, are better positioned to demonstrate what is at stake for them in signs such as nobility titles.

In developing a theory of anti-discrimination under Article 14 of the Convention, the Court should have taken into account the different starting points of men and women in relation to nobility titles. In failing to recognise that the succession rule of nobility titles is discriminatory, both the Spanish courts and the Strasbourg Court were held captive by the distorted perspective described above. Under this naturalistic fallacy, the 'is', the current state of things (nobility titles' succession rule), is mistaken for the 'ought': titles *should be* passed down from male to male because titles *have been* passed down like that for generations (see paragraph 10 of the rewritten judgment).

Finally, perhaps the campaign that the Spanish female applicants launched in vindication of their right to inherit nobility titles was perceived as transgressive in terms of both gender and class conventions. Their desire to position themselves as the primary bearers of the family's status symbol could be seen both as unfeminine (for women are socialised to defer their desires and needs and grant primacy for the needs and wishes of others[31]) and as unbecoming for a true aristocrat.[32] In short, it would be 'un-ladylike'. Caring for one's self-interest, especially when honour and prestige are concerned, may have been viewed by the courts (perhaps unconsciously) as an unappealing and unappreciated behaviour when conducted by women, let alone women who claim to have footing in aristocracy.[33]

Reciprocal anti-discrimination

As we have seen, the ECHR dismissed the significance of titles as 'merely symbolic'. But it used another important reasoning to reject the discrimination claim, namely, that applicants cannot rely on anti-discrimination law in order to gain access to something that is in itself inherently discriminatory. This Part focuses on this challenging reasoning, and examines it from the perspective of anti-discrimination theory.

---

[31] See J. S. Mill, *The Subjection of Women: A Critical Edition* (Edward Alexander ed., New Brunswick, NJ: Transaction Publishers, 2001 (1869)), p. 14; C. A. MacKinnon, 'Difference and Dominance: On Sex Discrimination', in C. A. MacKinnon, *Feminism Unmodified* (Cambridge, MA: Harvard University Press, 1987), pp. 32–45.

[32] The upper classes typically have a sense of ease and of entitlement to their high social rank, and therefore fighting such rank betrays them as not truly noble. See, generally, P. Bourdieu, *Distinction: A Social Critique of the Judgment of Taste* (Richard Nice trans., Cambridge, MA: Harvard University Press, 1984 (1979)).

[33] See, generally, C. Gilligan, *In a Different Voice* (Cambridge, MA: Harvard University Press, 1982).

What are reciprocal anti-discrimination arguments (RADARs)?

Spain argued, and the Court accepted, that nobility titles belonged to the 'old world' of arbitrary social hierarchies. Nobility titles, so runs the argument, create class distinctions that are foreign in their spirit to contemporary social egalitarian values, by which all are essentially equal before law and equal *vis-à-vis* others. From this followed, according to Spain, that:

> It would be contrary to the principle of the universality and equality of human rights to regard enjoyment of a nobiliary title as a right to respect for private and family life.

The argument then is one of a problematic lack of reciprocity on behalf of the applicants: the applicants sought non-discriminatory treatment, but were unwilling to reciprocate with such non-discriminatory treatment in their own relations with others, since they aspired, through nobility titles, to be socially superior to those others.

Part of Spain's reply to the Court discussed the idea of dignity. This reply illustrates the problem at hand nicely. Spain emphasised what it saw as a misuse of the idea of dignity in this application: how can the applicants argue that their own dignity was violated because they were being skipped-over as women in the succession line, when accepting their claim would contaminate the concept of dignity because it would create contingent distinctions between persons?[34]

Note that the violation of dignity that Spain is concerned about is the one resulting from the arbitrary distinction between nobility and common people – a distinction that results from the arbitrariness of social destiny. However, Spain is not concerned here with an equally arbitrary distinction of nature: the distinction between the sexes. What about the dignity of those who, due to their sex, are skipped over in the succession line?

In *Barcaiztegui* v. *Spain* before the UNHRC, Spain's argument was stated even more elaborately. Spain argued that sex-based discrimination is only the third form of discrimination that is entailed in the practice of passing on nobility titles:

> According to the State party these [succession] rules embody a first element of discrimination by reason of birth, since only a descendant can succeed to the title; a second element of discrimination lies in birth order, based on the former belief in the better blood of the firstborn; and lastly, sex constitutes a third element of discrimination. The State party contends that the author accepts the first two elements of discrimination, even basing some of her claims thereon, but not the third.[35]

---

[34] ECHR, *De La Cierva Osorio De Moscoso* v. *Spain*, 28 October 1999, p. 8.
[35] *Barcaiztegui* v. *Spain*, 30 March 2004, para. 4.7.

Women who, like the applicants, want to inherit titles without being discriminated against on the basis of sex, and yet at the same time cannot reciprocate
with sensibility to arbitrary class and age (i.e. primogenitary) distinctions, have
an incoherent position, according to Spain. Let me dub this type of claim 'the
reciprocal anti-discrimination argument', or, in short, RADAR. RADARs, then,
are arguments that serve to rebut a plaintiff's anti-discrimination claim by
asserting that the plaintiff itself is unwilling to reciprocate with non-
discriminatory practices. I find this reasoning intriguing, appealing and
challenging.[36]

The use of RADAR as a reasoning to deny anti-discrimination claims is
intriguing in that it posits a logic of *reciprocity* that is not commonly used in
legal anti-discrimination contexts: 'Do not ask the law for assistance regarding
your discrimination if you yourself participate in discriminatory practices in
your very appeal to the law.'

This reasoning is *appealing* because it represents, at least on its face, a holistic
approach to inequality. If the goal is to eliminate discrimination, then this goal
is best achieved when legal decisions are based on a deeper and larger conception of equality, and do not confine themselves to the narrow and formalistic
examination of discrimination as the plaintiff frames it (justifiably or not). We,
the Court, might solve your problem of discrimination, but, by doing so, we
would simultaneously exacerbate another form of discrimination.[37]

Another appeal of RADAR is that it echoes fairness arguments: if one expects
not to be discriminated and seeks legal remedy against one's discrimination,
then one should also refrain from discriminating or from relying on discriminatory structures. This reasoning can be analogous to the doctrine of 'unclean
hands' in private law.[38]

The reasoning is also appealing because the ECHR seems to be positing an
argument about the legitimising power of law: its decision suggests that if the

---

[36] For an elaborate exploration of RADAR, see Y. Tirosh, 'Reciprocal Antidiscrimination
Arguments' (2012) 6 *Law and Ethics of Human Rights* (forthcoming).

[37] But cf. *Barcaiztegui* v. *Spain*, 30 March 2004, where two dissenting opinions in the UN's
Human Rights Committee argued that, 'in deciding to find the communication
inadmissible on the basis of a supposed inconsistency between the author's claim and
the "underlying values behind" [*sic*] the principle protected by Article 26, has clearly ruled
ultra petita, i.e. on a matter not raised by the author. The author confined herself to
complaining of discrimination against her by the State party on the grounds of her sex; the
discrimination in the case before us was clear, and the Committee should have come to the
decision on admissibility on the strength of the points clearly made in the communication.'
Ibid., para. 4 of Individual Opinion by Committee member Rafael Rivas Posada. See also
Individual Opinion by Committee member Hipólito Solari-Yrigoyen, *ibid.*

[38] The doctrine of 'unclean hands' is a defence against a petition for equitable relief. To take
advantage of the doctrine, the defendant must show that the plaintiff did not act in good
faith with regard to his or her complaint. See T. L. Anenson, 'Limiting Legal Remedies: The
Doctrine of Unclean Hands' (2010–11) 99 *Kentucky Law Journal* 63.

petition is accepted, it might reify the significance of nobility titles in Spanish society – and this, again, is contrary to the egalitarian spirit of the application (and also of the Convention).

Moreover, the Spanish government (and this was not denied by the Court) expressed a worry that the very core constitutional values of equality and dignity would be diluted or compromised if they were to be applied in cases that deal with hierarchical institutions such as nobility titles:

> Accordingly, it would be paradoxical if a peerage could be acquired by succession not, as historical practice dictates, on the basis of the criteria which governed previous transmissions, but of other criteria, since that would amount to ascribing the values and principles enshrined in the Constitution, and which today have a substantive content within our legal order, to something which, because of its symbolic nature, does not have such content.[39]

Finally, this reasoning is *challenging* because it leaves many questions yet unanswered: what are additional cases in anti-discrimination doctrine in which this logic is applied by courts (a descriptive question)? How should courts determine when to apply this logic and when to refrain from applying it (a normative question)? And what is the vision of equality that should lie at the basis of judicial decisions when judges deny discrimination claims on the grounds that the claims are themselves discriminatory?

Despite their appeal, RADARs should be treated with caution. In what follows, I shall describe what I see as the pitfalls and shortcomings of RADARs. These shortcomings would lead me to conclude that the Court erred in using a RADAR to deny the application in *De Moscoso*.

Who is vulnerable to RADARs?

When courts use reciprocal anti-discrimination arguments to rebut an applicant's discrimination claim, they send the applicant back home empty-handed because his or her discrimination claim was not 'discrimination-free': it was flawed with discriminatory effects such that, if the applicant's discrimination claim were accepted, this would lead to discrimination for others.

The first and main question we should ask when encountering a RADAR is who is most prone, or exposed, to the usage of RADAR for blocking their discrimination claim. The answer is that RADARs can be invoked precisely against those groups which anti-discrimination law is crafted to assist (that is, individuals from traditionally discriminated groups, such as women, people of colour, the disabled, etc.). Here are three reasons for the heightened vulnerability of traditionally discriminated groups to RADAR claims.

---

[39] ECHR, *De La Cierva Osorio De Moscoso* v. *Spain*, 28 October 1999, p. 3.

First, as an almost trivial and self-evident empirical matter, generally speaking, the majority of discrimination plaintiffs are members of groups that suffer from discrimination.[40] Therefore, to tell discrimination plaintiffs that they need to 'purify' their discrimination claim from any adverse affects that their claim might have on other groups is to double their burden: not only should they prove that they were discriminated against, but they should now also prove that remedying their discrimination would not hurt anyone else.

Secondly, we should keep in mind that contemporary societies are imbued with unequal social and legal structures. Thus, invoking RADAR against plaintiffs in discrimination cases is an easy task – perhaps often too easy – and might lead to conservative outcomes in inhibiting the evolution of anti-discrimination adjudication. For example, RADAR could have been used against the black American citizens fighting for their suffrage in the United States before the Fourteenth Amendment: how could they fight for equal access to the vote when women were denied suffrage, thereby entrenching the vote as a deeply inegalitarian institution (just like nobility titles)? But this is clearly a paralysing claim that could hamper any effort to social reform.

In a deeply inegalitarian world, it would be hard to come by a discrimination claim that would be 'pure' and free of any 'contaminating' discrimination that might be peripherally attached to it. The ease of producing a RADAR to rebut discrimination plaintiffs should serve as a cautionary signal, because it means that almost any discrimination claim could potentially be blocked by a RADAR.

Thirdly, although RADARs could be formulated against almost any discrimination claim, coming either from members of underprivileged groups or from members of the dominant group, courts would be generally less prone to invoke a RADAR to rebut discrimination claims of the latter than of the former. Phrased differently, when members of the dominant group argue discrimination, they are less likely to encounter a RADAR as the argument that rebuts their claim.

---

[40] Indeed, rich literature teaches us that the picture is much more complex than that, and that, for example, it is the relatively privileged within the discriminated group that use those laws (e.g. strong and educated women use sex equality laws more than poor or uneducated women). We also know that, in some cases, the lack of plaintiffs from a particular group cannot serve as an indication that its members do not suffer discrimination. An example of this is Palestinian citizens of Israel, who, as data suggest, are constituently discriminated in the Israeli workplace, and yet refrain from suing in courts. See G. Mundlak, 'The Law of Opportunities in Employment: Between Equality and Polarization' (2009) 90 *Comparative Labor Law and Policy Journal* 213. We also know that members of the privileged group often use anti-discrimination law for their own purposes (e.g. when white students attack race-based affirmative action programmes in education): see C. A. Sullivan, 'The World Turned Upside Down? Disparate Impact Claims by White Males' (2004) 98 *Northwestern University Law Review* 1505. All that being said, still the majority of discrimination plaintiffs are those who come from traditionally discriminated groups.

I will illustrate this argument through the surname adjudication of the ECHR. The ECHR hears a fair amount of cases in which women or men argue that the patriarchal naming system regulated by their State violated their right to private and family life under Article 8 of the Convention, in conjunction with Article 14.[41] A woman could argue, for example, that she had a right to keep her pre-marital surname after marriage,[42] or a man could argue that his child should bear his surname after the mother remarried and had additional children with her new spouse, and wanted to change the surname of the child from the first marriage such that the entire family would bear the same surname.[43]

Examining these cases through the analytical lens of RADAR reveals that men and women are positioned differently when they argue for their right not to be discriminated against in the naming system. When men argue discrimination in the context of the naming laws, their argument is flawed in a very similar way to the weakness that the ECHR found in the applicants' claim in *De Moscoso*: they are asking to be treated equally within a discriminatory system from which they are the constant and primary beneficiaries. In other words, restoring equal treatment for them would not entail equal treatment for all, but rather would mean sustaining and even deepening the unequal treatment of women by the naming system.

And yet, throughout the extensive adjudication of the ECHR on surnames and gender, there has not been even a single case in which a man's claim was rebutted using a RADAR. That is, never did the Court say to a male applicant: 'You cannot come here and ask for our help because your hands are not clean; you ask for remedy against your own discrimination, but you are unwilling to reciprocate with non-discrimination of women in the very area in which you seek equal treatment.'

The case of *Burghartz* v. *Switzerland*[44] serves as a good example. Without entering into all its factual nuances, the case concerned a man, Alfred Schnyder, who took his wife's surname (Burghartz) upon marrying her, but, since he was an academic and was known in professional circles as Schnyder, he sought the

---

[41] See, generally, Y. Tirosh, 'A Name of One's Own: Gender and Symbolic Legal Personhood in the European Court of Human Rights' (2010) 33 *Harvard Journal of Law and Gender* 247.

[42] See e.g. ECHR, *Ünal Tekeli* v. *Turkey*, 2004; ECHR, *Hagmann-Hüsler* v. *Switzerland*, 1977.

[43] See e.g. the case of ECHR, *Petersen* v. *Germany*, 2001 (discussed at length in Y. Tirosh, 'A Name of One's Own: Gender and Symbolic Legal Personhood in the European Court of Human Rights' (2010) 33 *Harvard Journal of Law and Gender* 247 at 278–80).

[44] ECommHR, *Burghartz* v. *Switzerland*, 22 February 1994. For an elaborate analysis of the case, see Y. Tirosh, 'A Name of One's Own: Gender and Symbolic Legal Personhood in the European Court of Human Rights' (2010) 33 *Harvard Journal of Law and Gender* 247 at 270–6.

possibility to hyphenate his pre-marital surname in professional contexts such as academic publications (Schnyder-Burghartz). The European Commission of Human Rights[45] granted his application, finding that his right to private and family life under Article 8(1) of the Convention, in conjunction with Article 14, was violated. But, if we were to apply the RADAR logic of *De Moscoso* to *Burghartz*, the Commission should have rejected his application, on the grounds that, in wishing to maintain his pre-marital surname, the applicant sought equal access to a patriarchal naming system (that is, to a system that is imbued with sex discrimination and, in the eyes of many, represents an old and bygone value system).

I imagine most readers do not think Alfred Schnyder-Burghartz should have lost his case. Similarly, the applicants in *De Moscoso* should not have lost their case either.

Earlier, I noted that discrimination claims are likely to be imbued with residual discriminatory effects. Although this happens both to discrimination claims by members of underprivileged groups, and to discrimination claims of members of dominant groups, only the former tend to be exposed to RADARs as blocking their discrimination argument. Why this difference? Perhaps because in order to accept and remedy the discrimination claim of members of traditionally discriminated groups a much more radical change in the *status quo* is needed than that which would be required in order to accept and correct the discrimination claim of members of dominant groups. Removing an unfair treatment that is aimed against a member of the hegemonic group is like restoring things back to their natural state: these people are usually handled fairly, and, if something is wrong in the picture, it is a detail, a small section of the entire picture, that should and could be easily fixed. In contrast, when it comes to members of discriminated groups, the dynamics are different. They are usually embedded in a deep structure of discrimination, and changing any detail of this structure so that it will be free of discrimination is radical – both because it contradicts the rest of the picture, and because it might entail changing other parts of the picture as well, since working on the detail alone would not bring significant change. This might be why courts recognise more readily a reciprocal anti-discrimination argument when the plaintiff is a member of a generally discriminated group than when the plaintiff is a member of the dominant group.

I enumerated three reasons for why members of traditionally discriminated groups are particularly vulnerable to the invocation of RADAR against their discrimination claim. These reasons place RADAR-type claims in a less positive

---

[45] For an explanation of why the Commission and not the Court was the relevant instance in this case, and of the evolution of the procedures of the Court, see Y. Tirosh, 'A Name of One's Own: Gender and Symbolic Legal Personhood in the European Court of Human Rights' (2010) 33 *Harvard Journal of Law and Gender* 247 at 250 n. 9.

light than at first appeared. They should lead to caution in using RADARs in anti-discrimination cases, and they should have lead the ECHR to refrain from using RADAR in the current case (see paragraphs 7–8 of the rewritten judgment).

Who has the power to change the discriminatory reality?

Another question we should ask in order to assess RADARs as an instrument in rebutting discrimination claims is who has the power to change the residual discriminatory effect that the RADAR alerts us to – is it the plaintiff or the defendant? In our case, such a question would be formulated as follows: if nobility titles have a discriminatory effect in invoking a bygone world of social hierarchies, then who can mitigate this effect? The system of nobility titles, including their succession rules, lies beyond the control of the applicants. Conversely, the Spanish State recognises the titles in that it keeps a registered record of title bearers. It is somewhat odd that the same entity that registers the titles also argues that they are horribly inegalitarian and therefore women should not rely on an equality argument in order to gain equal access to them. If the 'inequality residue' of title bothers the Spanish government that much, it should have discontinued the registration of titles, rather than oppose the reform in their succession line as it did in *De Moscoso*. The State should thereby stop granting titles the official recognition that they have so far been receiving (see paragraphs 2 and 6 of the rewritten judgment).

These observations should not lead to the conclusion that RADARs are never a just argument for rebutting a discrimination claim. RADARs reflect a holistic understanding of discrimination, and therefore they might be appropriate in certain situations. However, as I showed here, they may unequally burden groups that are already burdened with discrimination, and therefore they should be used with caution.

The question of authenticity

One last issue regarding *De Moscoso* warrants critical attention: Spain's argument that changing the succession rule to a rule that would be sex-egalitarian would compromise the authenticity of titles as the historic relic that they are. Spain argued that the practice of nobility titles should be kept unmodified if it is to survive in the modern age. Here are some quotes from Spain's Constitutional Court on that matter:

> [P]eerages are now passed on as they stand by succession. In most instances, these are titles that were attributed under the Old Regime and were defined in the historical past to which, precisely, they now refer … Thus, the legal rule governing their transmission on death has, with time, itself become an inherent feature of nobiliary titles acquired by succession … If

the nobiliary title is not discriminatory and, therefore, not unconstitutional, the precedence [given to the male over the female line] is not either. In other words, since it is accepted that peerages are consistent with the Constitution owing to their purely honorary nature and their purpose, which is to keep alive the historic memory of their grant, a specific element of that institution – the rules governing their transmission on death – cannot be regarded as being exempt from the conditions laid down in the royal charter of grants.[46]

Modifying the way titles are passed down the generations, writes the Constitutional Court, would amount to altering a quality so inherent in titles that they could no longer fulfil even the purely symbolic function that they do now.

There is certainly logic, and even charm, to this reasoning. It reflects the Constitutional Court's general unease and ambivalence about the whole business of nobility titles. The Court is worried that, once it starts meddling with the titles so that they would fit contemporary mores about sex equality, it would then be required to fix the other misfits of titles to current moral sensibilities (namely, that they create class and primogenital distinctions). This would be an impossible mission, because class- and age-based distinctions lie at the basis of nobility titles – this is what they do: they give ranking to certain segments of the population, and, since they are indivisible, only the oldest offspring receives them.

Additionally, if the State or the Court embark on the task of trying to improve the flaws of nobility titles by making their succession rule more egalitarian, they would be perceived as embracing the value system that titles represent – an honour-based system that welcomes hierarchical and vertically stratified social distinctions – distinctions that are not based on merits but on the arbitrariness of fate or biology.

This reasoning is problematic. Recent history provides us with many examples of institutions that were originally imbued with discrimination based on sex, race or sexuality, yet they managed to march with time and adapt to increasing commitments to equality without endangering their very essence.

The last century and a half saw the entrance of women into politics, into universities,[47] into the professions[48] and (still to a limited degree) into the church.

---

[46] ECHR, *De La Cierva Osorio De Moscoso* v. *Spain*, 28 October 1999, pp. 2–3. Cf. Spain's similar argument before the UN's Human Rights Committee in *Barcaiztegui* v. *Spain*, 30 March 2004, para. 4.5.

[47] Recall Virginia Woolf's description of being informed at the entrance to the library at 'Oxbridge' that 'ladies are only admitted to the library if accompanied by a Fellow of the College or furnished with a letter of introduction'. See V. Woolf, *A Room of One's Own* (Mariner Books, 2005 (1929)), p. 8.

[48] See *Bradwell* v. *State of Illinois*, 83 US 130 (1873). See also K. D. Weisberg, 'Barred from the Bar: Women and Legal Education in the United States 1870–1890' (1977) 485 *Journal of Legal Education* 28.

Similar stories could be told about the entrance of non-whites or of gays into these institutions (still very much a work in progress). The point is that the entrance of women and minorities into these institutions is precisely what keeps them viable, since they adapt to the changing times.

This point was made very well by one of the dissenting opinions in *Barcaiztegui* v. *Spain*:

> The use of titles can be adapted to take account of the legal equality of women. Even within the tradition of a title, a change of facts may warrant a change in discriminatory rules. For example, in an age of national armies, it is no longer expected that a titleholder must have the ability to fight on the battlefield. (Admittedly, Jeanne d'Arc might suggest a wider range of reference as well.)[49]

Indeed, we do not feel the ambivalence that we do *vis-à-vis* nobility titles towards many of the institutions I just mentioned, because the latter have some intrinsic values that we cherish (universities promote knowledge and education, parliaments promote the democratic process, etc.). However, going back to our case, if Spain finds reasons to sustain the titles as a viable practice (if only due to symbolic reasons), then it ought not to be tight-fisted about changing the way they are passed through the generations (see paragraph 9 of the rewritten judgment).

Conclusion

This chapter examined *De Moscoso* through two theoretical perspectives: that of semiotics theory, and that of anti-discrimination theory. In analysing the case, my aim was to question some of the unstated assumptions on which the ECHR relied in denying the application admissibility, namely, assumptions on the nature and role of symbols such as nobility titles, identity, gender, reciprocity and authenticity.

The applicants in this case were presented, albeit in the subtext of the opinion, as dishonourable: as if by their very battle over nobility titles they prove themselves as unworthy of such titles. Noble persons, as members of the high class, supposedly have an inherent sense of ease in their social position; of entitlement in their rank in society.[50] Thus launching a legal campaign to chase a nobility title perhaps seemed to the Court as a deeply un-aristocratic endeavour. I hope that the analysis offered here succeeded in presenting the application as less petty and nobler than it might have initially seemed.

---

[49] *Barcaiztegui* v. *Spain*, 30 March 2004, Individual Opinion by Committee member Ms Ruth Wedgwood.
[50] See the discussion on p. 132 above.

Rewriting De La Cierva Osorio De Moscoso v. Spain

...

As to the law

...

1. . . . The Court observes, firstly, that it has on a number of occasions held that disputes relating to individuals' surnames and first names come within Article 8 of the Convention. Although that provision does not contain any explicit provisions on names, as a means of personal identification and of linking to a family, a person's name nonetheless concerns his or her private and family life (see, *mutatis mutandis*, the following judgments: *Burghartz* v. *Switzerland* of 22 February 1994, Series A no. 280-B, p. 28, § 24; *Stjerna* v. *Finland* of 25 November 1994, Series A no. 299-B, p. 60, § 37; and *Guillot* v. *France* of 24 October 1996, *Reports of Judgments and Decisions* 1996-V, pp. 1602–03, § 21). [Fragment deleted] **Indeed, the case law cited above concerns names and the instant case concerns nobility titles, but the cited cases can still serve to illustrate the nature and scope of the right protected under Article 8. Like names, nobility titles are a means of personal identification and connote linkage to one's family. The facts of this case suggest that nobility titles have symbolic significance for the aristocratic families, for individual family members who pass the titles down the generations, and for the Government as it recognises and monitors their succession.**

2. The fact that a nobiliary title may be entered on the civil register as an item of additional information facilitating the identification of the person concerned **indeed** cannot suffice to bring the debate within the scope of Article 8, **but it can serve as an indication of the importance of titles. If Spain partakes in sustaining nobility lines as a meaningful category in Spain's society and culture, and in monitoring that the titles are appropriately passed on, then it is hard to accept Spain's argument that the practice of title-bearing lacks meaning. Furthermore, even if we accept Spain's claim that titles are 'only' of symbolic significance, we stress that symbolic significance is still significance. That is, symbols maintain their symbolic function because they mean something to those for whom they are symbolic. Therefore, this Court sees Spain's participation in registering the title bearers and monitoring their succession as revealing in relation to the present-day significance of titles in Spanish society. Indeed, Spain's very insistence on objecting to the applicants' petition to change the succession order serves to attest that titles are still important and meaningful in the Government's view.**

The Court concludes that the applicant's complaint [fragment deleted] **can** be regarded as coming within the scope of application of Article 8 of the Convention. [Fragment deleted]

Spain did not provide any arguments to demonstrate that its interference in the private and family life of the applicants was necessary in a democratic society, therefore we conclude that Article 8 was violated.

3. The applicants also alleged a violation of Article 14 taken together with Article 8 of the Convention in that giving precedence to males in the transmission of peerages amounted to discrimination which pursued no legitimate aim and was in any event disproportionate.

. . .

The Court reiterates that Article 14 concerns only discrimination affecting the rights and freedoms guaranteed by the Convention and its Protocols. [Fragment deleted] **Since the Court has found that Article 8 has been violated, it should examine whether Spain discriminated against the applicants in setting unequal conditions for enjoying the right.**

4. As a preliminary note, the Court indicates that, even if it would have found that Article 8 was not violated (and the right to nobility titles was not part of the right to private and family life under Article 8), the applicants might still have an argument under Article 14. The prohibition of discrimination enshrined in Article 14 extends beyond the enjoyment of the rights and freedoms of the Convention. It applies also to those additional rights, falling within the general scope of any Convention Article, for which the State has voluntarily decided to provide. This principle is well entrenched in the Court's case law (see *Case 'Relating to Certain Aspects of the Laws on the Use of Languages in Education in Belgium'* v. *Belgium* (Merits), Judgment of 23 July 1968, Series A no. 6, § 9). The present case concerns facts that, if not falling within the core of Article 8 (and in our view they did), surely would have fallen within Article 8's ambit: In registering titles, Spain operates at least within the ambit of Article 8, and in providing for the right to inherit titles it cannot take discriminatory measures within the meaning of Article 14. The sole criterion that distinguishes the applicants from other competitors on the titles is their sex. Therefore, even if this Court had found that there had been no violation of Article 8 standing alone, it would still have found that Article 14 in conjunction with Article 8 is applicable in the present case.

5. The applicants demonstrate that female offspring receive the title only as a last resort, in the absence of a male heir. By this they have shown that the succession rule, on its face, arbitrarily discriminates against female offspring of nobility because it significantly reduces their chances of inheriting the title. It follows that the burden shifts to the respondent

to demonstrate that the sex-based distinction in the succession order of nobility titles did not violate Article 14 in conjunction with Article 8, in that it did not prevent women from equal enjoyment of their right under Article 8 (see ECHR (GC), *Şerife Yiğit* v. *Turkey*, 2 November 2010, para. 71, in which this Court has established that, 'once the applicant has shown a difference in treatment, it is for the Government to show that it was Justified').

6. The respondent State replies with two arguments. First, nobility titles are today merely symbolic and have no material or actual value. The Court cannot accept this argument as sufficient to justify a discriminatory allocation of the titles – as symbolic as they might be. As noted above, symbols have meaning; otherwise human societies would not have sustained and preserved them as symbols. If the titles are indeed insignificant as the respondent State argues, then it follows that *either* their succession order is insignificant as well, and should therefore be outside the interest of the State (and the respondent State would not object to a reform of their succession rule towards a more egalitarian rule that would comply with domestic and European law), *or* titles should be done away with altogether, as a practice that is no longer viable in this modern and more egalitarian era, in which democratic societies seek to minimise arbitrary hierarchies of rank and honour. The respondent cannot hold both ends of the stick by saying that nobility titles do not matter, *and* that they matter a great deal, thus the discriminatory inheritance rules remain untouched and receive State recognition.

7. The Government's second argument is that nobility titles are a historic relic of a bygone world, and part of sustaining their nature as such entails maintaining the original rules of passing them on from generation to generation. The applicants, continues the Government, could not simultaneously ask to remedy their alleged sex discrimination while at the same time sustaining the age and class discrimination that are embedded in the practice of nobility titles. Titles are inherently contradictory to the egalitarian values of the liberal State, and therefore, according to the respondent Government, it would be absurd to impose on them a constraint that belongs to the modern commitment to sex equality.

We find this argument unconvincing. Indeed, Spanish domestic courts deciding this case have recognised an inherent paradox in the argument that nobility titles should be passed down equally on the basis of sex. As relics of the old regime in which social hierarchies based on class and rank were accepted as natural, it might indeed seem paradoxical to argue for sex equality in the allocation of a rank that is passed on according to arbitrary criteria (whether one was born to the right family, and whether one is the oldest sibling).

However, if we were to decide about the values that underline nobility titles, we would have ruled *ultra petita* – on a matter that was not raised by the applicants. The application is confined to the sex based discrimination argument, and the Court should not decide based on grounds that fall outside its scope, such as the age or class distinctions that titles allegedly create. The *ratio decidendi* is limited to determining whether or not the applicants were discriminated against by reason of their sex, in violation of Article 14. The Court could not include in its decisions issues that have not been submitted to it because, if it did so, it would be exceeding its authority. A discussion of the age- and class-based distinctions inherit in titles should be conducted separately, if at all, and cannot be included in the present application.

8. Additionally, the Government's argument amounts to asking the applicants that they rid their discrimination claim from any hint of accompanying discrimination. The logic implied here is the logic of reciprocity: according to the Government, one cannot argue against one's discrimination if along the way there are other forms of discrimination that one's claim does not remedy. The Court is concerned by this logic of reciprocity, as it might lead to setting a very high bar that would block most discrimination claims. In the Court's view, to rebut a discrimination claim of a group that suffers from discrimination by saying that its discrimination claim suffers from discriminatory residue is to potentially block the chances of almost any discrimination claim from succeeding.

An analogy would illustrate this point. In *Burghartz*, mentioned above, this Court held that Switzerland's refusal to allow the applicant to keep his pre-marital surname for professional purposes despite the fact that when he married he took his wife's pre-marital surname as the joint family name, amounted to a breach of Article 8 and Article 14 taken together. Note that the applicant sought equal access to a patriarchal naming system (that is, to a system that was imbued with discrimination and, in the eyes of many, represented an old and bygone value system). Still, this Court did not block the applicant's discrimination claim by arguing that he sought equal access to a good that was imbued with discrimination. In other words, the Court did not require that the applicant reciprocate by demonstrating commitment to the principle of anti-discrimination.

9. If we accept the argument that the rules governing the transmission of nobility titles by death had themselves become an inherent feature of nobility titles, we might reach absurd conclusions that impede progress

towards social and legal equality between men and women. Many of the finest institutions in contemporary societies have been historically closed off for women, and only became open to them in the last century (for example, universities, the legal profession, the vote and the parliament, or the church clerkship). Still, we do not say that male monopoly is an inherent part of academia, law, politics, or the church. Social institutions change with time according to changing moral and legal commitments, and they survive such reforms. There is nothing unique in nobility titles in that regard. As this Court has stated repeatedly, 'the Convention is a living instrument which must be interpreted in light of present-day conditions' (see, for instance, ECHR *Tyrer* v. *United Kingdom*, 25 April 1978, para. 31).

10. In applying anti-discrimination clauses, courts should be careful not to allow prevailing norms to shape their view whether a particular practice is discriminatory or not. Accordingly, this Court takes into account that, throughout history, men have had an easier access to positions of prestige and public visibility (including to nobility titles), while women have been traditionally excluded from such positions. This state of affairs makes it harder for women to demonstrate what is at stake for them in gaining equal access to nobility titles – because they need to demonstrate the damage in being deprived of something that was never theirs. That nobility titles *have been* passed down from one man to the next for generations does not mean that nobility titles *should be* passed down in that manner.

We therefore hold that Article 14, in conjunction with Article 8, was violated.

11. Relying on Article 1 of Protocol No. 1 to the Convention, the applicants argued that the fact that they had been deprived of the peerages concerned had infringed their right to the peaceful enjoyment of their possessions, without any reasonable justification and without compensation. The titles concerned had not been merely of honorary value but also had a pecuniary value, for example, in the form of social advantages and increased prestige. Furthermore, assets from the family estate, especially immovable property, frequently reverted to the holder of the peerage by custom.

. . .

The applicants contended that in a country which, like Spain, recognises, regulates, protects and grants nobiliary titles, such titles are indisputably perceived as conferring a social advantage. As for the commercial exploitation of peerages, that was constant practice in Spain. On that point, the applicants referred to the well-known commercial exploitation of peerages in the wines and spirits sector, where they served as trademarks. Ultimately, the commercial, social and honorary use of a nobiliary title was an integral part of the estate of the person enjoying it, such that Article 1 of Protocol No. 1 was indisputably applicable.

[Fragments deleted]

Based on our earlier findings that nobility titles are part of the right to private and family life regardless of whether they are merely of honorary value or carry pecuniary implications, and that Article 8 was violated, we do not need to determine whether the right to peaceful enjoyment of possessions was infringed in this case.

For these reasons, the Court unanimously

[Fragment deleted]

1. Declares the application admissible;
2. Holds that there has been a violation of Article 8 of the Convention;
3. Holds that there has been a violation of Article 14 of the Convention taken in conjunction with Article 8;
4. Holds that it is not necessary to consider the complaint under Article 1 of Protocol No. 1 of the Convention, taken alone or in conjunction with Article 14.

6

From inclusion to transformation: rewriting Konstantin Markin v. Russia

ALEXANDRA TIMMER*

Introduction

At first sight, *Konstantin Markin* v. *Russia* might be an unlikely locus of concern for feminist legal scholars. The case revolves around the question whether military servicemen should be entitled to the same parental leave as military servicewomen. The applicant, a serviceman and primary care-taker of three young children, was refused parental leave by the Russian authorities and was told that only servicewomen qualify for such leave. *Konstantin Markin* is perhaps not the most obvious choice to redraft from the ECHR's docket, as, in many ways, this is a 'successful' gender equality case:[1] the First Section acknowledged that Markin is a victim of discrimination and found a violation of the European Convention on Human Rights ('the Convention'). Moreover, the Chamber judgment recognised that the discrimination of military service-men in the area of parental leave is a widespread problem in the Russian legal framework, which needs to be attended to.[2] Therefore, there are definitely cases that are more worrisome (and frustrating) from a gender justice perspective.[3]

Nevertheless, *Konstantin Markin* merits attention. First of all, at the time of writing the case has been referred to the Grand Chamber and thus promises to become a leading judgment on gender equality.[4] I chose this case, however, before the referral took place. The reason for choosing this case was that,

---

* Many thanks to my colleagues at the Human Rights Centre of Ghent University for sharing their ideas with me: Eva Brems, Maris Burbergs, Laurens Lavrysen, Saïla Ouald Chaib, Lourdes Peroni and Stijn Smet. The research for this paper was conducted within the framework of the ERC Starting Grant project 'Strengthening the European Court of Human Rights: More Accountability Through Better Legal Reasoning'.
[1] Elsje Bonthuys, 'Institutional Openness and Resistance to Feminist Arguments: The Example of the South African Constitutional Court' (2008) 20 *Canadian Journal of Woman and Law* 1–36 at 4.
[2] ECHR, *Konstantin Markin* v. *Russia*, 7 October 2010, para. 66.
[3] Prominently among these worrying cases is ECHR (GC), *A, B and C* v. *Ireland*, 16 December 2010, discussed in Chapter 4 of this volume by Patricia Londono.
[4] At the time of publication, the Grand Chamber judgment has been delivered. See ECHR (GC), *Konstantin Markin* v. *Russia*, 22 March 2012.

although the Chamber judgment holds promising gender justice potential, the Court falls short of handing down a truly transformative ruling. *Konstantin Markin* achieves *inclusion* – the right to parental leave should be extended to military servicemen according to the Court – but it embodies no *transformation*; the underlying framework that generates these gender inequalities is left untouched.[5] The contrast I make here between inclusion and transformation is inspired by Elsje Bonthuys and Catherine Albertyn, who have offered a thoughtful critique of the South African Constitutional Court's gender and sexual orientation jurisprudence. They suggest that an inclusionary judgment is one that 'expands the groups of people who can claim legal protection . . . [but] leaves the legal and social *status quo* largely intact', whereas transformative jurisprudence would locate gendered disadvantage within systemic inequalities 'and thus dislodge the underlying norms and structures that create and reinforce a rigid and hierarchical *status quo*'.[6]

This chapter is based on the premise that gender justice should entail transformation rather than inclusion. Concretely, this chapter seeks ways to draw out the transformative potential in *Konstantin Markin* by suggesting certain textual changes to the judgment that focus on disrupting the use of gender stereotypes. In what follows, I shall first outline the facts and the Chamber judgment. Next, I shall discuss the methodological tools with which I shall construct my analysis of the judgment; this entails grounding my project in the work of the Committee on the Elimination of Discrimination against Women ('CEDAW Committee'). Then I shall analyse the judgment. The question is what should be retained from the original judgment, what should be changed and why. After the Conclusion, this chapter closes with a redraft that endeavours to be a more transformative *Konstantin Markin* judgment.

Outlining the facts and the Chamber judgment

The applicant, Mr Markin, is a military serviceman who was divorced from his wife in September 2005. He became the primary care-taker of their three young children. Less than two weeks after the divorce, Mr Markin applied to the head of his military unit for three years' parental leave, but this request was turned down because leave of such duration could only be granted to female personnel. Mr Markin appealed this decision, but was unsuccessful at all subsequent

---

[5] Cf. Nancy Fraser, *Justice Interruptus: Critical Reflections on the 'Postsocialist' Condition* (New York and London: Routledge, 1997), p. 23 ('By transformative remedies . . . I mean remedies aimed at correcting inequitable outcomes precisely by restructuring the underlying generative framework').

[6] Elsje Bonthuys, 'Institutional Openness and Resistance to Feminist Arguments: The Example of the South African Constitutional Court' (2008) 20 *Canadian Journal of Woman and Law* 1–36 at 35, quoting Catherine Albertyn, 'Defending and Securing Rights through Law: Feminism, Law and the Courts in South Africa' (2005) 32 *Politikon* 217–37.

bodies of appeal. Eventually, he applied to the Constitutional Court, claiming that the provisions regarding parental leave as laid down in the Military Service Act were not compatible with the equality clause in the Constitution. The Constitutional Court rejected his claim. In its judgment, the Constitutional Court emphasised that military personnel have special duties involving the defence of the country and the security of the State, and that they therefore have a special legal status which involves a limitation on their civil rights and freedoms. The Constitutional Court justified the difference in treatment between female and male military personnel as regards their entitlement to parental leave as follows:

> Owing to the specific demands of military service, non-performance of military duties by military personnel en masse must be excluded as it might cause detriment to the public interests protected by law ... By granting, on an exceptional basis, the right to parental leave to servicewomen only, the legislature took into account, firstly, the limited participation of women in military service and, secondly, the special social role of women associated with motherhood.[7]

Mr Markin decided to take his case to Strasbourg and complained that the refusal to grant him parental leave constituted discrimination on the grounds of sex, on the basis of Article 14 in conjunction with Article 8. The majority of the Court ruled in favour of Mr Markin, as it found that the refusal by the Russian authorities to grant parental leave to servicemen constitutes discrimination on the basis of sex.

I will now briefly trace the Strasbourg Court's reasoning. To start, the Court reasons that, as parental leave allowances promote family life and have an impact on the way family life is organised, these allowances fall under the scope of Article 8. Subsequently, the Court divides the question as to whether, in relation to parental leave, the difference in treatment of military servicemen was justified; first, it assesses whether there is an objective and reasonable justification for the difference in treatment between men and women,[8] and next it assesses whether such a justification exists regarding the difference in treatment between civilian workers and military personnel.[9]

In examining the permissibility of the difference in treatment between men and women, the Court applies the 'very weighty reasons' test.[10] Thus, the Court considers that the difference in treatment is not justified by 'the special social role of mothers' since both parents are 'similarly placed' as regards the role of

[7] ECHR, *Konstantin Markin* v. *Russia*, 7 October 2010, para. 19.   [8] *Ibid.*, para. 47.
[9] *Ibid.*, para. 50.
[10] See also Alexandra Timmer, 'Toward an Anti-Stereotyping Approach for the European Court of Human Rights' (2011) 11 *Human Rights Law Review* 707–38 at 723.

taking care of the child in the period after childbirth and the period of maternity leave.[11] The Court makes a point here of departing from the case of *Petrovic v. Austria* (1998).[12] In *Petrovic*, the majority of the Court ruled that it was not discriminatory of Austria to award parental leave solely to mothers, as there was no European consensus on this point and Austria therefore possessed a broad margin of appreciation. The Court points out in *Konstantin Markin* that this consensus has since developed – 'society has moved towards a more equal sharing between men and women of responsibility for the upbringing of their children and ... men's caring role has gained recognition' – and it considers that it cannot overlook these developments.[13]

Next, the Court examines whether there exists an objective and reasonable justification for the special treatment of military personnel as compared to civilian workers (as both civilian men and women are entitled to parental leave). As to restrictions on the private and family life of military personnel, protected by Article 8, the Court notes that the States do not have a broad margin of appreciation. And, while the aim of 'ensuring operational effectiveness' is certainly legitimate, the means to pursue that aim must be proportional.[14] In the context of proportionality, the Court notes that the argument of the State – that allowing parental leave to military servicemen would have an adverse effect on the operational effectiveness of the army – is unconvincing because it is not substantiated with concrete evidence.[15]

The Court concludes, in paragraph 58, with some observations on the reasoning of the Constitutional Court. The majority of the Strasbourg Court makes clear that it does not accept the argument that the difference in treatment is justified by traditional gender roles; nor does it allow the State's argument that women are less numerous than men in the army and that therefore it is justified to give parental leave only to women. Lastly, the majority is not convinced by the argument that a military serviceman has the option to resign if he wants to take care of his children.

Drawing lessons from CEDAW

Preliminary notes on methodological issues

How can the deep structures of gender injustice be transformed through human rights law? And what generates these structures in the first place? In my view, one of the most promising approaches to these complex questions is developed by the CEDAW Committee. The legal arguments that I shall raise in this chapter, including the redraft, therefore rely in large part on the Convention on the Elimination of All Forms of Discrimination against Women[16] (CEDAW) and the CEDAW Committee. Indeed, one of the primary aims of

---

[11] ECHR, *Konstantin Markin v. Russia*, 7 October 7 2010, para. 48.
[12] ECHR, *Petrovic v. Austria*, 27 March 1998.
[13] ECHR, *Konstantin Markin v. Russia*, 7 October 7 2010, para. 49.   [14] *Ibid.*, para. 55.
[15] *Ibid.*, para. 57.   [16] 1249 UNTS 13.

this chapter is to show how the work of the CEDAW Committee can be integrated better into the legal reasoning of the ECHR. To be sure, the Strasbourg Court is already increasingly referring to the CEDAW Committee and other UN treaty bodies.[17] I applaud this development, but wish the Court would carry it still further.

Yet why choose a case with a male applicant (namely, Konstantin Markin)? History teaches us that gender justice can indeed be furthered using cases brought by male applicants.[18] Moreover, there is a growing awareness among feminists that dismantling gender stereotypes requires us to investigate both sides of the coin; we have to address stereotypes of both sexes.[19] I have selected *Konstantin Markin* deliberately, as the case is a good example of how gender-role stereotypes harm both men and women. But then why emphasise the relevance of CEDAW (also known as 'the Women's Convention')? I believe that the work of the CEDAW Committee is pertinent to this case, as the Committee is aware of the double-edged nature of the harm that gender stereotypes cause. In its recent General Recommendation No. 28, the Committee observes: 'The principle of equality between men and women, or gender equality, entails the concept that *all human beings, regardless of sex*, are free to develop their personal abilities, pursue their professional careers and make choices without the limitations set by stereotypes, rigid gender roles and prejudices.'[20]

Before proceeding to explore the CEDAW Committee's conceptualisation of equality more fully, I should add some comments of a practical nature. First, as the idea of this volume is to rewrite judgments of the ECHR, I shall redraft the Chamber judgment in *Konstantin Markin* rather than predict the Grand Chamber judgment which, at the time of writing, had not yet been delivered. Secondly, when the case was referred to the Grand Chamber, the President of the Court granted the Human Rights Centre of Ghent University permission to submit a third party intervention.[21] I have been actively involved in drafting

---

[17] See, for example, ECHR, *Opuz* v. *Turkey*, 9 June 2009; ECHR, *RR* v. *Poland*, 26 May 2011; and ECHR, *VC* v. *Slovakia*, 8 November 2011.

[18] This has been shown by the litigation work of Ruth Bader Ginsburg in the 1970s. See Cary Franklin, 'The Anti-Stereotyping Principle in Constitutional Sex Discrimination Law' (2010) 85 *New York University Law Review* 83–173.

[19] This is amply demonstrated by scholars who combine feminist legal theory with studies of law and masculinity. See e.g. David S. Cohen, 'Keeping Men "Men" and Women Down: Sex-Segregation, Anti-Essentialism and Masculinity' (2010) 33 *Harvard Journal of Law and Gender* 509–53. See also Nancy Levit, 'Feminism for Men: Legal Ideology and the Construction of Maleness' (1996) 43 *UCLA Law Review* 1037–1116. Actually, we also have to investigate the ways in which people who do not self-identify as either male or female are hurt by gender-role stereotypes. Regrettably, that subject falls outside the scope of this chapter.

[20] CEDAW Committee, General Recommendation 28 on the Core Obligations of States Parties under Article 2, 47th Session 2010, para. 22 (emphasis added).

[21] The President gave his permission in accordance with Rule 44 § 3 of the Rules of Court.

these written submissions. Accordingly, much of the present discussion draws on that work.[22] Finally, in my redraft I shall rely on sources that were available at the time of the original judgment of 7 October 2010, with one exception: I shall draw on the memorandums of the State and the applicant to the Grand Chamber, which were naturally drafted after the Chamber ruling was delivered.

CEDAW's thick conception of equality and the role of gender stereotypes therein

The CEDAW Committee has formulated its views on gender equality most clearly in General Recommendation No. 25.[23] In that Recommendation, the Committee observes that States are under an obligation to (1) ensure that there is no direct or indirect discrimination against women (formal equality); (2) improve the *de facto* position of women (substantive equality); and (3) address prevailing gender relations and the persistence of gender-based stereotypes (transformative equality).[24] As several scholars have noted, this is a rich conception of equality that goes much further than the injunction that men and women have equal rights, since it encompasses formal, substantive *and* transformative equality.[25]

The focus in this chapter will be on this last dimension of equality. I do, however, wish to emphasise that the way the CEDAW Committee conceptualises substantive equality – as an obligation to improve the *de facto* position of women – should preclude the Russian State from responding to a finding of a violation in *Konstantin Markin* by removing the entitlement of parental leave from military servicewomen, so that all military personnel are equally bereft of the benefit. This is the phenomenon of 'levelling down', meaning to bring 'the group that is better off down to the level of those worse

[22] Human Rights Centre, Ghent University, Written Submissions in *Konstantin Markin* v. *Russia*, Application no. 30078/06 (17 May 2011), available at www.ugent.be/re/publiekrecht/en/department/human-rights/publications/amicus.pdf.
[23] CEDAW Committee, General Recommendation No. 25: Article 4, Paragraph 1, of the Convention on the Elimination of All Forms of Discrimination against Women, on Temporary Special Measures, A/59/38 (2004).
[24] *Ibid.*, para. 7.
[25] Sandra Fredman, 'Beyond the Dichotomy of Formal and Substantive Equality: Towards a New Definition of Equal Rights', in Ineke Boerefijn, F. Coomans, Jenny E. Goldschmidt, R. Holtmaat and R. Wolleswinkel (eds.), *Temporary Special Measures: Accelerating De Facto Equality of Women under Article 4(1) UN Convention on the Elimination of All Forms of Discrimination Against Women* (Antwerp: Intersentia, 2003), pp. 111–18; Rikki Holtmaat and Jonneke Naber, *Women's Human Rights and Culture: From Deadlock to Dialogue* (Antwerp: Intersentia, 2011); Alexandra Timmer, 'Toward an Anti-Stereotyping Approach for the European Court of Human Rights' (2011) 11 *Human Rights Law Review* 707–38.

off'.[26] One of the results of a substantive underpinning of equality is that levelling down will not be seen as a viable solution to equality problems.[27]

Equality as transformation addresses the root causes of gender discrimination and gendered disadvantage. In the words of the CEDAW Committee: 'The position of women will not be improved as long as the underlying causes of discrimination against women, and of their inequality, are not effectively addressed.'[28] This requires 'a real transformation of opportunities, institutions and systems so that they are no longer grounded in historically determined male paradigms of power and life patterns'.[29]

The obligation to transform the underlying structures that generate gender inequality is grounded in Article 5 CEDAW.[30] Article 5(a) provides that States ought to take all appropriate measures:

> To modify the social and cultural patterns of conduct of men and women, with a view to achieving the elimination of prejudices and customary and all other practices which are based on the idea of the inferiority or the superiority of either of the sexes or on *stereotyped roles for men and women*.[31]

The CEDAW Convention has recently been critiqued for what is seen as its inability to further gender equality because it focuses 'narrowly and exclusively on women'.[32] This type of critique overlooks the fact that the wording of Article 5 clearly encompasses both women *and* men. Moreover, Article 5 is part of the general provisions of CEDAW and, as such, ought to play a role in the interpretation of the CEDAW Convention as a whole.[33]

---

[26] Deborah L. Brake, 'When Equality Leaves Everyone Worse Off: The Problem of Leveling Down in Equality Law' (2004) 46 *William and Mary Law Review* 513–618 at 515.

[27] Cf. Sandra Fredman, *Discrimination Law* (2nd edn, Oxford University Press, 2011), p. 10.

[28] CEDAW Committee, General Recommendation No. 25: Article 4, Paragraph 1, of the Convention on the Elimination of All Forms of Discrimination against Women, on Temporary Special Measures, A/59/38 (2004), para. 10.

[29] *Ibid.*

[30] For a thorough commentary on this Article, see Rikki Holtmaat, 'Article 5 CEDAW', in Marsha A. Freeman, Christine Chinkin and Beate Rudolf (eds.), *The Convention on the Elimination of All Forms of Discrimination against Women: A Commentary* (Oxford University Press, forthcoming, 2012), pp. 141–67.

[31] Emphasis added.

[32] Darren Rosenblum, 'Unisex CEDAW, Or What's Wrong with Women's Rights' (2011) 20 *Columbia Journal of Gender and Law* 98–194 at 100. See also Berta Esperanza Hernández-Truyol, 'Unisex CEDAW? No! Supersex It!' (2011) 20 *Columbia Journal of Gender and Law* 196–223.

[33] Rikki Holtmaat, 'Article 5 CEDAW', in Marsha A. Freeman, Christine Chinkin and Beate Rudolf (eds.), *The Convention on the Elimination of All Forms of Discrimination against Women: A Commentary* (Oxford University Press, forthcoming, 2012), pp. 141–67 at p. 143. See also Rikki Holtmaat and Alexandra Timmer, 'De SGP-Zaak Anders Bekeken.

The harm of gender stereotypes and their role in the Konstantin Markin judgment

At its core, the complaint of Mr Markin concerns the kind of gender stereotyping that CEDAW disallows. Gender stereotypes are preconceptions regarding the characteristics, roles or attributes that we assign, either descriptively or normatively, to men and women. Such stereotypes often target subgroups of men and women. Examples of gender stereotypes that have played a role in ECHR cases[34] include the notions that Muslim women are oppressed,[35] lesbian women are not good mothers[36] and married women are homemakers.[37] The harm that gender stereotypes cause is both pervasive and complex, in large part because stereotypes often operate unconsciously. 'Gender stereotypes tend to freeze gender identities and gender roles and make them appear as real, universal, eternal, natural, essential, and/or unchangeable.'[38] In this manner, they justify the *status quo*.[39] The harm of gender-role stereotyping is that this leads to disapproval of men and women, like Mr Markin, who do not conform to the traditional roles, and leads to men's greater power and authority and women's dependency.[40] Gender-role stereotypes construct men or women as inferior in certain spheres of life. I have argued elsewhere that gender stereotypes thus cause harmful recognition, distribution and psychological effects.[41]

Naar een Holistische Uitleg van Artikel 7 VN-Vrouwenverdrag' (2011) 36 *NTM/NJCM-Bulletin* 445–57 at 449.

[34] For a more comprehensive treatment, see Alexandra Timmer, 'Toward an Anti-Stereotyping Approach for the European Court of Human Rights' (2011) 11 *Human Rights Law Review* 707–38.

[35] ECHR, *Dahlab* v. *Switzerland*, 15 February 2001; and ECHR (GC), *Leyla Şahin* v. *Turkey*, 10 November 2005. Unfortunately, in these cases the Court reinforced those stereotypes concerning Muslim women. See also Carolyn Evans, 'The "Islamic Scarf" in the European Court of Human Rights' (2006) 7 *Melbourne Journal of International Law* 52–74.

[36] ECHR (GC), *EB* v. *France*, 22 January 2008. The Court did not refute this stereotype explicitly, but did rule in favour of the applicant.

[37] See e.g. ECHR, *Wessels-Bergervoet* v. *Netherlands*, 4 June 2002; and ECHR, *Runkee and White* v. *United Kingdom*, 10 May 2007.

[38] Rikki Holtmaat, 'Article 5 CEDAW', in Marsha A. Freeman, Christine Chinkin and Beate Rudolf (eds.), *The Convention on the Elimination of All Forms of Discrimination against Women: A Commentary* (Oxford University Press, forthcoming, 2012), pp. 141–67 at p. 147.

[39] John T. Jost and Aaron C. Kay, 'Exposure to Benevolent Sexism and Complementary Gender Stereotypes: Consequences for Specific and Diffuse Forms of System Justification' (2005) 88 *Journal of Personality and Social Psychology* 498–509.

[40] Janet K. Swim and Lauri L. Hyers, 'Sexism', in Todd D. Nelson (ed.), *Handbook of Prejudice, Stereotyping, and Discrimination* (New York: Psychology Press, 2009), pp. 407–30 at p. 413.

[41] Alexandra Timmer, 'Toward an Anti-Stereotyping Approach for the European Court of Human Rights' (2011) 11 *Human Rights Law Review* 707–38 at 715–16.

This account of the harm of gender stereotypes is no different in cases of so-called 'positive discrimination' or 'benevolent sexism' (the kind of sexism that rewards women for conforming to traditional gender roles). Psychological research suggests that benevolent sexism may play a significant role in justifying and maintaining gender inequality.[42] Benevolent sexism is often failed to be perceived as a form of prejudice, and therefore not challenged as an 'illegitimate cause of social inequalities'.[43] I emphasise this point because it has become one of the issues of dispute before the Grand Chamber: the State argues that providing parental leave to servicewomen is 'positive discrimination',[44] whereas the applicant argues there is nothing positive about the discrimination in question.[45] The applicant is right when he argues: 'While women have indeed been historically disadvantaged with respect to many types of opportunities . . . staying at home to care for children is not among them . . . [T]he policy choice . . . only perpetuates a stereotype that has been harmful to women.'[46]

What courts in general and the ECHR in particular should do, at a minimum, is to name gender stereotypes and the harm that they do. Diagnosing gender stereotyping as a wrong is essential to applying a cure.[47] Specifically relevant for the *Konstantin Markin* case is that harmful gender stereotypes should not be permitted to function as justifications for discriminatory conduct.

Assessing and improving the judgment

Praise

Many parts of this judgment, as well as the outcome, are worth retaining from a gender justice perspective. The first thing that stands out is the Court's

---

[42] Peter Glick and Susan T. Fiske, 'An Ambivalent Alliance: Hostile and Benevolent Sexism as Complementary Justifications for Gender Inequality' (2001) 56 *American Psychologist* 109–18; John T. Jost and Aaron C. Kay, 'Exposure to Benevolent Sexism and Complementary Gender Stereotypes: Consequences for Specific and Diffuse Forms of System Justification' (2005) 88 *Journal of Personality and Social Psychology* 498–509 at 499.

[43] Manuela Barreto and Naomi Ellemers, 'The Burden of Benevolent Sexism: How It Contributes to the Maintenance of Gender Inequalities' (2005) 35 *European Journal of Social Psychology* 633–42 at 633.

[44] Additional Memorandum of the Russian Federation Authorities on the Questions Posed by the European Court of Human Rights to Oral Hearings, Application No. 30078/06, *Konstantin Markin* v. *Russia*, Moscow, 28 April 2011 (on file with author), at 27. See in the same sense also the dissenting opinion of Judge Kovler in *Konstantin Markin* (further discussed below).

[45] Applicant's Memorandum on the Merits, Application No. 30078/06, *Konstantin Markin* v. *Russia*, 29 April 2011 (on file with author), pp. 6–7.

[46] *Ibid.*, p. 6.

[47] Rebecca J. Cook and Simone Cusack, *Gender Stereotyping: Transnational Legal Perspectives* (Philadelphia: University of Pennsylvania Press, 2010), pp. 39–45. See also Alexandra Timmer, 'Toward an Anti-Stereotyping Approach for the European Court of Human Rights' (2011) 11 *Human Rights Law Review* 707–38 at 720.

approach to parental leave. The Court emphasises correctly that, in contrast to maternity leave, both parents are 'similarly placed' as regards parental leave, as that leave is intended to enable a parent to stay at home and look after the child personally (retained in paragraph 49 of the redraft).[48] Additionally, the Court notes that there is now a consensus in Europe that fathers and mothers share the responsibility of the upbringing of their children. By emphasising that 'men's caring role has gained recognition', the Court pierces through the gender stereotype that men are not nurturing and that their role lies outside the house (retained in paragraph 50 of the redraft). In the meantime, the Court overturns *Petrovic v. Austria*, which proves that the dissenters in that case, Judges Bernhardt and Spielmann, were prophetic.[49] With all this, the Court shows that it does not fall for the separate-spheres mentality. The government tries to erect a barrier between the army and family responsibilities, between public and private, and this fails before the Strasbourg Court. The Court rightly notes that servicemen should not be 'forced to make a difficult choice between nursing their new-born children and pursuing their military career' (retained in paragraph 60 of the redraft).[50]

Also, even though the Court uses the word 'prejudices' instead of 'stereo-types' in paragraph 58, the essence of the idea that States cannot use stereotypes as justifications is found in the judgment. This is a view that I have advocated elsewhere,[51] and I believe this is an important addition to the Court's case law.[52] Its importance stems from the refusal of the Court to accept easy generalisations as reasons to interfere in the human rights of individuals. On a more profound level, the Court signals it will not take for granted the dominant gender ideology (or, for that matter, dominant racial, sexual or religious ideologies) and is willing to contest the social assumptions that construct women or men as inferior in certain areas of life (retained in paragraph 59 of the redraft).

---

[48] ECHR, *Konstantin Markin* v. *Russia*, 7 October 2010, para. 48.

[49] The dissenters claimed: 'It is in reality the traditional distribution of family responsibilities between mothers and fathers that gave rise to the Austrian legislation under which only mothers were entitled to parental leave allowance. The discrimination against fathers perpetuates this traditional distribution of roles and can also have negative consequences for the mother ... [T]raditional practices and roles in family life alone do not justify a difference in treatment of men and women.' Dissenting opinion of Judges Bernhardt and Spielmann, in ECHR, *Petrovic* v. *Austria*, 27 March 1998.

[50] ECHR, *Konstantin Markin* v. *Russia*, 7 October 2010, para. 58.

[51] Alexandra Timmer, 'Toward an Anti-Stereotyping Approach for the European Court of Human Rights' (2011) 11 *Human Rights Law Review* 707–38.

[52] The Court had on other occasions already ruled that neither 'negative attitudes' towards a particular group cannot form a justification (ECHR, *L and V* v. *Austria*, 9 January 2003, para. 52), nor can arguments that merely reflect the 'traditional outlook' (ECHR, *Inze* v. *Austria*, 28 October 1987, para. 44).

Finally, in the application of Article 46 of the Convention, the Court notes that: 'The Court's finding that the legislation in question is not compatible with the Convention discloses a widespread problem in the legal framework concerning a substantial number of people.'[53] The Court therefore suggests that the government amend its Military Service Act and the regulations on military service, in order to ensure effective protection against discrimination in the field of parental leave.[54] The Court does not often feel itself called upon to explicitly recommend a State to amend its laws, yet this is arguably in line with the role of the Court as envisaged by the Committee of Ministers. In its 'Resolution on judgments revealing an underlying systemic problem', the Committee invites the Court 'as far as possible, to *identify*, in its judgments finding a violation of the Convention, what it considers to be *an underlying systemic problem and the source of this problem*, in particular when it is likely to give rise to numerous applications, so as to assist states in finding the appropriate solution'.[55]

Because I agree entirely with the Court's observations regarding the application of Article 46, I have not redrafted that part of the judgment. I shall now turn to the question of how the Court could have done a more thorough job in identifying the 'underlying systemic problem and the source of this problem' in its consideration of the merits in *Konstantin Markin*.[56]

Troublesome aspects of the Court's reasoning

The fundamental problem with the reasoning in *Konstantin Markin* is that the Court employs a formal rather than transformative conception of equality. In what follows, I shall endeavour to show that the legal issue in *Konstantin Markin* is construed too narrowly, as purely formal discrimination on the ground of sex; the difference in treatment between men and women is elevated to the key issue to be ruled on. This reasoning is flawed. The formal difference of treatment is not the crux of the problem; it is rather a manifestation of the deeper underlying social assumptions that lock women into the home and men out of it.

---

[53] ECHR, *Konstantin Markin v. Russia*, 7 October 2010, para. 66.   [54] *Ibid.*, para. 67.

[55] Committee of Ministers, Resolution Res(2004)3 'on judgments revealing an underlying systemic problem', adopted 12 May 2004 (emphasis added). Though this resolution is most often cited in connection with the pilot judgment procedure – the Court's newest procedural tool to manage its caseload – I think that the text of the resolution as such supports my argument that the Court was right in *Konstantin Markin* to include, in the words of Antoine Buyse, a 'pedagogical element: not only indicating what is wrong, but also shedding some light on the correct path to be taken'. See Antoine Buyse, 'The Pilot Judgment Procedure at the European Court of Human Rights: Possibilities and Challenges' (2009) 57 *Nomiko Vima (The Greek Law Journal)* 78–90 at 85.

[56] Committee of Ministers, Resolution Res(2004)3.

The Court's resort to formal equality shows itself in three ways; these will be briefly discussed and criticised below. The main thrust of my argument is that the legal issue in *Konstantin Markin* encompasses the domestic authorities' reliance on gendered stereotypes of military servicemen and military servicewomen, and that the Court should address these stereotypes in order to protect a meaningful version of equality.

No context assessment: gender roles in the Russian military

Feminists and other critical legal scholars have long argued that courts should ground their reasoning in an appreciation of the historical, social and economic reality as experienced by disadvantaged groups, rather than in abstract and rigid legal concepts.[57] South African scholars, Catherine Albertyn and Beth Goldblatt, have succinctly described what such a contextual approach stands for: 'Our understanding of contextual analysis within a transformative equality jurisprudence entails locating the impugned act within real life conditions and understanding how these reinforce both disadvantage and harm.'[58] In my view, the Court has largely neglected to make such an analysis in *Konstantin Markin*, and in my redraft I shall therefore introduce some additional contextual information (see paragraph 58 of the redraft).[59]

In the case of *Konstantin Markin*, a contextual assessment means placing the rule that excludes servicemen from parental leave in the reality of gender-role expectations and gendered restrictions in the Russian army. Women have been able to enter the Russian military since 1991, when contract service was made available to them in order to supplement the failing system of conscription for men.[60] Unfortunately, it is nearly impossible to obtain sufficient English-language materials on their situation and on gender-role expectations in the Russian military. A few essential facts, however, can be garnered from the parties' submissions to the Grand Chamber. In their brief, the Russian authorities set great store by what they term the 'insignificant' number of female personnel in the Russian army and the fact that their duties are not directly linked to the

---

[57] See e.g. Katherine T. Bartlett, 'Feminist Legal Methods' (1990) 103 *Harvard Law Review* 829–88, in particular at 849–63; Martha C. Nussbaum, 'Foreword: Constitutions and Capabilities: "Perception" Against Lofty Formalism' (2007) 121 *Harvard Law Review* 4–97.

[58] Cathi Albertyn and Beth Goldblatt, 'Facing the Challenge of Transformation: Difficulties in the Development of an Indigenous Jurisprudence of Equality' (1998) 14 *South African Journal on Human Rights* 248–76 at 261.

[59] My position is far from unique. Rosemary Hunter, one of the editors of *Feminist Judgments*, notes that all the redrafts in their project introduce additional contextual material. See Rosemary Hunter, 'An Account of Feminist Judging', in Rosemary Hunter, Clare McGlynn and Erika Rackley (eds.), *Feminist Judgments: From Theory to Practice* (Oxford and Portland, OR: Hart Publishing, 2010), pp. 30–43 at p. 37.

[60] Jennifer G. Mathers, 'Russia's Women Soldiers in the Twenty-First Century' (2007) 1 *Minerva Journal of Women and War* 8–18 at 9–11.

combat-readiness of the army.[61] The Russian authorities state that women make up approximately 10 per cent of service personnel.[62] This amounts to approximately 110,000 women.[63] The authorities point out that 'female military servants hold strictly defined posts in the Armed Forces of the Russian Federation [which are], as a rule, unrelated to warlike equipment and armament operation and maintenance and to participation in an armed conflict'.[64]

The purpose of the authorities in making these points is to show why granting parental leave to servicemen, as opposed to servicewomen, would have devastating consequences for the combat-readiness of the Russian army. They clearly do not perceive that they only succeed in demonstrating the vulnerable position of women in the Russian army, a fact that is corroborated in academic literature.[65] Jennifer Mathers notes that women have fewer opportunities available to them in the Russian military than men, and that this has a lot to do with traditional perceptions of femininity and masculinity and the legal framework that puts restrictions on women's employment, especially when they have children.[66] She writes that: 'Russia's protective labour legislation actively harms the career prospects of its women soldiers.'[67] By belittling the contribution of women in the army, the State adds insult to injury and fails to justify their discriminatory practices. This is the point to which I shall now turn.

A too narrow conception of the problem: the importance of naming gender stereotypes

Because of the Court's narrow focus on the difference in treatment between servicemen and servicewomen, and their failure to place these legal rules in their context, the Court overlooks the deeper causes and wider implications of

---

[61] Additional Memorandum of the Russian Federation Authorities on the Questions Posed by the European Court of Human Rights to Oral Hearings, Application No. 30078/06, *Konstantin Markin* v. *Russia*, Moscow, 28 April 2011 (on file with author), p. 18 and also pp. 23 and 27.

[62] *Ibid.*, p. 23.

[63] Jennifer G. Mathers, 'Russia's Women Soldiers in the Twenty-First Century' (2007) 1 *Minerva Journal of Women and War* 8–18 at 11.

[64] Additional Memorandum of the Russian Federation Authorities on the Questions Posed by the European Court of Human Rights to Oral Hearings, Application No. 30078/06, *Konstantin Markin* v. *Russia*, Moscow, 28 April 2011 (on file with author), p. 18.

[65] Jennifer G. Mathers, 'Russia's Women Soldiers in the Twenty-First Century' (2007) 1 *Minerva Journal of Women and War* 8–18; Jennifer Mathers, 'Women, Society and the Military: Women Soldiers in Post-Soviet Russia', in Stephen L. Webber and Jennifer G. Mathers (eds.), *Military and Society in Post-Soviet Russia* (Manchester University Press, 2006); Aleksandr I. Smirnov, 'Women in the Russian Army' (2002) 43 *Russian Social Science Review* 61–71.

[66] Jennifer Mathers, 'Women, Society and the Military: Women Soldiers in Post-Soviet Russia', in Stephen L. Webber and Jennifer G. Mathers (eds.), *Military and Society in Post-Soviet Russia* (Manchester University Press, 2006), p. 211.

[67] *Ibid.*, p. 216.

the rule that allows parental leave only to servicewomen. At issue in this case is not just the position of military servicemen, but the gender stereotyping of both military servicemen and servicewomen (see paragraphs 47–8 of the redraft).

Elsewhere, I have emphasised the need for the ECHR to 'name' gender stereotypes, so that their harm might be exposed and their grip on us weakened.[68] In the words of Catherine MacKinnon: '[Y]ou can't change a reality you can't name.'[69] Therefore, the question: which gender stereotypes play a role in *Konstantin Markin* and what harm do they do? The most blatant stereotype is, of course, the one of woman-homemaker/man-breadwinner. The Russian Constitutional Court speaks of the 'special social role of women associated with motherhood'.[70] This contains both a descriptive and a prescriptive element: the Russian authorities imply that care-giving *is* (most often) done by mothers and *ought* to be done by mothers. That this is also partly a prescriptive stereotype is borne out in the memorandum of the State to the Grand Chamber. The State observes that '[t]he support of the child's interest require in fact the presence of his/her mother next to a child at least during the first year',[71] thus dictating that mothers should perform the care-giving role. Other stereotypes that play a role in this case concern the military more specifically. By belittling women's participation in the army, the State makes clear that it views military life as something masculine; the stereotype here is that women cannot be real soldiers.[72]

In its most recent 'Concluding Observations' on the periodic report submitted by the Russian Federation, the CEDAW Committee drew attention to the pervasiveness of gender-role stereotypes. The Committee emphasised that it is concerned 'at the persistence of practices, traditions, patriarchal attitudes and deep-rooted stereotypes regarding the roles, responsibilities and identities of women and men in all spheres of life. In this respect, the Committee is concerned at the State party's repeated

---

[68] Alexandra Timmer, 'Toward an Anti-Stereotyping Approach for the European Court of Human Rights' (2011) 11 *Human Rights Law Review* 707–38. See also Rebecca J. Cook and Simone Cusack, *Gender Stereotyping: Transnational Legal Perspectives* (Philadelphia: University of Pennsylvania Press, 2010), Chapter 2.

[69] Catherine A. MacKinnon, *Women's Lives, Men's Laws* (Cambridge, MA: Belknap, 2005), p. 89.

[70] ECHR, *Konstantin Markin v. Russia*, 7 October 2010, para. 19.

[71] Additional Memorandum of the Russian Federation Authorities on the Questions Posed by the European Court of Human Rights to Oral Hearings, Application No. 30078/06, *Konstantin Markin v. Russia*, Moscow, 28 April 2011 (on file with author), p. 26.

[72] Cary Franklin notes that '[i]t would be difficult to conceive of an activity more antithetical to the traditional conception of women's role than military service'. Cary Franklin, 'The Anti-Stereotyping Principle in Constitutional Sex Discrimination Law' (2010) 85 *New York University Law Review* 83–173 at 155.

emphasis on the role of women as mothers and caregivers.'[73] The Committee is of the opinion 'that a shift from a focus on women primarily as wives and mothers to individuals and actors equal to men in society is required for the full implementation of the Convention and the achievement of equality of women and men' (see paragraph 48 of the redraft).[74] In the words of Sandra Fredman, what is needed is 'a reconstruction of the public world ... so that child-care and parenting are seen as valued common responsibilities of both parents and the community'.[75]

Gender-role stereotypes injure all of us. This is the fundamental insight that is lacking in the Chamber judgment in *Konstantin Markin*. The Court condemns gender stereotypes only in so far as they have the effect of putting service*men* in the intolerable position of having to choose between their family life and their livelihood. But the Court neglects their counterpart, namely, that, at the same time, these gender stereotypes have the effect of restricting women's access to military careers (since women are only allowed into a few 'strictly defined' posts), of diminishing the quality of those careers, and of putting all the burden of child-care responsibilities on them.[76] This is a missed opportunity, as these reflections could have been quite easily incorporated (see paragraphs 48, 58, 59 and 61 of the redraft).

Disaggregation of military status and sex: integrating an intersectional analysis

Feminists have persuasively argued that courts often fail to examine how discrimination on more than one ground works, and how the interaction

---

[73] CEDAW Committee, Concluding Observations, Forty-Sixth Session July 2010, CEDAW/C/USR/CO/7, para. 20.

[74] *Ibid.*, para. 21.

[75] Sandra Fredman, 'Beyond the Dichotomy of Formal and Substantive Equality: Towards a New Definition of Equal Rights', in Ineke Boerefijn, F. Coomans, Jenny E. Goldschmidt, R. Holtmaat and R. Wolleswinkel (eds.), *Temporary Special Measures: Accelerating De Facto Equality of Women under Article 4(1) UN Convention on the Elimination of All Forms of Discrimination Against Women* (Antwerp: Intersentia, 2003), pp. 111–18 at p. 115.

[76] In contrast, in the so-called breastfeeding leave case, the European Court of Justice has condemned rules that withhold child-related leave from fathers because they worsen the employment situation of mothers. See ECJ, Case C-104/09, *Pedro Manuel Roca Álvarez v. Sesa Start España ETT SA*, 30 September 2010, para. 37: '[T]o refuse entitlement to the leave at issue in the main proceedings to fathers whose status is that of an employed person, on the sole ground that the child's mother does not have that status, could have as its effect that a woman ... would have to limit her self-employed activity and bear the burden resulting from the birth of her child alone, without the child's father being able to ease that burden.'

between several forms of discrimination marginalises many women.[77] Instead, when confronted with discrimination that is based on a combination of grounds, courts tend to separate the grounds and/or privilege one discrimination ground over the others. The Strasbourg Court acts no differently in *Konstantin Markin*, as the Court disaggregates military status from sex. The Court makes two sets of comparisons: one comparison regards the difference in treatment between men and women; and the other regards the difference in treatment between civilian workers and military personnel.[78] This is unfortunate, as the Court is obviously aware that this case concerns intersectional discrimination, since it observes: 'The denial of parental leave to the applicant was accordingly based on a combination of two grounds: military status plus sex.'[79]

The Court ought to appreciate the intersectionality of discrimination. Widely acknowledged in academic scholarship on equality and discrimination,[80] intersectionality is also recognised by the CEDAW Committee as a pertinent concept for understanding the scope of States Parties' obligation to eliminate discrimination. The Committee states that: 'States parties must legally recognize and prohibit such intersecting forms of discrimination and their compounded negative impact on the women concerned.'[81]

Whether the Court makes one intersectional discrimination analysis or two separate analyses, is not of solely technical interest. The problem is that, by disaggregating the discrimination on the basis of sex and discrimination on the basis of military status, the stereotypes concerning military servicewomen recede to the background. In the Chamber judgment, one set of comparisons concerns men and women in general and the other set concerns soldiers and civilians: thus, the concerns of military servicemen are but scantily recognised directly,[82] and what is at stake for servicewomen is not mentioned at all. By explicitly acknowledging the importance of an intersectional approach, and subsequently incorporating such an approach (see paragraph 46 of the redraft), my redraft explores the ways in which the impugned rule affects military

---

[77] There is a vast body of literature on intersectionality. Foundational work was done by Kimberlé Crenshaw. See e.g. Kimberlé Crenshaw, 'Mapping the Margins: Intersectionality, Identity Politics, and Violence Against Women of Color' (1990–1) 43 *Stanford Law Review* 1241–1300. In the European context, see Dagmar Schiek and Anna Lawson (eds.), *European Union Non-Discrimination Law and Intersectionality: Investigating the Triangle of Racial, Gender and Disability Discrimination* (Farnham: Ashgate, 2011).

[78] ECHR, *Konstantin Markin v. Russia*, 7 October 2010, paras. 47 and 50.

[79] *Ibid.*, para. 46.   [80] See the text accompanying note 76 above.

[81] CEDAW Committee, General Recommendation 28 on the Core Obligations of States Parties under Article 2, 47th Session, 2010, para. 18.

[82] The exception is found in para. 58, where the Court notes that servicemen are 'forced to make a difficult choice between nursing their new-born children and pursuing their military career'. ECHR, *Konstantin Markin v. Russia*, 7 October 2010, para. 58.

servicemen and servicewomen directly (see paragraphs 58 and 61 of the redraft).

Why the redraft makes a difference

As the outcome of my version of the judgment is the same as the Court's – a finding of a violation of Article 14 in conjunction with Article 8 – one may wonder what difference it makes. This is the moment to discuss the dissenting opinion by the Russian Judge Kovler in *Konstantin Markin*. Judge Kovler wrote what has turned out to be a powerful dissenting opinion, which the government uses in its submissions to the Grand Chamber. Judge Kovler did not vote in favour of finding a violation of the Convention, because, among other things, he thought that the impugned rule was 'a policy choice, motivated by women's special social role as mothers, to grant them entitlement to parental leave on an exceptional basis. The authorities' direct knowledge of their society and its needs means that they are in principle better placed than the international judge to appreciate what is in the public interest.'[83] From a transformative equality point of view, this reasoning is flawed. When it comes to stereotypes, the authorities' 'direct knowledge of their society' is *not* a good reason for the Court to grant a wide margin of appreciation. The Russian authorities are part and parcel of the same culture that has perpetuated the stereotype that men and women should stick to traditional gender roles, and that has spawned the applicant's complaint. The ECHR is there to give a 'much-needed external perspective' on discriminatory stereotypes.[84] Therefore, in cases that concern harmful stereotypes, the authorities' closeness to their society is a reason to narrow rather than widen their margin of appreciation.[85]

In Judge Kovler's opinion, 'this isolated case does not impose on the respondent State a legal obligation to implement appropriate general measures'.[86] Whether Judge Kovler could have been of another opinion if the majority had taken a more transformative approach to the judgment, I do not pretend to say. If, however, the Court had undertaken a more thorough equality analysis – as the redraft does – it would have laid bare the larger societal issues that are at stake and the pervasiveness of the harm of the gender stereotypes invoked by the government. That way, the dissenting opinion would have lost much of its force.

---

[83] *Ibid.* (dissenting opinion of Judge Kovler).
[84] Cf. The Honourable Madame Justice Claire L'Heureux-Dubé, 'Beyond the Myths: Equality, Impartiality, and Justice' (2001) 10 *Journal of Social Distress and the Homeless* 87–104 at 101.
[85] See also Alexandra Timmer, 'Toward an Anti-Stereotyping Approach for the European Court of Human Rights' (2011) 11 *Human Rights Law Review* 707–38 at 723–5.
[86] ECHR, *Konstantin Markin* v. *Russia*, 7 October 2010 (dissenting opinion of Judge Kovler).

Another difference that my redraft makes concerns the application of the *Konstantin Markin* reasoning in future cases. The Court's subsequent case law has shown that the holding of the Chamber judgment in *Konstantin Markin* risks being unduly narrowed. *Andrle* v. *Czech Republic* is a case concerning the Czech pension scheme, which provides for lower pensionable ages for women who have raised children than for men who have raised children. In that case, the Fifth Section of the Court explicitly distinguishes discrimination in the field of parental leave from discrimination in the field of pensions.[87] The Court held that, as opposed to amendments in the pension system, 'the amendments of the parental leave system referred to in the case of *Konstantin Markin* do not involve changes to the subtle balance of the pension system, do not have serious financial ramifications and do not alter long-term planning'.[88] For the Court, this was reason to diverge from the ruling in *Konstantin Markin* that the traditional perception of women as primary child-carers cannot provide a justification for a difference in treatment between men and women. In contrast to *Konstantin Markin*, the Court leaves a wide margin of appreciation to the State in *Andrle*.

The *Andrle* Court bypasses the fact that what both cases have in common is the States' reliance on the classic gender-role stereotype. The *Andrle* Court seems to suggest that the commitment to not let such stereotypes be a justification for discriminatory treatment only runs skin deep: if the socio-economic interests are too big then considerations about gender stereotypes can be discarded. If the Court in *Konstantin Markin* had been more thorough in its pursuit of gender stereotypes as an important source of discrimination and other harm, then it could have prevented this dangerous narrowing of its holding.

Conclusion

Although a few aspects of the Court's reasoning show laudable gender sensitivity, this chapter has argued that the Chamber judgment mistakenly reduces the wrong in *Konstantin Markin* to a case of formal sex discrimination, pure and simple. The problem in *Konstantin Markin* goes deeper than the difference in treatment between servicemen and servicewomen as regards parental leave; it lies in the State's reinforcement of harmful gender stereotypes. By focusing on the harm of stereotypes, the Court can promote a richer understanding of equality. Conceptualising equality as a transformative principle allows the Court to address the underlying structures of discrimination. In the redraft, I have attempted to show how this can be done.

Readers will have to determine whether the redraft is convincing, both in the sense that it achieves its purpose of expressing transformative equality (scholars

---

[87] ECHR, *Andrle* v. *Czech Republic*, 17 February 2011, para. 59.   [88] *Ibid*.

of diversity all know that transformation is difficult to achieve through the courts!) and in the sense that it appears like it could have been written by the ECHR. I am of the same mind as Denise Réaume, who apologised that 'I fear that you may be able to take the girl out of the academy, but you cannot entirely take the academy out of the girl'.[89] Through participating in this redrafting project, I appreciate the complexity of the judicial enterprise now better than ever.

Rewriting Konstantin Markin v. Russia

(i)   Applicability of Article 14 taken together with Article 8

. . .

(ii)   Compliance with Article 14

46. The Court observes that the applicant, being a serviceman, had no statutory right to parental leave. It is undisputed that civilians, both men and women, as well as servicewomen, are entitled to parental leave. The denial of parental leave to the applicant was accordingly based on a combination of two grounds: military status plus sex. **This is therefore a case of intersectional discrimination, in the sense that several personal traits intersect and produce a negative impact on a specific group of people who possess these traits. In this case, which concerns parental leave, military status and sex produce a combined impact that burdens servicemen in particular. The Court recalls that the CEDAW Committee has noted that intersectionality is a basic concept for understanding the scope of the obligation to eliminate gender-based discrimination (CEDAW, General Recommendation 28, § 18). The Court is in agreement with the South African Constitutional Court that 'discrimination must be understood in the context of the experience of those on whom it impacts' (South African Constitutional Court,*National Coalition for Gay and Lesbian Equality and others* v. *Minister of Home Affairs and others* (1999), § 35). Often, the experience of discrimination will not be limited to just one part of a person's identity – like one's sex, one's occupational status, one's religion, one's sexual orientation, or one's race. In this case, the Court has to examine whether, in relation to parental leave, the disadvantageous**

---

[89] Denise Réaume is one of the authors of the *Women's Court of Canada*, a project that is aimed at rewriting the Canadian Charter of Rights and Freedoms equality jurisprudence: Denise Réaume, 'Law v. Canada (Minister of Employment and Immigration)' (2006) 18 *Canadian Journal of Women and the Law* 143–88. More information on the Women's Court of Canada is available at www.womenscourt.ca.

treatment of military servicemen [fragment deleted] is acceptable under Article 14.

47. The Court [fragment deleted] reiterates that the advancement of the equality of the sexes is today a major goal in the Member States of the Council of Europe and very weighty reasons would have to be put forward before such a difference of treatment could be regarded as compatible with the Convention (see *Burghartz* v. *Switzerland*, 22 February 1994, § 27, Series A no. 280-B, and *Schuler-Zgraggen* v. *Switzerland*, 24 June 1993, § 67, Series A no. 263). **As a preliminary matter, the Court is of the opinion that, when considering the general meaning of equality and discrimination, it has to have regard to the provisions of more specialised legal instruments such as CEDAW (see *Opuz* v. *Turkey*, no. 33401/02, § 67, 9 June 2009). Equality of the sexes entails more than a purely formalistic obligation of equal treatment of women and men (CEDAW, General Recommendation 25, §§ 7–10). The Court notes that Article 5 CEDAW urges States to eliminate gender stereotyping. Gender stereotypes are preconceptions about the characteristics, attributes or roles that correspond to men and women (cf. Inter-American Court of Human Rights, *Case of González et al. ('Cotton Field')* v. *Mexico* (2009), § 401). The CEDAW Committee has remarked that 'the principle of equality between men and women, or gender equality, entails the concept that all human beings, regardless of sex, are free to develop their personal abilities, pursue their professional careers and make choices without the limitations set by stereotypes, rigid gender roles and prejudices' (CEDAW, General Recommendation 28, § 22).**

It is against this backdrop that this case, including the Government's arguments, needs to be examined. In essence, the Government has put two types of justifications forward for the difference in treatment between military servicewomen and military servicemen. The first justification concerns the special social role of mothers in the upbringing of their children. The second justification concerns the operational effectiveness of the armed forces. The Court will assess the merits of these arguments separately.

α. **The special social role of women associated with motherhood**

48. The Court is not convinced by the Constitutional Court's argument that, as far as parental leave is concerned, the different treatment of male and female military personnel is justified by the special social role of mothers in the upbringing of children (see paragraph 19 above). **By making this argument, the Government relies on gender-role stereotypes. In the first place, this is the traditional stereotype that women are homemakers and, its corollary, that men are breadwinners. Gender stereotypes such as these are harmful because they ascribe a certain identity to men and**

women, and prohibit the individualised evaluation of their capacities and needs (see, *mutatis mutandis, Alajos Kiss* v. *Russia*, no. 38832/06, § 42, 20 May 2010). The Court is convinced that this stereotype impairs both military servicemen and military servicewomen in their freedom to make important choices concerning their family life.

The Court notes that, in its Concluding Observations of its 2010 periodic report on Russia, the CEDAW Committee expressed its concern 'at the persistence of practices, traditions, patriarchal attitudes and deep-rooted stereotypes regarding the roles, responsibilities and identities of women and men in all spheres of life' and 'the State party's repeated emphasis on the role of women as mothers and care-givers'. The CEDAW Committee recommended that the Government no longer focus on women primarily as wives and mothers but instead focus on women as individuals and actors in society equal to men (CEDAW/C/USR/CO/7, §§ 20–21).

49. The Court [fragment deleted] observes that in contrast to maternity leave and associated allowances, which are primarily intended to enable the mother to recover from the fatigue of childbirth and to breastfeed her baby if she so wishes, parental leave and the parental leave allowances relate to the subsequent period and are intended to enable the parent to stay at home to look after the infant personally. Whilst being aware of the differences which may exist between mother and father in their relationship with the child, the Court considers that, as far as the role of taking care of the child during this period is concerned, both parents are 'similarly placed' (see *Petrovic*, cited above, § 36). **In addition, the Court recognises that making parental leave available to both parents can be a useful tool for promoting gender equality (see the report by the International Labour Organization, cited above, § 26). Such a measure enables men and women alike to achieve a work–family balance based on individual capacities, needs and wishes. It can serve the best interest of the family as a whole, including particularly that of the children, because child-care arrangements that best suit the family's circumstances can be created and because the children can enjoy the attention of both their parents (cf. Inter-American Commission on Human Rights, *Morales de Sierra* v. *Guatemala*, Case 11.625 (2001), § 44).**

50. The Court notes that, in the *Petrovic* v. *Austria* case, a distinction on the basis of sex with respect to parental leave allowances was found not to be in violation of Article 14. In that case a broad margin of appreciation was granted to the respondent State because of the great disparity in the 1980s between the legal systems of the Contracting States in the sphere of parental benefits. The Court held that at the material time there was no European consensus in this field, as the majority of Contracting States did not provide for parental leave or related allowances for fathers (see *Petrovic*, cited above,

§§ 38 to 42). However, in the more recent case of *Weller* v. *Hungary* the Court took a step away from the approach adopted in the *Petrovic* case and found that the exclusion of natural fathers from the entitlement to receive parental allowances, when mothers, adoptive parents and guardians were entitled to them, amounted to discrimination on the ground of parental status (see *Weller*, cited above, §§ 30 to 35). It is also significant that since the adoption of the judgment in the *Petrovic* case the legal situation as regards parental leave entitlements in the Contracting States has evolved. In an absolute majority of European countries the legislation now provides that parental leave may be taken by both mothers and fathers (see §§ 26 to 30 above). In the Court's opinion, this shows that society has moved towards a more equal sharing between men and women of responsibility for the upbringing of their children and that men's caring role has gained recognition. The Court considers that it cannot overlook the widespread and consistently developing views and associated legal changes to the domestic laws of Contracting States on this issue (see, *mutatis mutandis*, *Smith and Grady* v. *the United Kingdom*, nos. 33985/96 and 33986/96, § 104, ECHR 1999-VI). It follows that the respondent State can no longer rely on the absence of a common standard among the Contracting States to justify the difference in treatment between men and women as regards parental leave. [Fragment deleted] Accordingly, the Court concludes that **'the special role of women associated with motherhood' is not a convincing or weighty reason to justify the exclusion of servicemen from parental leave entitlements** [fragment deleted].

[Paragraph 50 deleted]

β. Operational effectiveness of the armed forces

51. The Court will now turn to the second argument brought forward by the Government, which centres on the specific demands of the military.

. . .

58. Further, [fragment deleted] **the Court is not convinced by the Constitutional Court's reliance on the limited participation of women in the military service as an argument to justify restricting parental leave for military servicemen (see paragraph 19 above). The Court notes that, in making the argument that granting parental leave to servicemen would jeopardise the operational effectiveness of the armed forces, the Government disparages the importance of the contribution that women make to the armed forces, both in terms of their number and in terms of the content of their positions. The Court regrets that this seems to confirm another gender stereotype, namely that real soldiers are manly. This stereotype risks devaluing the labour of military servicewomen,**

which is significant: women constitute approximately 10 per cent of the
Russian army personnel.

(iii)   Conclusion

59. [Fragment deleted] **The denial of parental leave to military servicemen such as the applicant** was founded on the traditional gender roles, that is
on the perception of women as primary child-carers and men as primary
breadwinners. These gender **stereotypes** ['prejudices' deleted] cannot, by
themselves, be considered by the Court to amount to sufficient justification
for the difference in treatment, any more than similar **stereotypes** ['prejudices' deleted] based on race, origin, colour or sexual orientation. Nor can the
fact that in the armed forces women are less numerous than men justify the
disadvantaged treatment of the latter as regards entitlement to parental leave,
as this argument is also grounded in harmful stereotypes.

60. The Court is particularly struck by the Constitutional Court's intima-
tion that a serviceman wishing to take personal care of his children was free
to resign from the armed forces. Servicemen are thereby forced to make a
difficult choice between caring for their new-born children and pursuing
their military career, no such choice being faced by servicewomen. The
Court reiterates in this respect the unique nature of the armed forces and,
consequently, the difficulty in directly transferring essentially military qual-
ifications and experience to civilian life. It is therefore clear that, if they
choose to resign from military service to be able to take care of their new-
born children, servicemen would encounter difficulties in obtaining civilian
posts in their areas of specialisation which would reflect the seniority and
status that they had achieved in the armed forces (see, *mutatis mutandis*,
Smith and Grady, cited above, § 92). In view of the above consideration, the
Court finds that the reasons adduced by the Constitutional Court provide
insufficient justification for imposing much stronger restrictions on the
family life of servicemen than on that of servicewomen. Accordingly, convincing and weighty reasons have not been offered by the Government to
justify the difference in treatment between male and female military personnel as regards entitlement to parental leave.

61. In view of the foregoing, the Court considers that the exclusion of
servicemen from the entitlement to parental leave, while servicewomen are
entitled to such leave, cannot be said to be reasonably and objectively
justified. **Gender stereotypes concerning the proper roles of servicemen
and servicewomen harm individuals from both these groups, and as such
are not acceptable under this Convention**. The Court concludes that [frag-
ment deleted] there has therefore been a violation of Article 14 taken in
conjunction with Article 8.

PART III

Religious minorities

7

Rethinking Deschomets v. France: reinforcing the protection of religious liberty through personal autonomy in custody disputes

RENATA UITZ

Introduction

Deschomets v. *France*[1] is an admissibility decision involving a custody dispute[2] between a divorced father who left a religious community (the Brethren movement) and a mother who decided to stay within the religious community. The religiously dictated, strict and puritan lifestyle of the mother, which she also imposed on the couple's children, met the father's disapproval. In addition to seeking a divorce, the father also started a long battle for custody of their children in order to rescue them from the daily regimen dictated by their mother's religious beliefs.

At first sight, such a custody dispute resulting from a religious disagreement between the parents appears to be a rather ordinary, if sad, conflict within a family. On a deeper level, however, such custody disputes touch upon the religious freedom of at least one parent, and a child or children, if not an entire family. The choice of religion and the decision to change one's religion are the most intensely protected aspects of religious liberty (i.e. the so-called inner core (*forum internum*)), and the manifestations stemming from this choice are not only protected in the context of various Convention rights, but also inhabit the private sphere (family homes). In addition, lawsuits arising from custody disputes of the *Deschomets* type centre around the best interest of children caught in the middle of the dispute, and ultimately turn into a highly sensitive balancing act about the versions of the good life a judiciary finds tolerable, easily leaving the parent who made a controversial choice somewhat behind. The European Court of Human Rights (hereinafter ECHR) tends to decide these disputes under Article 8 (right to respect for private and family life) in conjunction with Article 14 (prohibition of discrimination). While the current

---

[1] ECHR, *Deschomets v. France*, 16 May 2006 (decision, inadmissible).
[2] In this chapter, I use the term 'custody' broadly to cover parental rights over a child, where the parent retaining custody also retains the power to determine the habitual residence of a child. National legal systems in the Council of Europe differ in their definition of custody, guardianship and parental rights.

approach offers a neutral frame of judicial analysis, it seems to bypass the kernel
of the dispute: the religious freedom (Article 9) of the parent (and child) who
wishes to deviate from the mainstream in her beliefs and, also, in ensuing
lifestyle choices.

This chapter argues that the current framework of analysis based on Article 8
in conjunction with Article 14 would benefit from accounting more markedly
for the religious-liberty dimension of custody disputes triggered by religious
disagreement through the concept of the protection of 'personal autonomy', a
consideration often emphasised in Article 8 jurisprudence. As a matter of
principle, this approach would reinforce the premise that a religious way of
life is not an accident or a *vis maior*, but the result of conscious individual
decisions about the good life which are clearly protected under the
Convention.[3] As a matter of sheer practicality, by providing more detailed
and accessible guidance, the ECHR would assist national courts and petitioners
on the standards applicable in custody disputes which are triggered by religious
disagreement. The ECHR did not shy away from providing detailed guidance in
admissibility decisions on the nature and extent of protection under the
Convention before.[4] The ECHR gave better guidance on arguments and direc-
tions it preferred even in rather sensitive matters (like bans on religious
symbols).[5] In addition, through exposing the connection between the various
components of the Convention's rights protection system, the ECHR could
enable a more robust protection for the rights of members in vulnerable,
marginalised and disadvantaged communities living in multi-religious and
multi-cultural democracies. If national courts cannot maintain the image that
in cases involving religious liberty they decide in a neutral and impartial
fashion,[6] they do not only impair diversity, but also undermine trust in the
judiciary.

Deschomets and progeny before the ECHR

Deschomets v. *France* stems from a custody battle underscored by a religious
disagreement which led to a family crisis. Initially, both parents were members
of the Brethren movement. Subsequently, the father left the movement; the
mother continued to live with the children according to the precepts of the
movement. As the ECHR also described in the case, the Brethren movement is a
conservative evangelical Christian movement with nineteenth-century origins.

---

[3] ECHR, *Jehovah's Witnesses of Moscow and others* v. *Russia*, 10 June 2010.

[4] See e.g. ECHR, *Skugar* v. *Russia*, 3 December 2009 (decision, inadmissible).

[5] See e.g. ECHR, *Phull* v. *France*, 11 January 2005 (decision, inadmissible); ECHR, *El Morsli* v.
France, 4 March 2008 (decision, inadmissible); *Mann Singh* v. *France*, 27 November 2008
(decision, inadmissible).

[6] More broadly, see e.g. M. Evans, *Manual on the Wearing of Religious Symbols in Public
Areas* (Council of Europe Publishing, 2009), pp. 43 *et seq.*

Followers are required to adhere to the Scriptures, and keep their distance from harmful outside influences. Television, radio, computers and the Internet are regarded as harmful influences. In addition to a daily and weekly routine of religious observances, there are also strict rules on family life, including a prohibition on taking meals with non-believers. Work or school on Saturdays is prohibited, and Sundays are exclusively devoted to religious exercise.

Initially, the mother had custody of the couple's children, but, after a decade-long litigation, custody was granted to the father. From the beginning, the French courts took into account the nature and impact of the mother's beliefs. In the early period of the separation proceedings, the mother had custody and contested even limited access to the children on Sunday, arguing that 'it was a day set aside for religious devotion and that it would be abnormal for the children to be deprived of their Sunday observances because of the change in the father's beliefs'. In the separation proceedings, custody of the children was granted to the mother, with visitation rights granted to the father, as the separation was the result of the father's adulterous affair. Joint parental responsibility was rejected in the separation proceedings.

Three years after the separation, after the couple's divorce, in a separate custody proceeding the welfare report ordered by the first-instance court found that '[the mother's] way of life is not favourable to [the children's] opportunities for further education, to their integration into society in the broad sense or to their character development; the children live with a constant feeling of guilt whenever their aspirations diverge from her own. It was very clear during the two interviews with the children that they both wanted to change their way of life. A no longer wishes to attend Brethren meetings and is aware that his mother cannot change her lifestyle or religious practice. J would like to have greater freedom; he does not want to leave his brother but remains very attached to his mother.' When the court ruled in favour of joint parental responsibilities, it said that 'the children ... are currently torn between their father and mother, each of whom represents a different lifestyle; A and J do not adhere to [the applicant's] way of life, as they suffer from various taboos when they are with her, although they remain very attached to her.' The report added that 'the fact that [the applicant] adheres to a religious movement cannot in itself justify a change in the children's residence, as she provides them with a high standard of care and education that have made them well-bred children with good school results, and as the continuation of the children's schooling is not currently at issue.'

In 1999, the appellate court decided that the children should reside with their father. In its decision, it noted: 'Lastly, it is not for the court to decide whether or not the Brethren movement constitutes a sect, but simply to determine whether the constraints imposed on the children, because of the mother's affiliation to the movement, do not run counter to their interests. Contrary to what [the applicant] seems to believe, the moral values that have to be inculcated in children are not the prerogative of religions. Above all, the acquisition of such values does not depend on stringent religious observances and the imposing of prohibitions on children which have the effect of setting them apart from their non-believing peers, who are regarded as sinners.' In her appeal against the custody decision, the mother complained about religious discrimination. In 2002, the Cour de cassation dismissed her appeal, finding in particular that 'the Court of Appeal ... took into account the findings in the welfare report, together with the feelings expressed by the children, whose maturity was emphasised in that report, considered that the obligations and prohibitions imposed on them were harmful to their development and social integration'.

After losing custody in the national courts, the mother challenged the decision of the national courts as a violation of her right to respect for family life due to discrimination based on religion (Articles 8 and 14), and also a violation of her freedom of religion (Article 9). The ECHR declared the application to be manifestly ill-founded on the Article 8/14 ground, while it did not find an interference in the Article 9 complaint. At the time of the ECHR decision, the children were twenty and seventeen years old.

It is clear from the string of decisions in the national courts that the religious reasons behind the lifestyles of the children fade step-by-step as the case progresses in the national judicial hierarchy. While references to the daily routine and negative feelings of the children (infused by the mother's religious beliefs) were more prevalent in the initial stages of the judicial process, with the passage of time and the progress of the custody case, the development of the children together with concern for their social integration became prevalent. The decision of the appellate court clearly says that, instead of assessing the qualities of the Brethren movement as such, the task of the court is to assess the impact of the mother's beliefs on the interests of the children. One can clearly observe a shift of emphasis from the family's daily routine to the long-term interests of the children. In addition to introducing a sense of the long duration of the case, in 1999 the appellate court found it necessary to remind the mother who was deprived of custody that 'the moral values that have to be inculcated in children are not the prerogative of religions'.[7] While this reminder may be read as reassuring advice, it is also possible to see it as a slightly demeaning remark on the dubious contributions of her religious beliefs to the development of her children in French society.

When *Deschomets* was decided, the leading cases on religious discrimination in custody disputes were *Hoffmann* v. *Austria*[8] and *Palau-Martinez* v. *France*.[9]

---

[7] In the original French, this sentence reads: 'contrairement à ce que semble croire [la requérante] les valeurs morales qui doivent être inculquées aux enfants ne sont pas l'apanage des religions.'

[8] ECHR, *Hoffmann* v. *Austria*, 23 June 1993.

[9] ECHR, *Palau-Martinez* v. *France*, 16 December 2003.

Although these cases contain important pronouncements on the prohibition of religious discrimination in custody cases, they offer little practical guidance on how future cases should be decided by national courts. In *Hoffman*, the deeply divided panel (five to four) importantly held that: 'Notwithstanding any possible arguments to the contrary, a distinction based essentially on a difference in religion alone is not acceptable.'[10] To this, the *Palau-Martinez* judgment added the strong hint that it is problematic if a parent's religious affiliation is of decisive importance in a custody dispute.[11] It was also found questionable in the case that the national authorities considered the abstract teachings of the applicant's religion for the custody decision, and did not look into 'any direct, concrete evidence demonstrating the influence of the applicant's religion on her two children's upbringing and daily life'.[12]

Frugal and pragmatic as the guidance of the ECHR is, it turns out in practice that national authorities and domestic courts are not necessarily aware of what is expected of them in similar cases,[13] nor does the ECHR speak in one voice. At the time when *Deschomets* was decided, the ECHR had already received applications in two custody cases where applicants complained about religious discrimination in similar settings. In *Ismailova* v. *Russia*,[14] custody of two children was granted to the father, a seaman, instead of their mother, who was a Jehovah's witness, despite the fact that due to the father's frequent absences custody was in fact in the hands of the paternal grandparents. The custody agency as well as the lower level courts found it problematic that the mother's house was a place for meetings of strangers, belonging to Jehovah's Witnesses and also that the children, who attended these meetings, were affected by the religious teachings.

In *Deschomets*, the ECHR rejected the mother's application as inadmissible, and a divided First Section found that, while the applicant's religious affiliation was a factor for the custody decision, the national courts did take other factors into account (such as the size of the living quarters). Dissenting Judges Hajiev, Vajic and Steiner, however, were troubled by the tone of the national court judgments on the applicant's beliefs, pointing out that 'the national courts mainly balanced the financial situation of the father and the housing conditions he was providing to the children, on the one hand, and the mother's religious activities of which the family and villagers disapproved, on the other'. In the other case, *Gineitiene* v. *Lithuania*,[15] the applicant divorced her husband not

---

[10] At para. 36.   [11] See paras. 37–9.   [12] Para. 42.
[13] For a positive example, as an exception, see ECHR, *RR* v. *Romania (No. 3)*, 15 March 2011, para. 155.
[14] ECHR, *Ismailova* v. *Russia*, 29 November 2007.
[15] ECHR, *Gineitiene* v. *Lithuania*, 27 July 2010.

long after joining the Osho movement, and later lost custody of her two children. The ECHR found that, while the first-instance court observed that the Osho movement was controversial, 'the domestic courts did touch upon the applicant's religious affiliation. However, that text was an isolated reference and was unrelated to the applicant's ability to bring up her children.'[16]

Challenges in cases where national courts make comments about parental religious convictions, and the consequences thereof, continue to reach the ECHR. For instance, in *M and C* v. *Romania*,[17] in a protracted custody battle, a first-instance court made express comments on the notoriety of the 'Jehovah's Witness sect', to which the mother belonged but the father had left.[18] The ECHR found no violation on this account in the case, as the first-instance court's observations were not prejudicial to the mother's custody case on appeal.[19] In another custody battle, in *RR* v. *Romania*, the national courts, and ultimately the ECHR, had to assess (among many other factors) the impact of a mother's religious convictions on the upbringing of a child, including the mother's negative views of the biological father's sexual orientation.[20]

Without going into further details about these custody cases, it is striking that they all involve believers of minority, unpopular or lesser known religions who feel that they have been left behind by their national judiciaries. It is this sense of religious discrimination which leads them to the ECHR after a long and strenuous custody battle. The rewritten version of the *Deschomets* decision does not change the outcome of the case. It only offers more detailed reasons on how the conclusion was reached. Looking at the challenges faced by the national courts in custody cases arising from a religious disagreement, it seems that further guidance is needed from the ECHR, not only to assist national courts in their decisions, but also to strengthen trust in the neutrality and impartiality of judicial decision-making.

Religious disagreement in custody disputes: preliminary considerations

Religious disagreements in custody disputes present a deep-running conflict between competing fundamental human rights considerations: the family life dimension competes with questions concerning the scope of protection and limits of religious liberty in the private sphere, together with questions on the protection of children's interests and, additionally, by issues of the children's own religious liberty (also including the right to choose a belief), if any. The resolution of the dispute revolves around the manner in and extent to which the religious beliefs of a parent, and the lifestyle choices dictated by those beliefs, should be relevant for deciding whether this parent's rights to family life have

---

[16] *Ibid.*, para. 40.   [17] ECHR, *M and C* v. *Romania*, 27 September 2011.
[18] *Ibid.*, para. 62.   [19] *Ibid.*, para. 146.
[20] ECHR, *RR* v. *Romania (No. 3)*, 15 March 2011 (decision, inadmissible).

been breached by national authorities granting custody to the other parent. Therefore, before discussing developments in the jurisprudence, it is important to consider the nature of the religious liberty claim in the family life setting.

From the perspective of individual religious liberty, the choice of religion is part of the inner core (*forum internum*) which enjoys absolute protection and is not subject to any limitation.[21] Article 9(1) of the Convention is accepted to offer protection to the *forum internum* in the jurisprudence of the ECHR.[22] The right to bring up one's children according to one's own preferred religious or philosophical convictions is also widely recognised as a human right, and is deeply connected with the concept of parental rights and family life.[23] Parents receive protection against all types of State intrusion into this right before national constitutional courts and the ECHR. The Convention is generally seen by the ECHR as a safeguard against religious indoctrination by the State in the school environment, although with a broad margin of appreciation protecting national (majority) traditions.[24]

In custody disputes fuelled by the parents' religious disagreement, courts are invited to reflect on a child's upbringing due to a disagreement between parents who are otherwise not answerable to the State on this matter, and courts are meant to settle the custody issue without deciding the dispute about the good life. The real antagonist in these cases is not the government, but a former spouse or partner who decided to abandon his or her partner on a spiritual journey as a matter of an equally respect-worthy choice.[25] The primary concern in custody cases is the protection of the best interest of the child. Nonetheless, by focusing on the living conditions of the child, courts' attention easily shifts from the source of the dispute: one parent's (typically the mother's) choice of a religion and a religious way of life.

This last observation certainly leads to the fundamental preliminary issue of why freedom of religion should be protected at all. There are several competing

[21] On *forum internum* and international human rights law, see e.g. P. M. Taylor, *Freedom of Religion, UN and European Human Rights Law and Practice* (Cambridge University Press, 2005), pp. 24 *et seq.*

[22] C. Evans, *Freedom of Religion under the European Convention on Human Rights* (Oxford University Press, 2001), pp. 72–4.

[23] P. M. Taylor, *Freedom of Religion, UN and European Human Rights Law and Practice* (Cambridge University Press, 2005), pp. 200–1. Here I will not deal with further complications which may stem from rules of behaviour imposed upon parents towards each other and towards their children under religious legal systems.

[24] P. M. Taylor, *Freedom of Religion, UN and European Human Rights Law and Practice* (Cambridge University Press, 2005), pp. 200–1. See ECHR, *Kjeldsen, Busk Madsen and Pedersen v. Denmark*, 7 December 1976; and ECHR, *Folgero and others v. Norway*, 29 June 2007, para. 84(h). Cf. ECHR (GC), *Lautsi v. Italy*, 18 March 2011.

[25] The problem of horizontal effect is cloaked by the fact that family law governs matters of custody, and by the time a dispute reaches the ECHR the State will become a handy respondent.

explanations in this centuries-old debate, and the confines of the present project do not permit a detailed elaboration, which ultimately may not even be necessary as the present project is also mindful of certain limitations stemming from the jurisprudence of the ECHR. Among the popular non-religious justifications, Michael Sandel (who finds religious believers 'morally admirable'), for instance, forcefully argued that liberal theorists err when they argue on the basis of choice (personal autonomy) and State neutrality, because religious believers follow the 'dictates of conscience' and not 'decisions based on choices'.[26]

Note, however, that this justification does not square with the jurisprudence of the ECHR. When carefully reviewing the justifications underlying the protection of freedom of religion, Carolyn Evans duly noted that, although the ECHR has not elaborated its understanding on the underlying rationale,

> [t]he argument from autonomy seems to be the best approach for the Court to take to interpreting Article 9. It is broadly consistent with the ideas of pluralism, tolerance, and the importance of religion to believers that the Court has already adopted. It allows for an integrated approach to Article 9 and other important autonomy rights in the Convention, such as freedom of speech, freedom of association, and the right to family life, which recognize the importance of allowing a person to be the "author of his or her own life" . . . This approach emphasizes the dignity of all human beings and the importance of allowing them to make and live out decisions about the issues that are most important to them.[27]

For the rewriting exercise, an autonomy-based approach was adopted (starting with paragraph 27) exactly to this effect. This approach rests on the intimate connection between personal autonomy as expressed in religious liberty and decisions about private life in the family context, and is infused by a requirement of non-discrimination and State neutrality – all components drawn from ECHR jurisprudence. Consequently, this approach is believed to fit cosily with existing case law and the principles followed by the Court.

Religious discrimination in custody cases under the Convention

Although several provisions of the Convention would be *prima facie* relevant to questions of religious discrimination in custody disputes,[28] over the years the

---

[26] M. J. Sandel, *Liberalism and the Limits of Justice* (2nd edn, Cambridge University Press, 1998), pp. xii–xiv (preface to the second edition); the argument is illustrated by examples from US constitutional jurisprudence in his 'Freedom of Conscience or Freedom of Choice?', in J. D. Hunter and O. Guiness (eds.), *Articles of Faith, Articles of Peace: The Religious Liberty Clauses and the American Public Philosophy* (Brookings Institution Press, 1990).

[27] C. Evans, *Freedom of Religion under the European Convention on Human Rights* (Oxford University Press, 2001), p. 33.

[28] Article 2 of Protocol 1 ensures parents' right to have their children educated according to their own religious or philosophical preferences, but no parental rights beyond that. In

ECHR developed a strong preference for hearing these cases under the right to respect for private and family life of Article 8 read in conjunction with Article 14 on the prohibition of discrimination.[29] The standard pragmatic justification for this approach is that, once the claims are assessed as a violation of the right to family life due to discrimination on the basis of religion under Articles 8 and 14, the facts do not warrant separate consideration under Article 9 taken alone, or in conjunction with Article 14.[30] Indeed, as seen from numerous decisions, the approach adopted by the ECHR is clearly capable of addressing the religious-liberty dimension of such cases in the context of the religious discrimination claim under Article 14. The prevalent framework of Article 8 read in conjunction with Article 14 has the potential to more comprehensively appreciate the religious-liberty dimension of the disputes. This project argues that, within the current framework, the ECHR might find it practicable to provide further guidance for applicants as well as for national courts on the protection due to religious liberty in private and family life under the Convention.

Custody disputes follow the overall logic of discrimination cases under Article 14.[31] First, the ECHR assesses the alleged interference with the right to family life under Article 8. The concept of family life is autonomous under the Convention, and protection of family life does not cease when a parent does

---

addition, Article 5 of Protocol 7 provides for spousal equality in numerous affairs. The right to education exists *vis-à-vis* the State, while the spousal-equality provision was intended to regulate private relations, and does not apply in other fields of law as a general prohibition of discrimination. Pieter Van Dijk, Fried Van Hoof, Arjen Van Rijn and Leo Zwaak, *Theory and Practice of the European Convention on Human Rights* (4th edn, Intersentia, 2006), p. 986. Although it was mentioned *passim* in *Hoffmann* (at para. 35), it does not seem to be very influential in the ECHR's assessment of parental rights in custody cases. The ECHR appears to prefer to decide custody disputes on Article 8 grounds, thus mooting any further discussion under the spousal-equality provision of Article 5 of Protocol 7. See e.g. ECHR, *Kaplan* v. *Austria*, 18 January 2007; ECHR, *Chepelev* v. *Russia*, 26 July 2007.

[29] Often both grounds are invoked, as an alternative. See ECommHR, *MM* v. *Bulgaria* (Commission, ended in friendly settlement); also *Hoffmann*, at para. 38; *Palau-Martinez*, at para. 46; *Ismailova*, at para. 65; *Gineitienne*, at para. 44. The ECHR did consider the Article 9 claim in considerable detail in ECHR, *FL* v. *France*, 3 November 2005 (decision), but found the matter inadmissible.

[30] Note that, in the custody cases so far, the ECHR did not consider the religious freedom of the child directly, but typically takes this aspect into account in the proportionality analysis concerning the limitation on the applicant-parent's rights to family life. S. Langlaude, *The Right of the Child to Religious Freedom in International Law* (Kluwer, 2006), p. 219. When discussing the rights involved in the *Hoffmann* case, the van Dijk commentary does not discuss the religion aspect either: Pieter Van Dijk, Fried Van Hoof, Arjen Van Rijn and Leo Zwaak, *Theory and Practice of the European Convention on Human Rights* (4th edn, Intersentia, 2006), p. 697.

[31] See e.g. S. Greer, *The European Convention on Human Rights: Achievements, Problems and Prospects* (Cambridge University Press, 2006), p. 220.

not share a home with his or her biological children.[32] A parent who loses a custody battle is worthy of protection of his or her family life which clearly entails his or her relationship with his or her children under Article 8. A domestic court decision severing ties with a parent and thus altering custody rights is sufficient to interfere with the right to family life protected under Article 8.[33]

In order for the religious-liberty issue to be appraised, the applicant needs to show under Article 14 that she was treated differently from other comparably situated persons due to her religious freedom (i.e. a Convention right). This approach follows from the complementary nature of Article 14.[34] The difference in treatment can be justified 'with an objective and reasonable justification', showing a 'reasonable relationship of proportionality between the means and the aims sought'.[35] The margin of appreciation of the States in justifying differences in treatment has been consistently reinforced.[36] As the intended legitimate aim of the measure the ECHR accepts the protection of the best interest of the child/children,[37] or the health and rights of the children.[38] Ideally, the judicial decision should result in a solution which creates an environment where the worldviews of both parents influence the children and the parents retain joint parental authority.[39] In addition, the ECHR went as far as saying that, in case the interests of the child collide with those of the applicant-parent, the interests of the child should prevail.[40] In *Deschomets*, the government argued that the father and the mother were not treated differently, because the national courts treated their arguments equally: instead of concentrating on the mother's religion, the courts matched the living conditions of the

---

[32] ECHR, *Berrehab* v. *Netherlands*, 21 June 1988; and ECHR, *Keegan* v. *Ireland*, 26 May 1994, discussed in Pieter Van Dijk, Fried Van Hoof, Arjen Van Rijn and Leo Zwaak, *Theory and Practice of the European Convention on Human Rights* (4th edn, Intersentia, 2006), pp. 690–1.

[33] *Ibid.*, p. 697.

[34] In this context, this approach was explained in most detail in *Palau-Martinez*, paras. 29–31.

[35] *Hoffmann*, para. 33; *Palau-Martinez*, para. 31; *Ismailova*, para. 57; also in *Gineitiene*, para. 36.

[36] See *Palau-Martinez*, para. 31; *Ismailova*, para. 57; also in *Gineitiene*, para. 37.

[37] *Palau-Martinez*, para. 40; *Ismailova*, para. 58; *Gineitiene*, para. 39.

[38] *Hoffmann*, para. 34.

[39] *FL* v. *France*: 'La Cour observe en l'espèce que l'intérêt des enfants relevait principalement de la nécessité de maintenir et de favoriser leur épanouissement dans un environnement ouvert et apaisé, en conciliant dans la mesure du possible les droits et convictions de chacun de leurs parents, ceux-ci exerçant en l'occurrence conjointement l'autorité parentale sur les deux enfants.'

[40] *FL* v. *France*: 'La Cour réaffirme à ce sujet que lorsque sont en jeu les droits garantis aux parents par l'article 8 de la Convention et ceux d'un enfant, les tribunaux doivent attacher la plus grande importance aux droits de l'enfant. Lorsqu'une mise en balance des intérêts s'impose, il y a lieu donc de faire prévaloir les intérêts de l'enfant.'

children. The applicant (the mother), however, argued that the appellate court decided on the basis of the Brethren lifestyle in general, and ignored evidence that this way of life was not harmful to the children. In its decision, the ECHR found that in the decision of the domestic courts the best interest of the children was paramount. The ECHR added that the decision of the appellate court was 'based precisely on the effective consequences of their mother's lifestyle for them. Whilst that lifestyle stemmed from the applicant's religious practice, it does not follow that the domestic courts attached decisive importance to that practice or that they generally criticised the Brethren movement *per se*.'

In the ECHR's approach, thus, the religious-liberty issue is too easily subsumed in the discrimination analysis. In the words of the Court in *Hoffmann*, 'a distinction based essentially on a difference in religion alone is not acceptable' (also quoted above).[41] The *Hoffmann* court did not offer much guidance on what it considers to amount to 'a distinction based essentially on a difference in religion alone'. The ECHR found that the Austrian Supreme Court's decision is based on a difference in treatment on the basis of religion due to the 'tone and phrasing of the Supreme Court's consideration'.[42] If at all, a more detailed analysis of religious reasons may take part in the justification phase of the proportionality analysis, in the means/aims assessment.

This point of the judicial assessment on its face is completely capable of functioning as a neutral, or, at least, a non-prejudicial, setting for assessing the explanations (including religious motivations) on the behaviour of the persons affecting the outcome of the custody case. At the same time, it is also the phase where the assessment of factors may easily be tainted by misgivings or second thoughts about unusual decisions motivating parental choices. As a matter of taking into account the interest of the child, one has to be reminded that the national courts (as well as the ECHR itself) often consider actual as well as potential factors and threats, as the following paragraphs will demonstrate.

The concrete factors concern the living conditions and lifestyles of the family, with special regard to the children. The number of rooms, the daily routine of children as well as financial resources are clearly relevant. Note, however, that, by the time a case reaches an appellate court, and especially the ECHR, the judicial decision essentially concerns the emergence of a *status quo* and the costs (material as well as emotional) of altering it as a result of the judgment of the court. Passage of time and unsettling solidified – even if illegal – relations are rightly a matter of concern for the ECHR.[43] As an international court, it does not have any direct connection with the parties to the dispute, including the affected child: it typically does not meet the affected parties or witnesses, the

---

[41] *Hoffmann*, para. 36.   [42] *Ibid.*, para. 33.
[43] This aspect of the ECHR's decision-making is best illustrated by ECHR (GC), *Neulinger and Shuruk v. Switzerland*, 6 July 2010, paras. 136 *et seq*. Disrupting the settled *status quo* was also a key concern in *Palau-Martinez*.

procedure is written only, and, by the time the ECHR delivers its decision, the original dispute might be a decade old. In the maze of these factors, although it might have been the source of the custody dispute, the religious liberty dimension quickly – and somewhat conveniently – fades away. Therefore, it is all the more important for the ECHR to provide ample guidance to national courts on how to settle these custody disputes in a Convention-conforming manner.

While the impact of the passage of time is relatively easy to assess using reasonable criteria, the assessment of the impact of other factors is often a value-laden exercise in the course of which any court easily gets caught in cultural prejudices, leaving lesser known or unpopular minority religious communities at a disadvantage. In *Ismailova*, it was decisive for the applicant's case both on the national level and also in the ECHR that, once the applicant started to include her children (over whom she initially had custody after her divorce) in her religious exercise as a Jehovah's witness, the children became irrationally afraid of rain and wind as a sign of a 'Worldwide Flood'. The ECHR found it problematic that the applicant 'failed to protect' her children from the impact of her religious practices.[44] In another case, *FL* v. *France*, the ECHR found no problem with a custody scheme under Article 9 which explicitly banned the children in the custody of the mother from attending the meetings of a religious community with the mother, in order to protect the children.[45]

At this point, it is important to pay attention to how the judicial assessment on the hard facts of living arrangements is easily mixed with much softer considerations concerning the children's impression about their care-giver parents, the courts' perspective on their most likely future, and, ultimately, about the good life children are entitled to. When it comes to assessing the emotional turmoils of the affected children, and also predictions about the interests as well as the future of the children, stereotypes and mainstream cultural patterns often surface with compelling force. The above illustration on the fear of rain and floods comes as a telling example. Note, however, that, when placed on a broader plain of assessment, one will find that most mainstream world religions teach rather distressing, if not outright scary, lessons about those who do not adhere to their teachings. It is unlikely that the Catholic hell (or purgatory) is any more friendly in a child's imagination than a 'Worldwide Flood'. Still, it is highly questionable whether in the opinion of a European court Catholic parents would be under an obligation to protect their children from vivid images of hell (or crucifixion, and even resurrection for that matter) by telling them that it does not really exist. Similarly, parents are barely under an obligation to protect their children when they are afraid of centuries-old witches in traditional stories or the Nutcracker to whom many children routinely get exposed around New Year's Eve.

The potential factors assessed by courts in custody cases are wide-ranging and often involve long-term expectations or projections about the imagined

---

[44] *Ismailova*, para. 62.   [45] *FL* v. *France*.

consequences of a particular custody decision. In *Hoffmann*, the Austrian Supreme Court assessed 'the possible effects on their social life of being associated with a particular religious minority ... that is, possible negative effects of her membership of the religious community of Jehovah's Witnesses'.[46] The ECHR found this problematic due to the tone used by the Austrian Supreme Court. However, from the subsequent *Palau-Martinez* judgment, it seems that the ECHR can accept such a project on the possible consequences of the children's religious involvement. The ECHR noted there that a social inquiry report, which the national courts refused to commission despite the applicant's request, 'would no doubt have provided tangible information on the children's lives with each of their parents and made it possible to ascertain the impact, if any, of their mother's religious practice on their lives and upbringing during the years following their father's departure when they had lived with her'.[47]

The approach followed by the ECHR is an example of a judicial exercise where religious claims about the good life do not receive privileged treatment *per se*, nor do they get to be treated with suspicion or outright rejection due to their religious origins. This framework of judicial assessment places claims about religious liberty on the same foundation as other (often competing) claims about the good life, and, as such, it is best situated to offer a framework for a fair and neutral assessment. The newly inserted segments do not seek to loosen or undermine this framework. Rather, the suggested revision hopes to demonstrate how the religious-liberty dimension of these custody disputes can be accounted for in a manner which gives due respect to lifestyle choices dictated by religious beliefs.

In this respect, it is crucial to acknowledge that the judicial assessment of the consequences of custody decisions belongs within the broader framework of assessing the scope of the permissible exercise of fundamental human rights in the setting of private life, wherein parents make decisions concerning the good life for themselves as well as for their children. Lacking a custody dispute, parents would enjoy great freedom in making the exact same choices with the exact same consequence for their children without State or judicial interference. The ability to assess some of the actual and potential threats considered by the national courts in a manner which is sensitive to cultural differences is much needed in such settings. To begin with, there is a possibility that any court involved in such a case (including the ECHR) will essentially decide on the legitimacy of religious teaching, irrespective of whether such a decision is acceptable in a plural, multi-cultural and multi-religious democracy under the Convention. Furthermore, such decisions have the potential to marginalise minority and under-privileged groups in society even further.

---

[46] *Hoffmann*, para. 32.   [47] *Palau-Martinez*, para. 42.

Towards a novel approach

The approach followed by the ECHR in cases involving complaints about religious discrimination in custody cases is essentially a discrimination analysis carried out in the broader context of Article 8 protecting the right to family life. Although the *Hoffmann* judgment led several commentators to suggest that the ECHR applies 'strict scrutiny' (to use US terminology) in religion cases,[48] in light of more recent jurisprudence it is clear that – unlike in the case of several protected traits – the ECHR does not require 'very weighty reasons' to be offered for religious discrimination.[49] The analysis in its current form appears capable of accounting for a wide range of factors connected with the daily life and upbringing of a child whose custody is at stake. Since this approach does not involve passing judgment on a religious manifestation directly (as is often the case in the setting of Article 9 on religious liberty), it has the potential of reflecting on religiously motivated decisions about the good life in a broader framework of analysis which is capable of accounting for diverse factors affecting parental decisions on family life. Nonetheless, exactly because this framework of analysis is not geared towards reflecting on religious manifestations, decision-makers may easily become unaware or less sensitive of their own cultural or intellectual biases in the course of the assessment.

In order to enable the application of this framework of decision-making in a manner which is sensitive to religious liberty, the ECHR may find it appropriate to consider the religious-freedom rationale behind parental life-style choices through resorting to the concept of 'personal autonomy', an

---

[48] Pieter Van Dijk, Fried Van Hoof, Arjen Van Rijn and Leo Zwaak, *Theory and Practice of the European Convention on Human Rights* (4th edn, Intersentia, 2006), p. 1046, and p. 1048 n. 77; O. M. Arnardóttir, *Equality and Non-Discrimination under the European Convention on Human Rights* (Kluwer, 2003), p. 155; J. Schokkenbroek, 'The Prohibition of Discrimination in Article 14 and the Margin of Appreciation' (1998) 19 *Human Rights Law Journal* at 22.

[49] 'Very weighty reasons' are required for distinctions e.g. on the basis of illegitimacy (e.g. ECHR, *Mazurek* v. *France*, 1 February 2000, para. 49; ECHR, *Camp and Bourimi* v. *Netherlands*, 3 October 2000, paras. 37–8; ECHR (GC), *Şahin* v. *Germany*, 8 July 2003, para. 94; ECHR (GC), *Sommerfeld* v. *Germany*, 8 July 2004, para. 93), nationality (e.g. ECHR (GC), *Andrejeva* v. *Latvia*, 18 February 2009, para. 88), ethnic origin or race (ECHR, *Timishev*, 14 June 2007, para. 56; ECHR (GC), *DH and others* v. *Czech Republic*, 13 November 2007, para. 182; and ECHR (GC), *Oršuš* v. *Croatia*, 16 March 2010, para. 149), biological sex or gender (ECHR, *Abdulaziz, Cabales and Balkandali* v. *United Kingdom*, 28 May 1985, para. 78, and lately in ECHR, *Stec* v. *United Kingdom*, 12 April 2006 (GC), para. 52), sexual orientation (ECHR (GC), *EB* v. *France*, 22 January 2008, para. 98; and ECHR, *Karner* v. *Austria*, 24 July 2003, para. 36), mental disability (ECHR, *Alajos Kis* v. *Hungary*, 20 May 2010). Very weighty reasons were recently not required when Article 9 was applied in conjunction with Article 14 in ECHR, *Grzelak* v. *Poland*, 15 June 2010, para. 89.

approach used widely elsewhere in Article 8 analysis and also in other spheres of the jurisprudence. After all, as Jill Marshall expressed in an account of the ECHR's headscarf jurisprudence: 'Decisions to remain within, or convert to, a particular faith or way of life could be viewed as exercises of choice by the particular women who make them. Any view that presents these qualities as situations that happen to women, with no agency on their part, can be criticized for hindering women's ability to make these essential choices.'[50] Bringing the religious-freedom dimension home through an emphasis on the protection of personal autonomy is not that big a leap to make. This idea is expressed in the new segments of paragraph 27 in the rewritten decision.

This thought experiment should take into account general considerations which underscore the system of rights protection in the Convention as a whole, and also the application of Article 8. As the ECHR formulated it in *Pretty* v. *United Kingdom* a decade ago in the context of Article 8: 'The very essence of the Convention is respect for human dignity and human freedom. Without in any way negating the principle of sanctity of life protected under the Convention, the Court considers that it is under Article 8 that notions of the quality of life take on significance.'[51] Over the years, the ECHR was keen to emphasise that the protection of human dignity and human freedom also protects 'the right to establish details of ... identity as individual human beings',[52] and 'aspects of an individual's physical and social identity including the right to personal autonomy, personal development and to establish and develop relationships with other human beings and the outside world.'[53] Note that, in most of the cases where the ECHR spoke about the protection of personal autonomy in such robust terms, the petitioners were seeking protection for choices about the good life which were much less mainstream and, thus, more controversial than following the precepts of one's faith or religion.[54]

---

[50] J. Marshall, 'Conditions for Freedom? European Human Rights Law and the Islamic Headscarf Debate' (2008) 30 *Human Rights Quarterly* 652.

[51] ECHR, *Pretty* v. *United Kingdom*, 24 July 2002, para. 65 (right to die). Subsequently reinforced e.g. in ECHR (GC), *Evans* v. *United Kingdom*, 10 April 2007, para. 71 (right to become or not to become a genetic parent); ECHR, *Tysiąc* v. *Poland*, 20 March 2007, para. 107 (access to legal abortion); ECHR, *Ternovszky* v. *Hungary*, 14 December 2010, para. 22 (right to give birth at home); ECHR, *A, B and C* v. *Ireland*, 16 December 2010, para. 212 (termination of pregnancy).

[52] ECHR, *Goodwin* v. *United Kingdom*, 11 July 2002, para. 90; also ECHR, *I* v. *United Kingdom*, 11 July 2002, para. 70.

[53] *Evans*, para. 71; also ECHR, *Kalacheva* v. *Russia*, 7 May 2009, para. 27.

[54] See J. Marshall, 'Conditions for Freedom? European Human Rights Law and the Islamic Headscarf Debate' (2008) 30 *Human Rights Quarterly* 652 at 642.

Admittedly, the rewritten decision seeks to infuse Article 8 jurisprudence in religious discrimination cases in the family setting both by reiterating the relevance of protecting personal autonomy in the context of family life (paragraphs 27 and 28) and also through reinforcing the connection between neutrality and non-discrimination (paragraphs 29–33). Importantly, for bridging the gap between Article 8 and Article 9 on account of the protection of personal autonomy, recently the ECHR attributed overwhelming significance to the protection of lifestyle choice dictated by religious beliefs in *Jehovah's Witnesses of Moscow and others* v. *Russia*,[55] emphasising that:

> 118. . . . it is a common feature of many religions that they determine doctrinal standards of behaviour by which their followers must abide in their private lives . . . Jehovah's Witnesses' regulations on allowing sufficient time for religious activities and abstaining from celebrating non-Witnesses or secular events were in that sense not fundamentally different from similar limitations that other religions impose on their followers' private lives. By obeying these precepts in their daily lives, believers manifested their desire to comply strictly with the religious beliefs they professed and their liberty to do so was guaranteed by Article 9 of the Convention in the form of the freedom to manifest religion, alone and in private.
>
> 119. The Court further reiterates that the State's duty of neutrality and impartiality prohibits it from assessing the legitimacy of religious beliefs or the ways in which those beliefs are expressed or manifested. Accordingly, the State has a narrow margin of appreciation and must advance serious and compelling reasons for an interference with the choices that people may make in pursuance of the religious standard of behaviour within the sphere of their personal autonomy.

Thus, taking into account that parental choices affecting the daily life and upbringing of children are an aspect of religious liberty, and as such, are protected by the Convention, would not be that alien from the jurisprudence of the ECHR, and would not require a profound departure from the framework of analysis used currently for assessing the resolution of custody disputes resulting from religious disagreement. The last part of this chapter suggests that a more detailed approach along the lines outlined above will not change the outcome of the *Deschomets* decision. Nonetheless, such a more detailed and more reflected reasoning provides useful guidance for national courts in future cases, while also fostering coherence across different provisions of the Convention in plural societies.

---

[55] ECHR, *Jehovah's Witnesses of Moscow and others* v. *Russia*, 10 June 2010.

Rewriting Deschomets v. France[56]

...

The law

26. Having regard to the nature of the allegations, the Court observes from the outset that a right guaranteed by the Convention is in issue, that is to say the applicant's right to respect for her family life, and that the dispute falls within the scope of Article 8 of the Convention, taken in conjunction with Article 14, as has not been disputed by the parties.

27. The Court further points out that, in the enjoyment of the rights and freedoms guaranteed by the Convention, Article 14 affords protection against different treatment, without objective and reasonable justification, of persons in similar situations (see in particular *Hoffmann*, cited above, § 31). **States enjoy a certain margin of appreciation in assessing whether and to what extent differences in otherwise similar situations justify a different treatment (*Palau-Martinez*, para. 31). At the same time, the Court finds it important to reinforce that the notion of personal autonomy is an important principle underlying the interpretation of the guarantees of the Convention (*Pretty*, para. 61). Article 8 protects a right to personal development, and the right to establish and develop relationships with other human beings (*Pretty*, para. 61). The protection of personal autonomy also applies to relationships with others within family relations. This protection is of particular significance when national authorities or national courts interfere in a dispute concerning family life.**

28. **Individual decisions concerning the choice of religion are protected by the Convention (Article 9), and belong in the untouchable core of human personality. Closely related to it, the decision on the principles of upbringing of one's child is also a sensitive aspect of personal autonomy. In case of a dispute concerning the principles of upbringing of a child in a family, the State has to be particularly mindful of the significance of this decision for the autonomy of parties concerned.**

29. **When offering a justification for differences in treatment in a plural, multi-religious society the State shall be mindful that such justifications shall be compatible with its role to preserve public order, religious harmony and tolerance in a democratic society. Any justification which undermines equal respect for the autonomous choices of**

---

[56] The original judgment of the Court was delivered in the form of an admissibility decision. It thus came with few paragraph numbers. For the purposes of clarity, the author has added her own paragraph numbers during the rewriting exercise.

human beings due to the State's disapproval of their deeply held religious or non-religious beliefs is incompatible with the Convention.

30. **The Court recalls that** notwithstanding any possible arguments to the contrary, a distinction based essentially on a difference in religion alone is not acceptable (*Hoffmann*, cited above, § 36). **Furthermore, a decision based solely or predominantly on the alleged religious affiliation of either parent is unacceptable (*Palau-Martinez*, paras. 33–38; *Gineitiene*, para. 40).**

31. The Court should thus begin by determining whether the applicant is entitled to complain of such a difference in treatment.

The Court considers, like the parties, that the applicant and her ex-husband were in similar situations for the purposes of Article 14 of the Convention.

Such a difference in treatment is discriminatory in the absence of an 'objective and reasonable justification', that is, if it is not justified by a 'legitimate aim' and if there is no 'reasonable relationship of proportionality between the means employed and the aim sought to be realised'. The Court is of the opinion that the aim pursued in the instant case, namely, the protection of the children's interests, is legitimate (*Palau-Martinez*, para. 39; *Ismailova*, para. 57).

32. **In order to properly assess the relationship of the aims sought and the means employed, the Court reiterates that the national authorities cannot rely on the abstract teachings of religions, or the lack of State registration of religious communities. Instead, domestic courts shall consider the specific circumstances of each case, assessing the daily living conditions, the child's own preferences (where ascertainable depending on age and maturity), and the applicant's ability to bring up the child. To the extent feasible, the domestic courts should foster a solution which creates an environment where the worldviews of both parents guide the children and the parents retain joint parental authority (*FL* v.*France*).**

33. **In this assessment, the religious affiliation of either parent and the preferences of the child shall be taken into account as they influence the daily life of the child among other factors. The Court recalls that in the course of this assessment the national courts cannot pass judgment on the soundness or legitimacy of the religious beliefs of the applicant or of other persons involved in the assessment.**

...

Accordingly, the Court considers that in the present case the Court of Appeal, in assessing the actual interests of the children, gave a ruling *in concreto* based precisely on the effective consequences of their mother's lifestyle for them. Whilst that lifestyle stemmed from the applicant's religious practice, it does not follow that the domestic courts attached decisive importance to that practice or that they generally criticised the Brethren movement *per se*. On the contrary, the Court of Appeal explained that it was not for it 'to decide whether or not the Brethren movement constitute[d] a sect'. In the Court's opinion, the domestic courts gave their disputed rulings without any theoretical discussion, and therefore any value judgments, as to the applicant's conceptions and ideological practices (see *FL*, cited above, and contrast *Hoffman*, cited above, § 33, and *Palau-Martinez*, cited above, §§ 37 *et seq*.). In reality, those rulings were based on the children's best interests, taking into account their reactions to the lifestyles of both their parents, in conformity with the Court's case law, which has been inspired in particular by Article 3 of the United Nations Convention on the Rights of the Child (see, among other authorities, *Nuutinen v. Finland*, no. 32842/96, ECHR 2000-VIII).

In view of the foregoing, the order stipulating that the children should habitually reside with their father, and granting the mother a right of visiting and staying in contact, cannot be regarded as a difference in the treatment of the two parents on the ground of the applicant's religion.

It follows that this complaint is manifestly ill-founded and must be rejected in accordance with Article 35 §§ 3 and 4 of the Convention. Similarly, the complaint under Article 8 of the Convention, taken separately, is manifestly ill-founded, as the interference with the applicant's right to respect for her family life was not disproportionate in relation to the rights of others, within the meaning of paragraph 2 of that Article.

8

Mainstreaming religious diversity in a secular and egalitarian State: the road(s) not taken in Leyla Şahin v. Turkey

PIERRE BOSSET

Introduction

Just as it is, by definition and necessity, a matter of belief, religious freedom can be a matter of symbols, observance and rituals. Accordingly, the European Convention on Human Rights guarantees the right to manifest one's religion or beliefs in practice and observance, subject to the normal requirements of public safety, the protection of public order, health or morals, or the protection of the rights and freedoms of others.[1] International human rights law now accepts that such customs as 'the wearing of distinctive clothing or headcoverings'[2] are protected by freedom of religion. However, in recent years, a growing number of European and other Western countries have restricted the wearing of religious clothing in the public sphere.[3] The notion of a public sphere is inherently vague: some bans on religious clothing apply only within specific institutions, such as public schools;[4] others extend beyond, to what people may wear on the street.[5] The justifications invoked in support of such measures are

[1] European Convention for the Protection of Human Rights and Fundamental Freedoms, 4 November 1950, ETS No. 5, Article 9.

[2] United Nations Human Rights Committee, General Comment No. 22: The Right to Freedom of Thought, Conscience and Religion, CCPR/C/21/Rev.1/Add.4, 30 July 1993, para. 4.

[3] For an overview, see Laura Barnett, 'Freedom of Religion and Religious Symbols in the Public Sphere: Background Paper' (Ottawa: Library of Parliament, Publication No. 2011-60-E, 25 July 2011).

[4] See, for example, the French law on signs or clothes expressing a specific religious identity, Loi encadrant, en application du principe de laïcité, le port de signes ou de tenues manifestant une appartenance religieuse dans les écoles, collèges et lycées publics (France), *Journal officiel*, 17 March 2004.

[5] For prohibitions of full facial veils in public, Loi interdisant la dissimulation du visage dans l'espace public (France), *Journal officiel*, 12 October 2010; Loi visant à interdire le port de tout vêtement cachant totalement ou de manière principale le visage (Belgium), *Moniteur belge*, 13 July 2011. Similar bans are in force or are being contemplated in other countries, sometimes at a local level. See Laura Barnett, 'Freedom of Religion and Religious Symbols in the Public Sphere: Background Paper' (Ottawa: Library of Parliament, Publication No. 2011-60-E, 25 July 2011), pp. 8–11.

equally varied: it is not always clear whether such restrictions respond to concerns for gender equality, human dignity, public safety, secularism, or some combination thereof.[6] Such variants and ambiguities in national practice suggest there is a need for guidance from international human rights law.

In *Leyla Şahin v. Turkey*,[7] the European Court of Human Rights had an opportunity to set European standards in the matter of regulating the wearing of religious symbols in universities. The case also had the potential to provide national authorities and courts with detailed guidelines that might inform their choices and decisions concerning permissible and impermissible restrictions on the wearing of religious clothing in the 'public sphere'. For reasons discussed here, however, the Court took a general and abstract approach to the subject that now predetermines the outcome of similar cases and precludes any alternative reading of the substantive issues involved.

The facts and the judgment

The applicant, Ms Leyla Şahin, a fifth-year medical student, had been denied access to lectures, examinations and enrolment in a Turkish university, and was eventually suspended, because she was wearing a *hidjab* (veil or headscarf).[8] The Turkish administrative courts ruled that those measures could not be considered contrary to the Convention, since they had a statutory basis and complied with settled Turkish constitutional case law, according to which, in institutions of higher education, it was 'contrary to the principles of secularism and equality for the neck and hair to be covered with a veil or headscarf on grounds of religious conviction'.[9]

Ms Şahin filed an application before the European Court of Human Rights. A chamber found that the university regulations had interfered with Ms Şahin's right to manifest her religion.[10] However, the chamber went on to find that the interference was prescribed by law and pursued two of the legitimate aims set out in the second paragraph of Article 9 of the Convention, i.e. protecting the

---

[6] For example, the justifications invoked in support of the French ban on full facial veils constantly shifted between those elements until it was finally made clear by the Conseil d'Etat that a ban could only be justified on grounds of public safety: Conseil d'Etat, *Etude relative aux possibilités juridiques d'interdiction du port du voile intégral*, 25 March 2010.

[7] *Leyla Şahin v. Turkey* (GC), no. 44774/98, ECHR 2005-XI.

[8] A *hidjab* is a square scarf worn by women that covers the head and neck but leaves the face clear. It is different from the *niqab*, which covers the face but leaves the area around the eyes clear. It is also different from the *burqa*, which covers the entire face and body, leaving just a mesh screen to see through. For a useful visual representation of various types of female clothing often associated with Islam, see www.bbc.co.uk/news/world-europe-13038095.

[9] Turkish Constitutional Court, Judgment of 9 April 1991, *Official Gazette*, 31 July 1991 (translation); quoted in *Şahin*, at para. 41.

[10] *Leyla Şahin v. Turkey* (4th Chamber), 29 June 2004, paras. 66–116 (hereinafter the 'Chamber judgment').

rights and freedoms of others and protecting public order. Furthermore, the interference was justified in principle and proportionate to the aims pursued and could therefore be regarded as having been necessary in a democratic society.

Ms Şahin requested that the case be referred to a Grand Chamber, whose judgment will be discussed here. The Court dismissed Ms Şahin's claim that her freedom of religion guaranteed by Article 9 had been violated. An interference with freedom of religion was acknowledged, but, in view of the State's margin of appreciation and the principle of secularism enshrined in Turkey's constitution, the Court was of the opinion that the interference was justified in principle and proportionate to the aim pursued. Claims based on Article 8 (respect for private life), Article 10 (freedom of expression) and Article 14 of the Convention (non-discrimination) were also rejected by the Court, and so was Ms Şahin's claim based on Article 2 of Protocol 1 (the right to education).

Why Şahin?

The reasoning of the Court in *Şahin* is highly relevant to issues involving religious minorities, despite the fact that Ms Şahin, a Muslim 'in a country in which the majority of the population ... adhere to the Islamic faith',[11] clearly did not belong to a minority. *Şahin* has significantly influenced the outcome of other cases involving religious freedom and religious equality, including those where the alleged victim belonged to a religious minority.

The Court's case law concerning restrictions on religious clothing in public education, until *Şahin*, discussed admissibility issues and, therefore, did not directly address the merits of the cases.[12] In *Dahlab v. Switzerland*, decided four years before *Şahin*, the Court had declared that an application brought by a primary school teacher who had been sacked for wearing a headscarf was 'manifestly ill-founded'.[13] The applicant had taught for several years with a headscarf, without any complaint. Still, invoking the tender age of the children involved, who were between four and eight years old, the Court stated it could 'not be denied outright that the wearing of a headscarf might have some kind of

---

[11] *Ibid.*, para. 108.
[12] Isabelle Rorive, 'Religious Symbols in the Public Space: In Search of a European Answer' (2009) 30 *Cardozo Law Review* 2669 at 2678–80. See e.g. *Karaduman v. Turkey*, 74 DR 93 (1993), where the then European Commission of Human Rights, ruling on admissibility, had found that a university regulation prohibiting Muslim students from wearing a headscarf on identity cards did not reveal any interference with the right to manifest one's religion. The Commission considered that students who chose to study in a secular university had to abide by university regulations. Later, the Court would consider such cases admissible, although the interferences would be regarded as having been prescribed by law (see e.g. *Dogru v. France* (5th Chamber), no. 27058/05, 4 March 2009).
[13] *Dahlab v. Switzerland* (2nd Chamber), no. 42393/98, ECHR 2001-V.

proselytizing effect'. Without discussion or qualification, the Court also quoted the Swiss court's opinion that the headscarf was difficult to reconcile with the principle of gender equality. The case has been criticised for giving only cursory attention to a complex and sensitive issue.[14]

Having declared the case admissible, the Court in Şahin might have expanded on its reasons for apparently distrusting the headscarf. Instead, however, deferring to the State's national margin of appreciation, the Court turned the case into an abstract examination of the conformity of the principle of secularism with the values underpinning the Convention. The Court equated wearing the headscarf with a negation of secularism, a constitutional principle to be found in a number of European legal systems. The Court also equated wearing the headscarf with an alienation of women, a subject of concern for all members of the Council of Europe given that the advancement of the equality of the sexes is, by common agreement, a major goal for Member States.[15] Conflating secularism with gender equality, the Court wrote that secularism was so closely related to gender equality that it would be 'contrary to such [a] value'[16] to allow religious attire to be worn in institutions of higher education.

Şahin's impact on cases involving secularism has been momentous, and the case has truly been described as 'emblematic' and one of the cornerstones of the Court's jurisprudence on religious freedom in the public space.[17] In Kurtulmus v. Turkey, an admissibility case, the Court relied on the importance of secularism as expounded in Şahin and on Turkey's margin of appreciation in order to reject an application by a civil servant. The applicant, a university lecturer, had been sanctioned, and then fired for wearing a headscarf. The Court noted that upholding the principle of secularism was 'undoubtedly one of the fundamental principles of the Turkish State' and found that Turkey's decision to ban the wearing of headscarves by university lecturers (as opposed to the prohibition aimed at primary school teachers in Dahlab) fell within that State's margin of appreciation.[18] In Kervanci v. France, a chamber of the Court, quoting Şahin no less than nine times, found no violation of Article 9 in the fact that the applicant, a pupil in a French public school, had been expelled for wearing a headscarf in a gymnastics class. While ostentatiously relying on the French national margin of appreciation, the Chamber drew broad parallels with other secular countries. 'In France, as in Turkey or Switzerland', the chamber wrote, 'secularism [laïcité] is a constitutional principle that is supported by the whole

---

[14] See Carolyn Evans, 'The "Islamic Scarf" in the European Court of Human Rights' (2006) 7 Melbourne Law Journal 52.
[15] See Abdulaziz, Cabales and Balkandali v. United Kingdom, 28 May 1985, Series A no. 94, para. 78.
[16] Şahin, para. 116.
[17] Isabelle Rorive, 'Religious Symbols in the Public Space: In Search of a European Answer' (2009) 30 Cardozo Law Review 2669 at 2677–8 and 2680.
[18] Kurtulmus v. Turkey, no. 65500/01, 24 January 2006 (admissibility).

population, and its protection is of paramount importance.'[19] More
recently, the Court, in upholding the expulsion of a boy from a French
public school pursuant to the 2004 law forbidding religious clothing in
schools, saw 'no reason' to depart from the line of reasoning followed in
Şahin. The applicant, a fourteen-year-old Sikh pupil, had been expelled for
wearing a small and unobtrusive turban, known as a keski. Although,
compared with the ban in Kervanci, the interference applied to all school
activities, the Court contented itself with a finding that the ban was 'solely
motivated by the [aim of] safeguarding of the constitutional principle of
secularism'.[20]

Redrafting Şahin

In redrafting Şahin, my purpose is not to second-guess, let alone overrule, the
Court, but to introduce alternative approaches and concepts that might inform
the Court's reasoning in cases where religious freedom is involved. My concern
is not whether the actual outcome of Şahin was 'right', but whether it was
'rightly decided', i.e. with what I would consider to be a more substantial regard
for mainstreaming religious diversity. For the sake of redrafting the judgment, I
conveniently assumed that the facts of the Şahin case occurred today and,
therefore, within today's legal background. Thus, I had the luxury of considering recent post-Şahin developments. They include: Turkey's ratification of the
International Covenant on Civil and Political Rights,[21] the adoption of a
general comment on gender equality by the UN Committee on Economic,
Social and Cultural Rights,[22] and the examination of Turkey's latest periodic
report under the International Convention on the Elimination of All Forms of
Discrimination against Women.[23]

My redrafting of Şahin is based, first, on considerations that are relevant to the
European Convention as a whole: first, the necessity of ensuring harmony with
the rest of international human rights law; and, second, avoiding abstract issues
when examining cases. Then I add two considerations that are specifically

---

[19] Kervanci v. France, no. 31645/04, 4 December 2008, para. 72 (author's translation).

[20] Jasvir Singh v. France, no. 25463/08, 30 June 2009 (author's translation).

[21] International Covenant on Civil and Political Rights, 999 UNTS 171, ratified by Turkey on
23 September 2003 (i.e. after the facts in Şahin).

[22] International Covenant on Economic, Social and Cultural Rights, 993 UNTS 3, ratified by
Turkey on 23 September 2003. See United Nations Committee on Economic, Social and
Cultural Rights, General Comment No. 16: The Equal Right of Men and Women to the
Enjoyment of All Economic, Social and Cultural Rights, E/C.12/2005/4, 11 August 2005.

[23] International Convention on the Elimination of All Forms of Discrimination against
Women, 1249 UNTS 13, accession by Turkey on 20 December 1985. For the
examination of Turkey's report, see United Nations Committee on the Elimination of
Discrimination against Women, Concluding Observations (Turkey), CEDAW/C/TUR/
CO/6, 16 August 2010.

relevant to minority issues, namely: the need to accommodate diversity in the formulation and application of public policy; and the need for integrating a proper regard for the concepts of agency and intersectionality when examining complex issues of freedom and equality, such as those raised in *Şahin*.

Ensuring harmony with the rest of international human rights law

Ensuring harmony between the Convention and the rest of international human rights law has been an underlying concern throughout my redrafting. As a matter of principle, the Convention, as the Court stated in *Al-Adsani* v. *United Kingdom*,[24] should be interpreted 'in harmony with other rules of international law of which it forms part'.[25] In that case, the Court recognised that the Convention had to be interpreted in light of the rules set out in the Vienna Convention on the Law of Treaties,[26] of which Article 31(3)(c) indicates that account is to be taken of 'any relevant rules of international law applicable in the relations between the parties'. The Convention, therefore, should not be interpreted in a vacuum, especially considering that Article 53 provides that the Convention shall not be construed as limiting or derogating from any of the human rights and fundamental freedoms which may be ensured under any other relevant international agreement. This, in my mind, must be read as an invitation to the Court to take into account the protection that is being given to rights in other international human rights systems. In particular, the interpretation given to freedom of religion in the UN human rights system is a relevant factor in the interpretation of Article 9.

Throughout my redrafting, I tried to emphasise the desirability of ensuring harmony with the rest of international human rights law, especially UN law. This will not necessarily lead to radical departures from the Court's actual reasoning. For example, my references to UN law at paragraph 105 (the outward manifestations of freedom of religion) only add supplementary authorities to the already well-documented original judgment. At other times, however, the impact of referring to UN law can be more consequential. See, in particular, the new passages on proportionality (at paragraphs 125–35). In those passages, referring to UN law clearly induces, in my opinion, a different approach to proportionality, based on accommodating diversity and on the interdependence of rights.[27]

Avoiding abstract issues

Avoiding abstract issues was a second general consideration. In *Şahin*, the Court considered the notion of secularism, as elaborated by Turkey's

---

[24] *Al-Adsani* v. *United Kingdom* (GC), no. 35763/97, ECHR 2001-XI.   [25] *Ibid.*, para. 55.

[26] *Ibid.* See Vienna Convention on the Law of Treaties, 1155 UNTS 331.

[27] See below.

Constitutional Court, to be consistent with the values underpinning the Convention:

> [T]he Constitutional Court stated that secularism in Turkey was, among other things, the guarantor of democratic values, the principle that freedom of religion is inviolable – to the extent that it stems from individual conscience – and the principle that citizens are equal before the law. Secularism also protected the individual from external pressure. It added that restrictions could be placed on freedom to manifest one's religion in order to defend those values and principles.
>
> This notion of secularism appears to the [chamber] to be consistent with the values underpinning the Convention and it accepts that upholding that principle may be regarded as necessary for the protection of the democratic system in Turkey.[28]

With respect, there would be other ways of putting the issue before the Court. As a principle, secularism (*laïcité*) can be understood as separating the State from religions, so that each remains autonomous *vis-à-vis* the other in order to preserve freedom of conscience and religion. However, when implemented in specific national and historical contexts, the principle of secularism necessarily takes on various forms. Baubérot and Milot have identified no less than six ideal types of secularism, ranging from strict separation between the public sphere and the private sphere to an arrangement that accepts a measure of institutional cooperation between public and religious authorities; other ideal types may range from militant, anti-religious secularism to a recognition of the moral autonomy of individuals, consistent with the modern guarantee of human rights.[29] By turning the case into an abstract examination of the conformity of the 'principle' of secularism with the 'values' of the Convention (bowing to the State's margin of appreciation in the process), the Court in *Şahin* ignored the complexities of secularism and curbed its own autonomy in future cases, in which secularism will be pitted against freedom of religion. In fact, once it is accepted that the issue is whether the *principle* of secularism is consistent with the values of the Convention, the risk is that any measure taken *in the name* of secularism and which does not exceed a State's margin of appreciation will be considered as complying with the Convention. Thus, in *Şahin*, the Court apparently assumed that secularism must be understood as imposing obligations on the recipients of public services – a conception which, in view of its implications, would normally have deserved further explanation and

---

[28] *Şahin*, para. 114, quoting from the Chamber judgment at paras. 105–6.
[29] Jean Baubérot and Micheline Milot, *Laïcités sans frontières* (Paris: Seuil, 2011), Chapter III. As elucidated by Milot, the pillars of secularism are respect for the fundamental freedoms of conscience and religion and the equal treatment of citizens, the separation of Church and State, and the neutrality of the State *vis-à-vis* religions: Micheline Milot, *La laïcité* (Montreal: Novalis, 2008), pp. 17–21.

developments. Similarly, later cases, such as *Kurtulmus*, apparently ignore conceptions of secularism that may accept forms of religious expression by civil servants who deal with mature adults (e.g. university lecturers) or whose duties do not involve personal contact with the public.[30]

Two reasons explain why the issue faced by the Court in *Şahin* was not the conformity of the 'principle' of secularism with the 'values' underpinning the Convention (paragraph 114). First, if framed this way, the issue takes on a level of generality and abstraction that requires the Court to depart from its judicial role and act as political philosopher. Looking in such an abstract and *a priori* way at the issues raised in a case like *Şahin* is a rather peculiar approach to the Court's duty as guardian of the Convention. It seems difficult to reconcile such an approach with one of the central concerns underlying the Convention, which is to guarantee not rights that are theoretical or illusory 'but rights that are practical and effective'.[31] In addition, reasoning in such general terms ties the hands of the Court for eventual cases where the principle of secularism will be invoked in order to justify interferences on freedom of religion. In *Kervanci*,[32] for example, the Court contented itself with a general statement on the compatibility of the principle of secularism with the Convention: a fine statement perhaps, but one which clearly did not address the issue of whether and how the exclusion was actually justified, in that case, by safety or hygiene concerns, as was contended by the State.

Regarding the margin of appreciation, the case law of the Court makes it abundantly clear that religion and morals are, generally speaking, matters where no standard European conception exists, therefore justifying the existence of a national margin of appreciation.[33] The scope of that margin, however, is a crucial issue, and defining that scope is largely a matter of perspective. In *Şahin*, the Court, using comparative law, explained the wide margin of appreciation it was prepared to leave Turkey by the fact that European national laws on the wearing of religious symbols in the broad category of teaching institutions vary.[34] Eventually, however, the Court found that in only three European States (Turkey, Azerbaijan and Albania) was the wearing of religious

---

[30] In Canada, such a conception of secularism, as far as civil servants are concerned, has been proposed by the Consultation Commission on Accommodation Practices Related to Cultural Differences, set up in 2007 by the Premier of Quebec. See *Building the Future: A Time for Reconciliation* (Montreal, 2008), pp. 149–51. It recommended that civil servants be allowed to wear religious signs, except for judges, police officers and prison guards, who exert a coercive power on behalf of the State.

[31] *Airey* v. *Ireland*, 9 October 1979, Series A no. 41, para. 24.

[32] *Kervanci* v. *France*, no. 31645/04, 4 December 2008.

[33] E.g. *Otto-Preminger-Institut* v. *Austria*, 20 September 1994, Series A no. 295-A, para. 50; *Handyside* v. *United Kingdom*, 7 December 1976, Series A no. 24; *Evans* v. *United Kingdom* (GC), no. 6339/05, ECHR 2007-I.

[34] *Şahin*, paras. 55–65. The use of comparative law in *Şahin* was more substantial than in the Chamber's judgment, which commentators had criticised as being superficial. See

symbols banned in universities. In fact, as far as universities were concerned, non-regulation was the European standard, which should have significantly reduced the extent of Turkey's national margin of appreciation in Şahin.[35] Instead, the Court apparently allowed the doctrine of the margin of appreciation to obscure its role as ultimate interpreter and guarantor of the principles of the Convention. The Court's task in this case should have called for an *in concreto* examination, in light of the principles of the Convention, of the facts and circumstances that gave rise to interference on a protected right.[36] In her impressive dissenting opinion in Şahin, Judge Tulkens adopted that approach. Rightly, in my view, she took a sceptical view of arguments based purely on the *principle* of secularism. An intellectually more satisfying approach would have discussed the various possible meanings of secularism and questioned the application of that principle by the Turkish authorities, in line with the requirement of proportionality which is a crucial part of the Court's approach to violations of Convention rights. I have integrated the sceptic's approach in my redrafting (see paragraphs 117–20).

Proportionality may require accommodation

Applying the requirement of proportionality in cases like Şahin may require the Court to look into the possibility of individually accommodating the beliefs of an applicant. In several cases, particularly ones concerning freedom of religion under Article 9, alone or in combination with Article 14 (non-discrimination), the Court (and before it the Commission) have taken the position that if a law or regulation with an objective and legitimate purpose nevertheless restricts the liberty of certain individuals and that changes to it would avoid such interference without undermining this lawful aim, then this option should be chosen.[37] In other words, the least restrictive means should be adopted. The least restrictive alternative approach is somewhat similar to the arguments sometimes put forward by Canadian and US courts when they apply the concept of reasonable accommodation, a concept which North American courts consider as a corollary

Emmanuelle Bribosia and Isabelle Rorive, 'Le voile à l'école: une Europe divisée' (2004) 60 *Revue trimestrielle des droits de l'homme* 960.

[35] Şahin, Dissenting Opinion of Judge Tulkens, para. 3. This was also pointed out by Dominic McGoldrick, *Human Rights and Religion: The Islamic Headscarf Debate in Europe* (London: Hart, 2006), p. 168. See also Isabelle Rorive, 'Religious Symbols in the Public Space: In Search of a European Answer' (2009) 30 *Cardozo Law Review* 2669 at 2682.

[36] See *Bosphorus Hava Yollari Turizmve Ticaret Anonim Sirketi* v. *Ireland* (GC), no. 45036/98, ECHR 2005-VI, Joint Concurring Opinion, para. 2.

[37] This section draws from Pierre Bosset and Marie-Claire Foblets, 'Accommodating Diversity in Quebec and Europe: Different Legal Concepts, Similar Results?', in *Institutional Accommodation and the Citizen: Legal and Political Interaction in a Pluralist Society* (Strasbourg: Council of Europe, Trends in Social Cohesion No. 21), p. 37 at pp. 61–2. See e.g. *Thlimmenos* v. *Greece* (GC), 6 April 2000, no. 34369/97, ECHR 2000-IV; or *Glor* v. *Switzerland*, 30 April 2009, no. 13444/04.

of equality.[38] In some ways, proportionality and the least restrictive alternative approach play a role similar to that of reasonable accommodation when determining the compatibility with the Convention of restricting one's liberty.[39]

Conceptual differences continue to exist between European Convention law and its North American counterparts.[40] Thus, while the European Court of Human Rights has recognised the notion of indirect discrimination,[41] so far it falls short of recognising a corollary duty to accommodate individual differences. In practice, the Court appears to adopt a much more cautious approach than the North American courts to States' commitments and responsibilities with regard to equal treatment. The Supreme Court of Canada, for example, has not hesitated on a number of occasions to infer from a specific case that a reasonable accommodation would help to avoid differential treatment and that the competent authorities had a duty to remedy the situation by altering the relevant rule or standard. For example, in *Multani v. Commission scolaire Marguerite-Bourgeoys*, a Sikh boy was allowed to wear a *kirpan* at school, provided that basic security safeguards were observed.[42] The Canadian Court stressed that the limit imposed on freedom of religion in that case (a prohibition on the *kirpan*) was not proportionate to the aim pursued (ensuring safety), since an individual accommodation was available and, based on the evidence, would not have compromised the objective. In other cases, the Canadian Court went so far as to impose a duty to consider alternative approaches when actually drawing up standards, so that individuals do not have to bear the burden of asking for adjustments or exemptions.[43] The case law of the European Court reveals a much more cautious position, with States being given (as seen above) a considerable margin of appreciation, especially in religious matters.

---

[38] See *Ontario Human Rights Commission and O'Malley* v. *Simpsons-Sears* [1985] 2 SCR 536 at 554. José Woehrling, 'L'obligation d'accommodement raisonnable et l'adaptation de la société canadienne à la diversité religieuse' (1998) 43 *McGill Law Journal* 325–401.

[39] Eva Brems, 'The Margin of Appreciation Doctrine of the European Court of Human Rights: Accommodating Diversity within Europe', in David P. Forsythe and Patrice C. McMahon (eds.), *Human Rights and Diversity: Area Studies Revisited* (Lincoln, NE, and London: University of Nebraska Press, 2003), pp. 81–110.

[40] For an instructive comparative analysis, see Emmanuelle Bribosia, Julie Ringelheim and Isabelle Rorive, 'Aménager la diversité: le droit de l'égalité face à la pluralité religieuse' (2009) *Revue trimestrielle des droits de l'homme* 319. Frédéric Mégret argues that the Canadian approach complies with the 'spirit of international human rights law': F. Mégret, 'Le Canada à la pointe de la tolérance? L'accommodement raisonnable à l'aune du droit international des droits de la personne', in J.-F. Gaudreault-Des Biens (ed.), *Le droit, la religion et le 'raisonnable'* (Montréal: Thémis, 2009), pp. 263–302.

[41] E.g. *Zarb Adami* v. *Malta*, 20 June 2006, no. 17209/02, ECHR 2006-VIII (jury duty having a disproportionate impact on men).

[42] *Multani* v. *Commission scolaire Marguerite-Bourgeoys* [2006] 1 SCR 256.

[43] *British Columbia (Superintendent of Motor Vehicles)* v. *British Columbia (Council of Human Rights)* [1999] 3 SCR 868. However, see *Alberta* v. *Hutterian Brethren of Wilson Colony* [2009] 2 SCR 5567 (no duty to accommodate within legislation).

However, a general obligation to design public policy so as to mitigate its impact on fundamental rights may now be emerging in international human rights law. This obligation may exist quite independently from the doctrine of reasonable accommodation elaborated specifically under North American anti-discrimination legislation.[44] Empirical evidence of the trend in the specific area of headscarf bans may be found in the following recent developments:

- The UN Committee on the Rights of the Child has invited France, a State Party to the Convention on the Rights of the Child (UNTS, vol. 1577, p. 3, ratified by Turkey on 4 April 1995), to closely monitor the situation of girl pupils who might be expelled from public schools for not complying with a law that prohibits the wearing of conspicuous religious symbols in public schools. The Committee expressed its concern at the possible impact of the law on the possibility for those girls of having access to education. The State Party was recommended 'to consider alternative means, including mediation, of ensuring [the] secular character of public schools, while guaranteeing that individual rights are not infringed upon and that children are not excluded or marginalized from the school system and other settings'.[45]
- The UN Committee on Economic, Social and Cultural Rights, established to monitor the implementation of the International Covenant on Economic, Social and Cultural Rights (UNTS, vol. 993, p. 3, ratified by Turkey on 23 September 2003), has emphasized the obligation of States 'to develop monitoring mechanisms to ensure that the implementation of laws and policies aimed at promoting the equal enjoyment of economic, social and cultural rights by men and women do not have unintended adverse effects on disadvantaged or marginalized individuals or groups, particularly women and girls'.[46]
- In examining Turkey's latest periodic report under the International Convention on the Elimination of All Forms of Discrimination Against Women (UNTS, vol. 1249, p. 13, accession by Turkey on 20 December 1985), the UN Committee on the Elimination of Discrimination Against

---

[44] Principle 13 of the Declaration of Principles on Equality, sponsored by the Equal Rights Trust (see www.equalrightstrust.org) (2008). The Principles are said to be based 'on concepts and jurisprudence developed in international, regional and national legal contexts ... They might serve as a compass to orient legislative, judicial and policy efforts towards a more progressive set of equality norms and policies in the 21st century.' On 25 November 2011, the Standing Committee of the Parliamentary Assembly of the Council of Europe (PACE) adopted a Resolution and a Recommendation, welcoming and endorsing the Declaration.

[45] UN Committee on the Rights of the Child, 'Consideration of Reports Submitted by States Parties under Article 44 of the Convention (France)', CRC/C/15/Add.240, 30 June 2004, paras. 25–6.

[46] UN Committee on Economic, Social and Cultural Rights, General Comment No. 16: The Equal Right of Men and Women to the Enjoyment of All Economic, Social and Cultural Rights, E/C.12/2005/4, 11 August 2005, para. 21.

Women reiterated 'its concern about the absence of information and statistical data on the impact of the ban on the use of headscarves in the areas of education, employment, health and political and public life, such as the number of women excluded from schools and universities'. The Committee recommended Turkey 'to undertake studies to evaluate the impact of the ban on wearing headscarves in the fields of education, employment, health and political and public life, and to include detailed information regarding the result of the study and measures taken to eliminate any discriminatory consequences of the ban in its next periodic report'.[47]

The Court's discussion of proportionality in *Şahin* was influenced by Turkey's margin of appreciation and did not attempt to balance the competing interests of Ms Şahin and the State Party. I tried to fill in the gap by including the foregoing developments in my analysis of the proportionality test (paragraph 135). In particular, I took a critical look at the process of 'dialogue' that had been followed by the university authorities in *Şahin*. In my opinion, trying as they did to convince students of the merits of the ban on headdress did not change in any significant way the nature and severity of the interference on freedom of religion inherent in banning Ms Şahin's headscarf, considering that Ms Şahin was eventually barred from lectures, examinations and enrolment and even had to move abroad to continue her studies. While Ms Şahin apparently professed sincere faith in the principle of secularism, acknowledged that limitations on the right to wear a headscarf were possible and did not wear her headscarf in a provocative or proselytising way, no attempts were made to accommodate her, for example, by applying the ban only in cases where wearing a headscarf would exert pressure on others, or would provoke a reaction from others. The proportionality aspect was also problematic in view of its impact on Ms Şahin's right to education. The Court treated an eventual violation of the right to education (Article 2 of Protocol 1) as a separate issue from the alleged interference with freedom of religion. As I have pointed out in my redrafting (paragraph 108), balancing fundamental rights – a necessity in any democratic society, as the Court rightly wrote[48] – should take place bearing in mind that international human rights law now emphasises the interdependence of rights, whether civil and political or economic, social and cultural.[49]

---

[47] UN Committee on the Elimination of Discrimination against Women, Concluding Observations (Turkey), CEDAW/C/TUR/CO/6, 16 August 2010, paras. 16–17.

[48] *Ibid.*, para. 108.

[49] See World Conference on Human Rights, Vienna Declaration and Programme of Action, A/CONF.157/23, 12 July 1993, para. 5.

Agency and intersectionality

Şahin's view of the relationship between gender equality and the headscarf is rather straightforward: the latter is incompatible with the former. In future cases, concepts such as agency and intersectionality might, however, allow the Court to acknowledge and consider the complexity of issues of equality and religious freedom involved in cases such as *Şahin*.

Just as wearing the headscarf was equated with political extremism by the Court when discussing secularism,[50] it was equated in *Şahin* with the alienation of women when discussing equality. The Court indicated that limitations on wearing the headscarf may be regarded as meeting a pressing social need in a country in which the majority of the population adhere to the Islamic faith.[51] Thus, secularism and gender equality were inextricably linked. '[W]here the values of pluralism, respect for the rights of others and, in particular, equality before the law of men and women are being taught and applied in practice', the Court wrote, 'it is understandable that the relevant authorities should wish to preserve the secular nature of the institution concerned.'[52]

Yet, in view of the diverse social meanings and possible uses of the headscarf, discussing the relationship between gender equality and wearing a headscarf requires considerable caution. In contrast with the black-and-white world of concepts, gender and religion, in the real world, will often meet in flesh-and-blood individuals, thereby raising crucial issues for human rights: 'veiled women' are archetypal examples. In *Şahin* (as in *Dahlab*), the Court assumed that the headscarf is a symbol that goes against equality of men and women. But looking at the experience of women themselves, and hearing their voices, might warrant a different approach. A significant body of social science literature, from within critical or post-colonial feminist perspectives, suggests that wearing a headscarf cannot and should not automatically be equated with a symbol or instrument of the oppression of women. For example, wearing a headscarf may be an expression of legitimate personal piety and/or cultural identity; it may be a symbolic, ironic and even subversive challenge to the sexual exploitation of women's bodies; or, quite simply, and more prosaically, it may serve as a vehicle for interaction between women and the rest of society, thus facilitating Muslim women's participation and empowerment.[53] In discussing the

---

[50] *Şahin*, para. 115. This was uncharitable to Ms Şahin, who challenged neither the principle of secularism nor Turkey's constitutional order.

[51] *Ibid.*   [52] *Ibid.*, para. 116.

[53] See e.g. Homa Hoodfar, 'More Than Clothing: The Veil as Adaptive Strategy', in S. Alvi, H. Hoodfar and S. McDonough (eds.), *The Muslim Veil in North America* (Toronto: Women's Press, 2003), pp. 3–40. For critical appraisals of 'Western' views of 'veiled women', see Homa Hoodfar, 'The Veil in Their Minds and on Our Heads: The Persistence of Colonial Images of Muslim Women', *Resources for Feminist Research*, Winter 1993, pp. 3–10; or Lama Abu-Odeh, 'Post-Colonial Feminism and the Veil:

relationship between the headscarf and gender equality, my redrafting (paragraph 122) attempts to account for the multi-layered meaning(s) of the headscarf.

In view of the emphasis the Court puts on gender equality, it is regrettable, moreover, that the issue of discrimination was apparently 'underpleaded' by the parties during the proceedings and was given such short change in Şahin. The Court summarily stated that the reasons for validating the interference on the applicant's freedom of religion also applied to a possible violation of Article 14, apparently considering that only religious discrimination was involved in Ms Şahin's application. Here again, this may be over-simplifying reality. Discrimination can also be the result of a synergy between mutually reinforcing social markers – in this case, gender *and* religion. Thus, the experience of discrimination suffered by minority women will often differ, not only from discrimination suffered by men of the same minority, but from the experience of discrimination suffered by women in general.[54] When analysing 'headscarf issues', it is necessary to recognise that a headscarf ban can be discriminatory both from the perspective of veiled women versus non-veiled women (whose religious practices remain unaffected) *and* veiled women versus Muslim men (who are similarly unaffected). In the future, as a judicial organ whose role is to interpret the Convention as a 'living instrument'[55] and 'in the light of present-day conditions',[56] the Court should not ignore the modern insights into gender equality offered by intersectional approaches (paragraph 165).[57]

Considering the Differences' (1992) 26 *New England Law Review* 1527. For self-perceptions by women wearing a *hidjab*, see Ismahane Chouder, Malika Latrèche and Pierre Tevanian, *Les filles voilées parlent* (Paris: La Fabrique, 2008); or Farhad Khosrokhavar, *Le foulard et la République* (Paris: La Découverte, 1995).

[54] To put it bluntly, '[c]ategorizing such discrimination as primarily racially oriented, or primarily gender-oriented, misconceives the reality of discrimination as it is experienced by individuals': *Canada (Attorney General)* v. *Mossop* [1993] 1 SCR 554 at 645–6 (L'Heureux-Dubé J, Supreme Court of Canada). Thus, disregarding the specific character of the exclusion of minority women can be exclusionary: Carol Smart, 'The Woman of Legal Discourse' (1992) 1 *Social and Legal Studies* 29 at 30 ('to invoke an unproblematic category of Woman, while presuming that this represents all women, is an exclusionary strategy'). On the necessity of integrating such an approach into human rights theory, see Colleen Sheppard, 'Grounds of Discrimination: Towards an Inclusive and Contextual Approach', in *Les 25 ans de la Charte québécoise* (Cowansville: Yvon Blais, 2000), pp. 112–16.

[55] *Tyrer* v. *United Kingdom*, 25 April 1978, Series A no. 26, para. 31.

[56] *Marckx* v. *Belgium*, 13 June 1979, Series A no. 31, para. 58.

[57] Intersectionality is a methodology of studying 'the relationships among multiple dimensions and modalities of social relationships and subject formations': Leslie McCall, 'The Complexity of Intersectionality' (2005) 30 *Journal of Women in Culture and Society*

Finally, taking 'multiple identities' seriously, under an intersectional approach, would be consistent with a strand in the Court's case law, according to which there is a right to personal autonomy (or self-determination) inherent in certain provisions of the Convention.[58] Thus, in *Pretty* v. *United Kingdom*, the Court accepted that, under Article 8, the right to respect for private life protects individuals against treatments that would conflict with strongly held ideas of self and identity. The Court stated that the notion of personal autonomy was an important principle underlying the interpretation of the guarantees of Article 8.[59] Similar cases under the same Article also suggest an entitlement of individuals to live lives of their own choosing and to have their own identity.[60] In adopting this approach under Article 8, the Court is an intellectual heir to a philosophical and sociological tradition that emphasises the agency of individual actors, i.e. the capacity for willed or voluntary action, as opposed to the determinism of social structures.[61] The concept of agency would be a useful tool for dealing not only with cases under Article 8, but also cases where religious freedom is at stake and the free will of the individuals concerned is put in doubt (paragraph 123).[62] Certainly, wearing a headscarf for religious reasons, to borrow the Court's words in *Pretty*, reflects an individual's strongly held ideas of self and identity. Ms Şahin's determination to fight her way up to the European Court of Human Rights in Strasbourg was eloquent testimony to this. Transposed in the future to cases such as *Şahin*, involving religious freedom, an assumption of agency would not

---

1771–1800. The founding text on intersectionality is often considered to be Kimberlé Crenshaw, 'Mapping the Margins: Intersectionality, Identity Politics, and Violence against Women of Color' (1991) 43 *Stanford Law Review* 1241–99. On intersectionality as part of human rights doctrine, see Ontario Human Rights Commission, *An Intersectional Approach to Discrimination: Addressing Multiple Grounds in Discrimination Claims* (Toronto, 2001).

[58] This is pointed out in Judge Tulkens' admirable dissent in *Şahin* (at para. 12).

[59] *Pretty* v. *United Kingdom*, no. 2346/02, paras. 61 and 65–7, ECHR 2002-III.

[60] See *Dudgeon* v. *United Kingdom*, 22 October 1981, Series A no. 45; *X and Y* v. *Netherlands*, 26 March 1985, Series A no. 91; *Norris* v. *Ireland*, 26 October 1988, Series A no. 142; *Goodwin* v. *United Kingdom* (GC), no. 28957/95, para. 90, ECHR 2002-VI.

[61] Gordon Marshall, 'Agency', *A Dictionary of Sociology* (1998), Encyclopedia.com. 27 November 2011, www.encyclopedia.com. On the application of the concept of agency to Muslim women, stressing a need to 'think about the agency of the veiled woman without binding *a priori* the meaning of her veiling to the teleology of emancipation, whether feminist or anti-imperialist', see Sirma Bilge, 'Beyond Subordination v. Resistance: An Intersectional Approach to the Agency of Veiled Muslim Women' (2010) 31 *Journal of Intercultural Studies* 9–28.

[62] Jill Marshall, 'Conditions for Freedoms? European Human Rights Law and the Islamic Headscarf Debate' (2008) 30 *Human Rights Quarterly* 631–54. The author expands her views on autonomy in *Personal Freedom Through Human Rights Law? Autonomy, Identity and Integrity under the European Convention on Human Rights* (Leiden: Martinus Nijhoff, 2009).

only confirm the recognition of multiple identities underlying the intersectional approaches, it would also improve global coherence within the Court's jurisprudence.

Conclusion

Initially, the impact of the Court's judgment in *Leyla Şahin* v. *Turkey* might have appeared as if it was limited to Turkey's context. The Court noted the historical importance of the principle of secularism in the founding of the Turkish Republic. The judgment emphasises the protection of gender equality in a country where an overwhelming majority of the population is Muslim. And, although no link had been established between such movements and Ms Şahin herself, the Court recalled that 'there are extremist political movements in Turkey which seek to impose on society as a whole their religious symbols and conception of society'.[63] Mention was made of an earlier case, also involving Turkey, where the Court had affirmed a right for each State Party under the Convention to take action against such political movements 'in the light of its historical experience'.[64]

However, the Court's reliance on the 'principle' of secularism, the *a priori* distrust of headscarves and the wide margin of appreciation left to States all suggest that the impression of *Şahin* as contextually limited is misleading. In fact, as seen here, *Şahin*'s influence on later ECHR cases has extended beyond the Turkish context, to secular and egalitarian States with different backgrounds from Turkey's. Because of *Şahin*'s impact, it is regrettable, therefore, that the Court did not address the very substantial issues involved with greater sensitivity.

For better or for worse, the trend in an increasing number of secular and egalitarian countries, not only in Europe but elsewhere, seems to be towards restrictions on the wearing of religious clothing in the public sphere. The permissible extent of such restrictions, as well as the grounds for such measures including the relationship with secularism and gender equality, remain matters of controversy. Although *Şahin* gave the Court's blessing to the measure taken by Turkey against the applicant, the underlying reasoning of the Court was detached from contemporary research and remains intellectually unsatisfying. Given the current trend, the Court will likely be faced again with similar issues in the future. Hopefully, this will provide opportunities for revisiting the highly sensitive issues of equality and religious freedom that are at stake in such cases.

---

[63] *Şahin*, para. 115.

[64] *Refah Partisi (The Welfare Party) and others* v. *Turkey* (GC), 13 February 2003, no. 41340/98, ECHR 2003-II (quoted in *Şahin* at paras. 114–15).

Rewriting Leyla Şahin v. Turkey

. . .

Alleged violation of Article 9 of the Convention

. . .

4. 'Necessary in a democratic society'

. . .

(b) The Court's assessment
(i) General principles
. . .

105. While religious freedom is primarily a matter of individual conscience, it also implies, *inter alia*, freedom to manifest one's religion, alone
and in private, or in community with others, in public and within the circle
of those whose faith one shares. Article 9 lists the various forms which
manifestation of one's religion or belief may take, namely worship, teaching,
practice and observance (see, *mutatis mutandis, Cha'are Shalom Ve Tsedek
v. France* [GC], no. 27417/95, § 73, ECHR 2000-VII). **Freedom to wear
religious clothing is one of the various external manifestations of that
freedom (see United Nations General Assembly, Declaration on the
Elimination of All Forms of Intolerance and Discrimination Based on
Religion or Belief, GA Res. 36/155 (1981), Article 6; UN Human Rights
Committee, General Comment No. 22: The Right to Freedom of
Thought, Conscience and Religion, CCPR/C/Rev.1/Add.4, § 4).**
[Fragment deleted]

. . .

108. Pluralism, tolerance and broadmindedness are hallmarks of a 'democratic society'. Although individual interests must on occasion be subordinated to those of a group, democracy does not simply mean that the views of
a majority must always prevail: a balance must be achieved which ensures
the fair and proper treatment of people from minorities and avoids any
abuse of a dominant position (see, *mutatis mutandis, Young, James and
Webster v. the United Kingdom*, judgment of 13 August 1981, Series A no.
44, p. 25, § 63, and *Chassagnou and others v. France* [GC], nos. 25088/94,
28331/95 and 28443/95, § 112, ECHR 1999-III). Pluralism and democracy
must also be based on dialogue and a spirit of compromise necessarily
entailing various concessions on the part of individuals or groups of individuals which are justified in order to maintain and promote the ideals and
values of a democratic society (see, *mutatis mutandis, the United Communist
Party of Turkey and others*, cited above, pp. 21–22, § 45, and *Refah Partisi*

(the Welfare Party) and others, cited above, § 99). Where these 'rights and freedoms' are themselves among those guaranteed by the Convention or its Protocols, it must be accepted that the need to protect them may lead States to restrict other rights or freedoms likewise set forth in the Convention. It is precisely this constant search for a balance between the fundamental rights of each individual which constitutes the foundation of a 'democratic society' (see *Chassagnou and others*, cited above, § 113). **However, balancing fundamental rights is not an abstract exercise; as far as possible, care must be taken to respect the 'indivisible, interdependent and interrelated' character of all human rights (see World Conference on Human Rights, Vienna Declaration and Programme of Action, A/CONF.157/23, 12 July 1993, § 5).**

109. Where questions concerning the relationship between State and religions are at stake, on which opinion in a democratic society may reasonably differ widely, the role of the national decision-making body must be given special importance (see, *mutatis mutandis, Cha'are Shalom Ve Tsedek*, cited above, § 84, and *Wingrove v. the United Kingdom*, judgment of 25 November 1996, Reports 1996-V, pp. 1957–58, § 58). This will notably be the case when it comes to regulating the wearing of religious symbols in educational institutions, especially (as the comparative-law materials illustrate – see paragraphs 55–65 above) in view of the diversity of the approaches **that may be** taken by national authorities on the issue. **Generally speaking**, it is not possible to discern throughout Europe a uniform conception of the significance of religion in society (see *Otto-Preminger-Institut v. Austria*, judgment of 20 September 1994, Series A no. 295-A, p. 19, § 50), and the meaning or impact of the public expression of a religious belief will differ according to time and context (see, among other authorities, *Dahlab v. Switzerland* (dec.), no. 42393/98, ECHR 2001-V). Rules in this sphere will consequently vary from one country to another according to national traditions and the requirements imposed by the need to protect the rights and freedoms of others and to maintain public order (see, *mutatis mutandis, Wingrove*, cited above, p. 1957, § 57). Accordingly, the choice of the extent and form such regulations should take must inevitably be left up to a point to the State concerned, as it will depend on the specific domestic context (see, *mutatis mutandis, Gorzelik and others*, cited above, § 67, and *Murphy v. Ireland*, no. 44179/98, § 73, ECHR 2003-IX).

110. **However**, this margin of appreciation goes hand in hand with a European supervision embracing both the law and the decisions applying it. The Court's task is to determine whether the measures taken at national level were justified in principle and proportionate (see *Manoussakis and others*, cited above, p. 1364, § 44). In delimiting the extent of the margin of appreciation in the present case, the Court must have regard to what is at

stake, namely the need to protect the rights and freedoms of others, to preserve public order and to secure civil peace and true religious pluralism, which is vital to the survival of a democratic society (see, *mutatis mutandis, Kokkinakis*, cited above, p. 17, § 31; *Manoussakis and others*, cited above, p. 1364, § 44; and *Casado Coca*, cited above, p. 21, § 55). **The Court, however, should also be mindful of Article 53 of the Convention, which states that the Convention shall not be construed as limiting or derogating from any of the human rights and fundamental freedoms which may be ensured under any other relevant international agreement.** As previously stated by the Court, the Convention has to be interpreted in light of the rules set out in the Vienna Convention on the Law of Treaties of 23 May 1969 (see *Al-Adsani* v. *United Kingdom* [GC], no. 35763/97, ECHR 2001-XI, § 55). Article 31 § 3(c) of that treaty indicates that account is to be taken of 'any relevant rules of international law applicable in the relations between the parties'. The Convention, therefore, should not be interpreted in a vacuum, and the Court in applying its margin of appreciation doctrine should keep in mind the Convention's special character as a human rights treaty. As far as possible, the Convention should be interpreted in harmony with other rules of international law of which it forms part (*Al-Adsani*, cited above, § 55).

(ii)   Application of the foregoing principles to the present case

112. The interference in issue caused by the circular of 23 February 1998 imposing restrictions as to place and manner on the rights of students such as Ms Şahin to wear the Islamic headscarf on university premises was, according to the Turkish courts (see paragraphs 37, 39 and 41 above), based in particular on the two principles of secularism and equality.

Secularism

113. In its judgment of 7 March 1989, the Constitutional Court stated that secularism, as the guarantor of democratic values, was the meeting point of liberty and equality. The principle prevented the State from manifesting a preference for a particular religion or belief; it thereby guided the State in its role of impartial arbiter, and necessarily entailed freedom of religion and conscience. It also served to protect the individual not only against arbitrary interference by the State but from external pressure from extremist movements. The Constitutional Court added that freedom to manifest one's religion could be restricted in order to defend those values and principles (see paragraph 39 above). **The Chamber considered this notion of secularism to be consistent with the values underpinning the Convention (see paragraph 106 of the Chamber judgment).**

114. However, the issue faced by the Court in the present case is not the conformity of the 'principle' of secularism with the 'values' underpinning the Convention. Two reasons dictate why this is not the proper way of putting the issue before the Court. First, if framed this way, the issue takes on a level of generality and abstraction that requires the Court to depart from its judicial role and act, so to speak, as political philosopher. This would run contrary to the central concern underlying the Convention, which is to guarantee not rights that are theoretical or illusory but rights that are practical and effective (see *Airey* v. *Ireland*, 9 October 1979, Series A no. 41, § 24). In addition, reasoning in such abstract terms would, in effect, tie the hands of the Court in possible future cases where the principle of secularism will be invoked in order to justify interferences on freedom of religion. [Fragment deleted]
. . .

117. Rather, the Court's task in such cases calls for a case-specific or *in concreto* examination, in light of the principles of the Convention, of the facts and circumstances that gave rise to interference on a right guaranteed by the Convention (see, *mutatis mutandis, Bosphorus Hava Yollari Turizm ve Ticaret Anonim Sirketiv. Ireland* [GC], no. 45036/98, CEDH 2005-VI, Joint Concurring Opinion, § 2). In so doing, the Court will bear in mind that the term 'necessary', used in paragraph 2 of Article 9 of the Convention, does not have the flexibility of such expressions as 'useful' or 'desirable' (see *Chassagnou and others* v. *France*, cited above, § 112), and that, where limitations are imposed on freedom of religion, as on any other fundamental freedom, their necessity must be demonstrated by the State concerned (UN Human Rights Committee, General Comment No. 31: The Nature of the General Legal Obligation Imposed on States Parties under the Covenant, CCPR/C/21/Rev.1/Add.13, 26 May 2004, § 6).

118. The Chamber in the present case chose to emphasise 'the fact that there are extremist political movements in Turkey which seek to impose on society as a whole their religious symbols and conception of a society based on religious precepts' (see paragraph 109 of the Chamber judgment). This point is not challenged (see, for instance, *Refah Partisi (the Welfare Party) and others*, cited above). However, it does not address the issue of whether (and how) the behaviour, conduct or attitude of the applicant in the present case contradicted the principle of secularism, for example by creating a pressure on others to wear a headscarf. In fact, no evidence whatsoever has been produced to that effect. Neither does the Chamber's approach take into account the fact – undisputed by the Contracting Party – that the applicant acknowledged that 'the right to wear the headscarf will not always be protected by freedom of religion' (see paragraph 73 above) and that she explicitly professed her allegiance to

the principle of secularism. Finally, the argument assumes that the principle of secularism must be understood as extending beyond public servants, reaching the recipients of public services – a conception which, in view of its implications for the present and future cases, would normally deserve further explanation and development.

119. When determining whether the interference with freedom of religion in the present case was 'necessary in a democratic society', it is to be recalled that the Court must respect the margin of appreciation that is left to States in matters where no uniform European conception exists (see paragraph 109 above). As mentioned before, European practice concerning the wearing of religious symbols in teaching institutions varies significantly between individual Contracting States (see paragraphs 55–65 above). Still, only a very limited number of Contracting States have attempted to regulate the wearing of religious symbols in universities as such (see paragraph 55 above). Seen from that perspective, in fact, non-regulation seems to be the European standard. In the instant case, therefore, the Court should not allow the doctrine of the margin of appreciation to obscure its role as ultimate interpreter and guarantor of the principles of the Convention.

120. In view of the foregoing, the Court considers that the link between the interference on the applicant's freedom of religion and the principle of secularism has not been convincingly demonstrated in this case.

Equality

121. Just as wearing the headscarf was equated with political extremism by the Chamber when discussing secularism (see paragraph 116, above), it was equated with the alienation of women when discussing equality. The emphasis placed in the Turkish constitutional system on the protection of the rights of women was noted by the Chamber (paragraph 107 of its judgment). It is recognised by the Court as one of the key principles underlying the Convention and a goal to be achieved by Member States of the Council of Europe (see, *inter alia, Abdulaziz, Cabales and Balkandali* v. *United Kingdom*, judgment of 28 May 1985, Series A no. 94, § 78). In the present case, the Chamber went on to note that 'in a country in which the majority of the population, while professing a strong attachment to the rights of women and a secular way of life, adhere to the Islamic faith', limitations on wearing the headscarf may be regarded as meeting a pressing social need (paragraph 108 of the Chamber judgment).

122. However, because of the various possible meanings and uses of the headscarf, discussing the relationship between gender equality and wearing the headscarf requires considerable caution. A significant body of literature from the social sciences indicates that the headscarf should not simply be

equated with a symbol or instrument of the oppression of women.[65] Such literature suggests that, among other significations, wearing the head-scarf can also express legitimate personal piety and/or cultural identity; be a challenge to the sexual exploitation of women's bodies; or, simply, be a useful vehicle for interaction between women and society, promoting women's social participation and empowerment. The Court, as a judicial organ whose role is to interpret the Convention as a 'living instrument' (*Tyrer* v. *United Kingdom*, 25 April 1978, Series A no. 26, § 31) and 'in the light of present-day conditions' (*Marckx* v. *Belgium*, 13 June 1979, Series A no. 31, § 58), cannot and should not ignore such extrinsic evidence.

123. In view of the Court's earlier developments on the near absence of regulation of headscarves in the universities of Europe (paragraph 55 above), there seems to be no overwhelming reason, in the instant case, to automatically defer to the Contracting Party's national margin of appreciation over this issue. This is all the more so since the Court, in other cases, has recognised a right to personal autonomy that 'prohibit[s] any oppressive removal of a person's freedom of choice and action' (see, *mutatis mutandis*, with respect to Article 8 of the Convention, *Keenan* v. *United Kingdom*, 3 April 2001, no. 27229/95, ECHR 2001-III, § 92). In the instant case, respecting the personal autonomy and self-determination of adult women who wear headscarves, like the applicant, will ensure the consistency of the Court's case law.

124. The Court finds, therefore, that in the present case no unambig-uous link has been established between gender equality and the interfer-ence on the applicant's freedom of religion.

Proportionality

125. The Court must now determine whether in the instant case there was a reasonable relationship of proportionality between the means employed and the legitimate objectives pursued by the interference.

126. In applying the proportionality test, the Court finds it appropriate to refer to materials from human rights systems other than the Convention. This is consistent with Article 53 of the Convention and

---

[65] See. e.g. HomaHoodfar, 'The Veil in Their Minds and on Our Heads: The Persistence of Colonial Images of Muslim Women', *Resources for Feminist Research* (Winter 1993), pp. 3–10; or Lama Abu-Odeh, 'Post-Colonial Feminism and the Veil: Considering the Differences' (1992) 26 *New England Law Review* 1527; Ismahane Chouder, Malika Latrèche and Pierre Tevanian, *Les filles voilé esparlent* (Paris: La Fabrique, 2008); Farhad Khosrokhavar, *Le foulard et la République* (Paris: La Découverte, 1995). Disregarding the specific character of the exclusion of minority women can itself be exclusionary. See Carol Smart, 'The Woman of Legal Discourse' (1992) 1 *Social and Legal Studies* 29 at 30.

with the Court's obligation to interpret the Convention in harmony with other relevant rules of international law (see paragraph 110).

127. The International Covenant on Civil and Political Rights (UNTS, vol. 999, p. 171, ratified by Turkey on 23 September 2003), which recognises freedom of religion in terms similar to those of Article 9 of the Convention and provides for similar limitations, has been invoked in connection with the right to wear a headscarf at university in an application filed before the United Nations Human Rights Committee (*Hudoyberganova* v. *Uzbekistan*, application no. 93132000, 5 November 2004, (2004) *Revue universelle des droits de l'homme* 412). The Committee found a violation of Article 18 of the Covenant in that case, since the State Party had made no effort to justify the ban on the headscarf on the grounds specified in the Covenant, i.e. public safety, order, health, morals or the fundamental rights and freedoms of others.

128. In reviewing the periodic report of France under the Convention on the Rights of the Child (UNTS, vol. 1577, p. 3, ratified by Turkey on 4 April 1995), the Committee on the Rights of the Child has invited the State Party to closely monitor the situation of girl pupils who might be expelled from public schools for not complying with a law that prohibits the wearing of ostentatious religious symbols in French public schools. In its concluding observations, the Committee expressed its concern at the possible impact of the law on the possibility for those girls of having access to education. A recommendation was made to the State Party 'to consider alternative means, including mediation, of ensuring [the] secular character of public schools, while guaranteeing that individual rights are not infringed upon and that children are not excluded or marginalized from the school system and other settings' (see United Nations Committee on the Rights of the Child, Consideration of Reports Submitted by States Parties under Article 44 of the Convention (France), CRC/C/15/Add.240, 30 June 2004, §§ 25–26).

129. In examining Turkey's latest periodic report under the International Convention on the Elimination of All Forms of Discrimination Against Women (UNTS, vol. 1249, p. 13, accession by Turkey on 20 December 1985), the Committee on the Elimination of Discrimination Against Women reiterated 'its concern about the absence of information and statistical data on the impact of the ban on the use of headscarves in the areas of education, employment, health and political and public life, such as the number of women excluded from schools and universities'. The Committee recommended Turkey 'to undertake studies to evaluate the impact of the ban on wearing headscarves in the fields of education, employment, health and political and public life, and to include detailed information regarding the result of the study and

measures taken to eliminate any discriminatory consequences of the ban in its next periodic report' (United Nations Committee on the Elimination of Discrimination Against Women, Concluding Observations (Turkey), CEDAW/C/TUR/CO/6, 16 August 2010, §§ 16–17).

130. In its general comment on gender equality, the UN Committee on Economic, Social and Cultural Rights, established to monitor the implementation of the International Covenant on Economic, Social and Cultural Rights (UNTS, vol. 993, p. 3, ratified by Turkey on 23 September 2003), has emphasised the obligation of States 'to develop monitoring mechanisms to ensure that the implementation of laws and policies aimed at promoting the equal enjoyment of economic, social and cultural rights by men and women do not have unintended adverse effects on disadvantaged or marginalized individuals or groups, particularly women and girls' (United Nations Committee on Economic, Social and Cultural Rights, General Comment No. 16: The Equal Right of Men and Women to the Enjoyment of All Economic, Social and Cultural Rights, E/C.12/2005/4, 11 August 2005, § 21).

131. In the opinion of the Court, the foregoing developments are clear evidence of a concern in modern international human rights law, in the specific area of headscarf bans, for mitigating the unintended consequences of laws and policies on categories of persons who may be vulnerable. In conformity with the principles of indivisibility and interdependence of human rights (see paragraph 108 above), the above-mentioned materials also emphasise the interconnectedness of all human rights, whether civil and political or economic, social and cultural.

132. [Fragment deleted] It is common ground in the present case that practising Muslim students in Turkish universities are free, within the limits imposed by the constraints of educational organisation, to manifest their religion in accordance with habitual forms of Muslim observance. [Fragment deleted] It is true also that the resolution adopted by Istanbul University on 9 July 1998 shows that various other forms of religious attire are also forbidden on the university premises.

. . .

134. The Court is aware that [fragment deleted] the process whereby the regulations that led to the decision of 9 July 1998 were implemented took several years and was accompanied by a wide debate within Turkish society and the teaching profession (see paragraph 35 above). [Fragment deleted] The Court is willing to admit that throughout the decision-making process, the university authorities sought to adapt to the evolving situation [fragment deleted].

135. However, the Court cannot fail to note that the underlying assumption in the present case, and throughout the whole process, was that the dress requirements imposed by the university authorities would eventually have to be complied with – an assumption that was indeed borne out by facts later, since the applicant was actually barred from lectures, examinations and enrolment, and was later suspended, and eventually had to move abroad to continue her studies. No attempts were made to limit the ban to cases where the headscarf would be worn by the applicant so as to exert pressure on others, or to provoke a reaction. While showing a willingness to explain the reasons for the banning of the Islamic headscarf, that process of dialogue did not change in any way the nature and severity of the interference on freedom of religion inherent in banning the headscarf; neither did it demonstrate that the interference, especially in view of its impact on the applicant's freedom of religion and her right to education guaranteed in Article 2 of Protocol 1 of the Convention, was proportionate to the legitimate objective pursued.

Conclusion

136. In the light of the foregoing and [fragment deleted], **despite** the Contracting States' margin of appreciation in this sphere, the Court finds that the interference in issue **cannot be considered as either** justified in principle **or** proportionate to the aim pursued.

137. Consequently, **the Court finds that** there has been [fragment deleted] **a** breach of Article 9 of the Convention.

Alleged violation of Articles 8, 10 and 14 of the Convention

...

165. As regards the complaint under Article 14, taken alone or in conjunction with Article 9 of the Convention or the first sentence of Article 2 of Protocol No. 1, the Court [fragment deleted] **notes** that the applicant did not provide detailed particulars in her pleadings before the Grand Chamber. Furthermore, as has already been noted (see paragraphs 99 and 158 above), the regulations on the Islamic headscarf were not directed against the applicant's religious affiliation, but pursued, among other things, the legitimate aim of protecting order and the rights and freedoms of others and were manifestly intended to preserve the secular nature of educational institutions. **However, the Court cannot fail to note, also, that preventing Ms Şahin from wearing a headscarf in this case has resulted, based on the exercise of her religion, in her being excluded from higher education. Neither can the Court fail to note that, while the applicant was directly**

affected by the measure taken by the university authorities, male students were unconcerned by it, so that the measure appeared to be discriminatory not only on the basis of religion but also on the basis of sex. The Turkish authorities have tried to convince the Court that the said measure was justified in the name of the principles of secularism and gender equality, but, for the reasons elaborated earlier by the Court (see paragraphs 113–124), the link between either of those principles and the headscarf ban does not appear strong enough to be justified, even under the margin of appreciation Turkey was entitled to in this case. Consequently, the reasons which led the Court to conclude that there has been [fragment deleted] a violation of Article 9 of the Convention or Article 2 of Protocol No. 1 incontestably also apply to the complaint under Article 14, taken alone or in conjunction with the aforementioned provisions.

166. Accordingly, the Court finds that there has been a breach of Article 14 of the Convention.

9

Suku Phull v. France rewritten from a procedural justice perspective: taking religious minorities seriously

SAÏLA OUALD CHAIB*

Introduction

Religious manifestations have always been a complicated issue. Over the past decade, uncountable pages have been written about the headscarf and about the case law of the European Court of Human Rights[1] concerning this topic.[2] More recently, a worldwide debate was held about the crucifix case, *Lautsi v. Italy*.[3] The world press,[4] researchers from universities in Europe and across the

* I would like to thank several people who contributed to this work, each in their own way. First of all, I am indebted to my supervisor, Eva Brems, and to Stijn Smet for their comments on an earlier draft of this chapter. Further, I would like to thank my colleagues at the Human Rights Centre, especially my co-team members. I am also grateful to Maryam H'madoun and Kim Lecoyer for the inspiring discussions. Finally, a special mention goes to Mariam and Yasmina: they know why. The research for this paper was conducted within the framework of the ERC Starting Grant project 'Strengthening the European Court of Human Rights: More Accountability Through Better Legal Reasoning'.

[1] Hereinafter the 'Court' or the 'Strasbourg Court'.

[2] See, *inter alia*, P. Cumper and T. Lewis, '"Taking Religion Seriously"? Human Rights and Hijab in Europe – Some Problems of Adjudication' (2008–9) 24 *Journal of Law and Religion* 599; C. Evans, 'The Islamic Scarf and the European Court of Human Rights' (2006) 7 *Melbourne Journal of International Law* 52; J. Marshall, 'Conditions for Freedom? European Human Rights Law and the Islamic Headscarf Debate' (2008) 30 *Human Rights Quarterly* 631–54; I. Rorive, 'Religious Symbols in the Public Space: In Search of a European Answer' (2009) 30 *Cardozo Law Review* 2669–98.

[3] ECHR, *Lautsi v. Italy*, 3 November 2009; and ECHR (GC), *Lautsi v. Italy*, 18 March 2011.

[4] See, for example, 'School Crucifixes "Do Not Breach Human Rights"', at www.bbc.co.uk/news/world-europe-12791082; 'European Court of Human Rights Rules Crucifixes Are Allowed in State Schools', 18 March 2011, at www.guardian.co.uk/law/2011/mar/18/european-court-human-rights-crucifixes-allowed?INTCMP=SRCH; and S. Fish, 'Crucifixes and Diversity: The Odd Couple', 28 March 2011, http://opinionator.blogs.nytimes.com/2011/03/28/crucifixes-and-diversity-the-odd-couple (last accessed 29 January 2012).

Atlantic,[5] bloggers,[6] the Vatican[7] – everybody wished to have a say in the discussion. In many of these famous cases, I would probably also judge differently – and yet, this is not the kind of case I have chosen to rewrite.

My choice went to *Suku Phull* v. *France*,[8] a case about a Sikh who was compelled to remove his turban at a security check in the airport and who complained that this single fact violated his freedom of religion. Many people might not understand why Mr Phull was so much affected by having had to remove his turban that he hired a lawyer and contested this situation before the domestic courts and the Court in Strasbourg. Even the Court, which declared the case inadmissible, seems to consider this situation as an *a priori* clear-cut issue. It considers the claim as manifestly ill-founded, since security checks in airports are 'without any doubt' necessary to safeguard public safety. Of course, the Court is right about that; who could disagree with this safety concern? In fact, I am convinced that even Mr Phull cares about the safety in airports as much as I do, as much as France does and as much as the Strasbourg Court does.

This, however, is not the question that is at stake in Mr Phull's case. The issue at stake is whether the concern of public safety required the removal of Mr Phull's turban. This question, however, is not addressed by the Court, even though Mr Phull's argument had pointed at alternative measures for safeguarding public safety, such as the use of a manual detector or a walk-through scanner.

The main concern in this chapter is not to criticise the outcome of the case, but rather to assess the way the case was dealt with. In the first section, I will present the idea of procedural justice. Building on empirical findings concerning the link between the legitimacy of courts and the acceptance of their rulings on the one hand, and the way they deal with applicants and their arguments on the other, some normative guidelines have been developed. After outlining the *Phull* decision more extensively in the second section, the ruling will be checked against these procedural justice guidelines in the third section. In the fourth section, I will propose remedies for the problems that will have been identified. These include reframing the decision into a judgment, asking the right necessity question and proposing an alternative. This will be followed by some concluding remarks and by the presentation of the redrafted judgment of *Suku Phull* v. *France*.

---

[5] See, for example, (2011) 6(3) *Religion and Human Rights*. Almost the entire volume is dedicated to the *Lautsi* case.

[6] See, for example, A. Buyse, 'Grand Chamber Judgment in Lautsi: No Violation', 18 March 2011, at http://echrblog.blogspot.com/2011/03/grand-chamber-judgment-in-lautsi-no.html; L. Peroni, 'Lautsi v. Italy: Possible Implications for Minority Religious Symbols', 31 March 2011, at http://strasbourgobservers.com/2011/03/31/lautsi-possible-implications-for-minority-symbols; L. Zucca, 'A Comment on Lautsi', 19 March 2011, at www.ejiltalk.org/a-comment-on-lautsi/#more-3161 (last accessed 29 January 2012).

[7] www.uscatholic.org/news/2011/03/vatican-welcomes-european-court-decision-classroom-crucifixes.

[8] ECHR, *Phull* v. *France*, 11 January 2005.

Procedural justice

Social psychology research has revealed that, in their evaluation of their experience with the law, people do not only care about the outcome in their case, but also, and even more, about the way their case is dealt with.[9] Taking these findings seriously implies that judges should care not only about outcome fairness, but should pay particular attention as well to the fairness of the process as such. This means that the parties' views should be taken into account, that the judge should act in a neutral and unbiased way, that the parties should be treated with respect and that the Court's actors should show genuine care about the parties' concerns.[10] This idea forms the starting point of the rewriting exercise I undertake in this chapter.

Benefits of a procedural justice approach

Since the Court system is in the first place concerned with delivering fair decisions and not with pleasing the parties in a case, judges might ask why they should care about procedural justice.[11] Here are some arguments in favour of procedural justice in judicial procedures.[12]

The findings of Tyler and his associates indicate that procedural justice 'encourages decision acceptance and leads to positive views about the legal system'.[13] Treating individuals fairly thus enhances the legitimacy of courts and of the law in general. Moreover, 'once the perception that legal authorities are legitimate has been shaped, compliance with the law is enhanced, even when it conflicts with one's immediate self-interest'.[14] Hence, the integration of a procedural justice approach in its adjudication can strengthen the Court's position and enhance compliance with its judgments. Moreover, as Brems and Lavrysen argue,

---

[9] T. Tyler, 'Procedural Justice and the Courts' (2008) 44 *Court Review* 26–31; T. Tyler, 'What Is Procedural Justice?: Criteria Used by Citizens to Assess the Fairness of Legal Procedures' (1988) 22(1) *Law and Society Review* 103–36 at 121.

[10] See below.

[11] K. Burke and S. Leben, 'Procedural Fairness: A Key Ingredient in Public Satisfaction' (White Paper for the American Judges Association, 2007), p. 15; T. Tyler, 'Procedural Justice and the Courts' (2008) 44 *Court Review* 26–31 at 26.

[12] For a specific analysis of the importance of procedural justice for the Strasbourg Court, see E. Brems and L. Lavrysen, 'Procedural Justice in Human Rights Adjudication: The European Court of Human Rights', *Human Rights Quarterly* (forthcoming, manuscript on file with the authors), pp. 2–5.

[13] T. Tyler, 'Procedural Justice and the Courts' (2008) 44 *Court Review* 26–31 at 27; T. Tyler, 'Public Trust and Confidence in Legal Authorities: What Do Majority and Minority Group Members Want from the Law and Legal Institutions?' (2001) *Behavioral Sciences and the Law* 215–35 at 234.

[14] R. Paternoster, R. Brame, R. Bachman and L. Sherman, 'Do Fair Procedures Matter? The Effect of Procedural Justice on Spouse Assault' (1997) *Law and Society Review* 169.

regardless of its impact on legitimacy, procedural justice should matter for human rights adjudicating bodies 'simply because it is part of the value system they represent'.[15]

The way courts treat individuals also directly impacts on the individuals themselves. Research in economics has revealed that trust in the legal system is an important non-economic factor contributing to individuals' sense of well-being.[16] Moreover, in search of the reasons why individuals care about fair treatment by the authorities, Tyler and Lind developed the group-value model that is premised 'on notions of respect and trust between authorities and group members'.[17] According to this model, fair treatment communicates regard for the individual whereas unfair treatment signals marginality and exclusion.[18] Thus, treating individuals in a fair manner is beneficial for social cohesion in society. People who feel respected consequently feel part of the society the authority is representing.[19] Although this model applies to the relationship between a particular individual and an authority and despite the finding that members of both minority and majority groups care about procedural justice,[20] it can be argued that in a multicultural context procedural justice deserves extra attention.

To start with, research has proven that minority members are more than averagely distrustful towards authorities such as the police and courts.[21] Overcoming this distrust may require a particular focus on fairness in cases dealing with applicants belonging to a minority group such as in the present case. Moreover, treating a member of a minority in an unfair manner does not only communicate information about the position of this applicant as suggested by the group-value model, but it can also have an impact on the whole minority group.

---

[15] E. Brems and L. Lavrysen, 'Procedural Justice in Human Rights Adjudication: The European Court of Human Rights', *Human Rights Quarterly* (forthcoming, manuscript on file with the authors), p. 10.

[16] A. Aslam and L. Corrado, 'The Geography of Well-Being' (2011) *Journal of Economic Geography* 18–19.

[17] Y. Huo, 'Procedural Justice and Social Regulation Across Group Boundaries: Does Subgroup Identity Undermine Relationship-Based Governance?' (2003) *Personality and Social Psychology Bulletin* 345.

[18] *Ibid.*, p. 337.

[19] Y. J. Huo, K. R. Binning and L. E. Molina, 'Testing an Integrative Model of Respect: Implications for Social Engagement and Well-Being' (2010) 36(2) *Personality and Social Psychology Bulletin* 200–12.

[20] T. Tyler, 'Public Trust and Confidence in Legal Authorities: What Do Majority and Minority Group Members Want from the Law and Legal Institutions?' (2001) *Behavioral Sciences and the Law* 215–35 at 217 (with references); K. Burke and S. Leben, 'Procedural Fairness: A Key Ingredient in Public Satisfaction' (White Paper for the American Judges Association, 2007), p. 18.

[21] T. Tyler, 'Public Trust and Confidence in Legal Authorities: What Do Majority and Minority Group Members Want from the Law and Legal Institutions?' (2001) *Behavioral Sciences and the Law* 215–35 at 217 (with references).

In this context, it is noteworthy to refer to the letter by which Fazilet Partisi[22] – a political party that had been banned in Turkey – withdrew its case from the Court. It argued, *inter alia*, that the Court is 'not a fair tribunal' since 'it rejects constantly cases introduced by Muslims'. Fazilet Partisi also argued that the Court 'has prejudices against Islam' since the Court 'has formulated critique towards a universal religion about which [it] has no knowledge'. Fazilet Partisi concludes that, in light of the judgments held in the cases of *Refah Partisi* v. *Turkey*[23] and *Leyla Şahin* v. *Turkey*,[24] 'the Court has demonstrated to have prejudices against the Muslim community' and that therefore they have the conviction that they 'can have no trust in the justice of this Court'.[25] When dealing with a case concerning a member of a particular group, it is useful to be aware of the impact the case may have on the Court's perception within that group. For example, the Court's case law concerning Sikhs has been widely debated in the Sikh community.[26]

In conclusion, procedural justice is important for the legitimacy of the Court, for compliance with human rights, for social cohesion and for the well-being of individuals. This is applicable to both minorities and majorities. However, there are good reasons to pay extra attention to procedural justice in a diversity context.

The four procedural justice criteria

In the judicial context, procedural justice or procedural fairness concerns the perception people have of the way they are treated by courts and by the courts' actors. Empirical research has consistently shown that individuals evaluate this treatment according to four criteria: representation, neutrality, respect and trustworthiness.[27]

---

[22] ECHR, *Fazilet Partisi* v. *Turkey*, 27 April 2006.
[23] ECHR, *Refah Partisi* v. *Turkey*, 31 July 2001, where the Court, *inter alia*, stated at para. 72 that '[i]t is difficult to declare one's respect for democracy and human rights while at the same time supporting a regime based on Sharia'.
[24] ECHR, *Leyla Şahin* v. *Turkey*, 10 November 2005.
[25] ECHR, *Fazilet Partisi* v. *Turkey*, 27 April 2006 (author's translation).
[26] See, for example, 'European Court Rules Against the Sikh Turban in French Schools', where the author states that 'Sikhs feel let down once again in history, now by the European Court of Human Rights, the apex European judicial body supposed to be the guarantor of human rights and human dignity'. See www.examiner.com/europe-policy-in-national/european-court-rules-against-the-sikh-turban-french-schools.
[27] For literature specifically concerning legal authorities, see K. Burke and S. Leben, 'Procedural Fairness: A Key Ingredient in Public Satisfaction' (White Paper for the American Judges Association, 2007); T. Tyler, 'Procedural Justice and the Courts' (2008) 44 *Court Review* 26–31; J. Greacen, 'Social Science Research on "Procedural Justice": What Are the Implications for Judges and Courts?' (2008) 47(1) *Judges' Journal* 41; E. Brems and L. Lavrysen, 'Procedural Justice in Human Rights Adjudication: The European Court of Human Rights', *Human Rights Quarterly* (forthcoming, manuscript on file with the authors).

The first criterion, *representation*, refers to the need of applicants to express their views to the Court, before a decision is taken in their case.[28] This criterion is important irrespective of whether or not their views will influence the outcome.[29] Yet this should not be a *pro forma* act; the applicants' views should be taken seriously and the judge should genuinely listen to them.[30]

As Brems and Lavrysen argue, this criterion can be met by the Strasbourg Court by accurately representing the arguments of the parties in the judgment and by carefully examining the merits of each of the arguments.[31] This is particularly essential when it concerns an admissibility decision, as in the present case. In the situation where an applicant is told that his case will not be examined on the merits, the Court should sufficiently clarify, based on the arguments of the parties, that the application has been fully and sincerely considered.[32]

The second criterion, *neutrality*, might be seen as the most obvious one for court actors. This criterion requires judges to be impartial, independent and unbiased. The decisions they take should be based on an objective assessment of facts and upon the rules instead of their personal opinion.[33] The parties in the case should be treated equally, which might not always be obvious if the opposite party is a State. Furthermore, the equality of parties does not only matter in the framework of a particular case, but also in the context of the broader case law of the Court. The Court should be consistent across people, over time and across cases.[34] Equality across people requires the Court to treat all applicants in a similar respectful way, irrespective of their country of origin, their economic status, their ethnicity, etc. This requirement of equal treatment is especially important for members of minority groups.[35] Equality over time and cases implies that, when the Court overrules a certain line in its case law, this is sufficiently explained.[36] Another aspect of equality over cases is the

[28] T. Tyler, 'Procedural Justice and the Courts' (2008) 44 *Court Review* 26–31 at 30.

[29] K. Burke and S. Leben, 'Procedural Fairness: A Key Ingredient in Public Satisfaction' (White Paper for the American Judges Association, 2007), pp. 11–12; T. Tyler, 'Procedural Justice and the Courts' (2008) 44 *Court Review* 26–31 at 30.

[30] *Ibid.*; and T. Tyler, *Why People Obey the Law* (Princeton University Press, 2006), p. 149.

[31] E. Brems and L. Lavrysen, 'Procedural Justice in Human Rights Adjudication: The European Court of Human Rights', *Human Rights Quarterly* (forthcoming, manuscript on file with the authors), p. 12.

[32] *Ibid.*, p. 6.

[33] T. Tyler, 'Procedural Justice and the Courts' (2008) 44 *Court Review* 26–31 at 30.

[34] T. Tyler, 'What Is Procedural Justice?: Criteria Used by Citizens to Assess the Fairness of Legal Procedures' (1988) 22(1) *Law and Society Review* 103–36 at 105; T. Tyler, 'Procedural Justice and the Courts' (2008) 44 *Court Review* 26–31 at 30.

[35] See T. Tyler, 'Public Trust and Confidence in Legal Authorities: What Do Majority and Minority Group Members Want from the Law and Legal Institutions?' (2001) *Behavioral Sciences and the Law* 215–35 at 231–2.

[36] E. Brems and L. Lavrysen, 'Procedural Justice in Human Rights Adjudication: The European Court of Human Rights', *Human Rights Quarterly* (forthcoming, manuscript on file with the authors), pp. 12–13.

consistency in the reasoning between the cases that are dealt with under different fundamental rights. The Court should avoid creating the impression that some rights are more important than others.[37] Finally, in order to ascertain neutrality, transparency in adjudication is crucial.[38]

Also important is the third criterion, *respect*. A good basis for a respectful treatment is the understanding that 'people come to court about issues that are important to them, irrespective of the strength of their legal case'.[39] Not only the case, but also the persons claiming a violation of their rights, should be taken seriously, meaning that they must be respected in their dignity and always be treated well and politely.[40] Respect can also indirectly be shown through the text of the judgment. In several freedom-of-religion cases, the Court clearly fell short with regard to this criterion. Stating, for example, that the headscarf 'is hard to square with the principle of gender equality' and that '[i]t therefore appears difficult to reconcile the wearing of an Islamic headscarf with the message of tolerance, respect for others and, above all, equality and non-discrimination'[41] surely did not only affect the applicants who were respectively a school teacher and a university student in medicine, but at the same time stigmatised a whole group of women.

Finally, the last element consists of the *trustworthiness* of the judge. This criterion involves an appraisal of the judges' motivation; whether they are sincere and caring and whether they are 'honest and open about the basis of their actions; are trying to do what is right for everyone involved; and are acting in the interests of the parties, not out of personal prejudices'.[42] This might be reflected in a judgment when, for example, the Court does not agree with the applicant, but shows understanding towards the applicant's concerns. In *Lautsi*, for instance, the Court stated that 'it is understandable that the first applicant might see in the display of crucifixes in the classrooms of the State school

---

[37] See in this sense S. Ouald Chaib, 'Religious Accommodation in the Workplace: Improving the Legal Reasoning of the European Court of Human Rights', in K. Alidadi, M.-C. Foblets and J. Vrielink (eds.), *A Test of Faith? Religious Diversity and Accommodation in the European Workplace* (Ashgate, 2012); T. Lewis, 'What Not to Wear: Religious Rights, the European Court, and the Margin of Appreciation' (2007) 56 *International and Comparative Law Quarterly* 395–414; L. Vickers, *Religious Freedom, Religious Discrimination at the Workplace* (Hart Publishing, 2008), p. 101.

[38] E. Brems and L. Lavrysen, 'Procedural Justice in Human Rights Adjudication: The European Court of Human Rights', *Human Rights Quarterly* (forthcoming, manuscript on file with the authors), p. 6.

[39] T. Tyler, 'Procedural Justice and the Courts' (2008) 44 *Court Review* 26–31 at 31.

[40] *Ibid.*, p. 30.

[41] ECHR, *Dahlab* v. *Switzerland*, 15 February 2001, and repeated in ECHR (GC), *Leyla Şahin* v. *Turkey*, 10 November 2005, para. 111.

[42] *Ibid.* See also E. Brems and L. Lavrysen, 'Procedural Justice in Human Rights Adjudication: The European Court of Human Rights', *Human Rights Quarterly* (forthcoming, manuscript on file with the authors), pp. 6–7.

formerly attended by her children a lack of respect on the State's part for her right to ensure their education and teaching in conformity with her own philosophical convictions. Be that as it may, the applicant's subjective perception is not in itself sufficient to establish a breach of Article 2 of Protocol No. 1.'[43]

No empirical research has yet been done on the importance of these procedural justice criteria for the legitimacy and broader image of the European Court of Human Rights. Yet there can be little doubt about the relevance of procedural justice for the Court. Following Brems and Lavrysen, two levels can be discerned at which it could and should take procedural justice into account.[44]

First, the Court should be careful to act fairly during its own proceedings. And, secondly, the Court could also incorporate in its reasoning a procedural justice assessment of the way the case was dealt with at the domestic level. As Brems and Lavrysen argue, where small shortcomings of procedural justice are concerned, these should be taken into account in the proportionality analysis, whereas more serious shortcomings of procedural justice should lead to the finding of a violation of the Convention.[45]

Hence, the Court can set a good example by being neutral, trustworthy and respectful and at the same time act as a kind of watchdog over the national authorities' conduct with respect to these criteria.

Suku Phull outlined

Factual background

Mr Suku Phull, a UK national, was stopped by security guards at the Entzheim airport of Strasbourg when returning to the UK from a business trip. As a practising Sikh, he was wearing a turban. For inspection reasons, Mr Phull was compelled to remove his turban as he was making his way through the security checkpoint prior to entering the departure lounge.

Mr Phull alleges that the obligation to remove his turban violated his right to freedom of religion. He argues that it was not necessary to make him remove his turban since he did not object to passing through the walk-through scanner, nor did he refuse to be checked with a hand-held detector.[46]

---

[43] ECHR (GC), *Lautsi* v. *Italy*, 18 March 2011, para. 66.
[44] E. Brems and L. Lavrysen, 'Procedural Justice in Human Rights Adjudication: The European Court of Human Rights', *Human Rights Quarterly* (forthcoming, manuscript on file with the authors), p. 11.
[45] *Ibid.*, p. 29.
[46] The applicant also complained under Article 2 of Protocol 4 of a violation of his right to freedom of movement. According to the applicant, as a national of one of the Member States of the European Union, he should be exempted from security procedures of this type on the territories of the Member States. As the focus of this chapter lies on the freedom of religion, this part of the complaint will not be examined.

Decision

The Court declared the case inadmissible, stating that the claim was manifestly ill-founded.

The Court's reasoning consisted of two parts. In the first part, the Court acknowledged that an interference with the applicant's right to freedom of religion took place, accepted that this interference was prescribed by law and finally found that the interference 'pursued at least one of the legitimate aims listed in the second paragraph of Article 9 (guaranteeing public safety)'. Subsequently, the Court examined whether 'the interference was "necessary in a democratic society in the interests of public safety" within the meaning of the second paragraph of Article 9'.

For this necessity test, the Court referred to an earlier case, *X* v. *United Kingdom*,[47] in which a turban-wearing Sikh who failed to comply with safety regulations concerning the compulsory wearing of a motor helmet, alleged a violation of his freedom of religion. The European Commission of Human Rights ('the Commission') declared the claim manifestly ill-founded following the reasoning that 'the obligation to wear a helmet was a necessary safety measure and that any resulting interference with the applicant's freedom of religion was justified for the protection of health by virtue of Article 9 § 2'.[48] The Court transposed this reasoning to the case of *Phull* where it concluded that Phull's claim was manifestly ill-founded as 'security checks in airports are *undoubtedly* necessary in the interests of public safety' and since 'the arrangements for implementing them in the present case fell within the respondent State's margin of appreciation, particularly as the measure was only resorted to occasionally'.[49]

Suku Phull submitted to a procedural justice test

Taking each case seriously: examination on a case-by-case level

The first eye-catcher, when glancing at the decision in *Phull*, is the shortness of the text.[50] When a closer look is taken at the reasoning (or the absence thereof), one can only be puzzled by the brevity of the decision. This is problematic from the perspective of several procedural justice criteria.

Having a voice in the proceedings is, as explained above, essential for applicants in their relationship with courts. It must be clear from the decision

---

[47] ECommHR, *X* v. *United Kingdom*, 12 July 1978, http://strasbourgconsortium.org/document.php?DocumentID=4845.

[48] Translation provided by the Court in the case of *Phull*.

[49] *Suku Phull* v. *France* (emphasis added).

[50] See also Isabelle Rorive, 'Religious Symbols in the Public Space: In Search of a European Answer' (2009) 30 *Cardozo Law Review* 2669–98 at 2687–8.

that the applicant's concern has been taken seriously, and has been the subject of a genuine examination. In this case, however, the reasoning is minimal and mainly based on the reasoning in a previous case that is, factually speaking, not entirely comparable to the case in *Phull*. Apart from the fact that the applicants are both Sikhs, UK nationals and turban-wearers, no similarities between the cases can be discerned. In fact, the case of *Phull* concerned an occasional security check, while the applicant in the case of *X* v. *United Kingdom* was prevented in general from riding a motorbike due to safety regulations. Moreover, the safety concern in *Phull* affects a broad audience, whereas, in the case of *X*, his own health is the main concern. Such factual differences may lead to different outcomes in a proportionality analysis.[51] The Court used the same 'technique' in the later case of *El Morsli* v. *France*,[52] in which a Muslim woman refused to remove her veil in a French consulate during an identity check.[53] Declaring this case inadmissible, the Court said it saw 'no reason why it would deviate'[54] from the reasoning in *Phull*. Reference to previous similar cases is important from a consistency perspective, yet this cannot be done blindly. The Court should always treat a case on its own merits, taking into account the particular situation of the applicant.

Taking the applicant's arguments seriously

The most troublesome observation from a procedural justice perspective is the way the Court completely ignores the applicant's arguments. He argued that 'there had been no need for the security staff to make him remove his turban, especially as he had not refused to go through the walk-through scanner or to be checked with a hand-held detector'.[55] The relevance or adequacy of these possible alternatives is not addressed by the Court. The absence of an examination on this point is disrespectful towards the applicant and goes against the requirement of representation. The possible existence of less restrictive alternatives is, in my opinion, the key issue in this case, necessitating a thorough proportionality analysis in an examination on the merits. The question is whether public safety could be guaranteed without interfering with the applicant's rights or with a less intrusive interference than occurred in the present case.[56]

Hence, the first major adaptation in my redraft is declaring the case admissible and examining it on the merits. An examination on the merits and a

---

[51] In fact, other – maybe even stricter – considerations should be taken into account when assessing whether the interference is justified in the case of *Phull*.
[52] ECHR, *El Morsli* v. *France*, 4 March 2008.
[53] El Morsli argued that she was not opposed to an identity check, but only if it took place in front of a woman.
[54] ECHR, *El Morsli* v. *France*, 4 March 2008, p. 4 (author's translation).
[55] *Suku Phull* v. *France* (emphasis added).   [56] See below.

decent proportionality analysis would further equality between the parties in this case, as the interests of both parties would be weighed against each other. Two other procedural justice criteria that would be furthered by an examination of the merits are respect and trustworthiness. No matter what the outcome in this case might be, by examining it on the merits, the Court shows understanding towards the applicant's position, shows that his claim is taken seriously and shows respect for his religious conviction.

Taking the applicant's religion seriously

Ultimately, this case has to be framed in a broader debate concerning religion and the question of accommodating religious minorities in the mainstream society. The Court, however, does not show awareness of this broader issue in the decision. Although it starts with recognising that an interference with the applicant's freedom of religion took place, it does not seem to acknowledge how important this interference could be for the applicant. In light of the procedural justice concerns mentioned above, it can be argued that this position does not give a caring impression towards the religious conviction of the applicant and at the same time of all Sikhs who could be in a similar situation. On the contrary, it can be argued that the Court is banalising their religious concerns, by brushing away the applicant's arguments rather lightly.

Regarding this point, the case of *Phull* can be contrasted to the Canadian *Multani*[57] case concerning a pupil who was prohibited from wearing his *kirpan*[58] in school. After finding an infringement of the applicant's freedom of religion, the Canadian Supreme Court examines in *Multani* whether the infringement is reasonable and can be justified in a free and democratic society. According to the Supreme Court, 'the issue is whether the respondents have succeeded in demonstrating that an absolute prohibition is justified'.[59] Obviously, this is the question that is lacking in the Strasbourg Court's decision of *Phull*. In short, the Canadian Supreme Court concluded that the authorities failed to demonstrate that the absolute prohibition minimally impairs the applicant's rights.[60] According to the Supreme Court, '[an] absolute prohibition would stifle the promotion of values such as multiculturalism, diversity, and the development of an educational culture respectful of the rights of others',[61] and it concludes that a

> total prohibition against wearing a *kirpan* to school undermines the value of this religious symbol and sends students the message that some religious practices do not merit the same protection as others. On the other hand,

---

[57] *Multani v. Commission scolaire Marguerite-Bourgeoys* [2006] 1 SCR 256; 2006 SCC 6.
[58] 'A *kirpan* is a religious object that resembles a dagger and must be made of metal.' Description given by the Supreme Court of Canada in *Multani* case, *ibid.*, para. 3.
[59] *Ibid.*   [60] *Ibid.*, para. 77.   [61] *Ibid.*, para. 78.

accommodating Gurbaj Singh and allowing him to wear his *kirpan* under certain conditions demonstrates the importance that our society attaches to protecting freedom of religion and to showing respect for its minorities. The deleterious effects of a total prohibition thus outweigh its salutary effects.[62]

This case is a wonderful example of how a jurisdiction can acknowledge and respect the religious conviction of an applicant belonging to a religious minority and frame the issue in a broader societal context of multiculturalism.

With this goal in mind, I start the redraft by reiterating the settled principles in the Court's case law concerning the importance of religious freedom in the Convention. In addition to the well-known principles cited in paragraphs 1–5, I introduce a new principle stressing the importance of accommodating religious minorities in the broader context of a diverse society. This is important not only 'for the purpose of safeguarding the interests of the minorities themselves but to preserve a cultural diversity that is of value to the whole community'[63] (paragraph 5 of the redraft)

Having examined the decision of *Phull* through a procedural justice lens, I will now examine the case on the merits in the next section. I will propose an alternative reasoning that takes the particular situation of the applicant into account and that balances the interests at stake in the proportionality analysis.

Suku Phull examined on the merits

Avoiding theological assessments

The Court does not dispute that an interference with the applicant's freedom to manifest his religion was at stake.

While the finding of an interference is undeniable in this case, the Court's representation of the manifestation of religion at stake is not unproblematic. By stating that 'the Sikh religion requires its male followers to wear a turban', the Court goes one step too far. Irrespective of whether or not the turban is a strong obligation in Sikhism, it is not for the Court to draw conclusions about this. Just as it would be wrong for the Court to interpret what a religion does not require from its followers, it is also wrong for the Court to interpret what a religion does require from them. The Court should refrain from walking on this theological path.[64] This would avoid excluding from Convention

---

[62] *Ibid.*, para. 79.
[63] See, *mutatis mutandis*, ECHR, *Muñoz Diaz* v. *Spain*, 8 December 2009, para. 60.
[64] C. Evans, *Freedom of Religion under the European Convention on Human Rights* (Oxford University Press, 2001), pp. 123–5; D. Harris, M. O'Boyle and C. Warbrick, *Law of the European Convention on Human Rights* (Oxford University Press, 2009), pp. 433–4.

protection religious practices that are unfamiliar to the Court,[65] as well as marginalising minority voices within religious communities.[66] Hence, when considering a manifestation of religion, the Court should not assess on a general level whether or not a religion requires its adherents to follow a certain rule, yet should look on a case-by-case level whether the applicant accords authority to a particular requirement of his or her religion.[67] This is supported moreover by the need for consistency in the Court's case law. In the cases concerning the Islamic headscarf, the Court never stated that, 'since Islam requires its female followers to wear a headscarf, it works from the premise that an interference of the freedom of religion is at stake'. Instead the Court stated that, since '[the applicant] considered that Muslim women have a religious duty to wear the Islamic headscarf'[68] or since 'the applicant said that, by wearing the headscarf, she was obeying a religious precept and thereby manifesting her desire to comply strictly with the duties imposed by the Islamic faith',[69] it would proceed on the basis that the measures interfered with their freedom to manifest their religion. Hence, in the headscarf cases, the Court developed a consistent subjective approach towards assessing whether a manifestation of religion is at stake.[70]

In the turban cases, similar consistency is lacking. In *Mann Singh* v. *France*,[71] regarding the appearance of a turban on a driver's licence, the Court seems to apply a subjective approach similar to that adopted in the headscarf cases:

> *According to the applicant*,[72] the Sikh faith compels its members to wear a turban in all circumstances. It is not only considered at the heart of their religion, but also at the heart of their identity. Consequently, the Court notes that it consists of an act motivated or inspired by a religion or a conviction.[73]

---

[65] C. Evans, *Freedom of Religion under the European Convention on Human Rights* (Oxford University Press, 2001), p. 125; P. Edge, 'The European Court of Human Rights and Religious Rights' (1998) *International and Comparative Law Quarterly* 687.

[66] Compare to G. Bouchard and C. Taylor, 'Consultation Commission on Accommodation Practices Related to Cultural Differences "Building the Future: A Time for Reconciliation"' (Full Report, Quebec, 2008), pp. 175–7.

[67] E. Brems, 'Human Rights as a Framework for Negotiating/Protecting Cultural Differences: An Exploration of the Case Law of the European Court of Human Rights', in M.-C. Foblets, J.-F. Gaudreault-Desbiens and A. Dundes Renteln (eds.), *Cultural Diversity and the Law: State Responses from Around the World* (Brussels: Bruylant, 2010), p. 677.

[68] ECHR, *Kurtulmus* v. *Turkey*, 24 January 2006.

[69] ECHR (GC), *Leyla Şahin* v. *Turkey*, 10 November 2005.

[70] Isabelle Rorive, 'Religious Symbols in the Public Space: In Search of a European Answer' (2009) 30 *Cardozo Law Review* 2669 at 2674.

[71] ECHR, *Mann Singh* v. *France*, 13 November 2008.   [72] Emphasis added.

[73] ECHR, *Mann Singh* v. *France*, 13 November 2008 (translation by the author).

However, in two later cases, *Jasvir Singh* v. *France*[74] and *Ranjit Singh* v. *France*,[75] concerning Sikh pupils who wanted to wear a turban at school, the Court returns to the 'theological' position it also adopted in *Phull*:

> The Court recalls that it already held that the wearing of the turban by men of the Sikh faith could be considered as an act 'motivated or inspired by a religion or a religious conviction', *since the Sikh faith indeed imposes on them the wearing of the turban in all circumstances.*[76]

For the reasons mentioned above, I have in the redraft adopted a subjective approach similar to that of *Mann Singh* and the headscarf jurisprudence (paragraph 1 of the redraft).

To accommodate or not to accommodate?

As argued above, on the ground of procedural justice, the Court is required to undertake a decent proportionality analysis with a sincere consideration of the arguments raised by the applicant about possible less restrictive alternatives. This requires two corrections. First, the right necessity question will be asked; and, secondly, a necessity assessment will be undertaken.

Asking the right necessity question

By affirming that a security check at the airport is without any doubt necessary in a democratic society, the Court repeats the legitimate aim, namely, the protection of the public safety, but does not question whether the measure taken – obliging a Sikh passenger to remove his turban – is proportionate to this undisputed legitimate aim. Consequently, the Court is asking the wrong question: the question should not be whether a security check is necessary, but whether in this case the public safety necessitates the applicant removing his turban at the security check (paragraph 9 of the redraft).

Applying the necessity test

The necessity test implies that an interference should be relevant, sufficient and proportionate to the legitimate aim pursued[77] (paragraph 9 of the redraft).

---

[74] ECHR, *Jasvir Singh* v. *France*, 30 June 2009.
[75] ECHR, *Ranjit Singh* v. *France*, 30 June 2009.
[76] ECHR, *Jasvir Singh* v. *France*, 30 June 2009 (emphasis added; translation by the author).
[77] J. Schokkenbroek, *Toetsing Aan De Vrijheidsrechten Van Het Europees Verdrag Tot Bescherming Van De Rechten Van De Mens* (Zwolle, 1996), p. 200. Pieter Van Dijk, Fried Van Hoof, Arjen Van Rijn and Leo Zwaak, *Theory and Practice of the European Convention on Human Rights* (4th edn, Intersentia, 2006), p. 193. See, for example, ECHR, *Church of Scientology Moscow* v. *Russia*, 5 April 2007, para. 87; ECHR, *Dahlab* v. *Switzerland*, 15 February 2001; ECHR, *Moscow Branch of the Salvation Army* v. *Russia*, 5 October 2006, para. 77.

There is no doubt that removing the turban for inspection reasons can be relevant to the aim pursued, which is the protection of the public safety. As a general rule, Travellers have to remove pieces of clothing such as their jackets or shoes to facilitate security checks in airports. However, from a procedural justice perspective, it is important to acknowledge that religious headgear such as the turban cannot be seen as a simple piece of clothing; that might be experienced by the applicant as disrespectful and careless. Giving due account to this religious aspect in the judgment shows understanding towards the applicant (paragraph 10 of the redraft).

An element that should be taken into account in the proportionality analysis is the margin of appreciation the Court accords to States. In this case, the Court decides that the way States implement their security policies falls within the margin of appreciation, especially since these measures occur only occasionally. Indeed, it is not for the Court to judge the effectiveness of a public safety measure. I therefore agree with the Court that the national authorities are best placed to assess the situation (paragraph 7 of the redraft). Yet, this does not altogether do away with the supervision of the Court. Hence, the Court can still check whether the national authorities were sufficiently respectful of the applicant's religious freedom (paragraph 7 of the redraft).

As outlined above, the main issue in this case concerns the argument raised by the applicant about possible less restrictive alternatives.

Several authors favour including a 'least restrictive alternative' criterion in the proportionality assessment.[78] The Court repeatedly applied such a test in its case law. In a case on solitary confinement, the Court stated that 'a rigorous examination is called for . . . to determine . . . whether the measures taken were necessary and proportionate compared to the available alternatives'.[79] In a case on the preventive detention of protesters, the Court argued that 'the commission of that offence could not justify an interference with the right to liberty, especially as less intrusive measures could have been taken'.[80] Another interesting example concerns a Swiss citizen suffering from diabetes. The applicant was relieved from compulsory military duty and from civic service, but instead had to pay a tax. In this case, the Court literally states that a measure can only be considered proportionate and necessary in a democratic society, when no other measure exists that is less invasive to the fundamental right while permitting the

---

[78] See J. Gunn, 'Deconstructing Proportionality in Limitations Analysis' (2005) 19 *Emory International Law Review* 467 and 474; Pieter Van Dijk, Fried Van Hoof, Arjen Van Rijn and Leo Zwaak, *Theory and Practice of the European Convention on Human Rights* (4th edn, Intersentia, 2006), p. 340; S. Vandrooghenbroeck, *La proportionnalité dans le droit de la Convention européenne des droits de l'homme: Prendre l'idée simple au sérieux* (Brussels: FUSL/Bruylant, 2001). Compare also to the dissent of Judge Tulkens in ECHR (GC), *Leyla Şahin v. Turkey*, 10 November 2005.

[79] ECHR, *Ramirez Sanchez v. France*, 4 July 2006, para. 136.

[80] ECHR, *Schwabe and MG v. Germany*, 1 December 2011, para. 85.

achievement of the same aim.[81] This position is less nuanced compared to earlier case law where the Court finds that:

> [t]he availability of alternative solutions does not in itself render the … legislation unjustified; it constitutes one factor, along with others, relevant for determining whether the means chosen could be regarded as reasonable and suited to achieving the legitimate aim being pursued, having regard to the need to strike a 'fair balance'. Provided the legislature remained within these bounds, it is not for the Court to say whether the legislation represented the best solution for dealing with the problem or whether the legislative discretion should have been exercised in another way.[82]

Likewise, several authors argue that the existence of a less restrictive alternative cannot be considered sufficient in itself to conclude that a measure is disproportionate,[83] although such a finding can be seen as an indication that there might be a problem with the proportionate character of that measure.[84] During the proportionality analysis, due weight must also be accorded to the interests of the State, for which the less restrictive alternative may constitute a burden. In the case of *Phull*, France might for example have argued that accommodating Phull's claim would place too heavy a burden on the authorities with regard to costs or time constraints.

A similar approach is found in Canadian case law applying the principle of reasonable accommodation.[85] The Canadian courts have repeatedly been confronted with Sikhs claiming accommodation of their religious practices.[86] It is worth mentioning that the way the Canadian jurisdictions apply reasonable accommodation is very similar to the necessity test applied by the Strasbourg Court.[87] When an infringement of an individual's rights is established, any attempt to 'disregard the duty to accommodate must show that it is necessary, in order to achieve a legitimate and important legislative objective, to apply the

---

[81] ECHR, *Glor* v. *Switzerland*, 30 April 2009, para. 94.

[82] ECHR, *James and others* v. *United Kingdom*, 21 February 1986, para. 51.

[83] S. Vandrooghenbroeck, *La proportionnalité dans le droit de la Convention européenne des droits de l'homme: Prendre l'idée simple au sérieux* (Brussels: FUSL/Bruylant, 2001), p. 219; E. Brems, 'Human Rights: Minimum and Maximum Perspectives' (2009) 9(3) *Human Rights Law Review* 364.

[84] J. Schokkenbroek, *Toetsing Aan De Vrijheidsrechten Van Het Europees Verdrag Tot Bescherming Van De Rechten Van De Mens* (Zwolle, 1996), p. 200.

[85] See also Pierre Bosset, in Chapter 8, above.

[86] See, for example, *Multani* v. *Commission scolaire Marguerite-Bourgeoys* [2006] 1 SCR 256; 2006 SCC 6; and *Nijjar* v. *Canada 3000 Airlines Ltd*, Can. Trib., T497/1498 (1999), www.chrt-tcdp.gc.ca/search/files/t497_1498de_07_09.pdf.

[87] P. Bosset and M.-C. Foblets, 'Accommodating Diversity in Quebec and Europe: Different Legal Concepts, Similar Results?', in *Institutional Accommodation and the Citizen: Legal and Political Interaction in a Pluralist Society*, Strasbourg, Council of Europe (Trends in Social Cohesion No. 21), pp. 37–65 at p. 61.

standard in its entirety, without the exceptions sought by the claimant'. It must be shown that the application of a certain rule is a 'rational means' of achieving the objective and that 'no other means are available that would be less intrusive in relation to the rights in question (minimal impairment test)'. This minimal impairment test also implies an assessment of possible undue hardship for the supposed accommodator. Finally, as seen above, it must be demonstrated that 'there is proportionality between the measure's salutary and limiting effects'.[88]

Similarly, when applying a least restrictive alternative test, the Strasbourg Court could take the criterion of 'undue hardship' into account. In fact, in a recent freedom-of-religion case, *Jakóbski* v. *Poland*,[89] the Court appears to apply this principle, albeit without using the same wording. In this case, a Buddhist prisoner claimed a violation of his religious freedom after his request for a diet adapted to his religious needs had been refused by the authorities. The Court was not convinced that providing the applicant with an adapted diet would lead to a 'disruption of the management of the prison' and consequently found a violation of Article 9 of the Convention.

In *Phull*, the least restrictive alternative criterion cannot be applied without restraint, since the State enjoys a wide margin of appreciation and it is consequently not for the Court to decide whether the proposed alternatives are appropriate in this case. However, the Court can still apply a marginal check. Similar to the Canadian model used in reasonable accommodation cases, it can be argued that, since the applicant suggested possible less restrictive alternatives, the State can only justify the non-adoption of the alternatives by proving in a satisfactory manner that applying these alternatives would not be effective for the legitimate aim pursued or would entail an excessive burden. In this sense, I concur with the dissenting Judge Hedigan in the case of *Jasper* v. *United Kingdom*, who is of the opinion that, 'where the applicant can establish on a *prima facie* basis that such an alternative way exists, the onus shifts to the respondent to show why it cannot use or adapt such a way'[90] (paragraph 12 of the redraft).

---

[88] J. Woehrling, 'L'obligation d'accommodement raisonnable et l'adaptation de la société à la diversité religieuse' (1998) 43 *McGill Law Journal* 324–401 at 360 (translation).

[89] ECHR, *Jakóbski* v. *Poland*, 7 December 2010.

[90] ECHR (GC), *Jasper* v. *United Kingdom*, 16 February 2000, Dissenting Opinion of Judge Hedigan. A comparison can also be drawn with the *Multani* case where the Canadian Supreme Court observed that the prohibition on the wearing of the *kirpan* was absolute, while the applicant 'has never claimed a right to wear his *kirpan* to school without restrictions'. 'Thus', the Supreme Court continues, 'the issue is whether the respondents have succeeded in demonstrating that an absolute prohibition is justified.' *Multani* v. *Commission scolaire Marguerite-Bourgeoys* [2006] 1 SCR 256; 2006 SCC 6, para. 54. The formulation by the Supreme Court could be interpreted in a way that, when the applicant is open to other alternatives than an absolute ban, it is for the authorities to prove that the absoluteness of the ban is justified.

However, in the present case, it seems that the domestic authorities did not even consider the alternatives proposed by the applicant. In that case, the Court can even go a step further in its assessment by applying a strictly procedural approach to the least restrictive alternative criterion, requiring 'not *per se* that the least restrictive option be chosen but that evidence is provided that the national authorities have included a consideration of less restrictive alternatives in their decision-making process'.[91] This approach was repeatedly used in the Strasbourg Court's jurisprudence[92] (paragraph 13 of the redraft).

Consequently, in *Phull*, instead of assessing *in concreto* whether less restrictive alternatives are available, I only examine whether the authorities sufficiently took alternatives into account, especially since the applicant proposed several alternatives. In procedural justice terms, using this line of reasoning, I assess whether the domestic authorities took the applicant seriously (paragraphs 11–13 of the redraft).

In this case, it is not sufficiently proven that these alternatives were seriously considered by the State. Consequently, the State did not adequately show that the measure is necessary in a democratic society. Therefore, I cannot but conclude that France violated the applicant's right to freedom of religion by compelling him to remove his turban (paragraph 14 of the redraft).

Conclusion

The man who was obliged to remove his turban at a security check, the Sikh who could not drive without a motor helmet, and the woman who had to remove her Muslim headscarf while queuing for a passport in a consulate, have something in common: they all returned from Strasbourg with an inadmissibility decision in their hands and at the same time – if you allow me a guess – they possibly all went home with a bit less trust in the justice system or at least with a feeling of not having been understood.

---

[91] E. Brems, 'Human Rights: Minimum and Maximum Perspectives' (2009) 9(3) *Human Rights Law Review* 362.

[92] See, for example, ECHR, *Bartik* v. *Russia*, 21 December 2006, para. 48, where the Court finds that the authorities 'did not consider whether the restriction on the applicant's right to travel abroad for private purposes was still necessary for achieving the legitimate aim it had been intended to serve and whether a less restrictive measure could be applied'; and in ECHR, *Khudoyorov* v. *Russia*, 8 November 2005, para. 184: 'Given that the applicant's trial would not be able to begin for a considerable time owing to events wholly unrelated to his conduct . . . the authorities should either have considered having recourse to such alternative measures or at minimum explained in their decisions why such alternatives would not have ensured that the trial would follow its proper course.' Other examples include ECHR, *Smith and Grady* v. *United Kingdom*, 27 September 1999, para. 102; ECHR, *Supreme Holy Council of the Muslim Community* v. *Bulgaria*, 16 December 2004, para. 97.

In this chapter, I tried to demonstrate in light of the findings of procedural justice research that the outcome of a case that might be seen by a majority of people as an *a priori* lost case, is not always that clear-cut if one genuinely takes the claim seriously and assesses the case on its own merits. But, more importantly, what I tried to show in this chapter is that this outcome, although important, is not always the main concern of applicants. In fact, research has consistently shown that people accord even more importance to the way they are treated by courts than to the outcome in their case. Obviously, in the case of *Phull*, the Court has failed at this level. Not only did it dismiss Phull's claim in an ultra-short inadmissibility decision, but – adding insult to injury – it completely ignored the applicant's claim about alternative solutions that would not have infringed his freedom.

In my redraft, I have tried to redress this situation by issuing a judgment instead of a decision, because if the argument of the applicant is taken seriously it becomes clear that the ill-foundedness of the claim is not as manifest as the Court concludes. Instead, the proportionality analysis necessitates a thorough balancing exercise where possible less restrictive alternatives are taken into account.

That public safety is an important legitimate aim is not contested. However, a general interest should not serve as a blindfold obscuring individual freedoms. I argued that the Court should keep in mind that the stakes of procedural justice include its own legitimacy. Finally, I argued that procedural fairness towards applicants and their claims is especially important in cases dealing with minorities, since it conveys a message to the minority group to which the applicant belongs. This message involves understanding, respect and the place the Court accords to minorities in the mainstream society.

Rewriting Suku Phull v. France

. . .

Alleged violation of Article 9 of the Convention

The applicant complained of a violation of his right to freedom of religion by the airport authorities. He argued that there had been no need for the security staff to make him remove his turban, especially as he had not refused to go through the walk-through scanner or to be checked with a hand-held detector. He relied on Article 9 of the Convention.

. . .

I.   Whether there was an interference

1. [Fragment deleted] **Since the applicant considered himself to be under a religious duty to wear the turban,** the Court is prepared to work

on the premise that the disputed measure constituted interference with the applicant's freedom to manifest his religion or beliefs.

II. Whether the interference was prescribed by law and pursued a legitimate aim

2. [Fragment deleted] **The Court** further notes that the applicant did not allege that the measure was not 'prescribed by law' and finds that it pursued at least one of the legitimate aims listed in the second paragraph of Article 9 (guaranteeing public safety).

The Court must therefore determine whether the interference was 'necessary in a democratic society in the interests of public safety' within the meaning of the second paragraph of Article 9.

[Paragraphs deleted]

III. Whether the interference was necessary in a democratic society

(i) General principles

3. The Court reiterates that, as enshrined in Article 9, freedom of thought, conscience and religion is one of the foundations of a 'democratic society' within the meaning of the Convention. This freedom is, in its religious dimension, one of the most vital elements that go to make up the identity of believers and their conception of life, but it is also a precious asset for atheists, agnostics, sceptics and the unconcerned. The pluralism indissociable from a democratic society, which has been dearly won over the centuries, depends on it. That freedom entails, *inter alia*, freedom to hold or not to hold religious beliefs and to practise or not to practise a religion (see, among other authorities, *Kokkinakis* v. *Greece*, judgment of 25 May 1993, Series A no. 260-A, p. 17, § 31, and *Buscarini and others* v. *San Marino* [GC], no. 24645/94, § 34, ECHR 1999-I).

4. While religious freedom is primarily a matter of individual conscience, it also implies, *inter alia*, freedom to manifest one's religion, alone and in private, or in community with others, in public and within the circle of those whose faith one shares. Article 9 lists the various forms which manifestation of one's religion or belief may take, namely, worship, teaching, practice and observance (see, *mutatis mutandis, Cha'are Shalom Ve Tsedek* v. *France* [GC], no. 27417/95, § 73, ECHR 2000-VII). However, Article 9 does not protect every act motivated or inspired by a religion or belief (see, among many other authorities, *Kalaç* v. *Turkey*, judgment of 1 July 1997, Reports of Judgments and Decisions 1997-IV, p. 1209, § 27; *Arrowsmith* v. *United Kingdom*, no. 7050/75, Commission's report of 12 October 1978, Decisions and Reports (DR) 19, p. 5; *C* v. *United Kingdom*, no. 10358/83, Commission decision of 15 December

1983, DR 37, p. 142; and *Tepeli and others* v. *Turkey* (dec.), no. 31876/96, 11 September 2001).

5. Pluralism, tolerance and broadmindedness are hallmarks of a 'democratic society'. Although individual interests must on occasion be subordinated to those of a group, democracy does not simply mean that the views of a majority must always prevail: a balance must be achieved which ensures the fair and proper treatment of people from minorities and avoids any abuse of a dominant position (see, *mutatis mutandis, Young, James and Webster* v. *United Kingdom*, judgment of 13 August 1981, Series A no. 44, p. 25, § 63, and *Chassagnou and others* v. *France* [GC], nos. 25088/94, 28331/95 and 28443/95, § 112, ECHR 1999-III). Indeed, in today's pluralist society, the presence of religious minorities becomes more visible. This is a trend that should not lead to suppression, but instead the individual concerns of members of these minority groups should be respectfully considered, not only for the purpose of safeguarding the interests of the minorities themselves but to preserve a cultural diversity that is of value to the whole community. (see, *mutatis mutandis, Smith and Grady* v. *United Kingdom*, para. 60 and *Chapman* v. *United Kingdom* [GC], no. 27238/95, § 93, ECHR 2001-I).

6. Pluralism and democracy must also be based on dialogue and a spirit of compromise necessarily entailing various concessions on the part of individuals or groups of individuals which are justified in order to maintain and promote the ideals and values of a democratic society (see, *mutatis mutandis, United Communist Party of Turkey and others*, cited above, pp. 21–22, § 45, and *Refah Partisi (the Welfare Party) and others*, cited above, § 99).

7. Regard must be had to the fair balance that has to be struck between the competing interests of the individual and of the community as a whole; and in both contexts the State enjoys a certain margin of appreciation in determining the steps to be taken to ensure compliance with the Convention (see, *mutatis mutandis, Jakóbski* v. *Poland*, § 47). The Court's task, in exercising its supervisory jurisdiction, is not to take the place of the competent national authorities but rather to review under Article 9 the decisions they delivered pursuant to their power of appreciation. This does not mean that the supervision is limited to ascertaining whether the respondent State exercised its discretion reasonably, carefully and in good faith; what the Court has to do is to look at the interference complained of in light of the case as a whole and determine whether it was 'proportionate to the legitimate aim pursued' (see, *mutatis mutandis, Vögt* v. *Germany*). Particular care is called for when examining whether the reasons adduced by the national authorities to justify the interference with the applicant's freedom to manifest his religion under

Article 9 of the Convention were relevant and sufficient and whether the means employed were proportionate to the legitimate aim pursued (see *Larissis* v. *Greece*, para. 70).

8. The object of Article 9 is essentially that of protecting the individual against unjustified interference by the State, but that there may also be positive obligations inherent in an effective 'respect' for the individual's freedom of religion (cf., *mutatis mutandis*, the judgment of the European Court of Human Rights in the *Marckx* case, p. 15, para. 31).

(ii)   Application to the present case

9. The Court must determine whether the interference with the applicant's freedom of religion was 'necessary in a democratic society in the interests of public safety' within the meaning of the second paragraph of Article 9. The applicant argued that there had been no need for the security staff to make him remove his turban, especially as he had not refused to go through the walk-through scanner or to be checked with a hand-held detector. Consequently, the Court must examine whether the removal of the turban was necessary in the interest of public safety. Therefore, it must determine whether the measure taken was appropriate for achieving this legitimate aim, whether less restrictive alternatives were available and whether the measure taken was proportionate to the aim pursued.

10. Security checks in airports are undoubtedly necessary in the interests of public safety within the meaning of that provision. The Court acknowledges that the removal of certain clothing such as jackets, shoes or in this case headgear during security checks might in certain situations be relevant in the interest of public safety. However, the Sikh turban cannot be regarded as a simple headgear, since the turban carries for the applicant a religious meaning. Therefore, the authorities should be careful to respect the sensitivities of the situation. The mandatory removal of his turban constituted an interference with the applicant's religious freedom.

11. This interference must be necessary to achieve the legitimate aim pursued and should not be more intrusive than necessary for that purpose (see, *mutatis mutandis, Bartik* v. *Russia*). The Court reiterates that the choice as to the most appropriate means of achieving this aim is in principle a matter for the domestic authorities, who are better placed to assess the efficiency of the available security techniques (see, *mutatis mutandis, El Majjaoui and Stichting Touba Moskee* v. *Netherlands*, no. 25525/03, § 32, 20 December 2007). The authorities must balance the interests at stake and should make serious efforts to find solutions to attain the legitimate aim pursued with a minimal infringement of the individual's fundamental rights. The applicant suggested two alternative

measures to the removal of his turban, namely, the manual metal detector
and the walk-through scanner. He argued that these measures would
allow a full-fledged security check of his turban without the need to
take it off and hence without touching upon his religious freedom.

12. Since the applicant proposed measures, the walk-through scanner
and the manual metal detector, that *prima facie* seem to be valuable
alternatives, the burden of proof shifts to the State who must prove that
these measures are insufficient for guaranteeing the legitimate aim pursued or that the accommodation through these measures would lead to an
excessive burden for the State (see, *mutatis mutandis, Jakóbski* v. *Poland*;
and *Multani* v. *Commission scolaire Marguerite-Bourgeoys* [2006] 1 SCR
256; 2006 SCC 6 (Supreme Court of Canada)). Furthermore, even if the
insufficiency of these measures were to be established by the State, this
does not exempt the State from its positive obligations inherent in an
effective 'respect' for the individual's freedom of religion (cf., *mutatis
mutandis*, the judgment of the European Court of Human Rights in the
Marckx case, p. 15, para. 31). Consequently, it must be shown that
enough efforts were undertaken by the State to accommodate the applicant's religious needs.

13. However, the Court observes that the French authorities did not
even consider the alternatives proposed by the applicant and that it did
not convincingly show why these proposals were not fully considered
(see, *mutatis mutandis, Van Mechelen* v. *Netherlands*).

14. Having regard to the foregoing and despite the margin of appreciation left to the State, the Court concludes that the authorities failed to
strike a fair balance between the right to freedom of religion of the
applicant on the one hand and the general interest of the public safety
on the other hand. Therefore, the obligation to remove the turban
imposed on the applicant was not proven to be necessary for the achievement of the legitimate aim pursued.

The Court therefore concludes that there has been a breach of Article 9
of the Convention.

PART IV

Sexual minorities

10

Rewriting Schalk and Kopf: shifting the locus of deference

HOLNING LAU[*]

Introduction

Just over a decade ago, the Netherlands became the first country in the world to legalise same-sex marriage.[1] With that milestone anniversary so near, it is fitting to reflect on the current status and future trajectory of same-sex marriage. Thus, for my contribution to this book, I have decided to discuss the same-sex marriage case of *Schalk and Kopf* v. *Austria*,[2] which the European Court of Human Rights[3] decided in 2010.[4]

The case of *Schalk and Kopf* put in stark relief the deference that the Court continues to grant Contracting States. Deference drove the Court to reject the applicants' two main claims concerning Austria's refusal to allow same-sex couples to marry. First, the applicants contended that Austria violated the right to marry enshrined in Article 12 of the Convention.[5] The Court disagreed largely because it determined the scope of the fundamental right to marry by

---

[*] For helpful conversations on drafts of this chapter, I thank Laurence Helfer, Charles Strohm, Mark Weisburd and participants of the Williams Institute's works-in-progress workshop series. For research assistance, I thank Lorelle Babwah, Uttara Kale and Sergio VeLarde. I also thank Sergio VeLarde for helping to translate sources from Italian, Portuguese and Spanish.

[1] The Netherlands legalised same-sex marriage on 1 April 2001.

[2] ECHR, *Schalk and Kopf* v. *Austria*, 24 June 2010.

[3] This chapter will often refer to the European Court of Human Rights as 'the ECHR' or 'the Court'.

[4] The First Section of the ECHR issued its judgment on 24 June 2010. The Grand Chamber rejected the applicants' referral request on 22 November 2010. See Registrar of the ECHR, 'Court's Judgment Concerning Austrian Authorities' Refusal To Allow Marriage of Homosexual Couple Becomes Final', Press Release No. 906, 29 November 2010.

[5] *Schalk and Kopf*, para. 39. For the purposes of this chapter, the 'Convention' refers to the European Convention for the Protection of Human Rights and Fundamental Freedoms.

243

deferring to Contracting States.[6] Invoking its consensus doctrine,[7] the Court refused to view the right as protecting same-sex unions because too few Contracting States supported that position.[8] Secondly, the applicants argued that Austria violated Article 14's prohibition of discrimination, taken in conjunction with Article 8's protection of the right to respect for private and family life.[9] In addressing this non-discrimination claim, the Court granted Austria a wide margin of appreciation to determine whether its differential treatment of same-sex and different-sex couples could be justified.[10] As such, the Court accepted Austria's conclusion that the differential treatment did not amount to impermissible discrimination.[11]

The role of deference is the primary lens through which this chapter critiques and rewrites the *Schalk and Kopf* judgment. Specifically, this chapter focuses on the applicants' non-discrimination-based claim because deference in the non-discrimination context was particularly misplaced.[12] Austria is no better positioned than the Court to evaluate whether treating same-sex couples differently is justified. Instead of deferring on that question, my rewritten judgment actively reviews and rejects the possibility that differential treatment for marriage purposes is justified, concluding that same-sex couples have a right to marriage equality pursuant to Articles 14 and 8. While my judgment recognises this right to marriage equality, it also recognises that there are difficulties in implementing marriage equality overnight. Therefore, the redrafted judgment defers to Contracting States' consensus on how and when to implement incremental reform to achieve marriage equality. In this regard, the new judgment preserves judicial restraint, but shifts the locus of that restraint from determinations about *whether* a right should be protected to determinations about *how* and *when* to implement protections of that right.

The rewritten judgment enhances the Court's expressive power. The Court plays a more active role in norm-setting by clearly explaining that same-sex

---

[6] *Schalk and Kopf*, paras. 58–9. In addition to deferring to Contracting States, the Court considered the text of Article 12 and the historical context of the Convention's adoption. *Ibid.*, paras. 54–5.

[7] For background on the ECHR's consensus approach, see generally L. R. Helfer, 'Consensus, Coherence and the European Convention on Human Rights' (1993) 26 *Cornell International Law Journal* 133–64.

[8] *Schalk and Kopf*, paras. 58–9.   [9] *Ibid.*, para. 65.

[10] For background on the margin of appreciation doctrine, see generally E. Brems, 'The Margin of Appreciation Doctrine in the Case Law of the European Court of Human Rights' (1996) 56 *Zeitschrift für ausländisches öffentliches Recht und Völkerrecht* 240–314; C. Yourow, *The Margin of Appreciation Doctrine in the Dynamics of European Human Rights Jurisprudence* (Martinus Nijhoff, 1996).

[11] *Schalk and Kopf*, paras. 96–7 and 105–10.

[12] To be clear, this chapter also discusses the applicants' Article 12 claim, but only to the extent that the Article 12 claim is relevant to analysing the non-discrimination claim based on Articles 8 and 14.

couples have a right to marriage equality that requires legal protection. That articulation gently pushes States towards enacting laws to achieve marriage equality. The rewritten judgment stops short, however, of finding Austria in violation of the Convention. In this regard, the rewritten judgment and the original are similar. According to the rewritten judgment, Austria has not yet breached the Convention because the Court grants Austria a grace period for implementing marriage equality. As explained below, Austria does not breach the Convention unless it lags behind a minimum pace of law reform that is determined by consensus. Because Austria has enacted a substantial partnership registry for same-sex unions,[13] it is not lagging behind the minimum pace of reform for the time being.

The remainder of this chapter unfolds in four parts. It begins by providing additional background on the original *Schalk and Kopf* judgment. It then elaborates on why and how the rewritten judgment re-situates judicial restraint. Next, the chapter reflects on the difference between the rewritten and original judgments. Finally, the chapter concludes by commenting on how the redrafted judgment advances this book's goal of promoting diversity. The conclusion also includes the rewritten passages of the *Schalk and Kopf* judgment.

Background on the original judgment

The applicants in *Schalk and Kopf* argued that Austria's refusal to grant them access to marriage violated the right to marriage protected by Article 12.[14] The Court rejected this argument, reasoning that the Article's sex-specific language about the right of 'men and women' to marry supported interpreting Article 12 as obligating States to recognise different-sex marriages only.[15] The Court acknowledged existing case law that treats the Convention as a 'living instrument', an approach that allows the scope of rights to expand over time.[16] However, the Court suggested that it would not expand the right to marry unless there was a consensus among Contracting States to support that expansion.[17] With only six out of forty-seven Contracting States having legalised same-sex marriage, the Court stated that no such consensus existed.[18]

The applicants also argued that, even if they did not have a right to marry pursuant to Article 12, they had a right to marry pursuant to Article 14's prohibition of discrimination, taken in conjunction with Article 8's protection of the right to private and family life.[19] In response, the Court made several

---

[13] Austria's Registered Partnership Act came into force on 1 January 2010. *Schalk and Kopf*, para. 17.
[14] *Ibid.*, para. 39.   [15] *Ibid.*, paras. 54–6.   [16] *Ibid.*, paras. 57–9.   [17] *Ibid.*, paras. 58–9.
[18] *Ibid.*   [19] *Ibid.*, para. 65.

observations that weighed in favour of the applicants. The Court recognised that cohabiting same-sex couples fall within the scope of 'family life' under Article 8.[20] It also recognised that same-sex couples are similarly situated to different-sex couples.[21] Finally, the Court noted that it has held repeatedly that differential treatment based on sexual orientation requires 'particularly serious justifications'.[22]

Despite those observations, the Court rejected the applicants' non-discrimination claim for two main reasons. First, in a rather conclusory fashion, the Court stated that, because Article 12 does not protect a right to same-sex marriage, the Court cannot derive a right to same-sex marriage from Articles 14 and 8.[23] In this view, the narrow definition of marriage in Article 12 precludes relying on Articles 14 and 8 to expand marriage rights.[24] Secondly, the Court granted Austria a wide margin of appreciation to decide for itself whether its differential treatment of same-sex couples was justified.[25] Austria did not articulate any specific justification to the Court, but the Court deferred to Austria nonetheless, accepting Austria's bare assertion that differential treatment could be justified.[26]

It is worth recalling that, during the course of litigation, Austria established a partnership registry that affords same-sex couples official recognition.[27] The majority opinion was ambiguous on whether Contracting States are obligated to offer same-sex couples recognition through programmes such as Austria's partnership scheme.[28] In contrast, three dissenting judges argued that Austria violated Article 14, taken in conjunction with Article 8, because it failed to justify introducing its civil partnership programme at such a late date.[29] Like the majority opinion, however, the dissenting opinion did not find Austria to be in violation of the Convention for failing to grant same-sex couples access to full-fledged marriage.

---

[20] *Ibid.*, para. 94.   [21] *Ibid.*, para. 99.   [22] *Ibid.*, para. 97.

[23] *Ibid.*, para. 101. See also L. Hodson, 'A Marriage by Any Other Name? Schalk and Kopf v. Austria' (2011) 11 *Human Rights Law Review* 175 (calling the Court's statement about the relationship between Article 12 and Articles 14 and 8 'hasty and unsatisfactory for its lack of reasoning').

[24] *Schalk and Kopf*, para. 101.

[25] *Ibid.*, paras. 98, 105 and 106. The Court suggested that a wide margin of appreciation was appropriate because 'a wide margin is usually allowed to the State under the Convention when it comes to general measures of economic or social strategy'. *Ibid.*, para. 97.

[26] *Ibid.*, para. 110; see also *ibid.*, Joint Dissenting Opinion, para. 8 ('respondent Government did not advance any argument to justify the difference of treatment, relying in this connection mainly on their margin of appreciation').

[27] See note 13 above.

[28] See L. Hodson, 'A Marriage by Any Other Name? Schalk and Kopf v. Austria' (2011) 11 *Human Rights Law Review* 175.

[29] *Schalk and Kopf*, Joint Dissenting Opinion, paras. 8–10.

Redrafting the anti-discrimination analysis

The rewritten judgment focuses on the Court's anti-discrimination analysis. As this chapter's title indicates, deference is the primary lens through which I critique the original judgment. With that said, I also take issue with the original opinion's understanding of how Article 12 interacts with Articles 14 and 8. This section of the chapter elaborates on how the redrafted judgment reflects these critiques.

Justifying judicial review (redrafted judgment, paragraphs 96–100)

The rewritten opinion contends that the Court should not defer to Contracting States on whether differential treatment based on sexual orientation is justified. Accordingly, the rewritten opinion addresses sexual-orientation-based differentiation with heightened scrutiny.[30] Doing so builds on existing ECHR case law as well as democratic principles.

As the original judgment noted, 'the Court has held repeatedly that, just like differences based on sex, differences based on sexual orientation require particularly serious reasons by way of justification'.[31] For example, the Court has required particularly serious reasons to justify sexual-orientation-based differentiation with respect to tenancy succession rights in *Karner v. Austria*, and with respect to the age of consent for sexual activity in *Smith and Grady v. United Kingdom*.[32] This case law legitimates, if not necessitates, active judicial review of alleged sexual orientation discrimination. The requirement of 'particularly serious reasons' would be toothless if the Court lacked power to assess the seriousness of purported reasons for sexual-orientation-based differentiation. This point was made by the dissenting judges, who concluded that the case law's requirement of 'particularly serious reasons' weighed against granting Austria a wide margin of appreciation.[33]

Judicial review of sexual-orientation-based differentiation is warranted not only by the Court's existing case law requiring 'particularly serious reasons'. Judicial review, in lieu of deference, is also warranted by democratic theory.[34] At the conference that launched this book project, the primary objection raised

---

[30] For the purposes of this chapter, I use the term 'heightened scrutiny' to describe judicial review that is not deferential; courts that exercise heightened scrutiny of alleged discrimination evaluate whether the differential treatment is proportionately related to achieving important governmental goals. See note 44 below and the accompanying text.

[31] *Schalk and Kopf*, para. 97.

[32] ECHR, *Karner v. Austria*, 24 July 2003, para. 37; *L and V v. Austria*, 9 January 2003, para. 45. See also ECHR, *Smith and Grady v. United Kingdom*, 27 September 1999, paras. 89–90 (stating that Article 8 requires 'particularly serious reasons' to justify discharging members of the armed forces based on their sexual orientation).

[33] *Ibid.*, Joint Dissenting Opinion, para. 8.

[34] See notes 36–42 below and the accompanying text.

against the ECHR's judicial review was that, by engaging in judicial review, the Court usurps the democratic functioning of Contracting States.[35] This criticism does not apply, however, to judicial review of differential treatment based on statuses such as sexual orientation, race and sex. Laws that differentiate people based on these statuses often reflect flawed democratic deliberations. Accordingly, judicial review of such laws ameliorates democratic deficits instead of undermining deliberative democracy.

The democratic deficiencies associated with statuses such as sexual orientation manifest in two respects. First, as a minority group, gays and lesbians often lack the political power that is necessary to remedy discrimination through democratic channels. Drawing on the seminal works of John Hart Ely, Eyal Benvenisti has explained that, because democratic channels fail in this regard, the Court generally should not defer to Contracting States in cases concerning minority groups' rights.[36] According to Benvenisti, Contracting States' courts and legislatures are too often beholden to majoritarian politics and are, therefore, inadequate protectors of minority rights.[37] Secondly, beyond numerosity-based constraints on minority groups' ability to influence democratic deliberation, entrenched stereotypes further impair democratic deliberation. For example, as I have argued in previous writing, democratic deliberation is often tainted by gender stereotypes even though neither women nor men typically constitute a minority group.[38] While reason-giving conversations are a core requisite of deliberative democracy,[39] claims based on flawed stereotypes often overshadow reason-based arguments concerning issues that implicate gender roles.[40] Similarly, entrenched stereotypes about sexual orientation threaten democratic deliberation on matters concerning

[35] For a discussion on how the ECHR's judicial review interacts with Contracting States' democratic functioning, see e.g. M. Fyrnys, 'Expanding Competences by Judicial Lawmaking: The Pilot Judgment Procedure of the European Court of Human Rights' (2010) 12 *German Law Journal* 1247–8.

[36] See E. Benvenisti, 'Margin of Appreciation, Consensus, and Universal Standards' (1999) 31 *NYU Journal of International Law and Politics* 848–50, building on J. H. Ely, *Democracy and Distrust* (Cambridge, MA: Harvard University Press, 1980).

[37] 'Absent political influence and faced with prevalent resentment, minorities rely upon the judicial process to secure their interests. But because the national judicial process – itself dominated by judges of the majority – may fail to protect them, international judicial and monitoring organs are often their last resort and only reliable avenue of redress.' E. Benvenisti, 'Margin of Appreciation, Consensus, and Universal Standards' (1999) 31 *NYU Journal of International Law and Politics* 848.

[38] H. Lau, 'Gender Scripting and Democracy', in M. Fineman (ed.), *Transcending the Boundaries of Law: Feminism and Legal Theory* (Routledge-Cavendish, 2010); H. Lau, 'Identity Scripts and Democratic Deliberation' (2010) 94 *Minnesota Law Review* 915–29.

[39] For background on deliberative democracy, see e.g. A. Gutmann and D. Thompson, *Why Deliberative Democracy?* (Princeton University Press, 2004).

[40] See H. Lau, 'Gender Scripting and Democracy', in M. Fineman (ed.), *Transcending the Boundaries of Law: Feminism and Legal Theory* (Routledge-Cavendish, 2010), pp. 334–8.

sexual orientation.[41] Thus, while the Court has stated that deference to Contracting States makes sense when national authorities are in a better position to address a particular dispute,[42] Contracting States are not particularly well positioned to determine whether sexual-orientation-based differentiation is justified.[43]

In sum, even if the Court generally defers to Contracting States through consensus doctrine and the margin of appreciation, the Court ought to exercise heightened scrutiny in Article 14 cases concerning sexual orientation because such cases are exceptional. Existing case law has already designated sexual-orientation-based disparate treatment as exceptional circumstances that require particularly serious justifications. Likewise, discrimination based on sexual orientation and certain other statuses is exceptionally difficult to remedy through democratic channels.

Exercising judicial review (redrafted judgment, paragraphs 101–4)

Because a wide margin of appreciation is inappropriate for assessing sexual-orientation-based differentiation, the redrafted judgment actively evaluates whether such differential treatment is supported by 'particularly serious' reasons. Instead of deferring to Austria, the redrafted judgment evaluates the differential treatment with heightened scrutiny. It does so by examining whether the differentiation constitutes proportionate means for advancing important governmental goals.[44]

---

[41] See H. Lau, 'Identity Scripts and Democratic Deliberation' (2010) 94 *Minnesota Law Review* 915 at 947–8.

[42] See G. Letsas, 'Two Concepts of the Margin of Appreciation' (2006) 26 *Oxford Journal of Legal Studies* 721–4 (surveying and critiquing case law in which the Court sought to justify the margin of appreciation by arguing that Contracting States were 'better placed' to make certain decisions).

[43] It is worth noting that the original *Schalk and Kopf* judgment claimed that Contracting States are entitled to a wide margin of appreciation on matters of 'economic or social strategy', which allegedly includes marriage policies. *Schalk and Kopf*, para. 97. The Court has previously sought to justify this wide margin of appreciation by stating: 'Because of their direct knowledge of their society and its needs, the national authorities are in principle better placed than the international judge to appreciate what is in the public interest on social or economic grounds.' ECHR (GC), *Stec and others v. United Kingdom*, 12 April 2005, para. 52. However, for the reasons discussed in notes 36–42 above and the accompanying text, Contracting States' deliberations on economic and social strategy are all too often tainted by democratic deficits associated with sexual orientation. Thus, Contracting States are not particularly well positioned for evaluating economic and social strategy when sexual orientation is implicated.

[44] In addition to stating that legal differentiation based on sexual orientation requires 'particularly serious reasons by way of justifications', the Court has stated that there must be a 'reasonable relationship of proportionality between the means employed [i.e. differentiation employed] and the aim sought to be realized'. *Schalk and Kopf*, paras. 96–7.

As noted earlier, Austria did not articulate *any* reason for the differential treatment; it relied entirely on arguing for a margin of appreciation.[45] To understand how a State might attempt to justify differential treatment, we can look to recent litigation before other courts. Two recurring arguments are that excluding same-sex couples preserves tradition and that the exclusion promotes stable, healthy families.[46] The first argument should be rejected because answering the question 'why is the traditional definition of marriage justified?' with the response 'because it is traditional' is circular. Under heightened scrutiny, such circularity must fail.[47] The second argument – that excluding same-sex couples promotes stable, healthy families – also fails because existing evidence refutes that claim.

Opponents of marriage equality have suggested that legalising same-sex marriage would destabilise different-sex relationships by prompting different-sex couples to forgo marriage and procreation.[48] Empirical research, however, contradicts this speculation. Available data from Europe suggest that introducing recognition of same-sex couples to a legal system – either through marriage or marriage-like registration schemes – does not reduce marriage rates, increase divorce rates, or affect birth rates.[49] In a similarly flawed fashion, some States have argued that they restrict marriage to different-sex couples because

---

[45] See note 26 above and the accompanying text.

[46] Due to the restricted length of this chapter, it is unfeasible to catalogue all the arguments that have ever been made for excluding same-sex couples from marriage. This chapter limits itself to considering the most prevalent and noteworthy of those arguments. For a more extensive list of arguments, consider the recent United States District Court decision in *Perry v. Schwarzenegger*, which rejected six purported justifications for exclusion. United States District Court, Northern District of California, *Perry v. Schwarzenegger*, 704 F Supp 2d 921, 998–1002, 4 August 2010, stay granted pending appeal, No. 10-16696, 2010 WL 3212786 (United States Federal Court, 9th Circuit, 16 August 2010).

[47] In the United States, state supreme courts that have reviewed same-sex marriage bans under 'intermediate' or 'strict' scrutiny have roundly rejected the 'tradition' argument because it is tautological. See Supreme Court of Iowa, *Varnum v. Brien*, 763 NW 2d 862, 898, 3 April 2009; Supreme Court of Connecticut, *Kerrigan v. Commissioner of Public Health*, 957 A 2d 407, 478–9, 28 October 2008; Supreme Court of California, *In re Marriage Cases*, 183 P 3d 384, 451–2, 4 June 2008; and Supreme Court of Hawaii, *Baehr v. Lewin*, 852 P 2d 44, 61, 5 May 1993.

[48] Exercising heightened scrutiny, courts have examined and rejected these arguments. See e.g. *Varnum*, pp. 901–3; Constitutional Court of South Africa, *Minister for Home Affairs v. Fourie*, 1 December 2005, para. 111, citing Constitutional Court of South Africa, *National Coalition for Gay and Lesbian Equality v. Minister of Home Affairs*, 2 December 1999, para. 59; Court of Appeal of Ontario, *Halpern v. Canada*, 10 June 2003, para. 121.

[49] See M. V. Lee Badgett, *When Gay People Get Married* (NYU Press, 2009), pp. 65–80; W. N. Eskridge, Jr and D. R. Spedale, *Gay Marriage: For Better or For Worse?: What We've Learned from the Evidence* (Oxford University Press, 2006), pp. 91–129.

different-sex couples are better suited to raising children.[50] Peer-reviewed research on gay and lesbian parenting does not support this claim. Research suggests that children raised by gays and lesbians fare as well as other children in terms of health and well-being.[51] Interestingly, while empirical research does not support claims about same-sex marriage harming different-sex couples, an emerging body of research suggests that the well-being of same-sex couples could be enhanced by marriage.[52] Indeed, Austria's exclusion of same-sex couples from marriage does not advance the goal of promoting stable and healthy families.

The conclusion that banning same-sex marriage fails to advance serious government interests comports with decisions from constitutional courts that have reviewed same-sex marriage prohibitions under heightened scrutiny. For example, in the United States, the high courts of California, Connecticut and Iowa have all applied heightened scrutiny to marriage laws' differential treatment of same-sex couples and have concluded that the differential treatment is not sufficiently related to advancing any important government interests.[53] The Constitutional Court of South Africa and provincial appellate courts in Canada have reached similar decisions by applying proportionality tests that are similar to the heightened scrutiny that the redrafted opinion adopts.[54] In contrast, virtually all of the high courts that have rejected same-sex couples' challenges to marriage exclusion have exercised great deference to legislatures

---

[50] For examples of courts that have examined and rejected these claims, see e.g. *Varnum*, p. 899; *Halpern*, para. 123.

[51] For reviews of this empirical research, see M. Rosenfeld, 'Nontraditional Families and Childhood Progress Through School' (2010) 47 *Demography* 770; G. M. Herek, 'Legal Recognition of Same-Sex Relationships in the United States: A Social Science Perspective' (2006) 61 *American Psychologist* 611–14; J. Stacey and T. J. Biblarz, '(How) Does the Sexual Orientation of Parents Matter?' (2001) 66 *American Sociology Review* 164–7. See also *Perry*, pp. 980–1 ('Children raised by gay or lesbian parents are as likely as children raised by heterosexual parents to be healthy, successful and well-adjusted. The research supporting this conclusion is accepted beyond serious debate in the field of developmental psychology.').

[52] See *Perry*, pp. 969, 973 (concluding, based on evidence provided to the court, that '[s]ame-sex couples receive the same tangible and intangible benefits from marriage that opposite-sex couples receive'); H. Lau and C. Q. Strohm, 'The Effects of Legally Recognizing Same-Sex Unions on Health and Well-Being' (2011) 29 *Law and Inequality* 107–48 (reviewing relevant empirical research).

[53] See *Varnum* (Iowa), *Kerrigan* (Connecticut) and *In re Marriage Cases* (California).

[54] For the South African case, see *Fourie*. For examples of the case law from Canadian provincial courts, see *Halpern*; Court of Appeal of British Columbia, *Barbeau v. British Columbia*, 8 July 2003.

instead of adopting heightened scrutiny.[55] For the reasons described above, the redrafted judgment rejects such weak judicial review.[56]

Because the differential treatment at issue cannot be justified, the redrafted judgment concludes that same-sex couples have a right to marriage equality pursuant to Articles 14 and 8, even though a right to same-sex marriage does not derive directly from Article 12. Although the theoretical focus of this chapter is the role of deference in the Court's opinion, it is worth pausing to address an important secondary distinction between the redrafted opinion and the original: the redrafted opinion does not hold that a narrow reading of Article 12 precludes finding that the applicants have a right to marry based on non-discrimination principles.

The original judgment stated correctly that the Convention's provisions should be construed in harmony with each other. However, it was wrong to conclude that a narrow reading of Article 12 cannot be harmonised with a right to marriage equality based on Articles 14 and 8. To reconcile a narrow reading of Article 12 with marriage equality pursuant to Articles 14 and 8, we can think of Article 12 as only setting the floor for marriage rights. By applying the Court's evolutive[57] approach to Articles 14 and 8, we can construe those Articles to provide rights-protections that rise above the floor set by Article 12. For relevant persuasive authority, the Court can look to the United States. Some state supreme courts in the United States have found that same-sex couples have a right to marry pursuant to constitutional protections of equal rights, even though they did not find same-sex marriage to be included in the fundamental right to marry.[58]

---

[55] See e.g. Constitutional Court of Portugal, Ruling No. 359/2009, Case No. 779/07, 9 July 2009; Constitutional Court of Italy, Judgment No. 138/2010, 14 April 2010; Constitutional Council of France, *Mrs Corinne C et al. (Prohibition of Marriage between Persons of the Same Sex)*, Decision No. 2010–92, 28 January 2011; Supreme Court of Maryland, *Conaway v. Deane*, 18 September 2007; Supreme Court of Washington State, *Andersen v. King County*, 26 July 2006; Court of Appeals (High Court) of New York, *Hernandez v. Robles*, 6 July 2006. For a case where a high court purported to exercise a more active form of judicial review, but still upheld the exclusion of same-sex couples from marriage, see the Costa Rican supreme court's Resolution No. 2006–07262, 23 May 2006 (stating that the same-sex couples' exclusion from marriage satisfied the court's proportionality test). The Costa Rican decision is problematic because it relied on the circular reasoning discussed in note 47 above and the accompanying text.

[56] See the discussion above under the heading 'Justifying judicial review'.

[57] For background on the Court's evolutive approach, see S. Greer, *The European Convention on Human Rights: Achievements, Problems and Prospects* (Cambridge University Press, 2006), p. 214.

[58] Connecticut's Supreme Court protected the right to same-sex marriage based on equal protection doctrine; the court also stated that it did not need to address whether same-sex marriage is protected by separate constitutional doctrine on the fundamental right to marry. See *Kerrigan*, p. 412. Similarly, Iowa's Supreme Court protected marriage equality based on equality rationales, while choosing not to address the couple's argument regarding the fundamental right to marry. See *Varnum*, p. 873. In *Baehr*, Hawaii's Supreme Court

The original *Schalk and Kopf* judgment cited *Johnston* v. *Ireland* for the proposition that, if a right does not derive from a narrow Convention provision, then the right cannot be derived from a broader Convention provision.[59] However, the Court ought to distinguish that divorce case. The applicants in *Johnston* claimed that the right to marry in Article 12 should subsume a right to divorce, so that individuals can exit existing marriages to pursue new marriages.[60] The applicants also made a simple facsimile of that argument in the Article 8 context: the right to respect for family life should subsume a right to divorce, so that individuals can exit existing marriages to pursue new family lives.[61] It makes sense that the applicants could not overcome the flawed logic of their Article 12 claim by merely recasting the same logic in a broader context. The Court achieved consistency by rejecting both the Article 12 and Article 8 claims.[62] In contrast, the same-sex couple's non-discrimination claim in *Schalk and Kopf* is not a simple facsimile of the couple's straightforward right-to-marry claim. Their non-discrimination claim, based on Articles 14 and 8, focuses the Court's attention on comparing similarly situated families in a way that is absent from the Court's Article 12 analysis. Because the same-sex couple's two claims involved different logics, they need not be resolved identically. As such, the applicants' flawed Article 12 claim can be reconciled with a successful claim to marriage equality based on Articles 14 and 8.

Retaining judicial restraint (redrafted judgment, paragraphs 105–9)

The discussion so far has focused on enhancing the Court's judicial activity. The redrafted judgment is careful, however, to balance that judicial activity with judicial restraint. For pragmatic reasons, the redrafted judgment defers to Contracting States on the timeline for reforming laws to achieve marriage equality. Requiring Contracting States to legalise same-sex marriage overnight can be counter-productive for reasons described below. Therefore, while the redrafted opinion calls for marriage equality, it permits incremental reform towards marriage equality and it takes cues from Contracting States to establish the required pace of reform.

Demanding immediate achievement of marriage equality would be counter-productive because of enforcement problems. Unlike national courts, the supranational ECHR has very few tools for enforcing its judgments. The only sticks that the Council of Europe wields against Contracting States that fail to comply

---

rejected the same-sex couples' argument regarding the fundamental right to marry; nonetheless, the court concluded that same-sex couples could possibly have a right to marry pursuant to equality principles and remanded the case to a lower court to determine whether banning same-sex marriages could pass strict scrutiny. See *Baehr*, pp. 55–8.

[59] *Schalk and Kopf*, para. 101, citing ECHR, *Johnston* v. *Ireland*, 27 November 1986.

[60] *Johnston*, paras. 49–57.   [61] See *ibid.*   [62] See *ibid.*

with ECHR judgments are expulsion and suspension of voting rights.[63] The Council of Europe almost never uses these extreme and impractical measures.[64] Instead, the Court elicits State cooperation by cultivating friendly relationships. As previous commentators have noted, the Court develops friendly relationships by exercising restraint, only requiring States to implement legal standards that a critical mass of Contracting States has already adopted.[65] By taking cues from Contracting States in this fashion, the Court balances its supervision of States with a respect for their sovereignty, thereby cultivating cooperation. If the Court were to forgo judicial restraint and demand immediate implementation of marriage equality, it would risk alienating Contracting States, undermining their overall cooperation with the Court.[66] As Robert Wintemute has noted about *Schalk and Kopf*: 'If the court appeared to force the views of a small minority of countries on all 47 [Contracting States], it would risk a political backlash, which could cause some governments to threaten to leave the convention system.'[67]

In addition to undermining Contracting States' cooperation with the Court, requiring immediate implementation of marriage equality might not be ideal because stable and enduring social change is sometimes better achieved incrementally. European jurisdictions that currently recognise same-sex marriage generally changed through incremental steps, gradually increasing gay rights and offering same-sex couples limited forms of recognition before moving to

[63] Statute of the Council of Europe, Article 8 (providing for the suspension and expulsion of Contracting States).

[64] For characterisation of these measures as 'extreme' and 'counter-productive', see e.g. P. Egli, 'Protocol No. 14 to the European Convention for the Protection of Human Rights and Fundamental Freedoms: Towards a More Effective Control Mechanism?' (2007) 17 *Journal of Transnational Law and Policy* 18. In a rare instance, the Council of Europe temporarily suspended Russia's voting privileges in 2000. See L. R. Helfer, 'Redesigning the European Court of Human Rights' (2008) 19 *European Journal of International Law* 157. See also D. Raab, 'What Happens If We Defy Europe? Nothing', *Daily Telegraph*, 3 February 2011, available at 2011 Westlaw NewsRoom (WLNR) 2132442 (noting that 'no state has ever been voted out of the Council of Europe' because of non-compliance with an ECHR judgment).

[65] See R. St J. MacDonald, 'The Margin of Appreciation', in R. St J. MacDonald (ed.), *The European System for the Protection of Human Rights* (Kluwer Law International, 1993), p.123; E. Brems, 'The Margin of Appreciation Doctrine in the Case Law of the European Court of Human Rights' (1996) 56 *Zeitschrift für ausländisches öffentliches Recht und Völkerrecht* 240 at 300; L. R. Helfer and A. Slaughter, 'Towards a Theory of Effective Supranational Adjudication' (1997) 107 *Yale Law Journal* 317.

[66] Cf. E. Brems, 'The Margin of Appreciation Doctrine in the Case Law of the European Court of Human Rights' (1996) 56 *Zeitschrift für ausländisches öffentliches Recht und Völkerrecht* 240 at 297–8 ('Judicial restraint may also express a Court strategy aimed at self-preservation ... If the Court adopted a too activist approach, it would risk losing the confidence of the member states, and thus undercut its own position.').

[67] See R. Wintemute, 'Consensus Is the Right Approach for the European Court of Human Rights', 12 August 2010, www.guardian.co.uk/law/2010/aug/12/european-court-human-rights-consensus.

full-fledged marriage rights.[68] William Eskridge has argued that such incrementalism is a desirable form of pragmatic liberalism because gradual law
reform helps to cultivate inclusive social attitudes that prevent popular backlash
against same-sex marriage. Eskridge calls such incremental reform 'equality
practice', and has explained: '[T]he same-sex marriage movement teaches us
that process matters and that equality cannot be shoved down unwilling
throats, especially by the judiciary. So liberalism in operation cannot ignore
pragmatic features such as those entailed in equality practice.'[69]

In light of incrementalism's merits, how can the ECHR enforce incremental
reform aimed at marriage equality? It is unfeasible for the Court to require each
Contracting State to develop and adhere to a timeline for implementing public
education campaigns and deadlines for increasing the rights and responsibilities afforded to same-sex couples. The ECHR lacks the institutional capacity to
develop and monitor such rigid incrementalism. Unlike the mandate of institutions such as the European Committee of Social Rights, the ECHR's mandate
does not include reviewing annual reports regarding Contracting States' progress in implementing rights-protections.[70]

Due to the Court's limited capacity, the redrafted opinion relies on the Court's
consensus doctrine to set the minimum pace of reform. To be clear, the redrafted
judgment states explicitly that same-sex couples have a right to marriage equality.
However, the Court does not hold that Contracting States have an obligation to
implement marriage equality immediately. Instead, the Court recognises a grace
period and relies on consensus doctrine to set the terms of that grace period.
During the grace period, Contracting States maintain a margin of appreciation to

---

[68] See W. Eskridge Jr, *Equality Practice: Civil Unions and the Future of Gay Rights* (Routledge,
2002), pp. 115–18; K. Waaldijk, 'Small Change: How the Road to Same-Sex Marriage Got
Paved in the Netherlands', in R. Wintemute and M. Andenaes (eds.), *Legal Recognition of
Same-Sex Partnership: A Study of National, European and International Law* (Oxford:
Hart Publishing, 2001), pp. 437–64. When the Court decided *Schalk and Kopf*, six
Contracting States – the Netherlands, Belgium, Spain, Portugal, Norway and Sweden –
had legalised same-sex marriage, and Iceland subsequently joined that group. Prior to
legalising same-sex marriage, the Netherlands, Norway, Sweden and Iceland had enacted
partnership registries that granted almost all the rights associated with marriage. Belgium
and Portugal both passed laws allowing registered same-sex cohabitants to enjoy some of
the rights associated with marriage. In Spain, numerous local governments created
registration schemes for same-sex couples before same-sex marriage was legalised at the
national level. For summaries of these developments, see M. V. Lee Badgett, *When Gay
People Get Married* (NYU Press, 2009), p. 12; E. Aloni, 'Incrementalism, Civil Unions, and
the Possibility of Predicting Legal Recognition of Same-Sex Marriage' (2010) 18 *Duke
Journal of Gender, Law and Policy* 117–27.

[69] W. Eskridge Jr, *Equality Practice: Civil Unions and the Future of Gay Rights* (Routledge,
2002), p. 158.

[70] For background on the European Committee of Social Rights, see www.coe.int/t/dghl/
monitoring/socialcharter/Presentation/AboutCharter_en.asp (describing the Committee's
'monitoring procedure based on national reports').

determine details regarding law reform. However, there will be a minimum pace of reform that is dictated by consensus doctrine. For example, once a consensus-deeming[71] number of Contracting States enacts domestic partnership registries that confer particular rights to same-sex couples, the margin of appreciation regarding those rights will close; laggard States will be in breach of Articles 14 and 8, and they will need to catch up by establishing similar domestic partnership registries. Likewise, once a consensus-deeming number of States have achieved full marriage equality, laggard States will need to catch up with their peers by granting same-sex couples access to marriage.

While the grace period is novel in the context of the ECHR, similar grace periods have existed in some domestic courts (even though the courts have not used the term 'grace period' to describe their remedial delays). For example, in July 2011, the Colombian Constitutional Court ruled that the Colombian Congress had two years to legislate same-sex marriage.[72] In December 2005, the Constitutional Court of South Africa gave the South African Parliament one year to amend its marriage laws to achieve marriage equality.[73] Certainly, these remedial delays in Colombia and South Africa were different from the grace period that I propose for the ECHR because the grace period that I propose is not defined by a specific date. The United States Supreme Court provides an example of a domestic grace period that lacked a specific deadline. The United States Supreme Court directed defendant school districts in *Brown* v. *Board of Education* to desegregate their racially segregated schools with 'all deliberate speed', rather than stipulating a deadline for integration.[74] Commentators have noted that domestic courts' remedial delays have tempered the backlash that otherwise could have undermined the courts' overall abilities to effectuate socio-legal change.[75]

---

[71] The ECHR has defined consensus inconsistently, and has not developed a clear methodology for determining whether a consensus exists. It is beyond the scope of this chapter to propose how exactly the Court should define consensus. Rather, the chapter leaves for the Court to decide, in future jurisprudence, what constitutes a 'consensus-deeming' number of States. For background on the Court's inconsistency in this regard, see generally L. R. Helfer, 'Consensus, Coherence and the European Convention on Human Rights' (1993) 26 *Cornell International Law Journal* 133–64; I. Radačić, 'The Margin of Appreciation, Consensus, Morality and the Rights of the Vulnerable' (2010) 31 *Zbornik Pravnog fakulteta Sveučilišta u Rijeci* 604–8.

[72] See J. Zebley, 'Colombia High Court Sends Same-Sex Marriage Question to Congress', *Jurist*, 27 July 2011, http://jurist.org/paperchase/2011/07/colombia-high-court-sends-same-sex-marriage-question-to-congress.php; 'Colombian Court Says Congress Must Decide on Gay Marriage', CNN, 27 July 2011, http://edition.cnn.com/2011/WORLD/americas/07/27/colombia.gay.marriage.

[73] See *Fourie*, para. 156.

[74] See United States Supreme Court, *Brown* v. *Board of Education*, 349 US 294, 301, 31 May 1955.

[75] See e.g. T. Jacobi, 'Sharing the Love: The Political Power of Remedial Delay in Same-Sex Marriage Cases' (2006) 15 *Law and Sexuality* 11–38 (arguing that remedial delays can temper backlash in important ways and discussing remedial delays related to same-sex

The redrafted judgment for *Schalk and Kopf* uses consensus doctrine to define the terms of its grace period because of the Court's institutional constraints. Recall that, as a supranational institution, the Court needs to defer to Contracting States to elicit their cooperation.[76] The consensus doctrine is a means through which the Court achieves such deference.[77] It is possible that the pace of change resulting from consensus doctrine turns out to be unfortunately slow. Indeed, the grace period could theoretically extend indefinitely if States never reach a point of consensus on same-sex marriage. In redrafting the *Schalk and Kopf* judgment, I begrudgingly accepted these possibilities, despite their normative problems, due to the Court's institutional constraints. With that said, I was hopeful that change would not be too slow because, as the original judgment noted, legal recognition of same-sex couples has been developing rapidly in recent years.[78] In light of the consensus-based grace period's drawbacks, it is worth noting that the consensus-based grace period is a tool that is unfitting for domestic courts. Domestic courts can be more assertive than the ECHR in driving legal reform because the ECHR, as a supranational court, has greater institutional constraints.[79] Thus, generally speaking, if a domestic court chooses to adopt a grace period, it should specify a specific length for the grace period, as did the constitutional courts of Colombia and South Africa.[80]

The difference between the original and redrafted judgments

At first blush, the redrafted judgment may seem extremely similar to the original judgment because neither of them finds Austria in breach of the Convention. Moreover, both judgments rely on the consensus doctrine. A deeper comparison, however, reveals that the redrafted judgment enhances the Court's expressive power, allowing the Court to play a more significant role in shaping human rights norms on marriage equality.

It is worth emphasising that this chapter approaches the redrafting exercise from a realist perspective as opposed to utopianism. The redrafted opinion is informed by the Court's institutional constraints and, relatedly, the likely reality that a majority of judges would not adopt an approach to marriage equality that

marriage litigation in Massachusetts and Vermont); S. Goldberg, 'Marriage as Monopoly: History, Tradition, Incrementalism, and the Marriage/Civil Union Distinction' (2009) 41 *Connecticut Law Review* 1416–23 (arguing that courts should generally be reluctant to adopt incremental approaches to achieving equality, but acknowledging that in some cases incrementalism helps to prevent harmful backlash that outweighs the benefits of more immediate reform).

[76] See notes 65–7 above and the accompanying text.

[77] See notes 65–7 above and the accompanying text.   [78] *Schalk and Kopf*, para. 105.

[79] For an elaboration on why the ECHR's deferential consensus doctrine is inapposite to domestic courts, see H. Lau and D. Loh, 'W v. Registrar of Marriages: Misapplication of ECHR Jurisprudence in Hong Kong' (2011) 41 *Hong Kong Law Journal* 75–88.

[80] See notes 72–3 above and the accompanying text.

disregards those constraints. The redrafted judgment seeks to balance these realist constraints on the one hand with normative ideals on the other hand. It strikes this balance by gently pushing States in the direction of marriage equality, even though it stops short of obligating Contracting States to legalise same-sex marriage immediately. The redrafted judgment pushes States towards marriage equality by articulating the right to marriage equality and explaining the reasons that undergird that right.

The Court's articulation of a right to marriage equality is significant, especially in light of the ECHR's respected stature. As William Eskridge has explained:

> A court's or a legislature's announcement of an equality right serves an expressive function at the very least. In the international context, human rights are typically articulated and endorsed long before they can be fully implemented, yet the official announcement of such a right contributes to the creation of a public norm to that effect. Public values and norms can influence private as well as public conduct. More important, they can embolden their intended beneficiaries to demand better treatment from private as well as public authorities.[81]

By announcing the right to marriage equality, the Court helps to develop marriage equality as a human rights norm not only among Contracting States, but also in other parts of the world. Many courts beyond Europe turn to the ECHR for guidance, even though ECHR jurisprudence is not binding on them.[82] Indeed, John Attanasio once remarked that the ECHR 'may be becoming a sort of world court of human rights'.[83] As far away as Hong Kong, the ECHR is making an impact on domestic adjudication. As Albert Chen recently noted, case law on the European Convention, including that from the ECHR, 'has proved to be the single most important source of reference for the Hong Kong courts in construing and applying the ICCPR and [Hong Kong's] Bill of Rights'.[84] In jurisdictions such as Hong Kong, courts look to the ECHR as an important identifier of human rights. The ECHR has developed enough reputational capital that its articulation of the right to marriage equality would help to shape norms both inside and outside Europe.

It is worth noting that the redrafted judgment is also significantly different from the original dissenting opinion because the dissenting opinion stopped short of announcing a right to marriage equality. Arguably, the redrafted

---

[81] W. Eskridge Jr, *Equality Practice: Civil Unions and the Future of Gay Rights* (Routledge, 2002), p. 153.

[82] See A. Slaughter, 'Judicial Globalization' (2000) 40 *Virginia Journal of International Law* 1109–10.

[83] J. B. Attanasio, 'Rapporteur's Overview and Conclusions: Of Sovereignty, Globalization, and Courts' (1995–6) 28 *NYU Journal of International Law and Politics* 16.

[84] A. H. Y. Chen, 'International Human Rights Law and Domestic Constitutional Law: Internationalisation of Constitutional Law in Hong Kong' (2009) 4 *National Taiwan University Law Review* 247.

judgment is less demanding because the dissenting judges did find Austria in violation of the Convention. The dissenters stated that Austria was in violation because it failed to justify the pre-2010 situation in Austria, when registered partnerships were not yet available.[85] The dissenting judges were unhelpfully ambiguous, however, on what rights Austria was obligated to provide before 2010 and how that bundle of rights would be determined.[86] To avoid that ambiguity, in addition to avoiding a potential backlash against the Court, the redrafted judgment diverges from the original judgment's dissenting opinion.

Conclusion

In sum, the redrafted judgment announces marriage equality as a right pursuant to Article 14, taken in conjunction with Article 8; it recognises a grace period during which Contracting States are directed to implement law reforms to achieve marriage equality; and it employs the Court's consensus doctrine to establish the minimum pace of reform for achieving marriage equality. In doing so, the redrafted judgment takes a measured approach to effectuating change. It amplifies the ECHR's expressive power and wields that power to cultivate a human rights norm of marriage equality. By declaring that Contracting States must work towards legalising same-sex marriage, the redrafted judgment affirms that same-sex couples – and the gay and lesbian communities to which same-sex couples belong – deserve the same respect that is afforded to their straight counterparts. This affirmation of inclusiveness advances this book's goal of promoting diversity.

Rewriting Schalk and Kopf v. Austria

. . .

b. Compliance with Article 14 taken together with Article 8

[Original paragraphs 96–110 deleted]
  96. It is worth addressing, at the outset, the contention that a right to same-sex marriage cannot be derived from Article 14, taken in conjunction with Article 8, because same-sex couples do not have the right to marry under Article 12. This contention is unpersuasive. For the reasons

---

[85] *Schalk and Kopf*, Joint Dissenting Opinion, paras. 6–8.
[86] The dissenting judges stated, rather opaquely, that they did 'not want to dwell' on the 'particular features of this [Registered Partnership] Act'. *Ibid.*, para. 7. They also stated that '[a]ny absence of a legal framework offering [same-sex couples], at least to a certain extent, the same rights or benefits attached to marriage would need robust justification', but the vague phrase 'to a certain extent' is question-begging. See *ibid.*, para. 9.

discussed in the remainder of this section, same-sex couples have a right of equal access to marriage, pursuant to Articles 14 and 8, taken together. The Court will refer to this right as the right to marriage equality. In the spirit of the Court's evolutive approach to interpreting the Convention, it is certainly possible for the right to marriage equality to evolve and come to fruition in the context of Articles 14 and 8, taken together, even though the Court does not derive marriage equality from the text of Article 12. Several state supreme courts in the United States have similarly decided that rights to same-sex marriage can derive from constitutional provisions on equality, even though the very same courts did not find same-sex marriage to be included in the fundamental right to marry guaranteed by other constitutional provisions.[87]

97. The Court notes that the instant case is distinguishable from *Johnston and others*, cited above. In that case, the applicants claimed a right to divorce based on Article 12 as well as a right to divorce based on Article 8. The flawed logical bases of those two claims were so similar that, to be consistent, the Court needed to reject the Article 8 claim after having earlier rejected the Article 12 claim. In contrast, the applicants' discrimination claim in the instant case (based on Articles 14 and 8) is substantially different from their straightforward right-to-marry claim (based on Article 12). By casting their argument in terms of Articles 14 and 8, the applicants illuminated unjustifiable aspects of marriage laws that did not come to light during the Court's analysis of the applicants' Article 12 claim. Accordingly, the Court need not resolve the applicants' two claims identically.

98. The Court recalls that, in order for an issue to arise under Article 14, there must be a difference in treatment of persons in relevantly similar situations. While the parties have not explicitly addressed the issue of whether the applicants were in a relevantly similar situation to different-sex couples, the Court starts from the premise that same-sex couples and different-sex couples are indeed relevantly similar. Same-sex and different-sex couples are similarly capable of having healthy, committed relationships; they are also similarly capable of raising children in healthy manners. Social science research supports this factual premise.[88] One can also reasonably infer that marriage would enhance the health and well-being of many same-sex couples, just as marriage does for many different-sex couples.[89]

---

[87] See *Kerrigan v. Commissioner of Public Health*, 957 A 2d 407, 412 (Connecticut Supreme Court, 2008); *Varnum v. Brien*, 763 NW 2d 862, 873 (Iowa Supreme Court, 2009); *Baehr v. Lewin*, 852 P 2d 44, 55–58, 61 (Hawaii Supreme Court, 1993).

[88] See e.g. G. M. Herek, 'Legal Recognition of Same-Sex Relationships in the United States: A Social Science Perspective' (2006) 61 *American Psychologist* 607 at 607–13.

[89] See H. Lau and C. Q. Strohm, 'The Effects of Legally Recognizing Same-Sex Unions on Health and Well-Being' (2011) 29 *Law and Inequality* 107.

99. Differential treatment of similarly situated persons is discriminatory if it is not sufficiently justified. The Court has held repeatedly that, just like differences based on sex, differences based on sexual orientation require particularly serious justifications (see *Karner*, cited above, § 37; *L and V*, cited above, § 45; and *Smith and Grady*, cited above, § 90).

100. Whether there are particularly serious justifications for treating couples differently based on their sexual orientation is a question that falls within this Court's domain of review. While it is sometimes appropriate for the Court to leave a margin of appreciation to States, a margin of appreciation is ill-suited for assessing the purported reasons for differential treatment based on sexual orientation. The margin of appreciation doctrine is appropriate for problems that national governments are better-positioned to address. National governments, however, are not in a superior position with respect to the problem of sexual orientation discrimination. History illuminates the fact that stereotype-tainted reasoning often undermines national authorities' deliberations on matters of sexual orientation. History also shows that, as a minority group, gays and lesbians often lack the political power that is necessary to remedy sexual orientation discrimination effectively through States' democratic channels. As such, national authorities are not in a superior position to evaluate the strengths and weaknesses of alleged justifications for differential treatment based on sexual orientation.

101. To determine whether there are particularly serious justifications for differential treatment based on sexual orientation, this Court will assess whether there is a well-calibrated proportionality between the differential treatment on the one hand and important governmental aims on the other.

102. The Government did not advance any specific justification for its differential treatment of same-sex and different-sex couples; instead, it invoked a margin of appreciation. However, as described above (para. 100), the margin of appreciation doctrine does not apply to the assessment of purported justifications for the differential treatment in this case. Based on its own analysis, the Court concludes that the differential treatment is unjustified because it is not proportionately related to any important governmental aims.

103. This Court agrees with courts in Canada, South Africa and the United States that have reviewed bans on same-sex marriage under heightened scrutiny.[90] These courts referred to their judicial review

---

[90] See *Varnum* (Iowa, cited above); *Kerrigan* (Connecticut, cited above); *In re Marriage Cases*, 183 P 3d 384, 451–2 (California, Supreme Court, 2008) (subsequently superseded by constitutional amendment); *Minister for Home Affairs* v. *Fourie*, Case CCT 60/04 (South Africa, Constitutional Court, 2005); *Barbeau* v. *British Columbia*, 2003 BCCA 251 (British

with different terms (e.g. 'intermediate scrutiny', 'strict scrutiny' and the application of 'proportionality' tests); nonetheless, they all applied standards of review that were substantially similar to the proportionality analysis that we apply in this case (para. 101). They all concluded that excluding same-sex couples from marriage is not sufficiently related to any important governmental goals. This Court agrees. Three reasons for this conclusion are particularly noteworthy. First, the Court rejects the possibility that preserving tradition is, in and of itself, an important goal that justifies the differential treatment in this case. Invoking tradition alone is tautological: it is logically flawed to suggest that tradition is what justifies the traditional definition of marriage. Secondly, although promoting the stability of different-sex relationships is an important governmental aim, the Court rejects the notion that excluding same-sex couples from marriage advances this goal. According to data from European States that were early adopters of same-sex marriage or other registration schemes for same-sex couples, whether and how States legally recognise same-sex relationships has not affected overall rates of marriage or divorce.[91] These findings cast substantial doubt on the belief that legalising same-sex marriage destabilises different-sex relationships. Thirdly, the Court rejects the idea that marriage rights should be limited to different-sex couples because they are uniquely capable of raising healthy, well-adjusted children. As noted above (para. 98), social science research does not support such speculation.

104. Because there are no serious justifications for denying same-sex couples access to marriage, same-sex couples have a right to marriage equality pursuant to Article 14, taken in conjunction with Article 8. The differential treatment in the instant case is discriminatory, unduly denying same-sex couples respect for their family life. The applicants are discriminated against even though they can obtain legal recognition through Austria's registered partnership scheme because marriages and registered partnerships are similar, but not equal.

105. While the Court recognises that denying same-sex couples access to marriage is discriminatory, the Court hereby recognises a grace period for achieving marriage equality. During this grace period, Contracting States that have not implemented marriage equality are not yet in violation of their Convention obligations. The Court adopts this grace period because it recognises that stable and enduring social change is sometimes

Columbia, Court of Appeal, 2003); and *Halpern* v. *Canada*, 65 OR 3d 161 (Ontario, Court of Appeal, 2003).

[91] See e.g. M. V. Lee Badgett, *When Gay People Get Married* (NYU Press, 2009), pp. 65–80; W. N. Eskridge, Jr and D. R. Spedale, *Gay Marriage: For Better or For Worse?: What We've Learned from the Evidence* (Oxford University Press, 2006), pp. 91–129.

best achieved incrementally. Specifically, one can reasonably believe that marriage equality is best achieved through gradual reform of law and public policy. Contracting States can use the grace period to implement policies that help to shape social attitudes, cultivating an inclusive cultural climate to prepare for marriage equality.[92] For example, during the grace period, Contracting States may decide to implement relevant public education campaigns and gradually increase the recognition rights afforded to same-sex couples before fully recognising same-sex couples through marriage. The Court notes that the six Contracting States that have legalised same-sex marriage – the Netherlands, Belgium, Spain, Portugal, Norway and Sweden – all achieved marriage equality after incrementally increasing the rights of same-sex couples, albeit through varying degrees of incrementalism. The grace period established by this judgment allows other Contracting States to reform along similar lines.

106. The terms of the grace period will be informed by the Court's long-standing consensus doctrine. During the grace period, State authorities retain a margin of appreciation to determine how and when to introduce reforms of law and policy aimed at increasing the recognition rights of same-sex couples. However, the width of that margin narrows as consensus develops over time. Put differently, a minimum pace of reform will be established through consensus. For example, once a consensus-deeming number of States have enacted civil partnership registries that confer particular rights to same-sex couples, the margin of appreciation regarding those rights will close; laggard States that have not established similar partnership registries will be in breach of Articles 14 and 8. Likewise, once a consensus-deeming number of States have implemented full marriage equality, laggard States will need to catch up by granting same-sex couples full access to marriage. The Court notes that the tendency to legally recognise same-sex couples has developed rapidly over the past decade. The Court is hopeful that this brisk pace will continue.

107. The Court finds that the Government is currently not in violation of Article 14, taken in conjunction with Article 8, because it offers same-sex couples a registration scheme that confers most of the rights associated with marriage; Austria is not lagging behind its peers in reforming laws to grant same-sex couples legal recognition.

108. It is worth noting that the applicants argued, in part, that the Government was in violation of Article 14, in conjunction with Article 8, during the period of time prior to the establishment of the Registered Partnership scheme in 2010. This claim is moot. Whether Austria was

---

[92] For an elaboration on this point, see W. N. Eskridge, *Equality Practice: Civil Unions and the Future of Gay Rights* (Routledge, 2002).

earlier lagging behind in law reform has become a moot question because, having instituted its registered partnership scheme, Austria is now not lagging behind. The Court reiterates that in proceedings originating in an individual application, the Court must confine itself, as far as possible, to an examination of the concrete case before it (see *F* v. *Switzerland*, cited above, § 31). Given that at present it is open to the applicants to enter into a registered partnership, the Court is not called upon to examine whether the lack of any means of legal recognition for same-sex couples would constitute a violation of Article 14 taken in conjunction with Article 8 if it still obtained today.

109. In sum, denying same-sex couples the right to marry is discriminatory. Denying same-sex couples the right to marry while offering them legal recognition through an alternative registration system, such as the Government's registered partnership scheme, is still discriminatory. Pursuant to Article 14, taken in conjunction with Article 8, same-sex couples have a right to marriage equality. With that said, the Court finds that, for the time being, the Government is not in violation of Articles 14 and 8 because the Court grants Contracting States a grace period to work towards implementing marriage equality and the terms of the grace period are stipulated above.

11

The *Burden* of conjugality

AEYAL GROSS*

Rather than arguing that rights are fundamental and natural to the individual, we should try to imagine and create a new relational right which permits all possible types of relations to exist and not be prevented, blocked, or annulled by impoverished relational institutions.[1]

Introduction

The case of *Burden and Burden* v. *United Kingdom*, decided by the European Court of Human Rights (ECHR) in a chamber judgment by the Fourth Section in 2006,[2] and then its second round as the case of *Burden* v. *United Kingdom*, decided in a judgment given by the Grand Chamber in 2008,[3] presented the ECHR with the challenge of addressing the legal consequences of the relationships of two sisters who have always lived together. This chapter looks closely at the judgments in this case, and, after criticising them, suggests an alternative route that would have better respected diversity of forms of human life and of family structures. The discussion will proceed as follows. In the first section below, I will describe the facts of the case. The second section will include a description of the judgments of the Fourth Section and Grand Chamber. The

* I am grateful to Eva Brems for inviting me to participate in this project, to Mary Anne Case, Ayelet Blecher-Prigat, Sharon Shakargy and Zvi Triger for their comments on a previous draft of this chapter, and to Nadav Dishon for his excellent research work. I also benefited from conversations with Erez Aloni, Hadar Aviram, Janet Halley and Nancy Polikoff and from comments made and questions asked by the participants in the Mainstreaming Diversity conference, especially Judge Christos Rozakis and Helmut Graupner, who commented on my presentation. The chapter was also presented in the Faculty Workshop in Tel-Aviv University Faculty of Law, and I am grateful to the participants for their insightful comments.

1 Michel Foucault, in Gilles Barbedette, 'A Conversation with Michel Foucault', 6 *Christopher Street* (1982) 36 at 38.
2 ECHR, *Burden and Burden* v. *United Kingdom*, 12 December 2006 (hereinafter '*Burden* (Fourth Section)').
3 ECHR (GC), *Burden* v. *United Kingdom*, 29 April 2008 (hereinafter 'Burden (Grand Chamber)').

third section will include an internal critique of the reasoning in the two judgments. This will be followed in the fourth section in a discussion that puts the questions addressed in the *Burden* case in the broader perspective of the limits of the conjugality-centred approach to relationship and family life and will accordingly include a critique of the judgments from that perspective. Finally in the concluding part I will explain the alternative route that I suggest the ECHR could have taken in the *Burden* case. This will be illustrated in my suggested redrafting of some crucial paragraphs of the Grand Chamber decision, which is to be found at the end of this chapter.

The *Burden* case challenged the notion of equal recognition of different forms of relationship, and illustrates how opening the institution of family life to same-sex couples raises new questions of equality, which touch upon the very notion of what types of relationships are worthy of legal recognition and for which purposes. Because the case was litigated against the background of the introduction of 'civil partnerships' for same-sex couples in the United Kingdom, it raised significant questions about the nature of this institution, and more generally about the law's treatment of people who live together in forms of life which differ from the nuclear heterosexual family.

The facts of the case

The facts of the case as detailed by the ECHR were as follows. The applicants are unmarried sisters, born in 1918 and 1925 respectively, who have lived together all their lives, in what the Grand Chamber described as a 'stable, committed, and mutually supportive relationship'.[4] In the thirty-one years prior to the Grand Chamber's judgment they lived in a house built on land inherited from their parents and owned by the sisters in their joint names. Each sister had made a will leaving all her property to the other. They submitted that each sister's one-half share was worth more than the existing exemption threshold for inheritance tax.[5] The ECHR noted that the inheritance tax, in accordance with UK domestic law, is charged at 40 per cent, on the value of a person's property, including his or her share of anything owned jointly.[6]

---

[4] *Burden* (Grand Chamber), note 3 above, para. 9.

[5] *Ibid.*, paras. 9–12; *Burden* (Fourth Section), note 2 above, paras. 8–11.

[6] *Burden* (Grand Chamber), note 3 above, para. 13, citing to the Inheritance Tax Act 1984, c. 51 (England). There was controversy during the litigation concerning the financial situation of the Burden sisters. Brian Dempsey points to the fact that, contrary to press reports, the remaining sister would not have had to sell the house upon the death of her sibling in order to pay the tax. See Brian Dempsey, 'Burden v. United Kingdom: "Dissin" Lesbians or Decentring Marriage (Part 1)' (2009) 376 *SCOLAG Journal* 35 at 35. These questions and the role the privileged economic status of the Burden sisters should (or should not) play in addressing the case are explored in Rosemary Auchmuty, 'Beyond Couples' (2009) 17(2) *Feminist Legal Studies* 205. For the purpose of my discussion that deals with the principled question of privileging conjugality, this issue is immaterial.

The sisters complained that their rights were violated under Article 1 of Protocol 1 to the European Convention on Human Rights ('the Convention'), which protects the 'peaceful enjoyment of . . . possessions', taken in conjunction with Article 14, which determines that the 'enjoyment of rights and freedoms set forth in [the] Convention shall be secured without discrimination on any ground such as sex, race, colour, language, political or other opinion, national or social origin, association with a national minority, property, birth or other status'. They argued that when one of them died, the survivor would face a significant liability to inheritance tax, which would not be faced by the survivor of a marriage or civil partnership.[7] The UK Civil Partnership Act 2004[8] (CPA 2004) created a formal mechanism for the recognition and creation of legal effects of the relationships of same-sex couples, while conferring on them, in the words of the Grand Chamber, 'as far as possible, the same rights and obligations as entailed by marriage'.[9] A couple is eligible to form a civil partnership if they are (i) of the same sex; (ii) not already married or in a civil partnership; (iii) over the age of sixteen; and (iv) not within the prohibited degrees of relationship.[10] The latter category includes siblings.[11] The Grand Chamber noted that, during the passage of the Bill which became the CPA 2004, the House of Lords adopted amendments to the Bill which would have had the effect of extending the availability of civil partnership, and the associated inheritance tax concessions that it entails, to family members within the 'prohibited degree of relationship', if they were over thirty years of age, had cohabited for at least twelve years, and were not already married or in a civil partnership with some other person. However, the amendment was reversed when the Bill returned to the House of Commons.[12] The Grand Chamber cited a few speeches made in the House of Lords and the House of Commons where members argued that there is an arguable case for relief from inheritance tax for family members living together and caring for each other, but that the CPA 2004 was not the right piece of legislation to address this issue.[13]

The judgments of the Fourth Section and the Grand Chamber

Both instances dealing with the application rejected it. The Fourth Section, in a narrow four-to-three majority, pointed to the fact that States enjoy a wide margin of appreciation in the field of taxation, and it is for national authorities to make the initial assessment of the aims to be followed and means to be used,

---

[7] *Burden* (Grand Chamber), note 3 above, para. 14.
[8] Civil Partnership Act 2004, c. 33 (England), cited and discussed in *Burden* (Grand Chamber), note 3 above, paras. 16–20.
[9] *Burden* (Grand Chamber), note 3 above, para. 16.   [10] *Ibid.*, para. 17.
[11] CPA 2004, Sched. 1.   [12] *Burden* (Grand Chamber), note 3 above, para. 19.
[13] *Ibid.*, para. 20.

with the Court generally respecting the legislature's policy choice in creating and implementing taxation, as long as it does not discriminate in a way inconsistent with Article 14.[14] Article 14, it noted, safeguards individuals placed in similar positions from discrimination in the enjoyment of rights and freedoms protected by the Convention: a difference of treatment is discriminatory if it has no objective and reasonable justification, i.e. does not pursue a legitimate aim, or if there is not a reasonable relationship of proportionality between the means employed and the aim sought to be realised.[15]

The Fourth Section thus examined the applicants' claim that they were in a similar or analogous position to cohabiting married and civil partnership couples for the purpose of inheritance tax, and the UK's contrary argument that there is no true analogy in this situation because they were connected by birth rather than by a decision to enter into a formal relationship recognised by law.[16] The Court noted that, unlike previous cases that involved unmarried heterosexual cohabiting partners who chose not to marry, and whose discrimination arguments were rejected, in this case the Burden sisters did not have the choice to marry, or enter a civil partnership, which may raise the question of whether this lack of choice bears on the question of the analogy to married or civilly partnered couples.[17] The Court side-stepped this question by holding that, even assuming that the applicants can be compared to married or civil partnership couples, the difference in treatment is not inconsistent with Article 14.[18] In reaching this conclusion, the Fourth Section recalled its previous determinations that difference in treatment between unmarried and married couples can be justified, with 'marriage remaining an institution that was widely accepted as conferring a particular status on those who entered it', and thus '[t]he promotion of marriage by way of the grant of limited benefits for surviving spouses could not be said to exceed the margin of appreciation afforded to the respondent State'.[19] Based on the above, it accepted the position that the inheritance tax exemption for married and civil partnership couples pursues a legitimate aim, 'namely to promote stable committed heterosexual and homosexual relationship by providing the survivor with a measure of financial security after the death of the spouse or partner'.[20] The Fourth Section cited the right to marry protected in Article 12 and the fact that sexual orientation discrimination is covered by Article 14, and thus held that the UK 'cannot be criticized for pursuing, through its taxation system, policies designed to promote marriage' or for 'making available the fiscal advantages attendant on

[14] *Burden* (Fourth Section), note 2 above, para. 54.   [15] *Ibid.*, para. 55.
[16] *Ibid.*, para. 56.
[17] *Ibid.*, paras. 57–8, citing to the ECHR, *Shackell* v. *United Kingdom*, 27 April 2000; and the European Commission of Human Rights opinion in ECommHR, *Lindsay* v. *United Kingdom*, 11 November 1986.
[18] *Burden* (Fourth Section), note 2 above, para. 58.
[19] *Ibid.*, para. 59, citing to ECHR, *Shackell* v. *United Kingdom*, 27 April 2000.   [20] *Ibid.*

marriage to committed homosexual couples'.[21] The UK's choice in this matter is within its margin of appreciation.[22]

The Grand Chamber, in its judgment, given in a fifteen-to-two majority, emphasised that Article 14 complements other substantive provisions within the Convention and has no independent existence[23] and that for an issue to arise under Article 14 there must be a difference in treatment of persons in relevantly similar situations. Such a difference is discriminatory if it has no objective and reasonable justification, i.e. if it does not pursue a legitimate aim or if there is no reasonable relationship of proportionality between the means employed and the aim sought to be realised.[24] Addressing this question, the Grand Chamber remarked that the relationship between siblings is 'qualitatively of a different nature to that between married couples and homosexual civil partners', as '[t]he very essence of the connection between siblings is consanguinity, whereas one of the defining characteristics of a marriage or a Civil Partnership Act union is that it is forbidden to close family members'.[25] 'The fact that the applicants have chosen to live together all their adult lives, as do many married and Civil Partnership Act couples', added the Grand Chamber, 'does not alter this essential difference between the two types of relationship.'[26] To this, the Grand Chamber added, citing previous case law,[27] and recalling Article 12 which protects the right to marry, that marriage confers a 'special status' on those who enter into it, with its exercise giving rise to social, personal and legal consequences. The Grand Chamber noted that the holding in previous judgments, whereby the situations of married and unmarried heterosexual cohabiting couples was not analogous for the purposes of survivor's benefits because of the particular status of marriage still holds true.[28] The CPA 2004, noted the Grand Chamber, now gives homosexual couples the choice to also enter into a legal relationship corresponding to marriage.[29] The Grand Chamber found that, as civil partnership is something a couple 'expressly and deliberately' decide to enter, this type of relationship is distinct from other forms of cohabitation: 'Rather than the length or the supportive nature of the relationship, what is determinative is the existence of a public undertaking, carrying with it a body of rights and obligations of a contractual nature'.[30] The Grand Chamber noted that, just as there can be no analogy between married and civilly partnered couples on the one hand, and heterosexual or homosexual couples who choose to live together without marrying or entering civil partnership on the other hand, then the absence of such a legally binding agreement between the applicants renders their relationship of cohabitation, notwithstanding its duration, 'fundamentally different to that of a married or

---

[21] *Ibid.*   [22] *Ibid.*, paras. 60–1.   [23] *Burden* (Grand Chamber), note 3 above, para. 58.
[24] *Ibid.*, para. 60.   [25] *Ibid.*, para. 62.   [26] *Ibid.*
[27] *Ibid.*, para. 63, citing to ECHR, *B and L v. United Kingdom*, 29 June 2004, and ECHR, *Shackell* v. *United Kingdom*, 27 April 2000.
[28] *Ibid.*   [29] *Ibid.*, para. 64.   [30] *Ibid.*, para. 65.

civil partnership couple',[31] and thus the applicants cannot be compared for the purposes of Article 14 to a married or civilly partnered couple.[32]

The judgments: a critique of the reasoning

Difference and similarity between the judgments

Looking at the two judgments, we can see that, notwithstanding some overlaps, the two instances put the emphasis on different reasons for rejecting the application. The Fourth Section found it unnecessary to hold whether the Burden sisters can be compared to a married or civil partnership couple, holding that, even assuming that the applicants can be compared to such couples, the difference in treatment is not inconsistent with Article 14, putting the emphasis on the UK's margin of appreciation. The Grand Chamber did actually make a determination on this point, holding that the two *cannot* be compared to a married or civil partnership couple for the purpose of Article 14. But, notwithstanding the difference between the two instances, at the heart of both judgments is a rejection of the application based on a valorisation of marriage as enjoying a special status, now conferred apparently also on civil partnership. This is apparent in the Fourth Section determination about marriage remaining an institution that was widely accepted as conferring a particular status on those who entered it, and holding that its promotion by way of the grant of benefits is within the State's margin of appreciation as it pursues the legitimate aim of promoting stable committed heterosexual, and homosexual relationships. This statement resonates with the Grand Chamber's determination that marriage confers a 'special status' on those who enter into it, and that there can be no analogy between married and civil partnership couples on the one hand, and heterosexual or homosexual couples who choose to live together without marrying or entering civil partnership on the other hand, the latter being 'fundamentally different' to the first. So, while the Fourth Section emphasises the State's rights to promote marriage or marriage-like (i.e. civil partnership) relationships, and the Grand Chamber rather sees a big difference between cohabitation and a registration-based 'public undertaking' relationship, both end up prioritising marriage and civil partnership, or, in other words, conjugality.[33]

---

[31] *Ibid.*, para. 65.

[32] *Ibid.*, para. 66. For a discussion of the judgments which includes an elaborate discussion of the dissenting opinions, see Brian Dempsey, 'Burden v. United Kingdom: "Dissin" Lesbians or Decentring Marriage (Part 1)' (2009) 376 *SCOLAG Journal* 35; Brian Dempsey, 'Burden v. United Kingdom: "Dissin" Lesbians or Decentring Marriage (Part 2)' (2009) 377 *SCOLAG Journal* 59.

[33] The *Oxford English Dictionary* defines 'conjugal' as 'of or relating to marriage, matrimonial'. Technically, then, it would not apply to civil partnership, but, given the way civil partnership is treated in the law, in society and in the *Burden* case itself, I chose to use the term as incorporating both marriage and civil partnership. For a critique of such a

The reasoning of both instances seems to me to be flawed. When it comes to the Fourth Section judgment, at its root is what the Fourth Section considers the government's legitimate interest in promoting marriage, described by the court as promoting stable committed heterosexual or homosexual (now that civil partnership is allowed) relationships. Now, one can dispute whether or not this is a proper cause for the State to promote, but at this stage I want to point to the fact that, by bracketing the comparability question, the Fourth Section side-stepped the question of choice, as discussed in more detail below.[34] Recall that, in previous judgments cited by both instances, the ECHR held that unmarried couples could not claim the same rights as married couples.[35] The Fourth Section mentions these judgments, and points to the fact that the Burden sisters, unlike the opposite-sex couples in such cases, did not have the option of marriage. Nevertheless, it chose to bracket the question of the implication of this difference.

The bracketing of the question of choice and the limits of formal equality

In order to see the effect of this bracketing, consider the *Karner v. Austria*[36] case, mentioned by both instances only briefly: in this case, the Court held that non-married same-sex couples, who did not have the option of marriage, or for that matter civil partnership, should not be discriminated *vis-à-vis* opposite-sex couples, who were awarded the benefit in question regardless of whether they were married or not. In discussing the margin of appreciation the State is accorded with regard to Article 14, which in *Karner* was held to be violated in conjunction with Article 8, the Court held that, while the State's stated aim was the protection of the traditional family, its margin of appreciation in the circumstances was narrow, given that there was a difference in treatment based on sex or

use in the context of the discussion of the *Burden* case, see Brian Dempsey, 'Burden v. United Kingdom: "Dissin" Lesbians or Decentring Marriage (Part 2)' (2009) 377 *SCOLAG Journal* 59 at 63 n. 35. However, as Dempsey notes, the ECHR in *Burden* treated civil partnership and marriage as essentially a single category, although, as he notes, by doing so the majority paradoxically both embrace civil partnership *and* maintain the privileged position of marriage, *Burden* (Grand Chamber), note 2 above, para. 62. For a discussion of the relationship of civil partnership to 'conjugality', see Carl F. Stychin, 'Couplings: Civil Partnership in the United Kingdom' (2005) 8 *New York City Law Review* 543 at 562–7. For the way in which various expansions of the nuclear-family model to include informal heterosexual unions and same-sex relationships, even if they do not amount to the 'conjugal family', still reinforce the idea of what she calls the 'sexual family', see Martha Alberston Fineman, *The Neutered Mother, the Sexual Family and Other Twentieth Century Tragedies* (Routledge, 1995), pp. 143–4.

[34] Indeed, in their joint dissenting opinion, Judges Bonello and Garlicki pointed to the lack of possibility of choice given to other couples as putting the Burden sisters in a different situation from that of couples who were free to choose whether to marry or not, *Burden* (Fourth Section), note 1 above, Joint Dissenting Opinion of Judges Bonello and Garlicki, para. 3.

[35] See notes 17–19 above and the cases cited therein.

[36] ECHR, *Karner v. Austria*, 24 July 2000.

sexual orientation, and that such differences require particularly serious reasons by way of justification. The principle of proportionality, it was held, does not merely require that the measure chosen is in principle suited for realising the aim sought, but it must also be shown that it was necessary in order to achieve that aim to exclude certain categories of people – in *Karner*, persons living in a same-sex relationship – from the scope of application of the statute in question.[37]

So, whereas in *Karner* the Court accorded the State a narrow margin of appreciation, in *Burden* the Fourth Section granted the State a much broader one. On the surface, the difference is based on the fact that *Karner* dealt with discrimination based on sexual orientation (or sex), especially given that the rights in question were accorded also to unmarried cohabiting opposite-sex couples, whereas in *Burden* the basis of discrimination was between those living in conjugal relations and others. But one can look at these cases as raising a similar question. That would require framing the question at the heart of *Burden* – as well as *Karner* – differently: is it justified to discriminate based on marital status, between two persons who live together in a joint household where they share responsibilities, especially when they do not have the option of marrying? If we were to read *Karner* as giving a negative answer to this question, then its logic could have led to a different conclusion by the Fourth Section in *Burden*. But *Karner* was read by the Fourth Section in *Burden* narrowly to be about discrimination based on sexual orientation. This is not surprising, given the reasoning in *Karner* itself, and given the fact that indeed the couple in question in *Karner* would have had access to the rights in question had it been an opposite-sex unmarried couple. The outcome of this reading is that same-sex couples can now join opposite-sex couples in enjoying financial benefits, be it through holding that acting otherwise would amount to discrimination (*Karner*) or through the creation of same-sex marriage or parallel institutions (such as civil partnership in the UK). But it is this logic of *Karner*, with its emphasis on the special nature of sex and sexual orientation discrimination, which serves in *Burden* (Fourth Section) to exclude others from the benefits awarded to relationships. In the Fourth Section's – and for that matter also the Grand Chamber's – reasoning, once the sexual orientation issue was settled in the UK, by way of the CPA 2004, there is no more justified case of discrimination to be made on behalf of two persons cohabiting in a joint household, whether it is the State's legitimate aim to promote stable heterosexual or homosexual relationships (Fourth Section) or because they cannot even be considered to be in an analogous situation to heterosexual or homosexual couples (Grand Chamber). The result of this is an exclusion of relationships – such as that of the Burden sisters – which do not fall into the conjugal model.

---

[37] *Ibid.*, paras. 37 and 41.

In *Karner* (as in other similar ECHR cases on the rights of same-sex couples that followed its logic),[38] the ECHR refused to give preference to opposite-sex married or cohabiting couples where same-sex couples were excluded from the institution based on their sexual orientation. Now, when in the UK the door is open to *both* opposite-sex and same-sex couples to enter the institution(s) of marriage/civil partnership, the line is drawn in a different place in the sand: it is no longer between opposite-sex and same-sex couples, but rather between opposite-sex or same-sex couples on the one hand (i.e. those who are not precluded from entering marriage or civil partnership), and all other forms of relationship on the other hand. This new drawing of the lines is upheld by the court, to the exclusion of, among others, the *Burden* sisters.

It is important to note that this drawing of lines may actually leave same-sex couples outside when it concerns couples who do not have the civil partnership/ marriage option, and with regard to rights given only to those with this status (i.e. not awarded to cohabiting couples, even if they are of the opposite sex). This is apparent from *Estevez* v. *Spain*, where the Court held as inadmissible a claim that same-sex couples were discriminated with regard to access to social security, when the law awarded the benefit only to married couples.[39] The Court held that the distinction was within Spain's legitimate aim of the protection of the family based on marriage bonds – notwithstanding the fact that same-sex couples were at the time excluded from that institution and thus from the social benefits in question.[40] This proves that the Court's concept of equality with regard to couples remains a *formal* one, as same-sex couples are awarded equality only with regard to rights awarded to non-married opposite-sex couples. *Substantive* equality would require that the fact that same-sex couples are excluded from marriage, would require, at the very least, recognition of their rights to equal access to the rights awarded to married couples. Indeed, the line drawn between married or civil partnership couples and others, which leaves the Burden sisters outside access to the inheritance tax exemption, is one of *formal equality*.

The detrimental affects of the Burden judgments on same-sex couples

Two cases heard after *Burden*, and citing it, reinforce this point: in these cases, the ECHR held as inadmissible claims coming from the UK on discrimination with regard to the very same rights discussed in *Burden*, concerning issues that arose *before* the enactment of the CPA 2004, when same-sex couples did not have this option open. *Courten* v. *United Kingdom* involved the same issue as in

---

[38] *Karner*'s principle that non-married homosexual couples, who did not have the option of marriage, or for that matter civil partnership, should not be discriminated *vis-à-vis* opposite-sex couples was upheld in ECHR, *PB and JS* v. *Austria*, 22 July 2010, paras. 38–42, and in ECHR, *Kozak* v. *Poland*, 2 March 2010, para. 99.
[39] See ECHR, *Mata Estevez* v. *Spain*, 10 May 2001.   [40] *Ibid.*

Burden, that of inheritance tax. The case was brought before the Court after the CPA 2004 entered into force, but the surviving partner and the deceased who cohabited could not have entered civil partnership, as the deceased died shortly before the CPA 2004 entered into force. In holding the application inadmissible, the ECHR reiterated its previous statements, citing, *inter alia*, *Burden*, that, notwithstanding social changes, marriage remains an institution that is widely accepted as conferring a particular status on those who enter it and, indeed, is singled out for special treatment under Article 12. The Court noted that, while the Grand Chamber in *Burden* equated civil partnerships between same-sex couples with marriage, this was on the basis that in both situations the parties had undertaken public and binding obligations towards each other. The Court added that 'the Government cannot be criticized for not having introduced the 2004 legislation at an earlier date and thereby enabled the applicant to obtain the benefit of the inheritance tax exemptions conferred on the survivor of a civil partnership'.[41] The applicant in *Courten* made the argument that, while relationships based on consanguinity (such as was the case in *Burden*) could be distinguished from married couples and civil partners, this ground of distinction could not apply to cohabiting same-sex couples, and that therefore it was implicit in the Grand Chamber judgment in *Burden* that cohabiting same-sex couples would be in an analogous position to married heterosexual couples, especially given that at the relevant time same-sex couples had no choice about whether to enter an equivalent arrangement. The Court rejected this argument, stating that, while the Grand Chamber in *Burden* equated civil partnerships between same-sex couples with marriage, this was on the basis that in both situations the parties had undertaken public and binding obligations towards each other. 'The judgment', said the Court in *Courten* (referring to *Burden*) 'therefore is of no assistance in that respect to the applicant who lived with his partner in a long term but informal relationship'.[42] The Court ruled inadmissible another case that raised similar legal and factual issues, emphasising that *Burden* was about identifying the fundamental difference between personal relationships that are based on a legally binding agreement giving rise to certain rights and duties for the parties and those that are not.[43] Since some see making the case for the Burden sisters as potentially undermining the recognition of same-sex couples, by negating their special status as a couple analogous to the married couple,[44] it is important to note that *Burden* was actually used in these later cases to the detriment of same-sex couples excluded from civil partnership on a temporal basis in the UK itself, and may be used again in a similar way to exclude same-sex couples from equal rights in countries which exclude same-sex couples from marriage and do not

---

[41] ECHR, *Courten* v. *United Kingdom*, 4 November 2008.   [42] *Ibid.*
[43] ECHR, *MW* v. *United Kingdom*, 23 June 2009.
[44] See the discussion in notes 85–8 below and the accompanying text.

have civil partnership or a similar institution. The question remains whether in future cases brought to it concerning a contemporary situation in countries with no same-sex marriage or civil partnership law, the ECHR would decide the same, or whether it would find that discrimination in access to rights on the basis of sexual orientation through the exclusion of same-sex couples from marriage is prohibited. In the only case decided so far on same-sex marriage, the Court did not have to address this question, as the country in question, Austria, had by the time the case was decided introduced a registered partnership act, offering rights similar to, but not identical to, those of married couples. In *Schalk and Kopf* v. *Austria*, the Court thus rejected the application, relying to a large extent on the determination in Article 12 that the right to marry is that of 'men and women of marriageable age', and interpreting this language to imply that the right is only accorded as such to opposite-sex couples.[45] But, in the same case, the Court did recognise that the relationship of same-sex couples amounts to 'family life' under Article 8,[46] and held that they are in a relevantly similar situation to a different-sex couple as regards their need for legal recognition and protection of their relationship.[47] It emphasised that it is the fact that the applicants can enter into a registered partnership which gives a legal status equal or similar to marriage in many respects, which makes it unnecessary for it to examine whether lack of marriage for same-sex couples would amount to a violation of Article 14 in conjunction with Article 8,[48] and held that examining whether the differences that do exist between the registered partnership and marriage are justified remained beyond the scope of the case in question.[49] These determinations, together with the Court's discussion of 'an emerging European consensus toward legal recognition of same-sex couples', even if the area is still one of 'evolving rights with no established consensus',[50] indicate that the Court may possibly in further cases treat discrimination in access to rights, or lack of any recognition of same-sex couples, as prohibited under the Convention. Should that happen, then the line will be redrawn again, albeit only with regard to same-sex couples, given the ECHR's emphasis on the 'suspect' nature of sex or sexual orientation discrimination.

The valorisation of marriage and civil partnership

I will return to discussing the privileging of conjugality in the next section, but, at this stage, I would like to point to the following questions that arise when reading the *Burden* judgments: when it comes to the Fourth Section's judgment,

---

[45] ECHR, *Schalk and Kopf* v. *Austria*, 24 June 2010, paras. 54–63.

[46] *Ibid.*, paras. 92–4. The Court reiterated this position in ECHR, *PB and JS* v. *Austria*, 22 July 2010, paras. 27–30.

[47] ECHR, *Schalk and Kopf* v. *Austria*, 24 June 2010, paras. 99 and 109.

[48] *Ibid.*, para. 103.   [49] *Ibid.*, para. 109.   [50] *Ibid.*, para. 105.

we may wonder, if indeed the purpose which justifies the discrimination with regard to the inheritance tax is to promote stable relationships, then it seems that the Burden sisters certainly enjoyed such a relationship. In order then to further inquire into the connection between the purpose to be promoted and the legislative measures, one should ask what actually is at the heart of the declared purpose of promoting stable relationships. Is it having people care for and support each other in a reliable and durable way? Is it having people show commitment and trust? Assuming those are the purposes worth promoting in the eyes of the State, it seems that all of these purposes were fulfilled in the case of the Burden sisters. Shifting to the Grand Chamber's judgment, it seems that, unlike the Fourth Section, the Grand Chamber actually does *not* consider these purposes as important or worthy of special protection: in its judgment it states that it is *not* the length or supportive nature of the relationships that matter, but rather the public undertaking which carries, in the Grand Chamber's terms, a body of rights and obligations of a contractual nature.[51] From this statement, we can discern that the Grand Chamber does not seem to see the length or the supportive nature as the features which distinguish relationships, making them worthy of special protection, but rather the formal legal act of the public undertaking and the entailed rights and obligations. It is actually somewhat perplexing that the Grand Chamber sees these rights and obligations as being of a contractual nature, as marriage or civil partnership are clearly more than a contract: rather, they affect one's personal status and create statutory rather than just contractual legal obligations.[52] But it is especially because of the Grand Chamber's choice to emphasise the nature of marriage or civil partnership as formal legal institutions, rather than their presumed substantial content, that we can see how the Grand Chamber in a paradoxical way shares the Fourth Section valorisation of marriage: whereas the Fourth Section considered that marriage or civil partnership can be awarded a special status because of the stability, and thus, presumably, the long-term support, the Grand Chamber considers that marriage and civil partnership should be in any case awarded a special status, notwithstanding the question of stability or support, and maybe actually precisely because they are not necessarily based on those character-istics. The Grand Chamber is right in the sense that length or support are not pre-conditions for marriage and civil partnership: one can enter them very quickly, and be legally considered a couple for all purposes. So what I find fascinating about *Burden* is the choice, by *both* ECHR instances, to maintain the hierarchy between, on the one hand, the institutions of marriage and civil

---

[51] *Burden* (Grand Chamber), note 3 above, para. 65.
[52] On the complex position of marriage between 'contract' and 'status', and of the impossibility of maintaining a strict opposition between the two, see Janet Halley, 'Behind the Law of Marriage (I): From Status/Contract to the Marriage System' (2010) 6 *Unbound* 1 at 14–23.

partnership, and on the other hand relationships which are based on support and length rather than mere registration (a registration which entails legal rights and obligations), with the two instances doing this based on an almost contradictory understanding of these institutions. The fact that for each of the instances marriage/civil partnership represent an institution that is indeed, 'fundamentally different' from cohabiting, but that for each of them the difference is based on different, almost opposite reasons, attests to the fact that marriage/civil partnership are actually empty signifiers, statuses which can be attained by mere registration on the one hand but are presumed or imagined to signify stable relationship on the other hand.[53]

Recall that, in deciding the *Burden* case, the Fourth Section noted that the previous decisions, where differences in treatment between married and unmarried couples were found to be not in violation of the Convention,[54] were ones where the couples in question were free to choose whether or not to marry. But the Burden sisters did not have this choice, and their exclusion from any institution that accords legal recognition, as is given to a married or civil partnership couple, is at the heart of their complaint. Still, the Fourth Section chose not to address the question of whether lack of choice has any bearing on the question, because of its judgment that, even assuming the applicants could be compared to recognised couples, the difference in treatment is not inconsistent with Article 14.[55] This determination by the Fourth Section is not very convincing: The lack of choice accorded to the Burden sisters situates them differently than opposite sex couples who chose not to marry and whose complaint was rejected in previous cases, and puts them more similarly situated to same-sex couples who cannot marry in countries which do not have same-sex marriage (or a parallel civil partnership option), as was the case in *Karner*. Once again, we see how, by holding that the choice issue is irrelevant, the Fourth Section in *Burden* distanced the Burden sisters from the unmarried same-sex couple. Even more perplexing is the Grand Chamber's determination that there is a difference between marriage and civil partnership on the one hand, which couples expressly and deliberately *decide* to enter into, and cohabitation on the other hand, setting the two apart: to support this argument the Grand Chamber noted that, just as there can be no analogy between married and civil partnership couples, on the one hand, and opposite-sex or same-sex couples who 'choose to live together' but not to marry or become civil partners, on the other hand, 'the absence of such a legally binding agreement between the applicants renders their relationship of cohabitation,

---

[53] As Mary Anne Case notes of marriage, it licenses couples to structure their lives as best suits them without losing recognition for their relationship, without having their commitment or the legal benefits that follow from it challenged. See Mary Anne Case, 'Marriage Licenses' (2005) 89 *Minnesota Law Review* 1758 at 1772–3.

[54] *Burden* (Fourth Section), note 2 above, para. 46, referring to ECHR, *Shackell* v. *United Kingdom*, 27 April 2000, and ECommHR, *Lindsay* v. *United Kingdom*, 11 November 1986.

[55] *Burden* (Fourth Section), note 2 above, para. 58.

despite its long duration, fundamentally different to that of a married or civil partnership couple'.[56] This is a circular argument that does not provide any justification for the exclusion of the Burden sisters from the institutions to which they did *not* deliberately decide or choose not to enter. The reasoning is circular because the *Burden* sisters were excluded from any legal arrangement that would have accorded them equal rights when it came to the inheritance tax, and not out of choice, but out of lack of any such arrangement and out of the legislature's, rather than their own, choice.

Another route could have been taken by both instances, which would have accorded the lack of choice a central role, as will be shown in the sixth section of this chapter. But, beyond that, one must wonder whether the question of choice is relevant at all, in the sense of whether marriage and civil partnership should be given special status when the choice does exist, or should all choices about relationships be accorded equal status? This question will carry us over to the next section.

Consanguinity v. conjugality?

Revisiting choice

Should the question of choice or lack thereof matter? On the one hand, perhaps we should not privilege conjugality at all, and the question of the accordance of choice should not matter: couples should be accorded the same rights whether married or not, and our concept of couples, or of relationships, should go beyond the conjugality model altogether to include relationships such as that enjoyed by the Burden sisters. On the other hand, we may consider that the question of lack of choice is crucial: perhaps if the choice to enter some form of legally recognised relationship is accorded, and people actually choose not to enter it, this implies that it was not their intention to undertake the obligations, not only the rights, entailed in legally recognised relationships.[57] One way to get out of this conundrum, should we really not want to prioritise conjugality over other forms of relations (for reasons that will be explained below), is first to detach as much as possible rights and benefits from relationships. But, before exploring these options, I would argue that, in any case, even within current legal and social frameworks, when the choice does not exist on the one hand, and on the other hand the law accords benefits and rights to legally recognised registered relationships (traditionally only marriage but now also civil partnership), then not according these rights to people who *cannot* enter these relationships is discriminatory. Previously, it was discriminatory towards same-sex

---

[56] *Burden* (Grand Chamber), note 3 above, para. 65.

[57] See on this problem Sahar Lifshitz, 'A Potential Lesson from the Israeli Experience for the American Same-Sex Marriage Debate' (2008) 22 *BYU Journal of Public Law* 359 at 368–79.

couples. Today, this discrimination is overcome only partly, since as discussed above, it is not clear yet whether in jurisdictions which do not have same-sex marriage or civil partnerships, and which accord rights only to married (rather than cohabiting couples), the ECHR will mandate according same-sex couples equal rights. It rejected this path in *Estevez*, but perhaps its growing emphasis on the special nature of sex and sexual orientation discrimination, as well as some of its *dicta* in recent cases,[58] may hint at a different direction in the future. But, even if such a development does occur, it will relegate same-sex couples to an equal status with married couples even in jurisdictions with no registered partnership, but will leave cases like that of the Burden sisters outside the scope of protection.

Is civil partnership like marriage?

Can this be justified? While, as explained below, the CPA 2004 does not require there to be a sexual relationship, it was constructed upon the model of a same-sex couple which is assumed to be similar to the married couple. The prohibition on family relations entering a civil partnership which prevented the Burden sisters from accessing civil partnership and the benefits it entails is clearly modelled on the incest prohibition in marriage and assumes conjugal relations which must never be mixed with consanguinity. This prohibition goes to the heart of the incest taboo. This is the place to indeed ponder whether, in a similar case of cohabitation without on the one hand consanguinity but on the other hand with the two members of the unit not considering themselves a 'couple' in the romantic and sexual contexts, and not seeing themselves as a conjugality-based unit, the two could have entered civil partnership and enjoyed the benefits in question. On its face, it seems that nothing in the CPA 2004 would prevent them from doing so, even if the legislative debates indicate that the purpose of the CPA 2004 was to accord legal recognition to same-sex couples which are enjoying an intimate and presumably sexual relationship.[59] This open question points to the many tensions and contradictions within civil partnership. Carl Stychin, who discusses these tensions and contradictions, points to the fact that, while debates about the CPA 2004 assumed a civil partnership relationship is one that includes a sexual component, the CPA 2004 in fact does not require a sexual relationship, or cohabitation, from those who enter it.[60] 'It seems unfair, so opponents argue', says Stychin, 'that the

---

[58] In ECHR, *Courten* v. *United Kingdom*, 4 November 2008; ECHR, *MW* v. *United Kingdom*, 23 June 2009; and especially in ECHR, *Schalk and Kopf* v. *Austria*, 24 June 2010.

[59] Carl F. Stychin, 'Couplings: Civil Partnership in the United Kingdom' (2005) 8 *New York City Law Review* 543 at 548–54.

[60] *Ibid.*, at 554–60. Stychin points to incoherencies within civil partnerships along the binaries of marriage/not marriage; sex/no sex; status/contract; conjugality/care; love/

spinster couple cannot be civil partners – except, of course, that they can be, provided that they register and accept both the benefits and burdens of partnership. However, if they are spinster *sisters*, then they cannot register under this Act.'[61] Indeed, the question remains whether the *Burden* case is about discrimination of any two who are not in a conjugal (or conjugal-like) relationship (i.e. two friends living together and maintaining the same level of joint household and support), or only about discrimination of the two because of the consanguinity, as others – as long as they remain two – could enter into marriage (if opposite sex) or civil partnership (if same sex), with the latter being an easier option because of the lack of the legal presumption of a necessary sexual relationship.[62] In any case, as civil partnership – restricted under UK law to people of the same sex – could not presumably lead to co-biological parenthood, and also does not actually require sex *per se*, then the question that pops up – but was not asked by the ECHR – is why is it justified then to carry over the 'incest' prohibition into it by prohibiting consanguinity?[63] From this perspective, indeed civil partnership is both like and unlike marriage. Presumably, a holding for the Burden sisters by the Court would have made civil partnership too much *unlike* marriage, but holding against them makes it too much *like* marriage.

Indeed, the Grand Chamber judgment seems almost to conflate civil partnership and marriage. The result is privileging conjugality, through holding, in the Grand Chamber's words, that there is a 'fundamental difference' between couples who entered a legally recognised relationship, and those who haven't. Is there really a legitimate State interest in so privileging conjugality and making it the only basis for formal legal recognition that accords rights? Is there indeed *a priori* a fundamental – and relevant – difference which justifies distinction in rights and privileges between persons within this form of relationship and other persons?

money; responsibilities/rights. Concerning the issue of sex, Gaffney-Rhys points to the fact that, in contrast to the provisions of the Matrimonial Causes Act 1973, c. 18 (England), the CPA 2004 does not allow a partnership to be set aside on the basis of failure to enter into a sexual relationship or on the ground that the respondent was suffering from a communicable form of venereal disease when the partnership was formed; see Ruth Gaffney-Rhys, 'Siblings and Civil Partnerships' (2007) *IFLaw Journal* 84 at 86.

[61] Carl F. Stychin, 'Couplings: Civil Partnership in the United Kingdom' (2005) 8 *New York City Law Review* 543 at 557 (emphasis in the original).

[62] Unlike marriage, as discussed in note 60 above and the article cited therein.

[63] While the Court did not ask this question, Rosemary Auchmuty, in her discussion of *Burden*, asked with regard to the CPA 2004, 'if sex is not relevant, then why the consanguinity ban?' See Rosemary Auchmuty, 'Beyond Couples' (2009) 17(2) *Feminist Legal Studies* 205 at 211. The answer may indeed be that sex is somehow both relevant and irrelevant and that the CPA 2004 still remains captured within the 'sexual family' model, as argued by Fineman. See note 74 below and the accompanying text.

As mentioned above, I suggest that the purposes mentioned by the Fourth Section as justifying a different treatment, would actually justify also protecting relationships such as those of the Burden sisters at least for purposes such as the ones brought before the ECHR. If one accepts that my point about the circular nature of the Grand Chamber reasoning is then also reinforced: to hold that there is a difference just because of the public formal legal undertaking to which the Burden sisters are denied access, does not prove that they are not similarly situated: it rather just says what we already know, i.e. that they are excluded by law from the institutions in question.

The symbolic and material meaning of marriage

In order to understand the problematic nature of prioritising marriage, we should recall that marriage, as an institution, conveys the message that it is the most sacred form of human relationship and the ultimate fulfilment of the individual's personal life. Thus, the mere existence of marriage (at least so long as it is constructed around the couple that enters into it and thus commits to the obligations associated with it) sends a message of exclusion to all who do not or cannot participate in the institution (based on their choice not to participate in, or their lack of ability to do so, be it a legal impossibility, or factual circumstances, e.g. for lack of a willing partner). Consequently, although allowing same-sex couples entry into this institution or into civil partnerships which provide for equal or similar sets of rights expands marriage, it also reinforces the message that marriage is the ultimate form of human relationship, whether opposite- or same-sex.[64] Given the symbolic and material benefits associated with marriage, this message is discriminatory towards all who do not participate in it, specifically those who live in family units that are not based on couplehood: the single person, individuals with more than one lover, and other forms of human relationships.[65]

---

[64] Another effect of the privileging of marriage is addressed by Michael Warner, who argues that marriage has become the central legitimating institution by which the State regulates and permeates people's most intimate lives: it is the zone of privacy outside of which sex is unprotected. See Michael Warner, *The Trouble with Normal: Sex, Politics and the Ethics of Queer Life* (Cambridge, MA: Harvard University Press, 1999), p. 96.

[65] Sybil Burden said: 'We are looked upon for being single. We just want to be treated as equal citizens and given the rights we deserve. We've saved the government thousands by caring for our elderly sick relatives till they passed away and have never claimed a penny apart from the pension.' Tony Grew, 'Spinster Sisters Challenge Over Gay Tax Rights', www.pinknews.co.uk/ news/articles/2005-2407.html, 4 September 2006. In this context, it should be mentioned that one could argue that expanding legal recognition of relationships beyond conjugality will actually reinforce the privatisation of social and economic responsibilities by assuming caring is taking place within private units and is not the State's responsibility, in a way that may justify the diminishing of publicly funded programmes. Compare the discussion on a similar possible effect of same-sex marriage in Susan B. Boyd and Clare F. L. Young, "'From Same-Sex to No

For these reasons, drawing a legal line between conjugality (or conjugality-like) based relationship and other forms of relationships in a way that allocates different rights and privileges, should be considered a prohibited form of discrimination: it reinforces the exclusionary messages described above.

While civil partnership may not enjoy the symbolic connotation of marriage, extending it to same-sex couples in a way that does give them some symbolic State recognition, and then gives them full or almost full material recognition, may end the discrimination against them, and send a message of equal respect to the life of gay people, but at the same time does not undermine the practice of sending a stigmatising and inferior message to those who would not want to or would not be able to marry or enter civil partnership in the new legal regime. Again, this could include people who have no partner either because they do not want one or could not succeed in finding one, people who have less or more than one partner, or anyone whose patterns of relationship do not fit the marriage model, such as the Burden sisters. Given the message of inferiority that the existence and stature of marriage sends to all kinds of relationships – and sex – outside of its parameters, marriage must be understood as part of the heterosexual-patriarchal structure of society, which seeks to valorise a certain kind of human life, and also restrict sexual relationships to this structure. Moreover, while exclusion of same-sex couples (and others) from marriage may have been excused (if not justified) in its religious and historical connotations, and in the case of siblings based on the incest prohibition, what justification can there be to exclude people like the Burden sisters from civil partnership, or at least from the rights and benefits that come with it?

Beyond conjugality?

Brenda Cossman and Bruce Ryder point to the fact that the notion of conjugality is an irrational basis for the allocation of legal benefits and burdens.[66] While arguing that the distinction between conjugal and non-conjugal relations has become more elusive, and that sex, once the hallmark of conjugal relationship, became legally less relevant, they argue that it should become totally irrelevant, and more generally that conjugality should no longer be the marker or proxy for the legal regulation of adult personal relationships, that which is the marker for legal inclusion to unmarried cohabitants through ascribed spousal status. The

---

Sex?" Trends Towards Recognition of (Same-Sex) Relationships in Canada' (2002–3) 1 *Seattle Journal for Social Justice* 757 at 776–7. Additionally, Boyd and Young are concerned with the possibility that the more relationships are recognised by the State, the more State intervention will result in terms of regulating the way those relationships operate. On the other hand, see Martha Fineman's position regarding the importance of recognising relationships which are based on care-giving rather than on sex: see note 74 below and the accompanying text.

[66] Brenda Cossman and Bruce Ryder, 'What Is Marriage-Like Like? The Irrelevance of Conjugality' (2001) 18 *Canadian Journal of Family Law* 269 at 272.

distinction, they argue, is no longer normatively or legally viable. The search for marriage equivalence, they suggest, is a relic of an era when the law sought to bolster and regulate marriage as the only socially acceptable intimate relationship between adults. They suggest that conjugality or marriage-equivalence is a poor proxy for the relational attributes relevant to legislative objectives and that the law should avoid presumptions based on relational status and focus more on the actual existence of the kinds of economic and/or emotional interdependence relevant to particular legal objectives.[67] To ask whether a conjugal or marriage-like relationship exists is, they say, to ask the wrong question, as this existence is rarely relevant to the attainment of legislative objectives.[68] Instead, they suggest that the relationships that are relevant to State policies will involve varying combinations of four criteria: co-residence, duration, emotional interdependence, and economic interdependence.[69]

Cossman and Ryder's analysis and suggestion point to the deficiency of the *Burden* judgments. Indeed, the objectives upheld by the Fourth Section as justifying the difference in treatment which is within the State's margin of appreciation is irrational, even viewed from the stated purpose of promoting stable relationships. Tests such as those suggested by Cossman and Ryder seem much more relevant. Such tests also point to questions which actually may be relevant in considering whether the Burden sisters are similarly situated to couples protected under current legislation, with the actual existence of the relevant factors (see paragraph 62 of the redraft) being much more important than the form or status test preferred by the Grand Chamber – this being in addition to the fact that in any case they were denied access to the status (see paragraph 63 of the redraft).

Such a change would amount to recognition of all families' worth, as suggested by Nancy Polikoff, who is right to argue that '[m]arriage as a family form is not more important or valuable than other forms of family, so the law should not give it more value'.[70] Polikoff suggests that couples should have the choice to marry but never have to marry to reap specific and unique legal benefits.[71] Again, it is worth recalling that the Burden sisters did not even have a choice: discrimination against those who do not marry should be abolished,

---

[67] *Ibid.*, pp. 272–4.   [68] *Ibid.*, pp. 311–12.

[69] *Ibid.*, p. 315. The need to go 'Beyond Conjugality' towards the recognition and support of personal adult relationships that involve caring and interdependence, based on a principle of 'relational equality', was the topic of an extensive report by that title issued by the Law Commission of Canada in 2001: see Law Commission of Canada, 'Beyond Conjugality: Recognizing and Supporting Close Personal Adult Relationships' (2001), available at www.samesexmarriage.ca/docs/beyond_conjugality.pdf. For a discussion, see Nancy D. Polikoff, 'Ending Marriage as We Know It' (2003–4) 32 *Hofstra Law Review* 201 at 203–309.

[70] Nancy D. Polikoff, *Beyond (Straight and Gay) Marriage: Valuing All Families Under the Law* (Boston: Beacon Press, 2008), p. 3.

[71] *Ibid.*

especially if they are not even given this choice. Polikoff points to the case of the Burden sisters as one of many cases to which marriage is not the solution, as they are a long-term, interdependent unit which is a family and needs the financial advantages now extended only to spouses.[72] Advocating 'valuing all families', she argues that marriage should not be the rigid dividing line between 'who is in and who is out'.[73]

From the 'sexual family' to care-taking and friendship?

Taking the critique of marriage a step further, Martha Fineman exposes the limits of what she calls the 'sexual family', which, even when expanded from the traditional nuclear family to include informal heterosexual unions and same-sex relationships, still has at its core a sexual tie, and remains the baseline of what is considered a core family unit. Her suggestion to re-vision the family, in a way that redefines the legal core unit away from the focus on sexual or horizontal intimacy and that allows one to take account of care-taking,[74] points to the limit of the conjugal model which does not accommodate relationships such as the one enjoyed by the Burden sisters.

Some jurisdictions do actually recognise relationships which are 'beyond conjugality'.[75] Polikoff points to cities in the United States which defined domestic partnership based on mutual support, caring and commitment, in a way that could include non-conjugal relationships.[76] She suggests the option of a registration system whereby people would be able to identify someone considered a family member, and she points to laws in some states in the United States which include the option of designating a person for 'reciprocal beneficiaries'.[77] While addressing specific legal reforms of this sort is beyond the scope of this chapter, I would argue that, as long as the law does not provide such an option, benefits allocated based on conjugality should be considered as discriminatory to family units such as that of the Burden sisters.[78]

---

[72] *Ibid.*, pp. 4–5.

[73] *Ibid.*, p. 5. See also 'Beyond Same-Sex Marriage: A New Strategic Vision for All Our Families and Relationships', The Full Statement, available at www.beyondmarriage.org/ full_statement.html, 26 July 2006 .

[74] Martha Alberston Fineman, *The Neutered Mother, the Sexual Family and Other Twentieth Century Tragedies* (Routledge, 1995), pp. 1–9 and 142–50.

[75] For the *Oxford English Dictionary* definition of this term, see note 33 above.

[76] Nancy D. Polikoff, *Beyond (Straight and Gay) Marriage: Valuing All Families Under the Law* (Boston: Beacon Press, 2008), pp. 50–1.

[77] *Ibid.*, pp. 133–5.

[78] Thus, Auchmuty is right to point to the fact that the *Burden* case raises the question of why the government should recognise one kind of caring relationship and not another. Rosemary Auchmuty, 'Beyond Couples' (2009) 17(2) *Feminist Legal Studies* 205 at 210 and 217.

The discussion raises the question of how do we define family and kinship: the Burden sisters do consist of a biological family, but were not recognised as entitled to the inheritance tax exemption. The issue is of course broader, as there could be similar situations like that of the Burden sisters where the persons involved are not blood relatives. Although it seems that, in the UK, two persons of the same sex, similarly situated to the Burden sisters but who are not siblings, may be able to enter civil partnership, this will not solve the problem for two of the opposite sex, or of cases involving more than two persons. We should thus consider that an approach that values diversity would consider other forms of relationship which are not based on the traditional kinship models as also worthy of protection and possibly recognised as 'family'. A related question is whether all relationships that are awarded some recognition must fall into the notion of 'family', however broadly defined, or can 'friendship' be an alternative paradigm.[79]

Indeed, thinking of forms of kinship outside the heterosexual paradigm should lead us to think not only of the equality of same-sex couples, but also of non-marital kinship relations that emerge outside heterosexuality-based family ties and only partially approximate the family form in some instances.[80] Judith Butler has suggested (following David Schneider) that kinship is a kind of 'doing' that does not reflect a prior structure, but can only be understood as an enacted practice. Can kinship be distinguished from other communal and affiliative practices? Or is it just modes of enduring relationship? Butler points to the fact that, as a matter of fact, kinship ties that bind people to one another may or may not be based on enduring or exclusive sexual relations, and may well consist of ex-lovers, non-lovers, friends, and community members. This displaces the central place of biological and sexual relations from the definition of kinship: the complex multiple nature of kinship relations cannot be configured according to a universal structure of symbolical norms. As Butler notes, the various forms of kinship include not only single- and multi-parent families, but various caring and budding systems. But only some forms of kinship

---

[79] See Katherine Franke's suggestion to consider substituting 'friendship' for 'marriage' as the benchmark that grounds our reasoning about sexual and affective liberty. Katherine M. Franke, 'Longing for *Loving*' (2008) 76 *Fordham Law Review* 2685 at 2703–6. See also Laura Rosenbury's critique of the way the divide between 'friendship' and 'marriage' amounts to State support of the types of domestic care-giving associated with marriage and traditional gender roles, and her suggestion to consider recognising the care provided to and received by friends. Laura A. Rosenbury, 'Friends with Benefits?' (2007) 106 *Michigan Law Review* 198. While the Burden sisters, by way of being sisters, amounted to being 'family', their case raises question of the similar relationship of support which may exist between individuals who are not siblings or otherwise related, and thus Franke's and Rosenbury's discussions of friendship are relevant here.

[80] For a discussion of such forms of kinship, see Kath Weston, *Families We Choose: Lesbians, Gays, Kinship* (New York: Columbia University Press, 1991).

are established as intelligible and liveable ones.[81] The *Burden* case illustrates that it is only the heterosexual family, or a similar same-sex-based family, that is considered a form of kinship which is worthy of legal protection. Instead of this restrictive model, as Butler suggests, consensual affiliation may replace blood ties as the basis for kinship, when such affiliation is based upon responsibility, trust and commitment. The Burden sisters did have blood ties, but I suggest we take their case as one that should cause us to think of any type of relationship which is based upon these values, whether it is based on conjugality, consanguinity or neither of these.

Consider an arrangement which is much more open than the UK CPA 2004 discussed in *Burden*: The Belgian law on cohabitation determines that a declaration on cohabitation may be made by any two persons who are in a communal-living situation, who are not connected by marriage or by another legal cohabitation, and who are capable of contracting. Under Belgian law, the nature of the relationship between the two is not relevant, and they can be of different sexes or of the same sex, and they can be related, or not. Hence, the Burden sisters could have entered into such an arrangement, had it existed in the UK. Notably, in Belgium (where same-sex marriage is legal) legal cohabitation, is not equal to marriage but is, in an increasing number of cases, treated as its equivalent.[82] While discussing the Belgian model in detail is beyond the scope of this chapter, it is for our purposes interesting to contrast it to the UK model, which remains conjugality-based.

Graycar and Milibank describe the Domestic Relationships Act enacted by the Australian Capital Territory in 1994, which (similarly to the Belgian law) introduced a category of domestic relationship that did not require parties to be in a sexual relationship or to cohabit. The definition was of a 'personal relationship between [two] adults in which one provides personal or financial commitment and support of a domestic nature for the material benefit of the other'. However, later legislation in the Australian Capital Territory retreated from this broad approach. The 2003 same-sex reforms use the category 'domestic partner', but the definition in that legislation expressly requires the parties to be a cohabiting couple. Legislation in other territories on this matter is even narrower.[83]

---

[81] Judith Butler, *Antigone's Claim: Kinship between Life and Death* (New York: Columbia University Press, 2000); Judith Butler, 'Is Kinship Always Already Heterosexual?' (2002) 13(1) *Differences: A Journal of Feminist Cultural Studies* 14.

[82] Frederik Swennen and Yves-Henri Leleu, 'National Report: Belgium' (2011) 19 *American University Journal of Gender, Social Policy and the Law* 57 at 72–4. I am grateful to Erez Aloni for pointing out to me the relevance of the Belgian model.

[83] Reg Graycar and Jenni Millbank, 'From Functional Family to Spinster Sisters: Australia's Distinctive Path to Relationship Recognition' (2007) 24 *Washington University Journal of Law and Policy* 121 at 147–51. See also Jenni Millbank, 'The Changing Meaning of "De Facto" Relationship' (2006) 12 *Current Family Law* 2. For a legal decision that expanded the notion of family, see *Borough of Glassboro* v. *Vallorosi*, 529 A 2d 1028 (NJ Super. 1987)

Addressing the discussion of this issue in Australia, Graycar and Milibank point to the fact that, while the original conception of a non-couple category was intended as a progressive gesture, to make a break from a hierarchical pattern of relationship rights with marriage at the top, and having the potential to destabilise heteronormativity and the hetero-nuclear family itself, then later the use of and discourse around non-couple recognition has changed dramatically in Australia, and has been completely 'captured' by conservative opponents of gay and lesbian equality movements who now promote it – in a very different light – as their own reform agenda.[84] Also addressing some of the dissenting opinions in the *Burden* judgments and reactions to the case, Brian Dempsey points to the fact that some of the statements supporting the case of the Burden sisters implied a disparagement of the official acceptance of same-sex relationships and that right-wing religious groups opposed to gay rights viewed the Burden sisters' case favourably.[85] Indeed, conservative groups, in Australia, the United Kingdom and elsewhere, promote the agenda of the recognition of relations beyond conjugality out of opposition to the recognition of same-sex couples. Sometimes, they wish by promoting this agenda to make the case that same-sex couples are privileged versus others, the classic example being, even before *Burden*, that of the 'spinster sisters' and similarly situated non-conjugal 'couples'.[86] In other cases, it may simply be the fact that they would rather give rights to all people in some form of relationship as long as they do not have to explicitly recognise same-sex couples. In any case, I believe that this 'hijacking' of the argument should not deter us from considering that its original conception, as Graycar and Milibank describe it, indeed still holds.[87] The fact that conservative

(holding that a group of college students who lived together as roommates were the functional equivalent of a family unit within the meaning of a zoning ordinance).

[84] Reg Graycar and Jenni Millbank, 'From Functional Family to Spinster Sisters: Australia's Distinctive Path to Relationship Recognition' (2007) 24 *Washington University Journal of Law and Policy* 121 at 150.

[85] Brian Dempsey, 'Burden v. United Kingdom: "Dissin" Lesbians or Decentring Marriage (Part 2)' (2009) 377 *SCOLAG Journal* 59 at 61.

[86] The question of why 'spinster sisters' became the trope of the non-sexualised relations even before *Burden* requires further exploration. See Reg Graycar and Jenni Millbank, 'From Functional Family to Spinster Sisters: Australia's Distinctive Path to Relationship Recognition' (2007) 24 *Washington University Journal of Law and Policy* 121 at 150–7; See also Carl F. Stychin, 'Couplings: Civil Partnership in the United Kingdom' (2005) 8 *New York City Law Review* 543 at 557–8.

[87] Carl Stychin points to the way in which the conservative critique of the CPA 2004, according to which, if civil partnership is not marriage, then it should not exclude all those who care for each other in interdependent committed relationships, is not dissimilar to feminist and queer readings of the legislation, which argue that, if the State is going to recognise relationship forms outside the institution of marriage, then it should take the opportunity to consider real alternatives in which conjugality may be de-privileged: see Carl Stychin, 'Not (Quite) A Horse and Carriage: The Civil Partnership Act 2004' (2006) 14 *Feminist Legal Studies* 79 at 81.

forces may want the same for their own reasons does not change my position that extending rights to various forms of relationships, and not discriminating against single persons, is a worthwhile project from the perspective of equality and diversity.[88] This point goes beyond the question of recognition of diverse forms of relationships: consider, for example, spousal benefits, such as the claim that was made by the Israeli Supreme Court (with success)[89] and the European Court of Justice (with failure)[90] that employees of transport companies (respectively airlines and train companies) should be awarded free tickets or discounts to their same-sex partners that are awarded to married couples. Would it not be more right to determine that single persons should not be discriminated and that *all* employees will be able to get this benefit and assign it to *any* person of their choice, regardless of the nature of their relationship?[91]

Function or form?

In any case, conjugality then is not a prerequisite for a mutually supportive relationship, and thus it is not clear why it is justified to confine property-related entitlements to couples which fall under this category. Adopting a 'functional' approach to family life raises these questions, and, even if indeed it is hard to devise a law which will cater to the myriad of circumstances possible,[92] this does not mean that discriminatory consequences should not be remedied by courts entrusted with guaranteeing human rights. A functional approach would thus reject the 'form' approach taken by the Grand Chamber.[93] It will, rather than

---

[88] On *Burden* as setting back attempts at 'modern, rational, equality-based laws and policies' and instead continuing 'the privileging of people in very particular forms of state-approved, state-regulated relationships', see Brian Dempsey, 'Burden v. United Kingdom: "Dissin" Lesbians or Decentring Marriage (Part 2)' (2009) 377 *SCOLAG Journal* 59 at 62.

[89] HCJ 721/94, *El-Al Israel Airlines Ltd* v. *Danielowitz* [1994] IsrSC 48(5) 749.

[90] ECJ, Case C-249/96, *Grant* v. *South-West Trains Ltd* [1998] ECR I-621.

[91] I elaborate on this in Aeyal M. Gross, 'Challenges to Compulsory Heterosexuality: Recognition and Non-Recognition of Same-Sex Couples in Israeli Law', in Robert Wintemute and Mads Andenas (eds.), *Legal Recognition of Same-Sex Partners: A Study of National, European and International Law* (Oxford: Hart Publishing, 2001), pp. 391–414.

[92] See Gillian Douglas, Julia Pearce and Hilary Woodward, 'Cohabitants, Property and the Law: A Study of Injustice' (2009) 72(1) *Modern Law Review* 24 at 28–9. On the functional approach in the context of parenthood, and also its limits, see Brad Sears, 'Winning Arguments/Losing Them: The (Dys)functional Approach in Thomas v. Rubin Y' (1994) 29 *Harvard Civil Rights–Civil Liberties Law Review* 559. See also Jenni Millbank, 'The Role of "Functional Family" in Same-Sex Family Recognition Trends' (2008) 20 *Child and Family Law Quarterly* 1.

[93] It has been argued that putting the emphasis on cohabitation would return to 'form' rather than 'function', as cohabitation *per se* is not the only indication: see Gillian Douglas, Julia Pearce and Hilary Woodward, 'Cohabitants, Property and the Law: A Study of Injustice' (2009) 72(1) *Modern Law Review* 24 at 29. While this may be true, cohabitation can be an indication (rather than an on/off marker) of the functional role,

aiming to give a 'one size fits all' answer, examine the purposes of the benefit in question – in this case, inheritance law exemption, and will deem offering the tax waiver justified or not from the perspective of anti-discrimination law, based upon the relationship between the benefit in question and the purposes which it seeks to advance.[94] Applying such an approach to the facts of this case would warrant, in my opinion, awarding the applicants the tax waiver they requested (or avoiding discrimination in other possible ways described below, see paragraph 65 of the redraft), based upon the fact that the relevant factors of stability, commitment and mutual support (as well as economic partnership and co-dependency), which justify awarding it to married or partnered couples, exist also in this case. Such a reasoning would consider that the privileging of what Fineman calls 'the sexual family' not only discriminates against individuals such as the Burden sisters, but also perpetuates the privileging of certain forms of life over others without any valid justification.

Conclusion

In a way, one can say that the reasoning of the Fourth Section justified the difference in the allocation of benefits based on the functional role of support, whereas the Grand Chamber justified it based on a formal test of registration. But, as I have shown throughout this chapter, both answers are unsatisfactory. The Fourth Section's route does not actually go all the way with the functional approach, and does not examine whether relationships of the kind that the Burden sisters have fulfil, for the purpose in question, the relevant function. The Grand Chamber relies on the formal fact of registration, but neglects the exclusionary nature of the registration mechanism and the fact that this route was not open to the Burden sisters. An approach that respects the diversity of human relationships could be based on either form or function, but should do it in an egalitarian way: either by examining whether for the purpose in question the function is fulfilled; or, if based on form, by opening up the form of registration and not limiting it to relationships based upon the conjugal model. For the purpose of the *Burden* case, as my suggested rewriting of the judgment that follows shows, the implication would be a determination that the arrangement in question was discriminatory, and violates Article 14 (which prohibits discrimination based, *inter alia*, on 'birth' and on 'other status', the latter including for our purposes marital status) in conjunction with the right to property protected in Article 1 of Protocol 1, but, perhaps more importantly,

and should be distinguished from a status devoid of any necessary substantive practices like marriage or civil partnership.

[94] For a differentiated model of the functional approach, in relation to parenthood, which inspires my approach in the text, see Pamela Laufer-Ukeles and Ayelet Blecher-Prigat, 'Between Function and Form: Towards a Differentiated Model of Functional Parenthood' *George Mason Law Review* (2013, forthcoming) (on file with the author).

the right to private and family life protected in Article 8 (see paragraph 66 of the redraft). I suggest that the UK may remedy the violation in one of a variety of ways: it may remove the spousal exception to inheritance tax altogether, expand the menu of legally recognised and registered forms of relationships in a way that will abolish discrimination, or create parallel exceptions to *de facto* forms of personal and family relationships that will take into account cases such as that of the applicants (see paragraph 65 of the redraft).

But it should be noted that the *Burden* case is relatively easy in this regard. It involves two siblings of the same sex, and one can make the argument that there is no justified reason to exclude them from benefits awarded to those who entered a civil partnership. But, what if they had been two siblings of the opposite sex? Would we then have had to compare them to opposite-sex couples who may actually enter marriage? This would bring up the question of the incest taboo in a stronger way, as the prohibition on consanguinity in marriage seems, as discussed in this chapter, to be more strongly rooted than the parallel prohibition in the CPA 2004. We may further ask: what would have been the result if the case had not involved two siblings, but just friends who maintain the same kind of relationship that the Burden sisters have. Would that render it impossible to argue for their protection under the right to family life? We may consider that a way out of these problems may be found in arrangements such as the Belgian domestic partnership law, discussed in this chapter, which offers a model which allows two adults to enjoy legal recognition and protection which are not necessarily based on the conjugal model. However, this will bring up yet another question: what if the case involved more than two persons: for example three sisters, or three siblings of different genders, or just three, or more, friends? Should equality then require that we allow each person to designate only one other person as beneficiary for inheritance tax waiver, or should that person be able to enjoy multiple waivers? Luckily within this book I am only asked to rewrite the *Burden* judgment and not any other hypothetical case that may come before the ECHR in the future, so I will conclude by leaving this question open and offering my rewriting of the relevant paragraphs in the Grand Chamber's *Burden* judgment.

Rewriting Burden v. United Kingdom

. . .

Alleged violation of Article 14 of the Convention in Conjunction with Article 1 of Protocol No. 1

. . .

62. The Grand Chamber commences by remarking that the relationship between siblings is qualitatively of a different nature to that between

opposite-sex married couples and same-sex civil partners under the United Kingdom's Civil Partnership Act. The very essence of the connection between siblings is consanguinity; whereas one of the defining character-istics of a marriage or Civil Partnership Act union is that it is forbidden to close family members [references deleted]. **However, for the purposes of the question before us, this difference is not a relevant one.** The fact that the applicants have chosen to live together all their adult lives, **in a stable, committed, and mutually supportive relationship** as do many married and Civil Partnership Act couples, [fragment deleted] **makes this difference between the two types of relationship as not justifying different treatment.**

63. Moreover, the Grand Chamber notes that [fragment deleted] **in cases of family units and adult relationships, at least such that, as in the present case, are structured around cohabitation, a long duration, and mutual emotional and economic support, the situation can be considered as analogous for the purposes of survivor's benefits, and that holding oth-erwise would justify differential treatment based on the formal fact of marriage or civil partnership, rather than upon more relevant factors which are anchored in substance rather than form. Had the Burden sisters been accorded the option to enter some kind of formal arrange-ment that would convey their intentions in this regard but had declined to do so, it could have been argued that this renders them in a different position to couples who choose to enter marriage or civil partnership. But it is wrong to both deny them access to any such arrangement, *and* to deny them the benefits that are attached to it.**

64. Since the coming into force of the Civil Partnership Act in the United Kingdom, a homosexual couple now also has the choice to enter into a legal relationship designed by Parliament to correspond as far as possible to marriage (see paragraphs 16–18 above).

[Original paragraph 65 deleted]

65. **It is the presumed length and supportive nature of the relationship which is at the heart of recognising marriage and civil partnership as having a special status and as being awarded a body or rights and obligations. The absence of such a legally binding arrangement that the applicants can enter, does not change the fact that for the purposes that may justify the inheritance tax exemption, i.e. the support of a long-term and committed relationship of caring, there is no fundamental difference between the applicants' relationship of cohabitation and mutual support, to that of a married or civil partnership couple. The respondent State may cancel the spousal exception to inheritance tax altogether, expand the menu of legally recognised and registered forms of relationships in a way that will abolish discrimination, or create parallel exceptions to *de facto***

forms of personal and family relationships that will take into account cases such as that of the applicants. Each of these measures would be within its margin of appreciation. What does not fall within this margin is legislation that creates such discrimination which has no justification because of the irrelevance of the difference and also its very imposition upon the applicants.

66. In conclusion, therefore, the Grand Chamber considers that the applicants [fragment deleted] **can be compared for the purpose of Article 14 to a married or Civil Partnership Act couple. It follows there has been discrimination, and that as explained above this discrimination does not advance a legitimate purpose and is not within the State's margin of appreciation.** The discrimination may fall into a few of the categories in Article 14's non-exhaustive list, especially 'other status' which may include marital status, but also perhaps in this case birth. There has therefore been a violation of Article 14 in conjunction with Article 1 of Protocol No. 1. The Court notes that while the imposition of a tax is not a violation of Article 1 Protocol No. 1 as such, its discriminatory application can in cases such as this amount to a violation as explained above. Although the applicants argued their violations under these articles, the Court notes that there may have also been a violation of Article 14 in conjunction with Article 8. This option was suggested by dissenting opinions in the Chamber Judgment, both by Judges Bonello and Garlicki in their dissenting opinion and also by Judge Pavlovschi who justly stated that it was not just a piece of property that is at stake, but rather the applicants' home. However, while the dissenting opinions focused on the protection of the home in Article 8, we consider that this would have been relevant only if the applicants could have shown that the remaining sister would have to sell the home for the purpose of the payment of the inheritance tax. It is our opinion that actually it is the protection of private and family life accorded in Article 8 which may be, together with Article 14, of special relevance to this case and we consider that the case for the applicants could have been even stronger had they based it on Article 8 in addition to Article 1 Protocol No. 1. The Court recalls that it has held before that the notion of family under this provision is not confined to marriage-based relationships and may encompass other *de facto* 'family' ties. See e.g. case of Şerife Yiğit v. *Turkey*, § 94, and previous case law cited therein. But since we do find a violation of Article 14 in conjunction with Article 1 Protocol No. 1 and since the applicants did not base their arguments on Article 8, we do not find it necessary to make a finding on this point.

12

The public faces of privacy: rewriting Lustig-Prean and Beckett v. United Kingdom

MICHAEL KAVEY*

Introduction

In twin landmark judgments in September 1999, *Lustig-Prean and Beckett v. United Kingdom* ('*Lustig-Prean*') and *Smith and Grady v. United Kingdom* ('*Smith*'), the European Court of Human Rights[1] held that the United Kingdom had violated the 'right to respect for . . . private . . . life' under Article 8 of the European Convention on Human Rights[2] by investigating and dismissing four military service-members based on their sexual orientation.[3] The judgments triggered the swift collapse of the United Kingdom's long-standing anti-gay military policies, and raised the momentum and morale of the lesbian, gay and bisexual (LGB)[4] equal-rights movement worldwide.

* The author thanks Eva Brems, Mathilde Cohen, Cedo Radnic, Stijn Smet, Alexandra Timmer and Kenji Yoshino, as well as the panellists and participants at the Mainstreaming Diversity conference at the European Court of Human Rights. He also thanks his colleagues in Columbia Law School's Associates' and Fellows' Workshop.
1 Hereinafter, the 'ECHR' or the 'Court'.
2 European Convention for the Protection of Human Rights and Fundamental Freedoms, ETS No. 5, entered into force 3 September 1953 (hereinafter 'the Convention'). Article 8 of the Convention guarantees the 'right to respect for . . . private . . . life', except where the government shows that an interference with private life was in accordance with national law, had a legitimate aim, and was 'necessary in a democratic society' for one of various enumerated objectives, including 'national security'.
3 ECHR, *Lustig-Prean*, 27 September 1999, paras. 104–5; ECHR, *Smith*, 27 September 1999, paras. 111–12. The applicants in both cases brought claims under Article 8 standing alone and in conjunction with Article 14's non-discrimination provision. See *ibid.*, para. 116; *Lustig-Prean*, para. 109. The *Smith* applicants also brought Article 10 freedom-of-expression claims (alone and in conjunction with Article 14). See *Smith*, para. 123. This chapter principally addresses Article 8 issues, and touches on Article 10 and 14 issues as well. It does not analyse other claims brought by some or all of the applicants, such as the claims under Article 3.
4 The judgments did not expressly refer to bisexuals, but the policy at issue defined 'homosexual' to include bisexuals. See United Kingdom Ministry of Defence, *Report of the Homosexuality Policy Assessment Team* (February 1996), Appendix B, para. 1. In this chapter, I include bisexuality when referring to 'same-sex orientation' and 'homosexual orientation', except where the context otherwise makes clear. While this chapter briefly

While *Lustig-Prean* and *Smith* represent a momentous victory for human rights,[5] advocates as well as jurists have much to gain from a critical inquiry into their reasoning. Engaging in that inquiry here, and focusing principally on Europe and the United States, I explore how the judgments illustrate not just the benefits but also the pitfalls and perils of relying on privacy[6] arguments to advance LGB equality. Those who invoke privacy rationales to protect LGB people can easily end up marginalising and stigmatising them as well; this happens in part because jurists, advocates and others confuse or conflate arguments about LGB individuals' right to spatial and informational privacy with the notion that LGB orientation naturally *is and should be* relegated to a non-public and confidential private sphere (in some cases, the closet). Jurists and others also too often conflate sexual orientation with sexual activity, and rely on unnecessarily restricted conceptions of privacy. In elaborating on these points below, this essay differs from other recent and related critiques of the Court's LGB-related jurisprudence;[7] most importantly, I explore how some objectionable aspects of the Court's reasoning can be traced directly to arguments advanced by LGB equal-rights advocates themselves, including the *Lustig-Prean* and *Smith* applicants. The problems I discuss, in other words, will not be solved by pointing fingers at courts; academics and advocates must also scrutinise their own language to ensure they are not unwittingly perpetuating a potentially harmful discourse.

Taking a fresh look at *Lustig-Prean* and *Smith* is particularly appropriate in 2013, as the risks and drawbacks of relying on privacy rationales invoked in these judgments increasingly pose a challenge to LGB equal-rights advocates on

---

addresses some related issues of transgender equality, these issues do not form a central part of the argument, as they raise distinct questions that the chapter cannot, for reasons of space, adequately address. *Lustig-Prean* and *Smith*, moreover, reviewed military policies as they pertained to sexual orientation, not gender identity.

[5] The effects of the Court's judgments often extend beyond the respondent State, including in the LGB context. See L. R. Helfer and E. Voeten, 'Do European Court of Human Rights Judgments Promote Legal and Policy Change?' (draft manuscript) (2011), available at http://ssrn.com/abstract=1850526, pp. 1–3 and 10–11. This does not mean, however, that States are – or consider themselves – necessarily bound by ECHR judgments against other States. See S. Davli, 'Homosexuality and the European Court of Human Rights: Recent Judgments Against the United Kingdom and Their Impact on Other Signatories to the European Convention on Human Rights' (2004) 15 *University of Florida Journal of Law and Public Policy* 467.

[6] Except where the context otherwise makes clear, I use the term 'privacy' simply to mean 'private life'. I recognise that 'privacy' is sometimes used more narrowly to refer to only one aspect of 'private life' under Article 8, but I do not follow that usage here. See e.g. D. Morris, 'Assisted Suicide under the European Convention on Human Rights: A Critique' (2003) 1 *European Human Rights Law Review*, 76–7.

[7] See e.g. P. Johnson, 'An "Essentially Private Manifestation of Human Personality": Constructions of Homosexuality in the European Court of Human Rights' (2010) 10 *Human Rights Law Review* 67.

both sides of the Atlantic – and around the world – in a variety of legal and cultural contexts, including in disputes over relationship recognition and parenting matters, employment and public accommodations discrimination, military service benefits, and efforts to protect the rights and safety of LGB youth. Returning to scrutinise the judgments is also valuable in light of the United States' repeal in 2011 of its ban on openly LGB military service-members[8] and the ongoing debates regarding LGB service-members in other countries around the world.[9]

My argument proceeds as follows. After summarising the judgments and their immediate impact in the next section, I turn in the subsequent section to criticise the judgments' reasoning along the lines suggested above, focusing chiefly on the Article 8 reasoning, with some observations on the Article 10 and 14 issues as well. The final section explains the revisions I would make to *Lustig-Prean* to avoid the problems I have identified. (Because *Smith*, with respect to Articles 8 and 14, is virtually identical, word for word, to *Lustig-Prean*, my proposed revisions refer only to *Lustig-Prean*, with the understanding that I would similarly revise *Smith*.)

The applicants, the rulings, and the rest of the world

In the early 1990s, United Kingdom Royal Navy authorities received information that Duncan Lustig-Prean, a lieutenant commander, and John Beckett, a weapons engineering mechanic, were gay. During approximately the same period, Royal Air Force authorities received similar information about Jeannette Smith, an air force nurse and senior aircraftwoman, and Graeme Grady, a sergeant. Pursuant to a Ministry of Defence (MoD) policy requiring dismissal of any LGB personnel, the authorities initiated investigations to confirm the four service-members' homosexuality.[10]

The investigations were, to put it mildly, thorough: even after all four service-members had acknowledged their homosexuality, their inquisitors humiliated them with detailed, insulting inquiries into their sexual practices. Officials asked Smith, for instance, whether she and her civilian partner had sex with their sixteen-year-old foster daughter. Beckett, in turn, was asked whether he was the 'bitch' or the 'butch' in his first gay relationship; officials also

---

[8] See the Don't Ask, Don't Tell Repeal Act of 2010, Pub. L. No. 111–321, 124 Stat. 3515 (2010).

[9] See generally International Commission of Jurists, *Sexual Orientation, Gender Identity and Justice: A Comparative Law Casebook* (2011), available at www.icj.org/dwn/database/ Sexual%20Orientation,%20Gender%20Identity%20and%20Justice-%20A%20Comparative %20Law%20Casebook%5B1%5D.pdf, pp. 123–35.

[10] ECHR, *Lustig-Prean and Beckett* v. *United Kingdom* (Admissibility Decision), 23 February 1999, paras. A1–A2; *Smith and Grady* v. *United Kingdom* (Admissibility Decision), 23 February 1999, paras. A1–A2; see also *Lustig-Prean*, para. 42.

interrogated him about pornography, lubrication and sex aids. Shortly after their respective investigations, all four were dismissed based on their homosexuality.[11]

With the support of human rights attorneys, each of the four applied for judicial review of their dismissals and of the MoD's anti-LGB policy. British courts reluctantly rejected their claims,[12] and the claimants applied for relief before the ECHR, alleging violations of, *inter alia*, Article 8's 'right to respect for ... private ... life', taken alone and in conjunction with Article 14's non-discrimination guarantee.[13]

The United Kingdom did not seriously dispute that it had interfered with the applicants' private lives,[14] but it asserted, relying on Article 8(2), that the interferences were justified as 'necessary in a democratic society' to protect national security.[15] This argument relied mainly on a 1996 report from the government's 'Homosexual Policy Assessment Team', which had concluded that, if the government lifted the anti-LGB policy, the negative attitudes of heterosexual personnel towards LGB personnel, ranging from unease to hostility, would damage morale and undermine the military's fighting power.[16]

In separate[17] but largely identical judgments issued on the same day, the Court forcefully rejected the United Kingdom's Article 8 argument, holding that the government had interfered in the applicants' private lives without lawful justification, both by engaging in the intrusive investigations and, independently, by dismissing the applicants based solely on their sexual orientation. As detailed in my proposed revisions to the *Lustig-Prean* judgment, the Court held that the government could not rely on the anti-LGB bias of heterosexual service-members to justify the interferences.[18]

Having ruled for the applicants under Article 8 taken alone, the Court declined to rule on their discrimination claims under Article 8 taken in conjunction

[11] *Lustig-Prean*, paras. 11–21; *Smith*, paras. 11–28.
[12] While the British judges expressed sympathy for the claimants, they held that the deferential standard of review and their inability to directly enforce the Convention (a problem that subsequent legislation remedied) precluded them from ruling against the government. See *Lustig-Prean*, paras. 11–34 (summarising British proceedings).
[13] Article 14 provides: 'The enjoyment of the rights and freedoms set forth in this Convention shall be secured without discrimination on any ground such as sex, race, colour, language, religion, political or other opinion, national or social origin ... or other status.' Article 14 is not a stand-alone non-discrimination provision; rather, it must be invoked in conjunction with another Convention protection. See ECHR (GC), *EB* v. *France*, 22 January 2008, paras. 47–8.
[14] *Lustig-Prean*, paras. 63–4.   [15] Article 8(2); see also note 2 above.
[16] See *Lustig-Prean*, paras. 88–9; *Smith*, paras. 96–7.
[17] *Smith*, which also raised Article 3 and 10 issues (see note 3 above), was formally disjoined from *Lustig-Prean*, though the Court continued to review the cases together. See also *Lustig-Prean*, para. 8.
[18] See *Lustig-Prean*, paras. 64 and 89–105; *Smith*, paras. 71 and 96–112.

with Article 14.[19] The Court also declined to rule on Smith and Grady's Article 10 freedom-of-expression claims, and it rejected Smith and Grady's Article 3 degrading-treatment claims on the merits.[20]

The judgments' immediate impact was striking. Within weeks, the British government announced it would lift its ban on LGB military personnel, and, within a month, it had done so.[21] By the British government's own account, the MoD successfully implemented the changes without disruption.[22] By 2004, the military was actively recruiting LGB people to enlist.[23]

The judgments – and the government's rapid compliance – are particularly remarkable from a comparative perspective, especially as seen from the United States. In the years immediately prior to *Lustig-Prean* and *Smith*, multiple US appeals courts had upheld the infamous 'don't ask, don't tell' policy that barred openly LGB people from service in the US armed forces.[24] And, while numerous countries had repealed anti-LGB military policies by 1999, courts had not played nearly the direct and prominent role that the ECHR did in *Lustig-Prean* and *Smith*.[25]

Advocates and public authorities in other countries have since looked to *Lustig-Prean* and *Smith*, as well as the United Kingdom's compliance, in their

[19] See *Lustig-Prean*, paras. 108–9; *Smith*, paras. 115–16.

[20] See *Smith*, paras. 123 and 128; see also note 3 above.

[21] The ECHR's judgments became final in December 1999. The UK lifted its anti-gay policy in January 2000. See Council of Europe, Committee of Ministers, ResDH(2002)34, Appendix (2002).

[22] See Ben Summerskill, 'It's Official: Gays Do Not Harm Forces', *Observer*, 19 November 2000, p. 5.

[23] See Matthew Hickley, 'RAF in Drive to Recruit More Gays', *Daily Mail*, 27 August 2004, p. 27.

[24] See e.g. US Court of Appeals for the Second Circuit, *Able* v. *United States*, 155 F 3d 628, 23 September 1998; US Court of Appeals for the Fourth Circuit, *Thomasson* v. *Perry*, 80 F 3d 915, 5 April 1996. Challenges to anti-gay military policies had also failed before the Spanish Constitutional Court (see Tribunal Constitucional de España, STC 446/1984, 7 November 1984) and, of course, in British courts (see *Lustig-Prean*, paras. 11–34). Colombia's Constitutional Court is one of few national courts to invalidate an anti-gay military policy: see Corte Constitucional de Colombia, STC 507/99, 14 July 1999.

[25] On the other hand, the perceived likelihood that courts would invalidate anti-LGB policies has prompted several governments to 'voluntarily' reform their law, both before and after *Lustig-Prean* and *Smith*. See e.g. International Commission of Jurists, *Sexual Orientation, Gender Identity and Justice: A Comparative Law Casebook* (2011), available at www.icj.org/dwn/database/Sexual%20Orientation,%20Gender%20Identity%20and%20Justice-%20A%20Comparative%20Law%20Casebook%5B1%5D.pdf, p. 123 (observing, with references to Australia, Canada and the United States, that '[t]he impetus for legislative reform [of anti-gay military policies] has often originated in judicial or quasi-judicial processes'); US Department of Defense, *Comprehensive Review of the Issues Associated with a Repeal of 'Don't Ask, Don't Tell'* (2010), p. 90 (reporting that military officials in Australia and Germany had changed anti-LGB policies 'to head off adverse outcomes in pending court challenges').

own struggles and debates over anti-LGB military policies. The German military abandoned its defence of an anti-LGB policy shortly after the Court issued its judgments in *Lustig-Prean* and *Smith*.[26] The British experience has been widely cited, moreover, by those who successfully advocated for the repeal of the 'don't ask, don't tell' policy in the United States, as well as by those charged with overseeing the repeal's implementation.[27] About forty countries now allow openly LGB people to serve in the military.[28]

The public faces of privacy: a critique of the Article 8 and 14 reasoning

Article 8: the (missing) public faces of privacy

While the immediate and principal effects of *Lustig-Prean* and *Smith* were liberating, the judgments' reasoning contains some troubling counter-currents, particularly in the Court's attempt to explain the meaning and significance of 'sexual orientation'. Despite their LGB-supportive holdings, the judgments portray same-sex orientation as a characteristic that relates, above all, to hidden, confidential or secret sexual practices – or the desire to engage in such sexual practices. This secrecy-focused, sex-act-focused depiction of LGB orientation is stigmatising and marginalising, as it plays into stereotypes about the excessive importance that LGB people are believed to place on sex, overlooks the multitudinous ways in which orientation can more broadly shape a person's identity, relationships and family life, and obscures what LGB people have, or could have, in common with heterosexuals. Much of the problem lies in the judgments' narrow conception of the 'private life' interests at stake.

Of course, sexual orientation, according to virtually any definition, *does* relate closely to sexual conduct and desire.[29] Nevertheless, the Court's implicit but unmistakable suggestion that LGB orientation amounts to essentially

---

[26] See US Department of Defense, *Comprehensive Review*, note 25 above, p. 90.

[27] See e.g. *ibid.*, pp. 8, 42–3, 90–2 and 111; see also Suzanne B. Goldberg, 'Open Service and Our Allies: A Report on the Inclusion of Openly Gay and Lesbian Service-Members in US Allies' Armed Forces' (2011) 17 *William and Mary Journal of Women and the Law* 547 at 556–7, 564–5, 568, 572–3, 579–82 and 584–5.

[28] See US Department of Defense, *Comprehensive Review*, note 25 above, p. 89 (reporting that '35 countries . . . permit gays and lesbians to serve openly in their military'). This figure includes only countries in the North Atlantic Treaty Organization or the International Security Assistance Force; it does not include countries such as Colombia, Uruguay and Israel, which also permit openly LGB individuals to serve in the military. Nor does the *Comprehensive Review* count the United States, which still banned openly LGB service-members at the time of the report's release. See note 8 above.

[29] The leading set of international human rights principles regarding sexual orientation define 'sexual orientation' as 'each person's capacity for profound emotional, affectional and sexual attraction to, and intimate and sexual relations with, individuals of a different gender or the same gender or more than one gender'. Philip Alston *et al.*, *The Yogyakarta Principles on the Application of International Human Rights Law in relation to Sexual*

nothing more than confidential and spatially private sex acts or urges is demeaning, in that it ignores how orientation also relates to, and helps define, other important areas of individuals' lives.

To understand how these problems arise, we can first consider the Court's language describing same-sex orientation, and the cases on which the Court relies. In both *Lustig-Prean* and *Smith*, the Court initially attempts to distinguish between orientation and sexual behaviour: It holds that the government interfered with the applicants' private life by, first, investigating them 'on matters relating to their sexual orientation and [sexual] practices', and, secondly, by dismissing them 'on the sole ground of their sexual orientation'.[30] But the distinction between same-sex orientation and sexual conduct occurring in private begins to fray when the Court endeavours to explain what it understands 'their sexual orientation' to mean. Though neither judgment attempts a comprehensive definition of 'orientation', both judgments describe the applicants' 'sexual orientation' as 'a most intimate aspect of an individual's private life';[31] in *Smith*, the Court adds that the applicants' orientation is 'an essentially private manifestation of human personality'.[32] With one arguable exception, earlier judgments had not characterised sexual orientation in this (or any other) way,[33] though later decisions have repeated or relied on *Lustig-Prean*'s and *Smith*'s formulations.[34]

While the meaning of 'private' and 'intimate' vary, the words' arrangement into the two phrases quoted above, considered in context, leads them principally if not exclusively to convey notions of secrecy or confidentiality, spatial privacy and bodily intimacy. To appreciate why this is so – and why it is problematic – we can ask how identical phrases would sound as applied to *hetero*sexuality. On any given day, we may hear casual references to a person's different-sex spouse, girlfriend or boyfriend; walk by a different-sex couple holding hands; hear about a friend's or celebrity's latest (different-sex) romantic interest; see a co-worker's photo of a different-sex spouse on his or her desk; witness a heterosexual kiss goodbye at the train station; or learn about a heterosexual wedding attended by a friend – or, as occurred in early 2011, encounter endless media commentary about a heterosexual royal wedding in

---

Orientation and Gender Identity (2006), available at www.yogyakartaprinciples.org, p. 6 n. 1.

[30] *Lustig-Prean*, para. 64; *Smith*, para. 71; see also *Lustig-Prean*, para. 104; *Smith*, para. 111.

[31] *Lustig-Prean*, paras. 81 and 82 (citation and quotation marks omitted); *Smith*, paras. 89, 90 (citation and quotation marks omitted).

[32] *Smith*, para. 127 (citation and quotation marks omitted). Both judgments also refer to the applicants' sexual orientation as an 'innate personal characteristic': *Lustig-Prean*, para. 86; *Smith*, para. 93.

[33] See ECHR, *Laskey, Jaggard and Brown* v. *United Kingdom*, 19 February 1997, para. 36 ('sexual orientation and activity concern an intimate aspect of private life').

[34] See e.g. ECHR, *Kozak* v. *Poland*, 2 March 2010, para. 83.

the United Kingdom. In these moments, we are typically learning about, or witnessing a public manifestation of, somebody's heterosexual orientation. We do not, however, normally (if ever) react with the thought that the people involved have publicly exposed a 'most intimate aspect' of their (or somebody else's) private life, or that they have revealed an 'essentially private manifestation of human personality'.[35] If a newspaper, for example, offered to reveal the 'most intimate aspect[s]' of a politician's 'private life', readers would surely feel cheated to learn that the paper was referring only to the politician's heterosexuality. Similarly, a court judgment revealing the mere fact of someone's heterosexuality with the phrases used in *Lustig-Prean* and *Smith* would leave many readers scratching their heads, wondering if they had overlooked more salacious details in the judgment.

In short, heterosexuality is a pervasively *public* manifestation of human personality; it relates inextricably not just to erotic desire, or to sexual conduct in private spaces, or to other typically confidential matters, but also to parts of life that are publicly visible to – and often celebrated by – other people. By describing the applicants' (homo)sexual orientation in much narrower terms, the judgments create a crude, one-dimensional and hyper-sexualised image of LGB people and their lives.[36]

It is telling, moreover, that in characterising the applicants' 'sexual orientation' as a 'most intimate aspect' of private life and an 'essentially private manifestation' of personality, the Court cites and quotes from *Dudgeon v. United Kingdom*, a judgment in which the Court used virtually the *precise* same language, *not* to describe 'orientation', but to refer to homosexual 'activities', 'homosexual behaviour', 'homosexual practices' and 'homosexual acts'.[37] *Dudgeon* held that a Northern Ireland sodomy law violated the applicant's Article 8 rights insofar as the law criminalised sex between consenting adult males in private spaces such as the home.[38] Unlike in *Lustig-Prean* and *Smith*,

---

[35] Though the person in these hypothetical situations might be bisexual, my arguments still hold with respect to the public manifestations of his or her different-sex attractions and relationships.

[36] I do not discount the importance of sexual relationships to many or most heterosexual or LGB people. To quote Janet Halley, I support the project of 'building a social consensus that homosexual erotic acts are good'. J. E. Halley, *Don't: A Reader's Guide to the Military's Anti-Gay Policy* (Durham, NC: Duke University Press, 1999), p. 125. There is no inconsistency in arguing, however, that, while 'homosexual erotic acts are good', we should not define the lives or orientation of LGB people in solely erotic terms. I also recognise that 'sexual orientation' encompasses feelings that a person may, in theory, choose not to reveal. But, in the actual lived experience of heterosexuals, the mere fact that one's sexual and romantic feelings are oriented towards members of a different sex is rarely considered an 'essentially private' matter or a 'most intimate aspect' of private life. Same-sex orientation is not 'essentially' different.

[37] ECHR, *Dudgeon v. United Kingdom*, 22 October 1981, paras. 52 and 60.

[38] *Ibid.*, paras. 39 and 63.

where the government's policy required dismissal of the applicants solely based on their homosexual *orientation* (regardless of conduct),[39] the law at issue in *Dudgeon* targeted homosexual conduct, 'not homosexuality itself'.[40] The Court in *Lustig-Prean* and *Smith* does not explain why it finds the phrases from *Dudgeon* characterising 'homosexual acts' occurring in private spaces to be equally suitable to describe same-sex orientation generally; indeed, the Court offers no acknowledgment that it is applying *Dudgeon*'s language to new circumstances.[41] Subsequent decisions have continued to quote or paraphrase this language to refer to sexual orientation, sexual activity, or both.[42]

Lustig-Prean and *Smith* also stand out for the precedent they do *not* cite. Earlier judgments had not limited Article 8's protection of 'private life' to matters of a secret, hidden or physically intimate nature. Nor had the Court conceived of 'private' to mean merely 'out of public view' or 'without public knowledge'. Prior judgments had instead construed the right to respect for one's private life 'broad[ly]'[43] to encompass, *inter alia*, the right to moral, physical and psychological integrity,[44] and the right to individual autonomy in matters of self-definition. The Court had also applied Article 8's 'private life' provision to protect, for example, certain publicly visible relationships – even business relationships.[45] And, in applying Article 8 to matters of self-definition, the Court in *Burghartz* v. *Switzerland* held that a person's freedom to choose his or her *publicly registered* surname after marriage fell within the ambit of Article 8's 'private life' protection.[46]

Not only does the Court fail to rely on any comparably capacious understanding of 'private life' in *Lustig-Prean* or *Smith*, but it effectively declares in *Smith* that it does not understand same-sex sexual orientation to implicate public life in any fundamental way. The *Smith* applicants (unlike the

---

[39] See *Lustig-Prean*, paras. 42 and 86. [40] *Dudgeon* para. 39.
[41] It is also revealing that, in other ECHR judgments using the phrase 'most intimate aspect of private life' or something very similar, the Court is virtually always referring, if not to sexual orientation, to sexual conduct, sexual abuse or some other highly sensitive and typically confidential issue involving bodily privacy. See e.g. ECHR, *Porubova* v. *Russia*, 8 October 2009, para. 34; ECHR, *Sanchez Cardenas* v. *Norway*, 4 October 2007, para. 33; and ECHR, *YF* v. *Turkey*, 22 July 2003, paras. 32–4. In several other sections of *Lustig-Prean* and *Smith*, moreover, the Court uses the term 'private' as a synonym for 'secretive' or 'confidential', or to refer to acts occurring 'in' private. See *Lustig-Prean*, paras. 31, 79 and 84; *Smith*, paras. 44 and 91.
[42] See e.g. ECHR, *Kozak* v. *Poland*, 2 March 2010, para. 83.
[43] ECHR, *Raninen* v. *Finland*, 16 December 1997, para. 63.
[44] See ECHR, *X and Y* v. *Netherlands*, 29 March 1985, para. 22; see also ECHR, *Botta* v. *Italy*, 24 February 1998, para. 29.
[45] ECHR, *Niemietz* v. *Germany*, 16 December 1992, para. 29.
[46] ECHR, *Burghartz* v. *Switzerland*, 22 February 1994, paras. 24 and 29 (applying Article 8 with Article 14). Judgments post-dating *Lustig-Prean* and *Smith* have reinforced this broad understanding of 'private life'. See e.g. ECHR, *S and Marper* v. *United Kingdom*, 4 December 2008, para. 66.

Lustig-Prean applicants) pressed Article 10 freedom-of-expression claims in addition to their other claims, arguing that the MoD's policy 'forced [them] to live secret lives'.[47] While the *Smith* judgment does 'not rule out' that the MoD policy 'could' burden expression, the Court declines to analyse the issue in depth, reasoning that the case's 'freedom of expression element' is 'subsidiary to the applicants' right to respect for their private lives which is principally at issue'.[48] Thus, even where the applicants alerted the Court to the ways in which sexual-orientation discrimination constrained their freedoms in public life and forced them into the closet, the Court dismissed these concerns as merely 'subsidiary' to what is 'essentially' a 'private' matter. The analysis stands in stark contrast to cases like *Burghartz*, where the Court recognised a privacy interest precisely *because* the law at issue significantly burdened the (hetero-sexual) applicant's autonomy in shaping his own *public* identity.[49]

One might resist these criticisms by arguing that the passages in question refer to 'sexual orientation' *generally*, not to 'homosexual orientation' or 'homo-sexuality' specifically. I agree that a certain 'surface universalism' appears in these passages; they cannot, however, be fairly read to refer to heterosexuality in addition to LGB orientation.

By 'surface universalism', I mean the thin layer of universalising rhetoric that may make it appear, initially or superficially, that the Court is speaking about sexual orientation in universal terms. In the passages at issue, for instance, the court refrains from explicitly mentioning 'homosexuality', and it includes phrases painting a veneer of neutrality ('an *individual's* private life', '*human* personality'). Nevertheless, the surface universalism dissolves fairly quickly in light of other considerations, most of which I have discussed above: the factual context, the Court's quotation of and almost exclusive reliance on *Dudgeon*, the incongruity of the Court's statements with the reality of heterosexuality, and the fact that, even in these passages, the Court refers to the *applicants'* ('their') sexual orientation. Another factor, which I call the 'transparency' of hetero-sexuality, may also create an illusion of neutrality here; I address this issue in a separate section, below.

The judgments' surface universalism, moreover, may provide reason to cri-ticise, not to defend, the quoted passages. Because the language at issue, read in light of various considerations analysed here, conveys messages specifically about homosexuality, any nominally neutral gloss succeeds only in making the negative characterisations of LGB orientation more subtle and insidious.

---

[47] *Smith*, para. 126.

[48] *Ibid.*, para. 127. The Court holds that it is therefore unnecessary to rule on the Article 10 claim. *Ibid.*, para. 28.

[49] See ECommHR, *Burghartz* v. *Switzerland*, 22 February 1994, para. 24 ('[T]he applicant's retention of the surname by which, according to him, he has become known in academic circles may significantly affect his career. Article 8 . . . therefore applies.').

The surface universalism may deflect immediate attention from the trouble-some elements of the judgments, facilitating the propagation of similar ideas in other contexts and reducing the likelihood of productive critique.

That said, none of this means the Court was purposely deploying manipu-lative rhetoric, as I discuss in a later section. First, however, I offer some reasons to sharpen the critique.

Sharpening the Article 8 critique: naturalisation and new contexts

The Court's narrow portrayal of same-sex orientation is flawed not merely because it mis-describes the lived experience of many LGB people, but because it naturalises or normalises as 'essential' fact what is actually a highly contingent and oppressive social condition. The judgments do not adequately recognise that the need felt by many LGB people to remain closeted does not result from anything naturally or 'essentially' private about sexual orientation; rather, LGB people normally keep their orientation confidential because they would face some cost or punishment if they dared to reveal their orientation as freely as most heterosexuals do on a regular basis. This cost could include, for example, harassment, family and social ostracism, or violence – or, as in the case of the British military before late 1999, the loss of one's career. To a large extent, therefore, the MoD's policy violated Article 8 not because it interfered with what was intrinsically or 'essentially' a 'most intimate aspect' of the LGB service-members' private lives, but because it *coerced* (or played a major role in coercing) LGB service-members to *treat* information about their sexual orientation as a 'most intimate' and secretive aspect of their lives.[50] Capturing this point requires appreciation of how the policy operated in two seemingly contradictory – but in fact mutually reinforcing – ways: while investigations to enforce the policy may have wrenched LGB service-members out of the closet against their will, the policy's existence helped produce the conditions that locked LGB people inside the closet in the first place.

In failing to recognise expressly how oppressive social and legal conditions shape the need for secrecy in LGB people's lives, the judgments end up playing a role in perpetuating those conditions – notwithstanding the paradoxical fact that the judgments' immediate purpose and effect was the eradication of an anti-gay policy. The Court's pronouncement that same-sex orientation is a 'most intimate aspect of an individual's private life' has the force of law; and when the Court makes the striking declaration that the right of LGB people not to live 'secret lives' is 'subsidiary' to what is really a 'private' matter, it helps to

---

[50] Cf. J. Rubenfeld, 'The Right of Privacy' (1989) 102 *Harvard Law Review* 737 at 783 (arguing for a conception of privacy that 'look[s] away from what the law would keep us from doing and instead look[s] to what the law would have us do').

maintain the social conditions that give that declaration the appearance of objective truth.[51]

These conditions did not originate, of course, with the Court. But, by endorsing them, the judgments reinforce perceptions of LGB orientation that have often proven a nightmare for LGB equal-rights advocates. In a broad range of contexts, achieving equality and liberating LGB people from the closet require precisely that LGB orientation *not* be perceived as a 'most intimate aspect of private life' or an 'essentially private manifestation of human personality', and that it not be conflated with sexual activity.

While a full exploration of these contexts is beyond the scope of this chapter, a few examples can illustrate the dilemma. Consider, for instance, the efforts in many countries to protect the rights, health and safety of LGB youth, and to reduce prejudice among youth generally, by including discussions of LGB issues at school – whether in lessons on tolerance, or in the context of literature, history or science. In a disconcerting echo of the ECHR's reasoning, those who *oppose* LGB-inclusive school policies and curricula frequently argue that sexual orientation – or, more specifically, LGB orientation – is a 'most intimate' issue necessarily involving erotic acts or desires, and therefore not appropriate for discussion at school.

Using typical anti-LGB rhetoric, for example, a 2005 British newspaper editorial opposed plans to teach about LGB and transgender history at school, arguing that 'sexual preferences . . . are a private matter, not a badge to be worn nor a propaganda weapon with which to influence young minds'.[52] (To keep 'sexual preferences' a 'private matter', should schools edit the heterosexuality out of *Romeo and Juliet*?) And, in 2007, one of the most popular political commentators on television in the United States criticised a school for allowing students to select two lesbian classmates for the yearbook's 'cutest couple' feature. 'Private behaviour belongs in private settings', he argued, adding that 'you don't allow sexuality to intrude in your high school yearbook'.[53] Evidently, LGB equal-rights advocates should not further entrench this way of thinking by affirming that LGB orientation is, as *Lustig-Prean* and *Smith* stated, an 'essentially private manifestation' of one's personality or a 'most intimate aspect' of one's 'private life'.

---

[51] As Paul Johnson observes, the Court's case law and 'the incremental process of legal citation produce a "sedimenting" effect in relation to discourses of sexuality that entrench and normalize ideas about what homosexuality "is"'. P. Johnson, 'An "Essentially Private Manifestation of Human Personality": Constructions of Homosexuality in the European Court of Human Rights' (2010) 10 *Human Rights Law Review* 67 at 72.

[52] Editorial, 'Not Wanted', *The Sun*, 21 January 2005, available at www.thesun.co.uk/sol/homepage/news/sun_says/113697/Not-wanted.html.

[53] 'High School Lesbians Voted "Cutest Couple" for Yearbook', *The O'Reilly Factor*, 8 November 2007 (television transcript), available at www.foxnews.com/story/0,2933,309578,00.html.

An article in the *School Psychology Review* analysed similar attitudes in its study of LGB parents and schools: 'A pervasive obstacle to supporting sexual minority parents in [schools] is the popular misconception that a same-sex sexual orientation is more sexually focused than a heterosexual orientation and that, therefore, talking about sexual minority people means talking about sexual material that is embarrassing, private, or inappropriate to children.'[54] Evincing just this sort of bias and misconception, a US federal appeals court displayed an inability to separate sex acts from sexual orientation and anti-harassment education when it rejected the proposition that a school should teach children not to mock gays and lesbians: 'There is no simple way', the author of the decision commented, 'of explaining to young students why it is wrong to mock homosexuals without discussing the underlying lifestyle or sexual behaviour associated with such a designation.'[55] A second judge concurred, adding that 'school authorities' options' in responding to anti-gay harassment 'are limited by an understandable reticence about flagging issues of sex for children'.[56]

A similar pattern arises in LGB-related disputes all over the world regarding, among other things, child custody and adoption,[57] demonstrations and marches in support of LGB and transgender equality,[58] anti-discrimination legislation, and a host of other LGB-related issues. Opponents of LGB equality often support their position by portraying LGB orientation as a private issue pertaining to sex – an issue that therefore should not, they argue, be raised (much less celebrated) in public spaces, at the workplace, in school, or with one's children. Thus, even as *Lustig-Prean* and *Smith* liberated LGB service-members from discriminatory policies in the UK, their reasoning fed into a

---

[54] D. Ryan and A. Martin, 'Lesbian, Gay, Bisexual, and Transgender Parents in the School Systems' (2000) 29 *School Psychology Review* 210.

[55] US Court of Appeals for the Seventh Circuit, *Schroeder* v. *Hamilton School District*, 282 F 3d 946, 954, 11 March 2002.

[56] *Ibid.*, p. 958 (Posner J concurring).

[57] The Supreme Court of Chile held in 2004 that the government should remove three children from the custody of their lesbian mother. While purporting to recognise that the mother's homosexuality did not itself pose a risk to the children, the court held that, by *explicitly declaring* her homosexuality and by cohabiting with another woman, the mother had put her children at risk. See Corte Suprema de Justicia, 31 March 2004, 'López Allende, Jaime (recurso de queja)', custody, *Revista de Derecho y Jurisprudencia*, Sec. 2, Part 1, p. 143 (Chile). The mother later brought this case before the Inter-American Court of Human Rights, which ruled in her favour in 2012.

[58] While the ECHR has recognised the right to campaign publicly for LGB and transgender rights, rejecting Russia's argument that 'any form of celebration of homosexual behaviour should take place in private or in designated meeting places with restricted access' (see ECHR, *Alekseyev* v. *Russia*, 21 October 2010, paras. 51, 69 and 109), problems persist. See 'Moscow Authorities Ban Gay Pride Parade on May 28', Russia and CIS General Newswire, 29 May 2011.

pernicious form of privacy discourse that many people have exploited to impede progress towards LGB equality.[59]

Tempering the Article 8 critique: the advocates' role and the transparency of heterosexuality

The foregoing criticisms may appear harsh in light of the Court's courageous holding advancing LGB human rights. While a laudable outcome does not immunise a judgment from critical scrutiny, I agree that there are reasons to temper and perhaps partially redirect the critique I have set out above.

As an initial matter, while some of the Court's rhetoric plays into the hands of those who would keep LGB people closeted, this does not change the fact that the *holdings* of *Lustig-Prean* and *Smith* liberated LGB service-members from the closet. Crucially, the Court did not condition the rights of LGB service-members on any understanding that they would keep their sexual orientation a secret (even though the applicants appear to have assured the Court that they would never have come out if they had not been investigated).[60] Thus, to the extent the Court's reasoning provokes concern, it does so because of more subtle, indirect and long-term effects on legal and cultural debates over LGB equality, and because of the missed opportunity it represents to promote a more complete understanding of sexual orientation and homophobia.

Criticism should also be tempered because the Court's characterisation of LGB orientation comes directly from arguments long advanced by LGB equal-rights advocates, including the *Lustig-Prean* and *Smith* applicants. To some extent, the judgments simply follow the applicants' cue: according to the Court, the applicants in both cases complained about 'inquiries made into a *most intimate part of their private lives, namely, their sexual orientation*'.[61] The applicants also argued that their 'private lives … were indeed private and would have remained so but for the policy';[62] thus, the applicants appear to have assured the Court that they would have remained comfortably in the closet (as if that is where they belonged) were it not for the military's investigations. These arguments are consistent with those they advanced before the British courts. 'This case', the applicants' attorney declared in his opening statement before a court in 1995, 'is concerned with whether the Ministry of Defence can

---

[59] Privacy has also proven a double-edged sword in efforts to protect other traditionally disadvantaged and subordinated groups. Many scholars, for example, have addressed the dangers and drawbacks of privacy arguments in struggles for women's equality. See e.g. A. L. Allen, 'Privacy', in H. LaFollette (ed.), *The Oxford Handbook of Practical Ethics* (Oxford University Press, 2005), pp. 495–7; R. B. Siegel, 'The Rule of Love: Wife Beating as Prerogative and Privacy' (1996) 105 *Yale Law Journal* 2120.

[60] See note 62 below and the accompanying text.

[61] See Admissibility Decisions, note 10 above (emphasis added).

[62] *Lustig-Prean*, para. 77; *Smith*, para. 84.

adopt a policy that all homosexuals must be discharged from the forces, *however much they keep their sexual orientation off-base and in their private lives.*'[63]

This mentality, according to which it was both possible and presumably laudable to 'keep [one's] sexual orientation off-base' and out of other people's way, did not of course originate with the applicants any more than it originated with the ECHR.[64] Both the applicants and the Court inherited a mind-set that has plagued discussions about sexual orientation – even among LGB activists – for decades. While this chapter cannot fully explore the origins of this privacy discourse, I will offer two additional observations, each of which not only helps explain why jurists and others often speak of orientation in terms similar to the Court's, but also provides further reason not to criticise too harshly the Court's judges – or the applicants whose arguments supported the objectionable reasoning.

First, the struggle to eliminate 'sodomy' and 'buggery' laws has defined much of the modern LGB civil rights movement, particularly in the United States[65] – where much of the movement was born – and in Britain. That struggle has relied heavily – and understandably – on the assertion that the government has no business intruding into adults' consensual sexual activity in the bedroom. While debates over LGB issues increasingly encompass other issues more obviously implicating the public sphere, the sodomy debates have had an anchoring effect on the discourse: debates remain tied to a narrow form of privacy reasoning developed in response to criminalisation, even as the criminalisation issue itself has, in most of Europe and the United States, faded into the distance.

Despite its theoretical and political drawbacks,[66] it is difficult to break out of this 'bedroom privacy' discourse, particularly as a litigator, even if one sees its double-edged nature. The attorneys in *Lustig-Prean* and *Smith* had effectively no choice but to rely on sodomy cases to some degree if they intended – as any competent attorney would – to ground their arguments in the Court's jurisprudence. As Robert Wintemute observes, '[f]rom 1981 to 1999, the Court had

---

[63] 'Gay Military Officers Challenge Ban', *Agence France Presse*, 15 May 1995 (internal quotations omitted) (emphasis added).

[64] See K. Yoshino, *Covering: The Hidden Assault on Our Civil Rights* (New York: Random House, 2006), pp. 31–107 (analysing cultural and legal pressures on LGB people to 'convert', 'pass' and 'cover').

[65] See e.g. US Supreme Court, *Bowers v. Hardwick*, 478 US 186, 30 June 1986, overruled by US Supreme Court, *Lawrence v. Texas*, 539 US 558, 26 June 2003; see also notes 37–40 above and the accompanying text; and note 67 below and the accompanying text.

[66] Cf. E. K. Sedgwick, *The Epistemology of the Closet* (Berkeley, CA: University of California Press, 1990), p. 71 (observing that liberals protesting sodomy laws in the US had focused 'on the image of the *bedroom invaded by policemen* ... as though political empowerment were a matter of getting the cops back on the street where they belong and sexuality back into the impermeable space where *it* belongs').

only been asked to consider one form of sexual orientation discrimination: blanket criminalisation of all sexual activity between persons of the same sex.'[67]

Secondly, even where judicial and political actors intend to advance LGB equality, they are often affected by the 'transparency' of heterosexuality. That is, precisely because heterosexuality is such a deeply entrenched cultural norm, the presence of which pervades everyone's life on a near daily basis, we tend not to notice it. Even when it stares us in the face, we look right through it.[68] If a heterosexual couple walks by holding hands or appears on a magazine cover, for example, most people will not see a *heterosexual* couple; they will just see a *couple*. (Heterosexuality's pervasiveness may often make it transparent even to LGB people, despite the generally heightened awareness of sexual orientation that comes with being in the minority.) Because of this transparency, we sometimes think and speak as if 'sexual orientation' were something only LGB people have – even though, if pressed to think more carefully, we know that this is incorrect.[69] Unsurprisingly then, if a particular definition of sexual orientation (or homosexual orientation), like the one articulated in *Lustig-Prean* and *Smith*, contradicts a person's daily experience with or exposure to heterosexuality, the transparency phenomenon makes it unlikely that she will notice any contradiction, oddity or asymmetry, as she is not really thinking of heterosexuality at all. This phenomenon may have contributed to the narrow definition of (same-sex) orientation in *Lustig-Prean* and *Smith*.

Nevertheless, while this discussion provides reasons to temper criticism of the Court – and to re-examine the rhetoric of LGB equal-rights advocates – it cannot absolve the Court (or the applicants) of any and all responsibility. The Court had sufficient indication that at least two of the applicants – Smith and Grady – viewed the policy as infringing not just on a trait they wished to keep secret, but on their freedom to express their identities publicly. The Court also

---

[67] R. Wintemute, 'Strasbourg to the Rescue? Same-Sex Partners and Parents Under the European Convention', in R. Wintemute and M. T. Andenæs (eds.), *Legal Recognition of Same-Sex Partnerships: A Study of National, European and International Law* (Portland, OR: Hart Publishing, 2001), p. 718.

[68] I borrow the 'transparency' idea from Barbara Flagg, who speaks of the 'transparency phenomenon' in the race context. See e.g. B. J. Flagg, 'The Transparency Phenomenon, Race-Neutral Decisionmaking, and Discriminatory Intent', in R. Delgado and J. Stefancic (eds.), *Critical White Studies: Looking Behind the Mirror* (Philadelphia, PA: Temple University Press, 1997), p. 220 ('I label the tendency for whiteness to vanish from whites' self-perception the transparency phenomenon').

[69] Evidence of this tendency abounds in the press. For instance, news reports routinely describe an individual as the 'first' person in a field to reveal his or her 'sexual orientation' – an assertion that is entirely implausible unless we understand 'sexual orientation' to mean homosexuality. See e.g. G. Tyndale, 'Come Out with the Truth, Chris', *Sunday Mercury*, 6 February 2005, p. 22 (Birmingham, UK) (identifying former Cabinet Minister Chris Smith as 'the first MP to admit his sexual orientation').

had ample precedent at its disposal construing the 'private life' guarantee broadly, but it relied almost exclusively on *Dudgeon* instead.

Regardless of how much one can 'blame' any particular actor, the more important point is that re-examining *Lustig-Prean*, *Smith* and other LGB-related cases with these criticisms in mind may allow jurists, advocates and scholars to avoid similar mistakes in the future, in part by heightening their awareness of how a particular representation of LGB orientation or of the rights of LGB people could have harmful and unintended effects in other areas of struggle.[70]

Articles 8 and 14: equal respect for privacy

In light of the pitfalls and risks that accompany any reliance on privacy to advance LGB equal rights, the Court should have ruled in favour of the applicants on their combined Article 8/Article 14 claim as well. That is, the Court should have held that the government discriminated against the applicants in their private life on the basis of sexual orientation, in violation of Article 8 taken in conjunction with Article 14. Such a ruling could have reduced the possibility that some readers would, based on their background assumptions about homosexuality and some inevitable ambiguity in the concept of 'private life', interpret the judgments as offering some sort of *special* privacy protection based on LGB people's unique needs – that is, based on the 'essentially private' nature of LGB orientation. Of course, a properly framed Article 8 ruling would not have labelled same-sex orientation 'essentially private' or a 'most intimate aspect' of private life in the first place. Nevertheless, no matter how valiant the effort to define the relevant privacy interests broadly, deeply entrenched biases make it possible, if not likely, that even some sympathetic readers will view the judgments as offering special solicitude to a group whose unconventional sexuality mandates a heightened degree of privacy protection.[71] An equality rationale could help resolve this dilemma by emphasising that the applicants simply demand the same respect for private life that heterosexuals enjoy.[72]

---

[70] See e.g. notes 54–60 above and the accompanying text.

[71] Widespread homophobia may in fact require that LGB people receive special solicitude in some contexts, but the Court should be careful not to insinuate that this is because of their sexuality *per se*. In any event, what applicants requested in this case was primarily *equal* respect for privacy, not special privacy protections.

[72] This portion of my analysis arguably differs from an argument recently advanced by Kenji Yoshino. See K. Yoshino, 'The New Equal Protection' (2011) 124 *Harvard Law Review* 747. In *The New Equal Protection*, Professor Yoshino observes and tentatively endorses a shift from 'group-based equality' analysis to 'universal liberty' analysis as a way to safeguard and advance equality norms in constitutional law. (While he focuses on American constitutional law, his argument speaks broadly enough about 'liberty' and 'equality'

Even setting these particular concerns aside, however, the Court's failure to squarely address the Article 14 claims is difficult to justify. The Court's jurisprudence clearly allows for a judgment on an Article 14 claim even where an applicant has already prevailed under another Article, provided that 'a clear inequality of treatment in the enjoyment of the right in question is a fundamental aspect of the case'.[73] As argued in the 'Revisions' below, that was unquestionably the situation here. Every aspect of the case – the underlying law, its application and its justification – involved discrimination.[74]

In these circumstances, a decision resting solely on Article 8 is inadequate, as it fails to fully capture or convey the nature of the offence to human rights.[75] While the incorporation of equality rhetoric into *Lustig-Prean*'s 'private life' reasoning is helpful to LGB people, the Court drained some of the power from that language by refusing to channel it into an unequivocal holding on equality. The act of identifying the textual or doctrinal basis for a court's judgment sends a powerful message about how the Court views the issues. It may be too easy for readers to disregard the anti-discrimination language in an Article 8 analysis if the Court specifically declines to tackle the discrimination issue more directly when given the chance.[76]

principles – including in the LGB-rights context – to be relevant to my analysis here of the ECHR's jurisprudence.) Yoshino argues that, by foregrounding universal liberties instead of 'group-based' non-discrimination principles, the law 'stresses the interests we have in common as human beings rather than the demographic differences that drive us apart'. *Ibid.*, p. 793. While I agree with much of Yoshino's argument, *Lustig-Prean* and *Smith* remind us to be careful in defining what constitutes 'universal'-liberty reasoning, even in cases where the liberty claim prevails. Though *Lustig-Prean* and *Smith* were, on some level, couched in universal terms (given that they relied only on Article 8), they do not succeed in 'stress[ing] the interests we have in common', for reasons I have explored above.

[73] ECHR, *Airey* v. *Ireland*, 9 October 1979, para. 30.

[74] One might argue that the Court did not feel ready to break new ground in *Lustig-Prean* and *Smith* by holding for the first time that Article 14 encompassed 'sexual orientation'. But breaking this ground would hardly have been a radical step, given what we know about the development of the Court's case law. Three months after *Lustig-Prean* and *Smith*, the Court held in a custody matter that Article 14 covered sexual orientation. See ECHR, *Salgueiro da Silva Mouta* v. *Portugal*, 21 December 1999, para. 28.

[75] Commentators have criticised the Court for under-utilising its authority to rule on Article 14 discrimination claims. See e.g. R. S. Arinas, 'Artículo 14: Prohibición de discriminación', in I. Lasagabaster Herrarte (ed.), *Convenio Europeo de Derechos Humanos: Comentario Sistemático* (Madrid: Civitas Ediciones, 2004), p. 531.

[76] My concerns on this issue are influenced by the development of equality jurisprudence in the United States after the Supreme Court's landmark decision in *Lawrence* v. *Texas*, see note 68 above, which invalidated Texas's anti-gay sodomy law under the 'liberty' component of the Due Process Clause of the Constitution's Fourteenth Amendment. While the Court incorporated equality concerns and anti-discrimination rhetoric into much of its due-process analysis (by observing, *inter alia*, that the sodomy law demeaned the dignity of gays and lesbians), it declined to rest its actual holding on an equal-protection theory. Compare US Supreme Court, *Loving* v. *Virginia*, 388 US 1, 12, 12 June 1967 (holding that a law prohibiting interracial marriage violated both the Equal

Lustig-Prean revised

My proposed revisions to *Lustig-Prean* (the 'Revisions')[77] address this chapter's concerns through edits to the judgment's Article 8 reasoning as well as its Article 14 reasoning. Because the proposed edits to the 'private life' reasoning are more complex, in that they introduce five different 'conceptions' of 'private life', I begin the next section with some detailed background explaining the privacy edits. I then address the more specific changes I have made to both the Article 8 and Article 14 sections.

The multiple conceptions of privacy

To begin, the Revisions present the right to respect for 'private life' in terms that are both broader and more particularised than anything set forth in the original *Lustig-Prean* judgment. Specifically, the Revisions identify five overlapping but distinguishable conceptions, or dimensions, of privacy (or private life)[78] implicated by the investigation and dismissal of the applicants under the MoD's anti-gay policy: *spatial* (or *zonal*) privacy, *relational* privacy, *decisional* privacy, *bodily* privacy, and *informational* privacy (Revisions, paragraph 62*bis*).

As the Revisions make clear, this multi-dimensional understanding of 'private life' finds ample support in the ECHR case law (Revisions, *ibid.*). Scholarship on the Convention and on the ECHR's jurisprudence has, moreover, explored the multi-faceted character of 'private life' under Article 8.[79] In proposing the specific five-part framework outlined above and in the Revisions, however, I have also drawn in significant part from the law and scholarship concerning the right to privacy in American constitutional law, particularly with respect to the first three conceptions of privacy (spatial, relational, and decisional). While a full treatment of this literature lies beyond this chapter's scope, a brief sketch of some legal and theoretical highlights will help

---

Protection and Due Process Clauses of the Constitution's Fourteenth Amendment). As a consequence, some lower courts interpreting *Lawrence* have not taken the majority's anti-discrimination rhetoric seriously, observing that the Court clearly chose not to rule on the equality claim. See e.g. US Court of Appeals for the First Circuit, *Cook v. Gates*, 528 F 3d 42, 61, 9 June 2008 (holding that, because *Lawrence* 'explicitly declined to base its ruling on equal protection principles ... there is no basis for arguing that *Lawrence* changed the standard of review applicable to a legislative classification based on sexual orientation' (citation omitted)).

[77] As explained in the introduction to this chapter, I have proposed revisions only to *Lustig-Prean*, with the understanding that I would make similar changes to *Smith*.

[78] I use the term 'privacy' interchangeably with 'private life' in this chapter. See note 6 above.

[79] See e.g. X. Arzoz Santisteban, 'Artículo 8: Derecho al respeto de la vida privada y familiar', in I. Lasagabaster Herrarte (ed.), *Convenio Europeo de Derechos Humanos: Comentario Sistemático* (Madrid: Civitas Ediciones, 2004), pp. 260–6; J. Marshall, *Personal Freedom Through Human Rights Law? Autonomy, Identity and Integrity under the European Convention on Human Rights* (Leiden: Martinus Nijhoff, 2009).

contextualise and facilitate understanding of the Revisions – particularly given that the Revisions themselves do not cite these US sources.

In an influential 1992 article, Kendall Thomas identified 'three broad conceptions of the constitutional right to privacy in contemporary [US] case law and literature'; he called these 'zonal, relational and decisional'.[80] The right to zonal (or 'spatial') privacy refers to the right to a physical space – paradigmatically, the home – that is free from government intrusion and surveillance.[81] This conception of privacy, as Professor Thomas explains, 'comprehends a space of civil sanctuary from which [an] individual can exclude others, thereby preventing the outsiders from "seeing, hearing, and knowing" what goes on there'.[82] 'Relational privacy', in turn, refers to an individual's freedom to associate with others and to form relationships, including sexually intimate relationships, again without government interference or surveillance.[83] Spatial and relational conceptions of privacy together laid the foundation for one of the most important privacy decisions in the US Supreme Court's jurisprudence: the 1965 decision in *Griswold* v. *Connecticut*, which recognised a general constitutional 'right to privacy', even though the US Constitution – in marked contrast to the Convention – lacks any reference to 'privacy' or 'private life' among its expressly enumerated guarantees.[84] Invalidating a statute that prohibited the use and distribution of contraceptives, *Griswold* focused on the law's effect on married couples in their home: 'Would we allow the police', the Court asked rhetorically, 'to search the sacred precincts of marital bedrooms for telltale signs of the use of contraceptives? The very idea is repulsive to the notions of privacy surrounding the marital relationship.'[85]

The 'decision-based understanding of the right to privacy', Professor Thomas goes on to explain, 'finds its bearings in the idea of individual

---

[80] K. Thomas, 'Beyond the Privacy Principle' (1992) 92 *Columbia Law Review* 1443. Though Professor Thomas concludes that 'privacy' provides an inadequate conceptual foundation for understanding the constitutional issues raised by sodomy laws, his oft-cited three-part typology of privacy nevertheless provides a useful starting point for understanding the various 'pillars' that sustain constitutional privacy law, particularly as it pertains to LGB issues. *Ibid.*, p. 1448.

[81] Numerous scholars have noted the centrality of the home to the American law of privacy. James Whitman, for example, explores this feature of US law in an article drawing contrasts between American and Western European understandings of privacy. See J. Q. Whitman, 'The Two Western Cultures of Privacy: Dignity Versus Liberty' (2004) 113 *Yale Law Journal* 1151 at 1161–2, 1194 and 1211–15.

[82] K. Thomas, 'Beyond the Privacy Principle' (1992) 92 *Columbia Law Review* 1443 at 1444 (citation omitted).

[83] *Ibid.*, pp. 1445–6.

[84] US Supreme Court, *Griswold* v. *Connecticut*, 381 US 479, 29 March 1965.

[85] *Ibid.*, pp. 485–96; see also *ibid.*, p. 495 (Goldberg J concurring). *Griswold*'s focus on spatial and relational privacy may have been misguided, since the actual prosecution at issue did not involve any physical intrusion into any couple's home. The defendant was a physician who had made contraceptives available to a married woman.

autonomy'.[86] In the United States, courts have been particularly solicitous of claims sounding in decisional privacy where the alleged intrusion implicates spatial and relational privacy concerns as well. This includes matters involving family relationships, procreation, children, and the home. In one of the most quoted passages of American privacy jurisprudence, for example, the Court wrote in the 1972 case of *Eisenstadt* v. *Baird* that: 'If the right of privacy means anything, it is the right of the individual, married or single, to be free from unwarranted governmental intrusion into matters so fundamentally affecting a person as the decision whether to bear or beget a child.'[87]

With a strong and increasing emphasis on the decisional component of the right to privacy, the Court built on *Griswold* and *Eisenstadt* in affording constitutional protection to, among other things, a woman's right to terminate a pregnancy,[88] the right to (heterosexual) marriage,[89] and – belatedly in 2003 – the right to engage in sexual conduct in private with a person of the same sex.[90] The Court's concern for autonomy, or decisional privacy, is evident in the way it has framed these holdings.[91]

State courts within the United States have similarly relied on a multi-dimensional understanding of privacy, with an increasing emphasis on autonomy, in their interpretation of state constitutions. This has proven significant in the context of LGB equality: in 2003, the Supreme Judicial Court of Massachusetts ruled that the state constitution required recognition of

---

[86] K. Thomas, 'Beyond the Privacy Principle' (1992) 92 *Columbia Law Review* 1443 at 1449.

[87] US Supreme Court, *Eisenstadt* v. *Baird*, 405 US 438, 453, 22 March 1972.

[88] US Supreme Court, *Roe* v. *Wade*, 410 US 113, 153, 22 January 1973 ('Th[e] right to privacy ... encompass[es] a woman's decision whether or not to terminate her pregnancy.').

[89] US Supreme Court, *Zablocki* v. *Redhail*, 434 US 374, 384, 18 January 1978 ('[T]he decision to marry [is] among the personal decisions protected by the right of privacy.').

[90] US Supreme Court, *Lawrence* v. *Texas*, 539 US 558, 574, 26 June 2003 (noting 'the respect the Constitution demands for the autonomy of the person in making ... choices' regarding, *inter alia*, 'marriage, procreation, contraception, family relationships, child rearing, and education', and stating that '[p]ersons in a homosexual relationship may seek autonomy for these purposes, just as heterosexual persons do'); see also notes 68 and 76 above.

[91] Pointing to *Lawrence* and other recent cases, prominent scholars such as Jamal Greene have argued that the Supreme Court has abandoned reliance on the 'so-called right of privacy' in favour of a 'liberty' analysis under the Due Process Clause. See e.g. J. Greene, 'The So-Called Right to Privacy' (2010) 43 *University of California Davis Law Review* 715 at 717 and 718. While I agree with much of Professor Greene's analysis, I also believe that notions of 'privacy' continue to give shape to the 'liberty' that the Court protects under the Due Process Clause. See e.g. *Lawrence* v. *Texas*, 539 US 558, 567, 26 June 2003 ('[A]dults may choose to enter upon this relationship in the confines of their homes and their own private lives and still retain their dignity as free persons.'). In any event, regardless of whether and to what extent the US Supreme Court is shifting away from a privacy analysis, Article 8's explicit protection of 'private life' ensures that the ECHR will not do the same.

same-sex marriages; the court relied largely on a decisional conception of privacy encompassing 'the right to choose to marry'.[92] The state and federal marriage cases are especially valuable in demonstrating that courts need not conceptualise 'privacy' solely in terms of spatially hidden conduct or confidential information.[93]

With respect to the fourth and fifth conceptions of privacy outlined above – 'bodily' and 'informational' – I have not drawn significantly from US law or scholarship. While these conceptions (particularly the former) find protection in American constitutional law, the Supreme Court has not embraced them under the rubric of a 'right to privacy'.[94] Nevertheless, the ECHR's Article 8 jurisprudence leaves no doubt that bodily integrity and control over personal information are core Convention concerns;[95] evidently, therefore, they must form part of any framework to explain Article 8's 'private life' protection.

As the Revisions and this brief overview together suggest – and as more detailed academic inquiry confirms[96] – the historical, textual and doctrinal underpinnings of the American 'right to privacy' and the European right to 'private life' differ in important ways. However, the framework that I have derived in part from American law and scholarship – when used with caution, with appropriate grounding in (and citations to) Convention jurisprudence, and at an appropriate level of generality – may usefully be applied to the ECHR's 'private life' cases. It may be especially helpful in cases involving LGB issues, and, most importantly for present purposes, in the *Lustig-Prean* Revisions. Two benefits deserve emphasis here. First, by specifying five distinguishable yet overlapping conceptions of private life, the framework facilitates a more precise understanding of the values and interests at stake in Article 8 cases, and allows readers to draw conceptual links between Article 8 cases covering widely disparate subject-matter. Privacy and private life can be slippery, elusive concepts. Too often, the ECHR (and commentators) describe the right to private life merely by noting the concept's breadth and the difficulty of

---

[92] Supreme Judicial Court of Massachusetts, *Goodridge* v. *Department of Public Health*, 798 NE 2d 941, 957, 18 November 2003.

[93] This is not to say that courts have abandoned the spatial and relational conceptions of privacy. For example, in *Lawrence* v. *Texas*, in the 2003 decision holding that Texas' sodomy law unconstitutionally intruded into the 'private life of the individual', the Court relied on all three of the 'conceptual pillars' of privacy identified by Professor Thomas in his 1992 article. *Lawrence* v. *Texas*, 539 US 558, 562, 567 and 574, 26 June 2003; K. Thomas, 'Beyond the Privacy Principle' (1992) 92 *Columbia Law Review* 1443 at 1448.

[94] See e.g. US Supreme Court, *National Aeronautics and Space Administration* v. *Nelson*, 131 S Ct 746, 756 n. 6, 11 January 2011; US Supreme Court, *Cruzan* v. *Director, Missouri Department of Health*, 497 US 261, 279 n. 7, 6 December 1989; US Supreme Court, *NAACP* v. *Alabama*, 357 US 449, 462, 30 June 1958.

[95] See e.g. *S and Marper*, paras. 66–86; *X and Y* v. *Netherlands*, 26 March 1985, para. 22.

[96] See generally e.g. J. Q. Whitman, 'The Two Western Cultures of Privacy: Dignity Versus Liberty' (2004) 113 *Yale Law Journal* 1151.

'exhaustive' definition, and by providing an unstructured list of discrete rights and subject-matter to which the right applies. As one can glean from earlier parts of this chapter, I do not object to holdings underscoring the breadth of the right to private life; nor do I object to judgments that provide examples of the rights encompassed by Article 8. But, without a more thorough and *conceptually* structured exposition of what 'private life' means, the ECHR's common refrain that '"private life" is a broad term not susceptible to exhaustive definition' provides insufficient guidance to jurists, litigators and others, even if the Court's judgment also provides a laundry list of rights and topics that have previously fallen within the provision's ambit of protection.

Secondly, and more importantly for those concerned with LGB equality, an analysis that clearly sets out the distinct yet overlapping conceptions of private life helps bring into sharp relief that 'private life' may, *but need not*, refer to 'hidden life' or 'secret life'. By clarifying the conceptual distinction between, for example, spatial and informational privacy on the one hand, and relational and decisional privacy on the other, a reader can more easily appreciate that protecting the private lives of LGB people means more than securing their bedroom privacy: it also means respecting their 'private' decision to live their lives openly and to form relationships, including publicly visible relationships. As discussed above and in the Revisions, protection for the public faces of private life has a long and well-established pedigree in Convention jurisprudence. And, as demonstrated by the brief overview above of US privacy jurisprudence, protecting publicly visible decisions and relationships under the rubric of 'privacy' or 'private life' is not an ECHR anomaly, but a practice shared by one of the largest constitutional democracies in the world.

The Article 8 and 14 Revisions

Applying these ideas to *Lustig-Prean*, the Revisions begin by setting forth the five conceptions of privacy and by grounding them in the Court's jurisprudence – including but not limited to *Dudgeon* and other sodomy cases[97] (Revisions, paragraphs 62*bis* and 62*ter*). I have been careful not to suggest that these five conceptions are necessarily exhaustive, or that any particular combination is necessary to prevail on a 'private life' claim (Revisions, *ibid.*).

By defining the privacy interests in broader terms, the Revisions also articulate the specific *interferences* in broader terms, and paint a richer picture of

---

[97] Notwithstanding the concerns expressed in this chapter about an undue focus on sexual conduct occurring in private spaces, reliance on the Court's sodomy cases remains necessary. These are, after all, the only pre-*Lustig-Prean* cases in which the Court squarely addressed LGB issues. See note 67 above and the accompanying text. My objections to the original judgment, moreover, should not be taken to mean that I object to *any* mention of sexual conduct. See note 36 above.

LGB individuals' lives (Revisions, paragraphs 62*bis* and 82). For example, the Revisions highlight the detrimental effect of an anti-LGB policy on the development of personal relationships – without insinuating that the detrimental effects consist *only* in restricting sexual activity or in punishing sexual desire (Revisions, paragraph 82). The restrictions on consensual sexual conduct were, however, significant in and of themselves; the Revisions therefore recognise that these restrictions *independently* interfere with private life (Revisions, *ibid.*). And, unlike the original *Lustig-Prean* judgment, the Revisions incorporate the concept of moral integrity as an element of individual autonomy, and observe that the government demeaned the applicants' integrity by coercing them, on threat of discharge, to engage in evasion and deception about significant aspects of their lives (Revisions, *ibid.*).

I should stress here that while the Revisions' Article 8 analysis articulates the 'private life' issues more broadly than *Lustig-Prean*, it does not significantly widen the scope of Article 8 'private life' protections beyond the boundaries the Court has drawn in other cases, either before or after *Lustig-Prean*.[98] My purpose here was not to expand the Court's Article 8 jurisprudence as a general matter. Rather, I aimed to provide a conceptual framework to organise various relevant elements of the Court's earlier jurisprudence, which had both implicitly and explicitly recognised diverse facets of 'private life'; the Revisions then demonstrate how the applicants' claims fall comfortably – and for multiple reasons – into that multi-faceted framework (Revisions, paragraphs 62*bis*, 62*ter* and 82).

This reframing of the Article 8 analysis allows the reader to appreciate how the United Kingdom failed in numerous ways to respect the applicants' private lives, without endorsing the mistaken view that sexual orientation, or LGB orientation specifically, is naturally or 'essentially' a 'most intimate aspect' of private life. The Revisions thus avoid contributing to the dangerously narrow form of privacy discourse that can impede progress towards equality in other contexts involving LGB issues.[99]

The Revisions to the Article 14 section reinforce these objectives. As explained above, an Article 14 holding aids in emphasising the universal nature of the privacy interests; this in turn helps to counter any unintended insinuation or mistaken assumption that LGB identity is uniquely sexualised in a way that requires *special* privacy. The Revisions thus emphasise that the MoD policy limited everyday freedoms that heterosexuals continued to enjoy

---

[98] While the Revisions rely only on cases pre-dating *Lustig-Prean*, their broad understanding of privacy is consistent with later cases. See note 46 above.

[99] The Revisions alter the way the Court distinguishes an earlier case, ECHR, *Kalaç* v. *Turkey*, 1 July 1997, para. 25. The original *Lustig-Prean* distinguished *Kalaç* on the ground that *Kalaç* involved 'public conduct'. To avoid insinuating that sexual orientation pertains only to things one does 'in private', the Revisions delete the 'public conduct' reference and distinguish *Kalaç* on other grounds (Revisions, para. 86).

(Revisions, paragraph 109). On the other hand, in an effort to 'universalise' the judgment from a different angle, the Revisions also signal that anti-LGB bias can negatively impact *all* people; in paragraph 109, the Revisions point out that anti-LGB policies can create an atmosphere of insecurity and distrust for all service-members, since nobody is free from 'accusations' of homosexuality.[100]

To integrate the equality ruling, the Revisions draw on pre-1999 case law to explain why it is appropriate to rule on the Article 14 issue even though the Court has already found a violation of Article 8 (Revisions, paragraphs 108–9). The Revisions also set forth the basic standards for applying Article 14 (Revisions, paragraphs 110–11).

Post-*Lustig-Prean* cases establish that 'weighty reasons' are required under Article 14 to justify discrimination based on sexual orientation.[101] In writing the *Lustig-Prean* Revisions, I have assumed that those later judgments would still exist. In light of those judgments, and considering the breadth of the Article 8 reasoning I have already proposed in the Revisions, I considered it unnecessary (and imprudent, in terms of institutional overreach) to add a definitive ruling on the 'weighty reasons' issue to this judgment. The Revisions nevertheless gesture towards some explanations for why particularly 'weighty reasons' might be required (Revisions, paragraphs 111–12.);[102] they stop short of definitely resolving that question, since the Article 14 violation here would be plain in any event (Revisions, paragraphs 112–13).[103]

---

[100] Cf. J. E. Halley, *Don't: A Reader's Guide to the Military's Anti-Gay Policy* (Durham, NC: Duke University Press, 1999), pp. 2–3 (discussing the insecurity that 'don't ask, don't tell' imposed on service-members 'who "really [were]" heterosexual').

[101] See e.g. ECHR, *Karner v. Austria*, 24 July 2003, paras. 37 and 42.

[102] In suggesting why 'weighty reasons' might be required, the Revisions draw on an argument that post-*Lustig-Prean* cases hint at, but do not explain, namely, that a connection or similarity exists between sex and sexual orientation discrimination. See e.g. ECHR, *Kozak v. Poland*, 2 March 2010, para. 92; and ECHR, *Karner v. Austria*, 24 July 2000, paras. 33 and 37; cf. A. Koppelman, *The Gay Rights Question in Contemporary America* (University of Chicago Press, 2002), pp. 53–71 (arguing that sexual-orientation discrimination is a form of sex discrimination). The Revisions also draw on connections between freedom from discrimination and other Convention protections and values (Revisions, para. 112).

[103] Because Lustig-Prean and Beckett, unlike Smith and Grady, did not bring free-expression claims, the *Lustig-Prean* Revisions do not offer any language regarding Article 10. As discussed above, however, I take issue with the *Smith* judgment's disposition of the free-expression claims. *Smith* could and should have simply held that the applicants' rights were sufficiently vindicated by the Article 8 and 14 rulings, making additional commentary on Article 10 unnecessary. (Affirmatively ruling for the applicants on Article 10 would have risked judicial overreaching and backlash. *Smith*, moreover, may not have been a proper vehicle for an Article 10 ruling due to the applicants' arguably contradictory statements about whether they had wished to reveal their orientation prior to the investigations. Compare *Smith*, para. 84, with *Smith*, paras. 124 and 126.)

Conclusion: privacy's future

As compared to many social movements, particularly in Europe and the United States, the movement for LGB equality has progressed with unusual speed. Even so, *Lustig-Prean* and *Smith* are hardly ancient history. The characterisations of sexual orientation and the privacy rationales I have identified continue to play an important role in advancing LGB equality on some fronts, while hindering the movement for LGB equality in other areas.

Continued close attention to privacy's many faces is critical, including in the military context, as additional countries around the world consider removing formal restrictions on military service by LGB people or work to improve conditions for those who already serve. In the United States, we have already seen that military officials, in preparing for and implementing the repeal of 'don't ask, don't tell', have adopted a mantra that sexual orientation is a 'personal and private issue'; those precise words are repeated, arguably *ad nauseam*, in materials and reports regarding the repeal's implementation.[104] But it remains unclear what this means. Hopefully, it means that sexual orientation is not the military's concern, that the witch-hunts are over, and that officials and service-members should treat their comrades, superiors and subordinates with equal respect regardless of sexual orientation. On the other hand, identical statements are found in documents issued under 'don't ask, don't tell'.[105] In *that* context, the emphasis on privacy had a very different meaning: *stay in the closet*. Moving from one understanding of 'private' to another – while using identical language – will not necessarily be a seamless process; those involved must carefully scrutinise appeals to privacy to ensure that they are deployed to protect and not, however subtly, to suppress human rights.

The problems that can arise from thinking and speaking about LGB equality as a 'private life' issue also raise the question of whether the ECHR should de-emphasise or even abandon Article 8's 'private life' provision in judgments dealing with LGB issues. In *Lustig-Prean*, abandoning a 'private life' rationale was not a reasonable possibility given the state of the law, and, perhaps more importantly, the manner in which the applicants framed their claims. In future cases, however, I would agree, in view of the problems addressed in this chapter, that the Court should look, where reasonably possible, to ground decisions affirming LGB equality in something other than (or in addition to) the right to 'private life'.[106]

---

[104] A US Department of Defense report, for instance, repeats this precise phrase eight times in the span of thirty-two pages. See US Department of Defense, *Comprehensive Review*, note 25 above, pp. 45, 52, 53, 54, 58, 61, 70 and 77.

[105] See e.g. US Department of Defense Directive 1332.14(H), 21 December 1993.

[106] In some cases, the Court has already done so. In recent years, for example, the Court has, under Article 11, affirmed the right to participate in public protests in favour of LGB rights. ECHR, *Alekseyev* v. *Russia*, 21 October 2010, paras. 68–88. The Court has also

I do not believe, however, that the Court can or should abandon 'private life' holdings or rationales altogether. Important cases have arisen, and will continue to arise, in which the right to respect for 'private life' presents the only – or at least the strongest – basis for decision.[107] To cast aside reliance on 'private life' in the LGB context, moreover, would be to cast aside arguments that are firmly grounded in the Convention's text and in long-standing Convention jurisprudence. These arguments have, despite their drawbacks and perils, often formed the basis for crucial rulings in favour of LGB equality.

Thus, the connection between Article 8's 'private life' provision and the movement for LGB equality cannot and should not be broken. Rather, those concerned with the human rights of LGB people must be vigilant and cautious in how they articulate and deploy 'private life' reasoning. By consistently examining how privacy arguments can play out in vastly different ways depending on their formulation and the subject-matter at issue, jurists, advocates and others can build a stronger discursive and jurisprudential foundation for LGB equality.

Rewriting Lustig-Prean and Beckett v. United Kingdom

. . .

I.   Alleged violation of Article 8 of the Convention

62. The applicants complained that the investigations into their homosexuality and their subsequent discharge from the Royal Navy on the sole ground that they were homosexual, in pursuance of the Ministry of Defence's absolute policy against homosexuals in the British armed forces, constituted a violation of their right to respect for their private lives protected by Article 8 of the Convention . . .

**62bis. The 'right to respect for . . . private . . . life' under Article 8 is 'not susceptible to exhaustive definition' (*Raninen* v. *Finland*, no. 20972/92, §
63 [1997]). As reflected in the Court's prior cases, however, the 'notion of "private . . . life" is a broad one' (*ibid.*), and encompasses several overlapping aspects or conceptions of privacy, including the following:**

(i) *spatial* privacy, which protects against State intrusions into private or intimate spaces such as the home (see e.g. *Dudgeon* v. *United Kingdom*, no. 7525/76, §§ 40–41, 63 [1981] (holding that enforcement of a law that prohibited consensual and nonviolent sexual conduct between adult males, even when it occurred in private spaces, violates Article 8));

recognised that same-sex couples may form a 'family' for the purposes of Article 8's protection of 'family life'. ECHR, *Schalk and Kopf* v. *Austria*, 24 June 2010, para. 94.
[107] See e.g. *EB* v. *France*, 22 January 2008, paras. 43–51.

(ii) *relational* privacy, which concerns a person's right 'to establish and develop relationships with other human beings', in both the private and public sphere (*Burghartz* v. *Switzerland*, no. 16213/90, § 24 [1994]; see also *Niemietz* v. *Germany*, no. 13710/88, § 29 [1992] (explaining that 'activities of a professional or business nature' fall within the ambit of Article 8's 'private ... life' protection 'since it is, after all, in the course of their working lives that the majority of people have a significant, if not the greatest, opportunity of developing relationships with the outside world'));

(iii) *decisional* privacy, which concerns a person's right to make choices significantly affecting his or her autonomy, self-definition, moral integrity and dignity, even where these privately made choices have public manifestations (see e.g. *Burghartz* v. *Switzerland*, no. 16213/90, § 24 [1994] (holding that a married person's choice of surname falls within the ambit of 'private ... life'));

(iv) *bodily* privacy, which protects a person's right to physical integrity and the right to make important decisions that significantly involve or affect one's body (see e.g. *Dudgeon*; see also *X and Y* v. *Netherlands*, no. 8978/80, § 22 [1985]);

(v) *informational* privacy, which concerns the right to control certain personal information by, for example, withholding it from the public or the government (see e.g. *Dudgeon*, §§ 33, 41, 63).

62*ter*. The Court does not intend this list to be exhaustive; nor does it intend to suggest that an applicant's claim must touch on more than one (or on a particular combination) of the aforementioned aspects of 'private ... life' in order for his or her claim to fall within Article 8's scope.

On the other hand, where the State's action implicates privacy concern across several of the above dimensions, the interference with Article 8 rights may be particularly plain. Such was the case in several earlier decisions involving the equal rights of homosexuals and bisexuals. In the *Dudgeon*, *Norris* and *Modinos* cases, for example, the Court held that laws criminalising private consensual sexual conduct between adult males violated Article 8 (see *Dudgeon*, §§ 61, 63; *Norris* v. *Ireland*, no. 10581/83 [1988]; *Modinos* v. *Cyprus*, no. 15070/89 [1993]). In each case, the law at issue encroached on the applicant's right to make deeply personal *decisions* regarding intimate sexual *relationships* and *bodily* intimacy, even where the sexual activity occurred within the *spatial* privacy of the home; the public officers' investigations of criminal sexual activity in *Dudgeon*, moreover, improperly coerced the applicant to reveal private *information* about his sexuality and sexual conduct (see *Dudgeon*, §§ 33, 41).

A.   Whether there was an interference

. . .

64. . . . In these circumstances **and in light of the foregoing principles (see § 62 above)**, the Court is of the view that the investigations by the military police into the applicants' homosexuality, which included detailed interviews with each of them and with third parties on matters relating to their sexual orientation and practices, together with the preparation of a final report for the armed forces' authorities on the investigations, constituted a direct interference with the applicants' right to respect for their private lives **across all of the dimensions discussed above (see § 62*bis* above and the cases cited therein; see also § 82 below)**. Their consequent administrative discharge on the sole ground of their sexual orientation also constituted an interference with that right [references deleted].

B.   Whether the interferences were justified

65. Such interferences can only be considered justified if the conditions of the second paragraph of Article 8 are satisfied. Accordingly, the interferences must be 'in accordance with the law', have an aim which is legitimate under this paragraph and must be 'necessary in a democratic society' for the aforesaid aim (see the *Norris* v. *Ireland* judgment of 26 October 1988, Series A no. 142, p. 18, § 39).

. . .

67. The Court observes that the essential justification offered by the Government for the policy and for the consequent investigations and discharges is the maintenance of the morale of service personnel and, consequently, of the fighting power and the operational effectiveness of the armed forces (see paragraph 88 below) . . .

. . .

68. [Fragment deleted] **The Court must determine** whether the interferences in the present cases can be considered 'necessary in a democratic society' for the aforesaid aims.

. . .

80. . . . Given the matters at issue in the present case, the Court would underline the link between the notion of 'necessity' and that of a 'democratic society', the hallmarks of the latter including pluralism, tolerance and broadmindedness . . .

. . .

82. **By restricting military employment opportunities based on sexual orientation, the policy at issue has demeaned the applicants' dignity and has risked impeding the development and enjoyment of personal relationships that may be among the most important and meaningful in an**

individual's life. The policy has thus interfered substantially with various aspects of private life – particularly decisional and relational privacy.

The policy has also infringed applicants' decisional, relational, spatial and bodily privacy by interfering with decisions about private sexual conduct, [fragment deleted] 'a most intimate part of an individual's private life' particularly because the law extends to off-duty sexual conduct, even if it occurs within an individual's home.

The policy has also coerced applicants, under threat of discharge, to engage in deception or evasion if asked about important aspects of their identity, personal relationships, home and family. This affront to applicants' moral and psychological integrity has substantially infringed on, *inter alia*, their relational, decisional and informational privacy.

Given the serious nature of these multiple interferences with private life, there must exist 'particularly serious reasons' before such interferences can satisfy the requirements of Article 8 § 2 of the Convention . . .

83. It is common ground that the sole reason for the investigations conducted and for the applicants' discharge was their sexual orientation. [Fragment deleted] **In view of the serious intrusion into various aspects of private life that this entailed (see §§ 62 and 82 above)**, particularly serious reasons by way of justification were required . . .

. . .

86. . . . With regard to the Government's reference to the *Kalaç* judgment, the Court considers that the compulsory retirement of Mr Kalaç is to be distinguished from the discharge of the present applicants [fragment deleted]. **Mr Kalaç was dismissed from the military based on Turkish officials' assessment that he 'lack[ed] . . . loyalty to the foundation of the Turkish nation'** (*Kalaç* v. *Turkey*, no. 20704/92, § 25 [1997]). **States have broad discretion in the context of military employment to consider loyalty to the nation. Here, in contrast**, the applicants were discharged on grounds of their innate personal characteristics, **and the Government has offered no reason to question their loyalty to the United Kingdom; on the contrary, the Government concedes that the applicants were repeatedly lauded for their fine military service (see also § 89 below).**

87. Accordingly, the Court must consider whether, taking account of the margin of appreciation open to the State in matters of national security, particularly convincing and weighty reasons exist by way of justification for the interferences with the applicants' right to respect for their private lives.

88. The core argument of the Government in support of the policy is that the presence of open or suspected homosexuals in the armed forces would have a substantial and negative effect on morale and, consequently, on the fighting power and operational effectiveness of the armed forces. The Government rely in this respect on the report of the [fragment deleted]

Homosexual Policy Assessment Team (HPAT), established by the Ministry of Defence in order to undertake an internal assessment of the armed forces' policy on homosexuality . . .

89. . . . The Court finds that the perceived problems which were identified in the HPAT report as a threat to the fighting power and operational effectiveness of the armed forces were founded solely upon the negative attitudes of heterosexual personnel towards those of homosexual orientation. The Court observes, in this respect, that no moral judgment is made on homosexuality by the policy . . . It is also accepted by the Government that neither the records nor conduct of the applicants nor the physical capability, courage, dependability and skills of homosexuals in general are in any way called into question by the policy.

90. The question for the Court is whether the above-noted negative attitudes constitute sufficient justification for the interferences at issue.

The Court observes from the HPAT report that these attitudes, even if sincerely felt by those who expressed them, ranged from stereotypical expressions of hostility to those of homosexual orientation, to vague expressions of unease about the presence of homosexual colleagues. To the extent that they represent a predisposed bias on the part of a heterosexual majority against a homosexual minority, these negative attitudes cannot, of themselves, be considered by the Court to amount to sufficient justification for the interferences with the applicants' rights outlined above, any more than similar negative attitudes towards those of a different race, origin or colour (see also §§ 112–113 below).

. . .

97. . . . The Court . . . notes the evidence before the domestic courts to the effect that the European countries operating a blanket legal ban on homosexuals in their armed forces are now in a small minority . . .

. . .

104. In sum, the Court finds that neither the investigations conducted into the applicants' sexual orientation, nor their discharge on the grounds of their homosexuality in pursuance of the Ministry of Defence policy, were justified under Article 8 § 2 of the Convention.

. . .

II. Alleged violation of Article 14 of the Convention in conjunction with Article 8

106. The applicants also invoked Article 14 of the Convention in conjunction with Article 8 in relation to the operation of the Ministry of Defence policy against them . . .

[Original paragraphs 108–9 deleted]

108. Where an applicant prevails on his or her claim that a State has violated a Convention right, such as Article 8's 'private ... life' protection, the Court generally need not rule on any additional allegation that the State violated that right in conjunction with Article 14. 'The position is otherwise', however, 'if a clear inequality of treatment in the enjoyment of the right in question is a fundamental aspect of the case' (*Airey* v. *Ireland*, no. 6289/73, § 30 [1979]).

109. Inequality of treatment in the enjoyment of Article 8 rights is fundamental to this case. The applicants were investigated and then dismissed from the military based solely on their sexual orientation, pursuant to a policy that expressly excludes all homosexuals and bisexuals based on their sexual orientation.

The Court notes that, under the policy at issue, heterosexual military personnel do not suffer significant limitations (if any at all) on decisions regarding their self-identity or on their ability to establish and to speak about their personal relationships. They also do not face the same (if any) pressure as homosexuals and bisexuals under this policy to engage in evasion or deception when speaking about their lives. While some heterosexuals may experience negative effects of the policy, particularly due to the atmosphere of suspicion and insecurity that such anti-gay policies may engender (since nobody is entirely free from suspicions of homosexuality), it is not disputed that the policy's principal effect is to burden the basic rights and freedoms of LGB service-members alone. Because the policy singles out LGB service-members in this way, denying to them basic, everyday freedoms that others enjoy – and may even take for granted – this case presents not only a question of 'respect for ... private ... life'; it fundamentally concerns *equal* 'respect for ... private ... life'.

In defending the discriminatory dismissals and the underlying law before this Court, moreover, the Government relied primarily on the discriminatory hostility and bias of service personnel participating in the HPAT study.

In short, inequality and bias based on sexual orientation lie at the heart of this case.

Accordingly, the Court will consider the Article 14 claim.

110. A difference of treatment is impermissibly discriminatory under Article 14 if it 'has no objective and reasonable justification', that is, if it does not pursue a 'legitimate aim' or if there is not a 'reasonable relationship of proportionality between the means employed and the aim sought to be realised' (*Karlheinz Schmidt* v. *Germany*, no. 13580/88, § 24 [1994]).

111. The prohibited bases of discrimination enumerated in Article 14 are illustrative, not exhaustive. This is evident from the text itself (in particular, the words 'such as' and 'other status'), as well as from this

Court's case law (see *Engel and others* v. *Netherlands*, no. 5100/71, § 72 [1976]). Accordingly, the requirement of an 'objective and reasonable justification' applies regardless of whether Article 14 specifically enumerates the 'status' at issue.

In some circumstances, however, the Court has applied the 'objective and reasonable justification' test with particular strictness. Differential treatment based on Article 14's specifically enumerated traits, or closely analogous traits, may be especially suspect under the Convention; the Court has held, for example, that 'very weighty reasons would have to be put forward before the Court could regard a difference of treatment based exclusively on the ground of sex as compatible with the Convention' (*Karlheinz Schmidt*, cited above, § 24).

112. In light of several considerations – including but not limited to the frequent overlap between discrimination based on sexual orientation and discrimination based on sex, the relationship of discrimination based on sexual orientation to other freedoms protected by the Convention (see e.g. §§ 62, 82), and the values underlying the convention as a whole (see § 82) – the Court is inclined to hold that, like distinctions based on sex, distinctions that impose disadvantages based on sexual orientation must be justified by particularly weighty reasons to be compatible with Article 14.

In this case, however, it is unnecessary to rule definitively on this question. Because the Government's policy imposes such substantial burdens (see §§ 62, 84), and because the Government's primary defence has been to rely on the irrational anti-gay bias and hostility expressed by service personnel (see § 90), the Government fails the 'objective and reasonable justification' test regardless of the strictness of the review.

113. Accordingly, the Court holds that the Government's discrimination against the applicants based on sexual orientation violated their rights under Article 14 taken in conjunction with Article 8.

For these reasons, the Court unanimously

1. *Holds* that there has been a violation of Article 8 of the Convention;
2. *Holds* that [fragment deleted] **there has been a violation of Article 14 of the Convention** taken in conjunction with Article 8;

   . . .

PART V

Disability

13

Unravelling the knot: Article 8, private life, positive duties and disability: rewriting Sentges v. Netherlands

LISA WADDINGTON

Introduction

Article 8 of the European Convention on Human Rights ('the Convention') protects the right to respect for home, private life, family life and correspondence. The concept of private life found within this Article has been interpreted broadly to cover a wide range of areas and interests, ranging from police searches[1] and handcuffing,[2] the right to refuse medical treatment,[3] the right to choose one's own name,[4] legal recognition of the gender of post-operative transsexuals,[5] and freedom from environmental pollution.[6] Article 8 has also been invoked in a number of cases involving individuals with disabilities, where the Court has been asked to consider whether the Article is applicable where State action or inaction which exacerbates, or fails to limit, the consequences of an impairment or disability constitutes an interference with an individual's private life. On occasion the disadvantage at issue is caused by an interaction between the applicant's impairment and the environment, as in the case of a physically inaccessible infrastructure, and on occasion the disadvantage flows directly from the unmitigated impairment. In such cases, applicants have claimed that the State is under a positive obligation to take action to alleviate the burden or disadvantage at issue in order to protect their right to private life. However, in deciding Article 8 cases, the European Court of Human Rights (ECHR) is much more likely to find that direct interferences by the State with an individual's private life fall within the scope of the Article, than to find that the State is under a positive obligation to act where the interferences are linked to the consequences of impairment or disability. Nevertheless, the Court has accepted, in a number of cases, that State action or inaction with regard to

---

[1] ECHR, *Gaskin* v. *United Kingdom*, 7 July 1989.
[2] ECHR, *DG* v. *Ireland*, 16 May 2002, para. 105.
[3] ECHR, *Glass* v. *United Kingdom*, 9 March 2004.
[4] ECHR, *Stjerna* v. *Finland*, 25 November 1994.
[5] ECHR (GC), *Goodwin* v. *United Kingdom*, 11 July 2002.
[6] ECHR, *Lopez Ostra* v. *Spain*, 9 December 1994.

persons with disabilities in such circumstances *may* fall within the scope of Article 8, but it has rarely found in favour of disabled applicants in such cases.

On the one hand, the Court has found that States enjoy a wide margin of appreciation in such cases. However, in many cases such issues do not even arise, as the Court has found that the threshold that must be met to establish that an actual interference in private life has occurred has not been met. Therefore, in a series of disability-related cases, the Court has explored the requirements that must be met to establish that an interference with private life contrary to Article 8 has occurred, but then held that no such interference has actually taken place in the case at issue. However, these judgments, read in combination, are somewhat confusing, in that the reader is left unclear as to what standards must be met for an actual Article 8 interference to occur in the context of a disability-related positive obligations claim. Indeed, one is sometimes left wondering why the Court has not found that an interference with private life has occurred, as all the requirements set out in previous case law seem to be met. One such case is *Sentges* v. *Netherlands*,[7] which will be explored in this chapter.

Sentges concerned the claim by a young disabled man that the Netherlands was under a positive obligation to provide him with an expensive assistive device in order to increase his independence, and thereby ensure respect for his private life. Aside from the importance of this decision in the context of the line of disability-related Article 8 case law referred to above, the case is significant because it addresses the increasingly vexed issue of the level of support States are obliged to provide to individuals who are severely disabled. On the one hand, international human rights law, and in particular the United Nations Convention on the Rights of Persons with Disabilities,[8] recognises the right to live independently in the community, and that persons with disabilities should have access 'to a range of in-home residential and other community support services, including personal assistance necessary to support living and inclusion in the community'.[9] On the other hand, both the increasing costs of providing assistive support and devices, and the current climate of austerity in Europe, exert tensions on public expenditure, and lead to a tendency to restrict, at least in some respects, support provided to people with disabilities.

However, the overall goal of this chapter extends beyond an exploration of the *Sentges* case. Instead, the aim is to reflect on how the Court deals with cases relating to alleged interferences with private life under Article 8 experienced by people with disabilities, and claims that the State is under a positive obligation

---

[7] ECHR, *Sentges* v. *Netherlands*, 8 July 2003.
[8] Convention on the Rights of Persons with Disabilities, GA Res. 61/106, UN GAOR, 61st Sess. Supp. No. 49, UN Doc. A/RES/61/106/Annex II, at 65 (13 December 2006), entered into force 3 May 2008.
[9] Article 19(2) CRPD.

to take action to eliminate or reduce disadvantages or burdens linked to impairment or disability. By rewriting one such case, it is hoped that the threshold for establishing an Article 8 interference in this context can be clarified and, more generally, allow for reflection in this area.

The Court's case law: establishing an interference with the right to private life

Article 8 protects a number of aspects of an individual's private life. However, the limits of the concept of private life are rather difficult to pin down, and, in *Pretty* v. *UK*,[10] the Court acknowledged that 'the concept of "private life" is a broad term not susceptible to exhaustive definition'.[11] Having said that, a number of dimensions or elements to the concept of private life can be identified through the Court's case law.

In *Niemietz* v. *Germany*, the Court found that there can be an interference with private life when a search of business premises occurs, and held:

> The Court does not consider it possible to attempt an exhaustive definition of the notion of 'private life'. However, it would be too restrictive to limit the notion to an 'inner circle' in which the individual may live his own personal life as he chooses and to exclude therefrom entirely the outside world not encompassed within that circle. Respect for private life must also comprise to a certain degree the right to establish and develop relationships with other human beings.[12]

At a minimum, therefore, the notion of private life protected within Article 8 includes at least two elements: an 'inner circle' in which the individual may live his own personal life as he chooses; and the right to establish relationships with other human beings.

This latter element is particularly relevant in the context of disability-related cases concerning claims that the State is under a positive obligation to act to protect private life. Arguably, the right to establish relationships with other human beings in the way in which one chooses is based on the concepts of human dignity and personal freedom. Indeed, in *Pretty* v. *UK*, the Court held: 'The very essence of the Convention is respect for human dignity and human freedom.'[13] In the same judgment, the Court expanded on the concept of private life, and held:

> It covers the physical and psychological integrity of a person. It can some-times embrace aspects of an individual's physical and social identity . . . Article 8 also protects a right to personal development, and the right to

---

[10] ECHR, *Pretty* v. *United Kingdom*, 29 April 2002.   [11] Para. 61.
[12] ECHR, *Niemietz* v. *Germany*, 16 December 1992, para. 29.   [13] Para. 65.

establish relationships with other human beings and the outside world ...
Although no previous case has established as such any right to self-
determination as being contained in Article 8 of the Convention, the
Court considers that the notion of personal autonomy is an important
principle underlying the interpretation of its guarantees.[14]

In the later case of *Goodwin* v. *UK*,[15] the Court once again stressed that 'respect
for human dignity and human freedom' is the 'very essence' of the
Convention,[16] and noted the importance of personal autonomy in the context
of private life.[17] In this case, the Court viewed private life as involving an
individual freedom to determine the course of one's own life, including through
obtaining legal recognition of gender-reassignment surgery, and regarded
Article 8 as conferring a 'right ... to personal development and to physical
and moral security in the full sense'.[18]

In a recent disability-related case, *Shtukaturov* v. *Russia*,[19] the Court found
that the applicant's right to private life had been breached when the authorities
had deprived him of legal capacity. The applicant was placed under the guardianship of his mother, at her request, by a court. This had occurred without the
applicant's knowledge or consent. His guardian subsequently placed him in a
psychiatric institution, again without his consent. The applicant attempted to
appeal against the removal of his legal capacity, but was denied access to his
lawyer, and his appeal was unsuccessful. Before the ECHR, the applicant
claimed that the relevant legal capacity law was imprecise and did not clearly
identify the severity of the reduction in cognitive capacity that was called for, for
full deprivation of legal capacity to occur. In that sense, the law failed to protect
people who were mentally ill from arbitrary interference with their right to
private life. The law also did not allow for a partial limitation of legal capacity, as
is the case in many other European countries.

The ECHR found that the deprivation of legal capacity amounted to an
interference in the applicant's private life. The interference was very serious,
and he became fully dependent on his official guardian in almost all areas of
life. The removal of full legal capacity was for an indefinite period. The
procedure by which legal capacity was removed was flawed, and the applicant
did not have any possibility to take part in the proceedings or subsequently
challenge them. The Russian court that had removed the legal capacity did not
analyse the applicant's incapacity in sufficient detail, and the law only allowed
for full legal capacity or incapacity, with no 'tailor-made response' being
available. Finding that the interference with the applicant's private life was
disproportionate to the legitimate aim pursued, the Court held that Article 8
had been breached.

---

[14] Para. 61.   [15] ECHR (GC), *Goodwin* v. *United Kingdom*, 11 July 2002.   [16] Para. 90.
[17] Para. 90.   [18] Para. 90.   [19] ECHR, *Shtukaturov* v. *Russia*, 27 June 2008.

Based on a deeper analysis of the case law than has been carried out here, Paul Bowen[20] has developed a taxonomy of the protected interests covered by the right to private life in Article 8. He argues that the interests can be divided into six categories:

- Physical and psychological (or 'moral') integrity
- The right to autonomy or self-determination
- The right to identity and personal development
- The right to establish and develop relationships with other human beings
- The right to protection of private sphere and private space ('privacy')
- State action having financial consequences

Bowen notes that the first interest, covering physical and psychological integrity, can cover State action or inaction that exacerbates the consequences of impairment or disability.[21] However, other issues, such as the right to autonomy and self-determination, and the right to establish and develop relationships with others, can also arise in disability-related cases. Arguably, all these dimensions were at issue in the aforementioned case of *Shtukaturov*, although the Court did not explicitly explore such issues.

Having established that the concept of private life is broad, it is worth noting that it is naturally not without limits. In *Friend v. UK*,[22] the Court noted: 'A broad construction of Article 8 does not mean . . . that it protects every activity a person might seek to engage in with other human beings in order to establish and develop such relationships.' The Court has also returned to the limits of the concept of private life, as protected by Article 8, in a number of disability-related cases which are considered below.

This chapter will now proceed to consider how the Court has addressed claims concerning Article 8 and the right to private life in a number of prominent disability-related cases concerning claims that the State is under a positive duty to act.

---

[20] 'Article 8 and "Private Life": The Protean Right', ALBA Seminar, 2 March 2010, Paul Bowen, Doughty Street Chambers, available at www.adminlaw.org.uk/docs/ALBA%20Seminar%20% 20Article%208%20and%20private%20life.pdf (last accessed 22 November 2011).

[21] Mr Justice Munby has also concluded, on the basis of the Court's case law, and in particular *Botta*, that the concept of physical and psychological integrity includes the right of people with disabilities to participate in the life of the community and to have 'access to essential economic and social activities and to an appropriate range of recreational and cultural activities'. He notes that this is matched by the positive obligation on the State to take appropriate measures designed to ensure to the greatest extent feasible that a disabled person is not 'so circumscribed and so isolated as to be deprived of the possibility of developing his personality'. Mr Justice Munby, 'Human Rights: Transforming Services?, Human Rights and Social Welfare Law: The Impact of Article 8', Social Care Institute for Excellence, available at www.scie.org.uk/news/events/previousevents/humanrights06/ mrjusticemunby.pdf (last accessed 22 November 2011).

[22] ECHR, *Friend and Countryside Alliance and others* v. *United Kingdom*, 24 November 2009.

A selection of cases involving the right to private life, positive duties and disability[23]

First, it is worth noting that the Court has long held that the 'respect' for private life which Article 8 guarantees imposes on States Parties not merely the obligation to abstain from inappropriate interference but also, in some cases, certain positive duties or obligations.[24] In deciding whether a positive obligation exists, the Court frequently carries out a balancing exercise between the rights of the individual and the rights of the community. As a result, where positive obligations are at issue, the Court has generally found that there is a considerable margin of appreciation allowed to the State to decide how it regulates a particular area.[25]

In *Botta* v. *Italy*,[26] the applicant claimed that Article 8, and specifically the right to private life, had been infringed when the public authorities had failed to ensure that a private beach, in a place where the applicant was on holiday, was physically accessible to people with disabilities. The applicant, who used a wheelchair, claimed that he was unable to enjoy a normal social life that enabled him to participate in the life of the community and to exercise essential rights, on account of the State's failure to discharge its positive obligations to adopt measures and to monitor compliance with domestic provisions relating to private beaches.[27]

In response, the Court reiterated its previous case law that in some circumstances a State may be under a positive obligation to prevent or stop a third party from interfering with an individual's private life.

> While the essential object of Article 8 is to protect the individual against arbitrary interference by the public authorities, it does not merely compel the State to abstain from such interference: in addition to this negative undertaking, there may be positive obligations inherent in effective respect for private or family life. These obligations may involve the adoption of measures designed to secure respect for private life even in the sphere of the relations of individuals between themselves ... In order to determine whether such obligations exist, regard must be had to the fair balance that has to be struck between the general interest and the interests of the individual.[28]

---

[23] See also O. de Schutter, 'Reasonable Accommodations and Positive Obligations in the European Convention on Human Rights', in A. Lawson and C. Gooding (eds.), *Disability Rights in Europe: From Theory to Practice* (Oxford and Portland, OR: Hart Publishing, 2005), p. 36.

[24] ECHR, *Marckx* v. *Belgium*, 13 June 1979.

[25] ECHR, *Rees* v. *United Kingdom*, 17 October 1986, paras. 37 and 44; and *Hatton and others* v. *United Kingdom*, 2 October 2001.

[26] ECHR, *Botta* v. *Italy*, 24 February 1998.   [27] Para. 27.   [28] Para. 33.

The Court then acknowledged that 'a State has obligations of this type where it has found a direct and immediate link between the measures sought by an applicant and the latter's private and/or family life',[29] and referred to a number of cases[30] in which such positive obligations had been found to exist based on Article 8. The Court continued:

> In the instant case, however, the right asserted by Mr Botta, namely the right to gain access to the beach and the sea at a place distant from his normal place of residence during his holidays, concerns interpersonal relations of such a broad and indeterminate scope that there can be no conceivable direct link between the measures the State was urged to take in order to make good the omissions of the private bathing establishments and the applicant's private life.[31]

Therefore, whilst the Court acknowledged that Article 8 was capable of resulting in positive obligations on the State relating to the protection of private life, and seemed, potentially at least, willing to acknowledge that Article 8 could be infringed when disabled individuals were unable to interact with their environment and their community because of lack of physical access, it did not find that Article 8 had been infringed in the case at issue.

A somewhat similar set of facts arose in the later case of *Zehnalová and Zehnal* v. *Czech Republic*.[32] However, in this case the first applicant, who once again used a wheelchair, claimed that Article 8 had been breached because she was unable to access a considerable number of public buildings and buildings open to the public in her home town. She alleged that she was unable to enjoy a normal social life, allowing her to deal with her everyday problems in a dignified manner, and to practise her profession, because the State had failed to meet its positive obligations to adopt measures and monitor compliance with domestic legislation on accessibility of public buildings. The applicants argued that there was a direct, immediate and permanent link between the national authorities' inability to implement the legislation in force and the quality of their private life.

In response, the Court noted:

> The Court considers that Article 8 of the Convention cannot be taken to be generally applicable each time the first applicant's everyday life is disrupted; it applies only in exceptional cases where her lack of access to public buildings and buildings open to the public affects her life in such a way as to interfere with her right to personal development and her right to establish and develop relationships with other human beings and the outside world ... In such circumstances, the State might have a positive obligation to ensure access to the buildings in question. In the instant case,

---

[29] Para. 34. [30] These cases did not concern claims by disabled applicants.
[31] Para. 35. [32] ECHR, *Zehnalová and Zehnal* v. *Czech Republic*, 14 May 2002.

however, the rights relied on are too broad and indeterminate as the applicants have failed to give precise details of the alleged obstacles and have not adduced persuasive evidence of any interference with their private life. In the Court's view, the first applicant has not demonstrated the existence of a special link between the lack of access to the buildings in question and the particular needs of her private life. In view of the large number of buildings complained of, doubts remain as to whether the first applicant needs to use them on a daily basis and whether there is a direct and immediate link between the measures the State is being urged to take and the applicants' private life; the applicants have done nothing to dispel those doubts.

Therefore, once again the Court found Article 8 to be not applicable.

In a third accessibility-related case, *Marzari v. Italy*,[33] the disabled applicant complained that the local authorities had not provided him with suitable adapted accommodation. Once again, the Court seemed open to the idea that Article 8 could impose positive obligations on the State in such circumstances, and held:

> The Court considers that, although Article 8 does not guarantee the right to have one's housing problem solved by the authorities, a refusal of the authorities to provide assistance in this respect to an individual suffering from a severe disease might in certain circumstances raise an issue under Article 8 of the Convention because of the impact of such refusal on the private life of the individual.

However, the Court did not find in favour of the applicant based on the specific circumstances of the case.

In a further access-related case, *Mółka v. Poland*,[34] which concerned a claim that the State was under an obligation to render a polling station accessible to an individual with a disability, the Court summarised its case law in the context of Article 8 and 'disability-accessibility' cases and observed: 'the effective enjoyment of many of the Convention rights by disabled persons may require the adoption of various positive measures by the competent State authorities.' Nevertheless, as in the other access-related cases, the applicant in *Mółka* was not successful. The Court's reasoning in this case is explored further below.

However, in *Tysiąc v. Poland*,[35] a disabled applicant was able to rely on Article 8 in the context of protection for private life and positive State obligations.[36] This case did not concern a claim that the State was under an

---

[33] ECHR, *Marzari v. Italy*, 4 May 1999.
[34] ECHR, *Mółka v. Poland*, 11 April 2006. This case is discussed further below.
[35] ECHR, *Tysiąc v. Poland*, 20 March 2007.
[36] See also the recent case of ECHR (GC), *A, B and C v. Ireland*, 16 December 2010.

obligation to render the environment physically accessible, but related to the very different area of procedures to be followed following a request for a therapeutic abortion. The facts of the case reveal that in general abortion is prohibited in Poland, and doctors carrying out illegal abortions are guilty of a criminal offence. However, termination is lawful where the pregnancy poses a threat to the mother's health.

The disabled applicant in *Tysiąc* had been unable to obtain an abortion, even though there was a realistic possibility that continuing with the pregnancy would result in a further deterioration in her already poor vision. Following the birth of her child, her vision did indeed deteriorate, and she was classified as severely disabled. The applicant claimed that an interference in her private life had occurred, and that her physical integrity had been threatened. The ECHR found that the Polish law was not clear as to when the conditions for a lawful therapeutic termination had been met, and women who were denied an abortion had few possibilities to challenge this decision. There was also no independent body that could review the doctors' decision to refuse the termination. Consequently, the Court held that Polish law lacked any means of determining whether the conditions for a lawful abortion had been met in the applicant's case, the applicant suffered stress and fear and her physical integrity had not been protected.[37] As a result, the Polish State had breached Article 8 and had not complied with the positive obligations to safeguard the applicant's right to respect for her private life in the context of the controversy as to whether she was entitled to a therapeutic abortion or not.

Based on these judgments, one can conclude that the following requirements must be met before the ECHR will hold that a State is under a positive obligation to take action to protect the right to a private life (in the context of disability). These requirements overlap to some extent:

– there must be a direct and immediate link between the requested measure and the private life of the applicant;
– the claim must not concern interpersonal relations of such a broad and indeterminate scope that there can be no direct link between the measures the State is urged to take and the applicant's private life;
– Article 8 only applies in exceptional cases where the State's failure to act affects an applicant's life in such a way as to interfere with his or her right to personal development and right to establish and develop relationships with other human beings and the outside world;
– applicants must give precise details of the alleged obstacles and produce persuasive evidence that an interference with their private life has occurred;

---

[37] Para. 107.

– the Court is more likely to find that a positive duty exists if the applicant's physical integrity, in terms of state of health or level of impairment, has been threatened;[38]
– in all cases, the State has a margin of appreciation within which to act.[39]

Having discussed case law relating to Article 8, private life, disability and positive duties, attention will now turn to the case at issue in this chapter, which combines all these four elements.

The Sentges case

Facts

Nikky Sentges was a young man who had a disability[40] characterised by progressive muscle degeneration, loss of ability to walk and loss of lung and cardiac function. He was unable to stand, walk or lift his arms, and used an electric wheelchair to move around, and his life expectancy was limited. He received twenty-four-hour-a-day support, mainly from his parents, and was completely dependent on assistance from third persons for all his physical needs, including eating and drinking. In order to increase his autonomy, his parents requested that the health insurance fund provide their son with a robotic arm. Their request was supported by a rehabilitation specialist. The robotic arm would have allowed the applicant to carry out basic tasks, such as pouring drinks and drinking; picking up remote controls and using them; operating audio and video players; pressing lift buttons and door bells when visiting others; shopping; and picking up various items. It was estimated that the arm would reduce his dependence on the constant presence of carers by one to three hours a day. The total cost of the robotic arm was about €36 000. The health insurance fund rejected the request on the ground that the robotic arm was not covered by any relevant health or social insurance scheme or law.

Before the ECHR, the applicant argued that the right to respect for his private life, as guaranteed by Article 8, entailed a positive obligation on the State to provide him with, or pay for, the robotic arm. He argued that the concept of private life, as interpreted by the Court, encompassed notions pertaining to quality of life, including personal autonomy, self-determination, as well as the right to establish and develop relationships with others.

---

[38] Where issues related to right to life are at issue, a claim can also be based on Article 2 of the Convention. See e.g. *Nitecki* v. *Poland*, discussed in the case note by Eva Brems: E. Brems, Case Note on 'Sentges t. Nederland' in *European Human Rights Cases* (2003).

[39] It was on this last issue which the claims of both *Sentges* and *Mółka* failed. Eva Brems has suggested that applicants are more likely to succeed with a positive duty Article 8 based claim when the requested measure is not costly (and perhaps also relatively minor). E. Brems, Case Note on 'Sentges t. Nederland' in *European Human Rights Cases* (2003).

[40] Duchenne muscular dystrophy.

Sentges argued that quality of life could be lost where an individual was forced to live in a dependent manner, thereby losing personal autonomy. He argued that his dependence on others for every single act meant that he was unable to pursue the establishment and development of relationships with others, and that he was not free in his choice of persons with whom to establish and develop relationships. Sentges argued that his position was different from non-disabled people who, although also subject to some constraints, did not experience the same 'unacceptable' level of lack of freedom and choice. He was never able to withdraw and be alone, and his total dependence on family and friends forced him to establish and develop relationships with persons he might not have chosen had he not been disabled. The applicant argued that the robotic arm would have allowed him an increased level of self-determination, reduced his dependence on others, and allowed him to establish and develop relationships with persons other than for reasons of dependence. He submitted that no alternative device existed, and that there was a direct and immediate link between the measure sought and his private life.

Decision

The Court reiterated its previous case law that private life includes a person's physical and psychological integrity and that the guarantee afforded by Article 8 is primarily intended to ensure the development, without outside interference, of the personality of each individual in his relations with other human beings. It noted that there may be positive obligations inherent in the respect for private life, and that these obligations may involve the adoption of measures to secure respect for private life, even in the sphere of interpersonal relations. The Court referred to its previous case law in *Botta* and *Zehnalovà*, and reiterated that: '[i]t is incumbent on the individual concerned to demonstrate the existence of a special link between the situation complained of and the particular needs of his or her private life'. The Court then proceeded by stating: 'Even assuming that in the present cases such a special link indeed exists ... in the circumstances ... it cannot be said that the respondent State exceeded the margin of appreciation afforded to it.' The Court referred to the need to balance the competing interests of the individual and the community, and the wide margin of appreciation enjoyed by States, in reaching this conclusion.

Critical discussion of the decision

As can be seen from the above summary, the Court did not actually specify whether an interference had occurred in the applicant's private life, but rejected his claim on the ground that, *even if* Article 8 were applicable, the State had not exceeded its margin of appreciation in determining what steps to take to ensure compliance with the Convention. The Court therefore resolved the case based on the assumption that Article 8 was applicable, without actually finding this to be the case.

It is submitted that this decision can be criticised for three related reasons, which are explored below.

It is not clear whether Article 8 was applicable, and, if it was not applicable, why not

The applicant raised a number of arguments as to why he believed that the respect for his private life was at issue. On the face of it, his arguments and claims, which did not seem to be disputed, addressed the requirements which the Court had previously identified in *Botta* and *Zehnalovà*. His case involved issues of personal autonomy, personal development and the right to establish and develop relationships with other human beings and the outside world. He gave details of the alleged obstacles and produced evidence as to how the provision of the robotic arm would have addressed these barriers. However, instead of ruling on whether an interference in the applicant's private life had occurred, the Court jumped to the question of whether the decision not to provide the robotic arm fell within the State's margin of appreciation, and quickly found that it did.

By failing to rule on whether Article 8 was applicable in *Sentges*, and therefore whether the applicant's right to private life had been respected or not, the Court muddied the waters as to the requirements which must be met for an interference in private life to occur. If the requirements were met – and, based on an analysis of the criteria given in previous cases, it seems that they were – the Court could have clarified this, and then moved on to the discussion of the State's margin of appreciation. If the requirements were not met, the Court could have explained why, thereby developing the criteria needed for an interference in private life to occur. However, based on *Sentges*, it is simply not clear to readers why, and if, the applicant had established that an interference in his private life had occurred.

This confusion is reflected in academic commentaries. For example, Angus Campbell and Heather Lardy[41] state that Sentges' claim failed partly because there was no conceivable link with his private life. Other commentators note that the Court did not address this issue at all. Aart Hendriks writes that the Court 'does not apply any substantive test whatsoever',[42] and notes that the Court did not consider if the requested measure met the requirement that there be a direct and immediate link with the applicant's private life. The Court also

---

[41] A. Campbell and H. Lardy, 'Transsexuals – The ECHR in Transition?' (2003) 54 *Northern Ireland Legal Quarterly* 209–53, n. 55.

[42] A. Hendriks, Case Note on 'Gehandicapte heeft geen recht op Robottarm', *NJCM-bull.*, 2004, p. 54. Text in the original: 'Iedere inhoudelijke toetsing blijft aldus achterwege.' See also E. Brems, Case Note on 'Sentges t. Nederland' in *European Human Rights Cases* (2003).

failed to discuss the issue of the increase in Sentges' independence and autonomy in its assessment, although it did recognise, in the penultimate paragraph of the judgment, that the robotic arm would have led to improved autonomy and the freedom to establish and develop relationships. Olivier De Schutter,[43] in contrast, notes that Article 8 was held to be applicable, but not violated.

Since the Court did not rule on whether Article 8 was applicable or not, it was also not possible to consider Article 14

As is well known, Article 14 of the Convention, which provides that the enjoyment of the rights and freedoms set forth in the Convention shall be secured without discrimination, can only be relied upon in conjunction with another Convention Article. This does not mean that another Convention Article has to be breached before Article 14 is relevant, but that another Article must at least be applicable. Sandra Fredman has argued that '[i]t is when allied with the equality guarantee in Article 14 that Article 8 has constituted the most potent source of positive duties'.[44] In both *Botta* and *Zehnalová*, the applicants tried to rely on Article 14, in conjunction with Article 8. However, since in both instances the Court found that there had been no interference in their private lives, and therefore that Article 8 was not applicable, their claims were unsuccessful.

As stated above, in *Sentges* the Court simply did not rule on whether Article 8 was applicable or not. Hendriks has noted that, as long as the Court 'denies, or at least does not clearly acknowledge, that the provision of a robotic arm falls within the scope of Article 8 ECHR, it precludes the possibility of invoking [Article] 14 ECHR'.[45] In light of this pattern, Hendriks states: 'It is remarkable, that in this series of decisions as to admissibility, the Court does not deal with the question as to whether Article 8 is applicable *at all*. For the applicants it is *de facto* of little importance, but it may be relevant in cases where Article 14 is invoked.'[46]

As noted by Hendriks, in the absence of a ruling on the applicability of Article 8, there is no possibility to proceed with a parallel claim based on Article 14. Now, there is no evidence from the *Sentges* judgment that the applicant in fact made a claim based on Article 14. However, as noted below, such a claim

---

[43] O. de Schutter, 'Reasonable Accommodations and Positive Obligations in the European Convention on Human Rights', in A. Lawson and C. Gooding (eds.), *Disability Rights in Europe: From Theory to Practice* (Oxford and Portland, OR: Hart Publishing, 2005), p. 40.

[44] S. Fredman, *Human Rights Transformed: Positive Rights and Positive Duties* (Oxford University Press, 2008), p. 207.

[45] Text in original: 'Zolang het Hof ontkent, althans niet duidelijk erkent, dat het verstrekken van een robotarm ... onder de werkingssfeer valt van artikel 8 EVRM is het beroep op artikel 14 EVRM afgesloten.'

[46] Text in original: 'Opmerkelijk is dat het Hof in deze reeks niets-ontvankelijkheidsbeslissingen in het midden laat of artikel 8 EVRM *überhaupt* van toepassing is. Voor de klagers maakt dat *de facto* weinig uit, maar dit kan van belang zijn ingeval van een beroep op artikel 14.'

could have been potentially relevant. Nevertheless, the Court's lack of clarity on the applicability of Article 8 would have blocked such a claim.

The Court did not follow the 'bifurcation between the definition of scope and the review of justification'[47]

Janneke Gerards and Hanneke Senden have argued that an important aspect of the structure of fundamental rights is the bifurcation between the definition of scope and the review of justification. They argue that the ECHR does not always take this bifurcation seriously, and often fails to address issues of definition of scope or merges the two elements into a single test. They note that this is problematic for a number of reasons: it may hamper the effectiveness of the Convention and limit protection offered to individual citizens.

Amongst the many examples which Gerards and Senden give of cases in which the Court has failed to clearly distinguish between scope and justification is *Sentges*. However, they note a similar approach was also adopted in the above-mentioned case of *Mółka*. In *Mółka*, which concerned, *inter alia*, the question of whether Article 8 had been breached when the disabled applicant was unable to vote because his local polling station was physically inaccessible, the Court laid the groundwork for determining whether the right to private life had been infringed, and whether a positive obligation existed, but then actually failed to rule on the issue. This is in spite of the Court actually having raised the issue of the applicability of Article 8 on its own motion.

In *Mółka*, the Court noted that the case related to the applicant's involvement in the life of his local community and the exercise of his civic duties. The Court also accepted that it could be argued that the situation touched upon the applicant's possibility of developing social relations with other members of his community and the outside world, and was pertinent to his own personal development, and that the inability to enter the polling station and vote may have aroused feelings of humiliation and distress capable of impinging on the applicant's personal autonomy, and thereby the quality of his private life. Nevertheless, and after having identified the relevant principles derived from previous case law, the Court stated:

> Having regard to the above considerations, the Court does not rule out the possibility that, in circumstances such as those in the present case, a sufficient link would exist to attract the protection of Article 8. However, the Court does not find it necessary finally to determine the applicability of the Article in the present case since, for the reasons which follow, the application is in any event inadmissible on other grounds.

---

[47] J. Gerards and H. Senden, 'The Structure of Fundamental Rights and the European Court of Human Rights' (2009) 7(4) *International Journal of Constitutional Law* 619–53.

The Court went on to find that, in light of the need to strike a fair balance between the competing interests of the individual and the community as a whole, and the margin of appreciation enjoyed by States in this area, the claim under Article 8 was manifestly ill-founded.

As can be seen, this line of reasoning, which involves a failure to clearly find whether Article 8 is applicable or not, and a determination of the case based on the State's margin of appreciation, is very similar to that adopted in *Sentges*. Gerards and Senden, mirroring my own criticism of the *Sentges* judgment above, note:

> The vague indication that the Court would not rule on the possibility that the applicant's situation falls within the scope of article 8 is not helpful in providing clarity. The individual case might be solved: nonetheless, the Court's decision leaves the reader, at least, with the rather unsatisfactory feeling that no clear answer has been given to the question whether the applicant had a right protected under article 8.[48]

Consequently, whilst the Court acknowledged in both *Mółka* and *Sentges* that there was an issue at the definitional stage that should be addressed, it failed to actually do this.[49] Instead, in both cases, the Court proceeded to resolve the case based on 'an assumption of applicability'.[50] As noted, Gerards and Senden criticise the Court for adopting this approach, and argue that it is unclear how the Court can decide 'convincingly' whether the limitation of a certain Convention right was legitimate when the scope of the Convention right has not been determined in the first place.

> Merely supposing or assuming that an Article is applicable cannot take the place of paying proper attention to the definition stage; to proceed so is far too indefinite. The scope of a right provides an indication of the type of limitations that might be allowed. Moreover, it is necessary to determine the obligations of the respondent State before one can actually decide whether they have been violated. Thus, it is necessary to discuss and

---

[48] *Ibid.*, p. 630.

[49] A further example of such a case is *Pentiacova and others* v. *Moldova*. This concerned a complaint by a group of haemodialysis patients that the State was insufficiently funding their medical treatment and that, as a consequence, they were obliged to use large parts of their family's income to fund the treatment themselves. Once again, in deciding the case, the Court 'assumes' that Article 8 is applicable, and proceeds to deal with the complaint on the basis of the State's margin of appreciation. The Court stated: 'The Court is therefore prepared to assume for the purposes of this application that Article 8 is applicable to the applicants' complaints about insufficient funding of their treatment.' Referring, *inter alia*, to *Sentges*, the Court found that the State had acted within its margin of appreciation.

[50] J. Gerards and H. Senden, 'The Structure of Fundamental Rights and the European Court of Human Rights' (2009) 7(4) *International Journal of Constitutional Law* 619–53 at 631 (writing about the *Mółka* case).

establish the scope of a provision in order to provide a convincing and coherent answer to the problem caused by the case at hand.[51]

Rewritten decision

All of the above three criticisms of the *Sentges* decision turn on the Court's failure to find clearly whether Article 8 was applicable or not. For that reason, the proposed rewriting of the decision focuses on this issue, and clearly specifies that the necessary 'special link' has been established. As a consequence, in the rewritten decision, Article 8 is applicable. Given the wording of the decision, it is suggested that this matter can be addressed surprisingly easily.

Explanation: how the rewriting addresses the identified problems

It is clear that Article 8 is applicable

As noted above, the Court, in its decision, laid the groundwork for a finding of whether Article 8 was applicable or not, but then failed to rule on the issue. The Court provided the necessary background both by presenting the specific situation of Nikky Sentges, the relevant legal principles and earlier case law. It is submitted that this 'groundwork' could have laid the basis for a finding that Article 8 was applicable. For this reason, the rewritten decision does not expand further on why Article 8 is applicable – although it would have been possible to develop the decision in this way – but merely clearly establishes that a 'special link' between the requested measure and the right to private life does exist, and, consequently, that Article 8 is applicable (paragraph 24 of the rewritten decision).

Since Article 8 is applicable, it is possible to also consider the relevance of Article 14

Whilst Article 14 does not explicitly mention disability as a protected ground, in 2009 the Court found, for the first time, a violation of the Article on the grounds of disability. Interestingly, the case in question, *Glor* v. *Switzerland*,[52] also concerned Article 8, private life, and positive obligations, and is worth considering further.

In *Glor*, the applicant challenged the levelling of a special tax (service exemption tax) that was based on his failure to carry out military service. The applicant, who had diabetes, had been declared unfit for military service, and was consequently never called up or required to perform an alternative duty. Under Swiss law a man who does not carry out military or civilian service is liable to pay the service exemption tax, unless he has a disability that affects his 'physical and mental integrity ... to at least 40%'. The applicant was assessed as having a lesser degree of disability, and was consequently obliged to pay the tax.

---

[51] *Ibid.*, p. 621.   [52] ECHR, *Glor* v. *Switzerland*, 30 April 2009.

Before the ECHR, the applicant argued that Article 14, in conjunction with Article 8, had been breached. He submitted that the Swiss authorities had discriminated against him by, on the one hand, preventing him from carrying out military service, when he had been prepared to do so, and, on the other, by requiring him to pay the military exemption tax, when individuals with more severe disabilities were exempt from payment. The Court, referring to its previous case law on physical integrity, held that a tax levied by a State, 'which arises from a person's inability to serve in the army because of an illness, i.e. a factual situation which is outside the person's control, undoubtedly falls within the ambit of Article 8 ... even if the consequences of this measure are mostly financial in nature'.[53] Having found Article 8 to be applicable, the Court could then proceed to determine whether discrimination within the meaning of Article 14 had occurred.

In this respect, the Court found that the Swiss authorities had treated persons in similar situations differently in two ways: first, the applicant was required to pay the service exemption tax whilst people with more severe disabilities were not; secondly, he was unable to perform an alternative civilian service, which was reserved for conscientious objectors. Consequently, the Court found there to have been a breach of Article 8 in conjunction with Article 14, and held that there had been no reasonable justification for the distinction made by the Swiss authorities between persons who were unfit for service and not liable to the tax in question and those who were unfit for service but were nevertheless obliged to pay the tax.

It is noticeable that, in *Glor*, the Court found that the disabled applicant had been discriminated against in comparison with people who were more severely disabled. Now, in *Sentges*, no Article 14 based claim was made, and the evidence does not allow for a consideration of whether Nikky Sentges had been discriminated against, in comparison with other people with disabilities who received treatment and support under the health insurance scheme in the Netherlands. However, based on the later case of *Glor*, one can conclude that this may have been a matter worth investigating. Specifically, if Sentges had been able to identify other persons with disabilities who were in a similar position to him, and who did benefit from expensive treatment or specialised equipment, he may have been able to base his claim on Article 8 in combination with Article 14. However, the judgment strongly implies that other people with the same kind of impairment as Sentges were also not entitled to receive a robotic arm – meaning that the comparison would have had to be made with people with different kinds of severe impairments who needed different kinds of equipment. The facts may well have meant that this was impossible or unreasonably difficult; however, in the absence of a finding that Article 8 was applicable, no such argument could even be entertained.

---

[53] Para. 54.

Given that the evidence does not allow for a consideration of such a claim, the case has not been rewritten to include a consideration of Article 14. Instead, for the purposes of this chapter, it must suffice to note that this may have been an issue worth considering.

Clear 'bifurcation between the definition of scope and the review of justification'

The rewritten decision clearly distinguishes between the issue of whether the complaint falls within the scope of the right to private life protected by Article 8 (paragraphs 23–4 of the rewritten decision), and the justification for the failure to provide the requested measure (paragraphs 24–6 of the rewritten decision). The conceptual distinction between scope and justification is respected, and the review of justification, which is not questioned here,[54] is based on a prior finding that Article 8 is applicable.

Mainstreaming disability in Sentges[55]

The concept of mainstreaming, whether with regard to gender, disability or another disadvantaged group, has been widely discussed in academic and policy-making circles. Within the EU,[56] for example, there has been an ongoing debate around the role to be played by mainstreaming,[57] and, since the mid-1990s, EU policy has included a commitment to mainstreaming.[58] This approach seeks to promote equality by mobilising all areas of law and policy.[59] Rather than relying only on specific measures, such as ground-specific

---

[54] The issue of whether the Court correctly assessed the State's margin of appreciation in *Sentges* is interesting. It is suggested below that, in light of the CRPD, States' margin of appreciation in disability-related positive-obligation cases may be becoming narrower. Nevertheless, this issue of the decision is not considered in the rewriting. The primary focus in this rewriting is on the need to clearly establish the criteria for the applicability of Article 8 in disability-related cases concerning the right to private life. Space does not allow for a full consideration of the limits of the margin of appreciation in such cases, and this has therefore been left to one side.

[55] I am grateful to Professor Mark Bell of Leicester University for commenting on this section of the chapter.

[56] See also L. Waddington and M. Bell, 'Exploring the Boundaries of Positive Action: A Search for Conceptual Clarity' (2011) 48(5) *Common Market Law Review* 1503–26.

[57] E.g. Centre for Strategy and Evaluation Services, 'Non-Discrimination Mainstreaming – Instruments, Case Studies and Way Forwards' (Brussels: European Commission, 2007).

[58] M. Bell, *Racism and Equality in the European Union* (Oxford University Press, 2008), p. 45.

[59] There is a large body of academic literature on mainstreaming, e.g. T. Rees, *Mainstreaming Equality in the European Union – Education, Training and Labour Market Policies* (London: Routledge, 1999); M. Verloo, 'Gender Mainstreaming: Practice and Prospects', *Report EG* (1999) 13 (Strasbourg: Council of Europe, 1999); F. Beveridge, S. Nott and K. Stephen (eds.), *Making Women Count – Integrating Gender into Law and Policy-Making* (Aldershot: Ashgate, 2000).

anti-discrimination legislation, mainstreaming implies that equality needs to be pursued in all activities. In practice, this means that equality needs to be taken into account during policy formulation, implementation and evaluation.[60] With regard to mainstreaming related to policy, therefore, the goal is to take a general instrument, which applies to all, or a wide section of society, and ensure that provisions are included in that instrument which allow for the full involvement and benefit of certain (traditionally) excluded sectors of society, such as people with disabilities. Failure to take account of the specific needs of people with disabilities, in terms of, for example, accessibility, can lead to this group being effectively excluded from the benefits of any policy, and consequent discrimination.

In contrast, far less attention has been paid to the issue of mainstreaming within court judgments. Such decisions are of a very different nature to general policy instruments. A court decision necessarily relates to an individual, or a group of identifiable individuals. In the case of *Sentges*, the decision concerns a specific disabled individual and it is consequently a disability-specific decision. In that sense, one cannot argue that there is a risk of a general instrument excluding people with disabilities because the disability dimension has been ignored, since the disability dimension to the decision has been clear and prominent throughout. Mainstreaming must therefore take on a somewhat different meaning in the context of judicial decision-making than it does with regard to general policy making.

It is submitted that mainstreaming in the context of judicial decision-making must involve a recognition that the application of seemingly neutral rules, which do not single out a particular group for disadvantage, such as people with disabilities, can in fact lead to unequal results and reinforce pre-existing disadvantage. In a similar vein, Shaw has argued that mainstreaming in the context of judicial decision-making by the European Court of Justice should involve reference to 'real world' effects and a consideration of the wider socio-economic circumstances in which cases arise.[61] In the context of Article 8, persons with disabilities, as revealed by the line of case law described above, are a particularly vulnerable group with regard to the protection of private life. The physical inaccessibility of the public infrastructure is one reason for this. The infrastructure is designed, in general, with non-disabled people in mind and, as a consequence, such people are not denied the possibility to enter and use buildings, and questions of respect for private life simply do not arise. This is often not the case for people with

---

[60] See also European Commission, '*International Perspectives on Positive Action Measures: A Comparative Analysis in the European Union, Canada, the United States and South Africa*' (Luxembourg: Office for Official Publications of the European Communities, 2009), p. 27.

[61] J. Shaw, 'The European Union and Gender Mainstreaming: Constitutionally Embedded or Comprehensively Marginalised?' (2002) 10 *Feminist Legal Studies* 213–26 at 223.

disabilities. Similarly, non-disabled people are able to enjoy and exercise high(er) levels of personal choice and physical integrity, and the need for assistive devices, personal support or other forms of assistance do not arise – yet such forms of support do determine the quality of the private life of individuals who are severely disabled. It is submitted that mainstreaming, in the context of Article 8 and disability, involves a recognition by the Court of the peculiarly disadvantaged and vulnerable position of people with disabilities in the context of respect for private life. The Court's failure to clearly find that Article 8 was applicable, in *Sentges*, and in the other disability-related cases described above, fails to do justice to this situation. The rewritten decision, by recognising that Article 8 is applicable, and that an interference in private life has occurred, takes this into account.

Conclusion

The criticisms of the *Sentges* judgment may seem to relate more to substance than to form. However, cases relating to positive obligations and the right to private life are particularly important for people with disabilities. This is so for (at least) three related reasons. First, disability results from an interaction between an impairment and the environment, as evidenced by the experience of Mr Botta and Ms Zehnalová. As a consequence, people with disabilities experience barriers in ways which people without disabilities do not. Therefore, the existence of positive obligations on the State to create an accessible environment, and to protect private life, are of great significance for people with disabilities. Secondly, new assistive equipment and advances in medical treatment mean that some of the limitations related to impairment can be mitigated, when this was previously not the case. Finally, people with disabilities and their families have increasing expectations and demands relating to support for independent living, and the possibility to live in the community, rather than in segregated institutions. It is submitted that this is partly due to the recognition in Article 19 of the United Nations Convention on the Rights of Persons with Disabilities (CRPD) of the right to live independently and be included in the community, and to the large number of (Council of Europe) States which have ratified the Convention. The possibilities for both the provision of medical treatment and equipment, and support for independent living, as well as the obligations imposed on States Parties by the CRPD, arguably create potential positive obligations for States within the context of the Convention.[62]

---

[62] See also C. Parker and L. Clements, 'The UN Convention on the Rights of Persons with Disabilities: A New Right to Independent Living' (2008) 4 *European Human Rights Law Review* 508.

It is also important to note that the State's margin of appreciation, which was interpreted so widely in *Sentges*, may be becoming narrower in disability-related positive-obligation cases.[63] The ECHR's interpretation of the Convention is influenced by external developments in the field of human rights. Of particular importance in this context is the CRPD. The CRPD places significant obligations on States Parties with regard to both civil and political rights, and economic, social and cultural rights. Whilst these are early days for the CRPD, and for speculating on its relevance to the European Convention, the ECHR has frequently noted that the European Convention must be interpreted in light of 'present-day conditions'.[64] In the case of *Demir and Baykara* v. *Turkey*, the Court observed that 'it has always referred to the "living" nature of the Convention, which must be interpreted in light of present-day conditions, and that it has taken account of evolving norms of national and international law in its interpretation of Convention provisions'.[65] It was sufficient for the Court that 'the relevant international instruments denote a continuous evolution in the norms and principles applied in international law ... and show, in a precise area, that there is common ground in modern societies'.[66] The Court's interpretation of Convention provisions is therefore influenced by emerging international consensuses expressed, *inter alia*, through treaty law. The CRPD reflects such an emerging consensus. Of the forty-seven Council of Europe Member States, twenty-seven have ratified the CRPD and a further eighteen have signed it.[67] On a global stage, the CRPD attracted a high number of signatures and ratifications within a short period of time, and in November 2011 had 153 signatories and 108 ratifications. Whilst one cannot predict how the Court will draw on the CRPD in its future judgments, it is clear that the wide-ranging CRPD is potentially relevant to many Convention rights. More specifically, the CRPD may lead to the ECHR finding that States have a narrower margin of appreciation with regard to Article 8, to the extent that the right protected by Article 8 is also protected by the CRPD. In such a scenario, it will become even more important to establish whether Article 8 is applicable to a case.

---

[63] It is worth noting, in this respect, that the Court has already ruled that the respondent States had a narrow margin of appreciation in the disability-related cases of ECHR, *Alajos Kiss* v. *Hungary*, 20 May 2010, and ECHR, *Kiyutin* v. *Russia*, 10 March 2011. However, neither of these cases concerned positive obligations.

[64] See e.g. *Marckx* v. *Belgium*, 13 June 1979; and ECHR (GC), *Demir and Baykara* v. *Turkey*, 12 November 2008.

[65] Para. 68.   [66] Para. 86.

[67] Mental Disability Advocacy Center, 'Universal Suffrage for All', *Information Bulletin*, 1 March 2011.

Rewriting Sentges v. Netherlands[68]

...

The law

...

23. The Court has held that Article 8 may impose such positive obligations on a State where there is a direct and immediate link between the measures sought by an applicant and the latter's private life (see *Botta v. Italy*, para. 34). However, Article 8 does not apply to situations concerning interpersonal relations of such broad and indeterminate scope that there can be no conceivable link between the measures the State is urged to take and an individual's private life (see *Botta*, para. 35). The Court has also held that Article 8 cannot be considered applicable each time an individual's everyday life is disrupted, but only in the exceptional cases where the State's failure to adopt measures interferes with the individual's right to personal development and his or her right to establish and maintain relations with other human beings and the outside world. It is incumbent on the individual concerned to demonstrate the existence of a special link between the situation complained of and the particular needs of his or her private life (see *Zehnalovà and Zehnal v. the Czech Republic*).

24. ['Even assuming' deleted] **Accepting** that in the present cases such a special link indeed exists – as was accepted by the Central Appeals Tribunal –, regard must be had to the fair balance that has to be struck between the competing interests of the individual and of the community as a whole and to the wide margin of appreciation enjoyed by States in this respect in determining the steps to be taken to ensure compliance with the Convention (see *Zehnalovà and Zehnal*).

25. The margin of appreciation is even wider when, as in the present case, the issues involve an assessment of the priorities in the context of the allocation of limited State resources (see, *mutatis mutandis*, *Osman v. the United Kingdom*, judgment of 28 October 1998, *Reports* 1998-VIII, p. 3159, § 116, *O'Reilly and others v. Ireland* (dec.), no. 54725/00, 28 February 2002, unreported). In view of their familiarity with the demands made on the health care system as well as with the funds available to meet those demands, the national authorities are in a better position to carry out this assessment than an international court. In addition, the Court should also be mindful of the fact that, while it will apply the Convention to the concrete facts of this particular case in accordance with Article 34, a decision issued in an

---

[68] For ease of reference, paragraph numbers have been inserted by the author, based on the (unnumbered) paragraphs of the admissibility decision of the Court.

individual case will nevertheless at least to some extent establish a precedent (see *Pretty*, cited above, § 75), valid for all Contracting States.

26. In the present case the Court notes that the applicant has access to the standard of health care offered to all persons insured under the Health Insurance Act and the Exceptional Medical Expenses Act (see *Nitecki v. Poland* (dec.), no. 65653/01, 21 March 2002, unreported). It thus appears that he has been provided with an electric wheelchair with an adapted joystick. The Court by no means wishes to underestimate the difficulties encountered by the applicant and appreciates the very real improvement which a robotic arm would entail for his personal autonomy and ability to establish and develop relationships with other human beings of his choice. Nevertheless the Court is of the opinion that in the circumstances of the present case it cannot be said that the respondent State exceeded the margin of appreciation afforded to it.

14

Rethinking Herczegfalvy: the Convention and the control of psychiatric treatment

PETER BARTLETT

Introduction: why Herczegfalvy?

The decision of the European Court of Human Rights (ECHR) in *Herczegfalvy* v. *Austria*[1] has defined the approach of the ECHR to standards of care and treatment in psychiatric facilities for almost twenty years. The case has created considerable difficulties in bringing litigation under the European Convention on Human Rights ('the Convention') on these matters, with the result that, while a burgeoning jurisprudence now exists on detention in psychiatric institutions under Article 5,[2] the Court has had very little to say about care and treatment within institutions under Articles 3 and 8.

A reading of *Herczegfalvy* serves as a reminder of how views of people with mental disability[3] and their treatment have changed in the subsequent decades. In part, this involves categorisation of facts. The Court in *Herczegfalvy* considered the handcuffing of the applicant to a security bed for more than two weeks as a matter of medical treatment. It would now be viewed as restraint, and that is how it is considered in the redrafting. Other issues concern developments in the law. The jurisprudence of the ECHR has itself of course progressed, and no doubt this would result in different arguments arising, were *Herczegfalvy* to be litigated today. It is difficult to believe now, for example, that Mr Herczegfalvy would not have included a number of challenges to the guardianship regime to which he was subjected, based on the Court's decision in *Shtukaturov* v. *Russia*.[4] *Herczegfalvy* further predates the influence of key human rights instruments in the area. Within the Council of Europe, the Committee for the Prevention of Torture (CPT) did not publish its standards for psychiatric

---

[1] ECHR, *Herczegfalvy* v. *Austria*, 24 September 1992 (A/244), (1993) 15 EHRR 437. Hereinafter '*Herczegfalvy*'.

[2] For a summary of this case law, see P. Bartlett, O. Lewis and O. Thorold, *Mental Disability and the European Convention on Human Rights* (Martinus Nijhoff, 2007), Chapter 2.

[3] In this chapter, 'mental disability' is to be taken broadly as referring to people with psychosocial disabilities (mental health problems), learning or developmental disabilities, and mental disabilities associated with the end of life such as dementia.

[4] ECHR, 27 June 2008.

establishments until 1998,[5] and, since that time, their country reports have been extraordinarily influential in setting European norms of service provision. Further, the Committee of Ministers has published recommendations concerning the protection of the human rights and dignity of persons with mental disorders in 2004,[6] and concerning the legal protection of incapable adults in 1999.[7] Internationally, an array of instruments has been adopted. The most notable of these is the new United Nations Convention on the Rights of Persons with Disabilities (CRPD),[8] which was passed by the General Assembly in 2006 and entered into force in May 2008. Like the European Convention, the CRPD is a binding international treaty. All States Parties to the CRPD are required to submit periodic reports to a committee that comments publicly on them, and, for States Parties to the optional protocol, the committee considers individual complaints, much as a court would. Non-compliance with the CRPD will therefore be visible, as is non-compliance with the European Convention. This raises interesting and problematic prospects of conflicts between the two regimes.

The approach in *Herczegfalvy* is therefore ripe for reassessment. The redrafting focuses on issues of treatment and conditions in psychiatric facilities, the issue for which the case remains a landmark, but a number of the issues raised below apply to the Court's approach to mental health law more broadly – most notably, the need for the Court to ensure that clear and meaningful substantive standards are in place in domestic law. Indeed, *Herczegfalvy* itself was primarily a case about detention under Article 5. These issues are not included in the redrafting since they have faded into obscurity, although some aspects are mentioned in passing in the third section of this chapter. The redrafting does take into account the developments in European and international law, and the developing case law of the ECHR, but the temptation to launch into entirely new lines of argument (as, for example, a challenge to the guardianship law based on *Shtukaturov*) has been resisted. The facts and domestic law have been taken as they were twenty years ago, when the case arose. Some factual material required for the new analysis is not contained in the existing reasons of the Court and Commission, and the application of the proposed new law to the factual situation of the case is consequently problematic.

Substantive overview: the ECHR and mental disability

The need for substantive clarity

In dealing with cases of persons with mental disabilities, the ECHR has been relatively good on procedural justice, but not nearly so strong on substance. The

---

[5] Originally as a part of their 8th General Report, CPT/Inf (98) 12; reprinted periodically since that time, most recently as CPT/Inf/E (2002) 1 – Rev. 2009.
[6] Rec(2004)10.   [7] R(99)4.
[8] United Nations General Assembly, A/61/611, 6 December 2006.

Court's treatment of Article 5 provides a clear example of this. The Court has been quite good at insisting on the provision of appropriate procedural controls and review hearings, and defining the terms of those processes, but its approach to substance has been abstract. The *Winterwerp* criteria require that a 'true mental disorder' be present, of a severity 'warranting compulsory confinement',[9] and the Court has elsewhere made it clear that detention under Article 5 may be justified for reasons of dangerousness or in the interests of the individual's health.[10] The Court has delegated further refinement of these requirements to States Parties, however, referring merely to the general requirement originating in *Sunday Times* v. *United Kingdom* that a citizen 'must be able – if need be with appropriate advice – to foresee, to a degree that is reasonable in the circumstances, the consequences which a given action may entail'.[11]

The *Sunday Times* language provides an appropriate standard, although the implied characterisation of a person with mental disability, be it a psychosocial disability (mental health problem) or a learning disability, as a person rationally considering the outcome of conduct and seeking legal advice may be counter-intuitive in some of the factual contexts where the law will be applied. What is at least as important is that the persons administering the law will have sufficient guidance to ensure consistency in decision-making. Without that clarity, the decision regarding compulsory admission or compulsory treatment will depend to an unacceptable degree on the professional staff (sometimes a doctor alone, sometimes a doctor with other professionals) assessing the individual. That will in turn often depend on who is on duty when the individual is apprehended: detention, enforced treatment and human rights become a lottery.

Notwithstanding the routine citation of the *Sunday Times* standard, the ECHR does not necessarily criticise legislation that is remarkably weak on its substantive specificity. In *Rakevich* v. *Russia*, after citing the *Sunday Times* standard, the Court did not criticise the standard that 'the mental disorder is severe enough to give rise to a direct danger to the person or to others', noting the practical difficulty of articulating dangerousness specifically in legislation.[12] The difficulty is that dangerousness is very difficult to predict, and, when relying simply on their instincts, doctors vastly over-predict dangerousness, resulting in the detention of large numbers of people who would not actually have been the cause of significant harm.[13] The standard also begs the question

---

[9] See ECHR, *Winterwerp* v. *Netherlands*, 24 October 2979 (A/33), (1979–80) 2 EHRR 387, para. 39.

[10] ECHR, *Hutchinson Reid* v. *United Kingdom*, 20 May 2003, (2003) 37 EHRR 9, para. 52.

[11] ECHR, *Sunday Times* v. *United Kingdom*, 26 April 1979, (1979) 2 EHRR 245, para. 49.

[12] ECHR, *Rakevich* v. *Russia*, 28 October 2003, para. 32.

[13] For an overview of the literature regarding prediction of dangerousness in a psychiatric context, see J. Monahan, 'A Jurisprudence of Risk Assessment: Forecasting Harm among Prisoners, Predators and Patients' (2006) 92 *Virginia Law Review* 392–435, especially at

of how dangerous is dangerous? In *Rakevich* itself, the government's position was that the applicant was in an acute psychotic condition accompanied by confusion, fear and psychomotor excitation.[14] While the government thus makes a coherent claim that the applicant was mentally unwell, there is no suggestion that she was in any way violent. Was she a 'direct danger'? It seems at best doubtful, but how is one to know, given this standard? The ECHR goes on to find that the fact that all detentions were subject to judicial review was a 'substantial safeguard against arbitrariness', but this is entirely unconvincing. Why would an unclear standard protect against arbitrariness, merely because the unclear standard was administered by a court?

Even more startling is the case of *HL v. United Kingdom*.[15] In that case, a person lacking the capacity to decide on his own psychiatric admission was detained in a psychiatric hospital. The detention was outside the terms of mental health legislation, and was held *ex post facto* to rely instead on the common law doctrine of necessity. The domestic court found that the substantive criteria for this detention were '(i) there must be a necessity to act when it is not practicable to communicate with the assisted person and (ii) that the action taken must be such as a reasonable person would in all circumstances take, acting in the best interests of the assisted person'.[16] There was no particular history to these criteria: the *HL* case itself was the first time that they had been formulated in this way, and to suggest that they were established law relied upon by the hospital in this case is a judicial fiction. The criteria are also astonishingly open-ended, offering very little guidance to practitioners as to what they ought to do in practice.

The ECHR did find a violation of Article 5 based on the unlawfulness of the criteria, and there is, just possibly, some indication that the substance of the criteria might have been insufficient.[17] The focus of the Court's concern, however, was once again not on the substance, but on the process: who should be allowed to detain the individual, and following what assessments, and whether a representative for the patient needed to be appointed.[18] There is no doubt that process is important; but it is not a substitute for proper substantive standards that provide meaningful direction to those administering the legislation.

Certainly, it remains within the jurisdiction of States Parties in the first instance to regulate their own affairs; but, in the same way that we would not allow religious persecution merely because the procedures of domestic legislation were followed, so we must insist on a certain level of substance for the law

405–27; M. Grann, N. Langstrom, J. Yourstone *et al.*, *Psychiatric Risk Assessment Methods: Are Violent Acts Predictable? A Systematic Review* (SBU, 2005).
[14] *Rakevich*, para. 23; see further paras. 10–11 concerning the facts.
[15] ECHR, 5 October 2004, (2005) 40 EHRR 32.   [16] *HL*, para. 117.
[17] *Ibid.*, para. 119. The Court seems not to make a definitive finding on this point.
[18] *Ibid.*, para. 120.

relating to people with mental disabilities. Certainly, as the Court is frequently at pains to point out, legislative drafting in this area can be a challenging exercise, but the Court can insist on a significantly higher standard than is the case at present.

This discussion is relevant for the Court's approach to mental disability law generally, but also to *Herczegfalvy* in particular. In *Herczegfalvy*, the Court begins its jurisprudence by stating that, 'as a general rule, a measure which is a therapeutic necessity cannot be regarded as inhuman or degrading'.[19] While that position has its merits, it begs the question of how 'therapeutic necessity' is to be understood. A considerable part of the present redrafting of that case is an attempt to articulate how, as a matter of Convention jurisprudence, States should be expected to approach that.

The European Convention and the CRPD: conflicts of laws

The introduction of the CRPD has the potential significantly to alter the legal and human rights landscape for persons with disabilities, including persons with mental disabilities. Currently, all Member States of the Council of Europe except Liechtenstein and Switzerland plus the European Union have signed the CRPD, and thirty-five Council of Europe Member States have ratified it. The CRPD Committee will report publicly on States' compliance with the convention, and for countries ratifying the first optional protocol, the CRPD Committee will adjudicate complaints from individuals. Currently, twenty-eight Member States of the Council of Europe have signed this protocol, and twenty-three have ratified it.[20] Unlike many of the previous international law instruments on mental disability, this is binding international law, with an enforcement mechanism attached.

It is of course a new convention, and the committee created to interpret, oversee and enforce it has been fully functional only since the autumn of 2010, so definitive interpretations of the convention's terms are not yet available. Much of the CRPD concerns positive obligations that services be made available for persons with disabilities, and prohibiting discrimination in service provision on the basis of disability. Most significantly for people with mental disabilities, it provides rights to community living and community integration, and many of the umbrella services that make that possible: housing, education, social services and employment, for example. These issues can be perceived as separate from and lying alongside traditional areas of ECHR jurisprudence: there is no necessary conflict. Other areas, such as the right to freedom of expression in Article 21 of the CRPD, do overlap with European Convention rights, but will generally be

---

[19] *Herczegfalvy*, para. 82.
[20] A table of signatories and ratifications for the convention and the protocol may be found at http://www.un.org/disabilities/countries.asp?id=166 (last accessed 16 November 2011).

consistent with the direction of ECHR jurisprudence. While practical conflicts may of course arise as different decision-making bodies interpret similar but non-identical provisions, it seems unlikely that there will be significant difficulties of coexistence. In some areas, however, the terms of the convention, along with some of the early comments made about it, would suggest overlap with ECHR jurisprudence in ways that are quite different to that jurisprudence, and potentially inconsistent with it.

Article 14(1)(b) of the CRPD, for example, provides in part that 'the existence of a disability shall in no case justify a deprivation of liberty'. While the matter is not entirely free from doubt, the UN High Commissioner for Human Rights has taken the view that this does not merely mean that disability may not be the sole justification for deprivation of liberty, but that it may not be a factor at all.[21] Equally challenging is the High Commissioner's view that the insanity defence, based as it is on the mental disability of the accused, must be abolished in its current form.[22]

Article 12 of the CRPD governs equal recognition before the law, and provides that persons with disability enjoy legal capacity on an equal basis with others in all aspects of life. Legal mechanisms, with appropriate safeguards, must be put into place to ensure that they may realise this right, and restrictions are placed on measures which affect the exercise of this legal capacity. It is not entirely clear whether the CRPD will prohibit any kind of incapacity determination, opting for a system of universal capacity buttressed by supported decision-making, or whether some limitations to the exercise of legal capacity will be permitted,[23] but certainly issues of guardianship and capacity determination will be much more closely limited than is the case in many Council of Europe Member States. The ECHR has itself started to address some of these issues from a rather different direction, most notably in *Shtukaturov* v. *Russia*[24] and, concerning the right to vote by people under guardianship, *Kiss* v. *Hungary*.[25]

---

[21] Annual Report of the High Commissioner for Human Rights to the General Assembly, A/HRC/10/49, presented 26 January 2009, paras. 48–9. See also UN, Office of the High Commissioner for Human Rights, 'Persons with Disabilities' Dignity and Justice for Detainees Week, Information Note No. 4 (2008), p. 2, available at http://www.ohchr.org/EN/UDHR/Documents/60UDHR/detention_infonote_4.pdf (last accessed 26 July 2009). For a consistent view, see the interim report of the UN Special Rapporteur of the Human Rights Council on torture and other cruel, inhuman or degrading treatment or punishment, published by UN General Assembly, A/63/175 (2008), para. 64.

[22] Annual report, A/HRC/10/49, para. 47.

[23] Regarding Article 12, see A. Dhanda, 'Legal Capacity in the Disability Rights Convention: Stranglehold of the Past or Lodestar for the Future?' (2007) 34 *Syracuse Journal of International Law and Commerce* 429–62.

[24] Application no. 44009/05, judgment of 27 June 2008.

[25] Application no. 38832/06, judgment of 20 August 2010.

Article 25 of the CRPD provides that medical treatment is to be given based on 'free and informed consent', and Article 17 provides a right to respect for 'physical and mental integrity on an equal basis with others.' Certainly for people with the actual capacity to make the treatment decision in question, it seems likely that the CRPD will be very hesitant to deprive them of the right to consent to medical treatment. In particular, it seems likely that it will prohibit systems that allow for the compulsory treatment of people with mental disabilities in circumstances where people with physical ailments of comparable seriousness would be permitted by law to refuse treatment. It is likely to be the case, as reflected in the redrafted version of *Herczegfalvy* below, that life-saving treatments of detained persons will still be permitted by the CRPD, if such treatment would be imposed upon persons who do not have such a disability.[26] Article 17 and the relevant portion of Article 25 explicitly refer to integrity and consent rights on the same basis as to non-disabled persons, suggesting that the concern is on non-discrimination. It is when different rules apply to people with disabilities that Article 25 will bite.

The immediate question is how far the ECHR should take into account the developing law surrounding the CRPD. Certainly, there is an argument that the two systems are separate, and each should be allowed to develop in its own way. This is legally correct, and, at least in some cases, does not pose a theoretical problem. If the CRPD Committee takes the view, for example, that mental disability may not form any part of criteria for detention, no direct conflict would be created with the European Convention, as Article 5(1)(e) does not oblige States to detain persons of unsound mind, but merely permits them to do so. The effect would be that the part of Article 5(1)(e) of the Convention relating to persons of unsound mind would in practice become an irrelevance for States party to the CRPD. While this would be doctrinally consistent, it would be a surprising and disappointing result, as it would leave the ECHR, the most important regional human rights court in the world, with nothing to say about an important human rights concern.

When the conventions place conflicting duties onto States that are party to both conventions, there are potential problems. If the Convention were to require compulsory treatment of an individual, for example, in situations where the CRPD would prohibit it, States Parties would be left in an impossible position. It is fair to expect both treaty bodies to work to ensure that this does not occur.

Most cases before the ECHR will fall into neither of these categories. Many important cases – cases relating to guardianship, conditions of treatment (whether that is medical treatment, or institutional conditions generally), confidentiality, non-discrimination (a particular concern for countries ratifying Protocol 12 to the Convention) and so many other matters – will raise issues

---

[26] See para. 93 of the redrafted judgment.

under both the European Convention and the CRPD. Once again, the key here is likely to be to ensure that States Party are not placed under conflicting obligations, while at the same time ensuring that the field is appropriately covered. This is likely to prove a complex process for both bodies. In some of these areas, the ECHR has an established jurisprudence, and such jurisprudence can be difficult to change. In other areas (non-discrimination being perhaps the clearest example), the two bodies will each be developing jurisprudence from a relatively limited base, contemporaneously. While that provides the potential for coherence, it also has the potential for difficulties, as both bodies feel their way in new territory.

Thus far, the ECHR appears to be proceeding with caution. Certainly, litigants before the Court now cite the CRPD, and the ECHR fairly routinely cites the CRPD as part of the international law context of cases.[27] It has actually referred to the CRPD in its own analysis of ECHR law only twice. In both cases, the Court has referred to the CRPD as evidence of an international consensus that discrimination on the basis of disability is no longer acceptable, and that disability should therefore be included by implication in the open-ended list of prohibited grounds of discrimination under Article 14.[28] While this development is certainly welcome both in its own right and as an indication of overall harmonisation of international human rights law, it is consistent with the overall direction of ECHR jurisprudence, and did not require a significant change of course for the Court. It remains to be seen how the Court will deal with harder cases, where clashes with existing ECHR jurisprudence are unavoidable.

Herczegfalvy: the original decision

Mr Herczegfalvy was a Hungarian citizen resident in Austria, who was imprisoned periodically commencing in 1972, following conviction for a variety of assaults on his wife, public officials and clients of his television-repair business. Following numerous complaints by him about prison conditions, the Austrian authorities commissioned a psychiatric report about him, on the basis of which he was brought before a guardianship court (Pflegschaftsgericht) in 1977 and an 'advisor' (*Beistand*; hereinafter 'guardian'[29]) was appointed for him. While that court found Mr Herczegfalvy was only partly incapacitated (*beschränkt entmündigt*), it would seem that this guardian exercised control over all

---

[27] See ECHR, *Glor* v. *Switzerland*, 6 November 2009; ECHR, *Seal* v. *United Kingdom*, 11 April 2011; ECHR, *Jasinskis* v. *Latvia*, 21 March 2011; ECHR, *Kiss* v. *Hungary*, 20 August 2010; ECHR, *Kiyutin* v. *Russia*, 15 September 2011.

[28] See *Glor*, para. 53; *Kiyutin*, para. 57.

[29] 'Guardian' is selected because the individual in question does appear to have exercised real decision-making power over the applicant, an authority not implicit in the English term 'advisor'.

personal and property-related decisions concerning him. It would appear that the guardian was kept informed of, and agreed to, all the controversial acts imposed on Mr Herczegfalvy discussed below. Mr Herczegfalvy was eventually found not criminally responsible for these actions because of his mental disorder, and, at the end of his sentence, his detention was continued based on his apparent danger to the public.

Mr Herczegfalvy's place of detention alternated between the general prison system and institutions for mentally ill offenders – matters considered at some length in the original judgment, but not pivotal to the present discussion. It was established, based on the reports of three psychiatrists, that he had suffered since at least 1975 with paranoia querulans, and he behaved in an aggressive fashion on an ongoing basis during his detention. He himself denied that he was mentally ill in this period, and continued to press his case before the courts, initially with a view to challenging his convictions, and then challenging his ongoing detention. Again, these legal manoeuvres occupy considerable discussion in the original decision, but will not be considered in detail here as they are relevant to his detention, not to his compulsory medical treatment. He was eventually released from detention in November 1984.

Throughout the period he spent in institutions, Mr Herczegfalvy continued to complain of the conditions of his detention. He suspected that these complaints were not forwarded to the relevant authorities. These suspicions proved well-founded: with the agreement of his guardian, his complaints had been retained by the institutions, and were returned to him at the time of his discharge. They filled six binders. He had also been denied access to television at various times during his detention. These matters were also litigated before the ECHR.

The applicant had requested and been denied access to his files. While neither the Court judgment nor the Commission decision are entirely clear on the point, it would appear that this refers to files that he had created during his incarceration, not his clinical record or official administrative file. In response to the refusal to make these files available, and in a protest about his continued detention generally, he commenced a hunger strike on 2 August 1979. On 10 September, because of his weakened condition, an order was made that he be given nutrition by force. As he was refusing all medical examination and treatment, he was given sedatives against his will (three doses of 30 mg each of Taractan IM). On 14 and 15 September, he was tied to a security bed, the net and straps of which he successfully cut through. On 17 September, he was given a different neuroleptic, Sordinol. He ceased the hunger strike on 27 September, after being allocated a single room and being given some of his files. The hunger strike, however, recommenced on 26 November. He was fed by tube commencing on 13 December 1979, a process which continued on a periodic basis until November 1982. His consent to this intubation was disputed.

On 15 January 1980, he was injected by force with 90 mg of Taractan in order to bring about a state of somnolence, to make treatment with perfusions possible. Since he actively resisted this injection, an emergency team was required to overpower him. The Commission notes that the precise facts of this event are unclear, but he was transferred to the hospital's intensive care unit, where he was found to be suffering from pneumonia and nephritis. Upon his return to the closed psychiatric ward on 30 January 1980, he was handcuffed and a belt was placed around his ankles, apparently because of the danger of aggression and the death threats he was making. These restraints were not removed until 14 February 1980. It is not clear how frequently the position of the restraints was altered in this period.

The factual account and Court's approach to the case raise a number of concerns. The applicant was diagnosed with 'paranoia querulans'. This disorder is referred to briefly in the United Nations International Classification of Diseases (ICD-10) in its residual category of delusional disorders,[30] but no proper definition is provided. The academic literature identifies it as the psychiatric disorder associated with persistent complaining and vexatious litigation,[31] and the potential for abuse of this diagnosis had been noted by the time *Herczegfalvy* was considered by the Court.[32] It is precisely the sort of diagnosis that ought to trigger the concern of the Court, for, whatever its medical merits when properly applied, its potential to silence or marginalise legitimate complaints will be evident. Further, the subjects of those complaints may well be the medical staff responsible for making the diagnosis, a situation creating obvious conflicts of roles. It is therefore disappointing that the Commission and the Court did not interrogate more carefully what precisely the diagnosis meant in the current case. It is acknowledged in paragraph 84 of the redrafted judgment, where no decision is reached as to the accuracy of the diagnosis. This is in part because evidence is legitimately lacking in the factual history of the case, but it is also, again, strategic. In most cases, the existence of a mental disorder will not be seriously contested, and it seemed more helpful to proceed on that premise.

Was this in fact a disorder 'of a nature or degree warranting confinement'? Again, it is very difficult to tell from the factual account provided in the Commission decision and the Court's judgment. In paragraph 22 of the judgment, the Court summarises without criticism the decision of the Austrian Regional Court in February 1984 to order the continued detention of the applicant:

---

[30] This is essentially similar to the approach in ICD-9, in effect at the time *Herczegfalvy* was decided: see ICD-9, 297.8, 'Other Specified Paranoid States'.

[31] See I. Freckelton, 'Querulent Paranoia and the Vexatious Complainant' (1988) 11 *International Journal of Law and Psychiatry* 127–43; P. Mullen and G. Lester, 'Vexatious Litigants and Unusually Persistent Complainants and Petitioners: From Querulous Paranoia to Querulous Behavior' (2006) 26 *Behavioral Science and the Law* 333–49.

[32] See e.g. O. Stalstrom, 'Querulous Paranoia: Diagnosis and Dissent' (1980) 14 *Australian and New Zealand Journal of Psychiatry* 145.

Taking into account the opinions of the psychiatric expert and the director of the hospital, filed on 25 January 1984, it considered that there had been no fundamental change in Mr Herczegfalvy's mental state. He was still suffering from paranoia querulans, and if released would undoubtedly refuse to follow the necessary course of treatment; he would consequently be likely to bring numerous complaints or even carry out the threats he had made, in particular those against the prison staff.

However, in paragraph 23 of the judgment, it goes on to repeat uncritically the comments of the Regional Court in November of that year, ordering the applicant's release:

> The court found that the applicant's paranoia had admittedly worsened, but that it was primarily due to his detention (*Haftquerulanz*); the vexatious complaints and petitions (*Rechtsquerulanz*) did not constitute a danger within the meaning of Article 21 of the Criminal Code; since being detained the applicant had behaved with genuine aggressiveness on a few occasions only; although the possibility could not be excluded of his becoming aggressive in the event of frustration, his psychiatric history did not permit the conclusion that his abnormal personality would induce him to commit criminal offences; moreover, continued psychiatric treatment or treatment by drugs was not considered necessary by the expert, although it was recommended.

This raises questions about the initial and ongoing justifications for detention. The finding of the November court that the applicant had behaved with genuine aggressiveness only on a few occasions is startlingly inconsistent with the ongoing allegations of dangerousness and violence elsewhere in the case, undercutting the justification for the use of force and detention. Which characterisation is correct? Further, the applicant was a persistent complainer – a core symptom of his diagnosed disorder – but it is difficult to see why this constituted a justification for detention up to the end of 1984, and, according to the Court, not thereafter. And, insofar as the applicant was dangerous or violent, was this in fact a consequence of his mental disorder? How is the change in judicial approach in the domestic courts between the two hearings to be understood? It does seem, at the very least, that this is yet another case where the criteria of detention lack the clarity required to ensure reasonably consistent decision-making.

It also raises questions about the ECHR's consideration of Article 8 and of the control of the applicant's correspondence. Mr Herczegfalvy was periodically deprived of writing materials so that he could not file complaints, and such letters as he was able to write, unless addressed to his lawyer, his guardian or the Guardianship Court, were only delivered with the guardian's approval. Upon discharge, unsent letters returned to the applicant included those addressed to the police, the public prosecutor's office, and the courts.[33] The Court does find a violation of Article 8 on the basis that the statutory justification for the control of correspondence was insufficient, but the retention of letters directed to official offices of complaint is a matter particular concern, and it is unfortunate that the Court did not make that point with particular force. The issue concerns mechanisms of complaint, not the standards for involuntary medical treatment, so the issue is not dealt with in the redrafting, but it serves as a reminder how problematic *Herczegfalvy* is as a case.

Facts about the enforced neuroleptic medication are similarly unclear. Was it intended to address an underlying psychiatric condition, or was it prescribed for its sedative properties only? At times in the judgment, it appears to be the former, but this interpretation is not entirely consistent with other statements of fact in the judgment. Thus, for the hearing on 14 February 1984, the hospital director provided evidence, in the ECHR's paraphrase, that, because 'the treatment carried out, based on medication, had only a sedative effect, the possibility could not be excluded that if he were released, he would again become aggressive and dangerous'.[34] If the medication was provided solely to sedate the applicant, should it be considered medical treatment or restraint? If it is for restraint, in what sense would it be 'medically necessary'? Certainly, restraint may in some cases be necessary, and in some cases may be necessary for considerable periods of time; but that is not an argument to consider it medical treatment. This issue will be of particular relevance in cases concerning homes for the aged, social care homes, and homes for people with learning disabilities – contexts where there are periodic complaints that medication is used for control rather than treatment – but it arises in *Herczegfalvy* as well.

In the redrafting, it is assumed that the treatment with neuroleptic medications was provided for medical reasons – that is, that it was directed to his underlying condition, rather than for his restraint.[35] This choice was made primarily for pragmatic purposes. Some clearly sedative medication was given to the applicant; that is dealt with as restraint. Treating the neuroleptics also as restraint seemed to add nothing to that analysis. Further, overwhelmingly, psychiatric medication is prescribed with the intent of curing the individual, or, at least, significantly improving his or her condition, and *Herczegfalvy* has been taken to be a landmark case in the Court's approach to these issues. That question was thus pivotal to the redrafting project, and the factual interpretation was made accordingly, to provide an occasion for that analysis.

The Court's silence on the question of whether the applicant had an effective domestic remedy is similarly troubling. It does seem that there was jurisdiction for the Austrian Administrative Court (Verwaltungsgerichtshof) to determine the legality of the treatment received by Mr Herczegfalvy, and for

---

[33] *Herczegfalvy*, para. 37.   [34] *Ibid.*, para. 33.   [35] See para. 84 of the redrafted judgment.

the Constitutional Court (Verfassungsgerichtshof) to determine its constitutionality, but the Court notes that these mechanisms had never actually been used for
this purpose.[36] The Court declines to make a finding on the applicant's claim for a
consequent violation of Article 13, a refusal based on its finding that, for the issues
of control of correspondence and access to information (flowing from a denial of
access to television), violations of Articles 8 and 10 had already been found.
Interestingly, the Court does not refer to the issues of enforced treatment, where
Article 3 would be satisfied in cases of medical necessity, but where the Court
'must nevertheless satisfy itself that the medical necessity has been convincingly
shown to exist'.[37] If this is the standard chosen by the Court, it must surely be
appropriate to insist that a domestic remedy be available to ensure that it is met in
individual cases. It would seem that the Austrian courts were not used for this
purpose at the time, and that raises an Article 13 issue. It is disappointing, and
somewhat surprising given the Court's generally good record on matters of
procedure, that this was not explored much more closely. In particular, it is
hoped that the Court will focus both on the impartiality of such remedies, and
on the practicalities of gaining access to them, including the provision of information about remedies and access to legal counsel, with legal aid available when
necessary. Access to these remedies must similarly not lie within the control of a
guardian or similar figure.[38]

    As noted above, the bulk of the legal reasoning in the case concerns Article 5
issues. While some of the remarks made elsewhere in this chapter and in the
redrafting will apply to those issues, they are not the matters for which the case
is known, and they are not discussed in detail here. The case is instead known
for its approach to psychiatric care and treatment as it relates to Article 3. Those
issues form the core of the redrafting, and it is to those issues that this chapter
now turns.

Herczegfalvy and care and treatment in psychiatric institutions

Regarding the care and treatment of the applicant, the Commission had found a
violation of Article 3, based on the degree of force used over an excessively
prolonged period. The government in response claimed that the measures had
been urgent with a view to the deterioration in Mr Herczegfalvy's physical and
mental health, and because of his 'resistance to all treatment, his extreme
aggressiveness and the threats and acts of violence on his part against the
hospital staff'.[39] The government also noted that the measures in question
had been agreed by Mr Herczegfalvy's guardian, and were for the least length
of time reasonably possible.

---

[36] *Herczegfalvy*, para. 55.   [37] *Ibid.*, para. 82.
[38] See para. 90 of the redrafted judgment.   [39] *Herczegfalvy*, para. 81.

The Court's reasons are contained in paragraph 82 of the case:

> 82. The Court considers that the position of inferiority and powerlessness which is typical of patients confined in psychiatric hospitals calls for increased vigilance in reviewing whether the Convention has been complied with. While it is for the medical authorities to decide, on the basis of the recognised rules of medical science, on the therapeutic methods to be used, if necessary by force, to preserve the physical and mental health of patients who are entirely incapable of deciding for themselves and for whom they are therefore responsible, such patients nevertheless remain under the protection of Article 3, whose requirements permit of no derogation.
>
> The established principles of medicine are admittedly in principle decisive in such cases; as a general rule, a measure which is a therapeutic necessity cannot be regarded as inhuman or degrading. The Court must nevertheless satisfy itself that the medical necessity has been convincingly shown to exist.

On all relevant points, the Court finds there is insufficient evidence to disprove the government's position. Thus notwithstanding the Commission's expression of disappointment at the poor calibre of evidence concerning the events in January 1980 that resulted in the applicant's handcuffing, the Court was not prepared to look behind the government's submission that, 'according to the psychiatric principles generally accepted at the time, medical necessity justified the treatment in issue'.[40] As a result, no violation of Article 3 was found. Similarly, when it considers Article 8 on these points, it finds a lack of specific evidence sufficient to displace the government's view that the hospital authorities were justified in regarding the applicant's psychiatric illness as rendering him 'entirely incapable of taking decisions for himself'.[41] Both these findings are problematic. Regarding the physical restraints, the Council of Europe's Committee for the Prevention of Torture (CPT) took a different view in its standards for detention in psychiatric institutions, written only a few years after the *Herczegfalvy* decision:

> The CPT has on occasion encountered psychiatric patients to whom instruments of physical restraint have been applied for a period of days; the Committee must emphasise that such a state of affairs cannot have any therapeutic justification and amounts, in its view, to ill-treatment.[42]

Regarding capacity, it should be noted that the Austrian courts made a finding only of partial capacity of the applicant.[43] It is not clear from the ECHR judgment or Commission decision what specific decisions the domestic court considered that he could not make, and whether that situation had changed

---

[40] *Ibid.*, para. 83.   [41] *Ibid.*, para. 86.
[42] Extract from the 8th General Report, CPT/Inf (98) 12.   [43] *Herczegfalvy*, para. 10.

between the initial decision in November 1977 and the events of the case. It is further not clear whether the medical staff were relying on the court decision or on their own evaluation of the applicant's capacity, and, if the latter, what the legal parameters and status of that evaluation were.[44]

While this is not the place to launch into a detailed analysis of the evidential rules and practices of the Court, it is appropriate to note the considerable inequality of arms between persons detained in psychiatric facilities and the governments and staff who administer those facilities. In other contexts, such as where an injury occurs in a closed institution, the Court places an onus on the State to provide a credible explanation of the injury.[45] It is reasonable to hope that the Court will extend this onus to require explanations whenever force is used in institutions, and in particular whenever violations of Article 3 are at issue. This may, perhaps, be implicit in the Court's requirement that 'the medical necessity has been convincingly shown to exist', but a clearer statement of the evidential principle would be welcome. For purposes of the redrafting exercise, a different view of medical necessity of handcuffing has been taken, consistent with the CPT standards, and the issue of the applicant's ability specifically to consent to medical treatment has been left unresolved (paragraphs 94–8 of the rewritten judgment regarding handcuffing, and paragraph 90 regarding capacity). This last is in part a stylistic ruse to allow for discussion of compulsory treatment both in situations when the individual has capacity, and in situations when he or she has not; but it also reflects the facts of *Herczegfalvy* as reported: we really do not know whether or not he had capacity to make the relevant decisions.

The overall approach of the Court is to state that, when an action is 'medically necessary', it will not be a violation of Article 3.[46] The first difficulty with this standard is that it is not at all clear what 'medically necessary' means. It must be a higher standard than merely 'medically appropriate': the fact that an appropriate treatment is available should not mean that a State should be able to force people to undergo that treatment. 'Medical necessity' as intended by the Court presumably does not mean that without such treatment the patient will suffer death or serious physical injury, since, at least as regards the neuroleptic medication, it is not obvious that this would have been the result in *Herczegfalvy* itself. The degree to which treatment can be enforced in order to safeguard others in society is likely to prove a controversial point, and to raise serious

---

[44] These ambiguities are reflected at paras. 89–90 of the redrafted judgment.

[45] See, for example, ECHR, *Selmouni* v. *France*, 28 July 1999, (2000) 29 EHRR 403, para. 87; ECHR, *Aksoy* v. *Turkey*, 26 November 1996, (1996) 23 EHRR 553, para. 61; ECHR, *Ribitsch* v. *Austria*, 21 November 1995 (A/336), (1996) 21 EHRR 573, para. 34.

[46] For a detailed discussion of this phrase in an English context, see P. Bartlett, '"The Necessity Must Be Convincingly Shown to Exist": Standards for Compulsory Treatment for Mental Disorder under the Mental Health Act 1983' (2011) 19 *Medical Law Review* 514–47, available on open access at http://medlaw.oxfordjournals.org/content/19/4/514.full.pdf+html (last accessed 29 November 2011).

substantive arguments under the Convention. Is the degree of likelihood of success relevant – that is, even to prevent death, can it be said that a highly intrusive and painful treatment with a low probability of success is 'medically necessary'? These and many other questions are left unanswered by the standard articulated.

If the standard is going to be meaningful, therefore, it must be articulated in a much clearer fashion. Certainly, this is appropriately an area where a margin of appreciation should apply and domestic legislation should take the lead, but the issue of substantive clarity discussed above remains relevant: domestic legislation must establish real criteria, and those criteria must be defensible in human rights terms. The redrafting indicates some possible ways of approaching the issue (see paragraph 89 of the rewritten judgment). While the treating physician may be best placed to make an initial evaluation of the situation, it needs to be noted that he or she is too close to the situation for the process to end with him or her. Further, the scope of the State's right to impose treatment raises a variety of political, legal and social issues as well as medical ones. This is not a purely medical matter, and the process must allow for an independent review of the decision.

So, when, if at all, should compulsory treatment be permitted? The redrafting makes the case that mere detention in a psychiatric institution is not sufficient, nor, a fortiori, is the mere presence of a mental disorder. The redrafting makes the case that the actual capacity of the individual to make the decision will be relevant but not necessarily determinative in all cases (paragraphs 86–90 of the rewritten judgment).

It is difficult to imagine a matter more directly related to the right to physical and personal integrity and autonomy than the right to control the chemicals that are introduced into one's body. This is an important point, regardless of what the chemicals are, and this remains the case even if the medicines were unproblematic. An absence of adverse effects may well be relevant to whether an individual wishes to consent to medication, but it is not an argument for the removal of that consent. Many medications, most psychiatric medications included, are not unproblematic. Taractan, the neuroleptic prescribed for Mr Herczegfalvy, is the trade name of chlorprothixene. Its adverse effects include highly sedative properties, dry mouth, massive hypotension and tachycardia, hyperhidrosis, substantial weight gain and extra-pyramidal effects such as Parkinsonianism, dystonia (abnormal face and body movements), restlessness, and tardive dyskinesia (rhythmic, involuntary movements of the tongue, face, and jaw). These extra-pyramidal effects can be permanent. It should be emphasised that psychiatric medication can also have very positive effects; but benefits may well come at a cost. Psychiatric in-patients may also have long experience with prescribed drugs, and have firm and defensible views as to what, if anything, they wish to take for their condition based on what seems to them to provide the best balance of improvements and adverse effects.

The redrafting acknowledges the potential impact of the CRPD in matters of consent, and in particular the strong wording of the CRPD defending the right of people with disabilities to consent to treatment (paragraph 89 of the redrafted judgment). It does seem that the CRPD will take a very narrow view of incapacity, and deprivation of the right to consent to treatment on this basis will need to be very carefully circumscribed by national governments, if indeed the CRPD allows it at all.

All of this is overlaid by a policy of non-discrimination (paragraph 86 of the rewritten judgment). While the Court has not yet interpreted Article 14 in the context of mental disability, it has done so in the context of physical disability in sufficiently expansive terms to suggest that discrimination on the basis of mental disability will also be within the scope of Article 14,[47] and, by extension, Protocol 12. The CRPD similarly places great emphasis on non-discriminatory approaches in these areas. It is therefore likely to be the case that it will allow compulsory treatment of mental disorders if compulsion would also be allowed for physical disorders of comparable seriousness, and in cases of people without mental or other disabilities.

In essence, the argument regarding Article 3 is that meaningful substantive standards consistent with international law, as well as appropriate procedural standards, must be developed. What appears to be an almost off-hand reference to 'medical necessity' in the original *Herczegfalvy* case needs to be expanded to provide a real substantive standard; and the effects of compulsory and unwanted treatment on capable and non-capable people must be re-articulated within the framework of Article 3.

That, in turn, raises issues relating to Article 8. If, as is argued, non-consensual treatment is sufficient to bring Article 3 into consideration, it must also be sufficient to engage Article 8(1); and this is consistent with the existing jurisprudence on the point. To satisfy Article 8(2), however, actions must be 'in accordance with law', and, as discussed elsewhere in this chapter, that requires a certain degree of specificity. This approach found favour with the Court concerning the withholding of Mr Herczegfalvy's correspondence under Article 8 and the withholding of information from him (caused by removal of his access to television) under Article 10, and the Court provides a pointed dismissal of the government's attempt to rely on the Hospitals Law and the Civil Code:

> 91. These very vaguely worded provisions do not specify the scope or conditions of exercise of the discretionary power which was at the origin of the measures complained of. But such specifications appear all the more necessary in the field of detention in psychiatric institutions in that the persons concerned are frequently at the mercy of the medical authorities, so that their correspondence is their only contact with the outside world.

---

[47] See *Glor* v. *Switzerland*, 6 November 2009, e.g. at para. 53.

One must view these comments with enthusiasm; but it is inescapable to note that the aspects of those same laws that concern involuntary treatment are no more clearly defined; and yet the Court makes no comment on them. Is it really the Court's position that involuntary psychiatric treatment warrants less protection than access to television?[48]

Conclusion

The ECHR did not consider matters relating to mental disability for almost thirty years following its establishment. A trickle has now become, if not a flood, at least a determined stream, and there is much in the Court's record for it to be proud of. At the same time, people with mental disabilities remain the subject of stigma throughout the Member States of the Council of Europe, and the human rights issues relating to them remain real and pressing. The Court has been instrumental in bringing about procedural standards throughout the Member States of the Council of Europe, but, in the end, process is not enough. Substantial standards must be required, that ensure improved services, dignity and respect for the affected populations.

Rewriting Herczegfalvy v. Austria

. . .

IV.   Alleged violation of Article 3

79. Mr Herczegfalvy also complained of his medical treatment. In that he had been forcibly administered food and neuroleptics, isolated and attached with handcuffs to a security bed during the weeks following the incident of 15 January 1980 (see paragraphs 24–28 above), he had been subjected to brutal treatment incompatible with Article 3 . . .

80. The Commission considered that the manner in which the treatment was administered had not complied with the requirements of Article 3: the various measures complained of had been violent and excessively prolonged, and taken together had amounted to inhuman and degrading treatment, and even contributed to the worsening of the patient's condition.

81. In the Government's opinion, on the other hand, the measures were essentially the consequence of the applicant's behaviour, as he had refused medical treatment which was urgent in view of the deterioration in his physical and mental health . . .

82. The Court considers that the position of inferiority and powerlessness which is typical of patients confined in psychiatric hospitals calls for

---

[48]   These issues are considered at paras. 107–8 of the redrafted judgment.

increased vigilance in reviewing whether the Convention has been complied with. [Fragment deleted] While the Court acknowledges the complexities of administering psychiatric hospitals and similar institutions for people with mental disorders, such patients nevertheless remain under the protection of Article 3, whose requirements permit of no derogation. [Fragment deleted]

83. The Court considers that two broad issues arise. One relates to the use of force in the provision of food and medicine to Mr Herczegfalvy, and the other to the implementation of restraint and isolation upon Mr Herczegfalvy during his detention.

(a) Compulsory medical treatment

84. The applicant was treated without his consent at various times, with sedatives and, on an ongoing basis and certainly for several weeks following 15 January 1980, with neuroleptic medication. In addition, he was forcibly fed during his hunger strike, commencing when his malnutrition became pronounced. The sedation was not directed to treatment or cure of the underlying condition of the applicant, but rather to the control of the patient both to regain order on the ward and to subdue him so that treatment directed to his condition could take place. It will be considered as part of the applicant's restraint, rather than medical treatment. The treatment with neuroleptic medication and the force-feeding will be considered in turn.

Compulsory treatment must perforce be directed to a true medical disorder with which the individual is affected. Compulsory treatment of an individual who is not reasonably believed to be suffering from such a disorder will almost inevitably constitute a violation of Article 3. It is to be expected that diagnoses will be made in good faith, consistent with a reasonable standard of professional competence, and consistent with a recognised medical diagnostic manual such as the United Nations International Classification of Diseases (ICD-10). While they may turn out to be incorrect, they must be objectively and demonstrably credible at the time they were made.

This case creates some difficulties in this regard. The applicant was diagnosed with paranoia querulans. While this disorder is acknowledged in ICD-10 under 'Other paranoid states', no definition is provided. It would appear to be characterised by consistent complaining and vexatious litigation, precisely the behaviour that triggered the applicant's transfer from prison to hospital. The potential for abuse of this diagnosis by pathologising troublesome individuals has been acknowledged in the academic medical literature, and the enforced medication of an individual based on his or her merely being 'troublesome' rather than legitimately suffering from a mental disorder would certainly raise the

prospect of a violation of Article 3. Because of the Court's findings elsewhere in this judgment, it is not necessary to reach a firm conclusion on the accuracy of the diagnosis in this case, but it would reiterate that convincing objective evidence of a true mental disorder must be shown to exist when compulsory treatment is at issue.

Assuming the appropriateness of the diagnosis, the Court accepts that the treatments with neuroleptic medication were given under medical supervision and directed to the treatment of the mental disorder from which the applicant was suffering. The Court does not question their medical appropriateness. The established principles of medicine are decisive on this point, and had the applicant given free and informed consent to the treatments, no issue under Article 3 would arise. The potential issue under Article 3 is whether the compulsory or non-consensual nature of the treatment alters that position.

85. The case of *Kudła* v. *Poland* (Application no. 30210/96, judgment 26 October 2000, para. 92) provides guidance as to the scope of inhuman or degrading treatment:

> The Court has considered treatment to be 'inhuman' because, *inter alia*, it was premeditated, was applied for hours at a stretch and caused either actual bodily injury or intense physical or mental suffering. It has deemed treatment to be 'degrading' because it was such as to arouse in the victims feelings of fear, anguish and inferiority capable of humiliating and debasing them. On the other hand, the Court has consistently stressed that the suffering and humiliation involved must in any event go beyond that inevitable element of suffering or humiliation connected with a given form of legitimate treatment or punishment.

While any intent to degrade or treat in an inhumane fashion is relevant to a finding of a violation under Article 3, it is not a requirement: *Peers* v. *Greece*(Application no. 28524/95, judgment 19 April 2001, para. 74; *Price* v. *UK*, Application no. 33394/96, judgment 10 July 2001, para. 30).

86. The Court notes that behaviour must reach a minimal level of severity to fall within the scope of Article 3. It also notes that the control of one's bodily integrity, and the right to consent to or to refuse medical treatment, constitutes a fundamental aspect of bodily autonomy. The overruling of a refusal and the forced imposition of medical treatment, particularly when that treatment involves surgical or similarly intrusive physical intervention, or the use of strong medications, is bound to give rise to the feelings of fear, anguish and inferiority referred to in the *Kudła* decision. Treatment provided in such circumstances falls within the scope of Article 3. Treatment with neuroleptic medication is certainly sufficiently intrusive to meet this threshold, and any treatment with such medication without the consent of the patient is within the scope of

Article 3. That is the situation in the current case, and the Court therefore holds that the enforced treatment with neuroleptics falls within the scope of Article 3.

This therefore triggers Article 14 as an aid to interpretation of Article 3. Enforced treatment should not be discriminatory in its effect. This applies not merely on the basis of the articulated grounds contained in Article 14, but also on the basis of disability: *Glor* v. *Switzerland* (Application no. 13444/04, judgment of 6 November 2009). While that case refers specifically to physical disability, the same principles must apply to mental disability. The fact that an individual has a mental disability, therefore, will not of itself justify a lower standard for enforced treatment, and criteria which impact disproportionately on people with mental disability must be objectively justifiable.

While the capacity of an individual to make the relevant treatment decision will be relevant to whether a breach of Article 3 occurs, the fact that an individual lacks such capacity does not place the factual situation outside the scope of Article 3. The pivotal question, based on the language in *Kudła*, is whether the actions complained of are such as to cause the individual feelings of fear, anguish and inferiority. Those lacking mental capacity are not immune from these feelings. They are also among the most vulnerable in institutions, and their situation warrants the particular attention of the Court.

The Court must therefore consider whether there is a violation of Article 3 in this case.

87. The mere fact that an individual is detained in a psychiatric facility will not be sufficient to justify compulsory psychiatric treatment. The Court has elsewhere held that the detention of persons in psychiatric facilities under Article 5(1)(e) may be justified not merely for therapeutic reasons, but also for reasons relating to the danger posed by the person detained as a result of his or her psychiatric condition: see e.g. *Hutchinson Reid* v. *United Kingdom* (Application no. 50272/99, judgment 20 May 2003). The detention removes the immediate social danger posed by the individual; it does not follow that the State acquires a consequent right to treat the individual without his or her consent. Even if the individual is detained for the sake of his or her health, it does not follow that he or she may be compulsorily treated. It is a *non sequitur* to say that, because treatment is medically appropriate or even necessary, it may be given without consent. This is as true in a psychiatric context as it is for physical disorders.

This is consistent with the approach of the Committee for the Prevention of Torture, whose standards state:

> Patients should, as a matter of principle, be placed in a position to give their free and informed consent to treatment. The admission of a

person to a psychiatric establishment on an involuntary basis should not be construed as authorising treatment without his consent. It follows that every competent patient, whether voluntary or involuntary, should be given the opportunity to refuse treatment or other medical intervention. Any derogation from this fundamental principle should be based upon law and only relate to clearly and strictly defined exceptional circumstances. [CPT Standards, CPT/Inf/E (2002) 1, Rev 2004, p. 57, para. 41.]

88. The CPT standard falls short of stating that involuntary treatment may never be given to detained patients without consent. Other European and international instruments are similarly not absolutely prohibitive. The Recommendation of the Committee of Ministers to Member States concerning the protection of the human rights and dignity of persons with mental disorder, Rec(2004)10, similarly sets out different criteria for involuntary treatment and involuntary detention. The substantive recommendations concerning involuntary treatment are as follows:

Article 18 – Criteria for involuntary treatment
A person may be subject to involuntary treatment only if all the following conditions are met:

i. the person has a mental disorder;
ii. the person's condition represents a significant risk of serious harm to his or her health or to other persons;
iii. no less intrusive means of providing appropriate care are available;
iv. the opinion of the person concerned has been taken into consideration.

Article 19 – Principles concerning involuntary treatment

1. Involuntary treatment should:
   i. address specific clinical signs and symptoms;
   ii. be proportionate to the person's state of health;
   iii. form part of a written treatment plan;
   iv. be documented;
   v. where appropriate, aim to enable the use of treatment acceptable to the person as soon as possible.
2. In addition to the requirements of Article 12.1 above, the treatment plan should:
   i. whenever possible be prepared in consultation with the person concerned and the person's personal advocate or representative, if any;
   ii. be reviewed at appropriate intervals and, if necessary, revised, whenever possible in consultation with the person concerned and his or her personal advocate or representative, if any.

3. Member States should ensure that involuntary treatment only takes place in an appropriate environment.

89. States enjoy a margin of appreciation in their implementation of the Convention, and within the framework of the Convention and other international law. Nonetheless, a few points may provide guidance as to the Court's approach in this area.

The decisions of a competent individual warrant particular respect, and may be overridden only for the most compelling reasons, if at all. The United Nations Convention on the Rights of Persons with Disabilities includes an express provision that treatment is to be provided on the basis of 'free and informed consent' (UN A/61/611, Article 25(d)). This is coupled with an Article that maximises the number of people who have legal capacity (Article 12), and thus have the legal right to exercise that consent. Further, the logic of the Court expressed above notes that the degradation implied in enforced treatment flows from the violation of selfhood that is inherent in the removal of the right of an individual to control chemical interventions to his or her body. That violation is most pronounced in the case of an individual with capacity to make the relevant decision.

As the potential violation of Article 3 flows from the removal of an individual's control over his or her self, the availability of procedural challenges prior to such interventions will be relevant to the way in which the affected person will experience the intervention. Article 3 violations are therefore less likely to occur when the right of the affected person to challenge the decision to enforce treatment is available. Appropriate legal representation must be provided as required for such challenges, with particular attention accorded to the situation of persons lacking or of marginal capacity. The Court notes that the Recommendation of the Committee of Ministers includes provisions relating to such reviews and appeals (Article 25).

The fact that treatment is in the best medical interests of an individual will not be sufficient to justify its forced administration. The likelihood of an Article 3 violation will depend on a range of variables. Where the individual has capacity, as noted above, his or her refusal of treatment should be overridden only in extreme cases, as for example in cases of immediate necessity of treatment to preserve life, if at all. Additional possible factors include, but are not restricted to, the certainty of the medical practitioners as to the diagnosis, prognosis and appropriate treatment for the patient, the seriousness of the disorder to be treated, the probability of success of the course of treatment, the potential adverse effects of the treatment, the nature and availability of alternative treatments and of failure to treat the patient, the positive and negative experiences of the patient with similar treatments in the past, and the capacity of the patient to consent to the intervention. Where the individual lacks capacity, in addition to the factors noted above, the views of the individual when competent and the values that the individual would have brought to the decision will always be highly relevant. The degree and nature of the objection of individuals lacking capacity will also be relevant. The Court reiterates that for capable and incapable patients alike, different standards must not apply between psychiatric and other treatments of comparable invasiveness and severity, nor between psychiatric and other patients, regarding the criteria to be used in enforcing treatment: the criteria must be applicable without discrimination.

90. In applying these principles, the facts of the current case are insufficient in a number of pivotal aspects. The facts regarding the incident on 15 January 1980 remain unclear, notwithstanding the Commission's request for further particulars. Further, the Court notes that capacity is a decision-specific concept that may vary considerably over time: people may have capacity at some times and not at others, and have capacity for some decisions and not others. While it is clear that the applicant was subject to a guardianship order, it is not clear from the facts whether he was in fact competent to make relevant treatment decisions on 15 January 1980, and, if not, whether or at what point he became competent to make those decisions. Information was not provided to the Court about the potential adverse effects of the medications (although the Court notes that the adverse effects of many neuroleptic medications can be serious), nor likelihood and degree of success of the proposed intervention. The Court was not told the procedures by which the proposed course of action was adopted, and it is therefore unaware of the degree to which the views of the applicant were taken into account. While the facts are not entirely clear, it seems that there were no established criteria for these decisions, and that considerable discretion was left to doctors without meaningful guidance as to how that discretion was to be exercised. While considerable latitude must be accorded to the treating authorities in situations of emergency, as may have been the case on 15 January 1980, it is not clear that appropriate procedures were in place to be followed in the weeks following that time, during which the compulsory treatment continued.

The Court notes the limited mechanisms for the applicant to require review of these decisions. The acts of the hospital, like any administrative act, could in theory have been challenged as to its lawfulness before the Administrative Court (Verwaltungsgerichtshof) and as to its constitutionality before the Constitutional Court (Verfassungsgerichtshof); however, as noted in paragraph 55, there are no examples of such applications against psychiatric hospitals relating to situations analogous to those in the current case. The Court therefore questions the practicality of this mechanism. These doubts are buttressed by the fact that the hospital was already failing to forward complaints by the applicant to the courts. The Court therefore holds that meaningful challenge to the decisions of the hospital was denied to the applicant.

91. On this basis, the Court holds that the enforced treatment with neuroleptic medication over the objections of the applicant constituted inhuman or degrading treatment, and the Court therefore finds a violation of Article 3.

92. The forced feeding of the applicant should be analysed in broadly similar terms. The physical violation of bodily integrity that this intervention involved, over the active objection of the applicant, was sufficient to bring the actions within the scope of Article 3 (see *Nevmerzhitsky* v. *the Ukraine*, Application no. 54825/00, judgment 12 October 2005).

As to whether there was a violation of that Article, the Court notes the ambiguity of European and international human rights instruments as to whether a hunger strike should be permitted to continue. Thus, paragraph 63 of Recommendation No. R (98) 7 of the Committee of Ministers to Member States concerning the ethical and organisational aspects of health care in prison provides:

> 63. If, in the opinion of the doctor, the hunger striker's condition is becoming significantly worse, it is essential that the doctor report this fact to the appropriate authority and take action in accordance with national legislation (including professional standards).

The relevant extracts from Chapter III of the CPT Standards of 'Health care services in prisons' (CPT/Inf/E (2002) 1, Rev. 2004) and extracts from the 3rd General Report (CPT/Inf (93) 12) read as follows:

> 47. Every patient capable of discernment is free to refuse treatment or any other medical intervention. Any derogation from this fundamental principle should be based upon law and only relate to clearly and strictly defined exceptional circumstances which are applicable to the population as a whole.
>
> A classically difficult situation arises when the patient's decision conflicts with the general duty of care incumbent on the doctor. This might happen when the patient is influenced by personal beliefs (e.g. refusal of a blood transfusion) or when he is intent on using his body, or even mutilating himself, in order to press his demands, protest against an authority or demonstrate his support for a cause.
>
> In the event of a hunger strike, public authorities or professional organisations in some countries will require the doctor to intervene to prevent death as soon as the patient's consciousness becomes seriously

impaired. In other countries, the rule is to leave clinical decisions to the doctor in charge, after he has sought advice and weighed up all the relevant facts.

The *Nevmerzhitsky* case itself identifies the conflict between the potential Article 3 violation and the duty on Contracting States to protect the right to life:

> When, however, as in the present case, a detained person maintains a hunger strike this may inevitably lead to a conflict between an individual's right to physical integrity and the High Contracting Party's positive obligation under Article 2 of the Convention – a conflict which is not solved by the Convention itself (see *X* v. *Germany* (1984) 7 EHRR 152). [para. 93]

A violation of Article 3 was found in *Nevmerzhitsky* on the basis that, even if medically necessary, the treatment was provided in a fashion that violated the applicant's Article 3 rights, and that procedural safeguards followed. Similar comments apply in the present case, and the Court therefore finds a violation of Article 3.

93. This does not necessarily entail that enforced feeding will constitute a violation of Article 3 in all subsequent cases. The protection of life is the most compelling justification for enforced treatment, and the Court notes that domestic law can be phrased to ensure that such protections apply equally to people with mental disabilities and those without such disabilities. The Court would not wish to pre-judge future cases in this regard.

(b) Restraint and isolation

94. The applicant was subject to restraint on numerous occasions during his detention. On a number of occasions, he was subject to physical restraint. The most significant occurrence of such restraint occurred in a continuous period from 30 January to 14 February 1980, when the applicant was handcuffed to a security bed and had a belt placed around his ankles. He was also subject on various occasions to chemical restraint, including the forcible injection of 90 mg of Taractan on 15 January 1980, to induce a state of somnolence so that he could be given other psychiatric treatment. It would seem that the applicant was further subject to segregation from other patients at various times, although the duration and intensity of this isolation was a matter of dispute between the parties.

95. The Court acknowledges that restraint and seclusion will on occasion be necessary in institutions, including psychiatric institutions. Such measures are justified when reasonably necessary to protect the health and safety of the person detained, or of other persons. Such measures must not be used as a form of punishment, and must continue only for

the shortest time reasonably possible. They must also be of the least severity possible: *Ribitsch* v. *Austria*(Application no. 18896/91, judgment 14 November 1995, para. 38).

96. As noted above, the facts regarding the incident on 15 January 1980 remain unclear. It does seem that the applicant was that day in poor physical health, but nonetheless became extremely agitated and fell into a rage. An emergency squad was called in response. Thereafter, the applicant collapsed, and developed pneumonia and nephritis, which required urgent medical treatment elsewhere in the hospital. It would appear that all this restraint occurred under proper medical supervision.

97. The Commission concluded that the initial actions of the hospital were justified, but not the subsequent actions:

> 247. The overcoming of the physical resistance of a mental health patient lacking insight concerning the necessity of a particular treatment can, in certain circumstances, be regarded as necessary, especially if the treatment in question appears imperative. The Commission considers that the condition was at least initially met in the applicant's case. It is nevertheless doubtful whether in view of the applicant's reaction on 15 January 1980 it was really necessary to insist on the immediate administration of his compulsory treatment and apply massive force to this end, including overwhelming him by an emergency squad. The Commission notes in this context that the use of force seems to have contributed to the applicant's state of agitation and his complete physical breakdown. It does not appear that the medical authorities could foresee this development when the treatment was started. They should, however, have reconsidered the appropriateness of the measures taken to overcome the applicant's physical resistance once their effect on his state of health became apparent.

98. The Court would express its reservations regarding the first sentence of the Commission's view, at least in the un-nuanced way in which it is phrased. As noted in the previous section, the 'overcoming' of an individual who is objecting to treatment is a complex decision, containing a variety of factors. The Court does share the view in the remainder of the paragraph. It further notes the following comment from the CPT Standards concerning involuntary placement in psychiatric establishments (Extract from the 8th General Report [CPT/Inf (98) 12]):

> 48. Resort to instruments of physical restraint (straps, strait-jackets, etc.) shall only very rarely be justified and must always be either expressly ordered by a doctor or immediately brought to the attention of a doctor with a view to seeking his approval. If, exceptionally, recourse is had to instruments of physical restraint, they should be

removed at the earliest opportunity; they should never be applied, or
their application prolonged, as a punishment.

The CPT has on occasion encountered psychiatric patients to whom
instruments of physical restraint have been applied for a period of
days; the Committee must emphasise that such a state of affairs cannot
have any therapeutic justification and amounts, in its view, to ill-
treatment.

In this case, the applicant was held in physical restraints – handcuffs
and ankle belts – for a period of more than two weeks. As the Commission
notes, the effect on him was traumatic, inducing a complete physical
breakdown. In the view of the Court, this constituted a violation of
Article 3.

99. Mr Herczegfalvy was also restrained with sedative medication
commencing in January 1980. The most severe treatment of this sort
commenced on 15 January 1980, but it is not clear from the facts how
long sedation continued. It is also not clear the degree to which the
neuroleptic medication given to the applicant on an ongoing basis had
sedative (and therefore restraining) effects.

100. The Court acknowledges that some people may require sedation
for significant periods, and that some medication provided for therapeutic reasons over a considerable time may have sedative effects. The Court
acknowledges that the use of medications for these purposes may remove
the need for physical restraints, and may (depending on the physical
restraint and the medications in question) be less severe than physical
restraints. The same principles nonetheless apply to medications with
sedative effects as apply to other restraints: they must not be used as a
form of punishment, must continue only for the shortest time reasonably
possible, and must be of the least severity possible. Medical professionals
are thus required to revisit medicinal restraint, as they would physical
restraint, on a periodic basis to ensure that it remains justified.

101. The Court has already expressed its reservations about the calibre
of the evidence in this case. Nonetheless, it does note that the applicant in
this case had a history of violence that continued through most of his
psychiatric detention. While the Court would in the future expect clearer
evidence relating to the necessity of specific uses of chemical restraint, on
this occasion it is minded to find that the use of sedative medication was
justified.

102. The Court notes that the jurisdiction of the Austrian
Administrative Court (Verwaltungsgerichtshof) and Constitutional
Court (Verfassungsgerichtshof), while apparently available in principle
to challenge the legality and constitutionality of enforced psychiatric
treatment have never in fact been used for this purpose. The Court

must therefore question whether these are in fact real avenues of redress for people subject to involuntary psychiatric treatment, and question whether the requirements of Articles 6 and 13 are met. As the issue was not pleaded before us in these terms, no finding is made on this point, other than to note the obligation of States to ensure mechanisms of redress for persons whose rights under this Convention are at issue.

[Original paragraphs 83 and 84 deleted]

V.   Alleged violation of Article 8

103. Mr Herczegfalvy further alleged that by administering food to him by force, imposing on him the treatment complained of and refusing to send on his correspondence, the hospital authorities had also violated Article 8 . . .

[Original paragraph 86 deleted]

104. **The substance of the first two complaints has already been considered from the point of view of Article 3. Article 8, however, raises some technical points of relevance to these matters.**

105. **A compulsory medical intervention, even if slight, constitutes an interference with Article 8(1): YF v. _Turkey_ (Application no. 24209/94, judgment 22 July 2003). Such an interference will only be permitted if justified under Article 8(2). It will be clear from the foregoing discussion that, if non-consensual treatment is to be permitted under Article 3, it will only be because it has considerable and demonstrable therapeutic benefits (for the neuroleptic medication and the forced feeding), or is warranted as necessary for the protection of the patient or others (for the sedatives used for restraint). These would appear to be justified under Article 8(2) with reference to the protection of health (for the medications) and for the prevention of disorder or crime, the protection of health, and for the protection of the rights and freedoms of others (for the restraint).**

106. **Article 8(2) also requires, however, that any reliance on Article 8(2) be 'in accordance with the law'.** The Court recalls that the expression 'in accordance with the law' requires firstly that the impugned measure should have some basis in national law; it also refers to the quality of the law in question, requiring that it should be accessible to the person concerned, who must moreover be able to foresee its consequences for him, and compatible with the rule of law (see, _inter alia_, the _Kruslin and Huvig_ v. _France_ judgments of 24 April 1990, Series A no. 176-A, p. 20, paras. 26–27, and no. 176-B, p. 52, paras. 25–26).[49] **While the usual phrasing of this**

---

[49] These seven lines are actually taken from the discussion of the withholding of Mr Herczegfalvy's letters in the original case: see para. 88 of the original judgment.

requirement is that the law's consequences be foreseeable to the person whose rights are at risk, the Court would note that it is equally important that the law be sufficiently precise and comprehensible that those charged with its administration will be clear what is expected of them, and so that there will be consistency of decision-making between these individuals. The Court notes that such clarity is particularly important in psychiatric and similar contexts, where initial decisions may well be taken by non-lawyers and where the people affected will be particularly vulnerable, and consequently not necessarily be in a position (or consider themselves to be in a position) where they can press for their rights or challenge decisions made about them. Without such clarity, rights become a lottery.

107. If non-consensual treatment is to be permitted, therefore, it must be given a firm and clear basis in domestic law. A mere repetition of the criteria identified in the discussion of Article 3, above, without further clarification, will be insufficient. The margin of appreciation accorded to States Party to the Convention imports a corresponding duty onto the State to establish clear criteria that meet both the needs of the State and the terms of the Convention.

108. In this case, the Hospitals Law (Krankenanstaltengesetz) required patient consent only for 'special curative treatments including surgical operations'. The applicant had been found incapable of managing his affairs in 1975, and the Incapacitation Regulations (Entmündigungsordnung) coupled with relevant Articles of the Civil Code (Allgemeines Bürgerliches Gesetzbuch) and the law on the appointment of curators of handicapped persons (Sachwaltergesetz) gave his curator an unfettered discretion to consent on his behalf. No guidance is provided as to what non-consensual treatments are to be permitted. This cannot be considered sufficiently precise as to satisfy Article 8(2). Admittedly, as the government submits, it may not be possible to draft a law which will definitively determine all eventualities; but equally, it is necessary that appropriate procedures be established and meaningful guidance be provided on matters of substance. The impossibility of perfection in drafting cannot be the excuse for failing to bring about a vast improvement.

The Court therefore finds a violation of Article 8.

15

Rewriting Kolanis v. United Kingdom: the right to community living

MARIS BURBERGS*

Introduction

Kolanis v. United Kingdom[1] concerns a failure by the State to provide Ms Kolanis with community-based mental health care after a mental health care authority had determined that hospitalisation was no longer needed. As a result of the State's failure, Ms Kolanis was kept in the mental health hospital a year longer. She argued before the ECHR that her right to liberty protected by Article 5 of the European Convention on Human Rights ('the Convention') had been violated in this situation. Another claim that surfaces in the case, but was not brought before the Court, is the impact of unnecessary institutionalisation on her private life. To address this issue, one has to explore the developments in mental health care that concern the treatment of mentally disabled persons in community-based settings. Community-based care has gained considerable recognition in the world and has recently been established as a binding international human rights norm in the form of a right to community living.[2]

The right to community living (also called 'the right to live in the community'[3] or 'the right to community integration'[4]) is comprehensively described in Article 19 of the United Nations Convention on the Rights of Persons with Disabilities (CRPD) where one can see the many aspects of the right:

> States Parties to the present Convention recognize the equal right of all persons with disabilities to live in the community, with choices equal to

---

* The research for this paper was conducted within the framework of the ERC Starting Grant project 'Strengthening the European Court of Human Rights: More Accountability Through Better Legal Reasoning'.
[1] ECHR, *Kolanis v. United Kingdom*, 21 June 2005.
[2] See Article 19 of the United Nations Convention on the Rights of Persons with Disabilities (CRPD). The CRPD was adopted on 13 December 2006 and entered into force on 3 May 2008.
[3] Report of the Ad Hoc Expert Group on the Transition from Institutional Care to Community-Based Care (2009), available at http://ec.europa.eu/social/main.jsp?langId=en&catId=89&newsId=614&furtherNews=yes (last accessed 1 September 2011).
[4] P. Bartlett, O. Lewis and O. Thorold, *Mental Disability and the European Convention on Human Rights* (Martinus Nijhoff Publishers, 2007).

others, and shall take effective and appropriate measures to facilitate full enjoyment by persons with disabilities of this right and their full inclusion and participation in the community, including by ensuring that:

(a) Persons with disabilities have the opportunity to choose their place of residence and where and with whom they live on an equal basis with others and are not obliged to live in a particular living arrangement;

(b) Persons with disabilities have access to a range of in-home, residential and other community support services, including personal assistance necessary to support living and inclusion in the community, and to prevent isolation or segregation from the community . . .

Several of the aspects of the right to community living have been previously assessed by the Court under Article 8. For example, the issues of access to public places for leisure activities,[5] access to public buildings and buildings open to the public for daily life arrangements,[6] and the provision of suitable adapted accommodation[7] have been considered under the right to protection of a person's private life. But the Court has never looked into the issue of institutionalisation of the mentally disabled persons from the perspective of Article 8 in situations where community-based treatment would have been possible according to medical standards. It did not do so in the *Kolanis* case either. To date, the strongest moves in favour of assessing the issue under Article 8 have been the separate opinions of judges in the case of *Stanev* v. *Bulgaria*.[8] In their view, Articles 3, 5 and 6 did not cover the whole claim of the applicant, who argued that his inability to live in a community and the effects institutionalisation had on him concerned rights protected under Article 8.

Thus, through the *Kolanis* case, this chapter explores the possibility to introduce an aspect of the right to community living – community-based treatment for mentally disabled persons – under Article 8.

I have picked the *Kolanis* case because it represents the decades-long developments in the treatment of mentally disabled persons by States around the world. The facts of this case thus serve as evidence of developments in mental

---

[5] See ECHR, *Botta* v. *Italy*, 24 February 1998.

[6] See ECHR, *Zehnalová and Zehnal* v. *Czech Republic*, 14 May 2002.

[7] See ECHR, *Marzari* v. *Italy*, 4 May 1999.

[8] ECHR (GC), *Stanev* v. *Bulgaria*, 17 January 2012. Cf. ECHR, *Ashingdane* v. *United Kingdom*, 28 May 1985, where the Court acknowledges limits to the application of Article 5 in institutionalisation cases. The Court stated in para. 49 of the judgment that 'the applicant suffered, in human terms, an injustice in having to endure the stricter regime at Broadmoor for nineteen months longer than his mental state required. The Government themselves have expressed sympathy at his plight and their great regret at the events giving rise to the application. The problem of transfer from the "special" hospitals in England and Wales, which lay at the root of the present case, was undoubtedly a serious one for those affected. However, the injustice suffered by Mr Ashingdane is not a mischief against which Article 5 para. 1(e) of the Convention protects.'

health care, and support my argument that States have changed their practice, and that there are new standards for States regarding the care of the mentally disabled – standards that accord due respect to a person's private life. If the Court were to include those standards in its practice, it would give due recognition to the concerns of mentally disabled persons. It should be noted that, even though there has been a marked decrease in long-term institutional care over the last few decades, the extent of this development varies considerably among European countries.[9] The inclusion of this aspect of the right to community living into Article 8 would make the standards obligatory and assure the same level of protection of this crucial aspect of the private life of mentally disabled individuals in all Council of Europe Member States.[10]

First, this chapter will highlight important facts of the *Kolanis* case. Next, it will examine methods of introducing new interests under the protection of Article 8. The further sections will examine the possibility to protect the interest to community-based mental health care under Article 8. This starts with an examination of the impact of different mental healthcare settings on a person's daily life, continues with an examination of medical and scientific considerations, and concludes with an assessment of the international and European consensus in this field. The final section of this chapter is dedicated to the rewritten judgment.

The factual context and the judgment

Ms Kolanis, born in 1972, was convicted for causing grievous bodily harm with intent in 1998. She was found to be suffering from a mental illness and was

---

[9] See Report of the Ad Hoc Expert Group on the Transition from Institutional Care to Community-Based Care (2009), p. 10, available at http://ec.europa.eu/social/main.jsp?langId=en&catId=89&newsId=614&furtherNews=yes (last accessed 1 September 2011).

[10] With regard to the financial burden the States might encounter, it should be mentioned that the dominant findings are that there is no evidence that community-based models of care are inherently more costly than institutions, once the comparison is made on the basis of comparable needs of residents and comparable quality of care. Other studies argue that institutional care may in fact be more expensive than community care. See H. Ward, L. Holmes and J. Soper, *Costs and Consequences of Placing Children in Care* (London: Jessica Kingsley Publishers, 2008). The study claimed that the average unit cost for maintaining a child for a week in a residential placement was 4.5 times that of an independent living arrangement, 8 times that of the cost for foster care, 9.5 times that of a placement with family and friends, and more than 12.5 times that of a placement with own parents. See also World Health Organization, 'Improving Health Systems and Health Services', available at http://whqlibdoc.who.int/publications/2009/9789241598774_eng.pdf (last accessed 1 September 2011). The assessment of all direct and indirect costs, though, and of long-term benefits of increased social participation remains open to different interpretations. See: Report of the Ad Hoc Expert Group on the Transition from Institutional Care to Community-Based Care (2009), p. 13, available at http://ec.europa.eu/social/main.jsp?langId=en&catId=89&newsId=614&furtherNews=yes (last accessed 1 September 2011).

detained in a hospital under the Mental Health Act 1983. She applied to a Mental Health Review Tribunal (MHRT) for her discharge from detention in hospital. Following a hearing, the MHRT held that the applicant should be conditionally discharged, that she should live at home with her parents, be supervised by a social worker and a forensic consultant psychiatrist and comply with her prescribed treatment. However, her psychiatrist considered that he could not safely supervise the applicant in her parents' home and that she should be cared for in supported accommodation. Subsequently, the health authority was unable to find a forensic consultant psychiatrist in the region who was willing or able to supervise the applicant's care in the community. Following a new decision by the MHRT, Ms Kolanis was conditionally discharged from hospital to a resettlement project hostel.

More than a year elapsed from the moment of the first decision of discharge from the hospital until Ms Kolanis was able to start living in the community. Ms Kolanis claimed violations of Article 5(1), (4) and (5), and violation of Article 13. The Court found no violation of Article 5(1), violations of Article 5(4) and (5), and no reason to examine the complaint also under Article 13.

Regarding just satisfaction, Ms Kolanis claimed non-pecuniary damages, referring to her anxiety and distress at the confinement, loss of self-respect, general effects of loss of liberty, uncertainty, depression, loneliness, considerable weight gain, and distress caused by other patients and the death of a nephew during this period, when she was unable to be with her relatives. The Court responded to this by granting just satisfaction and stating that: 'It cannot be excluded on the facts of this case, however, that the applicant would have been released earlier if the procedures had conformed with Article 5 § 4 and therefore she may claim to have suffered, in that respect, a real loss of opportunity. Furthermore, it considers that the applicant must have suffered feelings of frustration, uncertainty and anxiety from the situation which cannot be compensated solely by the finding of violation.'[11]

To my mind, this part of the judgment reveals a whole new segment of Ms Kolanis' claim that could have been brought before the Court – the impact of unnecessary institutionalisation on a person's private life. I will thus explore in the following sections the possibility to bring the claim under Article 8.

Protecting new interests

Three methods

Put in more general terms, the claim of Ms Kolanis concerns the interest of a person to be treated in a community-based setting when expert advice suggests this as an appropriate solution. An interest, formulated as a right[12] or without

---

[11] ECHR, *Kolanis v. United Kingdom*, para. 92.
[12] See, for example, ECHR, *Ternovszky v. Hungary*, 14 December 2010.

such formulation,[13] can be included under the protection of an already existing Convention right using any of several methods that one can identify in the Court's case law. The first one is a method that could be called the 'of course' method. This method means that the inclusion of the interest is presented as an unproblematic move, without specific motivation. The Court used this method in the case of *Radio France* v. *France* to introduce the right to protection of one's reputation under Article 8:

> The Court would observe that the right to protection of one's reputation is of course one of the rights guaranteed by Article 8 of the Convention, as one element of the right to respect for private life.[14]

The *Radio France* case was the first case where the new right was introduced by the Court.[15] The use of 'of course' suggests that the Court regarded the protection of reputation under Article 8 as self-evident; no more explanation was needed.[16] Using this method, the Court could just proclaim that the claim of Ms Kolanis raises an issue under Article 8.

The second method accompanies the introduction of an interest with a few sentences of reasoning. The Court used this method, for example, in the case of *Ternovszky* v. *Hungary* in which it introduced the right of choosing the circumstances of becoming a parent. The applicant intended to give birth at her home, rather than in a hospital or a birth home, but alleged she had not been able to do so because health professionals were effectively dissuaded by law from assisting her as they risked being convicted. The Court reasoned that:

---

[13] See, for example, ECHR (GC), *Christine Goodwin* v. *United Kingdom*, 11 July 2002. In the *Goodwin* case, the Court refers to the claim as concerning an interest of the applicant (see e.g. para. 93). I choose to use the word 'interest' instead of 'right' in this chapter too, as it seems better suited when referring to one of many aspects of a more general right – in this case – the right to community living.

[14] ECHR, *Radio France* v. *France*, 30 March 2004, para. 31.

[15] The Court used the 'of course' method also in the case of *Chauvy and others* v. *France*: '[I]n the exercise of its European supervisory duties, the Court must verify whether the authorities struck a fair balance when protecting two values guaranteed by the Convention which may come into conflict with each other in this type of case, namely, on the one hand, freedom of expression protected by Article 10 and, on the other, the right of the persons attacked by the book to protect their reputation, a right which is protected by Article 8 of the Convention as part of the right to respect for private life.'

[16] One of the grounds for objection could be the fact that the drafters of the Convention had explicitly excluded the protection of reputation from the scope of Article 8. In these circumstances, the inclusion cannot be regarded as self-evident, and broader justification should have been given. 'Preparatory Work on Article 8 of the European Convention on Human Rights', Council of Europe, Strasbourg, 9 August 1956, paras. 7, *et seq.*, 1, 'Deletion of the words: "nor to attacks upon his honour and reputation"', available at http://www. echr.coe.int/library/colentravauxprep.html (last accessed 29 September 2011).

'[p]rivate life' incorporates the right to respect for both the decisions to become and not to become a parent (*Evans* v. *the United Kingdom* [GC], no. 6339/05, § 71, ECHR 2007-IV). The notion of a freedom implies some measure of choice as to its exercise. The notion of personal autonomy is a fundamental principle underlying the interpretation of the guarantees of Article 8 (cf. *Pretty* [v. *United Kingdom*]). Therefore the right concerning the decision to become a parent includes the right of choosing the circumstances of becoming a parent.[17]

If the Court were to use this method, it could reiterate that Article 8 grants rights to personal development,[18] to establish and develop relationships with other human beings and the outside world,[19] and the right to self-determination.[20] Furthermore, the Convention is to be interpreted and applied in a manner which renders its rights practical and effective, not theoretical and illusory.[21] That could lead the Court to conclude that the Article 8 rights mentioned above protect also the interest to treatment of mentally disabled persons in a community-based setting, when that is determined as appropriate by expert advice.

The third method is the one where broad considerations are made to include an interest under Article 8. The Court did so in the case of *Christine Goodwin* v. *United Kingdom*.[22] The case concerned the lack of legal recognition of the applicant's post-operative sex and the legal status of transsexuals in the United Kingdom. In previous similar cases, the Court had held that the refusal of the United Kingdom government to alter the register of births or to issue birth certificates whose contents and nature differed from those of the original entries concerning the recorded gender of the individual could not be considered as an interference with the right to respect for private life.[23] In the *Christine Goodwin* case, the Court recognised the interest of the applicant in obtaining legal recognition of her gender reassignment as falling within the scope of Article 8. In doing so, the Court paid attention to the applicant's situation noting the impact of State inaction on the person's daily life,[24] medical and scientific considerations,[25] international and European consensus,[26] and the Court also drew inspiration from other jurisdictions – the courts in Australia and New Zealand (see paragraph 91 of the rewritten judgment).[27]

---

[17] ECHR, *Ternovszky* v. *Hungary*, 14 December 2010, para. 22.
[18] ECHR, *Pretty* v. *United Kingdom*, 29 April 2002, para. 61.
[19] ECHR, *Niemietz* v. *Germany*, 16 December 1992, para. 29.
[20] ECHR, *Pretty* v. *United Kingdom*, 29 April 2002, para. 61.
[21] See ECHR, *Artico* v. *Italy*, 13 May 1980, para. 33.
[22] ECHR (GC), *Christine Goodwin* v. *United Kingdom*, 11 July 2002.
[23] See ECHR, *Rees* v. *United Kingdom*, 17 October 1986, para. 35, and ECHR, *Cossey* v. *United Kingdom*, 27 September 1990, para. 36.
[24] ECHR (GC), *Christine Goodwin* v. *United Kingdom*, 11 July 2002, paras. 76–80.
[25] *Ibid.*, paras. 81–3.   [26] *Ibid.*, paras. 84 and 85.   [27] *Ibid.*, paras. 56 and 84.

In the next sections, I will make use of the third method to include the interest to community-based treatment of mentally disabled persons under Article 8.

Protecting the interest to community-based treatment

Impact on a person's daily life

Ms Kolanis' statements when she claimed just satisfaction show the life situations she was not able to take part in and the different effects institutionalisation had on her. Testimonies of individuals in a similar situation to that of Ms Kolanis[28] attest to this impact on many crucial aspects of daily life, such as the ability to keep contact with relatives, to go shopping and choose one's own clothes, and to attend celebrations.[29] A statement of the American Psychiatric Association, which represents 36,000 American and international psychiatrists,[30] acknowledges the impact of institutionalisation on persons' daily lives: '[I]solations from community settings can have far-reaching effects in curtailing the life opportunities of individuals – including family relations, social contacts, work options, economic independence, educational advancement, and cultural enrichment.'[31] The Ad Hoc Expert Group on the Transition from Institutional Care to Community-Based Care[32] characterises institutional settings as involving de-personalisation, rigidity of routine, block treatment, social distance and paternalism.[33]

Taking into account the above-mentioned, the Court could be satisfied that institutional settings and community-based settings have different impacts on a person's autonomy, ability to participate in the life of the community and ability to perform daily life activities. And that the confinement of Ms Kolanis in a mental health hospital, which is an institutional setting, thus limited her daily life to a considerably greater extent as compared to living at

---

[28] See US Supreme Court, *Olmstead* v. *LC*, 527 US 581 (1999).

[29] See Atlanta Legal Aid Society, http://www.atlantalegalaid.org/impact.htm (last accessed 3 October 2011).

[30] See the official website of the American Psychiatric Association, http://www.psych.org (last accessed 6 January 2012).

[31] American Psychiatric Association, *amici curiae* in US Supreme Court, *Olmstead* v. *LC*, 527 US 581 (1999).

[32] The Ad Hoc Expert Group on the Transition from Institutional Care to Community-Based Care is a group of independent experts convened by the European Union Commissioner for Employment, Social Affairs and Equal Opportunities, Vladimír Špidla, in 2009 to address the issues of institutional care reform.

[33] Report of the Ad Hoc Expert Group on the Transition from Institutional Care to Community-Based Care (2009), available at http://ec.europa.eu/social/main.jsp?langId=en&catId=89&newsId=614&furtherNews=yes (last accessed 1 September 2011).

home or in a hostel, which were assigned to her by the MHRT and are community-based settings (see paragraph 92 of the rewritten judgment).

Medical and scientific considerations

Contemporary psychiatry has undergone major changes over the last fifty years which concern not only the development of certain research areas, new therapies, care settings and renewed legal frameworks, but its whole internal and institutional organisation.[34]

> At the beginning of the nineteenth century, psychiatry made its generalized appearance as a social and historical actor and established itself as a medical discipline through a set of legal, theoretical, and practical innovations centered on the key institution of the asylum. Paradoxical as it may seem from today's perspective, the birth of the asylum, which was then widely perceived as the symbol of an enlightened and progressive civilization that no longer ignored or maltreated its dependent mentally ill citizens, was also accompanied by a clear reformist spirit of nearly utopian traits and a broad consensus about the essential role of isolating the patient from the community in the work of recovery. One hundred and fifty years later, it was this very institution of the asylum and the practice of segregation that many mental health professionals and policy makers believed to be the most important obstacles to the realization of psychiatry's therapeutic commitments.[35]

However, it would not be true to say that institutional settings have to be abolished entirely. The American Psychiatric Association has stated:

> To say that the opportunity for community integration is generally an important personal and social good is not, of course, to say that it is the right result for everyone at all times. Some individuals, whether mentally retarded or mentally ill, are not prepared at particular times – perhaps in the short run, perhaps in the long run – for the risks and exposure of the less protective environment of community settings ... For such individuals, at such times, an institutional setting may be the best environment for care and treatment, often (though not always) for a temporary period leading to re-integration into community life ... Accordingly, an extreme position in either direction can be cruel and harmful to the individuals whose interests are at stake. On the one hand, isolation from community, when not justified by individuals' needs, is undoubtedly a serious

---

[34] H. L. Freeman (ed.), *A Century of Psychiatry* (London: Mosby-Harcourt, 1999), p. 234. On the history of psychiatry and community care, see also P. Bartlett and D. Wright, *Outside the Walls of the Asylum: The History of Care in the Community 1750-2000* (Athlone Press, 1999).

[35] Enric J. Novella, 'Mental Health Care and the Politics of Inclusion: A Social Systems Account of Psychiatric Deinstitutionalization' (2010) 31(6) *Theoretical Medicine and Bioethics* 411–27.

> deprivation for the individual ... On the other hand, relegation to the
> exposure of an insufficiently protective environment, when such protec-
> tion is needed, may be dangerous and destructive for the individual, as well
> as for society.[36]

The medical bases that support community-based care are found in medications used in psychiatry. The American Psychiatric Association has stated in
1999 that:

> [A]dvances in antipsychotic medications and in treatment programs have
> meant that most individuals who previously were institutionalized can be
> treated in community settings.[37]
>   For individuals able to manage the process, the ability to choose expo-
> sure to the world of opportunities that depend on community integration
> is invaluable. Indeed, in mental-health terms, the enhancement to such
> manageable opportunities is near the core of what treatment and 'habil-
> itation' are fundamentally designed to achieve.[38]

In the redrafted judgment, the Court takes into account the decades-long
advances in anti-psychotic medications and in treatment programmes which
have made it possible to treat mentally disabled persons in community-based
settings (paragraph 93 of the rewritten judgment).

International and European consensus

The care of mentally disabled persons in a community is one aspect of the right
to community living. Developments in international law concerning the right
to community living therefore could be of assistance to the Court. The Court
has previously stated that it will not interpret the Convention in a vacuum.[39]
Explaining in more detail its rules of interpretation, the Court has stated:

> In addition, the Court has never considered the provisions of the
> Convention as the sole framework of reference for the interpretation of
> the rights and freedoms enshrined therein. On the contrary, it must also
> take into account any relevant rules and principles of international law
> applicable in relations between the Contracting Parties.[40]

Article 19 of the United Nations Convention on the Rights of Persons with
Disabilities (CRPD) has already been described in the introduction of this
chapter. This legally binding provision describes the right to community living.
The CRPD has been signed by 153 States and ratified by 108 States. For
determining the European consensus, it should be noted that all Council of
Europe Member States, except Moldova, Switzerland and Liechtenstein, have

---

[36] American Psychiatric Association, *amici curiae* in US Supreme Court, *Olmstead* v. *LC*, 527
   US 581 (1999).
[37] *Ibid.*   [38] *Ibid.*   [39] ECHR, *Loizidou* v. *Turkey*, 18 December 1996.
[40] ECHR (GC), *Demir and Baykara* v. *Turkey*, 12 November 2008, para. 67.

signed the CRPD. Out of forty-four Council of Europe Member States who have signed the CRPD, twenty-nine have also ratified it. The European Union has also signed and ratified it.[41]

Now legally binding, Article 26 of the Charter of Fundamental Rights of the European Union states that:

> The Union recognises and respects the right of persons with disabilities to benefit from measures designed to ensure their independence, social and occupational integration and participation in the life of the community.[42]

Other documents that should be taken into account are the UN Standard Rules on the Equalization of Opportunities for Persons with Disabilities and the Council of Europe Committee of Ministers Recommendation to Member States concerning the protection of the human rights and dignity of persons with mental disorder. Both documents recognise the right to community living.[43]

There are other documents that show the decades-long international trend in mental health care. The Declaration of Caracas is aimed at promoting community-based health care in Latin America. It is stated there, *inter alia*,

---

[41] Data as at 27 December 2011. See signatures and ratifications at: http://www.un.org/ disabilities/countries.asp?navid=12&pid=166.

[42] Charter of Fundamental Rights of the European Union, Article 26, http://www.europarl. europa.eu/charter/pdf/text_en.pdf.

[43] The Council of Europe Committee of Ministers Recommendation to Member States concerning the protection of the human rights and dignity of persons with mental disorder provides: 'Article 8 – Persons with mental disorder should have the right to be cared for in the least restrictive environment available and with the least restrictive or intrusive treatment available, taking into account their health needs and the need to protect the safety of others. Article 9 – Facilities designed for the placement of persons with mental disorder should provide each such person, taking into account his or her state of health and the need to protect the safety of others, with an environment and living conditions as close as possible to those of persons of similar age, gender and culture in the community. Vocational rehabilitation measures to promote the integration of those persons in the community should also be provided. Article 10 – Health service provision Member States should, taking into account available resources, take measures: i. to provide a range of services of appropriate quality to meet the mental health needs of persons with mental disorder, taking into account the differing needs of different groups of such persons, and to ensure equitable access to such services; ii. to make alternatives to involuntary placement and to involuntary treatment as widely available as possible; iii. to ensure sufficient provision of hospital facilities with appropriate levels of security and of community-based services to meet the health needs of persons with mental disorder involved with the criminal justice system; iv. to ensure that the physical health care needs of persons with mental disorder are assessed and that they are provided with equitable access to services of appropriate quality to meet such needs.' The UN Standard Rules on the Equalization of Opportunities for Persons with Disabilities provides, at para. 26 of the Introduction: 'Persons with disabilities are members of society and have the right to remain within their local communities. They should receive the support they need within the ordinary structures of education, health, employment and social services.'

that the mental hospital, when it is the only mode of psychiatric care provided, creates unfavourable conditions that imperil the human and civil rights of patients.[44] In 1999, the Inter-American Convention on the Elimination of All Forms of Discrimination against Persons with Disabilities was adopted. The objectives of this convention are to prevent and eliminate all forms of discrimination against persons with mental or physical disabilities, and to promote their full integration into society. It is the first international convention that specifically addresses the rights of persons with mental disorders. In 2001, the Inter-American Human Rights Commission issued a Recommendation on the Promotion and Protection of Human Rights of Persons with Mental Disabilities, recommending that countries ratify this convention. The Recommendation also urges States to promote and implement, through legislation and national mental health plans, the organisation of community mental health services, in order to achieve the full integration of people with mental disorders into society.

Furthermore, in 2005 representatives of all Council of Europe Member States met in Helsinki, and developed and adopted the Mental Health Declaration for Europe.[45] In this declaration, the States note that many aspects of mental health policy and services are experiencing a transformation across the European region. Services are being provided in a wide range of community-based settings and no longer exclusively in isolated and large institutions. The States reaffirmed that this is the right and necessary direction, and took on the responsibility to develop community-based services to replace care in large institutions.[46] Still, it has to be noted that, even though there has been a marked decrease in long-term institutional care over the last few decades, the extent of these changes varies considerably, being far more pronounced in Western Europe than in Central and Eastern Europe (see paragraph 94 of the rewritten judgment).[47]

---

[44] The Declaration of Caracas, adopted in Caracas, Venezuela, on 14 November 1990 by the Conference on the Restructuring of Psychiatric Care in Latin America within the Local Health Systems convened by the Pan American Health Organization and the World Health Organization provides: '2. That the mental hospital, when it is the only mode of psychiatric care provided, hampers the fulfilment of the above-mentioned objectives in that it: a) isolates patients from their natural environment, thus generating greater social disability; b) creates unfavourable conditions that imperil the human and civil rights of patients.'

[45] World Health Organization, Mental Health Declaration for Europe (2005), available at http://www.euro.who.int/__data/assets/pdf_file/0008/96452/E87301.pdf (last accessed 5 January 2012).

[46] World Health Organization, Mental Health, 'Facing the Challenges, Building Solutions' (2005), pp. 10–11, available at http://www.euro.who.int/__data/assets/pdf_file/0008/96452/E87301.pdf (last accessed 5 January 2012).

[47] Report of the Ad Hoc Expert Group on the Transition from Institutional Care to Community-Based Care (2009), p. 10, available at http://ec.europa.eu/social/main.jsp?langId=en&catId=89&newsId=614&furtherNews=yes (last accessed 1 September 2011).

Concerning the newest statistical data regarding mental health, the World
Health Organization (WHO) has published the Mental Health Atlas 2011.[48] It
shows that, since 2005 (the year of the previous edition of the Mental Health
Atlas), State activity concerning the care of mentally disabled individuals and
community-based treatment has increased. Now, out of 184 States that submitted data, almost three-quarters (72 per cent) have a mental health plan,[49]
covering 95 per cent of the world's population. Among countries with a mental
health plan, three-quarters (76 per cent) report a shift of services and resources
from mental hospitals to community mental health facilities.[50]

Having regard to various international documents that concern the treatment of disabled people and bearing in mind the Convention, the Council of
Europe Committee of Ministers has stated that:

> We have moved from seeing the disabled person as a patient in need of care
> who does not contribute to society to seeing him/her as a person who needs
> the present barriers removed in order to take a rightful place as a fully
> participative member of society. Such barriers include attitudes and social,
> legal and environmental barriers. We therefore need to further facilitate
> the paradigm shift from the old medical model of disability to the social
> and human rights based model.[51]

Consequently, there has been a shift in many European countries to promote
active policies which empower the individual disabled person to control his or
her life.[52]

Taking into account these developments in international and European law
and policy, the Court could be satisfied that there exists a strong international
and European trend towards recognising the right to community living and the
interest of mentally disabled persons to be treated in a community-based setting
(see paragraphs 95 and 96 of the rewritten judgment).

In conclusion of the three-fold analysis for inclusions of the interest in
community-based care for mentally disabled persons, it can be stated that,

---

[48] World Health Organization, 'Mental Health Atlas 2011', available at http://whqlibdoc.
who.int/publications/2011/9799241564359_eng.pdf (last accessed 6 January 2012).

[49] Mental health plan: a detailed pre-formulated scheme that details the strategies and
activities that will be implemented to realise the objectives of the policy. It also specifies
other crucial elements such as the budget and timeframe for implementing strategies and
activities and specific targets that will be met. WHO, 'Mental Health Atlas 2011', p. 20.

[50] WHO, 'Mental Health Atlas', p. 20.

[51] Council of Europe Committee of Ministers, Recommendation Rec(2006)5 of the
Committee of Ministers to Member States on the Council of Europe Action Plan to
promote the rights and full participation of people with disabilities in society: improving
the quality of life of people with disabilities in Europe 2006–2015, available at http://www.
coe.int/t/e/social_cohesion/soc-sp/Rec_2006_5%20Disability%20Action%20Plan.pdf
(last accessed 5 January 2012).

[52] *Ibid.*

taking into account the impact of institutionalisation on the person's daily life, medical and scientific considerations, and international and European consensus, there exists a solid basis for the Court to be satisfied that, interpreting Convention rights in light of present-day conditions,[53] treatment of mentally disabled people in community-based settings – an aspect of the right to community living – forms part of a person's private life and is protected under Article 8 (see paragraph 97 of the rewritten judgment).

Conclusion

In the case of *Kolanis* v. *United Kingdom*, the Court was faced with a situation where a person was confined in hospital for more than a year after a mental health authority had determined her release and further treatment in a community-based setting. This chapter argued for inclusion of access to community care within the scope of Article 8.

This chapter argued that the Court should take into account advances in anti-psychotic medications and in treatment programmes that have meant that most individuals who previously were institutionalised can be treated in community settings.

By interpreting Article 8 in a way that would include access to community-based treatment, the Court would do justice to the concerns of mentally disabled persons, and put itself in line with present-day standards in the legal and political discourse in Council of Europe Member States. Consequently, it would enable mentally disabled people to enjoy due respect for their private lives, a sphere of utmost importance in human existence.

Ms Kolanis did not claim a violation of Article 8. I thus take on the possibility allowed in this rewriting exercise to imagine that an issue was raised under Article 8. I do it through an action from the Court's side, as it has the possibility to invoke an Article on its own motion.[54] The following paragraphs are a pure addition to the existing text of the judgment in the case of *Kolanis* v. *United Kingdom*.

Rewriting Kolanis v. United Kingdom

. . .

Alleged violation of Article 8 of the Convention

89. In respect of the applicant's allegation that she suffered loss of self-respect, loneliness, general effects of loss of liberty, and the loss of

---

[53] ECHR, *Tyrer* v. *United Kingdom*, 25 April 1978, para. 31.
[54] See, for example, ECHR, *Mółka* v. *Poland*, 11 April 2006.

opportunity to be with her relatives when her nephew died, the Court raises of its own motion a complaint under Article 8 of the Convention. This provision reads:

> 1. Everyone has the right to respect for his private and family life, his home and his correspondence.
>
> 2. There shall be no interference by a public authority with the exercise of this right except such as is in accordance with the law and is necessary in a democratic society in the interests of national security, public safety or the economic well-being of the country, for the prevention of disorder or crime, for the protection of health or morals, or for the protection of the rights and freedoms of others.

90. The Court reiterates that the notion of 'private life' within the meaning of Article 8 of the Convention is a broad concept which encompasses, *inter alia*, the right to establish and develop relationships with other human beings (see *Niemietz* v. *Germany*, 16 December 1992, § 29, Series A no. 251-B), the right to personal development (see *Bensaid* v. *United Kingdom*, no. 44599/98, § 47, ECHR 2001-I) and the right to self-determination as such (see *Pretty* v. *United Kingdom*, no. 2346/02, § 61, ECHR 2002-III).

91. To determine whether the issue falls within the sphere of private life and should be protected by the Convention, the Court will examine the applicant's situation noting the impact of the State's inaction on the person's daily life, medical and scientific considerations, and international and European consensus (see *Christine Goodwin* v. *United Kingdom* (GC), 11 July 2002, §§ 71–85).

92. Regarding the impact on the applicant's daily life, the Court notes that institutional settings and community-based settings have different impacts on a person's autonomy, ability to participate in the life of the community, and ability to perform daily life activities (see American Psychiatric Association, amici curiae in *Olmstead* v. *LC*, 527 US 581 (1999); see also the Report of the Ad Hoc Expert Group on the Transition from Institutional Care to Community-Based Care). The Court is satisfied that the confinement of the applicant in a mental health hospital limited her daily life to a considerably greater degree as compared to living at home or in a hostel, which were assigned to her by the MHRT and are community-based settings.

93. Regarding the medical and scientific aspects, the Court notes that advances in anti-psychotic medications and in treatment programmes have meant that most individuals who previously were institutionalised can today be treated in community settings (see American Psychiatric Association, amici curiae in *Olmstead* v. *LC*, 527 US 581 (1999)).

94. With regard to international and European consensus, the Court reiterates that the Convention is first and foremost a system for the protection of human rights, the Court must have regard to the changing conditions within the respondent State and within Contracting States generally and respond, for example, to any evolving convergence as to the standards to be achieved (see, amongst other authorities, *Stafford* v. *United Kingdom* [GC], no. 46295/99, judgment of 28 May 2002, ECHR 2002-, §§ 67–68). It is of crucial importance that the Convention is interpreted and applied in a manner which renders its rights practical and effective, not theoretical and illusory. A failure by the Court to maintain a dynamic and evolutive approach would indeed risk rendering it a bar to reform or improvement (see *Stafford* v. *United Kingdom*, judgment, § 68). Furthermore, the Court proposes to look at the situation within and outside the Contracting State to assess 'in the light of present-day conditions' what is now the appropriate interpretation and application of the Convention (see the *Tyrer* v. *United Kingdom*, judgment of 25 April 1978, Series A no. 26, § 31).

95. The Court notes the developments in international law regarding the recognition of the right to community living and community-based mental health care. The Court notes, in particular, the adoption of the UN Convention on the Rights of People with Disabilities in 2006, the Charter of Fundamental Rights of the European Union, the Inter-American Convention on the Elimination of All Forms of Discrimination against Persons with Disabilities, the Mental Health Declaration for Europe, the Declaration of Caracas, the UN Standard Rules on the Equalization of Opportunities for Persons with Disabilities, and the Council of Europe Committee of Ministers Recommendation to Member States concerning the protection of the human rights and dignity of persons with mental disorder.

96. Regarding the European consensus, the Court notes that, even though there has been a marked decrease in long-term institutional care over the last few decades, the extent of this development varies considerably, being far more pronounced in Western Europe than in Central and Eastern Europe (see the Report of the Ad Hoc Expert Group on the Transition from Institutional Care to Community-Based Care). However, the developments in national mental health policies (see Recommendation Rec(2006)5 of the Committee of Ministers to Member States on the Council of Europe Action Plan to promote the rights and full participation of people with disabilities in society: improving the quality of life of people with disabilities in Europe 2006–2015), and international commitments of the Council of Europe Member States (see signatures and ratifications of the UN Convention on the Rights of

People with Disabilities; see also the Mental Health Declaration for Europe) lead the Court to acknowledge that there exists a strong tendency among the Member States towards recognising the treatment of mentally disabled individuals in community-based settings.

97. Taking into account restrictions posed on the exercise of persons' daily life by institutional mental health settings, advancements in mental health care, and the strong international and European trend to recognize the right to community living and to commit to develop community-based mental health settings, the Court is satisfied that the interest of mentally disabled individuals to be treated in community-based settings falls within the scope of the right to protection of a person's private life under Article 8.

PART VI

Cultural minorities

16

Minority marriage and discrimination: redrafting Muñoz Díaz v. Spain

EDUARDO J. RUIZ VIEYTEZ

Introduction

The case of *Muñoz Díaz* v. *Spain*[1] in part concerns the situation of the most vulnerable minority in Europe: the Roma ethnic community. The Roma people constitute a traditional minority in Europe who have suffered from significant shortcomings in legal protection at both the legislative and judicial levels. In this context, the recognition of traditional Roma marriage customs within the European legal order is relevant to the analysis of this particular case. Because the ethnic component is the least-considered aspect of the case, the rationale of the European Court of Human Rights (hereinafter 'the Court' or 'the Strasbourg Court') becomes a particularly important issue for analysis, even more so than the final outcome of the judgment. The approach adopted by the Court appears to reference a more general idea of equality, or equity, paying relatively little attention to the minority status of the applicant. This approach is one of the main reasons for proposing a redrafting of this particular judgment. The case may be influential in the field of minority law, limiting some of the potentialities arising from the recent evolution of this particular field of human rights law, in particular when it is analysed together with the new trends in the field of anti-discrimination law.[2] A strict reading of the case as decided by the Court may lead to a significant restriction of a more pluralistic interpretation of the Convention rights, in particular with respect to traditional European minorities. Within the present context of the increasing cultural diversity in European societies, the adequate development of anti-discrimination tools is necessary to address conflicts arising from the cultural affiliations of the citizens involved. Therefore, this case offers an opportunity to redraft a judgment from a more inclusive and pluralistic perspective that emphasises the right not to be discriminated against, thereby introducing or promoting a more intensive, pro-minority approach to a relatively recent case. It is my opinion that the case

---

[1] ECHR, *Muñoz Diaz* v. *Spain*, 8 December 2009 (Application no. 49151/07).
[2] We refer in particular to the progressive acceptance of concepts like indirect discrimination or discrimination as a result of non-differentiation.

could have been handled by the Court from a more sensible, pro-diversity perspective. To substantiate this proactive approach, the Court could have referred to specific concepts in the field of anti-discrimination law, granting a more central and active role to the applicant's ethnic condition in its reasoning. This is the main perspective I advocate for in this chapter.

In addition, the case is relevant because of its importance for the fate of the Roma community. It can be considered the most recent significant decision of the Court concerning the rights of members of this traditional minority and, therefore, the judgment illuminates a particular path for the future interpretation of the Convention rights of Roma people. The importance of this case is illustrated by the great anticipation that the judgment provoked, not only in the country directly involved but in a much wider area, including significant coverage by the European media.

Within this chapter, I first describe the basic facts shaping the case, followed by a description of the position adopted by the Court. I then describe other possible lines of reasoning that the Court could have adopted from a pro-diversity perspective. Finally, I draw some conclusions before redrafting some key paragraphs of the judgment.

The case

The present case was brought before the Court by a female Spanish national, Maria Luisa Muñoz, born in 1956, who is a member of the Roma ethnic community. She alleged that a violation of Article 14 (the prohibition of discrimination) had occurred in conjunction with Article 1 of Protocol 1 (the protection of property), as well as a violation of Article 14 in conjunction with Article 12 (the right to marry). The basis for these allegations was the refusal of the Spanish authorities to grant her a survivor's pension from Spanish social security. In the applicant's view, she had the right to receive the pension that is provided to the widows of workers who contributed to Spanish social security over a number of years. The applicant defined her own civil status as that of the widow of 'MD'; she and MD, who was also a member of the Roma community, married in 1971 according to the traditional rituals of their ethnic group. However, from the perspective of the Spanish authorities, Ms Muñoz had not legally married because the Roma form of marriage was not and is still not recognised by the Spanish legal system. Consequently, Ms Muñoz was not entitled to a pension, which can only be assigned after previously achieving legally recognised married status.

At the time of Ms Muñoz's marriage to MD, Spanish legislation only admitted a religious, Catholic marriage as valid unless the parties had declared public apostasy or shown evidence of belonging to a different faith. In this case, it would only be possible to celebrate a marriage according to the Civil Code. In the current legal system, Spain permits civil marriage for everyone and recognises the civil effects of religious marriage performed according to the rituals of the religions that have signed an agreement with the Spanish State, namely, the Catholic, Evangelical, Islamic and Jewish religions. In no sense has Roma marriage been recognised as a valid marriage contract by Spain, although, from a sociological viewpoint, the members of this ethnic group recognise this kind of marriage and its consequences as valid within their own community.

It is relevant to this case that, although Roma ethnic marriages have never been legally recognised in Spain, Ms Muñoz and her husband received an official family book from the Spanish Civil Register, and their six children were registered as members of the family. Furthermore, the applicant and her family were granted first-category, large-family status by the Spanish authorities. Ms Muñoz was also named on her husband's social security card as the 'wife of the latter', with their six children mentioned in the same document. Ms Muñoz's husband died in 2000, and in 2001, she applied for a survivor's pension. This petition was rejected by the social security authorities on the basis that Ms Muñoz had not been married to the deceased, as required by Spanish legislation. This rejection was confirmed by a second administrative decision in the same year. Having exhausted her administrative appeals, the applicant filed a claim with the corresponding labour court. In 2002, this first-instance judicial authority recognised the right of Ms Muñoz to claim the pension on the basis that Roma ethnic marriages should be considered to have the same standing as civil marriages. However, this judicial decision was appealed by the Spanish social security board, and the Madrid Higher Court of Justice reversed the previous judgment, supporting the arguments of the administrative authorities.

The applicant then submitted an extraordinary '*amparo*' appeal before the Constitutional Court, alleging a violation of the principle of non-discrimination for reasons of racial and social condition.[3] However, the Constitutional Court dismissed the petition of the applicant in 2007, upholding the previous decision of the Higher Court of Justice, following a very formalistic approach to the situation and underlining the fact that the alleged marriage had no legal standing in the Spanish legal system.[4] According to the Constitutional Court, the relationship maintained by the applicant with her partner had to be seen as *more uxorio*.[5] Moreover, the Constitutional Court viewed the law requiring applicants to be formally married to gain access to a social security benefit as neutral from the ethnic point of view, invalidating the allegation of ethnic

---

[3] This extraordinary appeal may be filed exclusively on the grounds of a violation of the fundamental constitutional rights, namely, those proclaimed in Articles 14–29 of the Spanish Constitution. Article 14 of the Constitution includes the non-discrimination clause.

[4] Constitutional Court Judgment 69/2007 of 16 April 2007.

[5] *More uxorio* means a kind of cohabitation which is *de facto* analogous to marriage. The Latin term only refers to the female part of the couple (*uxor* = wife, married woman).

discrimination. Finally, the Constitutional Court strongly rejected the possibility of the doctrine of 'discrimination resulting from undifferentiated treatment' or a supposed right to different treatment. A dissenting opinion was appended to the judgment, referring to a previous case[6] concerning a survivor's pension for the widower of a civil servant. At that time, Ms Muñoz decided to bring her case before the European Court of Human Rights.

The judgment of the Court

According to the Court's case law, discrimination is defined as instituting different treatment, without an objective and reasonable justification, to persons in relevant similar situations.[7] In this regard, there is no objective and reasonable justification for a difference in treatment if it does not pursue a legitimate aim or if there is not a reasonable relationship of proportionality between the means employed and the intended aim.[8] In *Muñoz Díaz* v. *Spain*, the Court ruled that the refusal of the Spanish State to grant a survivor's pension constitutes discrimination because it implies an unreasonable, unjustified difference in treatment in situations that must be seen as equivalent. This discrimination occurs in light of Article 1 of Protocol 1 (the protection of property), in which access to a survivor's pension is the protected right. By contrast, the Court found no discrimination with respect to Article 12 (the right to marriage) because it recognises the margin of appreciation of the State to regulate the recognition of the civil effects of different kinds of marriage, considering that civil marriage is available to everyone with the same conditions.[9]

---

[6] Constitutional Court Judgment 199/2004 of 15 November 2004. In this case, the Constitutional Court had found a violation of the right to equality after finding that a marital relationship existed. However, a marriage did not legally exist because it had not been registered civilly; the parties had explicitly refused such registration of their marital relationship, which had been solemnised in a religious form. Unlike for Ms Muñoz, the Constitutional Court recognised an entitlement for the widower to receive a survivor's pension.

[7] See ECHR (GC), *DH and others* v. *Czech Republic*, 13 November 2007, para. 175, ECHR 2007-XII.

[8] See ECHR (GC), *Larkos* v. *Cyprus*, 18 February 1999, para. 29, ECHR 1999-I.

[9] A number of legal commentaries on the judgment have been published: R. Gaya Sicilia, 'El matrimonio gitano ante el Tribunal Europeo de Derechos Humanos: el caso Muñoz Díaz contra España (STEDH de 8 de diciembre de 2009)' (2010) 11 *Revista de Derecho (Universidad de Piura)* 539–51; C. Sánchez-Rodas Navarro, 'El Tribunal Europeo de Derechos Humanos y la pensión de viudedad en caso de unión celebrada conforme al rito gitano' (2009) 18 *Aranzadi Social*; B. Arp, 'La protección de la minoría romaní: Comentario al asunto Muñoz Díaz c. España, resuelto por el TEDH con sentencia de 8 de diciembre de 2009' (2010) 21 *Revista General de Derecho Europeo* 1–17; J. R. Bengoetxea, 'Diversidad Cultural y Diversidad de Derecho: una difícil relación', in E. Ruiz Vieytez and G. Urrutia Asua (eds.), *Derechos humanos en contextos multiculturales: ¿acomodo de derechos o derechos de acomodo?* (San Sebastián: Alberdania, 2010), pp. 163–80. See also note 20.

In principle, the prohibition of discrimination does not prevent Member States from introducing general policy schemes by way of legislative measures, whereby a certain category or group of individuals is treated differently from others, provided that the difference in treatment that results from being a member of a group can be justified under the Convention and its Protocols.[10] However, in deliberating on Ms Muñoz's application, the Strasbourg Court took into consideration three previous cases decided by the Spanish Constitutional Court in a significantly different way. The first comparison case is that of a valid religious marriage that could not be performed because a previous divorce was not legally possible. Thus, the Constitutional Court judgment no. 260/1988, among others, concerned entitlement to a survivor's pension when canonical marriage had not been possible because of the impossibility of a previous divorce.[11] A second situation arises in the Constitutional Court judgment no. 180/2001 that recognised the right to compensation for the death of a partner when a canonical marriage had not been possible on account of a conscience conflict, being (religious) marriage against the couple's beliefs (before the legislative amendment of 1981), that is to say, when a canonical marriage was not a valid option due to the conflict between freedom of conscience and the legal obligation to follow Catholic marriage rites except in cases of apostasy in accordance with the Spanish legislation in force before 1981.[12]

A third domestic case valid for comparison with *Muñoz Diaz* involves a valid religious marriage that had no civil standing because it had not been registered in the Civil Register.[13] Thus, the Constitutional Court recognised in its judgment no. 199/2004 a survivor's pension entitlement in the event of a canonical marriage where the statutory requirements were not met, because the parties had voluntarily omitted to register it in the Civil Register.

Using these domestic precedents as comparison references, the Strasbourg Court found no valid justification for the different treatment Ms Muñoz received, particularly in relation to the case decided by the Spanish Constitutional Court in its judgment no. 199/2004. The Court noted that, in the previous cases, unlike in Ms Muñoz's case, the Spanish authorities recognised the survivor's right to a pension. For the Strasbourg Court, these precedents are sufficient for establishing that the non-discrimination clause was violated, in the sense that Ms Muñoz was in a comparable situation. According to this premise, she received different treatment without being given a reasonable justification for the difference, and thus, she suffered discrimination.

---

[10] See ECHR (GC), *Ždanoka* v. *Latvia*, 16 March 2003, para. 112, ECHR 2006-IV.
[11] Constitutional Court Judgment 260/1988 of 22 December 1988; and Constitutional Court Judgment 155/1998 of 13 June 1998.
[12] Constitutional Court Judgment 180/2001 of 17 September 2001.
[13] Constitutional Court Judgment 199/2004 of 15 November 2004.

The arguments of the judgment concerning the ethnic identity of the appellant, contained primarily in paragraphs 56, 59 and 61, are not as relevant as they may seem at first glance. In these paragraphs, the Court underlines the importance of the fact that the applicant belongs to the Roma community, 'a community which has its own values that are well established and deeply rooted in Spanish society' (see paragraph 56), and acknowledges the vulnerable position of Roma, which calls for special consideration of their needs to be incorporated at both the regulatory and particular decision levels (paragraph 61). However, these arguments do not play a decisive role in the final outcome of the judgment. The Court would most likely have reached the same conclusion had the claim not been brought by a Roma person. Obviously, the fact that Ms Muñoz married in the Roma tradition is relevant, but only to the extent that it implies the factual quasi-impossibility of engaging in a civil marriage contract at the time (1971), when predominantly Catholic marriages were recognised by the Spanish State aside from cases of apostasy. This is why, in the analysis of the present case, it is not particularly relevant to allude to previous cases, such as *Chapman* v. *United Kingdom*[14] and *DH and others* v. *Czech Republic*,[15] in which the ethnicity (Roma) of the applicants was an important factor in the Court's reasoning (see paragraph 66 of the redraft).

In *Muñoz Diaz*, the central point for the Court is that the appellant engaged in a *de facto* marital relationship in good faith. In this respect, the case is similar to that of *Şerife Yiğit* v. *Turkey*,[16] although the latter was decided one year later and is considered to be substantially different by the Court, in particular with regard to proportionality.[17] The belief of Ms Muñoz was that her marriage had been considered valid by the Spanish authorities, and this belief was supported by these authorities' behaviour as if, at least implicitly, they recognised the full effects of that assumed marriage during her husband's lifetime. As opposed to the case decided in the aforementioned judgment no. 199/2004 of the Spanish Constitutional Court, the Strasbourg Court found no reasonable justification for an official negative response because in both cases (*Muñoz Diaz* and the case decided by the Spanish Constitutional Court in judgment no. 199/2004), the alleged marriage lacked official recognition as a result of not having complied with all of the legal requirements of civil law. Therefore, the less formalistic approach taken by the Spanish authorities in judgment no. 199/2004 should have been maintained in the particular case of Ms Muñoz unless the State could produce a clear justification for a different outcome. The Court insisted on the specific circumstances of the case and on the fact that the applicant's belief had been reinforced by the Spanish authorities' behaviour. This fact, and not her ethnicity, seems to be crucial to the final decision of the Court.

[14] ECHR (GC), *Chapman* v. *United Kingdom*, 18 January 2001.
[15] ECHR (GC), *DH and others* v. *Czech Republic*, 13 November 2007.
[16] ECHR (GC), *Şerife Yiğit* v. *Turkey*, 2 November 2010.   [17] *Ibid.*, paras. 85 and 86.

Therefore, this *ratio decidendi* by no means implies that the Strasbourg Court is seeking the general recognition of Roma marriage as a valid legal contract, even as it specifically concerns Spanish territory. For this case, the Court uses a line of reasoning that is based on the general principle of discrimination derived from a comparison with the treatments given in what it considers to be similar situations. Nevertheless, in this reasoning, the ethnic affiliation of the applicant is not, as mentioned above, particularly relevant. Also playing an important role in the Court's decision is the specific regulation of marriage that existed in Spain during the pre-democratic period, by which marriages had to be celebrated in accordance with the Catholic tradition unless extremely severe conditions were met (including the explicit renunciation of the Catholic faith by both partners). This fact, along with the recognition in the Spanish legal system of the legal standing of a plurality of forms of marriage (including multiple religious forms and the civil form), constitutes the main difference between this case and *Şerife Yiğit*. In the latter, according to Turkish legislation, only one marriage tradition (the one prescribed in the Civil Code) is legally recognised. In any case, the appellant's minority status can hardly be considered central to the *Muñoz Diaz* judgment based on this combination of factors.[18]

Alternative interpretations of the case from a diversity perspective

As outlined above, the Strasbourg Court's case was decided on the basis of the principle of non-discrimination. In this chapter, I explore other possible interpretations of the case from an active, diversity-sensitive approach and through an examination of the principle of non-discrimination. In this particular case, it is important to underline the applicant's status as a member of a significant and traditional ethnic or cultural minority. Two different resolutions can be imagined for this case. One could consider whether it is possible to defend the formal recognition of Roma marriage as a valid form of the marriage contract according to human rights standards. In this sense, Articles 8 or 12, for example, could be used as a legal basis to justify the need for the validation of Roma marriage customs, which would be the more progressive or open-minded alternative. However, one could also consider whether the applicant was discriminated against not only in comparison with previous specific cases but also because of her specific status as a Roma, a member of a particular minority. I view this second option to be easier to defend, and the final resolution of the case would remain the same as the resolution decided by the Court: a violation of Article 14

---

[18] On the legal relevance of the ethnic status of Roma citizens, see J. Kusters, 'Criminalising Romani Culture through Law', in M. C. Foblets and A. Renteln (eds.), *Multicultural Jurisprudence: Comparative Perspective on the Cultural Defense* (Oxford and Portland, OR: Hart Publishing, 2009), pp. 199–228.

in relation to Article 1 of Protocol 1. This option would make it unnecessary to find additional violations with respect to other Convention Articles.

A double solution arises within the first option for defending a legal validation of Roma marriage. It would be radical and far-reaching to argue for the general recognition of Roma marriage across Europe, considering the role of the Roma in the traditional cultural heritage of the continent and understanding Roma marriage as an expression of the particular lifestyle of this deeply rooted European minority. Under this scenario, European States would be obliged to make changes to their respective laws or legal interpretations to recognise a particular form of marriage widely practised all over the continent by a significant and historical minority. This option, although reasonable from a doctrinal perspective, strays too far from what is realistically possible when interpreting current Convention rights. More importantly, this solution would certainly provoke a degree of social alarm in many countries. As an alternative interpretation, I will only introduce the recognition of the legal status of Roma marriage in the affected country, Spain. The argument for this possible outcome would be based on discrimination because no State is in principle obliged to recognise the civil effects of non-civil marriages.[19] I stress the point of introducing a minority–minority comparison approach within a particular nation's legislation.

My main proposal is the second option, which is to modify the reasoning of the Court without changing the final outcome of the case. I will concentrate on the Court's interpretation based on ethnic discrimination. In redrafting this judgment, I consider that there are two ways of reasoning: one based on recognition of discrimination as a result of non-differentiation and a second based on indirect discrimination.[20] I will develop three alternatives to the Court's reasoning; they are not necessarily complementary. Each alternative may be presented individually in a potential judgment, and, obviously, the alternatives that do not require a modification of the outcome appear more

---

[19] This is why I would not find *Şerife Yiğit* v. *Turkey* relevant for comparison with *Muñoz Diaz*. When arguing for the discriminatory effect of recognising the legal status of some forms of marriage and not others, the comparison with the Turkish system becomes irrelevant. It is only useful from the perspective of the expectation in a *de facto* marital relationship of the social benefits of a fully recognised marriage. On this point, the proportionality analysis is critical in comparing the cases. In any case, *Şerife Yiğit* v. *Turkey* would affect the reasoning of what I call the A alternative if we could justify discrimination based on undifferentiated treatment in the aforementioned case.

[20] Very similar arguments were proposed by Professor Fernando Rey in his brilliant commentary on the judgment. F. Rey Martínez, 'La Sentencia del Tribunal Europeo de Derechos Humanos de 8 de diciembre de 2009, asunto "Muñoz Díaz v. España": ¿Un caso de igualdad en general o de discriminación étnica en particular?', *La Ley*, 7344 (2010). I express my gratitude to Professor Rey for his valuable comments and suggestions during the process of drafting this chapter.

viable than the alternative that does require such a modification. The three proposals are as follows:

(1) Alternative rationale without modifying the outcome (the violation of Article 14 in conjunction with Article 1 of Protocol 1):

 (A) Option A: discrimination resulting from undifferentiated treatment;
 (B) Option B: indirect discrimination.

(2) Alternative rationale modifying the final outcome (the violation of Article 14 in conjunction with Article 12):

 (C) Option C: discrimination in relation to the right to marry.

In relation to the submissions of the parties, only reasoning pertaining to Option A was effectively used by the applicant and partially by the Unión Romaní, acting as *amicus curiae*. Options B and C do not clearly appear in the formulations of the parties. The allegations of the violation of Article 14 in conjunction with Article 12 were primarily based on the historical establishment of Roma marriage within Spanish society, with both the applicant and the Unión Romaní arguing that the non-recognition under Spanish law of Roma rites as a form of the expression of consent to marry entailed a violation of the Convention. The applicant also refers to minority religious rites as a point of comparison with Roma marriage. Therefore, the reasoning that follows only partly reflects the main allegations made by the applicant. In particular, Option B constitutes an additional line of reasoning that the judgment and the parties' allegations could have adopted.

Discrimination resulting from undifferentiated treatment

As we know from the Court's settled case law, the right to not be discriminated against as guaranteed under the Convention is also violated when States, without an objective and reasonable justification, fail to provide different treatment for persons whose situations are significantly different[21] (see paragraph 63 of the redraft). The *Muñoz Diaz* case could have been addressed from this perspective because the Spanish authorities gave the same treatment concerning a particular welfare benefit (survivor's pension) to any person not fulfilling one particular condition: having maintained a marital relation legalised in accordance with the regulation on marriages contained in the Civil Code. Therefore, all couples not legally married in accordance with this regulation are treated in the same manner: they are denied the right to receive a survivor's pension (according to the previous Spanish legislation), regardless of the reasons that prompted them to fail to legally formalise their familial relations or presumed marriages (see paragraph 64 of the rewritten judgment).

[21] See ECHR (GC), *Thlimmenos v. Greece*, 6 April 2000, para. 44, ECHR 2000-IV.

In other cases, those couples who did not have a valid marriage according to the regulations of civil law were also denied the benefits of the survivor's pension. The same policy was applied by the Spanish authorities to the applicant's case on the ground that her marriage was not formally legal. From this perspective, the Court could have applied its '*Thlimmenos* judgment doctrine' to reach a similar conclusion but with more significant consequences. The Court could have considered that the reason the applicant (and possibly many other Roma couples) had not been married in conformity with Spanish civil legislation differed substantially from the reasons of many other couples. From this case, however, we know that Ms Muñoz believed in good faith that her marriage was legally effective. It is likely that the same perception is shared by many other Roma individuals in similar situations. Even if this misperception was not an issue, their membership in a deeply rooted cultural-ethnic minority group would be a relevant factor to consider when determining whether absolute equal treatment may constitute discrimination in this context.

Many members of the Roma community, because they are part of this minority group, and precisely because they need to conduct their lives in accordance with their own way of life and social rules, prefer to marry following the Roma ritual. As representatives of the Unión Romaní confirm, Roma marriage, for most members of the community, does not differ from any other type of marriage: 'Roma marriage exists when a man and a woman express their intention to live together and their desire to found a family' (see paragraph 41). The applicant's marriage was void not because she wanted it to be so but because she believed in good faith that her traditional Roma marriage was a valid marriage. Hence, the reason Ms Muñoz and MD were not married in accordance with the statutory regulations of the Civil Code is substantially different from the reasons cited by many other *de facto* couples who have freely and consciously decided not to formally marry (see paragraph 64 of the redraft).

The Court also gives legitimacy to these considerations by alluding to the Framework Convention for the Protection of National Minorities[22] and the emerging consensus on the need for protecting the identity and lifestyle of minorities, which add important value to the whole community (see paragraph 60). In this respect, the Court maintains that belonging to a minority does not create an exemption from complying with marriage laws. However, minority status may have an effect on the manner in which those laws are applied (see paragraph 61), a statement that is crucial to justifying this particular approach.

---

[22] Framework Convention for the Protection of National Minorities, signed in Strasbourg on 1 February 1995. Spain signed the Convention on the day that it was opened for signature and ratified it on 1 September 1995. The Convention entered into force in Spain on 1 February 1998.

Briefly, the reason many Roma couples are not married in accordance with the Spanish Civil Code has to do with the specific culture and way of life of this minority group. Therefore, this reason cannot be compared to, or considered under the same light as the reasons of those who do not want to be formally married, even if these couples maintain a permanent monogamous relationship with their respective partners. From this perspective, members of the Roma community who are married according to their own rituals should not be treated in the same way as those who opt for a non-formalised relationship, at least when applying for social benefits such as survivors' pensions. When international standards, such as the Framework Convention for the Protection of National Minorities, ask the parties to adopt positive measures to protect the way of life of their respective national minorities, they are suggesting the possibility of different treatment in situations when the reason for the inequality lies in the specific culture of a particular well-established group.[23]

From the doctrine of the Spanish Constitutional Court, it is clear that this complementary interpretation of the non-discrimination clauses has not been heeded in the Spanish legal system. As the Constitutional Court indicated, there is no right to different treatment within the right to equal protection in Article 14 of the Spanish Constitution. This view is obviously shared by the Spanish government, which did not even insist on this comparison. However, from the perspective of the ECHR, the doctrine developed in the *Thlimmenos* case (as well as in a number of subsequent cases[24]) provides enough grounds to claim discrimination in some specific situations involving minorities, and it would have fit perfectly well in *Muñoz Diaz*.

Indirect discrimination

A second possible line of reasoning in the judgment, also leading to the same final decision, would be to consider indirect discrimination on the grounds of racial or ethnic features. If reasoning through discrimination as a result of non-differentiation was based on the comparison of Ms Muñoz's case with the cases

---

[23] See the Framework Convention for the Protection of National Minorities, Articles 4.2 and 5.1. See also United Nations, Human Rights Committee, General Comment No. 23: The Rights of Minorities (Art. 27), 8 April 1994, CCPR/C/21/Rev.1/Add.5, para. 9.

[24] Among others, see ECHR (GC), *Chapman v. United Kingdom*, 18 January 2001; ECHR (GC), *Beard v. United Kingdom*, 18 January 2001; ECHR (GC), *Jane Smith v. United Kingdom*, 18 January 2001; ECHR (GC), *Coster v. United Kingdom*, 18 January 2001; ECHR (GC), *Lee v. United Kingdom*, 18 January 2001; ECHR, *Fretté v. France*, 26 February 2002; ECHR, *Pretty v. United Kingdom*, 29 April 2002; ECHR, *Posti and Rakho v. Finland*, 24 September 2002; ECHR (GC), *Nachova and others v. Bulgaria*, 6 July 2005; ECHR (GC), *Stec and others v. United Kingdom*, 12 April 2006; ECHR, *Zeman v. Austria*, 29 June 2006; ECHR, *Snegon v. Slovakia*, 12 December 2006; ECHR, *Dobal v. Slovakia*, 12 December 2006.

of other couples who were not formally married, this reasoning involves comparing the situation of the applicant with the situations of other widows who were married in conformity with the Civil Code stipulations and requested the survivor's pension benefit (see paragraph 65 of the redraft).

The position of the Spanish government regarding this possibility is formalistic, denying any kind of direct or indirect discrimination against the Roma community's members. From this point of view, the statutory requirement that there must be a legal marital relationship for a survivor's pension entitlement to be valid does not amount to discrimination because it is equally applied to all citizens regardless of their ethnic identity. Moreover, the aforementioned statutory requirement is supposedly not based on ethnic grounds and, in principle, shows no link with the traditions, customs or habits of any particular group.

However, if a valid marriage is a prerequisite for granting a particular social benefit, such as the survivor's pension, the negative or prejudicial effect that this requirement may have on a particular group may lead to indirect discrimination even though the requirement itself is not discriminatory. Because the Roma community has its own marriage rituals, which its members follow to gain social recognition within their group, and because these rituals are not recognised as a valid form of marriage by the State, those Roma couples who are married exclusively following the Roma rituals may be discriminated against when requesting a survivor's pension (see paragraph 68 of the redraft). At the same time, the Roma form of marriage could also be considered an expression of the Roma community's right 'to family life in accordance with identity' that derives from Article 8. All of these reasons may explain why some members of this community do not legally marry: precisely because they are members of a cultural minority that is deeply rooted in Spanish society and has its own rituals with which to formalise marital relationships.[25]

From this perspective, Ms Muñoz was discriminated against because she is a Roma, but the gender perspective should also be considered in this particular case. Ethnicity plays a decisive role because the applicant was compelled to marry according to her community's culture; thus, she dismissed the legal path to marriage.[26] At the same time, this situation is much more likely to affect

---

[25] Recommendation 1203 (1993) of the Parliamentary Assembly on 'Gypsies in Europe' included the recognition that Gypsies, as one of the very few non-territorial minorities in Europe, 'need special protection'.

[26] United Nations International Convention on the Elimination of All Forms of Racial Discrimination of 7 March 1966, Article 1; Committee on the Elimination of Racial Discrimination, General Recommendation No. 14, 22 March 1993, on the definition of discrimination: 'A distinction is contrary to the Convention if it has either the purpose or the effect of impairing particular rights and freedoms. This is confirmed by the obligation placed upon States parties by article 2, paragraph 1 (c), to nullify any law or practice which has the effect of creating or perpetuating racial

women than men because the survivor's pension is justified in the traditional separation (and disparity) of social roles between men and women, with the latter being in charge of the care of the family. These considerations result in an explanation with two elements for discrimination in the particular case of *Muñoz Diaz*: gender and ethnic group membership create the possibility of intersectional discrimination, which is a kind of discrimination based on a combination of two or more factors. However, to qualify as intersectional discrimination, the adverse effects must rely on the individual's membership in two or more protected categories; that is, the discrimination must be premised on a combination of elements (in this case, ethnicity and gender) rather than on any one of them alone.[27] Although, in my view, this reading of intersectional discrimination can be defended in the case of *Muñoz Diaz*, we could also argue that the very fact of the applicant's ethnicity was already decisive of the indirect discrimination effect. At least theoretically, the same situation could also have affected a Roma man whose partner had contributed to social security during her working life. In this respect, the nature of the institution of a survivor's pension is decisive, and it seems more than reasonable to consider that this social benefit was based on the traditional separation of social roles between the two genders. Nevertheless, by adopting a more easily accepted perspective when redrafting the judgment, the concept of intersectional discrimination will not be introduced within the proposed text, and I will limit the alternative reasoning to the indirect discrimination suffered by Ms Muñoz on the basis of her ethnicity.

Discrimination in relation to the right to marriage

Article 12 secures the fundamental right of a man and woman to marry and to found a family. The exercise of this right is subject to the national laws of the Contracting States, but the limitations thereby introduced must not restrict or reduce the right in such a way or to such an extent that the essence of the right is

discrimination ... In seeking to determine whether an action has an effect contrary to the Convention, [the Committee] will look to see whether that action has an unjustifiable disparate impact upon a group distinguished by race, colour, descent, or national or ethnic origin.'

27 On intersectional discrimination, see L. L. M. Makkonen, *Multiple, Compound and Intersectional Discrimination: Bringing the Experiences of the Most Marginalized to the Fore* (Institute for Human Rights, Abo Akademi, 2002); M. Verloo, 'Multiple Inequalities, Intersectionality and the European Union' (2006) 13(3) *European Journal of Women's Studies* 211–28; F. Rey Martínez, 'La discriminación múltiple, una realidad antigua, un concepto nuevo' (2008) 84 *Revista Española de Derecho Constitucional* 251–83; E. Grabham, D. Cooper, J. Krishnadas and D. Herman (eds.), *Intersectionality and Beyond: Law, Power and the Politics of Location* (Routledge-Cavendish, 2009); D. Morondo Taramundi, 'Un caffè da Starbucks: Intersezionalità e disgregazione del soggetto nella sfida al diritto antidiscriminatorio' (2011) 2 *Ragion Pratica* 365–83.

impaired (see paragraph 78). In the case of Spain, it is clear that civil marriage is also open to the Roma people under the same conditions of equality as to persons not belonging to that minority. However, at the same time, some other rituals of marriage (Catholic, Protestant, Jewish and Islamic) are given official recognition by the State in a scheme that the Spanish government considers to be within the purview of the national legislature (see paragraph 80 of the redraft).

In principle, Articles 12 and 14 cannot be interpreted as obliging a State to accept a particular form of expression of consent to marry purely on account of a community's social roots or traditions. It is, therefore, not contrary to Article 12 for a State to impose particular formalities for the expression of such consent (see paragraph 80*bis* of the redraft) or to restrict the recognition of particular ways of marriage. However, this approach ignores the fact that, in this case, the applicant's lifestyle as a Roma person widens the scope of Article 12 with regard to other Convention rights (namely, Article 8).[28] Belonging to a historically rooted minority is a relevant factor in the interpretation of certain Convention rights and the subsequent obligations of the State before them. In addition, the specific situation of this minority must be taken into consideration in the application of the different Articles of the Convention. In this case, I submit that the applicant's belonging to a historical minority group imposes a positive obligation on the part of the authorities to ensure that members of this group can enjoy their right to marry, as well as their private and family life, in accordance with their traditional lifestyle. In this respect, it is relevant to restate the historically weak and vulnerable condition of the Roma people, which the Court has recognised in previous cases[29] (see paragraph 80 of the redraft).

Within this context, the fact that Spain recognises certain religious groups' alternative rituals to the civil form of marriage has to be seen as a relevant element for comparison. Indeed, the Spanish legal framework does not recognise a unique ritual or form of marriage (e.g. civil marriage), but all religious marriages of those faiths that have some social rooting in Spanish society and that have signed a specific agreement with the State, which are presently the Catholic, Evangelical, Islamic and Jewish faiths.[30] However, because Roma marriage is not recognised or incorporated into the legal system, many Roma couples may be deterred from following other civil or religious rituals that are

---

[28] See ECHR (GC), *Chapman v. United Kingdom*, 18 January 2001, para. 96, ECHR 2001-I, Joint Dissenting Opinion of Judges Pastor Ridruejo, Bonello, Tulkens, Stráznická, Lorenzen, Fischbach and Casadevall, p. 8.

[29] Parliamentary Assembly of the Council of Europe: Recommendation No. 1203 (1993) on 'Gypsies in Europe' and Recommendation No. 1557 (2002) on 'The legal situation of Roma in Europe'.

[30] Agreement of the Spanish Kingdom with the Holy See (Concordat of 1979); Agreement with the Evangelical Federation under Law No. 24/1992 of 10 November 1992; Agreement with the Islamic Commission under Law No. 26/1992 of 10 November 1992; Agreement with the Jewish Federation under Law No. 25/1992 of 10 November 1992.

the only officially recognised ways to marry according to Spanish legislation. Some Roma people may regard these 'official' ways of marrying as incompatible with their own ethnic or cultural identity. It is particularly relevant to note that the Roma community enjoys a significantly long tradition in Spain and is more far-reaching in numerical and social terms than some of the officially recognised religious communities.[31] In fact, Roma marriage has existed in Spain for several centuries (see paragraphs 76 and 77 of the redraft).

Without contradicting any disposition of the Convention, Spain likely could have opted for restricting legal status to one particular form of marriage in accordance with the Civil Code. However, from the moment that Spain first recognised the civil status of some forms of religious marriage, it became necessary to consider whether this decision is made in a way that discriminates against any other minority group. This point is the main difference between our case and *Şerife Yiğit* v. *Turkey*,[32] which was decided by the Court one year after *Muñoz Diaz*. In the former, the argument concerned the validity and recognition of a religious (Muslim, therefore majority) marriage in Turkey, a country where only civil marriages are granted civil legal status. From this perspective, no discrimination *vis-à-vis* other minority marriages can be established in the Turkish case, even though Muslim marriage is widely performed in Turkey. The difference between this case and *Muñoz Diaz* is evident because the State's decision to recognise the status of a unique form of marriage open to everyone or to a plurality of the population falls within the margin of appreciation of each country. In this respect, Turkey was not adopting a discriminatory measure by giving legal status only to civil marriages. An opposite interpretation could also be defended but would deviate, in my view, too far from the existing standards.[33]

However, and unlike in the *Şerife Yiğit* case, the Spanish State has freely decided to recognise legal effects of other kinds of minority marriages. In this context, if different minorities are not treated in the same ways, and this difference cannot be justified on reasonable and proportional grounds, it is reasonable to assume discriminatory treatment against the Roma community, whose way of marriage is not validated, unlike the traditions of other minorities

---

[31] See R. Morán Martín, 'Los grupos gitanos en la historia de España', in J. M. Pérez-Prendes Muñoz de Arraco (ed.), *La violencia y los enfrentamientos de las culturas* (Madrid: Iustel, 2004), pp. 223–74; H. Sánchez Ortega, 'Los gitanos españoles desde su salida de la India hasta los primeros conflictos en la península, Espacio, tiempo y forma' (1994) 7 *Historia moderna* 319–54; J. B. Monleón, 'Apuntes para una historia gitana' (2003) 43 *I Tchatchipen: lil ada trin tchona rodipen romani – Revista trimestral de investigación gitana* 4–10; J. M. Aparicio Gervás, 'Breve recopilación sobre la historia del pueblo gitano: desde su salida del Punjab, hasta la Constitución Española de 1978. Veinte hitos sobre la "otra" historia de España' (2006) 55 *Revista interuniversitaria de formación del profesorado* 141–62.

[32] ECHR (GC), *Şerife Yiğit* v. *Turkey*, 2 November 2010.

[33] In *Şerife Yiğit*, the relevant Article is Article 8 (in addition to Article 14 in conjunction with Article 1 of Protocol 1), not Article 12 as in *Muñoz Diaz*.

which do not necessarily show a stronger social or historical rooting in the country. This reasoning would lead me, in this case, to the conclusion that a violation of Article 14 in relation to Article 12 has been committed. The fact that other minority marriages contain a religious element cannot be regarded as decisive because marriage constitutes the essence of a right in and of itself, and it does not necessarily imply a religious component. The relevant point from this perspective is in comparing the treatment given to other minorities and discovering the State's justification for the different treatment. This difference should be based on objective, reasonable and proportional criteria, and the religious or ethnic nature of a marriage does not seem to be sufficient when the social rooting and presence of the Roma community is at least as easily defended as that of other minor religious communities (see paragraph 80*bis* of the redraft).

This reasoning is very similar to that of the UN Human Rights Committee in the case *Waldman* v. *Canada*, adopted in 1999.[34] In the *Waldman* case, the Human Rights Committee reached the conclusion that discrimination had occurred by the refusal of the Ontario authorities to provide other religious minorities the same treatment given to (some of) the Catholic schools, whose protected situation had been foreseen at the constitutional convention of 1867. The fact that some specific rights had been constitutionalised (in this case, in favour of the Catholic minority in Ontario) did not prevent the Committee from viewing as discriminatory the fact that the authorities did not extend the same treatment to other minority groups (such as the Jewish community, to which the applicant belonged) living in comparable situations.

Conclusion

The European Court of Human Rights ruled in favour of the applicant in the *Muñoz Diaz* case by recognising a violation of Article 14 in conjunction with Article 1 of Protocol 1. Thus, the case had a positive outcome for the applicant, quashing the formalistic solution provided by the domestic courts. Nevertheless, the reasoning used by the Court is merely based on a general perception of discrimination, with little relevance given to the ethnic background of the applicant. This case offered a useful opportunity to develop clearer and more ambitious arguments, with the objective of advancing and defending a diversity or minority approach beyond the individual case by broadening the scope of what we understand about discrimination, and by detecting discrimination in the Spanish State's refusal to recognise Roma traditional marriage, unlike other religious forms of marriage practised by other minorities.

---

[34] United Nations Human Rights Committee case, *Waldman against Canada* (Communication no. 694/1996), CCPR/C/67/D/694/1996, Decision of 3 November 1999.

The final decision of the Court solved Ms Muñoz's particular problem fairly without giving rise to a broad application of the same reasoning to similar cases. However, the discourse of the Court will hardly be useful in handling cases that may share important similarities. It is obvious that a more minority-sensitive line of reasoning could have had important effects on the Roma community's situation, or at least on the recognition of the validity of Roma marriages. However, it seems that the Court was clearly determined not to engage in discussions that would consider further effects and was only willing to address the applicant's particular situation. Therefore, the present case can be considered, to some extent, as a missed opportunity in the necessary process of reinterpreting human rights (and, in particular, non-discrimination clauses) in accordance with the needs of culturally diverse societies. In this necessary process of pluralising the meaning of the rights provided by the Convention, giving more relevance within the reasoning of the Court to the applicant's membership in a minority group and the comparison to the treatment given to other minority groups may have been more productive.[35]

Rewriting Muñoz Díaz v. Spain

[As previously noted, the main alternative proposal corresponds to Part I of the rewritten judgment (violation of Article 14 in conjunction with Article 1 of Protocol 1); and the complementary justification of a possible violation of Article 14 in conjunction with Article 12 corresponds to Part II of the rewritten judgment.]

...

I. *Alleged violation of Article 14 of the Convention in conjunction with Article 1 of Protocol 1*

...

[35] On the complex relationship between the recognition of general human rights with cultural diversity, see the comprehensive analysis in R. Medda-Windischer, *Old and New Minorities: Reconciling Diversity and Cohesion: A Human Rights Model for Minority Integration* (Baden-Baden: Nomos-Eurac, 2009); M. C. Foblets and A. Rentlen (eds.), *Multicultural Jurisprudence: Comparative Perspective on the Cultural Defense* (Oxford and Portland, OR: Hart Publishing, 2009); M. Koening and P. Guchteneire (eds.), *Democracy and Human Rights in Multicultural Societies* (Aldershot: UNESCO Publishing/Ashgate, 2007); E. Ruiz Vieytez and R. Dunbar (eds.), *Human Rights and Diversity: New Challenges for Plural Societies* (Bilbao: Humanitarian Net, 2007).

3. Compliance with Article 14 of the Convention taken together with Article 1 of Protocol 1

(a) The Court's case law

47. According to the Court's established case law, discrimination means treating differently, without an objective and reasonable justification, persons in relevantly similar situations. The 'lack of objective and reasonable justification' means that the impugned difference in treatment does not pursue a 'legitimate aim' or that there is not a 'reasonable relationship of proportionality' between the means employed and the aim sought to be realised' (see *DH and others* v. *the Czech Republic* [GC], no. 57325/00, §§ 175 and 196, ECHR 2007-XII, with further references).

. . .

(b) Application of the case law to the present case

. . .

54. In view of the foregoing, the question arising in the present case is whether the fact that the applicant was denied the right to receive a survivor's pension reveals discriminatory treatment based on her affiliation to the Roma minority, in relation to the manner in which legislation and case law have treated similar situations where the persons concerned believed in good faith that they were married even though the marriage was not legally valid.

55. The applicant based her claim, firstly, on her conviction that her marriage, solemnised according to Roma rites and traditions, was valid, and secondly, on the conduct of the authorities, which had officially recognised her as the spouse of MD and had consequently accepted, in her submission, the validity of her marriage.

56. The Court takes the view that the two questions are closely linked. It observes that the domestic authorities did not deny that the applicant believed in good faith that she was really married. Her belief was all the more credible as the Spanish authorities had issued her with a number of official documents certifying her status as spouse of MD.

For the Court, it is necessary to emphasise the importance of the beliefs that the applicant derives from belonging to the Roma community – a community which has its own values that are well established and deeply rooted in Spanish society.

57. The Court observes, in the present case, that when the applicant got married in 1971 according to Roma rites and traditions, it was not possible in Spain, except by making a prior declaration of apostasy, to be married otherwise than in accordance with the canon-law rites of the Catholic Church. [Fragment deleted]

58. Admittedly, following the entry into force of the Spanish Constitution of 1978 and by virtue of Law no. 30/1981 of 7 July 1981 (paragraph 26 above), the applicant could have opted for a civil marriage. The applicant argued, however, that she believed in good faith that the marriage solemnised according to Roma rites and traditions produced all the effects inherent in the institution of marriage.

59. In order to assess the applicant's good faith the Court must take into consideration the fact that she belongs to a community within which the validity of the marriage, according to its own rites and traditions, has never been disputed or regarded as being contrary to public order by the Government or the domestic authorities, which even recognised in certain respects the applicant's status as spouse. The Court takes the view that the force of the collective beliefs of a community that is well-defined culturally cannot be ignored.

60. The Court observes in this connection that there is an emerging international consensus amongst the Contracting States of the Council of Europe recognising the special needs of minorities and an obligation to protect their security, identity and lifestyle (see paragraph 33 above, in particular the Framework Convention for the Protection of National Minorities), not only for the purpose of safeguarding the interests of the minorities themselves but to preserve a cultural diversity that is of value to the whole community (see *Chapman* v. *the United Kingdom* [GC], no. 27238/95, § 93, ECHR 2001-I).

61. The Court takes the view that, whilst the fact of belonging to a minority does not create an exemption from complying with marriage laws, it may have an effect on the manner in which those laws are applied. The Court has already had occasion to point out in the *Buckley* judgment (albeit in a different context), that the vulnerable position of Roma means that some special consideration should be given to their needs and their different lifestyle both in the relevant regulatory framework and in reaching decisions in particular cases (see *Buckley* v. *the United Kingdom*, 25 September 1996, §§ 76, 80 and 84, Reports 1996-IV; *Chapman*, cited above, § 96; and *Connors* v. *the United Kingdom*, no. 66746/01, § 84, 27 May 2004).

[Original paragraphs 62–8 deleted]

62. The Court notes that the law excluding unmarried persons from obtaining a survivor's pension (which was modified in Spain at a later date) did not distinguish between persons not being officially married as a result of the lack of recognition of their minority group's own marriage rituals and persons who (consciously) decided not to marry of their own free will. The applicant does not complain about the requirement to be married for gaining access to the right to receive a survivor's pension, but about the fact

that, in the application of the relevant law, no distinction is made between unmarried persons and persons married in accordance with the traditional rites of deeply rooted minorities. In this context, the Court notes that the applicant is a member of the Roma community, an ethnic or cultural group having its own institution of marriage. In essence, the applicant's argument states that she was treated like any other unmarried person without taking into consideration her conviction that the marriage rituals of her own minority group were equally valid.

63. The right to not be discriminated against in the enjoyment of rights guaranteed under the Convention is also violated when States, without an objective and reasonable justification, fail to treat persons differently whose situations are significantly different (see *Thlimmenos*, cited above, § 44). According to its case law, the Court will need to examine whether the failure to treat the applicant differently from other unmarried persons when asking to gain access to a survivor's pension pursued a legitimate aim. If it did, the Court will have to examine whether there was a reasonable relationship of proportionality between the means employed and the aim sought to be realised.

64. It is true that the authorities had no option under a formalistic approach to the law but to reject the applicant's request for the pension. However, this limitation cannot absolve the respondent State from responsibility under the Convention. The Court has never excluded the possibility that legislation may be found to be in direct breach of the Convention (see, *inter alia, Chassagnou and others* v. *France* [GC], nos. 25088/94, 28331/95 and 28443/95, ECHR 1999-III). In the present case, the Court considers that the State is engaging in discriminating behaviour when it is unable to treat differently those people married in accordance with traditional and rooted rituals in Spain in contrast with those who have not married by their own will or for other reasons. In fact, the reason why the applicant (and possibly many other Roma couples) had not been married in conformity with the Spanish civil legislation was significantly different from that of non-Roma couples.

As the representative of the Union Romani stated during the hearings, Roma marriage is, for many members of the community, not different from any other type of marriage. It should also be stated that the Spanish legal framework does not privilege one ritual or form of marriage (e.g. civil marriage) over another, but recognises the religious marriages of those confessions that enjoy some social rooting in Spanish society and have signed a specific agreement with the State. However, because Roma marriage is not recognised or incorporated into the legal system, many Roma couples are considered unmarried simply because they married exclusively through their own rituals. However, these Roma couples are pursuing the same goals as others in official marriages. This situation is very different from that of those who have opted to not marry or even from those marrying through rituals that cannot be considered either traditional or socially relevant in Spanish society. This demand for a different treatment in such a special situation is also supported by instruments such as the Framework Convention for the Protection of National Minorities, which asks the parties to adopt positive measures to protect the way of life of their respective national minorities.

65. Moreover, the refusal of the Spanish authorities to grant Ms Muñoz a survivor's pension may also be considered as an indirect form of discrimination in relation to the situation of other widows married in conformity with the Civil Code stipulations, who had lived in similar personal and social conditions as the applicant. Spanish regulation of the access to a survivor's pension that made being married a condition for receiving such a benefit may be considered neutral, not intending to discriminate against a particular group, e.g. the Roma community. However, this requirement, in fact, has a negative impact on a particular group: Roma widows married through their traditional cultural rites.

The Court reiterates that a difference in treatment is discriminatory if 'it has no objective and reasonable justification'; that is, if it does not pursue a 'legitimate aim' or if there is not a 'reasonable relationship of proportionality' between the means employed and the aim sought to be realised (see, among many other authorities, *Larkos* v. *Cyprus* [GC], no. 29515/95, § 29, ECHR 1999-I; and *Stec and others*, cited above, § 51). Where the difference in treatment is based on race, colour or ethnic origin, the notion of objective and reasonable justification must be interpreted as strictly as possible (see *DH and others* v. *Czech Republic* [GC], no. 57325/00, § 96, ECHR 2007-XII).

66. Racial discrimination is a particularly invidious kind of discrimination, even in its indirect ways, and, in view of its perilous consequences, requires special vigilance and a strong reaction from the authorities. As already noted, the vulnerable position of Roma members (widows, in this case) means that special consideration should be given to their needs and their different lifestyle, both in the relevant regulatory framework and in the consideration of particular cases (*Chapman* v. *United Kingdom* [GC], no. 27238/95, § 96, ECHR 2001-I; and *Connors* v. *United Kingdom*, no. 66746/01, § 84, 27 May 2004). In *Chapman* (cited above, §§ 93–94), the Court also observed that there could be said to be an emerging international consensus amongst the Contracting States of the Council of Europe recognising the special needs of minorities and an obligation to protect their security, identity and lifestyle, not only for the purpose of safeguarding the interests of the minorities themselves but to preserve a

cultural diversity of value to the whole community (see *DH and others v. Czech Republic* [GC], no. 57325/00, § 176, ECHR 2007-XII).

67. The Court has already accepted in previous cases that a difference in treatment may take the form of disproportionately prejudicial effects of a general policy or measure which, though couched in neutral terms, discriminates against a group (*Hugh Jordan* v. *United Kingdom*, no. 24746/94, 4 May 2001, § 154; and *Hoogendijk* v. *Netherlands* (dec.), no. 58461/00, 6 January 2005). In accordance with, for instance, Council Directives 97/80/EC and 2000/43/EC and the definition provided by ECRI, such a situation may amount to 'indirect discrimination', which does not necessarily require a discriminatory intent (see *DH and others v. Czech Republic* [GC], no. 57325/00, § 184, ECHR 2007-XII).

68. In the present case, the manner in which the legislation was applied in practice resulted in a disproportionate (negative) effect on the applicant because of her ethnic membership and the particular way of celebrating marriages in her community. The situation may have also affected other Roma widows in the same position, placing this group (Roma widows) at a significant disadvantage.

As it has been established that the relevant legislation (as applied in practice at the material time) had a disproportionately prejudicial effect on the Roma community members whose marriage was not recognised as valid by the legal order, the Court considers that the applicant, as a member of that community, necessarily suffered the same discriminatory treatment.

69. In [fragment deleted] view of the specific circumstances of the present case, the Court finds that it is disproportionate for the Spanish State, which issued the applicant and her Roma family with a family record book, granted them large-family status, afforded health-care assistance to her and her six children and collected social security contributions from her Roma husband for over nineteen years, now to refuse to recognise the effects of the Roma marriage when it comes to the survivor's pension.

70. Lastly, the Court cannot accept the Government's argument that it would have been sufficient for the applicant to enter into a civil marriage in order to obtain the pension claimed. The prohibition of discrimination enshrined in Article 14 of the Convention is meaningful only if, in each particular case, the applicant's personal situation in relation to the criteria listed in that provision is taken into account exactly as it stands. To proceed otherwise in dismissing the victim's claims on the ground that he or she could have avoided the discrimination by altering one of the factors in question – for example, by entering into a civil marriage – would render Article 14 devoid of substance.

71. Therefore, because it has been established that the relevant legislation may have a disproportionately prejudicial effect on the members of the Roma community, the Court considers that the applicant, as a member of that community, necessarily suffered the same discriminatory treatment. Consequently, the Court finds that in the present case there has been a violation of Article 14 of the Convention taken together with Article 1 of Protocol 1.

II.   Alleged violation of Article 14 in conjunction with
Article 12 of the Convention

. . .

79. The Court observes that civil marriage in Spain, as in force since 1981, is open to everyone, and takes the view that its regulation does not entail any discrimination on religious or other grounds. The same form of marriage, before a mayor, a magistrate or another designated public servant, applies to everyone without distinction. There is no requirement to declare one's religion or beliefs or to belong to a cultural, linguistic, ethnic or other group. **It is also true, however, that at the time Ms Muñoz married according to the Roma rites, only religious marriage existed in Spain and civil marriage was not possible except in cases of apostasy. The applicant, therefore, did not enjoy a non-discriminatory option for officially marrying. Moreover, her condition as member of the Roma community, in which she wanted to secure the full recognition and effects of her marriage, compelled her to use Roma rites because they were the only rites recognised by her community. The fact that the Spanish authorities (wrongly) seemed to recognise the full effects of her marriage probably caused the couple to believe they did not need to obtain a civil marriage after 1981, when the current legislation was adopted.**

80. [Fragment deleted] **The Court acknowledges** that certain religious forms of expression of consent are accepted under Spanish law. Those religious forms (Catholic, Protestant, Muslim and Jewish) are recognised by virtue of agreements with the State and thus produce the same effects as civil marriage, whereas other forms (religious or traditional) are not recognised. The Court observes, however, that, **according to the Spanish authorities**, this is a distinction derived from religious affiliation, which is not pertinent in the case of the Roma community. [Fragment deleted] **Civil marriage is open to the Roma people under the same conditions of equality as to persons not belonging to their community, and this scheme is considered by the Spanish government as a decision taken by the national legislature within its margin of appreciation.**

However, this approach ignores the fact that, in this case, the applicant's lifestyle as a Roma person widens the scope of Article 12, as it would happen with regard to other Convention rights (namely, Article 8). Article 12 of the Convention imposes a positive obligation on the part of authorities to ensure that the Roma people have a practical and effective opportunity to enjoy their right to marry as well as their private and family life, in accordance with their traditional lifestyle. Again, this Court reminds us that, as a result of their turbulent history and weak social condition, the Roma people have become a specific type of disadvantaged and vulnerable minority (see also the general observations in the Parliamentary Assembly's Recommendation No. 1203 (1993) on Gypsies in Europe, and point 4 of its Recommendation No. 1557 (2002), 'The Legal Situation of Roma in Europe'), that, as the Court has noted in previous cases, requires special protection. Therefore, their specific situation must be taken into consideration in the application of the different Articles of the Convention.

80*bis*. This Court agrees with the government's statement that Articles 12 and 14 of the Convention cannot be interpreted as obliging a State to accept a particular form of expression of consent to marry purely on account of a community's social roots or its traditions. It is, therefore, not contrary to Article 12 of the Convention for the State to impose particular formalities for the expression of such consent. Nevertheless, the fact that Spain recognises alternative rituals to the civil form of marriage of certain religious groups must also be considered as a relevant factor in the comparison. Spain recognises full civil effects of marriages held by those following the Catholic, Evangelical, Jewish and Muslim rituals. If the socially prominent presence of the Catholic Church and worship in Spain is widely known, the social rooting of the other religious forms accepted by the Spanish legislature is not so evident. Nothing prevents Spain from recognising the full effects of any kind of religious marriage. However, bearing in mind that some religious minorities have benefited, many of which have shown a shorter tradition of presence in Spain and have fewer members than the Roma minority, excluding the Roma rituals may be deemed discriminatory. Realising that the Roma community shows a historical and wide social presence in Spain, in some cases stronger than those of some of the aforementioned religious communities, the non-recognition of the Roma marriage by the Spanish authorities, without an objective and reasonable justification, constitutes discrimination in relation to Article 14 of the Convention. Denying recognition to a particular kind of marriage while accepting others of minority groups which are, at least, in a similar condition in respect to the Roma community constitutes a difference in treatment disproportionate in practice, and based on no reasonable justification. The fact that religious communities' members enjoy a right to the freedom of religion, protected by Article 9 of the Convention, does not interfere with this conclusion because marriage should not be necessarily linked with a religious expression, as the wording of Article 12 of the Convention indicates. Simultaneously, members of the Roma minority do enjoy the right to a private family life on equal footing with any other minority members, this Convention right being equally linked with marriage as the right protected under Article 9.

[Original paragraph 81 deleted]

81. Accordingly, the Court notes that the fact that Roma marriage has no civil effects desired by the applicant, whereas other forms of marriage with less social and historical rooting in the Spanish society do, constitutes a discrimination prohibited by Article 14.

17

Chapman redux: the European Court of Human Rights and Roma traditional lifestyle

JULIE RINGELHEIM*

Introduction

On 18 January 2001, in *Chapman* v. *United Kingdom*,[1] the European Court of Human Rights (ECHR), sitting in a Grand Chamber, ruled that the refusal to grant a Gypsy/Roma[2] woman planning permission to settle with her family on a caravan on her own land and her subsequent eviction from her property did not constitute a breach of the European Convention on Human Rights ('the Convention').[3] This judgment was seen by many as a missed opportunity for the Court to develop an effective protection of minorities' right to preserve their cultural traditions based on the Convention.[4] Paradoxically, the Court did acknowledge in this ruling that the Convention must be interpreted in light of

---

* This chapterer was written while I was a Visiting Fellow at the Centre for the Study of Human Rights of the London School of Economics. I wish to thank the Centre for its support.

[1] ECHR (GC), *Chapman* v. *United Kingdom*, 18 January 2001.

[2] Different terms are in use to refer to this community. Since the late 1990s, it has become the practice in European institutions to describe them as 'Roma'. But other terms are still used at national level by State authorities or by the members of these communities themselves, such as 'Gypsies', 'Travellers', 'Sinti' or 'Gitanos'. See J.-P. Liégeois, *Roma in Europe* (Strasbourg: Council of Europe, 2007). In *Chapman* v. *United Kingdom*, the Court, following the terminology which appears in British legislation, employs the term 'Gypsies'. But, in cases concerning Central and Eastern Europe countries, it uses the word 'Roma'. See e.g. ECHR, *Velikova* v. *Bulgaria*, 18 May 2000 (Application no. 41488/98); and ECHR, *DH and others* v. *Czech Republic*, 13 November 2007 (Application no. 57325/00). In this chapter, both the terms 'Gypsies' and 'Roma' will be used.

[3] Application no. 27238/95. The Court arrived at the same conclusion in four other cases on similar facts decided the same day: *Beard* v. *United Kingdom* (Application no. 24882/94), *Coster* v. *United Kingdom* (Application no. 24876/94), *Lee* v. *United Kingdom* (Application no. 25289/94), and *Smith* v. *United Kingdom* (Application no. 25154/94), 18 January 2001.

[4] In this sense, see F. Sudre, 'A propos de l'autorité d'un "précédent" en matière de protection des droits des minorités' (2001) 47 *Revue trimestrielle des droits de l'homme* 905–15, especially at 913–15; M. Levinet, 'Juges de Strasbourg, encore un effort si vous voulez devenir des défenseurs de l'identité minoritaire! Observation sur les arrêts Chapman, Beard, Coster, Jane Smith et Lee' (2001) 5 *L'Europe des Libertés* 2–5; F. Benoît-Rohmer, 'La Cour de Strasbourg et la protection de l'intérêt minoritaire: une avancée décisive sur le plan des

emerging international norms on minority protection, in particular the Framework Convention for the Protection of National Minorities (FCNM).[5] Yet, at the same time, it limited the practical impact of this principle and when reviewing the concrete facts at stake, it paid only lip service to the notion and goals of minority protection. The special importance of this judgment lies with the fact that it strikingly illustrates the ambivalence of the Court, and indeed of human rights themselves, towards the minority question. It highlights both the potential of classic individual rights in providing the foundations for the development of minority protection and the obstacles that often hamper the emergence of a minority-sensitive interpretation of these rights. Significantly, this ruling was highly contested within the Court itself: seven judges among seventeen dissented and argued that the facts did reveal a violation of the Convention. But *Chapman* is also very interesting to look at in a historical perspective: when examining the judgment today, ten years after it was issued, one realises how much has changed in the Court's case law as well as in the broader legal environment in which the ECHR operates. For all these reasons, this case seemed to me especially relevant for the redrafting exercise proposed by the editor of this volume.

In what follows, I will proceed in three steps. First, I will provide some background information on the case. Secondly, I will underline what I see as the three major flaws in the majority's reasoning, namely, the downplaying of the importance of minority rights, the individualistic reading of the facts and the formalistic approach to equality. Thirdly, I will present the alternative drafting of the judgment that I propose. In doing so, I will take a deliberately anachronistic approach: I will not try to ascertain how the judges could have dealt with the case at the time. Rather, I will discuss how the Court could handle a similar case today, taking into account the evolutions that have taken place in the ECHR's jurisprudence and in the European legal space more generally.

The background to the case

In Britain, as in other Western European countries, there lives a small Gypsy/ Roma community whose presence dates back to the sixteenth century.[6] Their traditional lifestyle, characterised by caravan-dwelling and travelling, has been profoundly affected by the development of planning legislation and policies

principes? (En marge de l'arrêt Chapman)' (2001) 48 *Revue trimestrielle des droits de l'homme* 999–1015, especially pp. 1001–2; D. Rosenberg, 'L'indifférence du juge européen aux discriminations subies par les Roms (En marge de l'arrêt Chapman)' (2001) 48 *Revue trimestrielle des droits de l'homme* 1017–33; J. Ringelheim, *Diversité culturelle et droits de l'homme. La protection des minorités par la Convention européenne des droits de l'homme* (Brussels: Bruylant, 2006), pp. 242–7.

[5] ETS No. 157.

[6] J.-P. Liégeois, *Roma in Europe* (Strasbourg: Council of Europe, 2007), p. 20.

since the 1960s.[7] In the UK, the Caravan Sites and Control of Development Act 1960 granted local authorities the power to close commons on which Gypsies were until then allowed to stop. This resulted in a drastic reduction of the number of lawful stopping sites available to them. Many families found themselves in breach of the law when stationing their caravans on lands on which they had been used to halt for years. Acknowledging the problem, the authorities adopted a new law in 1968, the Caravan Sites Act, which created a duty for local authorities to provide adequate accommodation for Gypsies residing in or resorting to their area.[8] Where the Secretary of State was satisfied either that a local authority had fulfilled this obligation or that it was not necessary or expedient to make such provision, it could 'designate' that district or county, which had the effect of making it an offence for any Gypsy to station a caravan within this area on any other land without the consent of the occupier.[9] This legislation did not have the expected results: only a minority of local authorities created the required stopping sites. A 1976 report by Sir John Cripps observed that, among the estimated 40,000 Gypsies living in England and Wales, three-quarters were still without the possibility of finding a legal stopping place.[10] In 1992, a study indicated that, among the 13,500 Gypsy families living in caravans, around 4,500 were still unable to find a legal stopping place.[11] Nonetheless, in 1994, the government decided to repeal the obligation for local authorities to provide accommodation for Gypsies while generalising the powers previously limited to designated areas.[12] Under the Criminal Justice and Public Order Act 1994, whether or not they had created caravan sites for Gypsies, local authorities were given the power to direct any person residing in a vehicle on land without the owner's consent to move.[13] Failure to comply with such direction became a criminal offence. Local authorities could apply to a magistrates' court for an order authorising them to remove caravans parked in contravention of such a

---

[7] On the evolution of legislation and policies relating to the caravan-dwelling lifestyle in England and Wales between the 1960s and the 1990s, see S. Poulter, *Ethnicity, Law and Human Rights: The English Experience* (Oxford: Clarendon Press, 1998), pp. 147–94; OSCE High Commissioner on National Minorities, *Report on the Situation of Roma and Sinti in the OSCE Area* (March 2000), pp. 111–16; S. Campbell, 'Gypsies: The Criminalisation of a Way of Life?' (1995) *Criminal Law Review* 8–37.

[8] Section 6 of the Caravan Sites Act 1968.

[9] Sections 10 and 12 of the Caravan Sites Act 1968.

[10] *Accommodation for Gypsies: A Report on the Working of the Caravan Sites Act 1968* (London: HMSO, Department of Environment, 1977), quoted in *Chapman v. United Kingdom*, para. 36.

[11] Study quoted by S. Poulter, *Ethnicity, Law and Human Rights: The English Experience* (Oxford: Clarendon Press, 1998), p. 173.

[12] S. Poulter, *Ethnicity, Law and Human Rights: The English Experience* (Oxford: Clarendon Press, 1998), pp. 179–80.

[13] Section 77 of the Criminal Justice and Public Order Act 1994.

direction.[14] The government argued that 'public provision of sites has now reached an acceptable level' and that it was not in the public interest 'to continue to maintain what has become an open-ended commitment to provide sites for all gypsies seeking accommodation at the public's expense'.[15] The right approach, in its view, was now 'to encourage more gypsies to establish their own sites through the planning system'.[16] However, the government did not take any initiative to counter the obstacles resulting from planning regulation to the placement of caravans on private properties by their owner. According to S. Poulter, in practice, '[t]he opposition encountered from local residents when coupled with environmental and traffic safety factors is usually sufficient to prevent the necessary permission being granted'.[17]

It is against this background that the predicament of Ms Chapman must be viewed. She was Gypsy by birth and had lived in caravans all her life. Unable to find a place on a public caravan site, she was constantly moved from place to place by the police or local authorities' representatives, which was detrimental to the health of her family and the education of her children. Hence, she decided to buy a piece of land with the intention of settling on it with her family in a mobile home. Yet, the district council refused her application for planning permission and served enforcement notices. Her appeal was dismissed by the planning inspector on the ground that the land was in the metropolitan green belt in which there is a general presumption against inappropriate development. While noting that there were no sufficient sites for Gypsies in the county, the inspector declared that he attached more weight to the fact that 'this site lies in an attractive setting of mainly sporadic dwellings in extensive grounds and in a designated Landscape Conservation Area ... [I]t was agreed that the area is popular for recreational walking and riding.'[18] After being fined twice, the family moved out of the land and returned to a nomadic life. They could not find any alternative place to live on and were constantly moved from place to place by council officials. The eldest children had to abandon the professional training they had started and the younger children could no longer attend school.[19]

The judgment

In her application before the Court, Ms Chapman claims a violation of her right to respect for her private life, family life and home (Article 8), her right to

---

[14] Section 78 of the Criminal Justice and Public Order Act 1994.

[15] Speech of the Parliamentary Under-Secretary of State, quoted in ECHR, *Connors* v. *United Kingdom*, 27 May 2004, para. 37.

[16] *Ibid.*

[17] S. Poulter, *Ethnicity, Law and Human Rights: The English Experience* (Oxford: Clarendon Press, 1998), p. 175.

[18] Quoted in *Chapman* v. *United Kingdom*, para. 17.   [19] *Ibid.*, para. 15.

property (Article 1 of Protocol 1) and her right not to be discriminated against (Article 14).

Thus, the first question the case raised was whether the ability of Gypsies to live in caravans according to their cultural traditions could be said to be protected under the Convention. In a previous judgment on similar facts, *Buckley* v. *United Kingdom*,[20] the Court disregarded the opinion expressed by the former European Commission of Human Rights that the traditional lifestyle of a minority may attract the guarantee of Article 8 as concerning the private life, family life and home:[21] The judges merely stated that the contested measures had affected the applicant's right to respect for her home and that it was unnecessary to decide whether her right to respect for her private life and family life was also at stake.[22] They therefore treated the issue as a banal problem of refusal of planning permission, eluding the cultural aspect of the case.[23] The *Chapman* ruling marks an important evolution in this respect: the Court this time acknowledges that 'the applicant's occupation of her caravan is an integral part of her ethnic identity as a Gypsy, reflecting the long tradition of that minority of following a travelling lifestyle'.[24] Accordingly, measures affecting her stationing of her caravans 'have an impact going beyond the right to respect for her home. They also affect her ability to maintain her identity as a Gypsy and to lead her private and family life in accordance with that tradition.'[25] Hence, her right to respect for her private and family life as well as home is in issue.[26] The Court, moreover, notes the emergence of an international consensus amongst Council of Europe Member States recognising the special needs of minorities and an obligation to protect their identity and lifestyle, 'not only for the purpose of

---

[20] ECHR, *Buckley* v. *United Kingdom*, 25 September 1996.

[21] ECommHR, *Buckley* v. *United Kingdom* (Application no. 20348/92), Report, 11 January 1995, para. 64. This position was first outlined by the European Commission in *G and E* v. *Norway*: ECommHR, *G and E* v. *Norway* (Application nos. 9278/81 and 9415/81), decision, 3 October 1983, DR 35, p. 30.

[22] *Buckley* v. *United Kingdom*, para. 55. The Court later concluded that the interference with the applicant's right was justified under Article 8(2).

[23] See O. De Schutter, 'Le droit au mode de vie tsigane devant la Cour européenne des droits de l'homme: droits culturels, droits des minorités, discrimination positive' (1997) *Revue trimestrielle des droits de l'homme* 64–93; and J. Ringelheim, *Diversité culturelle et droits de l'homme. La protection des minorités par la Convention européenne des droits de l'homme* (Brussels: Bruylant, 2006), pp. 225–7. On this case, see also J.-P. Marguénaud, 'La protection du paysage rural contre les caravanes des gens du voyage' (1997) 1 *Revue européenne de droit de l'environnement* 87–95, especially 90–1.

[24] *Chapman* v. *United Kingdom*, para. 73.   [25] *Ibid.*, para. 73.

[26] *Ibid.*, para. 74. About a year before, in *Noack* v. *Germany*, the Court had for the first time admitted that 'for the purposes of Article 8 of the Convention, a minority's way of life is, in principle, entitled to the protection guaranteed for an individual's private life, family life and home' (ECHR, *Noack* v. *Germany*, 25 May 2000).

safeguarding the interests of the minorities themselves but to preserve a cultural diversity of value to the whole community'.[27] Given the vulnerable position of Gypsies as a minority, special consideration should be given to their needs 'both in the relevant regulatory planning framework and in reaching decisions in particular cases'. To this extent, States Parties have a positive obligation by virtue of Article 8 'to facilitate the Gypsy way of life'.[28]

This judgment represents in this respect an important move in the direction of integrating minority concerns in the interpretation of the Convention. However, when examining whether the interference with Ms Chapman's rights was justified under the Convention, the majority of the Court returns to a 'minority-blind' approach, which contradicts the minority-sensitive perspective it seems to adopt initially. This allows it to easily conclude that the restriction could be deemed necessary in a democratic society to achieve a legitimate aim under the Convention, namely, the protection of the rights of others through the preservation of the environment. In contrast with the first part of the judgment, the reasoning held at this stage appears as a setback for minority protection. More precisely, the position of the majority presents three major problems: it trivialises the importance of minority rights, it is based on an individualistic reading of the facts and it relies on a formalistic approach to equality and non-discrimination.

The trivialisation of minority rights

After acknowledging the emergence of an international consensus recognising an obligation to protect minorities' identity and lifestyle, the Court, however, declares that this consensus is not sufficiently concrete to derive any guidance as to the conduct or standards which Member States consider desirable in any particular situation. In its view, the FCNM, adopted in 1995 and in force since 1998, merely sets out general principles and goals but the signatory States were unable to agree on means of implementation. The Court thus considers international norms on minority protection as no more than vague declarations of good intentions devoid of any concrete content. This enables it to deprive of any practical impact the recognition of an emerging international consensus on minority protection and to justify the granting of a wide margin of appreciation to State authorities.[29]

In addition, when commenting on the difficulties faced in general by Gypsies leading a caravan-dwelling lifestyle in Britain, the Court misrepresents the problem at stake. It states that it cannot accept the argument that, 'because statistically the number of Gypsies is greater than the number of places available on authorised Gypsy sites, the decision not to allow the applicant Gypsy family to occupy land where they wished in order to install their caravan in itself, and

---

[27] *Chapman* v. *United Kingdom*, para. 93.   [28] *Ibid.*, para. 96.   [29] *Ibid.*, para. 94.

without more, constituted a violation of Article 8'.[30] This 'would be tantamount to imposing on States an obligation to make available to the Gypsy community an adequate number of suitably equipped sites, a conclusion that cannot be supported as Article 8 does not recognise a right to be provided with a home'.[31] This, however, mischaracterises what is really at issue: Gypsies in Britain do not need to be provided with a home. Rather, the problem lies with the fundamental inequality of treatment of their traditional way of life compared to that of the majority which live in sedentary houses: planning legislation and policies only take into account the lifestyle of the majority, considered as the norm, and ignore the needs of the Roma minority. As a result, a substantial number of them are unable to find a place – either on public or on private land – where they are simply *allowed* to live. In short, because it does not take minority rights seriously, the Court's majority distorts the issue underlying the case and downplays the responsibility of State authorities in creating this situation.

An individualistic reading of the facts

In order to capture the seriousness of the measures taken against Ms Chapman, it was necessary to pay regard to the overall condition of the Roma minority living in caravans in Britain. For this general situation was a determining element in assessing the alternatives open to her once she had been expelled from her land. This situation was characterised by a persistent shortfall of sites where Gypsy families were allowed to reside. Importantly, public authorities had largely contributed to produce this state of affairs: whereas public lands on which Gypsies used to stop had been closed to them during the 1960s, the State had consistently failed to ensure that local authorities created a sufficient number of public caravan sites. Nonetheless, in 1994, the government repealed the obligation previously imposed on local authorities in this regard. And, despite declaring that Gypsies would from then on be encouraged to establish their own sites, no initiative was taken to remedy the tendency of local authorities to refuse planning permission submitted by Gypsies to place a caravan on private land.

In the case of Ms Chapman, it had been acknowledged during the procedure that there were no official Gypsy sites in the district. While some sites existed at the level of the county, it was recognised that they were insufficient and that there was no place available in them.[32] In such circumstances, given the factual and legal background described above, refusing to allow Ms Chapman to reside in a caravan with her family on her own land amounted to force her either to live in illegality or to abandon her traditional lifestyle against her will and assimilate to the majority. The Court's majority, however, seems to go out of its way to detach the case of Ms Chapman from its wider context and from the

---

[30] *Ibid.*, para. 98.   [31] *Ibid.*, paras. 98–9.   [32] *Ibid.*, para. 12.

global difficulties faced, in the whole country, by the minority she belonged to. This attitude is palpable when the Court states that:

> the issue to be determined by the Court in the present case is not the acceptability or not of a general situation, however deplorable, in the United Kingdom in the light of the United Kingdom's undertakings in international law, but the narrower one of whether the particular circumstances of the case disclose a violation of the applicant's – Mrs Chapman's – right to respect for her home under Article 8 of the Convention.[33]

To be sure, the Court admits that the legal and social context in which the measure was taken is a relevant factor.[34] But, despite the wealth of evidence indicating that public sites accessible to Gypsies were insufficient in Britain generally, and in the county where Ms Chapman lived in particular, the majority declares that 'it cannot be doubted that vacancies on official sites arise periodically'.[35] On this basis, it concludes that it is 'not persuaded that there were no alternatives available to the applicant besides remaining in occupation on land without planning permission in a Green Belt area'. It adds that 'Article 8 does not necessarily go so far as to allow individuals' preferences as to their place of residence to override the general interest'.[36]

This reading of the facts appears narrowly individualistic in two ways. First, notwithstanding its acknowledgment that caravan life holds an important place in Gypsy collective identity, at the end of the day the majority discards the cultural dimension of the issue and reduces the wish of Ms Chapman to live in a caravan to a question of mere *individual preference*. Secondly, it refuses to see her plight as one instance of a collective and systemic problem: the failure of public authorities to ensure the availability of a sufficient number of places, on public or private lands, where Roma pursuing a traditional lifestyle can lawfully reside.

A formalistic approach to equality and non-discrimination

Chapman was decided after *Thlimmenos* v. *Greece*, in which the Court acknowledged that the right not to be discriminated against under Article 14 is violated not only when States treat differently persons in analogous situations, but also when they fail to treat differently persons whose situations are significantly different, without objective and reasonable justification.[37] Nonetheless, in *Chapman*, the majority returns to a formalistic approach to non-discrimination and suggests that to accord Ms Chapman a different treatment from that accorded to any individual who has established a house unlawfully in a

---

[33] *Ibid.*, para. 100.   [34] *Ibid.*, para. 101.   [35] *Ibid.*, para. 111.
[36] *Ibid.*, para. 113. The Court in this last sentence reiterates a remark already made in *Buckley* v. *United Kingdom* (para. 81).
[37] ECHR (GC), *Thlimmenos* v. *Greece*, 6 April 2000, para. 44.

particular place would be discriminatory.[38] This statement overlooks the fact that Ms Chapman's situation differs in some crucial respects from that of any other individual who would have been refused planning permission: as a Gypsy living in a caravan and wishing to maintain her traditional lifestyle, her possibilities to find an alternative place to live were much more limited than those of people living in sedentary houses. Accordingly, the consequences of the decision to evict her from her land were much more serious than in the case of a house-dweller: she did not have anywhere else to which she could reasonably be expected to move. It was predictably impossible for her to find another place to live lawfully, unless she renounced her traditional way of life.

The dissenting opinion

Judging by the number of dissenting judges, one can surmise that the case sparked lively debates within the Court. Importantly, the dissenting opinion demonstrates that there is no necessary opposition between classic individual rights and minority rights. In contrast with the majority, the alternative reasoning it proposes does fully take into account both the concrete situation in which Ms Chapman was placed and the underlying question of respect for a minority lifestyle. But it also seems much more consistent with the principles asserted by the majority itself in the first part of the judgment, in particular that States have a positive obligation by virtue of Article 8 to facilitate the Gypsy traditional way of life. Crucially, for the dissenting judges, given the potential seriousness of an interference which prohibits a Gypsy family from pursuing its lifestyle at a particular location, 'where the planning authorities have not made any finding that there is available to the Gypsy any alternative, lawful site to which he or she can reasonably be expected to move, there must exist compelling reasons for the measures concerned'.[39] In their opinion, it is 'disproportionate to take steps to evict a Gypsy family from their home on their own land in circumstances where there has not been shown to be any other lawful, alternative site reasonably open to them'.[40] Hence, they conclude that the measures taken against Ms Chapman could not be deemed necessary in a democratic society.

Redrafting Chapman in 2011

Looking back at *Chapman* in 2011 and reflecting on how such a case could be dealt with nowadays allows us to take stock of the evolutions that have occurred

---

[38] *Chapman* v. *United Kingdom*, para. 95.
[39] Joint Dissenting Opinion of Judges Pastor Ridruejo, Bonello, Tulkens, Stráznická, Lorenzen, Fischbach and Casadevall, para. 3.
[40] *Ibid.*, para. 5.

in the case law of the Court and in the European legal space more widely. These developments, I would argue, have reinforced the approach that was defended at the time by the dissenting judges. But they have also enabled the Court to go beyond the dissenting opinion and to point out some further problems the case raises. In the Court's case law, these ten years have seen the rise of the non-discrimination norm as well as of the notion of systemic violation of the Convention. Outside the Court, this period has been marked by the development of the work of the Advisory Committee on the Framework Convention for the Protection of National Minorities, the emergence of the issue of the Roma right to housing in the European Committee of Social Rights's case law and the expansion of European Union non-discrimination law. All these evolutions are relevant to the interpretation of the Convention: indeed, as the Court has asserted repeatedly, the Convention is a living instrument which must be interpreted in light of present-day conditions.

Recognising a Roma right to traditional housing

Since 2001, a number of evolutionary strands have combined to reinforce the view that, in conditions such as those prevailing in Britain, the decision to evict a Roma family living in a caravan on their own land where there has not been proven to be any lawful alternative site reasonably available to them, should be considered a violation of the Convention.

In *Chapman*, the majority, while accepting that the adoption of the FCNM was to be taken into account when interpreting the rights guaranteed under the Convention, declared that this instrument only set out general principles but did not provide any guidance as to the standards required in particular situations. This stance was already highly disputable in 2001.[41] Article 5 of the FCNM, in particular, lays down the obligation of States to promote the conditions necessary for members of minorities to preserve the essential elements of their identity and to refrain from policies aimed at assimilation of persons belonging to national minorities against their will. At the time of the judgment, however, the Advisory Committee – the body of experts charged with supervising implementation of the FCNM and whose work contributes to clarifying the obligations stemming from it – had not issued any opinion on the United Kingdom. At the time of writing, two Committee opinions relating to the UK are available: the first was published in November 2001,[42] and the second in June 2007.[43]

---

[41] See *ibid.*, para. 3.
[42] Advisory Committee on the FCNM, First Opinion on the United Kingdom, adopted on 30 November 2001, ACFC/INF/OP/I(2002)006.
[43] Advisory Committee on the FCNM, Second Opinion on the United Kingdom, adopted on 6 June 2007, ACFC/OP/II(2007)003.

In the three opinions, the Advisory Committee clearly identifies the lack of caravan sites available for Gypsies throughout the United Kingdom as being problematic from the viewpoint of Article 5 of the FCNM: 'This combined with a range of legislative and administrative measures have the effect of inhibiting nomadism and effectively denying travellers the right to maintain and preserve or develop one of the important elements of their culture and identity, namely travelling.'[44] This problem was also highlighted by the Committee of Ministers in its 2002 Resolution on the implementation of the FCNM in the UK, stating that 'the implementation of the Framework Convention has not been successful as concerns Roma/Gypsies and Irish Travellers, *inter alia*, due to the lack of adequate stopping places'.[45]

The question of respect for Roma traditional lifestyle has also emerged in another institution of the Council of Europe, namely, the European Committee of Social Rights. Since 1998, this body is entitled to examine collective complaints alleging a violation of the European Social Charter.[46] In 2004, the issue of the Roma right to traditional housing was raised for the first time before it in *European Roma Rights Centre* v. *Greece*.[47] The Committee found that a State's failure to take due account of the specific needs of Roma or Travellers and to ensure that they have access to a sufficient number of appropriate caravan sites

---

[44] Advisory Committee on the FCNM, First Opinion on the United Kingdom, adopted on 30 November 2001, ACFC/INF/OP/I(2002)006, para. 42. The Second Opinion, adopted in 2007, notes that new legislation has been adopted aimed at remedying the shortage of adequate stopping sites for Gypsies and Travellers and the negative effect that this has on their ability to maintain their culture. However, 'delays in the implementation of the new legislation, and in some cases resistance to taking the necessary measures on the part of local authorities, mean that numerous Gypsy and Traveller families continue to live on unauthorised land and/or unauthorised encampments.' Second Opinion on the United Kingdom, adopted on 6 June 2007, ACFC/OP/II(2007)003, para. 17.

[45] Resolution ResCMN(2002)9 on the Implementation of the Framework Convention for the Protection of National Minorities by the United Kingdom, adopted by the Committee of Ministers on 13 June 2002. The Resolution adopted in 2008, following the Second Opinion of the Committee on the UK, observes that '[h]ostility among some people within the local population and the resistance of certain local authorities to improving the availability of authorised sites have contributed to the fact that a number of Gypsies and Travellers continue to live on unauthorised sites and may face eviction orders.' Resolution CM/ResCMN(2008)7 on the Implementation of the Framework Convention for the Protection of National Minorities by the United Kingdom, adopted by the Committee of Ministers on 9 July 2008.

[46] Additional Protocol to the European Social Charter Providing for a System of Collective Complaints, CETS No. 158, adopted in 1995 and entered into force in 1998. Adopted in 1961, the European Social Charter, which guarantees social and economic rights, was revised in 1996. The 1996 revised European Social Charter is meant to gradually replace the initial 1961 Convention. On this system, see O. De Schutter (ed.), *The European Social Charter: A Social Constitution for Europe* (Brussels: Bruylant, 2010).

[47] *European Roma Rights Centre* v. *Greece*, 8 December 2004 (merits), No. 15/2003.

constitutes a violation of the European Social Charter.[48] This conclusion was confirmed in two later cases, *European Roma Rights Centre* v. *Italy* and *European Roma Rights Centre* v. *France*, where the Court found a breach of Article 31, which guarantees the right to housing, as well as of Article E, which prohibits discrimination, combined with Article 31.[49] On a similar note, in its 2009 concluding observation on the periodic report submitted by the UK, the United Nations Committee on Economic, Social and Cultural Rights expresses concern about the shortage of adequate sites for Roma/Gypsies and Irish Travellers and recommends that the 'State party ensures the provision of sufficient adequate and secure stopping sites for Roma/Gypsies and Irish Travellers'.[50]

The housing problems faced by Roma and Travellers in Europe more generally, have attracted the attention of the Committee of Ministers of the Council of Europe. In a Recommendation adopted in 2005, it calls upon Member States to ensure that, 'within the general framework of housing policies, integrated and appropriate housing policies targeting Roma are developed'.[51] Significantly, it insists that Roma and Travellers must be guaranteed the freedom to choose to pursue sedentary or nomadic lifestyles: 'all conditions necessary to pursue these lifestyles should be made available to them by the national, regional and local authorities in accordance with the resources available and to the rights of others and within the legal framework relating to building, planning and access to private land.'[52]

These elements would have to be considered by the Court if it were to be asked today to decide on a case similar to *Chapman* (see paragraphs 94, 97 and 98 of the redraft). In fact, in *Connors* v. *United Kingdom* (2004), the Court itself seems to qualify some of the findings of *Chapman*: it incidentally recognises that 'the situation in England as it had developed ... placed considerable obstacles in the way of Gypsies pursuing an actively nomadic lifestyle' and that 'the authorities had to take some responsibility' for this[53] (see paragraph 97 of the redraft). The facts at stake were different from *Chapman* though: at issue here was the regime applicable to Gypsies renting a plot on a local authority public site. The Court found that the special power of local authority to evict tenants from

---

[48] *Ibid.*, paras. 46–7. The Committee found a breach of Article 16 of the Charter under which States undertake to promote the economic, legal and social protection of family life, *inter alia*, through provision of family housing.

[49] See *European Roma Rights Centre* v. *Italy*, 7 December 2005 (merits), No. 27/3004, para. 37; and *European Roma Rights Centre* v. *France*, 19 October 2009 (merits), No. 51/2008, paras. 40–1.

[50] UN Committee on Economic, Social and Cultural Rights, Concluding observations, United Kingdom of Great Britain and Northern Ireland, the Crown Dependencies and the Overseas Dependent Territories, E/C.12/GBR/CO/5, 12 June 2009, para. 30.

[51] Recommendation Rec(2005)4 on improving the housing conditions of Roma and Travellers in Europe, adopted by the Committee of Ministers of the Council of Europe on 23 February 2005.

[52] *Ibid.* [53] ECHR, *Connors* v. *United Kingdom*, 27 May 2004, para. 94.

these sites without the requisite procedural safeguards was not compatible with
Article 8.

Acknowledging the systemic nature of violations of the Roma right to pursue their traditional lifestyle

It was noted above that, in order to assess the seriousness of the interference
with Ms Chapman's rights, account needed to be taken of the overall situation
of Gypsies living in caravans in the UK. Today, however, the Court could tackle
more directly the general obstacles faced by Gypsies wishing to pursue a traditional lifestyle in this country. Indeed, in May 2004, as a response to the
increasing workload of the Court, the Committee of Ministers has expressly
invited the Court to identify, where it finds a violation of the Convention, what
it considers to be an underlying systemic problem, in particular when it is likely
to give rise to numerous applications.[54] Beyond the so-called 'pilot-judgment
procedure', this has had a significant impact on the way the Court exercises its
role: in a growing number of cases, the Court does not content itself with
finding an individual violation of the Convention. Where it deems it appropriate, it also highlights the systemic defect in the State's law or practice from
which the violation originates and which needs to be remedied.[55] This
approach, I believe, should be applied to a case like *Chapman*: the Court should
not only rule that the measures taken against the individual applicant were in
breach of the Convention, it should also acknowledge that this violation results
from a systemic problem in the UK's legislation and policies, which affects a
large number of Roma/Gypsies, who are unable to find a place where they can
lawfully reside in caravans. Accordingly, it should recognise that the UK needs
to adopt general measures in order to bring its legislation and administrative
practice into conformity with the right of Roma/Gypsies to respect for their
private and family life, as protected by the Convention (see paragraph 100 of the
redraft).

The discrimination question

It was observed earlier that the Court could have applied to the case of Ms
Chapman the principle asserted in *Thlimmenos*, according to which

---

[54] Resolution Res(2004)3 of the Committee of Ministers on judgments revealing an
underlying systemic problem, adopted on 12 May 2004. This resolution provided the
basis for the development of the so-called 'pilot-judgment' procedure. See A. Buyse, 'The
Pilot Judgment Procedure at the European Court of Human Rights: Possibilities and
Challenges' (2009) 57 *Nomiko Vima (The Greek Law Journal)* 1890–1902.
[55] See, among numerous examples, ECHR, *Hasan and Eylem Zengin* v. *Turkey*, 9 October
2007, para. 84; ECHR, *Dybeku* v. *Albania*, 18 December 2007, para. 64; and ECHR,
Slawomir Musial v. *Poland*, 20 January 2009, para. 107.

discrimination may arise where a State, without objective and reasonable justification, fails to treat differently persons whose situations are significantly different.[56] On this account, the Court could have acknowledged that the situation of Ms Chapman was not analogous to that of any other person who would have established a caravan or a house without planning permission: as a Gypsy leading a traditional lifestyle, her possibilities to find an alternative place to live were much more limited than those of any other person. Hence, refusing to take these differences into account could have been deemed to constitute discrimination.[57] Since January 2001, however, the Court's case law on the concept of discrimination has undergone further evolution. Under the influence of EU non-discrimination law, and in particular of Council Directive 2000/43/EC which prohibits racial and ethnic origin discrimination,[58] the Court has progressively integrated the notion of *indirect* discrimination: it now accepts that a general policy or measure that has disproportionately prejudicial effects on a particular ethnic group may be considered discriminatory even where it is not specifically aimed at that group.[59] Applying this notion, in *DH and others* v. *Czech Republic* (2007), the Court famously found that Roma children, who were unjustifiably over-represented in special schools for mentally disabled pupils, were the victims of indirect discrimination in access to education.[60]

In my view, the concept of indirect discrimination is better suited than the *Thlimmenos* principle to identify the discrimination at work in a case like *Chapman*. For it allows us to see that the individual measures taken against Ms Chapman and her family are part and parcel of a general policy which, taken

---

[56] *Thlimmenos* v. *Greece*, para. 44.

[57] This was hinted at by the dissenting judges in *Chapman*: '[W]e cannot agree with the view expressed by the majority that to accord protection under Article 8 to a Gypsy in unlawful residence in a caravan on her land would raise problems under Article 14 where planning laws continued to prevent individuals from setting up houses on their land in the same area ... This approach ignores the fact, earlier acknowledged by the majority, that in this case the applicant's lifestyle as a Gypsy widens the scope to Article 8, which would not necessarily be the case for a person who lives in conventional housing, the supply of which is subject to fewer constraints. The situations would not be likely to be analogous. On the contrary, discrimination may arise where States, without objective and reasonable justification, fail to treat differently persons whose situations are significantly different.' Para. 8. Nonetheless, the dissenters explain that they voted for non-violation of Article 14 of the Convention as, given their firm conviction that Article 8 had been violated, they considered that no separate issues remained to be examined. Para. 11.

[58] Council Directive 2000/43/EC of 29 June 2000 implementing the principle of equal treatment between persons irrespective of racial or ethnic origin, OJ L180 of 19 July 2000, p. 22.

[59] ECHR, *Hugh Jordan* v. *United Kingdom*, 4 May 2001, para. 154; ECHR, *Hoogendijk* v. *Netherlands*, 6 January 2005 (admissibility decision); ECHR (GC), *DH and others* v. *Czech Republic*, 13 November 2007, paras. 175 and 184.

[60] *DH and others* v. *Czech Republic*, paras. 208–10.

as a whole, has a disproportionately prejudicial impact on the Gypsy minority in the UK: it is because the overall planning legislation and policy largely ignores the needs and lifestyle of this community that many Gypsies, like Ms Chapman, face considerable obstacles in finding a place to settle lawfully. The indirect discrimination notion therefore permits us to pinpoint the fundamental inequality of treatment, within UK law and practice, of the Roma traditional lifestyle compared to the majority way of life. Given that this adverse impact cannot be objectively and reasonably justified, this legal framework should be considered to constitute discrimination, in violation of Article 14, read in conjunction with Article 8 (see paragraph 129 of the redraft).

Conclusion

The *Chapman v. United Kingdom* ruling quite clearly indicates that, compared to other international human rights institutions, the European Court of Human Rights has not been a leader in the defence of the Roma right to pursue a private and family life in accordance with their traditions. It is not too late to reverse this situation. The dissenting opinion in *Chapman* demonstrates that even at the time of the case it was possible for the Court to take a different road. There are even more reasons to do so today. Since 2001, several evolutions have reinforced the case for mainstreaming diversity in the Court's jurisprudence and affording more effective protection to the Roma right to maintain their traditional way of life. First, various circumstances indicate the rise of a 'European consensus' on the need for States to ensure that members of the Gypsy/Roma minority have real and concrete opportunities to live in caravans if they so wish. The Advisory Committee on the Framework Convention for the Protection of National Minorities has made clear that the FCNM entails an obligation to respect the Roma/Gypsy caravan-dwelling lifestyle and abstain from adopting measures which effectively deny this community the freedom to preserve or develop this aspect of its identity. The lack of caravan places in the United Kingdom, in particular, has been deemed to reveal an unsatisfactory implementation of the FCNM. The European Social Committee has ruled that similar situations in Italy and France disclose a breach of the right to housing under the European Social Charter. The Council of Europe's Committee of Ministers has recommended all Member States to create conditions necessary to guarantee 'Roma and Travellers' the freedom to choose to pursue sedentary or nomadic lifestyles. Were a case similar to *Chapman* to return to the Court, the right to respect for private life, family life and home under the European Convention on Human Rights would have to be interpreted in light of these new developments. Secondly, the Court nowadays could apply its post-2004 jurisprudence on 'systemic problems' and recognise that, beyond the individual violation of the rights of the applicant, the eviction of a family from its own land under the conditions arising in *Chapman* reveals a systemic defect in the State's law and practices, which needs to be remedied through general measures. Finally, relying on the concept of indirect discrimination, the Court could acknowledge that, where planning and housing legislation or policies have a disproportionately adverse impact on Roma/Gypsies, because they result in an especially high number of them being unable to find a place where they can lawfully settle, without objective and reasonable justification, they must be deemed to constitute discrimination.

Rewriting Chapman v. United Kingdom

...

Alleged violation of Article 8 of the Convention

...

2. The Court's assessment

...

93. The applicant urged the Court to take into account recent international developments, in particular the Framework Convention for the Protection of National Minorities, in reducing the margin of appreciation accorded to States in light of the recognition of the problems of vulnerable groups, such as Gypsies. The Court observes that there may be said to be an emerging international consensus amongst the Contracting States of the Council of Europe recognising the special needs of minorities and an obligation to protect their security, identity and lifestyle (see paragraphs 55–59 above, in particular the Framework Convention for the Protection of National Minorities), not only for the purpose of safeguarding the interests of the minorities themselves but to preserve a cultural diversity of value to the whole community.

[Original paragraph 94 deleted]

94. The work of the Advisory Committee on the Framework Convention on the Protection of National Minorities (FCNM) makes clear that this consensus entails an obligation for the State to take steps to ensure the availability of an adequate number of sites where Roma/ Gypsies or Travellers living in a caravan are allowed to stop or to settle, in order to enable them to maintain their traditional lifestyle if they so wish (first opinion on the United Kingdom, para. 42). In the same vein, the European Committee of Social Rights has acknowledged that the right to housing under the European Social Charter implies, in the case of Roma leading a traditional lifestyle, that adequate stopping places be provided (*European Roma Rights Centre* v. *Greece*, para. 25). More generally, Member States must take into account in their housing policies the

caravan-dwelling lifestyle and the special needs of Travellers, including settled Travellers (*European Roma Rights Centre* v. *France*, paras. 37, 40 and 60). Similarly, in its Recommendation Rec(2005)4 on improving the housing conditions of Roma and Travellers in Europe (23 February 2005), the Committee of Ministers states that 'Member states should ensure that, within the general framework of housing policies, integrated and appropriate housing policies targeting Roma are developed'. Importantly, Roma and Travellers must be guaranteed the freedom to choose to pursue sedentary or nomadic lifestyles: 'all conditions necessary to pursue these lifestyles should be made available to them by the national, regional and local authorities in accordance with the resources available and to the rights of others and within the legal framework relating to building, planning and access to private land.'

Article 8 of the European Convention must be interpreted in light of these developments. Seen in this light, it entails a positive obligation for Contracting States to ensure that Roma/Gypsies or Travellers *have a practical and effective opportunity to enjoy their right to respect for their home, and their private and family life, in accordance with their traditional lifestyle.*[61]

...

97. [Fragment deleted] It appears from the material placed before the Court, including judgments of the English courts, that the provision of an adequate number of sites [fragment deleted] on which [fragment deleted] **Gypsies** can lawfully place their caravans [fragment deleted] is something which has not been achieved.

[Original paragraph 98 deleted]

98. In evaluating the seriousness of the interference with the applicant's right, the Court must have regard to the alternative opportunities available to her to find a place where she could live lawfully in a caravan. *Having regard to the potential seriousness of an interference which prohibits a Gypsy from pursuing his or her lifestyle at a particular location,* the Court *considers that, where the planning authorities have not made any finding that there is available to the Gypsy any alternative, lawful site to which he or she can reasonably be expected to move, there must exist compelling reasons for the measures concerned.*

...

[Original paragraph 113 deleted]

113. *There was no indication in the planning procedures that the applicant had anywhere else to which she could reasonably be expected to move her*

---

[61] All sentences in italic in this redraft are taken from the dissenting opinion annexed to the original judgment.

caravans. The local authority had been found in breach of their duty to make adequate provision for Gypsies ... and had been under a direction from the Secretary of State to comply with their statutory duty, without any concrete improvement of the situation resulting since. In these circumstances, **the Court** *finds that the planning and enforcement measures exceeded the margin of appreciation accorded to the domestic authorities and were disproportionate to the legitimate aim of environmental protection. They cannot therefore be regarded as 'necessary in a democratic society'.*

[Paragraph 100 deleted]

113*bis***. The Court also observes that the violation of the applicant's rights under Article 8 originates in a systemic problem related to the lack of consideration for the needs of Roma/Gypsies and Travellers in housing and planning legislation and policies. In view of its findings in the present case, the Court considers that, in addition to individual measures, the UK should take general measures in order to bring its legislation and administrative practice into conformity with this provision of the Convention, by guaranteeing Roma/Gypsies practical and effective opportunities to lead their private and family life according to their cultural tradition. It is not for the Court to determine whether, as a matter of general policy, this should be achieved through the creation of more public caravan sites or rather through an increase in their possibility to settle lawfully on private sites. But plainly the present situation entails a breach of the Convention.**

. . .

Alleged violation of Articles 14 and 8 of the Convention

. . .

126. The applicant complained that she had been discriminated against on the basis of her status as a Gypsy, contrary to Article 14 of the Convention ...

127. The applicant submitted that the legal system's failure to accommodate Gypsies' traditional way of life, by treating them in the same way as the majority population, or disadvantaging them relatively to the general population, amounted to discrimination in the enjoyment of her rights under the Convention based on her status as a member of an ethnic minority. For example, Gypsies alone were singled out for special treatment by the policy which declared that Gypsy sites were inappropriate in certain areas, and unlike house dwellers, they did not benefit from a systematic assessment of and provision for their needs. Further, the application to them of general laws and policies failed to accommodate their particular needs

arising from their tradition of living and travelling in caravans. She referred, *inter alia*, to the Framework Convention on National Minorities, as supporting an obligation on the United Kingdom to adopt measures to ensure the full and effective equality of Gypsies.

128. The Government, referring to the Commission's majority opinion, found that any difference in treatment pursued legitimate aims, was proportionate to those aims and had in the circumstances reasonable and objective justification.

[Original paragraph 129 deleted]

129. The Court has accepted that a general policy or measure which is apparently neutral but has disproportionately prejudicial effects on persons or groups who are identifiable on the basis of an ethnic criterion, may be considered discriminatory notwithstanding that it is not specifically aimed at that group (see, *mutatis mutandis*, *Hugh Jordan* v. *United Kingdom*, no. 24746/94, § 154, 4 May 2001 and *DH and others* v. *Czech Republic*, no. 57325/00, § 175, 13 November 2007), unless that measure is objectively justified by a legitimate aim and the means of achieving that aim are appropriate, necessary and proportionate. Furthermore, discrimination potentially contrary to the Convention may result from a *de facto* situation.

The material before the Court reveals that the legislation in force and the planning policies applied by the central and local authorities in the United Kingdom result in a substantial number of members of the Gypsy community being, like Ms Chapman, unable to find a place where they are allowed to live according to their tradition. This policy therefore has disproportionate prejudicial effects on the Gypsy community to which Ms Chapman belongs. In view of its findings above (paragraphs 100 and 113), the Court deems that the means used to achieve the legitimate objective of regulating planning practices and protecting the environment were not proportionate. Accordingly, the Court considers that the applicant, as a Gypsy pursuing a traditional lifestyle, has been discriminated against in the enjoyment of her rights under Article 8. There has therefore been discrimination contrary to Article 14 of the Convention.

18

Erasing Q, W and X, erasing cultural differences[†]

LOURDES PERONI[*]

Introduction

Kemal Taşkın and others v. *Turkey*[1] concerns the refusal to register the applicants' Kurdish names on the basis that the letters 'q', 'w' and 'x' do not exist in the Turkish alphabet. At first glance, the case is just about names and letters. A thorough examination reveals, nonetheless, the great complexity and substance that may lie behind symbols. Three characters and eight names can embody power, culture and, of course, identity. This contention is far from being a novelty. Yet, it is remarkable to see fundamental challenges of diversity all at once in three letters. Recognition, private–public intersection and equality are only some of these challenges. It is hard to think of any other name case where the European Court of Human Rights[2] could have integrated a minority-sensitive perspective more naturally into its legal reasoning. Instead, the Court turned away from the real issues at stake and missed the chance to break new ground in its name case law.

[†] By using 'differences' (plural) instead of 'difference' (singular), I wish to avoid reaffirming what Martha Minow dubs 'unstated assumptions about the nature of difference'. M. Minow, 'Foreword: Justice Engendered' (1987) 101 *Harvard Law Review* 10 at 31. I believe that 'differences' (plural) stresses what Minow calls the 'relational' character of difference, which basically means viewing differences as 'expressions of comparison between people' rather than as 'intrinsic'. *Ibid.*, pp. 32 and 34–8. To my mind, 'differences' (plural) may also address another fundamental concern raised by Minow: adopting one (dominant) form as the 'unstated norm' against which some are deemed 'different'. *Ibid.*, pp. 38–45. In essence, with 'differences', the point of reference does not necessarily have to be the dominant one. In *Kemal Taşkın and others* v. *Turkey*, for example, it may be the Turkish-speaking majority or the Kurdish-speaking minority, as they are both different from each other.

[*] I am grateful to Eva Brems, Alexandra Timmer, Laurens Lavrysen, Maris Burbergs, Saïla Ouald Chaib and Stijn Smet for their comments on earlier versions of this chapter. The research for this paper was conducted within the framework of the ERC Starting Grant project 'Strengthening the European Court of Human Rights: More Accountability Through Better Legal Reasoning'.

[1] ECHR, *Kemal Taşkın and others* v. *Turkey*, 2 February 2010 (hereinafter, *Kemal Taşkın*).

[2] Hereinafter, 'the Court', 'the European Court' or 'the Strasbourg Court'.

If I had to capture my argument in one sentence, I would say this chapter seeks to make a case against the suppression of differences. The argument involves seeing, through the lens of names, what is ultimately at stake for members of ethnic and linguistic minorities. It further requires meaningfully scrutinising States' purposes behind name-related policies in search of any 'assimilationist bias'.[3] Albeit different, both routes cut in the same direction: they seek to protect what applicants regard as a distinctive symbol of their ethnic and cultural background. One entails recognising the importance of applicants' cultural particularities. The other involves unveiling unjustified attempts to suppress them.

My full argument will come into view through five proposals. I suggest introducing two of them in the analysis under Article 8 (right to respect for private and family life) and the other two in the assessment under Article 14 (prohibition of discrimination), together with Article 8. The fifth proposal cuts across both sets of analysis. My first suggestion seeks to bring the *cultural dimension* of minorities' names to the foreground of Article 8 analysis.[4] My second proposal, drawing on Kenji Yoshino's work, rejects attempts to turn the claim that a group can change a certain trait into the claim that it should do so without investigating why.[5] The other two proposals aim to expose the possible discriminatory implications of official language policies for members of linguistic minorities in plurilingual societies. These proposals attempt to draw attention to a common misconception under-lying governments' arguments: the neutral and innocuous character of such policies. They furthermore seek to show that in order for real *equality* to thrive, *particularities* sometimes need to be affirmed. My last and cross-cutting proposal highlights the need to pay greater attention to *context* and to the *group vulnerability* that arises from past and continuing disadvanta-geous practices.

In the following pages, I introduce and explain each of these elements and indicate why and how the Court should have integrated them into its analysis. First, I present the facts of the case, outline the Court's judgment and situate the decision in the wider name case law. Then, I examine what a cultural inquiry in

---

[3] I borrow the expression 'assimilationist bias' from Kenji Yoshino in K. Yoshino, 'Assimilationist Bias in Equal Protection: The Visibility Presumption and the Case of "Don't Ask, Don't Tell"' (1998–9) 108 *Yale Law Journal* 485.

[4] Julie Ringelheim emphasises this 'cultural dimension' of names: J. Ringelheim, *Diversité culturelle et droits de l'homme. La protection des minorités par la Convention européenne des droits de l'homme* (Brussels: Bruylant, 2006), p. 192.

[5] K. Yoshino, 'Assimilationist Bias in Equal Protection: The Visibility Presumption and the Case of "Don't Ask, Don't Tell"' (1998–9) 108 *Yale Law Journal* 485 at 506; and K. Yoshino, *Covering: The Hidden Assault on Our Civil Rights* (New York: Random House, 2007), p. 138.

minority name cases may look like. I underscore the relevance of historical context in assessing the significance that name changes may have for minorities and in evaluating the reasons lying beneath States' name policies. I next turn to the backdrop against which *Kemal Taşkın* should have been examined and, drawing on the Court's case law on 'vulnerable groups',[6] argue for including the Kurdish minority in Turkey among such groups. I subsequently underline the impossibility of neutrality of State language choices and their disadvantageous effects on linguistic minorities. Finally, after offering some brief conclusions, I attempt to show through the redrafted judgment how my proposals may unfold in practice.

Eight applicants in search of a Kurdish name: the arguments, the judgment and the case law

The parties' arguments

Following the lifting of legal naming restrictions in Turkey in 2003,[7] eight Turkish nationals of Kurdish origin attempted to register their Kurdish names containing the letters 'q', 'w' and 'x'. They were known by these names in their inner circles but were officially registered under other names due to restrictions in force at the time of their birth. The applications were rejected at the domestic level on the ground that the letters in the names they requested did not exist in the Turkish alphabet.[8] Law 1353, adopted on 1 November 1928, requires the use of the Turkish alphabet in official documents. All requests were therefore denied on this basis except for one of them, which was partly admitted. In this one case, domestic courts ordered the registration of the applicant's name as 'Baver' instead of 'Bawer', as originally written in Kurdish. The Kurdish 'w' was thus replaced by what the Turkish authorities considered its closest phonetic equivalent in Turkish. Following the registration refusals, the applicants turned to the European Court of Human Rights alleging a violation of their right to respect for private life (Article 8) and of the prohibition of discrimination on the basis of their affiliation to an ethnic minority (Article 14 in conjunction with Article 8). They argued that, whereas

---

[6] For a descriptive and normative assessment of the concept of 'vulnerable groups' as a heuristic device in the Court's case law, see A. Timmer and L. Peroni, 'Vulnerable Groups: The Promise of an Emerging Concept in European Human Rights Convention Law' (manuscript on file with the authors).

[7] Law 1587 on civil status registries prohibited the registration of names incompatible with the 'national culture'. The reference to 'national culture' was eliminated by Law 4928 of 15 July 2003. *Kemal Taşkın*, para. 26.

[8] Article 3 of the Turkish Constitution grants official status to the Turkish language.

non-nationals and dual nationals were able to register their names with characters which did not exist in the Turkish alphabet, they, as nationals of Kurdish origin, were denied such a possibility. The applicants further claimed that the letters 'q', 'w' and 'x' were also used in commercial products.

The Turkish government justified the restrictions on the applicants' right to respect for private life on the grounds of order and defence of the rights of others through the establishment of an official language. According to the government, the obligation to transpose the names following the rules of the national alphabet did not constitute a failure to respect the applicants' right to private life. In the government's view, the inconvenience suffered by the applicants was not of sufficient importance, as they could have simply transposed their names using the letters of the national alphabet – i.e. 'k', 'ks' and 'v' – which, when pronounced, produce the same sounds as the letters 'q', 'x', and 'w', respectively. As for the alleged discrimination, the Turkish government said that the rule requiring names to be registered with the letters of the Turkish alphabet was applied to all citizens without distinction. All other signs foreign to Turkish, the government claimed, were similarly rejected.

The Court's judgment

The Court did not find a violation of Article 8. The main reason was that, at the relevant time, the applicants did have the possibility of registering their Kurdish names provided that they did so in accordance with the Turkish alphabet. The Court pointed out that, thanks to the phonetic transcription, it was possible within the Turkish system to register names with letters whose exact written matches did not exist in the Turkish alphabet. Moreover, the Court remarked that there was no indication that the applicants' names, if spelled with Turkish letters, would acquire a vulgar or ridiculous meaning, likely to cause them inconvenience in their social life or create any obstacle to their personal identification. The Court did not find a violation of Article 14, together with Article 8, either. For the Court, nothing suggested that the Turkish authorities would have reached a different decision if the request to spell a name with letters non-existent in the Turkish alphabet came from non-Kurds. As for the inclusion in the civil registry of names of persons with civil status documents issued by other States with non-Turkish characters, the Court held that this practice was based on an international convention aimed at introducing uniformity in the matter, which in itself could not be considered an unreasonable aim. Moreover, the Court was not sure whether the applicants, as individuals wishing to change their names, were in a situation analogous to that of those with civil documents issued by other States under their own rules.

The Court's case law

Disputes over names, the Court has time and again affirmed, fall within the scope of Article 8 in relation to both 'private life' and 'family life'.[9] Not surprisingly, the applicability of this provision was not contested in *Kemal Taşkın*. The Court reaffirmed the principle that names, as means of personal identification and links to a family, concern private and family life.[10] *Kemal Taşkın* was, however, particularly challenging in that, like in other cases concerning the adaptation of names according to official language rules, name changes could not be dissociated from State linguistic policies.[11] In this respect, the Court's established principle is that each Contracting Party is 'at liberty to impose and regulate the use of its official language or languages in identity papers and other official documents' on condition that the Convention rights are respected.[12] Moreover, the margin of appreciation given to States in the area of recognition and regulation of names is particularly wide, as a range of historical, linguistic, religious and cultural factors in each of these countries influence the use of names.[13]

A rewriter in search of the real issues and reasons: cultural symbols and assimilationist bias (Article 8)

Preliminary considerations

The outcome in *Kemal Taşkın* does not come as a surprise. It is determined, in large part, by the wide margin of appreciation granted to States in the area. Even though Turkey has not signed the Council of Europe's Framework Convention for the Protection of National Minorities (FCNM), some may still go as far as arguing that the European consensus on minority protection is substantial enough to call for narrowing States' margin of appreciation. The Court has accepted in other areas of its minority case law the existence of an emerging international consensus amongst the Council of Europe's Member States recognising the special needs of minorities and an obligation to protect their security, identity and lifestyle.[14] While reducing States' discretion as a result of the growing European consensus may sound desirable, the actual application of this line

---

[9] See e.g. ECHR, *Burghartz* v. *Switzerland*, 22 February 1994, para. 24; and ECHR, *Stjerna* v. *Finland*, 25 November 1994, para. 37.

[10] *Kemal Taşkın*, para. 45.

[11] See e.g. ECHR, *Kuharec alias Kuhareca* v. *Latvia*, 7 December 2004; and ECHR, *Mentzen* v. *Latvia*, 7 December 2004.

[12] See e.g. ECHR, *Bulgakov* v. *Ukraine*, 11 September 2007, para. 43(a).

[13] See e.g. ECHR, *Kuharec alias Kuhareca* v. *Latvia*, 7 December 2004, p. 17; and ECHR, *Mentzen* v. *Latvia*, 7 December 2004.

[14] See e.g. ECHR, *Muñoz Díaz* v. *Spain*, 8 December 2009, para. 60.

of reasoning remains, however, unrealistic.[15] What is more, although in the past the Court has referred to the FCNM in its minority-name case law even when respondent States have not signed or ratified it, the reference has been merely formal.[16] The FCNM has become relevant in the Court's actual legal reasoning when it has been ratified by the respondent State.[17] Where ratification has not taken place, the FCNM has tended to remain background information.[18]

I, then, do not challenge the margin of appreciation standard in the Court's Article 8 name case law based on the consensus argument. My main disagreements in this first part lie with the Court's application in *Kemal Taşkın* of an instrumentalist approach to names (names as means of personal identification)[19] and with its disregard for historical/contextual elements in the proportionality analysis. Once the former is abandoned and the latter is embraced, it becomes clear that the implications for historically vulnerable minorities may be serious enough to amount to disproportionate interference with their private and family lives. *Kemal Taşkın* is not the first minority name case decided by the Court.[20] It is, however, one of the cases that has most clearly offered strong contextual elements to push for reconsideration of the Court's approach to ethno-linguistic minorities in its name case law. The judgment itself offers enough background information attesting the historical vulnerability of the

---

[15] In *Chapman* v. *United Kingdom*, decided in 2001, the Court did not view this consensus as 'sufficiently concrete' to draw any guidance and, as a result, remained reluctant to narrow the State's margin of appreciation. ECHR (GC), *Chapman* v. *United Kingdom*, 18 January 2001, para. 94. In the 2009 case of *Muñoz Díaz* v. *Spain*, although the Court no longer held that the consensus was 'not sufficiently concrete', it did not go on to discuss the implications of the consensus for States' margin of appreciation. ECHR, *Muñoz Díaz* v. *Spain*, 8 December 2009.

[16] See e.g. ECHR, *Kuharec alias Kuhareca* v. *Latvia*, 7 December 2004, pp. 9–10; and ECHR, *Baylac-Ferrer and Suarez* v. *France*, 25 September 2008, p. 8. France has not signed the FCNM and Latvia had not yet ratified it at the time the decision was handed down.

[17] See e.g. ECHR, *Bulgakov* v. *Ukraine*, 11 September 2007, para. 48. Of particular relevance for minority-name case law is Article 11 § 1 of the FCNM: 'The Parties undertake to recognise that every person belonging to a national minority has the right to use his or her surname (patronym) and first names in the minority language and the right to the official recognition of them, according to modalities provided for in their legal system.'

[18] See e.g. ECHR, *Kuharec alias Kuhareca* v. *Latvia*, 7 December 2004; and ECHR, *Baylac-Ferrer and Suarez* v. *France*, 25 September 2008.

[19] On understanding names beyond 'instrumental' or 'functionalist' concerns, see e.g. J. Ringelheim, *Diversité culturelle et droits de l'homme. La protection des minorités par la Convention européenne des droits de l'homme* (Brussels: Bruylant, 2006), p. 192; and Y. Tirosh. 'A Name of One's Own: Gender and Symbolic Legal Personhood in the European Court of Human Rights' (2010) 33 *Harvard Journal of Law and Gender* 247 at 300–6.

[20] See e.g. ECHR, *Kuharec alias Kuhareca* v. *Latvia*, 7 December 2004; ECHR, *Bulgakov* v. *Ukraine*, 11 September 2007; and ECHR, *Baylac-Ferrer and Suarez* v. *France*, 25 September 2008.

Kurdish minority in Turkey and casting doubts on the motivations underlying the restriction. For the same reasons, *Kemal Taşkın* made a strong case for broadening the analytical scheme applied in the name case law so as to expressly include cultural minority concerns alongside personal identity and practical ones.

What is at stake in a minority member's name?

At the heart of the applicants' complaints lies an attempt to maintain what they see as central to their cultural identity. The linguistic and cultural attachment to their names is clear from both the applicants' arguments and the historical context of the case. All of the applicants were originally registered under other names due to restrictions in force at the time of their birth. All of them requested the registration of their Kurdish names as soon as such restrictions were lifted. One of them, Doğan Genç, claimed that keeping his Kurdish name, 'Ciwan', as originally spelled would enable him to better affirm himself. The Court, however, fails to see that the impact of the restrictive measures goes beyond any practical difficulties, ridicule or personal identification problems. For the Court, the applicants did not succeed in demonstrating that their Kurdish names, if spelled according to the Turkish alphabet, would take a vulgar or ridiculous meaning likely to cause them inconveniences in their social life or to create personal identification obstacles. By focusing on questions that are simply not relevant in *Kemal Taşkın* (social inconvenience arising from ridicule/vulgarity or personal identification difficulties), the Court turns away from what is fundamentally at stake in the case.

Kemal Taşkın seems to pose what Yofi Tirosh calls 'legal challenges to the functionalist approach to names'.[21] In a study of the Court's name case law, Tirosh explains how applicants' more complex narratives are forced to fit into 'the available categories of legal reasoning'.[22] The author argues that, when 'the narrative does not fit, the Applicant loses'.[23] My sense is that this is exactly what happened in *Kemal Taşkın*. The framework applied by the Court in this case did not recognise the applicants' cultural attachment to their Kurdish-spelled names. The Court's fault thus lies with the application of an inadequate analytical scheme – that is to say, of an instrumentalist approach – to a more complex reality.[24] Perhaps, had the Court realised what was really at stake for

---

[21] Y. Tirosh. 'A Name of One's Own: Gender and Symbolic Legal Personhood in the European Court of Human Rights' (2010) 33 *Harvard Journal of Law and Gender* 247 at 300.

[22] *Ibid.*, p. 305.   [23] *Ibid.*

[24] For a critique of courts' reliance on rigid doctrinal categories 'in the face of complexity', see M. Minow, 'Foreword: Justice Engendered' (1987) 101 *Harvard Law Review* 10 at 82–6.

the applicants, it would have searched for alternative frameworks capable of addressing the core of the problem more adequately. Various cases in the Court's wider name jurisprudence show that a more complex framework is possible. In some instances, the Court has assessed applicants' personal attachment to a name.[25] In others, it has even shown itself sensitive to the name's affective dimension.[26] Minorities' linguistic or cultural attachment to their names remains, however, for the most part, unaddressed in the Court's case law.[27] At times, the Court simply overlooks the fact that applicants belong to a minority even though their claims are explicitly framed in those terms.[28] At others, the Court addresses but ultimately dismisses their ethnic identity concerns.[29]

Kemal Taşkın should thus serve to show that, where names are viewed by the applicants as indicators of their links with a certain ethno-linguistic community or as symbols of their cultural identity, the focus of the analysis should shift from names as mere means of personal identification to names as symbols of one's ties to an ethno-cultural community or as carriers of cultural meaning.[30] The crucial questions should revolve around whether the disputed measures impair or diminish applicants' ability to maintain what they claim to be their cultural identity and to lead their private and family lives in accordance with that tradition.[31] From this perspective, and especially in view of disadvantageous circumstances like the ones faced by the Kurdish applicants in the past, the symbolic value of respecting the original spelling of ethnic minorities' names may take particular significance.

The redrafted judgment intends to address this first concern by acknowledging the importance of what was truly at stake for the applicants, by

---

[25] See e.g. ECHR, *Stjerna v. Finland*, 25 November 1994, para. 43. In this case, however, the Court ends up holding that the applicant's ancestors 'lived so far back in time that no significant weight can be given to those links for the purposes of paragraph 1 of Article 8'.

[26] See e.g. ECHR, *Daróczy v. Hungary*, 1 July 2008, para. 33.

[27] See e.g. ECHR, *Kuharec alias Kuhareca v. Latvia*, 7 December 2004; ECHR, *Bulgakov v. Ukraine*, 11 September 2007; and ECHR, *Baylac-Ferrer and Suarez v. France*, 25 September 2008. One case showing a more minority-sensitive stance is *Güzel Erdagöz*. The outcome was favourable to the minority applicant but the reasoning did not revolve around minority concerns. ECHR, *Güzel Erdagöz v. Turkey*, 21 October 2008.

[28] See e.g. ECHR, *Baylac-Ferrer and Suarez v. France*, 25 September 2008.

[29] See e.g. ECHR, *Kuharec alias Kuhareca v. Latvia*, 7 December 2004, p. 17.

[30] Julie Ringelheim argues that surnames do not only have an instrumental role but also an affective and cultural dimension; just as they indicate individuals' link to a family, names can similarly point to links with a national or a cultural group. J. Ringelheim, *Diversité culturelle et droits de l'homme. La protection des minorités par la Convention européenne des droits de l'homme* (Brussels: Bruylant, 2006), p. 192.

[31] I draw on, *mutatis mutandis*, ECHR (GC), *Chapman v. United Kingdom*, 18 January 2001, para. 73.

bringing the cultural dimension of the name to the fore of the Article 8 analysis,[32] and by weighing it heavily in the balance in view of the historical disadvantage suffered by the Kurdish minority in Turkey (see paragraphs 71*bis*, 71*ter*, 72 and 73 of the redraft). I try to show that spelling changes in applicants' names – even though the modifications are minimal and even though the names retain their original pronunciation – may still be of such significance as to affect the cultural identity of members of ethnic minority groups. Keeping the original spelling may have a strong symbolic value for members of groups showing historical vulnerability, as I attempt to show in greater detail in the second part of this chapter.

What is behind the demand to fit?

In *Kemal Taşkın*, the Court does not only overlook what is really at stake for the applicants. It also stops short of inquiring into the government's reasons for demanding the changes in their Kurdish names. True, except for two of the applicants, the rest did not react to the Turkish government's argument that transposing their names according to the national alphabet would not constitute an inconvenience of sufficient importance, as certain letters of the Turkish alphabet produce the same sounds as the Kurdish letters 'q', 'w' and 'x'. At first glance, one may be under the impression that this was the reason behind the Court's reluctance to conduct any further inquiry: most applicants did not dispute the government's argument explicitly. A closer look at the Court's judgment reveals, nonetheless, that this first impression may not be completely right. First, two of the applicants did explain why they did not want to pursue the path suggested by the government. The first of them alleged that the new version of his name would take the meaning of 'appointment' or 'assembly'. The other applicant argued that his name, if spelled according to the Turkish alphabet, would be meaningless in Kurdish. Both of them mentioned the difficulties that the change would represent in their relations with other members of their ethnic group. In my view, the arguments of these two applicants gave the Court enough elements to engage in a more serious or substantive inquiry into the government's motives to demand the changes in the written versions of the applicants' names.

Secondly, and applicants' arguments aside, what ultimately seemed to stop the Court from going any further was the implicit confirmation of an idea embedded in the government's argument: the fact that applicants can change may suffice to justify the demand for change. American scholar, Kenji Yoshino, has identified different kinds of what he calls 'assimilationist bias' inherent in the

---

[32] J. Ringelheim, *Diversité culturelle et droits de l'homme. La protection des minorités par la Convention européenne des droits de l'homme* (Brussels: Bruylant, 2006), p. 192.

'immutability' and 'visibility' factors in US equal protection jurisprudence.[33] One of these biases, he claims, is 'converting', which in essence means asking members of a group to change defining traits.[34] 'The immutability and visibility factors', Yoshino explains, 'presume that legislation is less problematic if it burdens groups that can assimilate into mainstream society.'[35] As a result, courts are 'more likely to withhold heightened scrutiny from groups that can change or conceal their defining trait'.[36] Yoshino argues that groups' ability to assimilate should not stop courts from exploring the reasons behind demands to assimilate.[37] His main concern thus seems to be with 'state-sponsored assimilation that fails adequately to question whether the assimilation in question is appropriate'.[38] Although the possible 'assimilationist bias' in *Kemal Taşkın* may take a form different from the ones identified by Yoshino in the US equal protection context, it embeds a similar idea: those who can change may be required to do so without further questioning why they should do it. In order to avoid turning the 'descriptive claim' that applicants can assimilate into the 'normative claim' that they must do so, the Court should insist on asking why change is demanded.[39]

What is more, the historical context of *Kemal Taşkın* should have been enough to alert the Court to the need to take its inquiry further. A contextual analysis would have soon brought out a series of elements calling into question the credibility and relevance of the justification put forward by the government. In some cases, a contextual evaluation of the reasons given by the State to support its demand to conform may prove crucial to unveil any undue assimilationist attempt implicit in State naming policies affecting ethnic or linguistic minorities. As various authors show, assimilation or repression of minority groups' cultural identity may sometimes underlie State name practices in multi-ethnic societies.[40] Teresa Scassa, for example, maintains: 'Because names can reflect ethnic identity, governments reacting

---

[33] The 'immutability' and 'visibility' factors, Yoshino explains, comprise one prong of the heightened scrutiny test in US equal protection jurisprudence. These factors ask whether the classification in question relies on immutable and visible group characteristics, respectively. K. Yoshino, 'Assimilationist Bias in Equal Protection: The Visibility Presumption and the Case of "Don't Ask, Don't Tell"' (1998–9) 108 *Yale Law Journal* 485 at 493–8.

[34] *Ibid.*, p. 500.   [35] *Ibid.*, p. 504.   [36] *Ibid.*, p. 490.

[37] *Ibid.*, pp. 504–5. See also K. Yoshino, *Covering: The Hidden Assault on Our Civil Rights* (New York: Random House, 2007), p. 136.

[38] K. Yoshino, 'Assimilationist Bias in Equal Protection: The Visibility Presumption and the Case of "Don't Ask, Don't Tell"' (1998–9) 108 *Yale Law Journal* 485 at 506.

[39] *Ibid.* See also K. Yoshino, *Covering: The Hidden Assault on Our Civil Rights* (New York: Random House, 2007), p. 138.

[40] See e.g. T. Scassa, 'National Identity, Ethnic Surnames and the State' (1996) 11 *Canadian Journal of Law and Society* 167. Drawing mostly on examples from Canada and the US, Scassa demonstrates how State surname policies 'have tended to reflect certain national identity objectives' including assimilation. *Ibid.*, p. 167.

to ethnic minorities within their territory have often struck at names as a means of either heightening the stigma attached to the ethnic group or as a means of assimilation.'[41] In turn, in a study of the Court's name case law, Aeyal Gross shows how names regarded by the State as 'divergent' may be common among members of ethnic or linguistic minority groups.[42] Barring these names, he argues, 'may be a tool for the repression of cultural identity or reflect an attempt to maintain the hegemony of a certain culture in the face of the changing ethnic composition of a society'.[43]

In the rewritten judgment, I attempt to address this second concern by paying attention to context and by meaningfully inquiring into the government's reasons for its restriction (see paragraph 72 of the redraft). Thus, in the justification analysis, I look at the context within which the challenged measure was applied, weighing up a mix of elements taken from the background information offered by the judgment itself, from the applicants' submissions not disputed by the government, and from reports/resolutions issued by international organisations.

A rewriter in pursuit of cross-cutting paths: context and vulnerability

In my view, *Kemal Taşkın* begs for the examination of a crucial contextual factor: historical vulnerability affecting a particular ethnic group. The judgment itself contains sufficient elements to undertake a contextual approach and get a fuller understanding of the impact of the disputed measure on the applicants as nationals of Kurdish origin. For example, under 'Relevant Domestic Law and Practice', the Court includes legal background information, which clearly shows the restrictive character of the government's practices towards Kurdish names in the past.[44] Nevertheless, the Court does not attach any consequences to this contextual factor in the analysis of the merits.[45] The long ban on Kurdish names is a key contextual element, which shows that the restriction in question touches upon an area in which nationals of Kurdish origin have suffered significant disadvantage in the past as a consequence of the government's restrictive laws and practices.

---

[41] *Ibid.*, p. 174.
[42] A. M. Gross, 'Rights and Normalization: A Critical Study of European Human Rights Case Law on the Choice and Change of Names' (1996) 9 *Harvard Human Rights Journal* 269 at 274.
[43] *Ibid.*   [44] *Kemal Taşkın*, para. 26.
[45] In contrast, and in a remarkable concurring opinion, Judge András Sajó nicely incorporates in his analysis what is undoubtedly the most important element of the historical context in *Kemal Taşkın*: the past ban on Kurdish names and decrease of restrictive administrative practices. *Ibid.*, p. 21.

A quick look at international organisations' resolutions and reports, including those issued by the Council of Europe Parliamentary Assembly,[46] the European Commission[47] and the European Commission against Racism and Intolerance,[48] clearly point to the vulnerable position of the Kurds as a result of historically disadvantageous laws and practices aimed at suppressing the expression of their cultural identity. International non-governmental organisations have raised similar concerns.[49] Based on these reports and on the background information included in the Court's judgment, I suggest that it is necessary (1) to take into account the broader context of disadvantage affecting the Kurds in Turkey; (2) to explore the links between their historical disadvantage and their present vulnerability; and (3) to underscore the particularly harmful effects the disputed restriction may have on the applicants given their vulnerable status. Part of my analysis draws on the Court's case law on 'vulnerable groups', which, I must admit, has taken clearer shape in the months following the *Kemal Taşkın* judgment.

The Court has used the term 'vulnerable group' to refer to several groups, including the Roma minority,[50] persons with mental disabilities,[51] persons

---

[46] See e.g. Parliamentary Assembly of the Council of Europe Resolution 1256 (2001) concerning the Honouring of Obligations and Commitments by Turkey, para. 16(k); and Parliamentary Assembly of the Council of Europe Resolution 1380 (2004) concerning the Honouring of Obligations and Commitments by Turkey, para. 21.

[47] See e.g. European Commission, Turkey 2010 Progress Report accompanying the Communication from the Commission to the European Parliament and the Council, 9 November 2010, p. 20; Turkey 2005 Progress Report, 9 November 2005, p. 38; 2004 Regular Report on Turkey's Progress towards Accession, 6 October 2004, pp. 49 and 50. Particularly relevant for the case of *Kemal Taşkın* is the European Commission's 2003 Progress Report, stating: 'The Civil Registry Law was amended to permit parents to name their children as they desire, provided that such names are considered to comply with "moral values" and do not offend the public. The reference to "politically" offensive names has been removed from the law. However, a circular was issued in September 2003 restricting the scope of this amendment by *banning the use of names including the letters q, w and x, commonly used in Kurdish.*' European Commission, 2003 Regular Report on Turkey's Progress towards Accession, p. 37 (emphasis added).

[48] See e.g. European Commission against Racism and Intolerance (ECRI), Third Report on Turkey adopted on 25 June 2004, para. 78. In this report, ECRI recommended that the Turkish authorities 'combat the prejudice and stereotyping to which Kurds are subject'. *Ibid.*, para. 81.

[49] See e.g. Minority Rights Group International, 'Minorities in Turkey, Submission to the European Union and the Government of Turkey', July 2004, p. 24 (highlighting how restrictive name registration practices affected only Kurdish names); and Human Rights Watch, Report 'Questions and Answers: Freedom of Expression and Language Rights in Turkey', April 2002, available at http://www.hrw.org/legacy/press/2002/08/turkeyqa041902.htm (reporting prosecutions against families who had given their children Kurdish names).

[50] See e.g. ECHR (GC), *Chapman* v. *United Kingdom*, 18 January 2001, para. 96; and ECHR (GC), *DH and others* v. *Czech Republic*, 13 November 2007, para. 181.

[51] ECHR, *Alajos Kiss* v. *Hungary*, 20 May 2010, para. 42.

living with HIV[52] and, most recently, asylum-seekers.[53] Apart from asylum-seekers – whom the Court has regarded as vulnerable mostly because of their State-dependency status – the vulnerability of the rest of these groups has been mainly determined by one central factor: a history of discrimination.[54] Moreover, one fundamental consequence that group-vulnerability reasoning has carried in the Court's case law is the narrowing of States' margin of appreciation when it comes to restrictions or differentiations affecting these groups.[55] For example, the Court held in *Alajos Kiss* v. *Hungary*: '[I]f a restriction on fundamental rights applies to a particularly vulnerable group in society, who have suffered considerable discrimination in the past, such as the mentally disabled, then the State's margin of appreciation is substantially narrower and it must have very weighty reasons for the restrictions in question.'[56] Although the Court has not yet considered the Kurds in Turkey vulnerable, I believe the group certainly meets the history-of-discrimination criterion. As the international reports and resolutions referred to above show, they have been historically harmed by both stereotyping and suppression of aspects of their linguistic and cultural tradition. *Kemal Taşkın*, more concretely, concerns the latter type of discrimination: the one that operates to suppress and assimilate the group in question into the dominant mould.

The rewritten judgment could call for a narrower margin of appreciation with the argument that the interference in question affects a particularly vulnerable group: the Kurds in Turkey. Closer scrutiny would make particular sense in the discrimination analysis, as the historical context the Court usually looks at when assessing a group's vulnerability casts doubts on the differentiation in question. Another reasonable approach consists in simply including the historical context and the ensuing group vulnerability as elements of considerable weight in the proportionality analysis. In the redraft, I opt for this second approach not because I do not find the first one sensible but simply because I believe the second remains relatively unexplored. I thus include context and vulnerability in the proportionality assessment under Article 14 in conjunction with Article 8 – more precisely in the examination of the particularly harmful implications the differential treatment may have on the applicants (see paragraph 86 of the redraft) – and under Article 8 alone – particularly in the assessment of the symbolic value that preserving the original written name may have for the applicants (see paragraphs 71*bis* and 71*ter* of the redraft).

---

[52] ECHR, *Kiyutin* v. *Russia*, 10 March 2011, para. 63.
[53] ECHR (GC), *MSS* v. *Belgium* and *Greece*, 21 January 2011, para. 251.
[54] A. Timmer and L. Peroni, 'Vulnerable Groups: The Promise of an Emerging Concept in European Human Rights Convention Law' (manuscript on file with the authors).
[55] *Ibid.*   [56] ECHR, *Alajos Kiss* v. *Hungary*, 20 May 2010, para. 42.

A rewriter in search of substantive equality (Articles 14 and 8)

The choice of an official language, as several authors argue, is not a neutral choice.[57] In contexts of linguistic plurality, such a decision may favour some and disfavour others.[58] As Fernand de Varennes points out:

> One of the most frequent misconceptions involving non-discrimination is the belief that a State measure imposing a single language for all signifies that everyone is treated the same and that therefore no differentiation is made between individuals.[59]

This misconception is implicit in the Turkish government's argument in *Kemal Taşkın*. The government claimed that, in applying the rule requiring names to be spelled according to the Turkish alphabet to all citizens without distinction, it was treating everyone equally.[60] In fact, however, the identical application of the rule forced only non-dominant linguistic groups (like those of Kurdish origin) to use in their names letters of an alphabet that is not theirs while allowing the Turkish majority to keep their names' spelling in accordance with the letters of their own. This is not the first time a government claims to be applying its name-related policies to everyone equally when in effect it is not.[61] In *Kemal Taşkın*, the Court responded to this sort of claim by noting that there was no indication that the Turkish authorities would have reached a different decision had the requests to spell names with non-Turkish letters come from non-Kurds.[62] The Court, however, fails to ask why non-Kurds like the Turkish majority members would request to register names with letters that do not exist in Turkish. The fact that the Turkish majority will hardly suffer from this problem is then a factor that illustrates how the policy disregards the concerns of the Kurds (see paragraph 82 of the redraft). The policy is therefore not neutral regardless of how it would be applied to non-Kurds; it ultimately maintains the historical discrimination of the Kurds in Turkey.

---

[57] See e.g. F. de Varennes, 'The Protection of Linguistic Minorities in Europe and Human Rights: Possible Solutions to Ethnic Conflicts?' (1996) 2 *Columbia Journal of European Law* 107 at 114–15; and J. Ringelheim, *Diversité culturelle et droits de l'homme. La protection des minorités par la Convention européenne des droits de l'homme* (Brussels: Bruylant, 2006), p. 175.

[58] *Ibid.*

[59] F. de Varennes, 'The Protection of Linguistic Minorities in Europe and Human Rights: Possible Solutions to Ethnic Conflicts?' (1996) 2 *Columbia Journal of European Law* 107 at 111.

[60] *Kemal Taşkın*, para. 74.

[61] See e.g. ECHR, *Bulgakov* v. *Ukraine*, 11 September 2007, para. 56; and ECHR, *Baylac-Ferrer and Suarez* v. *France*, 25 September 2008, p. 13.

[62] *Kemal Taşkın*, para. 78.

A State's choice of a particular language does, then, involve a distinction on the basis of language.[63] The first stage is, therefore, confronting the fact that language choices inevitably involve favouring some over others in several respects.[64] This, of course, does not mean that any language-based distinction is discriminatory.[65] It will only be so if it is not objectively and reasonably justified. The next and closely interconnected stage is acknowledging the negative implications language policies may carry for linguistic minorities in practice. One central question that substantive equality asks is 'whether the effect of the law is to perpetuate disadvantage, discrimination, exclusion, or oppression'.[66] Among the several dimensions of substantive equality, Sandra Fredman identifies one that emphasises the need to remove the detrimental consequences attached to differences rather than differences themselves.[67] Substantive equality, as she puts it, 'does not therefore aim to treat all individuals identically, but to affirm and accommodate differences'.[68] The Court's Grand Chamber has embraced this rationale in the case of *Thlimmenos* v. *Greece* by requiring that different situations be treated differently, unless there are objective and reasonable justifications for not doing so.[69]

I attempt to introduce all these concerns in the redrafted judgment in the analysis under Article 14 in conjunction with Article 8 (see paragraphs 81–7 of the redraft). In my view, one set of comparison arising from *Kemal Taşkın* – besides the one between nationals of Kurdish origin and non-nationals/dual nationals brought up by the applicants – concerns Turkish-speaking-majority nationals and Kurdish-speaking-minority nationals. In all fairness to the Court, I must make clear that the applicants did not complain of the difference in treatment with regard to the Turkish-speaking majority. In a sense, then, the Court cannot be blamed for not having addressed this concern. Still, I include

---

[63] F. de Varennes, 'Ethnic Conflicts and Language in Eastern European and Central Asian States: Can Human Rights Help Prevent Them?' (1997) 5 *International Journal on Minority and Group Rights* 136.

[64] I am by no means arguing for 'linguistic disestablishment' – which various authors rightly call an 'illusion' – but rather, and more simply, for awareness of the non-neutral character of State language choices. See e.g. A. Patten and W. Kymlicka, 'Introduction: Language Rights and Political Theory: Context, Issues, and Approaches', in W. Kymlicka and A. Patten (eds.), *Language Rights and Political Theory* (Oxford and New York: Oxford University Press 2003), p. 32.

[65] F. de Varennes, 'The Protection of Linguistic Minorities in Europe and Human Rights: Possible Solutions to Ethnic Conflicts?' (1996) 2 *Columbia Journal of European Law* 107 at 112.

[66] R. O'Connell, 'Substantive Equality in the European Court of Human Rights?' (2009) 107 *Michigan Law Review First Impressions* 129 at 129.

[67] S. Fredman, *Discrimination Law* (2nd edn, Oxford University Press, 2011), p. 30.

[68] S. Fredman, 'Facing the Future: Substantive Equality under the Spotlight' (University of Oxford Legal Research Paper Series, Paper No. 57/2010, July 2010), p. 6.

[69] ECHR (GC), *Thlimmenos* v. *Greece*, 6 April 2000.

such alternative reasoning in the redraft, driven largely by a need to address what seems to be a recurrent and misconceived argument of respondent governments, including Turkey in *Kemal Taşkın*. An equally important reason that explains my inclusion of this alternative reasoning in the redraft has to do with the need to flag this sort of argument and invite the Court to confront it in its future case law. I leave out of my rewritten judgment the analysis of the alleged discrimination with respect to non-nationals/dual nationals, as this would have meant addressing a whole array of issues diverging from the primary concern and focus of this chapter. The analysis would have most likely revolved around the interpretation of a convention of a technical nature[70] and the subsequent comparability of the applicants' situation with that of non-nationals and dual nationals.

In my redraft, therefore, I first try to show that the government is in fact treating its nationals of Kurdish origin differently from its Turkish majority on the basis of language (see paragraphs 81 and 82 of the redraft). I then find the distinction unjustified (see paragraphs 84, 85 and 86 of the redraft). For the reasons indicated in the previous section, I do not propose to narrow the margin of appreciation usually left to States in this area. This does not mean I do not find this approach sensible. I believe that notwithstanding the Court's considerable deference towards States' language policy choices – in particular, towards those related to 'official language' designations[71] – an argument can be made against this wide margin of appreciation in cases where historically disadvantaged minorities are affected by a certain language policy. Name policies and official language choices may generally attract a wide margin of appreciation, but when a discrimination claim is at issue there may be additional elements justifying a narrowing of this margin. The historical disadvantage and discrimination explains why the Court should apply stricter scrutiny than would be the case under a wide margin of appreciation.

Conclusion

The concerns of minority applicants rarely surface in the Court's reasoning in its name case law. In this regard, the *Kemal Taşkın* judgment is no exception; the Court overlooks what is truly at issue for the Kurdish applicants and shows nearly complete disregard for their concerns when balancing the competing interests. In this chapter, I have offered various proposals in an effort to add a minority perspective to the Court's analysis in its name jurisprudence. None of them offers a drastic departure from fundamental principles of the Court's case

[70] International Commission on Civil Status (ICCS) Convention No. 14 on the Recording of Surnames and Forenames in Civil Status Registers, signed on 13 September 1973.
[71] See e.g. *Kemal Taşkın*, para. 57.

law. On the contrary, some of the suggested ways in which the Court could take minorities more seriously draw on its own jurisprudence. The Court's case law offers several analytical tools capable of ensuring that minority concerns are taken into account more adequately. The rewritten judgment is an attempt to bring some of them together and put them into practice. The proportionality analysis – under both Article 8 alone and Articles 14 and 8 together – is where most of my proposals play out.

In addition, I have sought to expose and challenge inadequate conceptual frameworks and problematic assumptions underwriting the Court's reasoning in *Kemal Taşkın* and its minority name case law more broadly. *Kemal Taşkın* is possibly one of the best examples attesting the inadequacy of a model to address the complexity posed by minority members' name claims. The alternative model I have outlined seeks to add a cultural dimension of names to the existing framework. I believe this expanded conceptual scheme, along with a greater commitment to substantive equality, holds potential to discern unjustified suppression of differences. Eliminating differences instead of the disadvantageous treatment attached to them is not what real equality is about.[72] The rewritten judgment that follows is a call for not making conformity 'a price for equal treatment'.[73]

Rewriting Kemal Taşkın and others v. Turkey[74]

. . .

Alleged violation of Article 8 of the Convention

. . .

2. Did the interference pursue a 'legitimate aim'?

. . .

55. [Fragment deleted] According to **the government**, considering the important role of the State's official language, the impugned interference primarily pursued the legitimate aims of protecting the rights and freedoms of others and the protection of order.

. . .

---

[72] S. Fredman, 'Facing the Future: Substantive Equality under the Spotlight' (University of Oxford Legal Research Paper Series, Paper No. 57/2010, July 2010), p. 6.
[73] Sandra Fredman argues that 'formal equality demands conformity as a price for equal treatment'. *Ibid.*
[74] The judgment is available in French only. The original paragraphs kept in the rewritten judgment are the author's own translation.

57. [Fragment deleted] The Court considers that the interest of each State in ensuring that its own institutional system functions normally is incontestably legitimate (*Podkolzina* v. *Latvia*, no. 46726/99, § 34, ECHR 2002-II). It has already held that most Contracting States have chosen to grant one or more languages the status of official language or State language and that they have recognised them as such in their constitutions (*Mentzen*, supra). The same holds for the choice of a national alphabet. This is a choice of the national legislature, linked to historical and political considerations that are particular to the State in question (*Baylac-Ferrer and Suarez*, decision cited above).

58. In the decision *Mentzen or Mencena* v. *Latvia* (no. 71074/01, 7 December 2004), the Court held that a language 'is not in any sense an abstract value. It cannot be divorced from the way it is actually used by its speakers. Consequently, by making a language its official language, the State undertakes in principle to guarantee its citizens the right to use that language both to impart and to receive information, without hindrance not only in their private lives, but also in their dealings with the public authorities. In the Court's view, it is first and foremost from this perspective that measures intended to protect a given language must be considered' (see also, *Bulgakov* v. *Ukraine*, no. 59894/00, 11 September 2007, § 43 b). In other words, the Court considers that, implicit in the notion of an official language is the existence of certain subjective rights for the speakers of that language (see, *Kuharec alias Kuhareca* v. *Latvia*, no. 71557/01, 7 December 2004, p. 16). Thus, in the majority of cases, it may be accepted that a measure intended to protect and promote a national language corresponds to the protection of the 'rights and freedoms of others', within the meaning of Article 8 § 2 of the Convention (see *Bulgakov* v. *Ukraine*, no. 59894/00, 11 September 2007, § 43b).

59. Accordingly, the Court concludes that the interference in question had as objectives the defence of order and the protection of the rights of others.

3.   Was the interference 'necessary in a democratic society'?

. . .

62.   For the government, the obligation to transpose the names according to the rules of the national alphabet does not constitute a failure to respect the applicants' right to private life given that the inconvenience suffered by them would not be of sufficient importance. In addition, it argues that certain letters of the Turkish alphabet, i.e. 'k', 'ks' and 'v', when pronounced, produce the same sounds as the letters 'q', 'x' and 'w', respectively. In particular, citing the example of Mr Sünbül, who was able to

register the name he asked to use – 'Bawer', spelled with a 'v' instead of a 'w', in accordance with the national alphabet – [the government] considers that the applicants could have transposed their names without any problem with the letters of the national alphabet.

63. The applicants Mr Taşkın, Mr Alpkaya and Mr Fırat did not submit observations on this point within due time. As for Mr Anğ, Mr Şimşek and Mr Sünbül, they submitted no argument about any inconvenience eventually suffered as a result of the refusal at issue (compare with *Daniela Fornaciarini, Claudio Gianettoni and Francesco Fornaciarini* v. *Switzerland*, no. 22940/93, Commission's Decision of 12 April 1996).

64. In what concerns Mr Genç and Mr Yöyler, they do not really contest the government's assertion that the Kurdish names can be written with the letters of the Turkish alphabet. However, they argue that this practice distorts the meaning of their names. For example, Mr Genç explains that the name 'Ciwan', which in Kurdish means 'beautiful and young', when transcribed into 'Civan' without using the 'w', takes the meaning of 'appointment' or 'meeting'. Similarly, Mr Yöyler argues that, when the name 'Xweşbin' ('optimistic' in Kurdish) is spelled with the letters of the Turkish alphabet as 'Heşbin', it becomes a term with no precise meaning in Kurdish.

65. Mr Genç also emphasises that, as a human rights activist, he is in permanent contact with people of Kurdish origin, who would reproach him, as a result of his Turkish-like name, for not being a proper Kurd. Mr Yöyler presents similar arguments. According to him, the refusal to register his name in Kurdish is an unjustified interference with his cultural and ethnic identity. This restriction, which requires him to use a name of Arabic origin, 'Celalettin', would aim to create an obstacle in establishing relations with other Kurdish groups. He refers to the Court's jurisprudence in the area of personal autonomy and affirms that the Kurdish language should benefit from increased protection.

66. Insofar as Mr Genç and Mr Yöyler allege that the refusal in question constitutes an unjustified interference with their ethnic identity, [fragment deleted] **the Court cannot overlook the fact that the use of Kurdish names has long been banned in Turkey. In such circumstances, the identity concerns of people, whose right to respect for private life has been restricted, are the more relevant and their sensitivities particularly important.[75] In view of the historical context, the inconvenience caused by the refusal to use the Kurdish characters in the applicants' names can be said to be real and relevant.[76]**

---

[75] This part draws on Judge András Sajó's concurring opinion in *Kemal Taşkın*, p. 21.
[76] This part draws on Judge András Sajó's concurring opinion in *Kemal Taşkın*, p. 22.

67. [Fragment deleted] The Court observes that, as illustrated in the case of Mr Sünbül where the 'w' has been replaced by a 'v', in the Turkish system it is possible to proceed, thanks to the phonetic transcription, to the inscription in the civil registry of names containing sounds, whose exact match does not exist in the Turkish alphabet (for other examples, see paragraph 30 above). **The applicants do not contest this thesis. The Court then accepts that the applicants' Kurdish names, if spelled with the best matching script of the Turkish alphabet, will not lose their phonetic value. The Court notes, however, that the applicants did not want to pursue this route. One of them, Mr Sünbül – whose name was registered as 'Baver' instead of 'Bawer' – appealed the decision. Two others, Mr Genç and Mr Yöyler, raised cultural identity concerns in an attempt to explain why they did not choose that path. The question is, therefore, whether the mere alteration to the original *written* version of the applicants' names – which would apparently not alter the original *oral* form – is *per se* sufficient to cause them identification difficulties or acquire a meaning likely to cause them inconvenience in their social relations.**

. . .

[Original paragraph 69 deleted]
69. The Court will first address Mr Genç's complaint. According to the applicant, his name 'Ciwan', which in Kurdish means 'beautiful and young', when transcribed into 'Civan' without using the 'w', takes the meaning of 'appointment' or 'meeting'. The government did not dispute this. The Court then concludes that Mr Genç's name, if spelled with the letters of the Turkish alphabet, would have a ridiculous meaning likely to cause him an inconvenience of sufficient importance in his social life. As for the other applicants, they have not demonstrated that the written modification of their names would represent either an obstacle to their personal identification or a basis for ridicule.[77]
. . .

71*bis*. Nevertheless, names do not only have an instrumental character but also an affective and cultural dimension.[78] **They may reflect a person's specific linguistic and ethnic background**[79] **and may thus be essential to lead her private and family life in accordance with what she sees as fundamental to her cultural identity. Therefore, the additional question the Court faces in this particular case is whether the changes in the graphical representation of the bearers' names may be said to be of**

---

[77] Paras. 70 and 71 are unchanged.

[78] J. Ringelheim, *Diversité culturelle et droits de l'homme. La protection des minorités par la Convention européenne des droits de l'homme* (Brussels: Bruylant, 2006), p. 192.

[79] T. Scassa, 'National Identity, Ethnic Surnames and the State' (1996) 11 *Canadian Journal of Law and Society* 167 at 167.

such importance so as to affect what the applicants claim to be their ethnic and cultural identity. From this perspective, the Court cannot deny the strong symbolic value that keeping the original written version of a name may have for members of a non-dominant group willing to express their ethno-linguistic affiliation and maintain their cultural heritage, especially when, according to numerous international organisations' resolutions and reports, such a group's cultural expression has suffered from past disadvantage as a consequence of the government's restrictive practices.

71*ter*. While the requirement to spell names in accordance with the Turkish alphabet enables people with a command of Turkish to pronounce the names concerned correctly and to include it effortlessly in phrases of everyday language, it inevitably entails an alteration to the names' written form (see, *Mentzen or Mencena* v. *Latvia*, no. 71074/01, 7 December 2004). On one side of the balance are then the rights of others – the majority of the population – to understand and use the official language correctly and without difficulties. This is reflected in the need to bring the written form of a name in line with its pronunciation in the official language. On the other side, are the rights of the applicants for whom, as members of a vulnerable group that have suffered considerable disadvantage in the past (see, *mutatis mutandis, DH and others* v. *Czech Republic*[GC], no. 57325/00, 13 November 2007, § 182; *Alajos Kiss* v. *Hungary*, no. 38832/06, 20 May 2010, § 42 and *Kiyutin* v. *Russia*, no. 2700/10, 10 March 2011, § 63), keeping the original Kurdish spelling may be all the more relevant in the preservation of what they regard as symbols of their cultural and linguistic tradition. With this in mind, the Court will now examine whether the official language and order considerations relied on by the government can be said to outweigh the cultural identity concerns claimed by members of a vulnerable group under Article 8 of the Convention.

[Original paragraph 72 deleted]

72. The Court first notes that the main reason offered by the government for demanding the alteration of the applicants' names is the possibility of changing their original spellings without major inconvenience. In this regard, the Court believes that the fact that applicants can easily change or adapt their names does not automatically mean that they should do so. The Court needs to further inquire into the motivation or rationale behind the government's demand to change. The government has articulated none, apart from the mere formal and general invocation of the protection of order and the rights of others through its official language. What is more, several contextual elements arising from both the facts of the case and international organisations'

resolutions/reports point to past and continuing discriminatory practices in the use of Kurdish names in Turkey. Unlike the Latvian government in *Mentzen or Mencena* and *Kuharec alias Kuhareca*, the Turkish government has not contended that spelling the applicants' names with the Kurdish letters would have any negative consequences in the preservation of the Turkish language. In addition, the Court attaches particular importance to the fact that the use of the letters 'q', 'w' and 'x' cannot be regarded as exactly 'new' in Turkey (see, *mutatis mutandis, Johansson* v. *Finland*, no. 10163/02, 6 September 2007, § 38). They are in fact used by the government itself (ministry websites), by commercial products (see paragraph 34 of the original judgment) whose presence is more visible in everyday life and, lastly, by dual and non-nationals who are allowed to keep their original written forms of their names even if they include unavailable letters. While it is true that the latter group is permitted such registration on different grounds based on an international convention, the example nonetheless serves, along with the others, to weaken the government's thesis that accepting the Kurdish letters will undermine the official language. With respect to the protection of order, the examples further serve to show that there is *de facto* no practical impossibility likely to disrupt such order. Under these circumstances, any prejudice caused by the Kurdish letters in the applicants' names to the Turkish language or order cannot be said of sufficient significance to outweigh the cultural identity concerns of members of a group whose names had been banned in the past and for whom keeping the original spelling may have a strong symbolic value.

73. In the Court's view, the official language and order considerations relied on by the government cannot outweigh the interests claimed by the applicants under Article 8 of the Convention. A fair balance has therefore not been struck. There has thus been a violation of Article 8.

Alleged violation of Article 14 of the Convention in conjunction with Article 8

74. The applicants also contend that the refusal violated Article 14 of the Convention, combined with Article 8. [Fragment deleted]

75. The Government contests this thesis. The rule questioned by the applicants applies to all citizens without distinction. According to the Government, all other signs or written characters foreign to the Turkish language are similarly refused.

. . .

78. [Fragments deleted] **The Court** recalls [fragment deleted] that, in its decision *Baylac-Ferrer and Suarez* (cited above), it has regarded as objective

and reasonable a justification based on the linguistic unity in the relations with the administration and public services.

...

Nationals belonging to the Turkish-speaking majority and nationals of Kurdish origin

1.   Whether there was a difference in treatment

81. The Turkish government contends that the rule questioned by the applicants applies to all citizens without distinction. The Court observes, however, that the rule requiring all names to be registered according to the Turkish alphabet in practice affects a segment of the national population (in this case, those of Kurdish origin) differently from the Turkish-speaking majority. The latter is not forced to take letters of an alien alphabet but allowed to spell their names with the letters of their own, i.e. the Turkish alphabet. At the same time, and unlike the majority of their co-nationals, citizens of Kurdish origin – whose alphabet contains the letters 'q', 'w' and 'x' and whose names are more likely to include these letters as a consequence – are the ones forced to either have their names spelled with characters of an alphabet other than their own or choose from a narrower set options, i.e. from a group of Kurdish names not containing the officially unavailable letters. The latter was not, however, an option open to the applicants who have already been known in their inner circles by their Kurdish names containing those letters.

82. In sum, the disputed rule does not proscribe Kurdish names or letters. Nor does it stipulate, in itself, different consequences for the nationals of Kurdish origin. The differentiation lies in the failure to make a distinction for nationals of Kurdish origin. As for the Turkish government's argument that all other signs and written characters foreign to the Turkish language are similarly refused, the Court would like to add that the chance that members of the dominant linguistic group (Turkish-speaking majority) will request the registration of names containing letters foreign to their own Turkish alphabet seems rather slim. Therefore, requests for registration of names with non-Turkish characters from members of the majority-speaking language are much less likely than requests from members of non-dominant linguistic groups whose names are more likely to contain letters non-existent in the Turkish alphabet.

83. The Court thus concludes that dissimilar treatment on the grounds of language exists in this case. But, since not all differentiation is necessarily discriminatory, the Court will now turn to the examination of

whether the distinction has in this case an objective and reasonable justification.

2. Whether the difference in treatment had an objective and reasonable justification

84. The Court has said that the right not to be discriminated against in the enjoyment of the rights guaranteed under the Convention is not only violated when States treat differently persons in analogous situations without providing an objective and reasonable justification but also when States, without an objective and reasonable justification, fail to treat differently persons whose situations are significantly different (see *Thlimmenos* v. *Greece*[GC], no. 34369/97, 6 April 2000, § 44). The Court will therefore examine whether the failure to treat the applicants differently pursued a legitimate aim. If it did, the Court will have to examine whether there was a reasonable relationship of proportionality between the means employed and the aim sought to be realised.

85. The Court recalls that, in its decision *Baylac-Ferrer and Suarez* (cited above), it regarded a justification based on the linguistic unity in the relations with the administration and public services as reasonable and objective. In the present case, however, such a basis cannot provide similarly valid justification. On the one hand, evidence shows that non-Turkish letters are already used by the government itself (ministry websites),[80] by commercial products and by non-nationals who are allowed to register their names as originally spelled even if they include unavailable letters. The example of the latter – even though they may not be in a comparable situation – serves however to show, along with the other instances, that letters foreign to the Turkish alphabet are already available and used in the Turkish administration and public life. Furthermore, the examples serve to indicate that there is *de facto* no impediment to incorporate the applicants' names' letters.

86. On the other hand, the Court notes that the restriction may have particularly harmful effects on the applicants. In fact, although the case at issue concerns the individual situation of the applicants, the Court cannot ignore that they are members of a non-dominant ethnic group who have become vulnerable as a result of disadvantage and discrimination in the past (see, *mutatis mutandis*, *DH*, *Alajos Kiss* and *Kiyutin*, cited above). Numerous organisations and institutions, including the Council

---

[80] See also Report of the Committee on the Honouring of Obligations and Commitments by Member States of the Council of Europe, 17 March 2004, para. 243. The report highlights that the 'w' must feature on the keyboards of Turkish computers to access the Internet and hopes the government will show some flexibility when registering names containing letters not available in Turkish.

of Europe, the European Commission and the European Commission against Racism and Intolerance, have consistently reported past restrictive and discriminatory measures against the Kurdish population, as a consequence of which they have become a particularly vulnerable group in Turkey. Furthermore, the areas in which nationals of Kurdish origin have been historically disadvantaged include precisely those of concern in the present case. The bans on Kurdish names, which had been in place for decades in Turkey, is exactly one example of such disadvantageous practices (see, paragraph 66 above). In view of this past disadvantage and of the group's increased vulnerability to further discriminatory harms, it thus seems reasonable to assume that the differential treatment to which they have been subjected has had particularly severe impact on the applicants.

87. For the reasons given above, the Court finds that the failure to treat different situations differently was not reasonably justified in the particular circumstances of this case. There has thus been a violation of Article 14, in conjunction with Article 8, with respect to the Turkish-speaking majority.

INDEX

470